Morning Glory, Evening Shadow

Yamato Ichihashi and His
Internment Writings,

1942-1945

ASIAN AMERICA

A series edited by Gordon H. Chang

The increasing size and diversity of the Asian American population, its growing significance in American society and culture, and the expanded appreciation, both popular and scholarly, of the importance of Asian Americans in the country's present and past—all these developments have converged to stimulate wide interest in scholarly work on topics related to the Asian American experience. The general recognition of the pivotal role that race and ethnicity have played in American life, and in relations between the United States and other countries, has also fostered this heightened attention.

Although Asian Americans were a subject of serious inquiry in the late nineteenth and early twentieth centuries, they were subsequently ignored by the mainstream scholarly community for several decades. In recent years, however, this neglect has ended, with an increasing number of writers examining a good many aspects of Asian American life and culture. Moreover, many students of American society are recognizing that the study of issues related to Asian America speak to, and may be essential for, many current discussions on the part of the informed public and various scholarly communities.

The Stanford series on Asian America seeks to address these interests. The series will include work from the humanities and social sciences, including history, anthropology, political science, American studies, law, literary criticism, sociology, and interdisciplinary and policy studies.

Edited, annotated, and with a
biographical essay by

Gordon H. Chang

MORNING GLORY, EVENING SHADOW

Yamato Ichihashi and His Internment Writings, 1942-1945

STANFORD UNIVERSITY PRESS

Stanford, California

Stanford University Press, Stanford, California
© 1997 by the Board of Trustees of the Leland Stanford Junior University
Printed in the United States of America

CIP data appear at the end of the book

Frontispiece: The handwritten inscription on the reverse of this photograph reads: "On June 18, 1931, I was promoted to a full professorship, the goal to reach which I had struggled for seventeen years. As a souvenir of this event I wish to leave this autographed photograph to Kei. Yamato." (Woodrow Ichihashi)

Acknowledgments

The interest and help of Woodrow and Alyce Ichihashi made this book possible, and I thank them for all that they have done and for their friendship. Many colleagues around the country provided invaluable intellectual and moral support, but I especially want to acknowledge the constant and unselfish assistance of Yuji Ichioka, a pioneer in the writing of Asian American history. Barton Bernstein, Albert Camarillo, Estelle Freedman, George Fredrickson, David Kennedy, and Valerie Matsumoto all gave of their valuable time to read various drafts of the manuscript and provided me with exceptionally useful comments. This book is certainly better because of them. I also wish to thank other colleagues and friends who read portions of the work or extensively discussed the Ichihashis' lives and times with me; these include Harumi Befu, John Johnson, George Knoles, Seizo Oka, Gordon and Louise Wright, and Richard Yuen. My Stanford colleagues Peter Duus, Jeffrey Mass, and Jim Ketelaar patiently and constructively responded to my queries about Japanese history and culture.

I also wish to acknowledge the help of others who made completing this difficult project easier. Thank you Kim de St. Paer, Mae Lee, Jing Li, Ron Nakao, Steve Pitti, Nancy Stalker, and Daishi Torii. Thank you, too, to all the students who contributed to the History of Asian Americans at Stanford Project and constantly uncovered fascinating gems of information about the University's history. I also express my appreciation to Stanford's Center for International Security and Arms Control, Center for East Asian Studies, and Humanities Center for financial support for this project. The Humanities Center, where I was a fellow for 1994–95, provided a most congenial environment for scholarly work. The Humanities Center, the Stanford Asian Pacific Alumni/ae Club, the Stanford Historical Society, and the Asian American Studies Center at the University of California, Los Angeles, allowed me to present ideas to them while this manuscript was a work-in-progress. I thank them and the many in their audiences who responded with valuable comments and leads for further investigation. Many Stanford nisei alumni were most generous with their time in helping me understand their long-ago college days. I thank them for their help and support.

The archivists and staffs at Stanford's Green Library and its Special Collections, the Hoover Institution Archives, and the Pacific/Sierra Branch of the National Archives were all extraordinarily helpful in locating documents that form the core of this work. I also want to make a special expression of gratitude to the wonderful staff and editors at Stanford University Press, but especially to senior editor Muriel Bell, who has been a joy to work with on this and other endeavors. Her intelligence, candor, and efficiency led to improvements on every page of this book. Even more important, her support for the Stanford University Press series in Asian American studies is making a contribution of lasting and profound significance.

And finally, I want to thank my many wonderful friends and loved ones, but especially Vicki, who have provided understanding and sustenance in so many different ways to help me see this project through to completion.

G.H.C.

Contents

Abbreviations

The following abbreviations are used in footnotes and end notes for some of the most frequently cited sources.

DSJ   David Starr Jordan Presidential Papers, SC 58, Green Library, Stanford University
This collection is to be distinguished from the collection of Jordan Papers at the Archives, Hoover Institution, which will be cited as Hoover Jordan Papers.

EER   Edgar Eugene Robinson Papers, SC 29B, Green Library, Stanford University

IP   Yamato Ichihashi Papers, SC 71, Green Library, Stanford University

JERS   Japanese American Evacuation and Resettlement Records, Bancroft Library, University of California, Berkeley

PJT   Payson J. Treat Papers, Archives, Hoover Institution on War, Revolution and Peace, Stanford University

RLW   Ray Lyman Wilbur Presidential Papers, SC 64A, Green Library, Stanford University
These are to be distinguished from the Ray Lyman Wilbur Personal Papers, SC 64B, Green Library, which will be cited as Wilbur Personal Papers, and from the Ray Lyman Wilbur Papers at the Hoover Institution, which will be cited as Hoover Wilbur Papers.

WRA   Records of the War Relocation Authority, Record Group 210, National Archives, Suitland, Maryland

B   Box
F   Folder

A Note on Names and Transliteration

The names of individuals principally identified with Japan are rendered in traditional Japanese form, with family name first and given name second. The names of individuals of Japanese ancestry principally identified with the United States are rendered in Western style, with the given name first followed by the family name. Thus, Yamato Ichihashi's father's name is rendered as Ichihashi Hiromasa. In addition, I use macrons, or long marks, for the long vowel sound for Japanese names and words but not for the names of Japanese Americans, who did not regularly use such lexigraphy.

There is a related matter; a number of Japanese names that were transliterated into English were done so incorrectly. For example, in the papers of David Starr Jordan one can find references to a "Katzuzo Nakasawa," who worked in the Jordan home. The individual's given name probably should have been spelled "Katsuzo" and the surname spelled either "Nakazawa" or "Nagasawa." I did not attempt to correct these infelicities but have rendered names as they were given in the English-language documents.

The morning glory

Has stolen my well-sweep today

Gift-water, pray.

—Lady Chiyo (1703–75)

Morning Glory, Evening Shadow

Yamato Ichihashi and His Internment Writings, 1942-1945

Introduction

Several years ago, when I was collecting material on Asian Americans at Stanford, I came across the personal papers of Yamato Ichihashi in the university's manuscript collection. I was acquainted with Ichihashi's classic text on the early history of Japanese in the United States, published in 1932. Other than desultory disclosures of his personal life in the book, though, I knew little about the man himself. He had been a professor at Stanford, and his office was just down the hall from mine. (His office occupied an honored position on the second floor at the apex of the central quadrangle's "History Corner," with a bust of Leland Stanford just outside his window.) I also knew that he had written about a variety of subjects: the experience of Japanese in America, international relations in the Pacific, and Japanese government and civilization. I discovered that not much had been written about him, even though he had been one of the most prominent early intellectuals of Asian ancestry in the United States.

Exploring his papers further stimulated my curiosity, for I found that he had left a large amount of material documenting his life during World War II, when he and his wife, Okei, were forced to "evacuate" Stanford and join 120,000 other persons of Japanese ancestry in federal "relocation centers," the government euphemism for these prison camps. Ichihashi, 64 years old at the start of internment, knew the historical significance of the trials before him and decided, even before leaving the campus, that he would record his experiences in order one day to write an account of his life in wartime America. He never com-

pleted his project, however, and after his death in 1963, his family donated his papers to the Hoover Institution; they were later transferred
to Stanford University's Green Library. Packed in storage boxes for over
25 years, his correspondence with colleagues during the war, his research essays on relocation, and portions of his personal diaries lay virtually untouched. What an oversight! They form perhaps the richest
extant personal account of internment, yet, despite the considerable attention focused on the Japanese American experience during World
War II in recent years, no one had given them serious attention.

After surveying the papers, I decided for a variety of reasons—my
wish to honor his memory, the contribution his papers make to understanding internment history, the deeply poignant human story contained in his documents—that I would try to organize his papers and
present them in such a way that his long-unfinished account of internment would, in a sense, finally see the light of day. I would like to think
that Ichihashi, if he was with us today, would forgive my presumption.

Part II of this volume, the documentary section, consists of the
chronological presentation of material originally written by Yamato and
his wife, Okei (far fewer documents by Kei, as she was called, survive),
which describe in the first person their three-year incarceration in federal camps. Their story is, to the best of my knowledge, the only existing
contemporaneous account of an entire relocation experience. Although
much of the material published here was in Stanford's Ichihashi manuscript collection, more than half of it was found in the personal papers
of others, principally his Stanford colleagues, and in his personal diaries,
which had been retrieved from the papers donated to the Hoover Institution by family members concerned about matters of privacy. Thanks
to the thoughtfulness and generosity of the Ichihashis' son, Woodrow,
who has been most cooperative throughout this project, the diaries are
once again part of the Ichihashi papers at Stanford; significant portions
of them are published in Part II of this book. The Ichihashi material
covers the entire period from Yamato and Kei's departure from Stanford
in May 1942 to their return in April 1945. I have added extensive anno-
tation and editorial material to set the context, provide explanation (and
some interpretation), and help clarify the narrative.

In the documentary section I have organized the Ichihashi material,
which comprises different types of writing, into one chronological "personal narrative," to present what might be described as the first first-
person account of an individual's entire internment experience in English—and perhaps in any language.[1] I say "might be described" since I
recognize the constructed and interpretive character of this "narrative":
there is no question that if Ichihashi himself had published his own ac-

count, as he had once planned, the final result would have been very different. Based on the several "research essays" in his papers that appear to be draft sections of a manuscript, I assume that his work would have been a largely autobiographical account, with significant amounts of more "objective" sociological material included, a combination characteristic of much of his scholarly work.

The "narrative" presented in Part II has been reconstructed from a variety of materials. Yamato's writings include *correspondence* with close personal friends (it appears that Ichihashi intended to use at least portions of some letters in his manuscript); *research essays* evidently written for a future public audience; and *diaries* of a personal nature that were never intended for publication. Kei's correspondence, presumably, was also never meant to be published. I acknowledge that presenting these varied materials as a single chronological narrative may trouble some readers, who will question the liberties I have taken as compiler. My hope is that the juxtaposition of disparate materials will be seen as enabling rather than hindering understanding, by presenting the internment experience from several personal vantage points and levels of intimacy.

As fascinating as the wartime material is, however, I found the story of the rest of Ichihashi's life and career equally intriguing. Part I, therefore, consists of a two-part biographical essay on Yamato's life up to the outbreak of war in 1941. Following Part II is an Epilogue, which discusses the Ichihashis' lives after World War II until their deaths, Yamato's in 1963 and Kei's in 1970. Unfortunately, I was unable to construct a comparably detailed biography of Kei and have discussed her life largely in the context of her husband's experiences. Extant source material on Kei, an interesting person in her own right, is scarce.

In the biographical essay, I present an interpretation of Yamato Ichihashi's life and times, focusing on aspects of his personality and career that I believe especially relevant to readers today. In particular, I have focused on Ichihashi's experience as one of the first academics of Asian ancestry in the United States. He was also one of the first "Asian Americanists"—that is, a scholar interested in the experiences of Asian immigrants and their descendants in the United States. At the same time, Ichihashi was a historian of Japan and a specialist in international relations. Since I, too, have studied the histories of international relations and of Asian Americans, I found his life especially intriguing. Though I had not yet been born at the time of Ichihashi's incarceration and though I never met the man, I discovered that much in his life resonated with aspects of my own and that I identified with many of the challenges he faced.

In sum, then, what follows in this volume does not fall neatly into traditional categories of historical writing. It is not the edited and annotated diary of a single person, although diary entries are used extensively. It is also not a biography as such, although it begins with a long biographical essay. Finally, it is not an autobiography, even though Ichihashi's wartime story is presented largely in his own words. I hope the results will justify the invention of this hybrid genre.

This book joins a literature on Japanese American experiences during World War II and internment that is extensive, but curiously uneven and incomplete. In the decade following the war, a number of studies written by sociologists, historians, and officials involved in administering the camps presented perspectives on the politics and operations of the camps and observed experiences of the Japanese.[2] Few Japanese in those years put anything on paper expressing their own views of what had happened to them, and the published material often contained only meager insight into their own "felt experiences." Little more was written about relocation until the late 1960's, when a number of accounts severely criticized the relocation policy and the government's treatment of the Japanese. With one or two exceptions, these works were attempts by third parties to write from the viewpoint of the interned Japanese, rather than from the "detached," scholarly position taken in much of the earlier material. The studies produced during this time of social upheaval in the United States damned the camps as products of American racism and political opportunism, the treatment of the Japanese as brutal, and the consequences for Japanese Americans as profoundly damaging.[3]

With few exceptions, Japanese Americans themselves did not speak, let alone write, about their internment experiences in the three decades after the war; it was not until the 1980's that several books were published based on the memories of their lived experiences. It seems that the cushion of 30 years provided the detachment necessary for many to unburden themselves at last.[4] At the same time, the camps became the subject of research that explores particular issues in intellectual, legal, political, or social history.[5] Despite all this new material, a specialist in Japanese American history and the camps recently noted the surprising paucity of serious, systematic studies of the attitudes and experiences of the Japanese Americans themselves.[6]

This volume, it is hoped, will contribute to our understanding of the internment experience by providing vantage points previously unavailable. It is principally the story of one person, who happened to be a distinguished social scientist, a senior Stanford professor, one of the most eminent Japanese Americans of his day, fully literate in English and

Japanese, and thoroughly versed in both American and Japanese life and culture. Though obviously singular in many ways, Yamato Ichihashi had much in common with the tens of thousands of other Japanese who languished in the relocation camps throughout the war. He was an *issei*, a first-generation immigrant from Japan to America, and retained deep cultural and ethnic loyalties to his homeland, though not necessarily to all its politics and actions. Most published memoirs, oral histories, and constructed accounts of the relocation camp experience are heavily weighted toward the more "Americanized" viewpoint of the *nisei*, the second generation, born in the United States, which was not necessarily shared by the many thousands of issei in the camps, many of whom retained nationalistic sentiments toward Japan.[7] At the same time, Ichihashi had lived his entire adult life in this country and was intimately familiar with its society and ways. His life had prepared him to be a uniquely qualified recorder and interpreter of the internment drama.

Other features of his wartime writing make his account particularly valuable. His writing conveys to us, as no other account does, the cut and drift and anxiety of everyday life in the camps. Reading the material today, we gain a feeling for both the grinding tedium of daily life in camp and the ever-present uncertainty, suspicion, and even fear that permeated the internees' existence. The reader gains understanding, too, of the divisions, and sometimes violent conflicts, that beset Japanese Americans, notably Ichihashi, in ways both personal and public. He and his family did not escape camp pressures, and Ichihashi frequently found himself the center of unwanted and sometimes dangerous attention. The bitter fragmentation of Ichihashi's own family was itself inextricably connected to relocation. Yamato's obdurate refusal to accept his son's marriage irrevocably divided the family and was a source of agony for Kei for the rest of her life. The deeply personal distress suffered by the Ichihashis during the war seemed to be universal among internees, as we learn from Yamato's diaries.

Ichihashi's documentation of his many meetings and discussions with others in camp also introduces us to a wide variety of personalities and viewpoints of Japanese Americans and helps us see beyond what sometimes seems an undifferentiated and impersonal mass of people. We are introduced to George Danzuka, for example, who was living with his wife, a Native American, and their nine children on an Indian reservation in central Oregon when the relocation order came. He asked Ichihashi to help him find a way to return to his home, which was, after all, on federally controlled property. We also meet Kenneth Yasuda, a college student at the time and a lover of poetry. Ichihashi encouraged his interests, and Yasuda went on after the war to become a noted scholar of

Japanese literature and a playwright who composed, among other pieces, a tribute to Martin Luther King in the style of the traditional Japanese *noh* drama. One wonders about the connection between internment and Yasuda's sensitivity to racial injustice.

Ichihashi's wartime writing also portrays the several different institutions where he was incarcerated: the Santa Anita race track Assembly Center, the Tule Lake Relocation Center, the Sharp Park Immigration Detention facility, and the Amache Relocation Center in southeastern Colorado. He documents his encounters with administrators (including the director of the Tule Lake camp, who he discovered had been one of his students at Stanford) in all these facilities, and his private comments about their attitudes, policies, and treatment of the Japanese are especially telling in their candor.

Most of all, Ichihashi's account is distinguished by the immediacy of its observations. The mediating influence of intervening years or anticipated public audiences is minimal. In contrast, many other accounts of the relocation experience rely heavily on material generated after the event, sometimes decades later. Although oral history or autobiography can be a powerful and useful source, recollection is also selective and shaped by the passage of time. Many of those now telling us their stories were adolescents or young adults at the time of relocation. Ichihashi's account, one must keep in mind, was composed literally day by day as he, Kei, and the tens of thousands of other Japanese lived out their internment. They did not know what the next day would bring. They did not have decades in which to reflect on their experience and decide what was important to communicate to us, more than 50 years later. We can view relocation only in hindsight; the value of Ichihashi's record is that he had neither that burden nor, certainly, that luxury.

In addition, this volume, taken as a whole, should also speak to those interested in international history. Too frequently, the foreign relations of the United States are thought of as being "external," while matters such as "ethnic" history are "domestic" or "internal." Clearly, in speaking about the experience of Japanese Americans, and Asian Americans more generally, the international dimensions of the story are essential. Conversely, U.S. relations with other countries have often been profoundly affected by what happened within the formal borders of the country. Moreover, the history of international relations is often equated with diplomatic history, the account of the formal, political relations between nations. But the experience of nations and peoples with other nations and peoples obviously goes far beyond that of officials and diplomats. And the story of the interactions of countries, with consequences good and bad, cooperative and conflicting, is only partially understood by examining diplomacy and the exercise of power at the highest state levels. Yamato Ichihashi's life and thoughts help us to understand the often tortuous, frequently emotional, and at times tragic story of the more personal side of Japan-U.S. relations. It is a story that continues to be written today.

Parts I and II of this volume—the biography and the collected documents—can be read separately. Since the documentary section was annotated so it could be read and understood on its own, there is some duplication of material from Part I.

One final explanation before proceeding: the title of this volume. The Ichihashis, like many other Japanese, were fond of the morning glory plant. Propagated by seed, it is an annual vine that from early spring to autumn produces brilliantly colored blossoms that open wide in the early morning's light and then fade and shrivel in the afternoon warmth. It has been a favorite element in Japanese poetry, where it is used to suggest a variety of meanings. One uncharacteristically cheery poem entitled "Morning Glories" goes

> In the dewy freshness of the morning,
> They smile respectful greetings
> To the goddess of the Sun.[8]

More often, the flower symbolizes the fragile beauty and transitory nature of life. But there is another side to the morning glory. As a vine, it is tenacious and hardy; it sprouts rapidly and is adaptable. It has even been used as a metaphor for the Japanese navy.[9] "Japanese people love flowers for what they mean," wrote an early Japanese American author favored by Kei Ichihashi.[10]

The Ichihashis, like many others in the camps, planted morning glory seeds, and the flower became one of their favorites. Accounts and photographs of gardens Japanese internees cultivated around their barracks include morning glories in abundance. At Amache, where the Ichihashis lived, trees the internees planted were "morning-glorified," set off "by masses and banks of brilliant blue morning-glories."[11] The Ichihashis continued to raise them once they returned to Stanford. The morning glory was also the subject of one of Yamato Ichihashi's favorite poems, the epigraph for this volume, which he used in essays and lectures.[12]

The morning glory, then, may suggest the fleeting, tragic quality of life or brilliant success followed by unhappy decline, as does the epigraph to Part I.[13] It may also represent the tenacity of the human spirit. Contradictory meanings, perhaps, but in their interpretive ambiguity, they may in fact properly capture the quixotic quality of Ichihashi's profoundly conflicted and enigmatic life, as the reader will see in the following pages. Finally, in the evening the morning glory, unlike most flowering plants, displays no colorful blossoms but fades into obscurity. So too did Ichihashi's life in its evening, as the shadow of internment lay across his final years.

In a morning glory

today I seem to see

—my life, alas.

      —Moritake (1473–1549)

Yamato Ichihashi: A Biographical Essay

"A Man of Whom the University Can Be Proud"

Soon after he returned to his home on the Stanford campus in April 1945, after having been forced to spend three years in federal relocation centers, Yamato Ichihashi informed an old friend who, like himself, was a specialist in international relations, that he hoped "to write a history of the evacuation of Japanese from the West Coast states." He said he planned to draw from his own personal experiences to tell the story.[1] Ichihashi had gathered extensive research materials and recorded what had happened to him in detail from the moment of his ordered "evacuation"[2] from the Stanford area in the spring of 1942 to his return three years later. He had realized the drama that lay ahead of him—and the other 120,000 persons of Japanese ancestry incarcerated by the United States government a few months after the attack on Pearl Harbor—

would be a story of deep historical significance, and he understood that he was in a unique position to record that history.

Yamato Ichihashi in 1941, when the United States entered the war in the Pacific, was one of the best-known, certainly one of the most eminent, Japanese in the country. At a time when the Japanese American population was overwhelmingly rural, with a minuscule business and professional class, Ichihashi was a distinguished 64-year-old professor of history at Stanford University who had over 30 years built an international reputation as an authority on Japanese history and United States–East Asian relations. He had published respected books and scores of articles and reviews about Japan and East Asian security issues, written both in English and in Japanese. (See the listing in the Appendix.)

For some reason, however, Ichihashi never completed his project on relocation, and his accumulated research materials and draft essays languished in his files. Perhaps he was too embittered by his wartime experiences, public and personal, to reopen them through his writing; or perhaps those arduous years had simply worn him down and made him unable to concentrate on sustained scholarly work. He left no clue as to his reason. He published virtually nothing during the last twenty years of his life, after the internment, slipping into inactivity in his home near the center of the Stanford campus.

Ichihashi was a man of many and sometimes contradictory facets. There is an enigmatic quality about him as well. None of his contemporaries claimed to know him well. He was a pioneer in American academia, being one of the first professors of Japanese ancestry in the United States and an early specialist in United States–East Asian relations; but he was far from modern in many of his views of life, which tended to the Victorian, and in his formal politics, which were moderate to conservative even by the standards of his day. He was a lifelong critic of discrimination against Japanese and was one of the first specialists in what is now called Asian American studies. But his friendships were almost exclusively with whites on the Stanford campus, and in his adult life he increasingly shut himself off from the Japanese community. He claimed to be devoting himself to humanistic scholarship and service to his fellow Japanese in America; yet he privately developed an arrogant disdain for them and their plebeian ways even before the war years forced him into uncomfortable contact with those "undisciplined rustics." He prided himself on being an "objective" social scientist and an opponent of racial prejudice; but he was chauvinistic toward other Asians and became a virtual apologist for Japan's imperialism in Asia in the immediate prewar years. He was a moralist who constantly berated parents in the relocation camps for providing insufficient nurturing and guidance to their children; yet his own marriage and family life were difficult and unhappy. There was even a suggestion of a sexual scandal just before the war. And Ichihashi virtually ended all contact with his only child after Woodrow's 1943 marriage to a woman Ichihashi disapproved of, and to his dying day in 1963 he refused to meet his own grandchildren.

For his contemporaries, Ichihashi was not a completely admirable or easily likable man—he was often seen as stiff, self-centered, officious. But he was also known to have been charming on many occasions, a popular teacher, and giving of himself during the internment ordeal. Moreover, he did have an acute sense of the historical importance of much that he personally experienced throughout his life. And because of this sensitivity, he left a remarkable, even singular legacy. His writing and research on the early history of Japanese in America remain invaluable and indispensable in their detail, quality, and firsthand observations, and they continue to be cited by scholars.[3] The constructed chronicle of his life during wartime, Part II of this volume, is the only first-person, contemporaneous record of an individual's entire relocation experience that exists in any language.[4]

Yamato Ichihashi left a unique intellectual and personal legacy, but his life story has been largely neglected.[5] Even though he had occupied the very first endowed chair at Stanford, was one of the longest-serving faculty members in the history of the university, had been acting chairman of the History Department, and became the department's second professor emeritus, the Stanford community had nearly forgotten him by the 1990's. The reasons for his lapse into historical obscurity appear evident. For those interested in the mainstream of American intellectual and academic life, his work seemed marginal. East Asian studies and U.S.–East Asian relations remain esoteric and specialized subjects for many in American universities, as is the study of early Japanese immigrants. At the same time, for the growing number of persons interested in the minority experience in America, and in particular in the everyday experience of Japanese Americans, Ichihashi's life as a Stanford social scientist appeared atypical, disconnected from that of the Japanese community. Moreover, the relatively young field of Asian American studies, which has been dominated by the "new social history" with its focus on the lives of the "voiceless," has yet to examine the intellectual history of Asian Americans.

But Yamato Ichihashi's life has been overlooked for other, perhaps less obvious reasons. The study of race relations in the United States and racial minority experiences has been principally concerned with black-white relations and Americans of African descent. The lives of other minorities have not attracted as much attention, nor do they easily fit the prevailing paradigms about race developed from the examination of black-white interaction. And when they are included, most writers have looked for the "representative" experience or the "ethnic" leader.[6] Ichihashi's life does not fall neatly into either of these categories.

Ichihashi was an unusual person. He may have been Stanford's first nonwhite professor. This alone would make him a figure of historical interest; but there is more to him than that. He was a man who felt oddly out of place wherever he was. He was neither fully Japanese nor American, an uncomfortable condition he grappled with his entire life. And he faced other identity contradictions—personal, professional, political, moral. In many ways, he can be said to be a "postmodern" figure, one who does not conform to an accepted, defined national historical pattern. Seen in this way, perhaps he is more akin to the "trans-Pacific" population, whose numbers have grown steadily in this century as the putative Asia-Pacific region has become increasingly integrated in human, political, and economic terms. His life dilemmas, the ambiguities in his identities, his conflicts with the world around him, the circumstances of his joys and sorrows—examining all these offers an intriguing vantage point to understand previously obscured corners of the past, as well as aspects of a disorienting present where many set notions of racial and national identity are eroding.

Yamato Ichihashi's family background and childhood in Japan are difficult to reconstruct, in part because Ichihashi himself deliberately obscured important details of his early life for reasons about which one can only speculate. According to family registry records in Japan and his own later listings, Yamato Ichihashi was born in the city of Nagoya, Aichi prefecture, in central Honshu, the main island of Japan, on April 15, 1878, to Ichihashi Hiromasa (d. 1927) and Mizuno Ai (d. 1925). He was their third son. The shipboard manifest for his landing in America in 1894 lists him as sixteen years old, which would be correct for an 1878 birth date. Although I believe 1878 to be correct, other documents that he later completed, including his application to Stanford, show different years for his birth, variously 1882, 1883, or 1884.[7] All these dates, of course, make him out to be several years younger than he actually was. Such a claim might have been quite useful when there was outcry on the West Coast against Japanese male students being considerably older than their white public school classmates, especially the women. Many years later, when Ichihashi had retired, his inconsistently listed birth dates even generated problems for the funders of his pension.[8]

His father's predecessors included retainers to the nobility of the strategically located Owari domain, part of the region under the Tokugawa family that dominated feudal Japan. His family is registered in Japan as being from the "samurai class." The exact occupation of his father, though, is not altogether clear: according to various sources, he was a former samurai who had turned to teaching martial arts with the decline of the aristocracy after the Meiji Restoration of 1868, a tax collector, or a schoolworker. Whatever the case, it seems the family was somewhere between poor and well-to-do. But it was the aristocratic lineage that Ichihashi proudly invoked throughout his life to friends and family and that seemed fundamental both to his own sense of self-importance and to his acute sensitivity to personal and racial slights.[9]

The official family registry in Japan lists eight siblings for Yamato Ichihashi, and his son recalls conversations about several uncles. In registration forms the United States government required him to complete in relocation camp, however, Ichihashi named only a younger sister, Shizuko, a graduate of Palo Alto High School and Stanford, who later became secretary to the president of Tokyo University, and a brother, Akira, who was described as a schoolteacher. Ichihashi did not include the names of brothers who were military officers, no doubt suspecting that the information would attract unwanted attention during the war. In fact, however, the FBI knew of his family connections to the Japanese military.[10]

He attended public school in Nagoya and arrived in the United States on September 5, 1894, on board the ship *Belgic*, entering through the port of San Francisco. In a sketchy and incomplete autobiographical note probably written before World War II, he described himself as a "sickly young man" who had originally come to the United States for health reasons on the advice of his parents and family doctor. This draft autobiography claimed that he had planned to stay for only a year, but, in his words, he "became so well under the beautiful climate of sunny California" that he began to attend school here instead of returning to Japan. While he did have a weak constitution—he complained of illnesses throughout his life—he actually entered the United States on a student visa and his arrival card shows that he could read and write.[11] On the other hand, a confidential investigatory biography of Ichihashi compiled by the FBI in 1942 described him as having graduated from high school in Japan, applying for entry into the Japanese Naval Academy but failing the medical examination, and coming to the United States for his health.[12]

Other evidence suggests another possible version of the emigration story. His 1932 book on Japanese in America contains a passage that describes how many early Japanese immigrants first became aware of and attracted to the United States. It may have been autobiographical, at least in part, for himself or a brother who had preceded him to the United States. Ichihashi wrote that many young men from Japan were inspired by emigrant stories of economic opportunity in America, so-called "golden stories," and that one individual, Miyama Kan'ichi, was especially influential.[13] Miyama was

> a well-known student-immigrant among early Japanese residents in California, [who] returned to Japan in 1885 and visited many places in that country telling young men what splendid opportunities for education were open to them in the United States. . . . As a result of [this and other campaigns], hundreds of young Japanese emigrated to this country. These we know as Japanese "school-boys," who worked mornings and evenings in order to attend school in the daytime.[14]

In 1877, Miyama helped found the Japanese Gospel Society, or Nihonjin Fukuinkai, the first Japanese immigrant group in San Francisco; he also formed branches of the group in Japan to help prospective emigrants. According to Gospel Society records, one Ichihashi Shun'nosuke (b. 1871), Yamato's eldest brother, joined the Gospel Society around 1894 and studied in Palo Alto in 1895–96. It is not clear why Shun'nosuke came to the United States or went to Palo Alto, or what subsequently happened to him. Yamato Ichihashi is listed as a member of the Gospel Society in 1896, and his draft autobiography mentions that he joined an older brother here in America.[15]

Whatever the particular circumstances surrounding his emigration, in 1896 Ichihashi began to attend Adams Cosmopolitan Grammar School, located at Van Ness and Polk streets in the center of San Francisco; he stayed for three years. His school records show him as having lived at 725 Geary Street, with a Mrs. W. A. Douglas as his guardian.[16] Mrs. Douglas must have considered her ward something of a curiosity. Few other Japanese were here at that time—in 1890 there were some 2,500 Japanese in the entire United States, about half of them in California. Forming the first wave of Japanese immigration, most of these early immigrants came from small business or farming families in Japan and hoped to learn enough English and an occupational skill to embark on a more promising career upon their return to Japan. The several hundred Japanese in San Francisco in the late 1880's were, like Ichihashi, so-called student-laborers, who worked part-time and attended school part-time.[17]

During the years of Ichihashi's residence in San Francisco, the city saw a rapid growth in anti-Japanese sentiment and became the center of anti-Japanese agitation in the United States. Years later, in his Harvard doctoral dissertation, Ichihashi recalled the hostility toward Japanese, including some specific incidents while he was in school. He cited two dramatic anti-Japanese incidents that occurred in 1899 (the year was actually 1900): the first confrontation arose because many whites blamed the Asian residents of San Francisco, both Japanese and Chinese, for the outbreak of bubonic plague in the city; the second was an anti-Japanese rally called by organized labor groups.[18] At this rally James D. Phelan, the mayor of San Francisco, Edward A. Ross, a well-known sociologist from Stanford, and several labor leaders called for the exclusion of Japanese from America because of their alleged competition with white workers for jobs. From 1901–10, approximately 55,000 Japanese were admitted into the United States; most were laborers, not students, as they had been in the first years of immigration. But there was also a clear element of racial animosity in the San Francisco anti-Japanese agitation. Phelan's view was blunt: "The Chinese and Japanese are not bona fide citizens. They are not the stuff of which American citizens can be made." Ichihashi recalled that the agitators even demanded the expulsion of Japanese children from the public schools. "I was then one of the grammar school pupils and stayed out of the school, sensitive of humiliation and fearing possible violence."[19]

Despite the intimidation, the young Ichihashi persisted in his studies and became one of the most distinguished of these early immigrant students: he performed well enough to attend San Francisco's prestigious Lowell High School, entering in 1899 and graduating in June 1902 with a fine record in a college-preparatory course of study that included Latin and Greek. He applied to Stanford and was accepted for a fall 1903 matriculation date.[20]

Founded by Leland and Jane Stanford in 1891, the university had already established itself as a major institution of higher learning in the western region of the United States. Leland Stanford, railroad baron and former governor of California and U.S. senator, liberally donated money to attract a strong faculty and built a handsome campus on 9,000 acres of land he owned amidst farms and ranches 40 miles south of San Francisco, adjoining the towns of Mayfield and Palo Alto. From its beginning, the university's leaders had high aspirations for its future and were "world-minded," according to Ray Lyman Wilbur, who served as Stanford's third president from 1916 to 1943. He attributed the university's broad vision to the fact that from the start, in his telling words, "it was made up of cosmopolitan people—from the Founders and the president down through the faculty and students to the Chinese cooks and the Japanese houseboys."[21]

It is not known how or why Ichihashi first became interested in

Stanford, but he may have heard about the school even before he left Japan. The university had quickly established a positive reputation there thanks, at least in part, to the direct efforts of its first president, David Starr Jordan, who had come from Indiana University. As an ichthyologist, he had conducted research in Japanese waters and had made many friends in the academic and business communities there. He developed a strong fondness for the country and its people. Japanese students were among the members of Stanford's inaugural class in 1891, and they continued to form an important part of the Stanford community up through the years before World War II.

But the university in these early years was not an altogether welcoming place for Asians. Sociologist Ross, who had arrived at Stanford in 1893, was an outspoken "socialist" who attacked capitalists and Orientals with equal vehemence. He feared the "fecundity of Oriental races," whom he believed had to be kept out of California, if necessary by violence. His 1900 tirade in San Francisco, which Ichihashi recalled in his doctoral dissertation, so provoked Jane Stanford that she, fearing his radicalism and politics, had him fired from the university. His dismissal became a *cause célèbre* in academia, overshadowing the memory of his Japanophobia.[22]

Chinese and Japanese were in evidence at the university from the start. They worked as ranchhands on Leland Stanford's estate, as custodians in the dormitories, and as cooks in faculty homes and in dormitories. There was even a Chinese restaurant set up in the center of the school to feed workmen and students following the 1906 earthquake, which destroyed much of the campus. But Asians as workers and as students were two very different social phenomena. In 1916, white students at Encina Hall, the dormitory for men, refused admittance to a Chinese student, establishing the widespread belief for many years that Asians were not allowed in university housing. As a consequence, the Chinese and Japanese communities in the vicinity raised funds to establish the Chinese Clubhouse and the Japanese Clubhouse as residences for their respective students, American and foreign-born alike.[23]

Ichihashi later wrote that he "enjoyed a congenial life" at Stanford, but his transcript shows that he struggled through his four years of study. His initial grades were mediocre, mainly Bs and Cs, and even a few Ds. Not until his senior year did he finally receive a couple of As. His major was economics, which he thought would lead to an attractive career back in Japan, and he graduated with a bachelor's degree in May 1907 at the age of 29 (although Stanford believed he was no more than 24).

Columbia University rejected Ichihashi's application for graduate work, but he was accepted into the master's program in economics at

Stanford. The record of his work for a master's degree, including the course "Economic Factors in Civilization" with the famous social theorist Thorstein Veblen, was considerably stronger than for his undergraduate years, and he received his master's degree in a year. His record was deemed good enough to have him voted into the Phi Beta Kappa honor society. The austere Ichihashi probably found himself in much intellectual agreement with Veblen, author of *Theory of the Leisure Class*, which sharply criticized the extravagant consumption and waste of America's business elite.[24]

About this time, Ichihashi's younger sister, Shizuko (b. 1884), came from Japan for her own education. She attended Palo Alto High School from 1907 to 1911 and then entered Stanford, graduating with a degree in botany in 1916. She was the first Japanese woman to graduate from Stanford. Ichihashi served as guardian for his sister during her stay in the United States. After working for a few years, she returned to Japan around 1920. Ichihashi remained close to her throughout his life; with his brothers, he had almost no contact.[25]

At Stanford, Ichihashi undoubtedly passed easily as younger than his actual 29 years. He was small in stature, no more than 5 feet 4 inches, and he weighed less than 125 pounds. His face was broad and long, with prominent features and a serious expression. According to professors who worked with him, he had a pleasant and attractive disposition and was described as outgoing and friendly. His English writing ability was virtually as good as that of a native speaker.

During his undergraduate years at Stanford, Ichihashi had drawn the attention of President Jordan, who was keenly interested in linking the young university on the Pacific Coast with Asia, particularly with Japan, which, in his eyes, was fast becoming a country of major importance for America. Jordan was a social Darwinist, as were many intellectuals in his day, and assumed without question both the existence of a racial hierarchy of humanity, with the "white races" at the pinnacle, and the value of eugenics, the study of ways to improve alleged racial characteristics. Even though the Japanese, while "colored," were industrializing and modernizing their country in the late nineteenth century, their self-strengthening achievements did not undermine Jordan's beliefs about race and human civilization. Just the opposite: the Japanese had been successful, he believed, because they were not genuine Orientals but, in fact, had "white blood" in them and were thus a race superior to other peoples of color. As president of Stanford, Jordan once wrote publicly that he understood that the Japanese had nothing in common linguistically or racially with the Koreans and Chinese, the latter having affinities with the people of Mongolia, "from which region the Huns once swarmed through what is now Austria and Hungary." In his view, the origins of the Japanese were very different.

> The earliest records, bits of statuary and the like in Japan, represent a white people. These supposititious white people are called in Japanese, Yamato, which I suppose means mountaineer. They were characterized by light complexion, long faces, slender and wiry build. This type is now represented largely among the upper classes and the student classes of Japan. . . .
>   It is thought by many that the Yamato Japanese were derived from the races of the country of the Euphrates, allied therefore to Persians and to the people of the old civilization of Baghdad and Ninevah. This is not proved, but probable.[26]

At the same time, Jordan was liberal in his thinking on many other social and international issues of the day. He was an anti-imperialist and opposed the virulent anti-Japanese campaigns in California on the grounds they were unfair to the Japanese and detrimental to American interests in Asia. Agitation on racial issues seemed to rankle the personal sensitivities of the educator, too: racial discrimination was contrary to America's civilization. He once argued, "this is the white man's country but it is a gentlemen's country first." He thought quiet diplomacy with Japan, not remonstration against and persecution of its citizens here, was the way to keep large numbers of Japanese from entering the country.[27]

At the university, Jordan personally promoted the careers of many Japanese students, the most prominent being Ichihashi, who had come to Jordan's attention as a result of his leadership activities among the international students on campus. Ichihashi had been founder and president of the Cosmopolitan Club, an organization of students primarily from countries other than the United States. By his senior year, Ichihashi and Jordan had forged a close disciple-mentor relationship, and the two periodically visited in person as well as corresponding. Once they even spoke together at a public forum in Palo Alto condemning racial prejudice. Jordan took an active interest in shaping the young man's life, while Ichihashi was only too happy to have the attention and backing of such an eminent man. On his part, Ichihashi actively helped Jordan better understand Japan and the Japanese people, even serving as an interpreter for the university president on several occasions and translating some of Jordan's articles—scientific and social commentary—for publication in Japanese. Jordan was especially important in influencing the young Ichihashi to see the possibilities of devoting his life to the advancement of U.S.-Japan relations, which included helping to enhance the American public's knowledge of Japan and of the Japanese in America.[28]

Ichihashi's first published article, written just after he received his bachelor's degree, displayed these interests. *The Outlook*, an influential national weekly journal with a liberal Christian orientation, published Ichihashi's "Japanese Students in America" in October 1907. It was a racially charged time, but *The Outlook* had published controversial articles on race issues before, including several by W. E. B. Du Bois.[29]

These years following the end of the Russo-Japanese War of 1905 witnessed a surge in anti-Japanese sentiment in the United States. The Japanese victory over Russia inspired fears of Japanese power in the Pacific and of their influence even in California. The *San Francisco Chronicle* declared in November 1906, "The Japanese who come here remain Japanese. Their loyalty is to the Japanese Emperor. Every one of them, so far as his service is desired, is a Japanese spy."[30] Just the month before, the San Francisco School Board had decided to segregate Japanese students along with the Chinese, who were already forced to attend a separate school away from white pupils. The decision helped ignite an international crisis that was ultimately resolved only by the intervention of President Theodore Roosevelt. After months of wrangling in 1907 and 1908, Washington and Tokyo concluded the Gentlemen's Agreement whereby San Francisco dropped its segregation order and Japan agreed to stop issuing passports to Japanese laborers who wanted to come to the continental United States. Japanese immigration dropped dramatically. Diplomatic historian Thomas A. Bailey noted that tensions between the United States and Japan had risen to such a degree from 1906 to 1909 that, in a half-dozen or so situations, "under different circumstances and treatment" they could "easily have resulted in war."[31]

In his article, which *The Outlook* prominently advertised on its cover, Ichihashi spoke for his fellow Japanese students in America against what he believed were prejudices and hostility rooted in ignorance. Japanese students came to the United States, Ichihashi explained, for technical training but also "discovered in America opportunity for character-building." Japanese students learned not just skills but American values and civilization, which Ichihashi warmly praised. And once the students returned to Japan ("Of course we go back to Japan. There we are citizens; here we are refused citizenship"), they used the knowledge and experience gained in America for their country, but as "the faithful friend of the United States." They had paid their own way and deprived America of none of its own riches, he pointed out. Lastly, it was not only Japan that felt the positive effect of American education through the returned students, but the whole of Asia, since, "it is the mission of Japan to bring the East and West into harmony." A close and friendly relationship between Japan, the country of his ancestry, and the United States, the country for which he developed a genuine and profound admiration, should and therefore could be truly mutually beneficial.[32]

Jordan had helped Ichihashi get his essay published, and he urged Ichihashi to continue writing in the same vein to help educate Americans about aspects of life in Japan. Jordan suggested Ichihashi write an article about the Japanese educational system and then helped Ichihashi with the submission of an essay about Japanese women. The article on women was never published, but as a result of these promptings, the encouragement of other Stanford professors, notably Allyn A. Young, chair of the Economics Department, and the positive response he received from this work, Ichihashi began to see the possibility of a life in academia. He decided that he wanted to pursue a doctoral degree, somewhere in the eastern United States. "I am convinced," he wrote Jordan in the spring of 1908, that with proper training, "I shall be able to help in bringing about a better understanding between the West and East. Such is the object of my life."[33]

To help Ichihashi before he found a place to continue his education, Allyn Young hired him as a research and teaching assistant in the Economics Department. About the same time, Harry Alvin Millis,[34] also of the Stanford Economics Department, hired Ichihashi as a research assistant. Millis was engaged in research for the Congressional Joint Commission on Immigration, known popularly as the U.S. Immigration Commission. Congress had established the body in 1907 to complete a comprehensive study of immigration to the United States and the living and working conditions of recent immigrants. The Commission planned to present its extensive findings and policy recommendations to Congress in 42 volumes in late 1910.[35]

Later in his career, Ichihashi claimed that he had worked as a "special agent" for the Commission and that his responsibility "as its agent was to look into the Japanese immigration situation" in California.[36] In his work, Ichihashi had the valuable opportunity to study firsthand the local conditions of most of the Japanese communities in California as well as the census and other statistical records, but the historical record is unclear on whether he actually worked for the Commission or was simply one of Millis's personal assistants. The *Official Register of the United States*, which lists military and civilian personnel of the federal government for this period, does not include Ichihashi's name.[37] Ichihashi also worked for Wesley Claire Mitchell, a political economist at the University of California, Berkeley, who was head of the Immigration Commission's investigations in the western region.[38]

His work for the Commission lasted two years, which gave him an extraordinary opportunity to conduct fieldwork among the Japanese in California. As he later wrote, in these years he "personally investigated practically all the important Japanese activities in all the important places including such cities as San Francisco, Los Angeles, Sacramento and Watsonville, and such rural districts as the valleys of the Sacramento, San Joaquin and the Pajaro and Santa Clara Valley and Vaca Valley." He visited Japanese fishermen in Monterey, sugar beet farmers in Salinas, and "the vineyards of Fresno and potato and asparagus fields of Stockton."[39] Such travels provided him with insights into the conditions of life for the Japanese in California that few, if any, could match. His manuscript collection contains notes and reports from these field trips.

Although Ichihashi failed in an attempt to enter the doctoral program at the University of Wisconsin, by the spring of 1910 his efforts were rewarded by acceptance into the doctoral program of Harvard's Graduate School of Arts and Sciences. Deeply grateful for the support of David Starr Jordan and professing personal loyalty, a stance he would take throughout his life in his relations with influential sponsors, Ichihashi wrote the Stanford president shortly before leaving California: "I shall never forget what you and Stanford have done for me. You will be the source of my inspiration as long as [I] live. I shall try to be a useful man. Yours very affectionately, Yamato Ichihashi."[40]

Ichihashi moved to Cambridge in the fall of 1910 and for the next two years pursued course work principally in economics, which at the time included aspects of history, sociology, and politics. His main adviser was William Z. Ripley, a professor of political economy and specialist in management and industrial organization, especially railroads. Ripley took a liking to Ichihashi, who did so well in his first year's course work that Harvard awarded him the prestigious H. B. Rogers Memorial Fellowship, which W. E. B. Du Bois had held when he was a student at Harvard in 1891. "Mr. Ichihashi is highly thought of by the Department," the chairman of the Economics Department and proponent of laissez-faire and free trade theories, Frank William Taussig, stated in the recommendation letter to his academic dean. ("I was rather surprised at the appointment," Ichihashi wrote Jordan, "for I learned that the competition for it was very keen.") Frederick Jackson Turner, the famous historian who studied the American West and the influence of "the frontier" on American civilization, along with Ripley and Thomas Nixon Carver, formed Ichihashi's dissertation committee. Turner had just moved from Wisconsin to Harvard and had little contact with Ichihashi. Ichihashi's interest in the influence of the Far East—especially the immigration of its people—on the West complemented Turner's focus on the movement of Euro-American peoples from the east coast across the continent.[41]

In this pre–World War I heyday of Western nationalism and interest in big power politics, many at Harvard, like much of American academia, were concerned with race, national character, and nation formation. Ichihashi probably found the Harvard environment both stimulating and congenial to his own scholarly sensibilities, which were themselves highly political and proudly nationalistic. But he may also have been troubled by the prevailing assumptions of scientific racism, which assumed a biologically based racial hierarchy of humanity. Ichihashi's own dissenting views were akin to those of Franz Boas, an anthropologist at Columbia who had also worked for the Immigration Commission, studying immigrants in New York City. Boas argued that history and culture, not biology, formed the critical element in understanding differences between the races. Though busy with his studies, Ichihashi still found time to involve himself in the anti-imperialist movement in which Jordan played a prominent role and maintained active contact with his mentor. In late 1911, Ichihashi consented to act as an interpreter for a man named Shimada, a leader of the peace movement in Japan, during his speaking tour of the United States.[42]

By early 1912, Ichihashi had completed his course work, passed his qualifying examinations, and had got "all that I wanted" from Harvard, as he wrote Jordan. The ambitious Ichihashi boldly asked his longtime benefactor whether Stanford might not consider hiring him to teach a course in Japanese civilization and another one in sociology? He was not asking for a permanent position, he said, nor was he "particular about rank or salary so long as I get an opportunity to teach and [earn] a living," so he could support himself while completing his doctoral dissertation. The degree was important to him, of course. He told Jordan that if he was to remain in the United States, as he was encouraged to do by two of his former Stanford professors, he needed to establish himself as a scholar *before* becoming a permanent teacher. He had seen too many others begin work before they were qualified. Moreover, "I am a Japanese and must, therefore, be above the average." He hoped that his failure up to that point to obtain a permanent position in the United States had not had anything to do with his race.[43]

Once again, good fortune seemed to come Ichihashi's way. Jordan immediately responded to Ichihashi: "I would advise that you plan to return here," he wrote from Stanford. He made no specific promises to Ichihashi, but he informed Millis of his wish to have the Economics Department employ Ichihashi. Ichihashi also knew that Jordan, during a summer 1911 trip to Japan, had interested prominent Japanese business-men in the possibility of funding a permanently endowed chair in Japa-nese studies for Stanford. Ichihashi had hoped to accompany Jordan on the trip as a guide and interpreter, but the money had failed to materi-alize. Nevertheless, Jordan informed Ichihashi that he, Jordan, had his protégé in mind for the possible endowed position. Ichihashi also knew that Millis had been working simultaneously with Japanese merchants in San Francisco to fund a position in the Economics Department for a specialist in economic conditions in Asia. Thus in the late summer of 1912, Ichihashi left his Oxford Street home near Harvard and moved back to a rooming house at 1804 Sutter Street, in the familiar surround-ings of the Japanese quarter in San Francisco, eagerly anticipating that he would soon assume a position at Stanford University.[44]

By the fall, however, no progress had been made on the endowment from Japan, and Ichihashi concluded that his prospects for staying in the United States had died. Dejectedly, he informed Jordan, "I shall have to return to Japan. I have no aspiration other than an academic career, but it is denied me here in America because I am a Japanese. America is evidently no place for educated Japanese. Thus though it is against my will, I am compelled to go home." He asked Jordan for letters of intro-duction and recommendations to "prominent men" in Japan for a posi-tion in a university or even in business. "It does not really matter what kind of work I am to do, so long as it affords me a living and a leisure. I expect to devote my life to scholarship."[45]

The effusive praise for Ichihashi in the many letters Jordan sent to Japan reveal the extraordinarily high regard in which he held him. Ichi-hashi, Jordan wrote to Baron Iwasaki, the head of the Mitsubishi Com-pany and one of the wealthiest men in Japan, "is one of the best students with whom I have ever come in contact" and was well qualified for "a professorship in any university." Jordan wrote that Stanford had hoped that Ichihashi would be able to stay to "receive an endowment as a Pro-fessor [of] Japanese History and Ideals." Jordan concluded a letter to the secretary of the Bankers' Association in Tokyo with the comment that Ichihashi "is a man of whom Stanford has a right to be proud and we hope Japan also."[46]

Ichihashi, as it turned out, did not return to his native land but re-mained in San Francisco, where he entered one of the most productive periods in his life. While he continued to write his doctoral thesis for Harvard in absentia, he also became active in the Northern Califor-nia Japanese community, motivated by his distress over the ugly anti-Japanese mood in the state. Commissioned by the Japanese Association of America, a federation of local Japanese immigrant societies in California (and closely associated with Japan's Foreign Ministry), Ichihashi published in May 1913 a widely distributed and influential booklet entitled, *Japanese Immigration: Its Status in California*, with an introduction by David Starr Jordan certifying the author's credentials and abilities. Another essay, "The California Alien Land Law," was published in *The American Citizen*, which called itself "a national magazine of protest against prejudice and injustice." Ichihashi's articles aimed to correct distorted and prejudiced notions about the Japanese, argued the case for their assimilability and worthiness to live in America, and criticized the anti-Japanese movement as inhuman, contrary to American democratic principles, and injurious to America's own self-interest. The *San Francisco Chronicle* ran an article about the pamphlet just after its publication, and then a week later printed virtually the entire piece as an advertisement.[47] A 1915 expanded version of the piece was widely distributed, and California newspaper reviews described it as "unbiased" and "valuable."[48]

The two pieces are very different: the booklet is judicious, claims objectivity, and relies on statistical evidence to argue that the Japanese were certainly no worse, and in many ways were considerably better, than other immigrants in education, wages, acquisition of English, and other measures. The *American Citizen* essay, on the other hand, exhibits a dramatic flair and appeals to the American heart. The Japanese in America, Ichihashi wrote in this article, would not be daunted by the passage of the 1913 Alien Land Law that aimed to prohibit Asian aliens (in particular Japanese) from owning land in California. "We [Japanese] can assure America that we shall not and will not remain menial laborers forever because we are Japanese. We are a part of humanity. Humanity demands that we should struggle to rise." California's legislators, Ichihashi concluded, may want to keep the Japanese down, "but the people of California and the United States demand that we shall not be slaves." He argued that the Japanese should be treated no differently than any other immigrant group and should be accorded the right to naturalization.

In addition to his scholarship and writing for the popular press, Ichihashi also scrambled to create employment for himself at Stanford. This was not an easy task, for he had not only to sustain the attention of the administration at Stanford, where President Jordan had announced in the spring of 1913 his intention to step down, but also to cultivate close ties with Japanese officials in San Francisco who were central to locating Japanese funding for the proposed position at Stanford. Fortunately for Ichihashi, Tokyo at that moment was deeply troubled by the continuing anti-Japanese sentiment on the West Coast, and though such sentiment was directed immediately against her emigrants, the Japanese government feared wider consequences. Troubled by the rivalry with European powers over the division of East Asia, Tokyo had made the forging of amicable relations with the United States a priority in its foreign policy. Therefore in May 1913, the Japanese government launched a campaign to improve popular understanding of Japan and Japanese immigrants in America. Establishing professorships in Japanese studies was one way of achieving this goal, and Ichihashi was to be a direct beneficiary of this effort.[49]

On May 19, 1913, California Governor Hiram Johnson signed the so-called Alien Land Act passed by the legislature earlier that month. Japanese owned only about 30,000 acres of California land in 1913, but their success in farming had raised concern among white competitors. The land bill prohibited "aliens ineligible for citizenship," which included Japanese and Chinese immigrants, from purchasing agricultural land and drastically limited other land rights as well. In a letter dated the very next day, the Japanese consul in San Francisco, Numano Yasutarō, informed Jordan that a group of Japanese businessmen were willing to donate money to cover the salary and book expenses of an instructor in Japanese history and government at Stanford for a one-year trial period. University officials believed the gift to be the product of several years' fund-raising efforts spearheaded by Jordan toward that specific end; but the timing of the gift and the immediate political situation were undoubtedly important as well. Numano informed Jordan that donors represented by executives of the Oriental Steamship Company (Toyo Kisen Kaisha) and the Yokohama Specie Bank had donated the money; in fact, however, the funds, totaling $1,400, appear to have come from the Japanese Foreign Ministry. The fact that Japanese private citizens were named as the source of the money, and not a foreign government interested in peddling influence, certainly made it easier for Stanford to accept the donation. Jordan immediately offered the position to Ichihashi, whom Numano also supported.[50]

Although he had hoped for a permanent post, Ichihashi accepted the Stanford offer, while pursuing his efforts to obtain a long-term position elsewhere, including the University of Wisconsin, with the help of his Harvard friends. But as he approached the end of his first year of teaching at Stanford, he was gratified by the progress he had made in his career. He had issued two major publications on Japanese immigration, completed and submitted his doctoral thesis for Harvard, and successfully taught two courses on Japan at Stanford. Now, apparently in good favor with powerful benefactors in Japan (if not the Foreign Ministry itself), he had even brighter career prospects ahead of him. Within a year, the Japanese Foreign Ministry, again using the names of private citizens, contributed another $5,000 to support Ichihashi's reappointment for an additional three years, from 1914 to 1917.[51]

Here it may be useful to examine Ichihashi's doctoral dissertation for Harvard. Entitled "Emigration from Japan and Japanese Immigration into the State of California," Ichihashi's project examines the history of migration from Japan from premodern times to the Japanese settlement in California in the early twentieth century. The thesis relies principally on Ichihashi's "actual field work," as he describes it, but also draws on English-language and Japanese primary and secondary sources. Straddling traditional boundaries of three academic fields—Japanese history, contemporary international relations, and American immigration studies—the thesis displays Ichihashi's own unique combination of intellectual interests and scholarly abilities and provides insight not just into his thought but into his personal sensibilities as well.

This first major intellectual effort by Ichihashi reveals features that continued to mark his work for the rest of his life. First, he closely linked his scholarly work to his life experiences. In the introduction to his thesis, he explained that his interest in Japanese immigration was provoked almost in the moment of his arrival in the United States. When "I landed at San Francisco," he wrote, "there was a cry, 'Japs must go.' My first impression of America was naturally that America was hostile to Japan. My second thought was to discover the cause or causes underlying this hostility." Living in the San Francisco area, the center of anti-Japanese agitation in the country, he had "been personally through the thick and thin of the movement." But having had the opportunity also to live in the academic environment of Stanford, he believed he had "been able to take an 'objective' interest in the matter." And so it was for the rest of his life: Ichihashi explored issues in which he felt a particular personal stake, be it Japan's foreign policy in Asia in the 1930's or the relocation experience. In contrast, his decades' long effort late in life to complete a more traditional academic project, the cultural history of eighth-century Japan, amounted to virtually nothing.[52]

Ichihashi's doctoral thesis also displays an overriding, even consuming, sensitivity to racial discrimination or, more precisely, to what he believed was the unjustified prejudice against Japan and the Japanese in America. He acknowledged that other racial minorities suffered varieties of discrimination as well (he also held his own racial and ethnic prejudices, but more on this later), but he devoted his attention to refuting what he saw were the false and injurious assumptions about and allegations against the Japanese. Thus he devoted considerable attention in his thesis to arguing that the Japanese possessed all the fine and sober attributes ostensibly desired by Americans. Disputing the arguments of the anti-Japanese agitators, he argued that Japanese immigrants were not harmful to American labor or business interests but were fully capable of becoming assimilated and decent citizens if they were given the chance to prove themselves. He wrote, "the Japanese as a race have a peculiar power to assimilate and to be assimilated." The Japanese were hardworking, polite, and artistic ("racial traits possessed alike by the educated and uneducated"), and were "not inferior to any of the best European immigrants."[53] Anti-Japanese sentiment was therefore based purely on racial animosity, inherited in part from the American experience with the earlier Chinese immigrants—who, Ichihashi offered, were indeed socially and culturally less desirable than his fellow Japanese. (In this respect, his views were similar to those of other Japanese immigrant leaders who felt the Japanese were decidedly superior to other Asians.)[54] To him, it was not so much that anti-Japanese prejudices were morally wrong, but simply that they were without legitimate biological, social, economic, or political foundation.

It was his expressed intention, not to condemn the United States, but rather to try to improve relations between Japanese and Americans by promoting mutual understanding and appealing to the basic self-interest of each, which he believed to be compatible. "Professional agitators," especially demagogic labor leaders, were the source of the problem, according to Ichihashi, and he appealed to his readers: "No American would think it desirable that California should be made the constant ground of quarrels between the two countries just to satisfy [the] selfish motives of a few unscrupulous men. The United States and Japan have larger interests that are mutual."[55]

He was confident in the power of intellectual persuasion and believed that foolish and hateful ideas could be dispelled by those educated, dispassionate, and higher classes of men, among whom he counted himself, who had command of the "facts." This assumption, derived from the Enlightenment tradition, was closely linked to a final noteworthy theme that appears in his thesis, his emphasis on the unquestioned "objectivity" of his own work. He made no effort to present his views as simply detached scholarship, but neither did he relinquish the claim that his work was "objective" and without political or partisan bias. Such was the prevailing norm of American scholarship at the time, of course, but one has a clear sense that Ichihashi respected the standard and took pride in being an accomplished social scientist who relied on quantitative material as the basis of his informed opinions. For him as an unquestioning positivist, truth could be found in the accumulated information gathered through careful and precise research. For Ichihashi, the search for "objective truth," advocacy on vital social and political issues of the day, and even involvement in social activism were not incompatible, philosophically or personally.

One-third of Ichihashi's thesis examines the history of Japanese emigration, imperial emigration policy, and patterns of colonization and emigration throughout the world, especially to other parts of Asia and to Latin America, since the Meiji Restoration of 1868. The middle third of his thesis draws on his study of Japanese immigration to California based on his personal fieldwork and statistical research and presents one of the first comprehensive examinations of the occupational and social profile of the Japanese in California. He completes his study with explorations of the sources of the anti-Japanese movement in the United States and of the broader implications of Japanese immigration for America and Japan. He concludes with the specific recommendation that the United States extend naturalization rights to the Japanese, which he deemed essential if they were to assimilate and if there was to be a political counterweight to the anti-Japanese agitators. For Japan, he recommended that it control emigration, especially of those with the *dekasegi* or "birds of passage" mentality, who, in his view, sought only short-term material gain and took no interest in their adopted home. Such emigrants, who "are not wanted anywhere," cause only unnecessary prejudice and friction.

In May 1914, Ichihashi took leave from Stanford to undergo his final oral examination for his Harvard degree, presumably before at least Ripley, Turner, and Carver.[56] And though prospects for an American academic career were bright, Ichihashi himself was ambivalent about his future course. In his almost twenty years of life in America, he had come to be fond of the country and his life here, yet he also felt out of place. He could not become a U.S. citizen because of his ancestry (U.S. law permitted naturalization only of white persons and persons of African ancestry),[57] and his own "racial stigma," as he had once described it confidentially to Jordan, contributed to making Ichihashi self-conscious teaching at Stanford. A colleague observed that Ichihashi felt "social ostracism," from which he had "suffered much" at Stanford. He had difficulty renting a home in the Stanford area, and he had little social life. Ichihashi's colleagues reported to Ephraim Douglass Adams, the chair of the History Department, about Ichihashi's living situation that, "the social discrimination which must be experienced by Japanese" in California was deeply regrettable. Ichihashi thought seriously about returning to Japan permanently and gave many of his Stanford colleagues the impression that he was looking forward to doing so.[58]

Japan, on the other hand, also appeared distant to him in many ways. As an observer of events in Asia, Ichihashi was sympathetic to Japan's effort to expand its influence over neighbors such as China. The growing Japanese political and economic presence on the mainland was a stabilizing and civilizing force, he wanted to believe, and Tokyo would not resort to military intimidation to advance its interests. At the same time, he was not confident he even knew the politics and passions of the land of his birth. "Japan will be an enigma," he had written to Jordan in October 1913.[59] Ichihashi was also aware that the career record of the students educated in America who returned to Japan was mixed. Some succeeded in attaining positions of major importance in government, the professions, academia, and even the military, but others were not so lucky. One such man was Michitaro Sindo, himself a Stanford undergraduate schoolmate of Ichihashi, who had dropped out of the university, returned to Japan, and found himself unexpectedly out of place. Sindo had been Jordan's research assistant on several occasions.

The experience of Sindo, who like Ichihashi was educated largely outside Japan, was commonplace for returned students. "Many a foreign educated Japanese, on account of his too long continued absence from Japan, has lost touch on the ever-changing social ideas [of the country]," Sindo wrote to David Starr Jordan in 1908. Upon return to Japan, the student often "failed to fit himself into a right position where his ability could be applied to the best advantage, nor had he sufficient influence to crush the prejudice which surrounded him." Sindo candidly explained,

> Some worthy men were subjected to this humiliation and agony, and have either been compelled to sacrifice their pride and independence, or turned into bitter cynics. This in spite of their excellent training and splendid mental power, which, were they the natives of the country where they were educated, would have won for them positions of high usefulness and respect. They were expatriated by their foreign education and suffered the natural consequence.[60]

Linked to the issue of country of residence was another quandary that faced Ichihashi. He had to decide on his own intellectual focus. Would it be Japanese history or economics? He had specialized in economics and sociology, fields in which the United States pioneered, with an eye to returning to Japan to teach. "Over there [in Japan] my specialization in Japanese history has no value, yet as an economist I have every prospect of securing an agreeable position," he told his department chair in 1914.[61] Moreover, economics, not history, seemed to be his continuing passion. Ichihashi "is primarily interested in Economics. He really would prefer to be doing that kind of work," his friend, officemate, and fellow Asian specialist Payson Treat reported to Adams.[62] But now at Stanford he was sought after as one who could teach things Japanese, and there was little interest in him as an economist. Adams pressed Ichihashi to continue teaching in the United States, arguing that the demand for instruction in the history of Japan and Japanese civilization was growing. "Under such a demand," he told Ichihashi, "you have a distinct advantage, simply because you *are* a *Japanese* student of ability." But Ichihashi was well aware of his limitations as an Asianist. In his own words, Japan was a "strange subject" for him to teach as a "beginner," and, as Payson Treat observed to a colleague, Ichihashi, in teaching Japanese history, was "doing something in which his whole heart is not enlisted." He felt much more confident and happy teaching economics. Paradoxically, the ancestry that caused his social isolation was also what Stanford colleagues emphasized in trying to get him to reshape his career for their own reasons.[63]

Thus, in early 1914 Ichihashi decided he had to return to Japan for a visit, to reacquaint himself with his land of ancestry. He asked the Stanford administration whether he could take a leave with pay, drawing on the special funding for his teaching position. Releasing the money for his trip caused a small flap within the History Department, since its understanding had been that the funds were to go to advance Japanese studies at the university. Since Ichihashi had not yet decided whether he was even going to stay in the United States, let alone continue to develop his talents as an Asianist, the department wanted him to choose before advancing the funds. In fact, Ichihashi hoped that during the trip he could investigate other career opportunities as well as acquire books and research material for himself and Stanford.[64] He did not want to sacrifice his training as an economist and his prospects in Japan for the uncertain chance of a position in Japanese studies in the United States. Stanford University had given him no guarantee that there would be a permanent place for him there even if he transformed himself into an Asianist. Finally, in frustration, Ichihashi promised to refund the advanced money to the Japanese donors if he decided to remain in Japan or to return there as a result of his trip.[65]

After successfully completing his doctoral examination at Harvard in the spring, Ichihashi went on leave from Stanford and began what would be a six-month visit to Japan. His Stanford colleague Payson Treat saw him off at the San Francisco dock with a farewell gift, as Ichihashi set sail for Yokohama on the *Shin'yō Maru* on June 6. On board also was the eminent scholar of Japanese religion Anesaki Masaharu, who had been

lecturing at Harvard. Treat hoped that Anesaki would convince Ichihashi to stay in the United States to teach Japanese history and to "heave
all his economics overboard," as he told a friend. Anesaki and Ichihashi
did become and remain good friends.[66]

    Ichihashi's closest and most enduring friendship—with Payson Jack-
son Treat—also began at this time. Treat, who was about the same age
as Ichihashi, was educated at Wesleyan, attended graduate school at
Stanford from 1903 to 1905, and in 1910 earned his doctoral degree
from Stanford, the first issued from its History Department. He became
a member of the department soon afterward. Treat spent most of his
career at Stanford, serving as chair of the History Department from
1922 to 1929, but also held visiting appointments at Harvard, Johns
Hopkins, Columbia, and the University of California at Berkeley. He
retired in 1945 and remained a fixture on the Stanford scene until his
death in 1972. His major field of study had been the land system in early
U.S. history, but while he was still a graduate student completing his
thesis, Jordan and Max Farrand, then head of the History Department,
cajoled him into becoming an Asianist. (Radically switching fields of
study was more common in those days than at present—E. D. Adams
had started out as a Europeanist and later became a specialist in recent
American history.) Stanford University sent Treat on a grand tour of the
Far East in 1906–7, during which he developed a fascination with Japan.
He began teaching Far Eastern history after his return and became the
first professor of Far Eastern history in the United States, although he
never learned any Asian language. By the time Ichihashi joined the department, Treat already had accumulated six years' teaching experience,
and Jordan asked him to take Ichihashi under his direction. He and Ichihashi quickly developed a genuine fondness for one another.[67]
    Their friendship lasted an extraordinary 50 years. They shared intel-
lectual interests: both were deeply committed to their scholarship and
to the objective of improving U.S.-Japan relations and the position of
Japanese in America.[68] Both were unabashed Japanophiles. They were
devoted Stanford alumni and professors. And both had taken unusual
career paths: neither started out as an Asianist, but both became intellectual pioneers in what at that time in the United States was an exotic
field of study.
    They were also a strangely contrasting pair. Treat was a vigorously
physical man who liked gardening, hiking, and camping in California's
scenic wilderness. Ichihashi was constantly formal, aloof, and of weak
constitution, although he also liked the outdoors. Treat was known as a
considerate individual and teacher. He and his wife, Jessie McGilvray, a

Stanford alumna whom Treat married while he was a graduate student, often entertained students and colleagues in their comfortable campus home; many of his former students, including many Japanese and Japanese Americans, maintained close contact with him long after their graduation. Treat took an active personal interest in them and in his own relatives (he had no children) and was generous with his time and money. Ichihashi, on the other hand, socialized infrequently, had few friends, and was penurious. He did not marry until he was 40 years old, and he kept his distance from his own relatives. While he could be caustically opinionated, Ichihashi also maintained a high degree of formal deference and loyalty toward those who helped him through the years. One senses that Yamato Ichihashi felt he occupied an uncomfortable, if not uncertain, professional and social position throughout his entire life, even after he had established his career. He never had the personal security and professional satisfaction that Treat evidently enjoyed.

During his six-month stay, Ichihashi toured the length and breadth of Japan—Yokohama, Tokyo, Sapporo, Hakone—and was kept busy by meetings with his elderly parents, who had moved to Sapporo on Hokkaido, and other family members, academics, government officials, businessmen, and prominent persons everywhere he went. He used both the Stanford and Harvard networks in Japan to develop his contacts. But to his undoubted surprise, Japan often seemed like a new country to him, and he a stranger in the land. Some twenty years had passed since he had last seen his homeland. He wrote back to Payson Treat expressing wonder at things he observed. "I was much amazed at the smallness of Japanese *kisha* [narrow-gauge steam trains]," Ichihashi wrote Treat; like a first-time tourist to Japan, he wrote about the "picturesque" scenery and the "hard, laboring, peasant women" transplanting rice in the fields. The noise of the *geta* (wooden clogs) in the Tokyo train station impressed him but, as he wrote, "nothing surprised me more . . . than [the] extravagant dresses in which men but especially women appeared. I could hardly realize at the sight of them that Japan was a poor country." [69]

In Tokyo, his hosts put him up in a Japanese-style inn, "but one night was enough for me," Ichihashi confessed to Treat and, as he put it, "I was compelled to seek a real hotel." Even the Imperial Hotel, the best Tokyo had to offer, "is not very satisfactory," Ichihashi wrote, "according to the American standard." A high point in his Tokyo stay was dining at the "elegant home" of an acquaintance where he, to his "great joy," had a "European luncheon."

It was not just the physical surroundings that seemed to accentuate

Ichihashi's "foreignness" in Japan; its politics and passions disoriented him as well. He was impressed by the degree that Japan's "spiritual civilization" had already become Westernized and favorably reported to Jordan that the Japanese "thinking public" was "fast democratizing." But then Japan's shifting attitude toward the Great War in Europe, which broke out in the summer of 1914, shocked him. In August, he had assured Jordan, a longtime antimilitarist activist, that "Japan remains cool" in the crisis and that it would "maintain peace in the Far East." But after Japan entered the war against the Entente because of its alliance with Great Britain, he wrote Treat, "The whole world seems to have gone crazy, including my own poor country." He thought America fortunate in staying out of the bloodletting. One of his brothers, an army captain, had to depart for battle before Ichihashi could see him. "Probably will never see him," Ichihashi lamented,[70] though his brother did survive the war. (As the conflict dragged on, however, Ichihashi eventually came around to write supportively of the Japanese government's involvement. Japan, he later said before an audience celebrating the 1918 semicentenary of the founding of the University of California, Berkeley, was in "the war for principle and for nothing else." One is not sure whether Ichihashi actually believed his gloss.)[71]

All in all, though, it seems that Ichihashi was pleased by his trip to Japan. A few months after his return to Palo Alto, he wrote to Japanese Consul Numano Yasutarō in San Francisco,

> I feel that the sojourn of six months in Japan benefitted me immeasurably. I have seen [the] Japan of today. I have met the representative men of today at home. I have learned their ambition. Besides, I have brought back with me more than three hundred volumes of "authoritative" Japanese books. These will form the nucleus of our Japanese library, and will render me invaluable service. I now lecture with confidence which I did not possess before.[72]

Ichihashi returned to Stanford after the end of the fall semester of 1914–15 more secure, though still not completely settled, about his future prospects in the United States. He continued to divide his energies between the History Department, where he taught courses on Japanese history and civilization, and the Economics Department, where he presented Economics 54, "Immigration and the Race Problem," a popular course that attracted over 60 students in the spring of 1915. He described the course as "a study of immigration as a phenomenon of population, and the social and economic significance of the ethnic composition as affected by it, with special reference to the United States." He taught the course for several years.[73]

It is not clear whether Ichihashi was aware that the entire funding for his teaching position at this time came from the Japanese Foreign Ministry or believed, as the university did, that the money came from private donors in Japan who used the Japanese consul in San Francisco simply as a transfer agent. Stanford officials expressed no hesitation in accepting the funds; they understood they were to be used to support an instructor who would advance understanding of Japanese civilization, history, or current life and government. The Japanese donors placed no restrictions on the specific courses to be taught, let alone intimated what preference they had with regard to the content or point of view. At the same time, the donors were pleased that Ichihashi was selected to receive the funds since he had established a reputation as one of the leading defenders of the Japanese in America and was personally known to the Japanese consular officials.[74]

Although Japanese officials and Stanford administrators seemed satisfied with the arrangement, Ichihashi's position remained awkward, to say the least. He was happy that he was able to teach at Stanford and that the prospect for a permanent position remained strong. At the same time, he found himself laden with new obligations and tied to the Japanese government. Twice a year, at least for the years 1915–17 and perhaps beyond, Ichihashi submitted confidential reports directly to the Japanese Consul General in San Francisco on his activities. These reports, which eventually wound up in the central files of the Japanese Ministry of Foreign Affairs, described his teaching, professional, and public speaking activities.[75] Most of the reports, typed in English on Stanford History Department stationery, resemble those that recipients of scholarly grants submit to benefactors telling them how their money is being used. Ichihashi's reports tell of the courses he taught, the number of students in his classes, his public speaking and assistance to visiting Japanese dignitaries, and research work; they close by inviting criticism and suggestions. This material is innocuous. Other material in the reports, especially the later ones, however, would have shocked his Stanford colleagues and would have ended any prospect of an academic career for him in the United States if they had been disclosed. Not only do the reports show that Ichihashi was a highly opinionated person who bluntly criticized his fellow Japanese in America, specific individuals in the Japanese community, and inept government representatives from Tokyo, they also unintentionally reveal him to have been a fiercely ambitious person willing to ingratiate himself with Japanese diplomats and their political purposes. Publicly, Ichihashi, steadfastly denied throughout his life that he had ever been on the payroll of the Japanese Foreign Ministry.[76]

Ichihashi's tone in these reports varied from that of a dutiful humble servant to that of an eager professional trying to attach himself to the rich and powerful. His reports speak to the consulate general of "our work" and "our purposes," which Ichihashi defined as seeking to "bring about a situation where Japanese subjects and Japan's interests may be better guarded and improved." In his report on the fall 1915 semester, he offered that he had "handled some eighty students in a way that they will at least remember me. And the personal contact and relationship thus made and formed will be of value to me and therefore to Japanese interests sometime or [other]. I am trying to build a circle of friends, and I feel that my students will form the nucleus of such a circle." [77]

A month later, Ichihashi sent a long letter to Consul General Numano, who was about to return to Japan. Ichihashi said he wished to take the opportunity to expand on his views on the character, mentality, and habits of the Japanese in America, so that Tokyo might adopt policies more clearly in its interests. As he reminded Numano, the "presence here of 100,000 Japanese may injure or benefit the general diplomatic relations between America and Japan and likewise their commercial relations." And in his view, the Japanese in America left much to be desired: despite being in the United States for several decades, 90 percent of them still dreamed of returning home to Japan rich, and thus they lived only for shortsighted "pecuniary gain"; the result was that they remained poor. They were also "blindly passive" and required guidance and education from above so that they could know their best interests; the Japanese Associations, the most important immigrant organizations, were run by "inefficient (often ignoramus)" social climbers; and they were unenlightened politically. Ichihashi argued that the Japanese in America were "by nature" not democratic, and in fact were "at least twenty years behind the intelligent Japanese at home, and the lord only knows how [many] years they are behind the intelligent Americans." Ichihashi urged the Japanese government to take a more active role in directing the lives of his fellow Japanese in America since, "if these 100,000 Japanese are left alone to conduct their affairs they are bound to fail since they have no requisite intelligence, power and strength to struggle with. . . . Most of the Japanese resemble juiceless pulps. They have been squeezed right and left." [78]

Five months later Ichihashi turned from deprecating his fellow Japanese in America to promoting the value of his own work for the Japanese government. He reported that his course on "Immigration and the Race Problem" had attracted eighty students in the spring, which gratified him since "I thought that each student who studies under me regardless of the nature of subjects is to become a more or less pro-Japanese American citizen. Hence the larger the number of students I have, the greater my influence over them. This might eventually become a social force in favor of Japan."

Ichihashi's purpose was to press the consul general again on raising funds to support a position in Japanese studies at Stanford. In arguing for this, Ichihashi revealed his class bias as well as his own elevated sense of self. He baldly appealed to the official by waving the banner of national promotion, an interest held by many Japanese at this time:

> Why do we covet this University position (I am speaking objectively) so much? You and I agree that one of the serious difficulties we constantly meet with here on the Pacific Coast, in California and especially in San Francisco, is the entire absence of real representative Japanese who enjoy and could enjoy "social position." Our so-called representative Japanese here are far below the accepted social standard, and in my humble opinion many years must be consumed before they can attain that social standard. In other words, there are no qualified spokesmen in fact on behalf of the Japanese and their interests here and at home. Now, university professors though financially poor enjoy social position. I despise self-advertisement, but even [though I am] a Jap, because of my university position I enjoy social position and take advantage of it in carrying [on] my campaign of education. No one seems to refuse to take me in. This fact convinces me that the securing of social position is the fundamental pre-requisite before a positive campaign of any sort could effectively be conducted.

Although he acknowledged the obvious, that is, that he would be the beneficiary of the funding of a position in Japanese studies at Stanford, Ichihashi denied he sought such funding for purely personal reasons. He offered that "I am not so selfish as to consider my own interest first." Still, it seemed that Tokyo's interests and his own coincided nicely. He ended the letter inquiring whether Tokyo might consider providing financial and logistical support for a "party of university professors and their wives" from the West Coast to travel to Japan. He wanted to organize such a group to introduce them to the country. "Their familiarity means conscious and unconscious dissemination of a knowledge of Japan among their colleagues, students and friends. They constitute the cream of their respective communities."[79] Curiously, while his American friends thought that Ichihashi seriously contemplated returning to Japan for personal reasons, he gave Japanese officials the impression he was more than willing to stay in the United States for the Japanese national good.

At the end of the academic year 1916–17, his three-year funding from Japan was renewed for another three years, and the university promoted him to the rank of assistant professor. While happy to continue his work at Stanford, Ichihashi was frustrated that he had still not attained a regular teaching post.[80] He did receive a salary increase, with the university for the first time contributing to his salary from its own budget.[81] Ichihashi had to remain patient for a while longer.

He could probably appreciate the position of the university. Japanese studies was a new field in American academia, and having a Japanese on the faculty had already proved highly controversial. The university had come under criticism from various anti-Japanese agitators, one being a well-known journalist, Montaville Flowers. Flowers had long singled out Ichihashi by name in his published diatribes against the Japanese. "California must now take the offensive!" Flowers wrote in 1919 in *The Grizzly Bear*, a rabidly anti-Asian publication; its declared purpose was to help "Californians to keep this State, this Nation, a land for the white races" and combat the "'peaceful invasion' of California by the Asiatic hordes." Flowers declared that the people of the state must "expose the Japanese propagandists . . . the names—Kawakami, Iyenaga, Kasai, Inui, Ichihashi—must become familiar as originators of pro-Japanese and anti-American propaganda in this country."[82] Flowers wrote,

> The citizens of the State and the patrons of Leland Stanford University and every student there should know that a Japanese, Ichihashi, has occupied for several years the sensitive and powerful place of teacher of immigration, poisoning popular opinion at the spring, by instilling into the minds of our youth as fundamental principles of national honor, that Japanese should have equal privilege with other people to enter and populate our country, to become citizens, and to participate in the government.[83]

Although his career was still unsettled, in 1918 Ichihashi turned his attention to his personal life. In March, after what may well have been months, if not years, of preliminaries and negotiation, a *baishakunin*, or matchmaker, in Japan had successfully found a bride for him.[84] Okei Maki, born in February 1892 and fourteen years Ichihashi's junior, came from Niigata, a town on the west coast of the main island of Honshu and a center of Christian missionary activity. The match appeared to be proper and promising: the Maki family was also descended from former samurai; Kei, as she was later known, was educated at Tokio Joshi Daigaku or Tokyo Women's College, a Christian school founded by missionaries, and had completed graduate work there in Japanese and English literatures. Friends she later made at Stanford believed that her family was related to one of the first Japanese to be ordained as a Christian minister in Meiji Japan, and her father was rumored to have been a bodyguard to an early convert. Kei too became a Christian, joining many of the other converts in Japan who were from former samurai families.[85]

Little is known about her childhood and early life, but a book that she kept in her library after her marriage to Yamato may give us some idea of her early experiences. Etsu Inagaki Sugimoto, the author of *A Daughter of the Samurai*, in many ways was like Kei. She had a father who was a former samurai; she was approximately the same age as Kei, converted to Christianity as an adolescent, learned English at a Christian school in Tokyo, came to America because of an arranged marriage, and lived in an academic environment. In a memoir about her life in Japan, Sugimoto wrote about the strict, feudal upbringing of young girls. "Samurai daughters were taught never to lose control of mind or body— even in sleep," when they were physically to "curve into the modest, dignified character *kinoji*, which means 'spirit of control.' " From an early age, girls learned to value duty over feeling, especially in relation to men. Sugimoto recalled her grandmother's admonition, "Loyalty to your husband; bravery in defence of his honour. It will bring you peace." (How terribly ironic these words later would be when Kei's troubled marriage to Yamato brought her deep unhappiness!) [86]

Though she had been taught, as with "all Japanese people, that woman is greatly inferior to man," Sugimoto developed resentment of this "injustice," as she described it, and discovered a rebelliousness and independence of spirit within her. Much of Sugimoto's life then became a discovery of how to exhibit such traits without, in her words, destroying her desired "gentle womanhood." Nevertheless, Sugimoto remained deeply appreciative of the love and nurturing of her father and family and respectful of the strength Japan's cultural tradition gave her, even as she made a new life for herself in America, where she eventually would teach Japanese at Columbia University. [87]

Kei Maki was a striking and attractive woman of about the same height and weight as Yamato. It is unlikely there had been any courtship between Kei and Yamato before their marriage; indeed, they probably had not set eyes on each other before her arrival in America. [88] Although the engagement was probably arranged, Kei was not a "picture bride." Most Japanese women who came to this country in these years, were picture brides—families would arrange for a young woman in Japan to marry a bridegroom in absentia in America; she would then travel across the ocean to meet her mate, who may have known her only through a photograph. So controversial in America was this activity—"immoral" is what many Euro-Americans believed—that just a few years later, in March 1920, the governments of the United States and Japan effectively ended the emigration of such prospective brides to America. Japanese men still outnumbered Japanese women four to one in 1920. [89]

Okei Maki, identifying herself as a *single* female student, English-speaking, arrived on board the *Ten'yō Maru* in San Francisco on February 17, 1918. She listed Eizo Osawa as her friend in America and his home on Ashbury Street in San Francisco as her local address. Osawa had been one of the earliest Japanese students to come to America, arriving in 1886 and attending Wesleyan College in Illinois. He was a well-known Christian, securities broker, and publisher.[90] Exactly two months after her arrival, on April 17, Yamato and Okei were married in San Francisco. Dr. Harvey H. Guy, a professor of the philosophy of religion and Chinese history at the Pacific School of Religion, missionary in Japan in the 1890's, and active defender of Japanese rights in America, presided over the ceremony. Guy had also been president of the Japan Society of America. Mr. Osawa and his wife served as witnesses.[91] Yamato and Kei then settled in at Yamato's residence at 1010 Emerson Street, Palo Alto, on the edge of what was called "Professorville," where many Stanford faculty members lived; it was also not far from the commercial center of the local Japanese community. They lived there for two years before moving to an attached house near the center of the Stanford campus at 523 Salvatierra Street, where, except for the years of internment, they would live the rest of their days together. In December 1918, Kei gave birth to a son, Woodrow Tsutomu, their only child. They named him in honor of the liberal internationalist president of the United States who was at the moment preparing to attend the Versailles Peace Conference ending World War I. (Many Japanese admired Wilson because of his espousal of the equality of nations.)[92] Yamato with his infant, as photographs show, was an awkward and emotionally restrained father. Woodrow was one of just under 30,000 nisei in 1920.

Although the number of Japanese families living in the Palo Alto area was not large in absolute terms, persons of Japanese ancestry had become the largest racial minority in the town, exceeding in number the Chinese who had arrived in the area in the 1870's. Japanese migrant workers, farmers, shopkeepers, and craftsmen began settling in the Palo Alto area around the turn of the century. The 1890 census of Santa Clara County reported only 27 Japanese residents, the first ever listed in the records; the number climbed to 2,981 by the 1920 census. These Palo Alto Japanese formed part of a growing Japanese community in Santa Clara County, which included the farming area of nearby San Jose.[93] By the second decade of the twentieth century, several hundred Japanese lived in Palo Alto, with about seventy children enrolled in public schools as compared to only ten Chinese youngsters. Some two hundred adult Japanese also were day laborers and lived in crowded camps in the fields surrounding the town. Advertisements in the local newspaper from the Japanese Labor Association offered to provide Japanese workers at 75 cents an hour or $4.00 a day in 1919. Domestics and other service workers seemed to be in demand as well.[94]

Stanford University itself employed Japanese as custodians in the men's dormitories, and many Stanford administrators and faculty, including David Starr Jordan and Payson Treat employed Japanese as domestics. They, along with Chinese, were the favored home workers of the town—the cook for the Jordan household for some forty years, for example, was a man named Katzuzo Nakasawa (who was forced to relocated in 1942); and Ray Lyman Wilbur employed a Chinese cook, Wah Chuck, for six years at the President's house.[95]

The town Japanese congregated along a portion of Ramona Street, in an area just a few blocks south of University Avenue, which was the city's main thoroughfare. By the late 1910's, the Japanese community was sufficiently large to support a Japanese-language publication, a language school, Christian missions, and even a special Red Cross chapter to care for Japanese influenza victims. Annual spring parades and Japanese-language plays customarily brought out large crowds. But the Japanese presence was not welcomed by everyone. Organized anti-Japanese groups agitated against the Japanese from the moment of their arrival. In 1906, for example, the San Jose Chamber of Commerce and a farmers' group launched a self-described "gigantic advertising scheme" to attract 5,000 white families to Santa Clara County in order to supplant the hundreds of "yellow skinned pickers by substituting the children of the people who will move here." The plan failed since Japanese workers proved to be more productive than child laborers.[96]

About the time of Woodrow's second birthday, the local chapters of the American Legion and the Native Sons of the Golden West, the Palo Alto Chamber of Commerce, and the Carpenters' Union, called for the Palo Alto Japanese and other "Orientals" to segregate themselves residentially and commercially in a specially designated district and actively discourage further Asian settlement in the area. In return for accepting this "generous" proposal, its sponsors promised to "work for a more harmonious feeling between whites and Japanese." Anti-Asian sentiment was common throughout the West at this time. Representatives of the local Japanese community rejected the offer, arguing that they desired assimilation and that the proposal worked against such an end. The *Palo Alto Times*, which vociferously endorsed the segregation idea, condemned the decision of the Japanese, who, in the opinion of the newspaper, only hurt their own interests. "Socially and biologically," the newspaper concluded its editorial, "the two races [white and Japanese] are non-assimilable. All dealings must proceed from realization of this fundamental fact."[97]

Woodrow grew up in this atmosphere, attending the local schools, but still recalls his youth with fondness. It seemed clear that from his earliest days Woodie, as he was called, led a very different life than that wished by his parents. He had a rambunctious personality and enjoyed roaming the hills near the Stanford campus with his buddies, mostly sons of other faculty. When Woodrow was six, Yamato spoke about him to a researcher interested in race relations. Ichihashi worried that Woodrow and other young Japanese Americans faced a difficult future in America since, as he said, "the racial mark of the Mongolian face is going to stand against them and I am not very hopeful of a solution in the immediate future." For that reason, Yamato said he was going to encourage Woodrow to "learn the Japanese language so that he can go to Japan if he meets too many obstacles here." But then Ichihashi's observations, given from the porch of his home to the interviewer, displayed his anxiety about a cultural gap that was much closer to home, a gap that had already opened between Woodrow and himself:

> My boy has always had American playmates and so he considers himself as one of them. A short time ago he came home from school and reported that he had played with some Japanese boys in school that day—he said it as if he had gone outside of his group to play with some other children. He is not growing up as a Japanese. Just look at him now as he is pushing the lawn mower. It would not do for the son of a man in my position to push a lawn mower in Japan, but here he will not get that idea. I suspect that it will not be long before he will be calling attention to my English and other things about me that are not just exactly like the Americans.[98]

But fatherhood was not high on Yamato Ichihashi's personal agenda and he spent little time with his family during the next several years. He entered a heady time in his career and became directly involved in the high-powered world of international conferences and politics.

Just three months after Woodrow's birth, Ichihashi requested a leave of absence from Stanford for the entire academic year of 1919–20, not to be with his young family but to travel to Asia again for professional reasons. He wanted to see if he could secure permanent Japanese funding for his position at Stanford since the latest three-year arrangement terminated in June 1920.[99] But in early October 1919, the Japanese government asked Ichihashi to join its delegation to the first International Labor Conference of the League of Nations, which was to meet in Washington, D.C., in November.[100] He accepted the invitation with enthusiasm, prepared by studying labor issues in America and Japan, and found himself in controversy even before the conference began. Labor leaders in Japan condemned the delegation selection as representing only the interests of the employer class. Ichihashi himself was listed in the conference literature as a professor from Stanford and one of the nine advisers to the two representatives of the Japanese government. The two other delegation members nominally represented capital and labor.[101]

Although the United States did not send a formal delegation, since it was not a member of the League of Nations, Americans played prominent roles as officers in the meeting, with Samuel Gompers, founder of the American Federal of Labor and longtime proponent of excluding Asians from the United States, the unofficial representative of American labor. The principal item before the conference was the proposal to recommend acceptance of the 8-hour day and 48-hour week for the industrial world. This also provoked some of the most heated discussion involving the Japanese delegation. The Japanese delegates formally representing the government and capital argued that an exception should be made for Japan, considering that its economic development was still in its infancy and capital could not be as liberal in its labor policies as its counterparts in the more industrially developed countries. The Japanese labor delegate vehemently protested and asked that no exception be made, condemning the proposed exemption as only strengthening the hand of an autocracy over the workers of Japan. The labor delegate's position was not accepted by the Conference.[102]

After the conference, Ichihashi briefly returned to Stanford. But in the spring of 1920, he left home again to assist a group of leading Japanese businessmen host the visit to Japan of a high-powered delegation of Americans headed by Frank A. Vanderlip, president of the City Bank of New York, head of the Japan Society of New York, and former assistant secretary of the Treasury. The Japanese group, calling itself the Welcome Association, was led by Prince Tokugawa Iyesato, and included Baron Shibusawa Ei'ichi, Viscount Kaneko Kentarō, several bank presidents and directors, and more than a dozen other of Japan's most prominent dignitaries and business leaders. Vanderlip's group included leading American financiers and former high government officials.[103]

In early April 1920, Ichihashi met part of the American delegation in Chicago to accompany them on the long journey by train and ship to Japan. In Japan, Ichihashi traveled with the Americans to Japan's major cities and cultural sites for three weeks and helped in the translations during the extensive private meetings that explored ways to improve U.S.-Japan relations. A member of the delegation in his account of the trip praised Ichihashi for his "unusual talent in rendering Japanese speeches into excellent and often eloquent English." The so-called Vanderlip delegation was even honored by a luncheon hosted by Japan's Taishō Emperor and attracted widespread attention in both Japan and the United States.[104]

After three months in Japan, Ichihashi traveled to Europe, where he reportedly conducted scholarly research in Paris, attended sessions of the League of Nations Association in Geneva in June 1921 (the Association was organized as a public support group for the League's ideals), and lectured at the Université Internationale in Brussels in August. Before leaving Europe, he visited London, where he met with British naval officials.[105]

The time in Europe was critical for Ichihashi's career. During his visit, Ichihashi had ample opportunity to consolidate his relationship with leading Japanese officials and dignitaries who were visiting Europe during these busy days following the Versailles Peace Conference and the establishment of the League of Nations. One of the most important of these men was someone he had worked with in Japan, Shibusawa Ei'ichi, chairman of the Japanese League of Nations Association, prominent philanthropist, and for years a leading figure in private efforts to advance the U.S.-Japan relationship.[106]

Whatever Ichihashi did overseas, it seemed to help his career at Stanford. In August 1920, he informed the chair of the History Department that he had learned that Japanese donors would give $37,500 to endow a permanent position for a "Japanese scholar" to teach Japanese studies at Stanford. While the gift was substantially less than the $100,000 he and the Stanford History Department had hoped for, it was enough for Stanford to commit itself. The university agreed to match the annual interest from the Japanese gift; the combined amount would then be sufficient to cover the annual salary of an assistant professor. By the end of the year, Shibusawa formally tendered the offer, supposedly on behalf of other unidentified donors, to Stanford President Ray Lyman Wilbur. All the evidence, however, shows that in fact Shibusawa acted nominally, with the money actually coming again from the Japanese Foreign Ministry. The Ministry apparently had been pleased with Ichihashi's work in improving understanding of Japan in the United States. In December 1920, the Japanese Consul General in San Francisco, formally "representing Shibusawa and the Japanese donors," handed a check for $37,500 over to the Stanford treasurer. In early 1921, the University trustees appointed Ichihashi to a regular position as assistant professor in the Department of History, his endowed chair being the very first in Stanford's history.[107]

Was the university aware that most if not all of the endowment had secretly come from the Japanese Foreign Ministry? There is no evidence to show that the university ever made an effort to uncover the identity of the chair's actual benefactor; rather it comfortably accepted the money with no questions asked. Curiosity about the source of the money, however, lingered in some people's minds for decades.[108]

In addition to helping establish his professional life at Stanford, Ichihashi's European stay had perhaps even greater implications for his later life, although he was probably unaware of it at the time. His activities had drawn the attention of United States intelligence agencies. After a long eighteen months abroad, Ichihashi finally reentered the United States on board the Cunard Line SS *Aquitania* on September 9, 1921, arriving in New York. He was traveling under a Japanese diplomatic passport and under the watchful eyes of the FBI and Naval Intelligence. His close association with Japanese officials in Europe, his inclusion in the high-level Japanese delegation to the international Conference on the Limitation of Armament that would open in Washington in two months, and growing tensions between the United States and Japan in Asia were among the reasons for the intelligence agencies' interest in Ichihashi.[109] But naval agents became suspicious because of one particularly bizarre episode, almost theatrical as described in the surviving intelligence reports.

It seems that in the summer of 1921, Ichihashi and other persons connected to the Japanese official presence in Paris had made contact with a wealthy American named Peter Cooper Hewitt, vice president of the Naval Consulting Board and inventor of some "very important" military-related devices, including an "aerial bomb." Hewitt was the son of a former mayor of New York City and the inventor of the mercury vapor lamp. At one meeting with Hewitt, Ichihashi allegedly expressed interest in purchasing the plans of some of his work but was rebuffed. At that point, Ichihashi "became very insistent and Mr. Hewitt forced [Ichihashi] from his apartment at the Hotel Ritz." Soon afterward, Hewitt became seriously ill, and a British nurse, a Miss Elizabeth Kelly, was hired to attend to him at the American Hospital in Paris. She became "very anxious," however, when she learned about the sensitive nature of private papers Hewitt had brought with him to the hospital. Intelligence agents, according to the secret report, then "discovered that she was in close communication with the same YAMATO ICHIHASHI who had approached Mr. Hewitt at the Hotel Ritz. It was also discovered that this same nurse was found in a room in the Hotel Plaza, Boulevard Malesherbes, Paris, with the [other] Japanese." More suspiciously, after Hewitt's subsequent death, Nurse Kelly pressed Mrs. Hewitt to sell some of her husband's inventions to the Japanese but then suddenly disappeared with thousands of francs of the Hewitts' cash. Next, Ichihashi himself "approached Mrs. Hewitt and offered her a large sum of money for certain drawings" of Mr. Hewitt's but failed to persuade the widow.

After booking passage on the SS *Aquitania* to bring her husband's remains back to the United States for burial, Mrs. Hewitt discovered that Ichihashi had arranged passage on the very same voyage. (Also to the consternation of American officials, Mrs. Hewitt surrounded herself with five mysterious attendants and companions, all British subjects who were thought to be "representatives of the British Secret Service," including one man about whom there were "some very unwholesome rumors concerning his relations with Mrs. Hewitt.") Ichihashi, with a letter from the Japanese Embassy in Paris, succeeded in attaining an entry visa to return to the United States directly from the U.S. Embassy in Paris without the knowledge of the American Passport Bureau, which was usually responsible for such matters. But when Mrs. Hewitt learned that Ichihashi would be on board with her, she immediately made contact with American diplomatic and naval officials in Paris and demanded that Ichihashi's visa "be revoked or that his sailing be held up for that vessel." She said that she was carrying valuable papers of her husband's and feared "personal violence from the Japanese during the ocean passage." The officials informed Mrs. Hewitt that they could not accommodate her, but it was finally decided that she would leave the papers in secure storage in Paris and that naval command would be informed of her concerns about the sailing situation. One alarmed naval intelligence report concluded saying that Ichihashi was probably "trying to steal" the Hewitt papers and that he was "a dangerous character and would bear watching." Reports on Ichihashi were forwarded to local FBI offices in New York and Los Angeles.[110]

Upon Ichihashi's arrival in New York, federal and military agents watched his every move, recorded all his associations, and attempted to eavesdrop on his conversations for the next ten days. The field reports included all possible detail, including this description of his person:

About 5'5"; 43 years of age, slim build; round shouldered; about 130 lbs; clean shaven; black hair; blue flannel suit, with dark stripe; olive green velour hat, black oxford ties, soft collar, blue tie with white stripe about 1/8 of an inch in width; carried greenish brown cane.

During his few days in New York, Ichihashi stayed at the Pennsylvania Hotel in Manhattan, associated with several local Japanese, visited the Japanese consulate, and attended a Giants baseball game at the Polo Grounds. (One cannot be sure whether Ichihashi really enjoyed the sport or just wanted to get away from his tail and have a private conversation with his colleagues!) Other than these activities and his sleeping and meal habits, there was nothing sufficiently noteworthy to attract the agents' interest. Their reports were routine.[111]

On September 14, Ichihashi took a train to Washington, D.C., where federal agents again followed him all day. Despite detailed instructions, some agents wound up observing wrong individuals on the train, including one person who turned out to be "a tall, stout, gray haired Jew," according to the FBI agent's field report. After spending most of the day with members of the Japanese embassy and sending a telegram, the contents of which the FBI agent tried unsuccessfully to have the Western Union clerk reveal, Ichihashi departed for San Francisco. FBI agents at stops all along the way verified that Ichihashi was still on board. Finally back in San Francisco on September 19, the FBI ended its surveillance after agents were satisfied that Ichihashi was returning to his Palo Alto home. He was reunited with Kei and Woodrow, who had spent the summer in San Francisco living at 158 27th Avenue, near Golden Gate Park. Whether Ichihashi ever knew he had captured the attention of U.S. government agents from Europe to California, we do not know.[112]

Even though the reports reveal embarrassing sloppiness in the FBI's work—Ichihashi's name itself is misspelled a dozen different ways—the Bureau had developed a good idea of who Ichihashi was by late 1921. The reports on his activities and the interviews with what appear to be associates and friends of Ichihashi (the released FBI documents are still heavily elided and the identities of the informants concealed) seemed to convince the FBI that Ichihashi was not worth continued close monitoring. In fact, one last report in 1921, apparently from Ray Lyman Wilbur himself, praised him as a teacher and a scholar, discounted the accusation he was a propagandist, and provided detailed information about the propriety of the funding of his position at the university.[113] Still, Ichihashi remained a highly suspicious person to the FBI, whose internal reports labeled him a "Japanese suspect" and a "propagandist" for Japan. These damaging reports on him lay quietly for twenty years until the tense days before the attack on Pearl Harbor in 1941 when all the old security intelligence on Japanese in America was dredged up by federal agencies.

Ichihashi's return to teaching at Stanford in October 1921 was brief, for in early November he, Kyutaro Abiko, a leading member of San Francisco's Japanese American community, and U.S.-based writer, Kiyoshi K. Kawakami, whose books Ichihashi used in his Japanese foreign relations course, joined a group of dignitaries from Japan, which included Baron Shibusawa, to travel once again to Washington, D.C. There, they joined the Japanese delegation to the Conference for Limitation of Armament and Pacific and Far Eastern Problems, popularly known as the Washington Conference, which had been convened by President Warren G. Harding.[114] Attending the conference became a high point of Yamato's life, and he never tired of regaling friends and acquaintances with his experiences there even years later. It became the subject of his first book, *The Washington Conference and After: A Historical Survey* (1928).[115]

The Conference was indeed a spectacular gathering of major European states, Japan, and other Asian nations. The first conference of world powers held in the United States, it was also the first modern effort to control weaponry in the pursuit of international stability. Its successful outcome helped promote the popular hope in the 1920's and early 1930's that disarmament and peace could be achieved through big-power negotiations. The Conference met in the midst of international tensions stemming from problems that the Versailles Peace Conference had left unresolved or had even aggravated. The three great naval powers at the time, Britain, the United States, and Japan, were then engaged in a vigorous and costly naval arms race, which threatened to disrupt the tenuous balance of power that followed World War I. Moreover, Japan's aggressive demands on China and its conflicts with the United States and European powers over numerous territorial, commercial, and military issues in the Pacific and Far East heightened fears of war. United States–Japan relations were also strained because of American domestic politics—the court case of Takao Ozawa, a Japanese immigrant who had been prevented from becoming a naturalized citizen because of his race, highlighted years of discriminatory treatment of Japanese immigrants in the United States. Challenging the lower court ruling, Ozawa brought his case all the way to the Supreme Court, which would decide on the matter in 1922. In this charged atmosphere in Washington, D.C., Yamato Ichihashi no doubt felt that he was stepping onto the stage of world history.

Ichihashi attended the conference formally as an "expert" attached to the large Japanese delegation, led by the four official delegates: minister of the navy Admiral Baron Katō Tomosaburō, who was the actual political leader of the delegation; Baron Shidehara Kijūrō, ambassador to the United States; Prince Tokugawa Iyesato, son of the last shogun, president of the House of Peers, and nominal head of the delegation; and Hanihara Masanao, vice minister of Foreign Affairs and former consul general in San Francisco. In San Francisco, Hanihara had had frequent contact with Ichihashi and had helped arrange the funding of his teaching position. At the Conference, Ichihashi played a role much more conspicuous and important than that suggested by the simple public description of his position, acting as the personal secretary to Baron Katō himself and as his interpreter during all public and official functions, including the high-level meetings with American and British officials.[116] On November 21, a *New York Globe* reporter gave this account of Ichihashi's presence:

> Among the effective orators of Washington is Yamato Ichihashi, who translates for Admiral Baron Kato, chief of the Japanese delegation.

Mr. Ichihashi is a professor [of] Far Eastern history at Stanford University in California. At the last plenary conference he was brought in to deliver in English Admiral Kato's speech, which he did with great skill.

Ichihashi has made himself a necessity to Admiral Kato who, according to his colleagues, grows extremely nervous and anxious when his California interpreter is out of his sight, especially if Americans are present.[117]

Patrician political figures from around the world attended the Conference, with President Harding himself giving opening and closing addresses. Secretary of State Charles Evans Hughes led the American delegation, which included Senator Henry Cabot Lodge, former Senator and former Secretary of State Elihu Root, and Senator Oscar W. Underwood. From Britain came Foreign Secretary Arthur Balfour, from India Srinivasa Sastri, from China Alfred Sze and Wellington Koo, from France Aristide Briand, and unofficially representing Korea, then under Japanese occupation, Syngman Rhee. After working sessions of hard diplomatic bargaining, the various governments hosted "social functions" where dignitaries appeared in official regalia. Ichihashi joined the glittering formalities, where, in his words, "gold-braided uniforms and decorations were abundantly utilized."[118]

After ten long weeks of deliberation, the Conference produced agreements that restrained the naval arms race (symbolized by establishing the capital ship ratio of 5-5-3 for the United States, Great Britain, and Japan), affirmed, at least on paper, the policy of the "Open Door" for China and its territorial integrity, and established understandings that led to further temporary reductions of tension in Asia. The Conference won important concessions from all the powers involved, most significantly from Japan, which in turn was finally accorded status as one of the great world powers. Many in Japan believed that the Conference was the fruit of years of effort to improve relations with the United States. As judged at the time and in historical retrospect, the Conference "was clearly a landmark in history" and helped postpone the outbreak of war between the United States and Japan for twenty years.[119]

Yamato Ichihashi in his Stanford office. (Special Collections, Green Library, Stanford)

Below: Stanford Japanese students with university president David Starr Jordan, about 1905. Ichihashi is second from the right, top row. (Special Collections, Green Library, Stanford)

This 1916 photograph includes, in the front row, left to right: Steven Ivan Miller, Jr. (economics); Kiyoshi K. Kawakami, journalist; Ephraim Douglass Adams (history); Yamasaki Heikichi, acting consul general of Japan, San Francisco; Murray Shipley Wildman (economics); Arley Barthlow Show (history); Goroku Ikeda, journalist. Back row, left to right: Morioka Shohei, vice-consul; Yamato Ichihashi; (?) DeVries; Thomas Maitland Marshall (political science); Percy Alvin Martin (history); (?) Young; Payson J. Treat (history); Joh Tomoji, vice-consul; Kuwashima Kazue, vice-consul; Frederick Benjamin Garver (economics); Eugene Ellis Vann (history); Willard Hotchkiss (political science); Kyutaro Abiko, newspaper editor. All faculty were at Stanford. (Payson J. Treat Papers, Hoover Institution Archives)

Adml Tomosaburo Kato, head of the
Japanese Delegation, whose attitude
on Naval ratio, as between Japan
and the other powers, is the
subject of keen speculation in the
Conference. Photographed as he left
his hotel this morning accompanied
by his secty and a member of the
Secret service.
11/20/21 yamato Ichihashi #16978

The handwritten identification of Ichihashi was added in 1994. (Library of Congress)

Kei and Woodrow Ichi-
hashi, 1919. (Woodrow
Ichihashi)

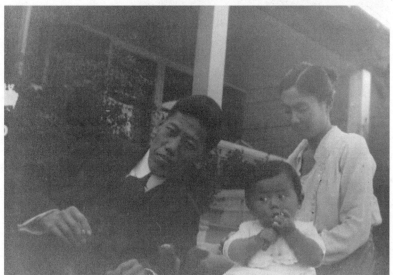

The Ichihashi family, 1920. (Woodrow Ichihashi)

Above: Woodrow and Kei
in the backyard of their
campus home, early 1920s.
(Woodrow Ichihashi)

Right: Woodrow Ichihashi,
1921. (Woodrow Ichihashi)

Shizuko Ichihashi, front left, Payson and Jessie Treat, center, and President
Nagayo Matao of Tokyo Imperial University, in front of his official residence,
December 1936. (Payson J. Treat Papers, Hoover Institution Archives)

President Ray Lyman Wilbur with students on the steps of the Japanese Club-
house on the Stanford campus, May 13, 1941. Front row, left to right: Paul Ya-
mamoto, Yoshio Okumoto, Wilbur, Ichihashi, Matsuye Takeshita. Second row:
Yoshio Oishi, Setsuo Dairiki, Alan Yamakawa (?), Cornelius Chiamori, Kay Ki-
tagawa, Ichiro Nagai, Takeo Omori. Third row: Pete Ida, Kazuyuki Takahashi,
Goro Oishi, Thomas Kawahara, Iwao Bando (?), Paul Fujii. Fourth row: Harold
Arai, Roy Nakagawa, Neil Kosasa, Wataru Takeshita, Tohru Inouye. Top row:
Elmer Tanase, George Kitagawa. (Special Collections, Green Library, Stanford)

Stanford faculty panelists at the October 2, 1941, Memorial Hall discussion of world conflict. Left to right: Karl Brandt, Philip Buck, Ray Lyman Wilbur, Yamato Ichihashi, Vladimir Timoshenko, Ralph Lutz, Shau Wing Chan, Graham Stuart, Rudolf Holsti, and Albert Guerard. (Special Collections, Green Library, Stanford)

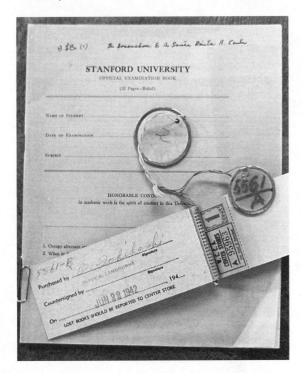

Cover of Yamato Ichihashi's first "Blue Book" diary, his ticket book, and his identification tag from the Santa Anita Assembly Center. (Yamato Ichihashi Papers, Special Collections, Green Library, Stanford)

Above: Page 1 of Yamato Ichihashi's first "Blue Book" diary. (Yamato Ichihashi Papers, Special Collections, Green Library, Stanford)

Right: Directive, baggage tag, and coupon book from Santa Anita Assembly Center. (Yamato Ichihashi Papers, Special Collections, Green Library, Stanford)

Above: A few of Yamato Ichihashi's mementos from Tule Lake. (Yamato Ichihashi Papers, Special Collections, Green Library, Stanford)

Right: A postcard announcing a meeting of the Stanford Faculty Club, forwarded twice to Ichihashi. (Yamato Ichihashi Papers, Special Collections, Green Library, Stanford)

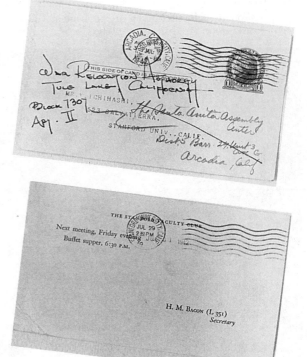

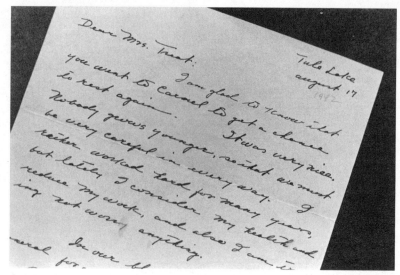

Kei Ichihashi's letter to Jessie Treat, August 17, 1943, from Tule Lake. (Payson J. Treat Papers, Hoover Institution Archives)

Woodie Ichihashi leading his jazz band at Tule Lake, November 1, 1942. (Record Group 210, National Archives)

2

"Son of the Rising Sun"

During his career at Stanford, Yamato Ichihashi developed special ties with the Japanese government and maintained a strong loyalty toward his land of origin. Examining his attachment helps us understand aspects of race and international relations in the early twentieth century as well as the possible reasons for the U.S. government's suspicion of him during World War II.

There seems little doubt Ichihashi had established a close relationship with Tokyo that accrued important benefits both to him and to the Japanese government. Ichihashi's own job at Stanford resulted from Tokyo's effort to counteract anti-Japanese sentiment centered in California. The racist agitation was highly insulting to the Japanese; they were charged with "stealing" jobs away from white workers, endangering white racial purity, and engaging in unsavory social practices and vices, such as the importing of "picture brides" and excessive gambling. The hostility toward Japanese immigrants—not to mention the exclusionary immigration laws directed against them—was so great that the Japanese government repeatedly raised the issues of racial equality for all peoples and of decent treatment of its citizens overseas as prominent concerns at the Versailles Peace Conference and at the labor and disarmament conferences attended by Ichihashi.[1] Eliot Grinnell Mears, a Stanford professor who studied race relations in the 1920's, explicitly linked domestic politics and foreign policy when he observed, "The attitude of California and Californians has largely determined American foreign policy toward the Oriental."[2] He did not exaggerate.

Thus the Japanese government believed money to support Ichihashi and others like him who were sympathetic to Japan was money well spent. For years, Japan had been actively engaged in expanding its influence in the Pacific region, including the United States. Its emigrants, trade, and culture were all seen as peaceful ways of advancing its national interests and prestige.[3] Just before the funds came to endow the Stanford chair in Japanese studies, a former minister of home affairs and foreign minister, Baron Gotō Shinpei, confidentially reported to the Japanese foreign ministry that Ichihashi had been "an effective agent who is supported by the Imperial Government to engage in indirect propaganda."[4]

What kind of "indirect propaganda" (Gotō's term) did Ichihashi produce? What kind of "propagandist" (the FBI's label) was he for Japan at this time?

In examining Ichihashi's published work in the late 1910's and 1920's, one certainly finds that he wrote sympathetically about Japan and Japanese immigrants. His approach was effective for an American audience, but in a way that was neither blatantly partisan nor transparently apologetic or self-serving. His work, for example, deeply impressed Stanford presidents David Starr Jordan and Ray Lyman Wilbur, both among the most prominent educators and public intellectuals of their day. They in turn openly promoted his work. In a letter to President William Howard Taft opposing congressional consideration of legislation that discriminated against Japanese immigrants, Jordan once appended an essay written by Ichihashi, whom Jordan described as a "highly educated Japanese gentleman," to present a "fairly typical" Japanese point of view for the President's consideration. An "admirable paper" "written in good form" Wilbur wrote to Ichihashi about his 1913 pamphlet on Japanese immigrants and recommended that he send copies to President Woodrow Wilson and Secretary of State William Jennings Bryan. Ichihashi's basic argument was simply that Japanese immigrants deserved fair treatment, equal to that which other immigrants received, and that the allegations against the Japanese stemmed from demagoguery, misinformation, or simple race prejudice. He argued that immigrants from all countries should be placed on a quota and that the right of naturalization be extended all immigrants. With such a right, he maintained, Japanese immigrants "will make contributions to American civilization as its loyal citizens." He ended the 1915 revision of his tract with a typical American appeal: "Give them a chance."[5]

For their part, Ichihashi publicly urged Japanese immigrants to "Americanize." They should assimilate as "the first step for their success," he maintained, and then by "contributing to the national interests of America they could attain their own economic development." They should not live a sojourner life, planning to make quick money and return to Japan, but rather should accept America as their permanent home. In these views, he associated himself with his longtime friend Kyutaro Abiko, the publisher of the *Nichibei Shimbun* (Japanese American news), the leading Japanese-language newspaper in America. Abiko had arrived in San Francisco in 1885, joined the Gospel Society, as had Ichihashi, and attended the University of California from 1892 to 1896. He founded his newspaper in 1899 and worked on it with Hachiro Senoo, a Stanford graduate. Ichihashi respected Abiko, but also considered him impractical and "an idealist."[6]

As for Japanese politics, Ichihashi identified himself with what he saw as the emerging Western-oriented, educated, modern, and democratic elite of Japan. Ichihashi's public talks and essays in these years emphasized the rapidly changing nature of Japanese society, and he wrote positively of the Westernization of many aspects of society and culture and of its political democratization. "The Westernized political life of New Japan is now a vital part of her organic existence," he noted. "Destroy it, and Japan will be no more."[7] Some others in Japan were much less welcoming of the changes overtaking their country. Ultraconservatives considered the West venal and corrupt and opposed its influences.[8]

Japan possessed a "peculiar type of civilization and culture, conspicuous for its hybrid character," as Ichihashi put it. "It was neither distinctly Oriental nor Occidental," and was especially capable of assimilating "exotic things" from others. In this respect, Ichihashi sincerely believed, other nations could learn from Japan. He, in other words, was clearly proud of being a modern, progressive (meaning, in favor of change and "modernization") Japanese and considered it his responsibility to help others understand his mother country as accurately and as positively as possible. Throughout his career, he wrote for periodicals with popular audiences and frequently spoke at events that reached beyond a narrow, scholarly audience.[9]

At the same time he promoted understanding of Japan and its image in America, he was deeply respectful and admiring of America. He not only wrote favorably about its educational institutions, system of government, economic might, and material culture, but also commended its "spiritual civilization," from which he believed Japan could learn much. He liked America's openness, its democratic aspirations (if not always its practice), its generosity, and its practicality. Following the devastating 1923 Tokyo earthquake and American humanitarian help in its aftermath, Ichihashi profusely praised the American people in an article in the travel magazine *Japan*. His home country, he assured his American readers, would rebuild from the rubble of the earthquake with America's generous material help and example. America helped motivate the people of Japan, who would build a "newly inspired spiritual civilization," he wrote. On another occasion in 1925, he stated that "the Westernization of material aspects of Japanese life is not so important as the Westernization of intellectual and emotional aspects of her life." Ichihashi, who regarded the "spiritual" or ideological life of a society as most important, was never a cultural exclusivist.[10]

Moreover, Ichihashi saw no substantive reason, such as fundamentally different national interests or ambitions, for enmity between the two countries. "The interests of America and Japan do not clash," he wrote in 1922, soon after the Washington Conference. "Prosperity for one means prosperity for the other. Both are actuated by the same desire for peace and friendship." Troubles that did exist between America and Japan resulted, in his mind, largely from ignorance and racial prejudice on the American side and from feudal narrowness on the Japanese side. "True understanding, sincere sympathy and active cooperation will never fail to cure international ills of any kind," Ichihashi optimistically wrote in 1922 about United States–Japan relations. Japan and the United States should collaborate in the modernization of Asia.[11]

In contrast to America, countries such as Russia, Germany, and China—with all of which Japan had been at war in the last two decades—drew few kind words from Ichihashi. He believed that Chinese immigrants in America, though they suffered from racial prejudice, were nonetheless responsible for many of their troubles in this country. He described China as backward, chaotic, and responsible for its low standing among nations. In his view, Japan's aggressive involvement in China was a legitimate quest for economic gain and political stability. A history full of wars and the civil disorder following the 1911 Revolution proved, in his view, that "the Chinese have not been and are not a peaceable people." His attitude toward China was a mixture of chauvinism and genuine conviction that Japan's modernity and power could uplift downtrodden China and the rest of Asia, which had suffered under European colonialism.[12]

Even though he wrote from a consistently sympathetic view toward Japan, Ichihashi was not above the rare public criticism of Tokyo's politics. "Infamous," "notorious," and "an epoch-making diplomatic blunder" is what he called the so-called "twenty-one demands" raised by Japan against China in 1915, which sought naked imperialist privileges for Japan in China.[13] He criticized certain political factions in Tokyo as "bureaucratic" or "militarist" or "aristocratic," identifying himself with what he believed were the rising, forward-thinking forces of the country. But his criticisms were limited, and he never publicly confronted the growing contradiction in Japan between peaceful liberalism and imperialism. Ichihashi never took a stand against Japan's designs on China in the late 1920's and 1930's and did not seem to understand that Japan's growing military might and aggressive nationalism were antithetical to his own professed visions of a peaceful international order.

In general, Ichihashi's writings reflected his dedication to the life work he had chosen for himself when he became a graduate student— that is, to improve the mutual understanding between East and West, and more specifically between Japan and the United States. He subordinated himself to this grand task, perhaps even to the extent of obviating his own political good sense and, given that he once actively identified with David Starr Jordan's antimilitarist views, his own erstwhile principles. Perhaps there was also an aspect of opportunism on his part—Ichihashi was profoundly ambitious. Yet one also must remember that he was acutely aware that he was a *Japanese citizen* and by law prohibited from becoming naturalized in the United States. As with first-generation immigrants of all nationalities, he retained pride in his ancestry, but the racial prejudice and isolation that Japanese experienced in America further encouraged him to cultivate close attachments to the motherland.[14] Finally, Ichihashi, as an international relations specialist, felt particular responsibility—and was frequently explicitly given the task by his American colleagues—to present the "Japanese point of view" on foreign policy issues to the American public, whose fear and suspicion of Japan's policy in the Pacific mounted in the 1920's and 1930's. Ichihashi never forgot, and he was often reminded, that he was a Japanese national, with aristocratic blood in his veins.

Following the flurry of semigovernmental activity and international conferences in the early 1920's, Ichihashi settled into an active academic life at Stanford. He never again flirted with the heady life of international diplomacy, perhaps because he simply preferred the stable, predictable routine of a college professor. He worked steadily to complete *The Washington Conference and After*, which Stanford University Press published in 1928. The book, dedicated to his old mentor David Starr Jordan, was immediately accepted as an authoritative account and was respected as such for years.

Stanford University Press thought highly of Ichihashi's work—an editor publicly promoted it by saying that "only two other living men, [Lord] Balfour and [Charles Evans] Hughes, could tell more about the gathering." The press also vigorously defended the book against some American reviewers who cast the work as presenting a Japanese point of view of the Conference. "It is no such thing," a Stanford Press newsletter argued:

> Dr. Ichihashi is a historian. He tells the story of the Washington Conference, tells it thoroughly and completely, tells it without prejudice of any sort. His book would have been written no differently had he been an American, a German, or a Fiji Islander. He was able to write the book he wrote because he is a scholar. . . . His is the best book yet written on the subject.

The editor ended his praise of Ichihashi by pointing out that Japanese critics had expressed "deep regret" that his book, in fact, did not present "a defense of Japan" at the Conference. Regardless, the press and David Starr Jordan held the work in such high esteem that in 1929 Jordan presented a specially bound copy as a gift to the Emperor of Japan.[15]

Around the time of the book's publication, Ichihashi's career as an academic was confirmed when Stanford promoted him to associate professor with lifelong tenure. He attempted to maintain relations with Japanese officialdom—he regularly entertained Japanese government officials on campus and periodically traveled to Japan—but after the Washington Conference he no longer cultivated ties with Tokyo to the extent he once had. He never again acted in any official capacity or joined any delegation for Tokyo. The choice, however, may not have been entirely his. As a later FBI report on Ichihashi speculated, it may have been that the Japanese reception of his book on the Washington Conference was not altogether positive, though the book was seemingly sympathetic and supportive of the Japanese government's point of view. The FBI learned of rumors that because his book did not express "a proper appreciation" of Japan's position, the Tokyo government gave Ichihashi no further official appointments. Another possible explanation is that he may have come to be identified with the naval faction in Japanese politics, which eventually lost out to the more aggressive and ultranationalist forces around the imperial army who believed that the Washington Conference had confirmed Western domination over the world.[16]

In any event, family needs and local demands kept him extremely busy. Like many other Stanford professors, Ichihashi believed that civic responsibilities accompanied his social position. He also wanted to be a good citizen of his home country and played a leading role in local efforts to raise humanitarian relief for the many victims of the devastating Tokyo earthquake of September 1923, which killed more than 100,000 people. The response was gratifying to him, and as noted he publicly praised American generosity toward Japan, writing that "the Japanese now know what the true American heart is—what the true Christian heart is."[17] In the 1920's and 1930's, he regularly spoke before civic groups interested in Japan and Pacific affairs, his lecture topics ranging from "Women Writers of the Tenth Century in Japan," for the Stanford Faculty Women's Club, to "The London Naval Conference," for the Commonwealth Club of San Francisco on May 2, 1930. Ichihashi seems to have represented himself and Japan well in these events; those whites who met him invariably recalled him favorably. He impressed them as a refined, cultured man on a par with any American of like station.[18]

Ichihashi also became a much sought-after contributor to the rapidly growing academic fields of international studies and race relations. He regularly wrote reviews of scholarly works on Japanese economics and politics and presented papers to convocations of specialists interested in current international problems. One of the more important of these occasions was the founding conference in July 1925 in Honolulu of what became known as the Institute of Pacific Relations (IPR). Twenty years later, after World War II, the IPR became a favorite target of archconservatives in their witch-hunt against suspected leftists in government and academia, but in 1925, the IPR, though a bold nongovernmental attempt to improve international understanding, was far from controversial.[19] Its first chairman was Stanford's Ray Lyman Wilbur, himself a confirmed Republican with close personal and professional ties to party leaders like Herbert Hoover, an active Stanford alumnus and soon to be U.S. president.

The Hawaii conference became the first of many in the pre–World War II years that brought together on an unofficial basis leading citizens and prominent academics from countries in the Pacific area to discuss common problems and seek ways to avoid conflict. On the way to Japan for a visit in 1925, Ichihashi attended the first meeting of the IPR as a member of the Japanese delegation, which included his friend Anesaki Masaharu, professor of religion at Tokyo University. Much of the discussion during the two-week meeting focused on issues of racial prejudice, immigration, and Western colonialism in the Pacific. The Japanese delegation specifically raised the problem of discriminatory legislation in the United States directed against Japanese, as manifested in the 1924 Immigration Act, which effectively ended Japanese immigration to the United States and confirmed their status as "aliens ineligible for citizenship." Ichihashi himself had fought passage of the bill and was embittered when President Calvin Coolidge signed it into law.[20] In contrast to the hostile American attitude toward Japanese, Japan welcomed the dramatic changes in its social, intellectual, and political spheres, according to Ichihashi. His lecture to the IPR, on "The Westernization of Japan," a favorite topic of his, hailed the changes brought to his land of ancestry. In his assessment, Japan and the West, the United States in particular, were becoming increasingly similar, which he hoped would help persuade Americans that friendlier, not more distant, relations were in order. It was a theme he reiterated at conferences throughout the later 1920's and 1930's. Ichihashi regularly attended IPR meetings in the prewar years.[21]

But the subject that most often commanded his attention remained the experience of Japanese immigrants in America, the focus of his early research activities and his doctoral dissertation. Even as he worked on problems of international diplomacy, he never ceased his involvement in opposing the virulent anti-Japanese movement that plagued California. He regularly met with immigration officials and even leading anti-Japanese agitators, like newspaper publisher V. S. McClatchy of the Japanese Exclusion League, to dispute and debate their anti-Japanese biases.[22]

Japanese Americans in the interwar years suffered social isolation and widespread discrimination. Some had attended college and became professionals in urban areas, but the vast majority remained tied to agricultural work and menial occupations. One embittered college graduate, Kazuo Kawai, who had studied under Ichihashi wrote in 1926, the year he began his doctoral work at Stanford,

> Our community is not self-sufficient. We can't stand off and live our own lives. We've got to find a place in American society in order to survive. And yet, no matter what our qualifications may be, evidently the only place where we are wanted is in positions that no Americans would care to fill—menial positions as house-servants, gardeners, vegetable peddlers, continually "yes, ma'am"-ing.[23]

As late as 1940, for example, almost 60 percent of Japanese males in Los Angeles still claimed agriculture as their area of work. They were engaged as farm laborers, tenant and family farmers, nurserymen, gardeners, and florists; in the retail trades they ran small produce shops.[24]

In 1922, Ichihashi joined the first major academic study of the Asian population in America. Stanford president Ray Lyman Wilbur headed the effort, known as the "Survey of Race Relations: A Study of the Oriental on the Pacific Coast," initiated by the Institute of Social and Religious Research in New York. Its stated purpose was "to discover and interpret some of the chief facts about relations between Orientals and whites on the Pacific Coast." The study went on for three years, when it ran out of funding, and involved dozens of researchers, including the well-known sociologist Robert E. Park of the University of Chicago, research director of the survey, and Eliot Grinnell Mears of Stanford, who later published much of the survey's findings in his 1928 *Resident Orientals on the American Pacific Coast*. Ichihashi participated in research panels and spoke before a convocation of 150 college presidents, leading academics, and political figures who had gathered at Stanford in March 1925 to learn the tentative findings of the survey. His talk, "The Awakening of the Orient," reviewed Japan's role in Asia and encouraged Japanese-American cooperation.[25]

Stanford had been an important center for research into Asian Americans since its earliest years. In the 1890's Mary Coolidge, a sociologist, had taught a course at the university on race problems, and in 1909 she published her classic book, *Chinese Immigration*, which remains the most comprehensive study of the conditions and status of the Chinese in the United States in the nineteenth and early twentieth centuries. Her work explicitly opposed the anti-Chinese movement. It is not known whether Ichihashi had had any contact with Coolidge at Stanford before she moved to Mills College in Oakland. But after joining the Stanford faculty, Ichihashi became an indispensable colleague in race relations research at Stanford and helped establish Stanford as a leading center of study of Asians in America. In addition to his earlier work with H. A. Millis and Mears,[26] he also worked with psychologist Edward K. Strong, Jr., who wrote three books about Japanese Americans;[27] and Reginald Bell, a former student and research assistant of Ichihashi's, who wrote extensively about the education problems of American-born Asian Americans, including *Public School Education of Second-Generation Japanese in California*, published in 1935. The early work of Ichihashi's History Department colleague Thomas A. Bailey,[28] who became one of the country's leading diplomatic historians, was also directly related to Ichihashi's interests. In the early 1930's, Bailey published "Japanese Protest Against the Annexation of Hawaii," and "California, Japan, and the Alien Land Legislation of 1913," and in 1934 the book *Theodore Roosevelt and the Japanese-American Crises: An Account of the International Complications Arising from the Race Problem on the Pacific Coast.* Sociologist Walter Greenwood Beach produced *Oriental Crime in California: A Study of Offenses Committed by Orientals in That State, 1900–1927* (1932), while sociologist Charles N. Reynolds, who had studied white attitudes toward Asians in Santa Clara for his Stanford doctoral dissertation, undertook a comprehensive study of Californians' attitudes toward Filipinos in the early 1930's.[29] Payson Treat, too, included research on Japanese Americans as part of his ongoing work on U.S.-Japan relations. And Ichihashi assisted the graduate work of students interested in race relations in addition to those who focused on Asia.[30]

In 1927, not long after completing his manuscript on the Washington Conference, Ichihashi renewed his field studies of the Japanese population in California and worked on the revision of his doctoral dissertation on Japanese immigrants. With the help of a two-year grant from the Social Science Research Council at Stanford, he produced in 1932 his classic and still frequently cited study, *Japanese in the United States: A Critical Study of the Problems of the Japanese Immigrants and Their Children.*[31] The work, over 400 pages in length, though still containing elements of his doctoral dissertation, substantially developed his earlier work on Japanese immigrants. It first surveys the international migration of Japanese, including their migration to the Hawaiian Islands, and then concentrates on four aspects of their life on the U.S. mainland: "the coming of the Japanese"; an analysis of the social, economic, and cultural aspects of their lives; "a historical examination of anti-Japanese agitation"; and last, a "survey of the so-called second-generation problems." The book is historical in that its author reviews the developments of the past, but its principal intent is to give the reader an understanding of the current condition of Japanese in America. It accomplishes this through heavy use of statistical evidence gathered from government reports and Ichihashi's own field research. Clearly and explicitly sympathetic to the Japanese, the study is nonetheless judicious, and its essential arguments are carefully substantiated.

The book is an interesting amalgam of several different elements, all characteristic of Ichihashi's intellectual style. First there is the core of the work, what was then considered careful, dispassionate sociology. Ichihashi hoped meticulous statistical and demographic work would present "an accurate, objective" (his words) profile of the Japanese in America and disprove a number of prejudiced assumptions about them. For example, he carefully reviewed Japanese and U.S. government figures on passports, visas, and registered entries into the country and methods of tabulation to show that, in fact, the Japanese had *not* flocked to the United States in "hordes" in the critical decade of 1901–10, as their detractors had charged. The commonly accepted figures, he showed, had been inflated. Nor had the Japanese formed any possible threat to dominate any occupation or trade, as had also been feared. They had simply tried to make an honest living; as he showed with figures gathered from employment agencies and his own investigations, Japanese domestic workers had not undercut anybody—Chinese, Filipinos or whites—and had been paid roughly comparable wages. If anything, the complaint against the Japanese might have been that they had been more diligent, intelligent, or ambitious than others in the same circumstances. He reminded the reader, for instance, of "the common complaint of housewives, still dreaming of old-fashioned servants no longer to be had, that their Japanese servants are often too intellectual and philosophical."[32]

A second element of Ichihashi's intellectual style is also evident in this book. He included personal impressions and observations gathered during his field research, principally in 1927–30, when he traveled to Fresno, Walnut Grove, Los Angeles, and Watsonville in California, and to Salt Lake City. Not only did such evidence give credibility to his work, it also intrigued the reader, especially when Ichihashi discussed issues far removed from the rarefied air of academia and polite society. Ichihashi included firsthand reports of rough migrant labor camps in California's Santa Clara Valley, of the flower-growing industry in Oakland, of segregated "Oriental" schools in the Sacramento delta, and of the operations of open-pit copper mines in Utah. While this material distinguished his work from that of other investigators, who lacked his access to the Japanese communities, he made far less use of this personal material than he could have, or would have had he been writing today, when we are more intrigued by such felt experiences and personal testimony. He may have assumed that this evidence was too "soft," too impressionistic, to be convincing to his fellow academics whose confidence was in numbers.[33]

Finally, alongside traditional discussion of other scholarly work in English and Japanese, Ichihashi employed a peculiar argumentative device. He frequently relied on long quotations from other published work. Their authors were virtually always white men (usually his colleagues such as Millis, Mears, or Treat), and he utilized them, it seems, as authoritative voices to substantiate points he feared would be taken as special pleading on behalf of the Japanese if he made them in his own words. As he added after one of these cumbersome block quotes, he could have formulated his own statement but preferred to rely on "American authorities." Ichihashi was never free of his self-consciousness at being an alien ineligible for citizenship in the United States, a fact that he pointedly included on the very first page of the book to establish his relationship to the subject matter and that he continued to remind the reader of throughout the book.

Ichihashi seems to have been unaware of any tension or contradiction between his sensitivity to the perceived subjectivity arising from nationality and his own claim to objectivity. Moreover, he saw no problem with adopting a didactic tone at times, as in the passages when he pontificates that young Japanese Americans should be optimistic, apply themselves, learn from their elders, and be mindful that they will have to work harder than whites if they are to compete successfully. He urged white Americans (he calls them simply "Americans") to adopt "a more kindly and sympathetic attitude toward these unfortunate sons and daughters of Japanese descent" and give them an opportunity to prove themselves.[34]

The general impression about Japanese Americans the reader takes away from the book is that they are a hard-working, intelligent people, comparable in ability to any other immigrant group in America. (Ichihashi reserved his caustic comments about the moral and intellectual qualities of his fellow Japanese, especially the American-born *nisei* for more private circumstances.) The Japanese sought assimilation as much as anyone. Yet Ichihashi wanted to leave no rosy picture—his investigations, in fact, had left him deeply troubled. The future of the Japanese in America, in his eyes, was complicated and not without dangers.

In his chapters on the second generation, Ichihashi observed that many of the young American-born children of Japanese immigrants were quickly leaving their parents behind culturally; they had even "developed a contemptuous attitude toward things Japanese, and in consequence parental and school discipline became more and more difficult." Was he speaking from personal experience? As he revealed, "The writer, as the father of an American-born boy, is perfectly familiar with this perplexing [social and legal] situation. Even in the child's prattle the father is reminded: 'I am an American and you are a Japanese.'" And yet the second-generation Japanese were still not full Americans, Ichihashi pointed out. "The Japanese children retain enough physical markings to be ranked as aliens, and are treated accordingly. There is the same social and racial prejudice against these Japanese-Americans as there is against their alien parents." As a result, he observed, many second-generation Japanese Americans, as they grow older and themselves encounter prejudice and social restriction, develop bitterness and resentment toward things *American*. They then tend "to rectify their former contemptuous attitude toward Japan and things Japanese" and begin even "to idealize the country of their parents." He warned that "these young Japanese-

Americans constitute a social problem not only for their parents but also for Americans."[35]

In hindsight, these observations painfully anticipate the wrenching and sharply conflicting mix of Japanese American reactions to internment a decade later. They also sound prescient about some of the perverse rationales given to justify relocation itself. While Ichihashi thought that drawing attention to the "social problem" of young Japanese Americans' feelings about Japan and America would help prompt white Americans to improve their racial attitudes, he could not know how his words would return to haunt him. After Pearl Harbor, federal officials, including Chief Justice Harlan Fiske Stone of the Supreme Court, used words similar to Ichihashi's observations of a decade earlier to label Japanese Americans security risks, endorsing relocation and internment. In an argument that justified victimizing the victim, Stone upheld internment on the grounds that the history of discrimination against Japanese in America may have made them resentful of, and thus dangerous to, the United States. They were therefore deserving, in his view, of incarceration.[36]

In his private research notes, Ichihashi revealed serious concern about a related situation facing Japanese Americans. During his fieldwork, he found deep divisions splitting the community. He saw that the California-born, Hawaii-born, and Japan-born Japanese each had contempt for the others. The California-born, he observed, felt superior to the other two communities because they felt the wealth of the American and Occidental tradition behind them; the Japan-born believed they were culturally superior to the others, who were seen as crude; and the Hawaiian Japanese felt superior to both since they understood the cultures of both East and West. Ichihashi wondered what would happen to these people if war came between the United States and Japan. Which side should they turn to for protection? They were in a perplexing situation, he conceded, and he had no answers.[37] The divisions, which did erupt later during relocation, often resulted in far-reaching and bitter consequences, documented by Ichihashi himself in his diary and research essays.

Taken as a whole, Ichihashi's book was without doubt the most important book then written about the Japanese in America, and it remains authoritative to this day. His statistical work has never been seriously challenged, and his reportage was never duplicated. The book received uniformly good reviews in the professional journals at the time.[38]

The publication of *Japanese in the United States* helped confirm Ichihashi as a leading member of the academic community. He was promoted to full professor at Stanford in 1931, and for the rest of the decade played an active role in the Pacific Coast Branch of the American Historical Association, becoming one of the first members of the board of editors for the *Pacific Historical Review*, the organization's scholarly journal.[39] At Stanford, he and Payson Treat carried the teaching responsibilities for Asian Studies, with Ichihashi presenting courses on Japanese history, government, civilization, and foreign relations, and his friend focusing on American relations with Asian countries and Chinese history. His colleagues in the department were principally international relations specialists, men such as E. D. Adams and Ralph Lutz, both of whom, along with Treat, helped build the Hoover Library. Another associate was Lynn White, Jr., who became a distinguished European medievalist, was named president of Mills College in 1943, and finished his career at UCLA.

Ichihashi and Treat built Stanford into a leading center of Asian Studies, a field still in its infancy in the United States. They, along with Ka-n'ichi Asakawa at Yale, were among the first Asianists in the United States. (Yale, however, did not promote Asakawa to the professorate until many years after Ichihashi joined the Stanford faculty.) But Ichihashi was not satisfied with the results. The field in the United States was far from professionalized, in his view, dominated as it was by individuals who had picked up knowledge of Asia informally through personal experiences, during travel or residence as members of missionary families, trade, or diplomatic work. Even Treat and Ichihashi were not formally trained as Asianists, although Ichihashi was able to conduct research into Chinese and Japanese texts. Ichihashi complained that Stanford students interested in Asia learned principally about Far Eastern politics and diplomacy, areas in which English-language materials could be used. The cultural side was not offered at Stanford or at most other institutions. The reason for this was simple, he observed: most American scholars teaching in the field were unacquainted with any Asian language. They therefore shied away from teaching about Chinese or Japanese civilization, culture, and literature. As he once complained to a colleague, "To attempt to teach Japanese and Chinese civilization without a knowledge of the languages involved is academically futile; it is like an attempt to teach Greek civilization without a knowledge of Greek." Ichihashi urged that Stanford hire faculty to teach Japanese and Chinese in order to train a new generation of scholars who could work in the original languages, build its Asian library collection, and allocate resources for students to study abroad. His recommendations were all gradually realized, though not until after World War II.[40]

Years later, after he retired, Ichihashi could be proud of his contribution to the development of Asian Studies. He and Treat had worked with many students, some of whom became important specialists in the histories of Japan and China and in Asian politics and diplomacy. They included Delmer Brown, Charles Nelson Spinks, Donald Nugent, Paul Clyde, Kazuo Kawai, Meribeth Cameron, Reginald Bell, and Stanford undergraduate Arthur F. Wright, whom Ichihashi characterized in 1937 as "the most brilliant young student" he had known. Wright later received his doctorate from Harvard and returned to Stanford to become an eminent scholar of Confucianism. Gordon Wright (no relation to Arthur) was also deeply influenced by Ichihashi, served as his teaching assistant for one quarter while a graduate student, and at one time thought seriously about teaching in Japan.[41] He became a distinguished historian of modern France and European diplomatic history. Although Ichihashi himself did not leave a rich legacy in research and publication on Japanese history—few historians of Japan today associate him with their field—he helped train a new generation of American scholars who would make important contributions. Ichihashi once calculated that, all in all, some 33 of his students went on to teach at institutions of higher learning in the United States.[42] Some of Ichihashi's former graduate students remember him with affection; others recall that he was a difficult mentor.

Ichihashi reached the high point of his career in the 1930's, when many considered him perhaps America's leading authority on Japanese politics. At the same time, he found himself in an increasingly controversial position because of events in Asia, sparked by what we know as the Manchurian Incident. On the night of September 18, 1931, units of the Japanese army stationed in Manchuria surreptitiously blew up property of the Japanese-controlled South Manchurian Railway. Blaming the Chinese for the explosion, Tokyo used the event as pretext to invade the northeast provinces of China. Japan rapidly occupied the whole of Manchuria, withdrew from the League of Nations after that body condemned Japan's aggression, established the puppet regime known as Manchukuo, and absorbed the rest of northern China into the Japanese empire. In January 1932, Japanese forces attacked Shanghai, killing thousands of civilians before withdrawing. Japan's march toward ultranationalism and militarism was confirmed, and in the view of many later historians, World War II had begun. By 1937, Japan would launch an all-out effort to conquer China.

The United States, though not a member of the League, formally protested Japan's actions in Manchuria, and American public opinion swung strongly in favor of the beleaguered Chinese, with prominent figures like President A. Lawrence Lowell of Harvard calling for a boycott of Japanese goods. Ichihashi's old friend Hanihara Masanao, the former Japanese consul general in San Francisco and now the ambassador to Washington, forcefully defended Japan's actions. Ultimately, Washington issued only moral condemnations and stopped short of taking any substantive steps.

Ichihashi now faced the most serious crisis in U.S.-Japan relations yet, but it seems to have posed no observable personal dilemma for him. It was not that he had favored the military in Japan; shortly before the Manchurian Incident, in fact, he had expressed optimism about Japan's development toward a two-party democratic system of government despite the growing political turbulence in the country. In his view, Japan was moving from autocracy and bureaucracy toward liberalism. The Japanese, he was certain, "will succeed in avoiding revolution. Whatever further political progress is to be attained, will be done through evolutionary processes in which extreme conservatism . . . and extreme radicalism . . . will be mutually modified." Whether Ichihashi really believed in such a rosy assessment or wrote to please an American audience wanting to indulge in wishful thinking, we do not know. In practice, he became virtually an apologist for expansionist Japan.[43]

Ichihashi publicly hailed the coronation of Henry Pu Yi as the new emperor of Manchukuo on March 1, 1932. And several months later, in the fall of 1932, Ichihashi took a sabbatical leave from Stanford to travel to Japan and the Far East for eight months, taking Kei and Woodrow, his now adolescent son, with him. Seven years had passed since he and Kei last visited Japan, both his parents had now passed away, and he was a well-known and respected professor in his homeland. In the letters he sent regularly to Payson Treat and to Edgar Robinson, the chair of the History Department, an influential presence at the university and a close friend, Ichihashi reported that he was kept very busy, busier even than when he was on the job at Stanford. "Tokyo," he wrote in a letter soon after arriving in Japan, "makes me feel like a rustic. Modernity knocks me down." He was kept busy with numerous speaking invitations and meetings with old friends in Tokyo and was relieved finally to flee to Nara, where he spent most of his time engaged in research. The beauty of that city and its surrounding countryside charmed him and touched a poetic nerve: the "flute-like calls for mates" of the famous Nara deer reminded him of the "love songs of old," he wrote Treat. He represented Stanford University at the fiftieth anniversary of the founding of Waseda University in Tokyo and delivered fifteen lectures at Tokyo University in the spring of 1933. While his letters to Treat and Robinson were warm and personable, asking them regularly to convey his greetings to the rest of his "history family," he made only vague comments about what he saw in Japan and about his specific activities. He wrote nothing about sensitive issues such as the effect of the worldwide Depression on Japan's economy and society or the political turmoil caused by the rising fascist movement. Political assassinations wracked the country. In May 1932, just before Ichihashi's arrival in Tokyo, a group of extremist military officers attempted to spark a military coup d'état. Though unsuccessful, they killed the country's premier and set the stage for the ascendance of the army over the civilian government in the following years.[44]

The most telling record of Ichihashi's thinking during his stay in Japan are the published talks and lectures he gave. In these, Ichihashi presented his assessment of the domestic scene in the United States and the state of relations between the United States and Japan. One would think that the talks Ichihashi presented before sympathetic audiences of his countrymen would be more candid than his presentations in the United States and that appears to have been the case. And yet Ichihashi was ever the deeply cautious person—even his published remarks are carefully presented and avoid anything that might have been controversial for the Japanese. He made no comment about Japanese politics, for example.

At a dinner party on October 14, 1932, Ichihashi spoke before a group of Japanese international relations specialists on the situation in the United States and American attitudes toward Japan. His comments, which reveal interesting insights into his personal feelings about America and Americans, began with a description of the magnitude of the Great Depression and the human suffering it had caused—in all his years in the United States, he had never seen an economic downturn on this scale. He told of job seekers who came to his home asking for work every day. But Americans were a very proud and individualistic people, having honor and self-respect, and they did not like to resort to receiving government relief. He admired their pragmatism but was angered by their unreasonable attitudes about race. They were essentially a conservative people, typified by Herbert Hoover, who he expected would be reelected in November, even though he believed Franklin D. Roosevelt possessed superior family and political credentials. But Americans were not as "progressive," he said, as the Japanese, who were more receptive to change. As for international relations, he observed, America emerged from World War I triumphant, with Europe now having to follow America's lead. The United States enforced its Monroe Doctrine over Latin America and pursued an Open Door policy toward Asia to advance its own interests; in its domestic life, though, it followed a "closed door" policy, by shutting off immigration and mistreating Japanese immigrants. On U.S.-Japanese relations, Ichihashi presented a sober picture of American feelings toward Japan. He spoke in an interestingly comparative way: he characterized the relationship as competitive, even adversarial, in Asia. Both were rising, vigorous countries—the Spanish-American War marked America's entrance onto the world stage, just as the Sino-Japanese War of 1895 did for Japan. And now the two countries were the leading powers in the Pacific. He feared that greater conflict, though short of war, was unavoidable.[45]

Ichihashi advised his academic audiences that they should understand the reasons for America's hostile reaction to Japan's advance into Manchuria and seek to improve their understanding of America generally. The common view in America was that Japan was strong and China weak, the underdog—and Americans traditionally favored the underdog, he pointed out. Furthermore, Chinese propaganda was very effective in getting the Chinese point of view across to American audiences, whereas Japan's case had been poorly presented. For Ichihashi, the issue was one of improving Japan's public relations, not one of Tokyo's policy. He concluded his talk with what had become his standard advice: he encouraged his colleagues to better Japan's image by promoting appreciation of Japanese culture in America. He himself was going to do so by writing a study of the city of Nara, an ancient political and cultural capital of Japan.[46]

In an essay published in Japan during his stay, Ichihashi made some uncomplimentary, but revealing, observations about Americans and their attitude toward the world. In his view, Americans were divided into four sorts of people with regard to international relations. One group mainly pursued their economic interests and promoted trade; another consisted of idealists, who had grand visions for remaking the world and promoting world peace. A third group, the most influential in Ichihashi's estimation, were isolationists; they were decisive in American history, as shown by the U.S. rejection of membership in the League of Nations. The fourth and last group was the general public. Though the majority, it was largely "ignorant" and easily influenced by propagandists, from either the left or right; basically, though, they too were isolationist in Ichihashi's view.[47]

Following his return to the United States, though, Ichihashi spoke not about cultural matters, but about politics. He generated a steady stream of material defending Japan's policies in China, which were a frequent subject of discussion in the Stanford campus and local newspapers: "Japan is not seeking hegemony, but co-operation in China," Ichihashi wrote in April 1934 in support of what was called Japan's Monroe Doctrine for Asia. It did not seek to monopolize or exploit China but only wanted to save it from the fate of Africa, carved up by the European powers. In the *Palo Alto Times* in August 1934, he claimed that the military did not dominate Japan and that it had brought unprecedented peace to Manchukuo. And in December 1935, before a conference of international relations specialists, in a talk he described as presented from a strictly "objective view . . . from a realistic standpoint," Ichihashi asserted that

> History shows that . . . Japan has struggled not only for her own security, but also for the preservation of peace in the Far East. She is firmly convinced that all the foreign wars that she fought had the single objective of stabilizing chaotic conditions, political, economic, social, and intellectual, in order to make the maintenance of peace possible in the territories concerned. If proof of this statement is needed, one may examine the conditions that now prevail in Formosa, Korea, and even Manchukuo. . . . In brief, Japan assumes the responsibility of keeping peace in the Far East.[48]

Ichihashi's view, in fact, was little more than a parroting of Tokyo's rationale for its empire, the so-called "Greater East Asia Co-Prosperity Sphere," as later articulated by Tokyo. Privately, to Treat, he even dismissed the American demonization of the Axis powers of Germany, Italy, and Japan as overreaction.[49]

Many Japanese in America held views similar to Ichihashi's, because of their attachment to their homeland. Historian Yuji Ichioka has observed that the outbreak of the Sino-Japanese War in 1937 "fully crystallized" the nationalism of the issei, who developed "an intense patriotic identification" with Japan and lent much "moral, financial, and material support to Japan's war effort."[50] But not all Japanese in America supported Tokyo's policies. In contrast to Ichihashi was the respected historian Kan'ichi Asakawa at Yale, who spoke against the rise of Japanese militarism in the 1930's. Asakawa came from a similar class background, was educated at Dartmouth College, took his doctorate at Yale in 1902, and wrote for a short while on contemporary Japanese foreign policy. In 1907, he was named curator of Yale's East Asian library collection and eventually became a tenured professor and distinguished scholar of medieval Japanese history at Yale. (Although Asakawa and Ichihashi never met, Asakawa thought enough of Ichihashi in 1930 to recommend him to Marc Bloch, the eminent French historian, as a possible contributor to *Annales d'histoire économique et sociale*, one of the profession's most influential journals.)[51]

To be fair to Ichihashi, it should be said that his ideas at this time, though contrary to those of many Americans, were not without some support among whites. The campus newspaper occasionally carried opinion pieces consistent with Ichihashi's views. In fact, some of his Stanford colleagues such as Payson Treat agreed with his defense of Japan's actions in China and were untroubled by political developments in Japan. As late as March 1936, Treat, speaking before a Stanford student gathering, declared that "The Japanese army is a people's army and to serve in it is both a duty and an honor." He added, "The army has never interfered in the constitutional framework of the state. The army has never supported any Fascist party." By the 1930's Stanford University itself was dominated by what one might call a patrician conservatism. Herbert Hoover, Stanford president Ray Lyman Wilbur, who had served as Secretary of the Interior in the Hoover cabinet, and Treat were all staunch Republicans. The student body was now largely drawn from California's privileged families. For some of them, like other Americans preoccupied with their own social and economic problems, Asia was distant, Japan's talk of peace, stability, and the legitimacy of its interests as a great power seemed reasonable; and communism, not fascism, appeared to be the greater threat.[52]

For the next two years, Ichihashi traveled up and down the West Coast presenting his views to popular and academic audiences alike. Among other engagements, he spoke at Stanford alumni conferences in San Francisco, Los Angeles, Sacramento, and Seattle and at the Commonwealth Club in San Francisco. In 1935 he addressed the Nippon Society of Portland, Oregon, the Northwestern Institute of International Relations at Reed College, and the Second America-Japan Student Conference at Reed College. In August 1936 he attended the Institute of Pacific Relations Conference in Yosemite's Ahwahnee Lodge, where he joined the Japanese delegation to debate the Chinese group headed by Hu Shih, the well-known intellectual and later Chinese ambassador to the United States. And in January 1937 he spoke before the annual dinner of San Francisco's Japan Society. He found some listeners sympathetic to his message, but many in his audiences (like a steadily increasing number of Americans in the 1930's) sided with the Chinese in the Sino-Japanese conflict. A Chinese American attending one of his talks was not at all impressed and found Ichihashi's denial that Japan had invaded north China without foundation and "hypocritical." Ichihashi's speaking engagements reduced his time for scholarly writing; he completed only a few commentaries and book reviews during these years.[53]

Then in August 1937, after briefly serving as acting chairman of the History Department, he again sailed to Japan, this time alone, for four months of research and vacation. He arrived in Japan at a critical moment in history: Japan had begun its invasion south from Manchukuo into the rest of China.[54]

In Japan, Ichihashi tried to stay away from Tokyo, traveling for rest to the Izu Peninsula, a beautiful resort area. He then went on to Kyoto,

Japan's other great ancient cultural center, where he tried to study Japanese art. Everywhere he went, though, he complained about the disturbances to his research by constant demands on his time for meetings and talks. He visited with, and was feted by, his graduate students studying in Japan. In late September, the America Japan Society hosted a luncheon for him and the new American envoy to Japan, Charles R. Cameron. Prince Tokugawa, head of the society, introduced Ichihashi by fondly recalling their time together at the Washington Conference in 1922 and praised him for his work in promoting "amity and cooperation between America and Japan."[55]

To Ichihashi's surprise, he found that war had little disturbed Japanese society. There was no "war atmosphere," he observed, and no anti-American feeling, despite Washington's condemnation of Japanese aggression in China. "To be sure, more soldiers and their paraphernalia are in evidence," he wrote Treat. "Stations are crowded by cheering crowds whenever soldiers depart. Otherwise the people are surprisingly calm and attend [to] their businesses in a usual manner." Ichihashi did not elaborate, guarded person as he was. As he told Treat, a fuller report about Japanese life would have to await his return, since "it is not judicious to talk or write about it."[56]

What more he did in Japan we do not know, but after returning to the United States in December 1937, he was more vociferous than ever in supporting Japan's war against China. His unpopular position led to a decisive public shift in attitude against him within the Stanford community, which had become increasingly sympathetic to the Chinese victims of Japanese aggression.

On the evening of January 5, 1938, Ichihashi addressed a record crowd of 1,100 listeners in Memorial Hall, the largest auditorium on campus. They had come eager to hear one of their own professors, advertised as recently returned from Japan, speak on "Observation of Japan in Time of War." What they heard angered many in what was described as a "rapt audience." The next day the *Stanford Daily* reported that some persons left the hall indignant; others felt cheated. Ichihashi's talk, according to the *Daily*, was simply a "rehash of the opinions given by Japan's consul," who had spoken at Stanford recently. Ichihashi claimed that China began the war; "inspired by Russia, China is using anti-Japanism to effect national unification." What is more, Japan had "no territorial ambitions in China or elsewhere" and had accepted the moral support of Germany and Italy only in its desire to rid the Far East of communism. "Japan is not interested in Nazism or Fascism," he was reported as saying. "The Japanese are all individualists. They want to maintain their economic security, to further their industrial development and trade expansion." He expressed his hope that the United States would remain neutral in the conflict.[57]

The editors of the *Daily* published an indictment of Ichihashi that undoubtedly cut deeply when he read it the day following his talk. Not only did he find his efforts to help the Stanford community understand Japan being ridiculed, but he also saw his integrity as a scholar impugned. Some students might have had high expectations, the *Daily* editorial read under the provocative heading "Son of the Rising Sun." "A Stanford man had gone abroad, as professors do," and students thought "he would give an impartial survey of a burning world question." Instead, the editors pointed out, students should not have been surprised to hear Ichihashi hold forth as he did, since "little else could be expected of a man whose country was at war. An American would uphold his country in the same situation. God is always on 'our' side." Then, the dig: the editorial ended, "One thing stands out. Although Mr. Ichihashi is an American professor and scholar, a student of history and international relations, he is even more a Son of the Rising Sun."[58]

To Ichihashi, it seemed that the Stanford community, which had been his adopted home for more than 30 years and of which he considered himself a loyal member, had rejected him. He was humiliatingly reminded again of his alien status. During the following week, students debated Ichihashi's speech in the *Daily*, with a few coming to his defense. The *Daily*, however, had the last word and reiterated its criticism of Ichihashi, even adding a crudely sarcastic aside that Ichihashi would probably cut the ears off a well-known Chinese cook on campus if the two ever encountered each other. For the next two years, the Stanford *Annual Report of the President*, which listed the faculty's activities and publications as submitted by them and which had included Ichihashi since 1913, carried not a word about him. After that, in the three years before his relocation in 1942, there is only the briefest mention of him. Embittered, Ichihashi himself probably stopped submitting his annual report.[59] More than 50 years after Ichihashi's talk, Kazuyuki Takahashi, who had attended the lecture as an undergraduate, still distinctly recalled the uproar it ignited.[60]

The *Daily's* invidious characterization of Ichihashi negated all that he had tried to accomplish in his professional life. Over the years, Ichihashi had developed a genuine fondness for and dedication to his alma mater and employer, Stanford University, which prided itself at that time on being a genteel and personal community, detached from the hubbub of the real world. He thought he had found his refuge there. He had taken his undergraduate and master's degrees at the school and devoted his entire professional life to the institution. By the late 1930's, he and Kei had lived in the same house on campus for some twenty years and had raised their son there. He had no close friends, Japanese or otherwise, off campus. Moreover, Ichihashi was a dedicated and enthusiastic Stanford alumnus. After Robert "Bones" Hamilton, an all-American football player at Stanford, took one of his classes and introduced him to the sport, Ichihashi became an enthusiast and regularly purchased season tickets for the home games. When Payson Treat traveled overseas, Ichihashi kept him abreast of the fortunes of the Stanford football team, with details about the players' health and other tidbits.[61] Ichihashi decorated his home, which was furnished in modest American style, with Stanford banners and looked forward to his son's attending his alma mater.

As for his personal life in the late 1920's and 1930's, Yamato gradually settled into a domestic routine now that his career was established. Though he prided himself on being progressive on social and political issues—he supported the political democratization of Japan, opposed feudalism and national exclusivity, endorsed Westernization, and claimed sympathy for women's rights—he was rigidly traditional at home.[62] He was the "boss" in the family whose word was law, and family life revolved completely around his schedule. Kei deferred to her husband even among close friends. He insisted on giving 8:00 A.M. classes (one student recalls he even held the early class on a Saturday morning of the Big Game between UC Berkeley and Stanford), returned home for lunch, and constantly applied himself to his work away from his family. He rarely socialized and seemed to enjoy his seclusion. Not until his family doctor told him that if he did not lighten his workload he would die early did Yamato take up hobbies such as fly-fishing and tennis. He commandeered graduate students to drive him up to the Sierras during the summer, where he would camp and fish alone for up to six weeks at a time. In fact, he, Kei, and Woodrow were often separated for long periods: he traveled back to Japan every few years for months, sometimes without them, as in 1925 and 1937. Kei visited her family in Japan for six months by herself in 1926. The two maintained separate bedrooms and work areas in their campus home, although such an arrangement was less uncommon in those days than today.

Yamato had few friends besides Payson Treat and some other colleagues in the History Department. Occasionally, he invited them over for dinner at his home or joined them at the faculty club for a meal, but he rarely ventured off campus, except for his professional activities and his summer fishing trips. Once in a while, he and Kei traveled to San Francisco to attend functions honoring dignitaries from Japan.[63] Sometimes he visited the Japanese Clubhouse, the residence for Japanese students on campus near his home, but even these students had few contacts with the man.[64] As for off-campus Japanese friends, he had virtually none; he had cut himself off almost entirely from the Japanese community, which in nearby San Francisco had developed into a vibrant ethnic, social, and business center. He attended services at the university chapel infrequently, and while he claimed he was a Christian, Woodrow recalls him saying that he was a Buddhist. Whatever the case, he went to few organized religious services. For relaxation at the end of the day, Yamato listened to news of the world on the radio and comedies like "Amos 'n' Andy." On occasion, he would sip some Johnny Walker Red Label Scotch and smoke a pipe. He was fond of eating fish and loved noodles, especially *udon* and *soba* during the summer months. He prided himself on his cooking ability.[65]

The Ichihashis' home was plain, even spartan. Half of a duplex, it was old and rickety even at that time, with three bedrooms, three floors, and a porch. Their American-style furniture, purchased around the time of World War I, did not change for 40 years. Ichihashi himself was orderly, even meticulous, in the words of his son. He organized everything, including the assortment of loose nails in the basement workshop. The family had a blue Plymouth that was rarely used; when it was, it was usually driven by Ichihashi's students. He had them take him and the family to Golden Gate Park in San Francisco for an excursion or to a hot spring in Gilroy, south of San Jose. Their neighbors were all Stanford faculty and staff.[66]

At home, Yamato and Kei spoke to each other in a mixture of Japanese and virtually unaccented English, but with Woodrow they used English almost exclusively, believing that, since he was an American by birth, his first language should be English. Because Yamato refused to send Woodrow to Japanese-language school for fear he would be adversely influenced by youngsters from a lower social position, Yamato and Kei attempted to teach him Japanese at home. Their efforts failed miserably.

Kei Ichihashi was also a very private person. Never during her marriage did she work outside the home; rather, she devoted her time to preparing the meals—a mixture of Japanese and Western foods—tending to the house, cultivating her Japanese-style garden, and raising her son. She enjoyed quiet activities such as reading (she collected a large library of English-language classics, including books by Austen, Twain, Dickens, the Brontës, and the like), sewing and knitting, and flower arranging in the traditional Japanese manner. She was a talented ceramicist, enjoyed playing the piano, played a little golf, and was a member of the Stanford Faculty Women's Club. Although a Christian, Kei too rarely attended church services. More socially inclined than Yamato, Kei occasionally visited the campus homes of her friends, the closest being Jessie Treat, Payson's wife, and Lisette Fast, who was an administrator in the History Department and at the Institute of American History and the companion of Edgar Robinson.[67] (By strange coincidence, Lisette's future sister-in-law, Ethel Barker, became the personal secretary of Dillon S. Myer, the director of the War Relocation Authority, responsible for managing the World War II internment centers.) Occasionally Kei ventured to Palo Alto to shop or see a movie on her own. Her friends described her as dignified, polite, cultured, and lonely.[68]

Although she spoke excellent English and always wore Western-style clothing, Kei retained much of her Japanese heritage. She accepted the subordinate status of a Japanese wife and even dutifully walked behind Yamato around campus, in the recollection of one of her close friends, Louise Wright, wife of historian Gordon Wright. She talked only about "feminine" things and never shared family, let alone personal, matters with friends. While those at Stanford today who knew the Ichihashis invariably describe Yamato as haughty, even arrogant, they recall Kei with fondness and sympathy. She was a sensitive person who, in the sad recollection of contemporaries, suffered a domineering husband. Woodrow recalls feeling the distance between his parents during his childhood.[69]

Woodrow's recollection of his parents and childhood convey the sense that a large cultural and social gap existed in the family. He remembers his father as always keeping his "head low, close to the ground" and continuing to work hard since in Yamato's experience, there had always been someone around to beat him down. While Woodrow does not recall any overt acts of discrimination against himself as a child on campus, he knew that his father had suffered when he had stepped off campus. In contrast, Woodrow fondly recalled his school days in Palo Alto. He was a lively youngster who liked to roam the hills behind Stanford, climb the rafters of university buildings with his friends, and flirt with girls. He chafed under his father's strictures and was often grounded for disciplinary infractions. His father very much wanted him to follow in his footsteps and was outraged that Woodrow's school performance failed to meet his high expectations. Woodrow joined the Boy Scouts, had a dog, and played water polo in school. Before life in the internment camp, 99 percent of his friends were Caucasian, Woodrow recalls. Symbolic of the generational and cultural gap between him and his parents was the conflict Woodrow and his father had over music. After hearing Benny Goodman perform on the radio one day, Woodrow was transformed and took to playing jazz. His father was appalled. Classical, symphonic music was acceptable to Ichihashi, but jazz? Woodrow came to favor the jitterbug music of Jimmie Lunceford, an African American musician in the tradition of Count Basie and Duke Ellington. A Japanese American childhood friend of Woodrow's remembers his being fun-loving, fond of "American" girls, and not shy, unlike the other nisei young men. Woodrow, according to the acquaintance, was a "typical American boy." [70]

As Woodrow recalls, he rebelled against his father's discipline and the pressures to mold him into something he did not want to be. Ichihashi's reputation, too, was a shadow on Woodrow, and he felt liberated when he left the Stanford area to attend Reed College in Oregon. There he felt he could finally become his own person. In his new environment, Woodrow tried to avoid mentioning his father's name or identity among other Japanese, wanting to be free of that heavy legacy. Later, when he resettled out of the Tule Lake relocation camp, he was thrilled, not only because it was an escape from incarceration, but also because it was a release from his father's dominating presence. As Woodrow remembers, he felt wonderful when he arrived in Chicago because the whites there had never heard of his father and did not really care who he was anyway. That was just fine with Woodrow; he never moved back to California.

Here it may be worthwhile to step back a moment and reflect upon Ichihashi's personal and professional life and some themes that thread through his experience. Certainly, his was an unusual personality; one can hardly say that Ichihashi was typical or representative of a broadly shared experience. Yet at the same time, he faced life issues, dilemmas, and challenges that transcended the particular and that, examined in a certain light, speak to continuing aspects of the experiences many other Asian Americans, particularly those connected to the academic world, faced and continue to face many years after Ichihashi grappled with them. In no way are these offered as defining or characteristic; they are advanced simply as possibilities for pointing toward the larger meanings and implications of Yamato Ichihashi's life and times.

The first unmistakable and fundamental theme that runs throughout Ichihashi's life is what one may call the dilemma of racial circumstance. The contemporary Asian American writer Frank Chin has observed that a minority writer, a minority generally, in America is "not an individual, not just a human being" because of the deeply ingrained racial assumptions of society. A person of color can never simply disappear. [71] Such was Ichihashi's life. He had to bear, as he once told David Starr Jordan, a racial stigma.

In addition to the social discrimination and discomfort he always felt personally, Ichihashi's race affected his life in another basic way: his ancestry, more than his deliberate intellectual choice or emotional preference, influenced the choice of his life's focus. He could never simply become an economist, a historian, a scholar—he knew that the modifier "Japanese" always preceded. He was expected to be, as he complained on different occasions, "an encyclopedia japonica"; it was an "inescapable fate," in his own words, of his professional position and, he could have added, of his racial circumstance.[72]

His ancestry, his race, accompanied him, draped around him as a "racial uniform," using the phrase of the sociologist Robert E. Park, who knew Ichihashi through the Survey of Race Relations and the Institute of Pacific Relations. "The trouble is not with the Japanese mind but with the Japanese skin," Park wrote in 1928 in a study of whites' attitudes about race. "The Japanese, like the Negro, is condemned to remain among us an abstraction, a symbol—and a symbol not merely of his own race but of the Orient and of that vague, ill-defined menace we sometimes refer to as the 'yellow peril.'"[73]

But Asia was also something to be studied in American universities, and Ichihashi's racial uniform was also the "right" color for the work Stanford wanted. "A historian of Japanese blood" was what the University should seek to replace Ichihashi, Thomas A. Bailey, chair of the History Department in 1953, advised Stanford President Wallace Sterling, a decade after Ichihashi had retired. Later in the year, Bailey, who was a friend of Ichihashi's, was even more blunt: "get a Jap prof" he scribbled on a memo to Gordon Wright concerning Ichihashi's empty endowed chair.[74]

As noted, Ichihashi's original intellectual interest was economics, and later he was excited by problems of large political concern, such as international relations, but he was always nudged back to teaching and speaking about Japanese history and culture. Neither his land of ancestry nor his adopted home wanted anything less—or more—from him. Ichihashi himself spoke repeatedly throughout his life of being "compelled to camouflage myself," and though he was referring to being known principally as a historian rather than as an economist, his self-characterization was apt: his race was a vestment, which defined as well as hid his self.[75]

And while he could not identify and empathize with the Japanese dirt farmers in America, his racial circumstances constantly forced him to reassociate himself with them. Relocation and his planned history of that relocation formed the poignant capstone on his career: they were emblematic of the imprint his racial uniform had on his entire life.

Connected to the condition of racial circumstance was the dilemma Ichihashi faced in deciding on his life role, his life position. As an ambitious man who was politically inclined, Ichihashi thought constantly, especially in his early professional years, about how he might situate himself in his intellectual activity to the maximum advantage for his career. He faced the quandary of what may be called the challenge of social marginality. Put in another way, his racial position offered him, as it did W. E. B. Du Bois, the great African American intellectual, the "gift or curse of marginality."[76]

From one perspective, marginality seemed to face Ichihashi no matter where he turned. If he had returned to Japan after graduate school, he might well have found himself on the fringes of academia there. While it is true that he had the advantage of training in Western economics, he had spent many years away from Japan and had few personal contacts in the tight-knit academic and business communities. He felt out of place in Japan during his 1914 visit, as we have seen. And of course in America he was acutely aware of his place in the racial hierarchy and understood the marginality of Japanese Americans, even well-educated ones, here. Moreover, his life was peripheral to the daily experience of most Japanese Americans. He played no role in community politics, rarely published for Japanese American audiences, and steadily reduced his personal contact with other Japanese Americans over the years until World War II.

Yet social marginality was unacceptable to him personally during his active years, as was the detached life of complete immersion in academia. And so he resolved the tension between his ambition and his given circumstances by, in a sense, turning his limits into what he believed were very real advantages. By so doing, he shifted himself from the social margin to a position he believed was closer to the center of modern cosmopolitan society. Some might mistake his solution as one of becoming a facilitator, a bridge, between East and West, a role that was often assumed by early Asian American writers.[77] Kazuo Kawai, Ichihashi's student, for example, wrote in 1924, when he was undergraduate:

> I thought of myself, racially a child of the Orient, culturally a child of the Occident, embodying within me the clash and the adjustments and the synthesis of the East and the West, a microcosm reflecting the macrocosm of the world problem of race and culture. I am both East and West made into one whole. . . . My life work would be that of an interpreter of East to the West and of the West to the East.[78]

But Ichihashi did not see himself as a passive conduit between two important civilizations or even as an interpreter; in that sense, he did not play a simple "bridge" role. Rather, Ichihashi aspired to a more ambitious position: it was at the center that he wished to be, essential to both societies, or at least to those occupying positions of power and influence.

He subscribed to and encouraged the view that Asia was becoming increasingly vital to American interests and that Japan was the gateway to Asia as the most powerful and Westernized country in the region and the country with ostensibly the most in common with America. In turn, the United States was the most important country in the world to Japan, not only for geopolitical reasons, but for reasons having to do with civilization and modern culture. His own role, then, as a promoter and interpreter of U.S.-Japan interaction and accord was critical. Thus, he became not marginal but uniquely placed to advance the work of Pacific cooperation.

He once offered his activist philosophy to a colleague in Japan. Soon after the passage of the discriminatory 1924 Immigration Act, Ichihashi wrote to Anesaki Masaharu in Japan that new methods had to be devised to advance U.S.-Japan relations. Appeals to "American friends" had not worked for Japan, nor had the good efforts of the executive branch in Washington that had opposed the most onerous portions of the Act. "An alliance of intellectuals" in Japan and the United States, Ichihashi proposed, might be the way to improve the situation since they were best positioned to "awaken the young generations as to better ways of creating and maintaining international friendship."[79]

Japan remained his land of principal identification throughout his entire life; he never ceased being self-consciously "Japanese" in a cultural sense and took chauvinistic pride in the accomplishments of Japanese civilization (see below). At the same time, Ichihashi held a genuine affection for America, which persisted despite the resentment, even bitterness, that he harbored because of racial discrimination, capped by his three-year internment. As has been noted, he admired what he called the "spiritual" aspects of American civilization: its democratic ethos and aspirations, its practicality, and its capacity for generosity. And for Ichihashi, what counted most in judging a people was their "spirit." Japan, he maintained throughout his life, could learn much from America. He applauded the postwar constitution for Japan: "It is the most revolutionary of monarchical constitutions known to me," he wrote to a friend in 1946, "and is doubtless a product of the American mind and ideal." He gave it his stamp of approval: "It is most satisfying to liberals like myself." And though America's penchant for conspicuous consumption bothered him, offending his frugal nature, he always appreciated its material accomplishments. A year after returning from camp and not long after the end of the war, he wrote a former student in the United States Army, "When we think of the existing conditions all over the world, those of us who are in the U.S.A. ought to be thankful, and most of us are."[80]

But Ichihashi's lifelong effort to situate himself at the "center" in international relations was made untenable by the events of the late 1930's and then ultimately smashed by the attack on Pearl Harbor. His effort to escape the margins brought him sad consequences. We do not know what decisions, if any, Ichihashi may have lamented late in life as he reflected on the past, but he was aware that perhaps he had made some unwise choices. "Unwittingly I served two masters simultaneously," Ichihashi confessed to an audience in Tokyo in 1953 about some of his institutional connections, occasionally with the Japanese government. Obliquely, he continued, "This fact proved, at times, to be rather embarrassing. For instance, during the war my wife and I with our son had to live in veritable concentration camps for three years." [81] Perhaps the acute ambiguity of his social position is captured by the contrast in two of his last major life decisions: Ichihashi refused to become an American citizen when it became possible to do so after 1952, but he also rejected the idea of returning to Japan to live out his remaining days.

Ichihashi faced another tension related to his life's calling, the tension between being an engaged intellectual or remaining a detached scholar. Ichihashi was never a political activist, but there was always a part of him that was drawn to public life, such as public speaking, despite his fondness for the tranquillity of the Stanford campus. In epistemological terms, Ichihashi faced the challenge of reconciling scholarly "objectivity" with his political inclinations. Like most social scientists in his era, he was an unquestioning positivist: he believed solutions to any problem could be found if persons of education, culture, and rationality would coolly examine the facts, and the facts, he believed, resided in the results of empirical and statistical investigations. He respected academic detachment and always prided himself on honoring its ideals.

Yet society, because of his racial uniform, continually pressed him to be engaged; to maintain his humanity he had to attend to the problems of race in America and speak to the injustices that Japanese Americans faced. Throughout his life he called attention to discriminatory laws, such as the California Alien Land Act, and the problems faced by the nisei, the American-born Japanese. In the 1930's, he felt obliged to speak regularly at their college student conferences and meetings, and he developed a reputation as a mentor. At a Stanford conference in April 1938, for example, he spoke on the "Nisei College Student." (While his credentials impressed the students, his stuffiness did not always endear him to the younger generation. In turn, in private moments, Ichihashi often expressed impatience with, sometimes even contempt for, the nisei, who did not retain the hard-working, self-reliant, and puritanical virtues he and others from his background most valued.) [82] During internment, he consistently tried to play a constructive role in ameliorating camp conditions and policies.

Ichihashi has been called an "attorney for the defense" in his scholarly work regarding Japanese Americans. The appellation may be fitting, since trial lawyers conjure the appearance of objectivity even as they work as advocates for their client, and most attorneys seem to be able to do so without moral or philosophical qualms. Although some of his contemporaries saw a contradiction between his adherence to the standards and ethics of "scientific" investigations and his efforts on behalf of his fellow Japanese in America, he never betrayed any sense that he felt such tension. For him, "objective" scholarship and engagement made an unproblematic mix.[83]

Another striking theme or tension in Ichihashi's life is what might be called his "multiple face." All persons present different aspects of themselves to others, but Ichihashi seems to have been perceived in sharply contrasting ways by those around him, and in ways that fall roughly along racial lines. In accounts of him from whites, either contemporary or retrospective, Ichihashi appears to have been formal, dignified, aloof, intelligent, and on occasion difficult and arrogant. He was also remembered as a caring teacher and humane person. While some of his Japanese American students recall him in similar terms, others who knew him well stress that he was egotistical, sometimes petty, and even mean-spirited. One old acquaintance of his recalls that many in the Japanese community did not care for him because of his bluntness.[84]

Compare some of the following comments about Ichihashi. Carolyn Strouse Baer, Stanford '25, took the trouble to write to Ichihashi in camp in 1942, "in the hopes that it might bring some small measure of pleasure to you in what must be most miserable and dreary times." She expressed her appreciation for Ichihashi's college instruction, and "so, belatedly but affectionately, I do want to tell you that your course in Japanese Civilization was the most interesting and inspiring of any I took at Stanford. I remember what you said in that course better than I remember anything else in the whole four years; and it has come back to me, over and over again, on countless occasions." Baer concluded, "I trust that the gentle spirit and artistry and sensitiveness which you conveyed to us all will be the one that wins in the end.... If you ever despair, please do remember how much you mean to your former students, and always will." Later in the same year in camp, Ichihashi received a letter from another alumnus, Oliver Coe Smith, praising him as "one of the finest Christian gentlemen it has been my pleasure to meet."[85]

Several Japanese American alumni recall him differently, describing Ichihashi as "mean and petty" and even a "son-of-a-bitch."[86] And a most telling recollection comes from Tamotsu Shibutani, who in 1942 was a UC Berkeley graduate and staff member on a famous project that studied relocation. Shibutani, who later became a professor of sociology at the University of California, Santa Barbara, remembers:

> I had only one encounter with Mr. Ichihashi, but it was an unforgettable one. As you know, I was employed in Dorothy Thomas' Evacuation and Resettlement Study. I think it was in the autumn of 1942 that she decided to have a staff meeting at Tule Lake and came with her husband, W. I. Thomas. Because of Professor Ichihashi's eminence she decided to make a courtesy call and brought her research assistants (Billigmeier, Miyamoto, Najima, Sakoda, and myself). Ichihashi talked almost continuously during the half hour or so that we were there—mostly about prominent people he knew and the nice things they had said about him or done for him. His remarks were addressed exclusively to the Thomases. No one else in the room, including his wife, seemed to exist. When we left, after we had turned the corner and were out of earshot, Dorothy burst out laughing. The rest of us were so astonished that we did not know what to do. He said little about the evacuees. As I recall, his attitude was that of an aristocrat living among beggars. . . . I'm sure none of us has forgotten that day."[87]

Without denying that an individual unflattering impression of Ichihashi might reflect a personality clash, one might understand the differing impressions of him in social context, as consequences of the racial hierarchy of society and of Ichihashi's social position. He understood where power lay in society, and it was not with Japanese Americans; he was also sensitive to the way he was perceived by members of the dominant society and that he was, in some way, representative of his "race." He felt responsibility for presenting what he thought was the best that Japanese culture had to offer to white America, and because of his class bias, which was connected to his cultural chauvinism, he also looked down on the plebeian origins of many Japanese Americans.

An insightful interpretation of Ichihashi is given by Noboru Shirai, who knew Ichihashi well. Originally from Hiroshima, Shirai was a graduate student at Stanford in 1942 and was reassociated with Ichihashi at Tule Lake. He taught at the University of Pennsylvania for a short time after the war before returning to Stanford and later became a successful businessman in southern California. In a 1981 memoir published in Japan, Shirai described Ichihashi as one of the most notable early Japanese in America and ascribed his success at least partially to Ichihashi's social skills among white Americans. Ichihashi, according to Shirai, knew how to appeal to white Americans; he could be modest, polite, and unassuming (the meeting with Thomas not withstanding!). But among Japanese, according to Shirai, Ichihashi's manner changed completely. He became unapproachable and unfriendly, and as a result his popularity suffered among Japanese Americans. Shirai, though, expressed sympathy for Ichihashi, who was, he said, really a decent fellow once one got to know him. According to Shirai, Ichihashi was actually a lonely person.[88]

Finally, there is the matter of Yamato Ichihashi's "bourgeois nationalism," which itself was a mix of upper-class prejudices and Japanese ethnocentrism. There was a continuing tension in Ichihashi's life between his ardent public defense of his countrymen and celebration of their claimed cultural strengths and his private scorn, even disdain, for the Japanese American common folk. It was a tension he never fully resolved in his life, bound up as it was with his own peculiar national chauvinism.[89]

Without question, Ichihashi reveled in his aristocratic background and fully expressed throughout his life a snobbery toward Japanese he believed were of lower station. He admired successful people, whether Japanese or American, and looked down on the poor. In his mind, social and economic position indicated a person's value. In this respect he was similar to others from the same background in his immigrant cohort, as well as many other Americans who had matured during the Victorian age and accepted its class notions. Seen in one light, Ichihashi's views were consistent with those of W. E. B. Du Bois in his early career. Du Bois had been a confirmed elitist who held that the fate of a race was determined by its talented, exemplary, and leading minority, to whom the majority should defer. "It is right and proper to judge a people by its best classes," Du Bois wrote in 1899 in his first book, *The Philadelphia Negro*. In turn, the elite should serve as the strict moral and intellectual guide for the masses, whose behavior, Du Bois adjudged, was often profane and corrupt.[90]

During relocation, Ichihashi himself sometimes seemed to object about equally to the abysmal living conditions and to his forced proximity to those he called "rustics" and "Okies," his fellow internees. (In fairness, we should note in the internment documents occasional comments that are perceptive and sometimes very sympathetic about the social and psychological plight of those internees.) He was also vehement in his negative opinions of other nationalities, who were decidedly lacking in his mind. "Hawaiians," he once wrote, are "an undisciplined people, unsuited to any type of sustained effort"; as for the Chinese, they were "notorious gamblers," and the Filipinos "famous brawlers."[91]

But while his views may resemble those of social Darwinists of the day who believed in a genetic, racial hierarchy of humanity, Ichihashi did not subscribe to such views. As racially prejudiced as they may sound, his views were inseparable from his own *class* outlook on laboring classes generally, and were not rooted in any explicit notion about innate, biological racial superiority and inferiority as white racial thought usually was. Koreans were drinkers, he wrote, but added they "drink just as well as Japanese." Drinking, gambling, and brawling were, in his words, all "human vices common to certain classes of all races of mankind." [92]

On at least one occasion, he specifically discussed the notion of "racial superiority" in a brief talk. His notes show that he began by conceding that virtually "every race" had developed some myth of its own superiority, but at that historical moment it was the "White race" that was touting its own dominance because of its admittedly advanced material culture. But Ichihashi immediately objected to the validity of any claim of white racial supremacy and, conversely, to any other group's alleged "racial inferiority." The reasons, he argued, were first, there was "no such thing as a pure race"; second, culture and social environment, not heredity, were the primary relevant factors in evaluating peoples; and finally, Ichihashi maintained, all cultures had positive points and their own particularities. Who was to say which was "superior?" He asked rhetorically, "If the West is interested in materialism and the East in spiritualism, . . . which should be looked upon as a mark of superiority or of inferiority?" [93]

If anything, Ichihashi tended to favor racial and cultural intermingling. Making a fetish of racial "purity" was probably anathema to him, for he was of the opinion that the two peoples he most admired on earth, Americans and Japanese, were in fact "hybridized" peoples. Citing a French authority for support, Ichihashi claimed in 1932 that the "Japanese nation" was a combination of "the Caucasian, the Mongolian, the Malay, and even, in the south, a slight tinge of Negrito from the islands of the Pacific." [94] How Ichihashi reacted to the Japanese militarists' claim and glorification of Japanese racial purity we can only imagine.

Yamato Ichihashi's controversial speech to the Stanford community in 1938 was a turning point in his life. He became alienated from students and colleagues alike as he continued to speak out in support of Japan's aggressive policies in China. According to reports the FBI gathered on Ichihashi in 1942 from Stanford informants who were clearly very familiar with the man (but whose identities are not revealed in the documents released to me), he had become almost "belligerently pro-Japanese." There is no evidence, though, that he ever supported Japan in its eventual open warfare with the United States. Although he had formerly been quite popular as a teacher, enrollment in his classes dwindled and his students became, in the FBI report's words, "generally irritated rather than convinced by his efforts to make them appreciate Japanese culture and to understand the Japanese political position." He grew increasingly resentful of his isolation on campus in the years immediately preceding Pearl Harbor.[95]

One of Ichihashi's last public speaking appearances was again in Memorial Hall on the Stanford campus. Like his previous talk, this one was also not favorably received. In the afternoon of October 2, 1941, just two months before the Japanese attack on Pearl Harbor, Ichihashi and eight other professors addressed a large crowd during a convocation entitled "The Aims of the Nations in the World's Conflict." President Wilbur had the difficult job of serving as moderator. The occasion was the celebration of the fiftieth anniversary of the founding of the university and the dedication of the newly constructed Hoover Tower housing the Institution's library on international relations.[96]

Ichihashi again found himself the center of attention. He staunchly defended Japan's policies on two grounds: first, that Japan, after suffering years of racial discrimination at the hands of the West, was simply trying to create an "Asia for Asiatics," which would include China; and second, that Japan was fighting to protect Asia from communism. The audience was not persuaded and gave an enthusiastic reception to Professor Shau Wing Chan, a Chinese American colleague, who defended China's position "in refutation" of Ichihashi, in the words of the *Stanford Daily*. Later in the symposium, Ichihashi also clashed with a Stanford colleague, Karl Brandt, who condemned Nazi Germany's aggression and argued that Japan was simply furthering Germany's global ambitions. Ichihashi chafed at the suggestion that Japan was anything less than an equal player in international affairs.[97]

Yamato's personal life was also tumultuous in these years. Woodrow, having been admitted to Stanford, did poorly in school, in part because of an attack of appendicitis, and he had to withdraw after one quarter, angering—and no doubt embarrassing—his father. He attended Menlo Junior College for a short while and then reentered Stanford on probation. Yamato required Woodrow to audit his course on Japanese cultural history. But Stanford held no appeal for Woodrow, and, in the fall of 1938, he moved to Oregon to attend Reed College, leaving home for good as it turned out. Away from his father and Stanford, Woodrow felt more comfortable, even liberated. Ichihashi's FBI file contains information that relations between Woodrow and his father had soured.[98]

In late September 1941, Kei herself moved to Eugene, Oregon, ostensibly to visit Woodrow, who had transferred from Reed to the University of Oregon to study architecture. Her visit, though, seems not to have been meant to be short-term. She enrolled in ceramics classes for adults and moved into a small house, while Woodrow lived nearby in a boardinghouse. In Eugene, Kei visited Gordon and Louise Wright, who were then at the university there, but they never learned why she had moved. It is doubtful that it was for happy reasons.[99]

Increasingly isolated and embittered, Ichihashi was no doubt harder than ever to live with. Now in his sixties and despite years of preaching to his fellow Japanese to behave virtuously, Ichihashi appears to have become infatuated with a young Japanese American woman student who had enrolled in his classes. According to several sources, Ichihashi definitely had more than "just a passing interest" in the woman; he even visited her at her parents' home in California's Central Valley one summer. The FBI later learned of the matter, too. According to the statement of an undisclosed informant made in 1942, Ichihashi had "made improper advances" to the student, had "tried to get her to live with him, and made numerous attempts to separate her from her fiancé." The specific accusations were not substantiated by any other FBI information, and Stanford Japanese students, other than those immediately involved, did not seem aware of the allegations. Ichihashi continued to have their respect.[100] This strange episode, though, exemplifies Ichihashi's enigmatic, even contradictory, personality—he himself advocated strict, conservative Victorian morals and even once claimed, in praise of his fellow Japanese immigrants, that "the control over sexual instinct is carried out far more successfully among the Japanese race than among some other races."[101]

Whatever the particulars, Yamato and Kei were not long separated. On December 7, 1941, Japanese forces attacked Pearl Harbor, an act which Woodrow's mother thought was "appalling" and "crazy," according to her son's recollection. Neither could believe the news. Ichihashi, too, was shocked. In his first letter to his sister after the war, written in Japanese, Ichihashi stressed how much the outbreak of war between Japan and the United States had taken him by complete surprise. He wrote that he deeply regretted Japan's starting the war and blamed it on the overconfidence of the military, whose action outraged and saddened him.[102]

The atmosphere on the Pacific Coast quickly became hostile toward Japanese Americans, and Ichihashi decided his wife should return to Stanford. Woodrow, with a letter testifying to their identities in hand from Donald Erb, the president of the University of Oregon, drove his mother back to Palo Alto and then returned to Oregon. He had thought that he had finally gotten his studies and life together and wanted to finish college. He had even joined the campus ROTC. But the war changed everything for him, and he never finished his education.[103]

Yamato Ichihashi and his family were soon to endure their greatest test as a family and as Japanese Americans. The experience was to cast an indelible shadow over the Ichihashis for the rest of their lives, leaving them estranged and permanently scarred in professional and, most of all, in profoundly emotional ways. The excitement of Yamato Ichihashi's career as a pioneering Japanese American intellectual in the academic world would be left far behind and his accomplishments largely forgotten.

The Internment Documents, 1942–1945

Editor's Note

The documents that follow include letters, diary entries, and essays. The originals were found in a number of places.

Typed carbon copies or handwritten drafts of most of the letters written by Yamato Ichihashi are located in his papers now in the Special Collections of Stanford University's Green Library. The papers of his various Stanford correspondents, which are kept in Green Library or the Hoover Institution's Archives, contain the remaining letters. Checking these against references to letters written recorded in his diary indicates that the correspondence held at Stanford constitutes the vast majority of the letters Yamato Ichihashi wrote during the war years; it is doubtful that many others remain in existence.

The correspondence of Kei Ichihashi and Woodrow Ichihashi was found in the Payson Treat Papers at the Hoover Institution. Though Kei made references to other letters she wrote, it is not known to whom she may have written or how extensively. Efforts to locate more material written by her have been unsuccessful.

Yamato Ichihashi's internment diaries were of two sorts. The material from 1942 was handwritten in several Stanford University examination "blue books" that Ichihashi took with him to the camps; these blue books are now in the Ichihashi Papers at Stanford. For the remaining war years Ichihashi made his entries in commercially published blank year-books that were sent to him by Payson Treat at the end of 1942 and subsequent years. Ichihashi customarily made entries in these books several times a day, and this habit explains the running account of the weather and other events within each day. These diaries also had a section at the end of each month for "special data," in which he often wrote brief essays on a particular topic.

Ichihashi continued to keep a diary on a daily basis until just before his death in 1963. Among his papers donated to the Hoover Institution soon after his death were twenty diary books, but these were later reclaimed by Kei Ichihashi. In 1992, they were found in the possession of the Ichihashis' son, Woodrow, who subsequently redonated them to the Ichihashi Papers in the Special Collections of Green Library.

A large portion of the remaining papers donated to the Hoover Institution was discarded, because archivists believed that much of the material consisted of lecture and class notes and hence held little value. On the advice of Thomas C. Smith, a historian of Japan who taught at Stanford after the war, however, the Hoover did keep four linear feet of the material, which was transferred to Stanford's Special Collections in 1966. This material was then organized and made available to the public in 1970. It is also highly likely that the original donated papers represented only a small part of Ichihashi's accumulated personal papers, for the current collection includes virtually no correspondence for the years before World War II and very little material written in Japanese. It seems probable that most such material was destroyed by Ichihashi or his family after the attack on Pearl Harbor.[1]

The final type of document consists of research essays that Ichihashi periodically completed while in camp, combining a record of his personal experiences with analyses of camp life. The exact date of these essays is not always clear, although they were evidently composed within days—and at most within two months—of the events discussed. Ichihashi may have intended these materials to form part of the book on relocation that he planned to write after his return to Stanford.

The documents have been organized to create a chronological narrative. I had once thought of grouping the material by author, mainly in hopes of conveying a better sense of Kei Ichihashi's personality and experience, but it soon became evident that such an approach would require the reader to make repeated efforts to understand the sequence of events and would disrupt the narrative flow, with all its drama and surprise.

I have selected approximately one-third of the extant writings of Yamato Ichihashi from the war years, based on their considered historical value and contribution to the story of camp life. Part of this selection was determined by my decision to edit the material to eliminate both redundancy and details that I consider of marginal interest to the non-specialist. The diary entries and letters included all appear in their correct chronological order. I have interspersed Ichihashi's research essays among the letters and diary entries where I thought they best complemented a narrative reading.

The diary entries, research essays, and correspondence generally did not differ significantly in tone, attitude, or conclusion, although Ichihashi was occasionally more caustic about events and individuals in his diary than in comments he shared with his Stanford correspondents. As one would expect, the diary also contains significantly more detail about family matters and personal activities than does his correspondence.

Establishing the chronological order of the documents was complicated by the fact that many of them were undated. In some instances letters were incorrectly dated by their recipients; other documents were misfiled by archivists.

When there was duplicate material, such as a carbon copy of a typewritten outgoing letter, I usually relied on the recipient's copy, since Ichihashi often added handwritten marginalia or postscripts to the letters he sent out. On occasion, however, he also made notations for himself on the copies of the letters he retained.

Editing the individual documents presented a different set of problems. Ichihashi's handwriting, as he himself periodically admitted with embarrassment, was "awful." Deciphering some words or phrases in his draft letters, essays, and diary entries was frustrating and at times simply impossible. In addition, misspellings, grammatical errors, mispunctuation, and typographical errors abound in his and Kei's writings. One can attribute many of these to the difficult conditions under which they wrote, and of course to the fact that English was their second language. In Yamato's case, these problems may also have been aggravated by eye ailments he suffered in camp. I minimized grammatical editing in Kei's letters in order to retain the charm of her expression and because her meaning is usually evident. Both Ichihashis occasionally used Japanese phrases, either in Japanese characters or in romanization that sometimes varied from the standard transliteration system. I have italicized such terms, but these were not given any special treatment in the original documents.

In preparing the materials for publication, I have adhered to the following editing guidelines:

1. Where important words are missing or indecipherable in the original document, I have selected what I believe to be appropriate words to convey intended meaning; these interpolations are en-

closed by square brackets, [ ]. I include a question mark within the bracket when I am not confident in my choice. The Ichihashis sometimes used parentheses in their writing, but never brackets.

2. After words that seem inappropriate or unclear in meaning in the context of the original, I have placed a question mark in brackets. A question mark in brackets is also used where I believe words may be missing in the original but cannot be guessed from the context.

3. I have spelled out abbreviations at their first use and subsequently when I thought they would not be easily recognizable.

4. I have enclosed in brackets the initials of some individuals whose complete names are indecipherable in the original or whose identity should be protected.

5. I have corrected obvious misspellings, including in transliterations, and typographical errors. I have occasionally inserted punctuation for clarity. I have also corrected some grammatical errors (such as incorrect verb tenses, misplaced modifiers, etc.). Changes of this sort are not indicated in the text. Finally, I have sometimes added a minor word or words for which the need was obvious; these words are enclosed in brackets.

6. I use ellipses to indicate omissions, particularly in the diary material. Where a full paragraph or more has been omitted, ellipsis points are set as a separate line. I tried to keep omissions to a minimum in the correspondence.

My aim throughout has been to retain as much as possible of the feeling of the original material and to allow it to speak unencumbered, while framing it in a way that makes it accessible to a reader now 50 years removed from the events described. Even with the editing described above, the syntax of the published text is sometimes awkward, and I have let stand minor grammatical errors to retain the flavor of the writing. As noted, only about one-third of the internment material was used, in the interest of keeping this volume to a manageable length. For purposes of clarification, I have added material in brackets to translate Japanese phrases, explain references, and briefly identify persons or events. Lengthier explanations are given in footnotes. I also use endnotes for citations, extended identifications, and occasional commentary.

I have, as appropriate, interspersed the documents with commentary that summarizes correspondence received by the Ichihashis, clarifies the context of the documents that follow, or discusses an interpretive issue. The beginning and end of each of these sections is marked by a typographical ornament. And each document is preceded by a heading that names the correspondent or identifies it as diary material, research essay, or some other form.

The reader is invited to compare a sample of edited text to the original. Note 2, to this paragraph, contains the unedited transcription of the diary selection that appears on pp. 101–3.[2]

A comment about the nature of diary keeping.

Ichihashi's diary keeping was somewhat idiosyncratic. Much of what he wrote conforms to what one historian of Japan has described as the "documentary diary," that is, a record of public events and formal ceremonies kept on a daily basis. Little or no personal comment, and scant literary effort, is found in such diaries. In his study of the first mission of Japanese emissaries to the United States, Masao Miyoshi found that Japanese diaries usually did not employ the perspective of the "isolated first person" commonly found in Western diaries; they often used the passive voice, ambiguous pronouns, and uncertain points of view.[3] Ichihashi's diaries bear some resemblance to these. But they also include a record of his own daily activities and occasionally his personal reflections. He records, however, less clearly "confessional" and introspective material than some readers might expect in a prison camp diary. There is no evidence to suggest that Ichihashi later edited his diaries nor that he wrote them with an eye to future readers. Ichihashi was, however, a cautious man, and he most likely entertained the possibility that he might lose control of his diaries during internment. This concern, even if it was not prominent in his mind, may account for his sometimes cryptic expression, particularly in his comments on developments in the war.[4]

One last comment. I have tried to identify as many of the individuals mentioned in the Ichihashi documents as possible, even though most do not seem to play major roles in the lives of Kei and Yamato. I have done so, especially for those in the internment camps, to try to provide some individual identity, albeit woefully incomplete, to those who were incarcerated because of race. I also believe many Japanese Americans will be able to identify some of the people mentioned by Ichihashi, and thus even such a brief identification may be especially evocative for these readers. For help in identification, I relied on two publications that reprinted camp directories: H. Inukai, ed. and comp., *Tule Lake Directory and Camp News* (1988) and Paul Rodriguez, ed., *Amache* (1992).[5] The directories, which are admittedly not complete or accurate, are organized alphabetically, generally according to the name of the male head of household. A brief entry provides names of family members, camp address, and home location.

Stanford–Santa Anita–
Tule Lake
May 26, 1942–
August 19, 1942

T he lights were off, and Yamato Ichihashi's Stanford campus house was dark and quiet on the evening of Sunday, December 7, 1941. On Monday, December 8, the day after the Japanese attack on Pearl Harbor, the senior professor peered into his Stanford classroom and asked apprehensively, "Shall I come in?" The students applauded and welcomed him.[1] The outbreak of war between Japan and the United States stunned him, even though just two months before he had expressed fear of an eventual clash between the two countries. Though unquestionably sympathetic to the people of his homeland, he condemned the Japanese military for starting the conflict and began monthly purchases of $100 U.S. war bonds.[2]

Despite the understanding of his students, Ichihashi, feeling betrayed and disgraced by his homeland, was too distraught to continue teaching.

He visited Edgar Robinson,[3] then the chair of the History Department and a lifelong friend, and talked about what he should do. He thought he might continue to teach until the end of the quarter, only a few weeks away, and then take a sabbatical leave. He said he did not want to "embarrass" the University. After the meeting, Robinson wrote in his private diary that Ichihashi had been "the gentleman" he had always been but that he tragically had also seen "the death of all his hopes and his life." Ichihashi then went to see Ray Lyman Wilbur,[4] president of Stanford, and submitted his resignation. But the supportive and insistent president persuaded him to reconsider, urging that he take a paid leave of absence instead. Ichihashi resisted the idea of remaining on the payroll, but finally accepted the argument that his leave could be considered comparable to those given for unusual medical needs. On December 9, Wilbur confirmed that Ichihashi would be given a leave with full salary for the remainder of the academic year 1941–42. In addition, Wilbur left open the possibility of granting Ichihashi a special "sabbatical leave" for the following, and of course completely uncertain, year to come.[5]

Despite ugly anti-Asian agitation in the late nineteenth and early twentieth centuries in Palo Alto, the Stanford vicinity in recent years had not been known to be particularly anti-Japanese in climate, and the university itself had been a relatively hospitable place for students of Japanese ancestry. Still, the outbreak of war ignited popular fears, and suspicions about the Japanese who lived in the area quickly mounted, as they did throughout the rest of the country. On December 8, the Palo Alto police, on instructions from the FBI, began to stop and question "any Japanese observed motoring to determine their identity and business." Nationally, within days the FBI took into custody 1,500 *issei* (first-generation Japanese immigrants), many of them community, business, and religious leaders, as suspect or dangerous enemy aliens. The *Palo Alto Times*, however, called on the surrounding community to reject "indiscriminate animosity" toward the local Japanese: "We are at war with Japan but not with our Nipponese neighbors, many of whom have proved their loyalty and most of whom can be counted on for self-sacrificing devotion to this country, which they have adopted or where they were born."[6]

Many local Japanese Americans immediately felt it necessary to affirm publicly their loyalty to the United States. The Palo Alto Japanese-American Association did so within days of the Pearl Harbor attack. On campus, the Stanford Japanese Student Association officers wrote Wilbur an open letter, saying: "As American citizens of Japanese ancestry, we have been prepared to assume and discharge our duties and responsibilities which have been placed upon us. Yet little did we dream that we would be called upon to prove our loyalty under the circumstances in which we now find ourselves." They concluded by pledging their full support to the American war effort. On December 10, President Wilbur pointedly included a call for "tolerance" toward Japanese students in an address to a convocation of 3,500 persons from the Stanford community. "They are just as good Stanford people as we are," he counseled.[7]

Ichihashi endured the immediate crisis alone. Kei, his wife, had been away in Oregon since September, helping their son, Woodrow, settle in at the University of Oregon.* She soon returned to Stanford, however, to face with Yamato the mounting pressures for the ordered removal of Japanese from the West Coast. On February 19, 1942, President Franklin D. Roosevelt signed Executive Order 9066, which authorized the War Department to form security zones from which designated people could be excluded. The army soon organized Military Zones 1 and 2, a continuous zone, 200–300 miles deep, along the coastal and border areas of Washington, Oregon, California, and Arizona and began planning the mass exclusion of persons of Japanese ancestry from the zones. From that point on, restrictions mounted rapidly. In early March, the head of the Western Defense Command, General John L. DeWitt, advised all persons of Japanese ancestry to move themselves voluntarily to areas outside the sensitive military region. The Ichihashis, unlike some 10,000 other West Coast Japanese, did not avail themselves of this opportunity, but remained on campus instead. (After the war, Ichihashi claimed that he had forgone the chance to move in order to be of service to his fellow Japanese and to experience the war as they did.[8] If he had wanted to do so, he would have had little difficulty arranging affiliation with a university in the Midwest or the eastern United States as a senior professor.)

On March 27, however, the military reversed itself and ordered all persons of Japanese ancestry to remain in place in the restricted zone until government plans were completed for their controlled evacuation. From that day on, the forced removal of residents of Japanese ancestry from the zones was quickly and methodically carried out, district by district. By November 1942, over 120,000 persons of Japanese ancestry, citizen and alien alike, were forcibly moved from their homes and incar-

---

*Woodrow Tsutomu Ichihashi was born in Palo Alto on Dec. 22, 1918, grew up on the Stanford campus, and graduated from Palo Alto Union High School in 1936. He attended Reed College from 1938 to 1940 and then transferred to the University of Oregon, where he was a member of the ROTC. His parents had named him for President Woodrow Wilson, but his middle name was not Wilson, contrary to what many believed. Personal statement, IP, B8, F2; author's interview with Woodrow Ichihashi, April 5, 1992.

cerated first in temporary "assembly centers" and later in "relocation camps." In 1942, the total population of persons of Japanese ancestry in the continental United States was 127,000. Over 60 percent were citizens.

Although the army claimed that evacuees would receive approximately one week's notice before they had to depart, the Ichihashis officially learned of their evacuation order less than three days before they were to leave. On Saturday, May 23, 1942, just days before the end of the academic year, notices were posted on the Stanford campus ordering Japanese Americans to bring only what they could carry. The Ichihashis hurriedly tried to arrange their household affairs, including having a gardener and neighbors care for their home, with its well-tended yard, graced by tall bamboo, a maple tree, lavender and begonia plants, and a fishpond. The couple lived in one half of a semidetached, three-story Victorian row house, close to the center of the Stanford campus at 523 Salvatierra Street. Two elderly sisters, the Stoltenbergs, lived in the other half of the house, and promised to help the Ichihashis rent their home during their absence.[9] Ichihashi, however, did not have the time, or perhaps the inclination, to return the hundreds of books he had checked out from the Stanford Library over the years. The History Department locked his office to keep it as he left it, and on Ichihashi's request, opened a special account to hold the funds from his salary to await his return. When that might be, of course, no one knew.[10]

Just after three o'clock on Monday, May 25, Yamato Ichihashi went to the president's office to see his old friend and colleague Ray Lyman Wilbur. The two men had known each other and worked together for almost 30 years, their association beginning even before Wilbur became Stanford's third president in 1916. Ichihashi wanted to say good-bye and leave his forwarding address. He and Kei were required to go to the Santa Anita racetrack, outside Los Angeles,[11] the largest of fifteen assembly centers for the evacuees, even though the closest assembly center would have been the Tanforan racetrack, just one half hour's drive north of Palo Alto. The next morning, on Tuesday, May 26, the Ichihashis left their Stanford home for the departure site from Palo Alto. A member of the local meeting of the American Friends, which lent moral support and comfort to the relocating Japanese, recalls seeing the Ichihashis that day. She sensed "the humiliation he must have been feeling," and remembers "how he sat quietly half way down on the left side of the bus, very disciplined and remote from his fellow passengers. We thought how he was from a different social class than most of them, how he was the most distinguished of all."[12] Incongruent with the setting, Yamato was wearing knickers.[13]

The May 26 edition of the *Stanford Daily* marked the departure of the Japanese from Stanford in a small article buried on page three: "Farm Japanese To Leave Today" ("Farm" being a nickname for the university campus). "At noon today the last remaining Japanese students will leave the campus and their organization will be closed," the paper reported. In addition, several university staff members and faculty housekeepers, including those of the widow of David Starr Jordan, Stanford's first president, of the Wilbur family, and of fellow historian Payson Treat, also departed. The article did not mention Professor Yamato and Kei Ichihashi.[14]

Just before "evacuation," Payson Treat, Yamato Ichihashi's best friend, and his wife Jessie, received the following poignant message:

Dear. Mr. and Mrs. P. Treat:

Within a very short time, we shall be leaving our work, our friends, our homes, and our church.

In many ways our evacuation is not a pleasant thing to contemplate, but we feel that it is a necessity brought on by the circumstances of war, and we shall cooperate to the utmost. Above all, we shall remain true to the best traditions of our American citizenship.

The church that we shall have to abandon for the duration has meant a great deal to us, not only as a sanctuary of worship, but as a symbol of American-Japanese friendship in this community.

As we take leave, we thank you for your past kindness. Wherever we may go, we shall take with us the memory of your Christian friendship.

Farewell, and may God Bless You abundantly.

> Faithfully yours,
> PALO ALTO JAPANESE CHURCH
> Grace Yoshida
> Secretary[15]

Yamato, age 63, and Kei, age 50, were among the 144 Japanese Americans from the Palo Alto area who faced the uncertain future. When asked whether he would like to return to Palo Alto someday, an unnamed Stanford graduate who was quoted in the local newspaper on the day of relocation shrugged his shoulders and answered, "Yes, but who knows?"[16] ◼

DIARY[17]

Through Hideo Furukawa of the Palo Alto [Japanese] Service Committee,[18] [we] learned of the evacuation announcement Saturday morning (May 23, 1942) at 11:00 A.M. Summoned for registration at San Jose State College gym [on Sunday] at 8 A.M., [we] learned that

Tuesday was the day of evacuation; I tried to negotiate for a one-day postponement; the office personnel were unanimous in approving, including Lieutenant Holmes, Jr., the military provost, but the Central Office at S.F. said nothing doing.

So K and I busied ourselves in packing our luggage and arranging the house which was left in the care of the University. A complete set of keys was left with the Stoltenbergs and Lois Ruth Bailey.[19] Left the house at 11:00 A.M. Tuesday (May 26th); Sam Anderson[20] drove us to Mayfield where we assembled at the Japanese Language School, 472 Sheridan Avenue [in Palo Alto]. We were supposed to leave there at 12:00, but due to the inadequacy of trucks to carry luggage, we were detained until after 1 P.M.; we did not reach San Jose until 2:00. A medical examination was held and we did not get on the train until 3:00. It was a hot day, but we had to walk quite a distance with heavy luggage; it was cruel hardship on old people like ourselves. All this was done at the San Jose Freight Depot.

We entrained at 3:00; the cars composing this train were all old day coaches, dirty and smelly—no light in the lavatory which people, especially children, dirtied in no time. Upholstered chairs showed moth-eaten spots. Basket supper [with] sandwiches, 2 cupcakes, an orange and milk at 6:00 P.M. This was repeated for breakfast (Wednesday). At night, heat was turned on and it got too hot, so that electric fans were turned on; thus passengers suffered either from heat or draft. This was the worst-managed train [I] experienced in the U.S., in addition to the above characteristics. Each car was guarded by an armed soldier. Beside him there was a doctor and a nurse.

All these people were nice and sympathetic. The train was supposed to reach the destination at 6 or 7 A.M. the following morning. But alas, it did not reach the Santa Anita Assembly Center till 12:30. It was a most trying trip—hot, dirty, very uncomfortable. But who were responsible for all this remains a question. At any rate, the delay was in part due to detention at Los Angeles when an electric motor had to be substituted for a steam engine; we reached Los Angeles at 7:00 A.M. but were detained until 11:30. We missed lunches. K and I got exhausted in finding our luggage and [trying] to have the same delivered to our woodshed. We had to stand in heat 2 1/2 hours. When we got to our dwelling-to-be after 3 hours, we were shocked to discover that it was empty except *mutsuki* [diapers] drying which belonged to the [people] next door. Luggage was piled up; at 5:00 [our] much hoped for "supper" was to be had. We were assigned to the Mess Hall (Red) in the Main Building. As we approached it, we heard a terrific noise (later found [out it was] the handling of used meal apparatus—metal plates designed like Stanford Union Blue Plates, a cup, a tea-spoon and a fork). Here thousands [eat] at 3 intervals. For our supper we got cherries compote[?] (white) 1/2 dozen, a small quantity of baked spaghetti, a small boiled potato, rice and water to drink.

Thus far we saw the shed and food, both of which made us feel very sad; it was an awful come-down. But when we returned to the shed, we found two dangerous wooden cots and we were told to pack bags with straw for mattresses. This was too [much]. By negotiations, I succeeded in obtaining two iron cots with mattresses, which are de luxe equipment as compared with the former. Having not slept a wink the previous night, we slept soundly in this hideous sleeping place, if it is fit to so designate.

. . . .

May 28

From Thursday noon, our Mess Hall was changed to "White." Food and dining service is much better in every respect. China wares are used, but the one fork and one spoon rule still prevails. Instead, uncouth boys, girls wait on tables. Foods are served abundantly, and, considering the number of persons served, are generally prepared satisfactorily and seasoning is quite acceptable. . . . Time of eating is arranged as follows:

Breakfast:	I from	6:30;	II from	7:00;	III	7:30
Dinner:	" "	11:30;	" "	12:00;	III	12:30
Supper:	" "	4:30;	" "	5:00;	III	5:30

The number served in the Mess Hall is about 3,500 or 4,000.

One has to stand in line at least 1/2 hour for each meal in order to enter the Hall. Sugar is rationed: a tea-spoonful for coffee (breakfast); no sugar for tea, which is served at dinner and supper along with water.

Foods served here are limited in kind and simple in character, but the cooking on the whole is fair, as far as we have experienced.

But I am informed by 12 persons that foods served at present show a vast improvement over what was formerly served. The first evacuees reached here 2 months ago (counting from May 30); these were given foods impossible to eat. Hard army bread and water. But the individuals were allowed to prepare and eat foods in their own sheds. There were bad foods served twice: once canned salmon and once canned spinach which both caused bowel troubles (*geri*) [diarrhea]. These created a havoc in lavatory facilities. Foods were served by contractors who are said to have indulged in [graft] by reducing to a minimum both the quantity and quality [of food]. On May 30th, it is said that the army has taken over the work of inspection; such inspectors appeared at the Mess Halls.

Each district is provided a lavatory which is kept in order and cleaned by care-takers; some of the users are careless. There is no privacy. Pots are arranged in a row and are open. Washing is provided with cold water only. The men's shower place only is provided with hot water. . . .

As regards soiled clothes, no professional or paid laundry facilities are allowed; individuals must do their own washing—everything including sheets. This is hard on the people who are not used to or physically unable to do. What then are the washing facilities provided in the camp? There is only one washing place in a territory as extensive as the Stanford campus; everybody is compelled to carry his or her soiled clothes, and since there is not enough space, many must wait in line; . . . there were 60 such persons when I visited there early this morning. [They] then carry [their clothes] back in order to dry them around their sheds, since many things disappeared when hung in public drying places located near the washing shed.

The major portion of evacuees are housed in newly constructed barracks (wood-sheds), but thousands are housed in stables which retain smells of the animals. A stable which housed a horse now houses from 5 to 6 humans, its ventilation is poor due to the absence of windows. A stable is generally partitioned into 2 parts, the back-part is dark. These are not only unsanitary, but mentally and morally depressive; they are bound to produce evil results and therefore should be condemned. The present occupants should be removed. . . . [21]

In a small section of a barrack, the government provides beds (mostly iron cots with mattresses), but again thousands are still sleeping on shaky wooden cots with cotton bags which are [packed] with straw (these are mattresses). [In addition], each shed is supposed to be given a broom and bucket (we have been here a week, but no bucket has come). Instructions as regards house-keeping mention dry mopping, but most of us have no materials necessary to improvise a mop. But Japanese, being clever artistically and cleanly in habit, have rendered the wood-sheds habitable in a sense, meaning on the basis of the lowest standard of life imaginable. The camp will be described in detail elsewhere.

Incidents Learned (May 27–June 2)

On May 14, 1941, [camp chief] Administrator H. Russell Amory issued an order to confiscate all the foods (canned or otherwise) and all the cooking utensils (electric appliances), but as usual without giving reasons or stating the purpose.[22] Many of the evacuees came as early as in the beginning of April, and these as well as later arrivals were allowed to bring in anything and everything as regards foods and utensils. These were essential as the camp lacked everything, including foods. At any rate, hardships that followed the deprivation of the above were soon realized, so the residents got together to draw up a petition for cancellation of the order on the grounds that the foods served in the Mess Halls are unsuitable for the aged and small children (foods are standardized according to the army diet for soldiers). Thereupon the order was modified and those who have children and the aged were allowed to keep and use foods and appliances until June 15th.

Old residents, 1 dozen men and women, said: foods served at first were extremely [bad] both as regards quality and quantity. As mentioned previously, there were two cases of universal poisoning ([valid?] cases of ptomaine). The mess halls were run under contract. White cooks were hired out of the per diem per capita allowance of 54 cents made by the army. Thus the allowance was reduced, beside inevitable graft was indulged in by the contractors. Consequently, residents had to suffer and became bitter. The situation became such that whites were discharged and experienced Japanese cooks were gradually substituted so that at the time of my arrival all the cooks are Japanese except the chief-cook. What "white" cooks were or are paid is, of course, kept secret. Japanese are supposed to be paid $12.00 per month. Japanese workers are classified as (1) professional (2) skilled and (3) unskilled. The class 1 are to be paid $16.00; skilled, $12.00; and unskilled, $8.00. The chief cook in each mess hall remained the agent of the contractor and his interests conflicted with those of the Japanese cooks; the former represented graft interests, while the latter were interested themselves on behalf of the evacuees.

Out of these conflicting interests, there developed many troubles which resulted once in the resignation of all the Japanese cooks in a Mess Hall. This strike was settled by the naming of a new white cook, and once in another Mess Hall, where one day the chief-cook . . . became rough with a waitress with a vile expression, [and] about 100 men eating there formed a circle armed with forks and spoons. This was a culmination of bitterness he had caused to de-velop; he knew it and got scared and ran away from the scene. He disappeared and has not been seen since; and so it is concluded that he must have resigned.

Foods served varied from day to day, sometimes fair, sometimes bad. Wednesday (June 3rd) both dinner and supper were bad at the "White" Mess Hall, and consequently many developed diarrhoea (*geri*), including myself. The same day 2 girls and a man fainted— mild cases of sun-stroke while waiting in line to gain entrance to the Hall. [The wait is] 30 minutes regularly; twice 55 minutes within a few days for us. It was said on the same day that [1/2 pint of] milk would be served everybody, but none was available for adults at sup-per; nothing is certain. On June 5th, I inquired of the "Carnation Milk" truck diver [and he] told me he brought 25,800 1/2 pint bottles that morning. Concerning efforts to bring about improve-ment . . . one Dr. Ishimaru played a conspicuous [role]. For this, however, he was forced out of the camp and ordered to proceed to Parker Dam (June 4th).* It looks [like] autocracy prevails; it cannot stand criticism. The military is afraid of information reaching the outside. Propaganda, including dramatized films are prepared and sent out, but the other side is carefully sealed [off] and there are rea-sons for all this, as it is well-known.

◻ The Ichihashis' closest friends were Payson and Jessie Treat. Payson Jackson Treat, a Wesleyan undergraduate and a Stanford Ph.D., began teaching at Stanford in 1905. Although he was trained in early American history, Treat became fascinated with East Asia and, after a trip to Asia, chose to specialize on the region. At Stanford he taught Chinese and Japanese history and international relations in the Pacific and helped pioneer the field of Asian studies in the United States. By World War II, Treat was one of the most important specialists on Japan and had a repu-

---

*The center administration claimed that Ishimaru, an optometrist, was moved to the Poston [Parker Dam] camp simply because he was needed there. Nevertheless, center res-idents circulated a slogan, "Remember Dr. Ishimaru," to protest what they believed to be an injustice. See Ichihashi to Treat, June 7, 1942, below, and Girdner and Loftis, *Great Betrayal*, p. 180.

tation as a Japanophile, although he never learned the Japanese language. Considerate and unassuming, he was very popular with Stanford students, including many Japanese Americans who wrote regularly to him about their relocation experiences. He worked against racial discrimination for much of his life. Treat first met Yamato Ichihashi when the latter was completing his Master's degree at Stanford in 1907. After the two shared an office during Ichihashi's first years of teaching at Stanford beginning in 1913, they became lifelong friends.[23]

Jessie McGilvray Treat was a graduate of Stanford, where she had met Payson when he was a graduate student. She played an active role in the Stanford community and had become friends with Kei Ichihashi in the course of her work among the spouses of Stanford faculty. The Treats had no children.

The correspondence between the Ichihashis and the Treats reveals an extraordinary intellectual and personal friendship, as the reader will discover. Yamato Ichihashi intended his letters to form part of the documentation for his planned history of internment.

Soon after their arrival at Santa Anita, before writing the following letter, the Ichihashis had sent a postcard with their address and a short note to the Treats. ◗

YAMATO ICHIHASHI TO
PAYSON AND JESSIE TREAT [24]

> Santa Anita Assembly Center
> District V, Barrack 29, Unit 3,
> Ave. G.
> Arcadia, California
> [June 1, 1942]

Dear Chief[25] and Madam:

Lest an ax fall on my neck, I hasten to keep my promise in dropping you a line despite the lack of a table and a chair. As I notified, we arrived here safe and sound, although I must confess that the train ride was the worst I have experienced here or abroad. The cars were dirty, uncomfortable day-coaches in which we were supposed to sleep. A few succeeded in doing so; I did not sleep a wink. We went without lunch the day we arrived here; at 5 p.m. much hoped for supper came. But alas the Mess Hall sounded like a battle, with booming and banging of metal dining service; the worst was yet to come: the supper consisted of a small quantity of baked spaghetti, a small potato, a little rice and water. What a come down even for a professor! Our living quarter is a small portion of wood-shed of cheapest type, very poorly constructed; we hear everything that goes in on either side and more. There is no privacy of any kind. In short the general conditions are bad without any exaggeration; we are fast being converted into veritable Okies.

Criticisms are being raised among some Americans who received communications from inmates of this place; the management has started to defend [itself]. Neither is truthful. Yesterday the new arrivals were filmed, which will doubtless impress the public favorably; but it was dramatized for the purpose. Soldiers appeared on the train platform and assisted the aged and young. When we arrived, we were forced to hunt for our luggage scattered on a half-mile long platform and not a soul to help. We stood there before our luggage was carried to our shed. What a difference! Why not film the true picture? No American visitors are permitted to enter the camp; interviews are held outside. The conditions cannot stand inspection.

Dear Madam:

From this point on I am acting as Kei's secretary. Mr. Ichihashi has written about some aspects of our experiences during our terrible trip from San Jose to Santa Anita. We were vaccinated and inoculated on Thursday, a day after our arrival; Mr. Ichihashi has thus far escaped from any suffering; but I developed a fever and suffered. I am much better now, although I cannot still use my right hand. It is a [marvelous?]²⁶ experience, though mostly painful to say the least. Now I get down to business and ask of you a favor in purchasing and sending (by parcel post) the following articles which we need very badly:

1) a card table; 2) two folding chairs (light and comfortable); 3) a pair of sun-glasses for Mr. Ichihashi; 4) a small radio without short-wave equipment; 5) a washing basin (enameled metal one); 6) three bunches of laundry ropes (lines); 7) a ball of cord like one enclosed; and 8) two shower caps (for Kei).

Please select the above articles according to your own judgment because it is difficult for me to describe them in detail. Mr. Ichihashi and I will write you from time to time because we have already learned many things pertaining to the Camp life.

Very sincerely yours,
Yamato and Okei

P.S. Enclosed please find a check; if there be a balance, please hold [it] for we may have to bother you again.

KEI ICHIHASHI TO JESSIE TREAT [27]

Arcadia, California
June 5th [1942]

Dear Mrs. Treat:

Thank you very much for your kind letter.[28] Since we have already been here 9 days, in the morning it is rather foggy and cool, but in the afternoon it is warmer, [even] quite hot. Yesterday the thermometer went up to 90 degrees, but due to pleasant sea breeze, we did not suffer.

How we get home-sick when we recall our campus house! Our present living quarter is a woodshed 19 1/3 feet deep 7 1/3 feet wide and 6 feet high, it is very ugly to say the least; it has no ceiling but a roof. I concealed my bed by hanging a sheet. The bed is my table and the hat box is my chair. I piled four suitcases and put the small mirror on their top. This is my dressing table. I read here, write here, dress here. Life is very simple.

The meals are very simple, too, a breakfast is at 7 a.m.; a dinner at 12 noon, a supper at 5 p.m. but every body eats too fast so that I can not stay at table long enough to chew, and I have indigestion already.

Foods are often very bad. I call this a "fishing trip" but without trouts, however with cooks;[29] therefore it is not so bad after all.

The other day Mr. Ichihashi wrote a letter to you for me in which we [were] forced to trouble you. I am very sorry for that.

I thank you for your kindness thinking of our house. Mr. Ichihashi wrote a letter explaining how we stand on the proposal; we would naturally like to have tenants.

A week ago I had the injections for typhoid, and the second one yesterday, so I do not feel well today once more. Tomorrow I hope that [I] will be all right again.

Very sincerely yours
Kei

DIARY [30]

June 6th

Continues to be hazy and cool until noon then the sun appears; it then becomes hot. The day's important event is the publication of election returns.[31] The medical records show the total population to be exactly 18,400 (June 6th); the number eligible to vote (21 and older both sexes and citizens and aliens) is said to be 10,365. (Therefore the minors number 8,035 whose exact age distribution can not be determined at present; other details are not available.) Of the voting population, 5924 or 57% cast ballots (unofficial). The elected are both citizens [and] aliens and both sexes. However, males dominate.

. . . .

Again, hazy and cool or even cold.

Packages of articles ordered via Treats arrived in the afternoon. Election returns were published: winners and followers-up. It is said that the Issei[32] numerically dominate the elected; four women elected.

No milk for dinner and supper, despite the customary allegation.

[June] 7th

Still hazy and cold. Wrote a lengthy letter to Payson telling something of this place. Nothing unusual. Looked over the sections beyond the Mess Hall. Kei had diarrhoea; my stomach still upset and no smoking.

YAMATO ICHIHASHI
TO PAYSON AND JESSIE TREAT[33]

June 7, 1942

Dear Friends:

Yesterday afternoon, the four packages reached us intact after having been inspected; the radio is working and its tone is very nice. For all these articles we are very grateful for your careful selection and quick dispatching.[34] Our wood-shed palace is gradually being converted into a habitable place I hope in time. Your former maid will get the magazine and soaps as soon as we reach her. Many, many thanks for your kindness.

This is our 12th day here, and of course I have used all my spare time (very limited because of numerous visitors) in looking over the Camp as well as in obtaining as much reliable information possible. I have already learned a great many interesting things concerning the community life, including even gambling and commercial vice, which are said to have now been suppressed. One has to be even careful of his own immediate neighbors. Here goes my first story touching on matters which, I think, will interest you.

First of all, whether it was so intended or not, the Wartime Civil Control Administration[35] under the Army's authority, has established in this Center a truly classless community (a Soviet ideal unrealized as yet in Russia). Residents (inmates more appropriately) are not recognized as individuals; we are numbered for identification and are treated exactly alike, except babies one year and younger as regards foods. We are fed, quartered and forced to do our own washing, including sheets, shirts, and what not. Washing facilities are wholly inadequate. They do not allow to have washing done by a laundry outside. Why I do not know. Criticisms relative [to] any matter are not tolerated by the management; a few days [ago] a doctor was railroaded from here because he, as a scientist, has tried to bring about improvements. It is very dangerous for any individual to try [not to go] along the line.

The Camp has a population of 18,400, each of which is numbered for identification; for instance I am No. 5561A, which is required for every transaction in the Camp; of course aside from mails, we have no contact with the outside world. The above number [of residents] has been mostly drawn from Southern California; the first batch reached here on April 3rd from San Diego and Long Beach; others followed from southern counties, and a month later from San Francisco; those from Santa Clara were the last to arrive here thus far. More are said to be coming, but from what places I do not know. At no time was the Camp prepared to receive evacuees; each arrival faced many hardships which could have been avoided; in particular their feeding was undescribably bad, and that was our experience, although we are informed by older residents that general conditions have been vastly improved in more recent days. The population is mixed: citizens and enemy aliens; they are differentiated in the Camp; it is an impossible combination. Many of the youngsters have been appointed [to administrative positions], and they act like petty bureaucrats—the word most commonly heard is *order*. More on this later.

In management of the classless community, the government has apparently adopted the lowest conceivable standard of treating human beings; thousands are still housed in stables; a stable for one animal is now occupied from five to six persons. They are still odorous and poor of ventilation. Of course, barracks are constructed exactly like our old fashioned wood-shed; each barrack is partitioned into six sections so that inmates have 4 walls, all constructed of rough pine boards nailed in a manner so that on the average [there is] 1/2 inch spaces between these wall boards; you can not only hear what goes on in the barrack, but can see, if you want, what goes on next door. There is no privacy anywhere; we have become veritable animals as far as our living is concerned. In addition, to be thrown into a community mostly composed of lowly, uncouth rustics, is in itself very painful for cultured persons. Some times these intangibles are more difficult to bear; but despite all, we are determined to be philosophic about everything; this is easy to talk about, but extremely difficult to face as realities.

A little more prosaically, meals served consist mostly of vegetables and rice, and meat or fish is very rarely served; when the latter is served it is done in very small quantities. Butter is not used with bread; nor do we get fats and oils and already our skin shows the result. Because of the coarseness of foods, digestive organs have a hard time in functioning properly. Diarrhoea is very prevalent, often causing panics in the lavatories, and this is no exaggeration.

Yet we are forced to face the shortage of medics and drugs and other necessary elements: there is one doctor to each 3,000 persons and only 3 dentists and some nurses. One need not observe more [than] the length of a line formed by those waiting in front of the hospital or the dental clinic to appreciate the inadequacy of facilities along these lines. Emergency cases are frequent. So far one death has occurred, but babies are born every day, often three to four; there are 800 potential mothers among the inmates. Physicians are [over]worked. I do not understand why the management fails to take advantage of the doctors present in the Camp; there are a number of unemployed ones.

There naturally exist a number of things which require reform or elimination in order to correct the general condition. But politics and graft prevent any efforts along these lines, according to older residents; for the time being, these must be seen as rumors; I have no means of verifying one way or other. They say that the Army allows 54 cents per diem for the food, if this be true, the residents are getting the benefit of such an appropriation.

I must now proceed to the mess hall 1/2 hour ahead [of time] so as to join the line in order to get into the hall on time, so I had better to put an abrupt end here, since there is no real end no matter [what] you write.[36]

Very affectionately.
Yamato

Remember us kindly to Madam.

DIARY [37]

[June] 8th

A 2nd trip made to the Stable District; some are in a fair condition, while others are in a bad state; the 1st row is provided with a number of small toilets. Water drainage is bad in many places. The variation of conditions due to the control exercised by residents; streets are dirt unlike those in this vicinity, which are covered with fine gravel and [?] with oil, making them hard and less dusty.

[June] 9th

Continues to be hazy and cool. . . . Visited Dr. Norman T. Kobayashi, head of the hospital. Nothing unusual happened. Continued to suffer from stomach trouble.

. . . .

[June] 10th

Learned that 50 cents per capita–per day is appropriated [from the government], which is sub-divided under 3 categories as follows: 40 cents for meals, 6 cents for room, and 4 cents for "miscellaneous" (unknowables).

The area of the camp is estimated at a little less than 100 acres (less than a mile square).

Toilets in my section are kept orderly and clean; others are not, even showing the evidence of leakage into streets (14 paces wide). Barracks and toilets are closely located. Waste water from showers and washing forms a large quantity, but is run in an open ditch which runs in the middle of the camp. It emits odorous gas very bad. It is said sludge boxes are being constructed for the discharge of water "into cess pools extending down but not below the natural underground flow of water." Army engineers are designing.

Arts and craft exhibition held on 9th and 10th: some handicraft are cleverly made.

Canteens allege that they will carry more items of goods; hitherto only candies, snacks and newspapers.

Shoe-repairing made possible outside the camp, prices determined and paid in the camp before such shoes are sent. No laundry or barber services are provided as yet.

Camouflage net-making (no aliens) is being done by citizens (the pay being $8.00 as unskilled); workers are supposed to be volunteers, but were practically drafted. When unwilling to do the job, many were threatened by the Japanese intermediaries. Conditions under which the work is done are bad; the materials used are poisonous and yet masks are only partially provided. [Camp administrator] Amory declares that the work has come directly from the Army; no private contract is involved and therefore no profit. He denies the drafting or "black-listing"; workers are merely but urgently asked to volunteer. In order to secure a necessary number of workers for this job, those already engaged in other tasks are being shifted.*

[June] 11th

. . . Continued to be hazy and cold in the morning and early afternoon.

There are 5,500 units based on the *Pacemaker*† circulation. Since each barrack is formed into 6 units, there appear to be 5,500 ÷ 6 or 906[?] or so; but there are stables, each being made into a unit; the stables are divided into the Districts I and II; while barracks are divided into the Districts III, IV, V, VI and VII. The District V consists of A21–K48 inclusive. 100 acres including the race track and the grand-stand. There is an additional unoccupied 150 acres which are in the immediate vicinity; this track is expected [to be turned] into a cultivated field.

[June] 12th

No milk for dinner and supper. Hazy and cold. Everett Chapman and [Edward J.] England, Service and Recreation Directors respec-

---

*For several months, residents at the Santa Anita center completed more than 22,000 nets that ranged in size from 22′ square to 36′ square. Issei, technically Japanese nationals, were not employed on the project since the Army wanted to avoid any appearance that it was using the forced labor of prisoners of war, which would violate provisions of the Geneva Convention. General John DeWitt claimed that the savings to the government through the use of evacuee labor more than offset the cost of feeding the entire camp. Girdner and Loftis, *Great Betrayal*, p. 179.

†The Center newspaper published by the residents.

tively, called and asked that I act as an adviser or consultant; accepted on the condition of 50-50 basis.[38] . . . It appears that American employees of the Centers are anxious, for obvious reasons, to convert this place into a permanent settlement. In the field of education and recreation there is the problem of handling about 4,400 minors below 16, i.e. 1–16 [years of age]. Those over 16 are urged to work on camouflage nets (drafted with a good deal of pressure); at present about 1,270 women are engaged and more are needed. Consequently education for these older boys and girls is out of the question—a serious problem. Some of the teachers have been drafted. No more school on Saturdays.

[June] 13th

Gave a talk to 120 teachers. Made 2 suggestions: (1) the formation [of] teacher-training courses to improve teaching ability of those who are teaching; most of these according to their own testimony lack necessary qualifications, and (2) [formation] of a P.T.A. in order to appeal to parents for more responsible care of their own children while out of the "school."[39]

Today I saw an organized campaign [under?] the Service Directors for getting more men and women to "volunteer" for net work. Pressure was brought to bear and a majority present at the meeting responded favorably as naturally expected. Advised England and Chapman against "forcing" persons to work; many do not desire because they are already engaged in some other projects. As far as recent arrivals are concerned, there are no jobs except this particular work. Psychological effect of "discrimination" is bad; there is a strong undercurrent.

A considerable shifting can be made; for example, a large number of boys in the mess halls can be taken out for net work and girls be substituted; there are other instances. Why this is not done, is difficult to understand. To show favoritism on the basis of early arrival is unjustifiable. This problem should be solved at once.

The "self-government" is now instituted by the 49 elected men and women; the committee of seven [was] elected, whose chairmanship has not been solved satisfactorily, Muraoka* reported. If the government is to function properly, it is O.K. But alas! Is it another propaganda? A mere form for the benefit of an uninformed public.

---

* Unidentified.

KEI ICHIHASHI TO JESSIE TREAT [40]

Arcadia, California
June 13 [1942]

Dear Mrs. Treat:

Thank you for your kind letters dated 4th and 9th of June. Last
Saturday we received four packages safely, as Mr. Ichihashi had written to you. I am very grateful for your kindness. The table is nice
and very steady, and the chairs are very comfortable; after meals we
sit and enjoy smoking on these de lux chairs.[41]

It was very nice of you to send me such a beautiful cushion; it is
too pretty to use in this wood shed. When I came here I brought a
shower cap, but I lost it the second day in the shower room. I heard
that somebody lost her clothes there, I don't know how she went
back to the barrack. We have a very strange life here, so we have to
be very alert in every way. We have no barbers, no beauty shops and
no home laundries here, so we have to wash even our own sheets.
At present the laundry accommodation is inadequate and very
crowded. We have only one laundry for the entire community of
18,400. There is a very nice and spacious place near the laundry for
drying. But often such clothes disappear, so that people bring back
their washed clothes, sheets and towels etc., to their barracks and
hang them around them. Every day one sees pants, slacks, shirts,
sheets, diapers and bibs surrounding the barracks. The appearance
is terrible; they are real "Okies" all right. In early mornings, sometimes at 5:30 A.M. mothers and daughters carry their washtubs and
washing boards and clothes on *kiddy wagons* to and fro the distant
laundry; these make terrible noises. Very often they have to wait for
a long time in front of the laundry because of a multitude. Women
occupy the laundry from morning till night, its closing hour being
at 8:00 P.M. It is a hard job; people say women work harder here than
men. I think this is especially of women who have little children.

We have heard from Woodrow; he is at Tule Lake, California,
and has a good job, so that we decided not to call him to this center.[42]

We may ask you to send us vitamin pills sometime later, but
please do not send us foods, because they do not allow us to have
any such food articles. Meals are still very bad except breakfasts. We
can't get enough nourishment.

Mr. Ichihashi has been and still is suffering with a headache. . . .

Affectionately yours
Kei

DIARY [43]

[June] 14th

Continues to be hazy and cool. An usual train of visitors; called on Mrs. Noro, a sick woman. Made another observation tour, and listened to a series of complaints along usual lines.

[June] 15th

The "government" was finally organized; its chairman, Sashihara, reported on this fact. As stated before, the camp was divided into 7 election "districts," each of which is subdivided into 7 "sections," which elects its representative, or 49 in all. These 49 constitute the so-called "Santa Anita Assembly Center Self-Government Assembly." Each district['s] representatives (7 in number) then elected one from among their number as the district representative; thus there are 7 of these who constitute the council presided over by a chairman elected from among these seven; he is the mayor, Sashihara. He, accompanied by Muraoka, requested that I become an "unofficial" advisor to this government, and speak before its first meeting on Wednesday next (June 17). Consented. Various committees have been named to handle matters.

A petition is being circulated (i.e., to secure signatures) for publication of a paper in Japanese; [I] signed but on the condition that it be presented to the government. My position is that this channel should be used in all cases of "public" matters in approaching the Center management.

Wrote letters to Stoltenbergs and Wilbur.

Received letters from Treat dated May 28, Wilbur in re: [sabbatical] leave and another, [from] Lynn White.[44]

[June] 16th

Continues to be hazy and cool with 12 [noon] and after rather [hot?]. Net workers struck: the grounds (1) inadequate food; (2) conditions under which they work are very bad; (3) for increase of the wages; $8.00 per month at present. Learned from Chapman: no formal education possible, only "informal;" i.e., the set-up to continue for those 16 and under—those over 16 "must" work in making nets (voluntary but high pressure applied.) Teachers classified as "P" (professional teachers), "S" (assistants and trainees). "Until the fall," is the time limitation[?].

[June] 17th

[I] was to give a talk before the 1st meeting of the Government, but the meeting was postponed because of Wilkinson's illness.* Received a letter from Wilbur, asking for further information. The public was pre-occupied in discussing the "strike" of yesterday. Further clarification is needed before truth can be learned. Over-zealous Japanese foremen (loyalty, obedience) seem to be a vital source of [dis?]satisfaction because they seem determined to carry out "orders" inflexibly.

. . . .

[June] 18th

Continues to be hazy in the morning, but hot from noon on. There began a sudden improvement in food both as regards quality and quantity. However the character of mess services continues to be the same. The management promises to better the conditions under which net workers labor; so far nothing materialized. In the government meeting, a hot debate took place as regards the proposal to "invite" the Spanish minister to inspect here.† A well known communist named Matsui opposed the idea, but trouble began. After the meeting he and another communist were badly beaten up; they have been on the spot for they have been alleged to have acted as *mikkō-sha* [informers] in L.A.[45] No one has been arrested, and the matter was made to [?] by the police. The victims are in the hospital. A sad incident at the best. Heard from Woodie and Edgar [Robinson].

---

*In his June 23 letter to Treat, below, Ichihashi identifies Wilkinson as the Personnel Director who oversaw the camp "self-government."

†The Spanish consul in San Francisco, Francisco de Amat, formally represented the Japanese government in matters concerning its interned nationals during the war.

[June] 19th

Hazy and cool in the morning, but rather hot in the rest of day. One Oyama, a councilman, reported in regard to the mess matters: graft being alleged. Service needs to be reformed. The same situation as regards the general condition remains except the sewer ditch is being cleaned so that water runs more or less. There prevails a general complaint about the behavior of residents as well as the indifference of the management.

YAMATO ICHIHASHI TO JESSIE TREAT [46]

June 19, 1942.

Dear Mrs. Treat:

Many apologies for not having written to you much sooner; the only excuse for that has been that I have been suffering from a series of headaches due to the peculiarly oppressive weather—hot and moist. . . .

The general condition in the Camp continues the same, but becomes less vivid and less shocking as you get accustomed to it. I have recently [been] summoned by the "Director of Services" under whom "education" is also conducted. He asked me to become his *unofficial* adviser; I have consented to do so. The "Self-Government" was recently instituted, and it asks me to act as its adviser; I shall see about this. I was asked to speak at its first meeting last Wednesday, but the meeting [was] postponed on account of the illness of the American representative. The management faced its first real headache on the 16th; "camouflage net" workers struck. Newspapers made a joke of it, saying that the workers objected to sauerkraut served at lunch, it being a German dish. This is a lie. First, the workers are supposed to [be] volunteers, but [were] "drafted" by the application of high pressures; these are boys and girls over 16 years of age (at present about 1,500 are working). Immediate causes were (if I am correct): 1) the Wednesday lunch consisted of 2 small wieners (meat) with sauerkraut, bread without butter as usual and brown water called tea; 2) they are paid $8.00 per month (in reality, none has received a penny so far); other workers have been here more than 2 months [without pay?]; and 3) conditions under which they work are bad: hot, dusty and poisonous, protective measures are lacking or wholly inadequate.[47]

I have already warned my "boss" of the existence of undercurrents everywhere, and if they are not alert, these might burst forth and create more headaches for the management. Supplies including food stuffs very often disappear in quantities. There is a general belief that graft exists everywhere, causing shortages of all kinds. The Santa Clara evacuees have not received buckets which are supposed to be furnished.*

My chief interest at present is in the schooling of children; there are more [than] 2,000 below [the age of] 16, and most of these are wild rustics and difficult to discipline. I have suggested a training course so as to improve the character of teachers and organization of a P.T.A. in order to reach parents so that they be made to cooperate. Children must be better controlled. I am not sure how we can do along this line.

By the way, Dr. Wilbur wrote me four times in a touching manner, although I wrote him [only] once. He asks me to keep him posted on what goes on and I shall do so for we certainly need outside help. Nothing unpleasant is allowed to go [out] there, and there are reasons for this. No one is permitted to come in; all interviews are held outside the Camp.

The Camp is noisy due to the presence of undisciplined rustic adults, and wild youth and children. 18,500 are huddled in an area of less than 100 acres in thousands of stables and barracks. Kei mentioned of the rolling of kiddy cars piled [with] washing equipments: metal tubs, [etc.]; they make noise unimaginable between 5:30 A.M. and 8:00 or 9:00 P.M., day after day. The inmates are officially checked at 6:00 A.M. and 9:30 P.M.; lights are supposed to be out at 10:00, but noise continues till mid-night. At about 8:30 searchlights, about a dozen in number, are played so that we have a continuous lightning effect, a source of disturbance at night. Such is our plight! Finally in regard to [your] kind consideration as regards "eatables," it is against the rule to possess any food articles which require cooking. Thus far all canned goods are forbidden; candies and crackers only are permitted. Even these, if brought by visitors are confiscated, but depending on cops or soldiers. At present, we have candies and crackers to last for a while. When we find [it] necessary, we will ask you to send us a few articles.

In the meantime, we are hoping for a general improvement all

---

*Santa Clara County, where Stanford University and Palo Alto are located.

around; one excuse of the management is "we are here temporarily." In fact, soon some thousands are to be removed to relocation centers. The population is kept moving so that a batch of "citizens" are to be imported to work on nets. Uncertainty prevails. Please tell Payson that I will write him soon (after I shall have met the "government").

> With best wishes to you and Chief, I am,
> Very Sincerely,
> Yamato Ichihashi

My typewriter is out of order, but it will be repaired. Then you will be spared of my awful hand-writing.

◻ The war in the Pacific had gone poorly for the United States since the bombing of Pearl Harbor. From December 1941 through the spring of 1942, Japan enjoyed an unbroken run of victories, seizing the Philippines, the Malay Peninsula, Burma, the Dutch East Indies, Hong Kong, and a number of British Pacific Islands. It had reduced the territory under the effective control of the Chinese Nationalist government to just the remote western region of the China mainland. Korea, Manchuria, Taiwan, and Indochina had already been incorporated into the Japanese empire. Japan's leaders believed the creation of the Greater East Asia Co-Prosperity Sphere, Japan's designation for its empire of puppet states ostensibly liberated from Western colonialism, was achieving even greater success than anticipated.

But the spring of 1942 witnessed a dramatic reversal of Japanese imperial ambitions. First in the battle of the Coral Sea in April–May and then in the battle of Midway in early June, the Japanese navy suffered strategic defeats that placed Japan on the defensive at sea and in the air. Ichihashi, as one can gather from his diary notations, cryptic though they usually are, and his clippings from the *San Francisco Examiner*, the *San Francisco Chronicle*, and the *Palo Alto Times*, tried to kept abreast of war developments. It is clear that he did not share American enthusiasm for the prosecution of the war against Japan and had sympathies for his homeland, but he also did not identify himself with the evacuees who agitated in favor of the Japanese militarists. He devoted his attention principally to the immediate human drama of internment, of which he was both participant and observer. ◼

DIARY [48]

[June] 20th (25th day)

Climate is the same, but temperature rose to 91 degrees. This combined with moisture made the day very disagreeable. Gave a second talk to "teachers" and advised, appealed, and demanded that parents exercise better control and discipline over their children. [They must] refrain from conduct that will make wild kids even worse.[49]

Two Tenrikyō preachers, one [an] aged woman, who had been released from the concentration camp and sent here were re-arrested and sent to a camp in Texas; [three?] others met the same fate.*

A Salvation Army captain paid me a visit and stated that, among other things, he is not allowed to preach in streets. He mentioned cases of moral evil; apprehensive of future fatherless children. In particular, he detailed the condition inmates of *yōrō-in* [old people's home] have to live; there are already 54, including 4 women. They are housed in stables which are difficult to keep in sanitary conditions because they are helpless. No special conditions are given them. Fleas and lice abound. Washing difficulty; underwears are lacking. I asked him to submit a written report.

---

*Tenrikyō, a Shinto sect, was founded in the nineteenth century by a female shaman and is known for its focus on faith healing. It became popular among the laboring classes of Japan.

"Concentration camps"—also called "internment camps" at the time—referred to special prisons run by the Department of Justice; enemy aliens (including Japanese diplomats) it considered "dangerous" were arrested by the FBI and placed in these camps. One of the largest was at Crystal City, Texas. These camps are not to be confused with the "relocation" camps or centers where most Japanese Americans were sent. The exact number of Japanese detained in these special camps and the length of their detentions have been difficult to establish. One estimate places the number, including resident men, women, and children at 7,000. The Justice Department operated the camps in a manner consistent with the 1929 Geneva Convention provisions on the treatment of prisoners of war. See Tetsuden Kashima, "American Mistreatment of Internees During World War II: Enemy Alien Japanese," and John J. Culley, "The Santa Fe Internment Camp and the Justice Department Program for Enemy Aliens"; both in Daniels, Taylor, and Kitano, eds., *Japanese Americans*, pp. 52–71.

[June] 22nd

Very hot, reaching over 100 degrees.

The postponed meeting of the Government was again postponed due to the penalty imposed on the individuals involved in the Thursday [June 18] incident—14 railroaded, including the "mayor."*
This was the work of the F.B.I. The management insisted on its innocence; autocracy prevails; the councilmen were indirectly intimidated. Harmony is difficult to attain under the existing set-up. Everybody in the administration appears to be more concerned about the defense of his post and duty: "passing the buck" is the order [of the day] and the residents are rendered helpless. Some even do not hesitate to say that the Japs are "prisoners of war" with no rights whatsoever; most of those in charge appear to be l. gr. pol. [low grade politicians?] and incapable to understand human problems—ignorant and vulgar.

[June] 23rd

Very hot again.

Dishwashers (in "White") struck at dinner and supper times, as well as Japanese policemen.† Fundamental causes appear to be the method of forcing these and other men into various services and the inability of the divisional service supervisors to handle them tactfully; the latter are ignorant but with the newly acquired sense of authority. Besides, the pay scales are also the source of irritation $16-$12-$8; gradation is often illogical. But bureaucracy of the worst kind prevails through the whole system—with its reflection on the most unimportant employees. This necessarily produces irritation among the adults whom these attempt to rule in conjunction with the Administration.

Sanitary equipments get out of order very often and repairs are very slow. Showers are one faucet; hence it is often too hot, [or] the hot water is often unavailable. A few days [ago] a leper was caught taking a shower. Athlete-foot is getting common; it is contracted in

---

*This incident is described in detail below in Yamato Ichihashi's June 28 letter to Payson Treat.

†Japanese American police handled some internal security tasks in the Center.

the shower. Some 15 odd young girls are said to be pregnant, a serious moral problem. . . .

This note closes the 4th week after we left home.

[June] 24th[50]

Continues to be hazy and then hot but not so [bad] as on the previous day. The meeting of the government was postponed again; will it die even before it is properly instituted? Likely. The strike in White Mess Hall was lost. The police decided to walk out, 250 in number. Its immediate cause was as follows: the Superintendent [England?], an American executive, failed to signal at a cross road; a Japanese cop called [this to] his attention, but he was punished instead of the culprit for unknown reasons. Whereupon the cops demanded the granting of certain authority to the Self-Government, so that the cops too might share in necessary power in order to function. This was denied whereupon they decided to resign as a body—"a walkout" to take effect on the 25th. Besides, the above course was intensified by their dissatisfaction as regards the pay of $8.00; they feel that there should be no grading and that there should be a flat rate of $16.00 for all employees, including cops.

Since it has been expected that the government should be the proper channel for complaints and suggestions in respect to the community desire for improvements along certain specific lines, I have been awaiting in vain for the actual operation of this channel. Nothing has been done. In fact, the situation is growing worse; "undercurrents" may result in manifold outbursts. It is too bad that the management is apparently unaware of such an eventuality. A group of Hawaii-borns was railroaded to the city court for [roughhousing?]; the rumor[?] was these boys formed a musical band aboard the military truck carrying them. As they were about to emerge from the "Gate," they played and sang the "Aloha" [song] to the great amusement and amazement of the crowd that gathered to see them off. They came back the same evening and nothing has been learned of what had happened to them since. These events seem to make it more vivid that the present setup of the community is illogical and impossible; this is made more so by the attitude and handling of affairs by the management—autocracy enforced by a veritable Gestapo.

KEI ICHIHASHI TO JESSIE TREAT [51]

Arcadia
June 24 [1942]

Dear Mrs. Treat:

Thank you for the soap and cream. You don't know how glad I am to get them; at present we can't buy anything in this center. There are 3 canteens, but they carry cigars, cigarettes, cheap 5 and 10 cent candies and ice cream, sometime apples and oranges. So every body is trying to be very thrifty, saving everything, scraps of paper, inches of string, even crooked nails etc.

In the next room, our neighbor has 3 children, 6 and 3 year old girls and a baby boy 14 months old. They make noises from morning till evening; besides these babies, there are many little children around here, so it is terrible sometimes. In these three weeks we have learned to adapt ourselves to this strange world so disturbing to mind and body; still we can take naps from time to time. Isn't it queer?

Lately meals have improved very much, if they keep up these menus, we need not worry about nourishment. Anyhow we lost our weight a bit already.

Today it was very hot and everybody was staying out in the shade to keep cool. The thermometer went up to 93 degrees at 3:00 P.M., but Mr. Ichihashi and I are quite well, so please do not worry about us.

Affectionately yours,
Kei

YAMATO ICHIHASHI TO EDGAR ROBINSON [52]

June 25, 1942

Dear Edgar:

Thank you for the kind letter; I have been trying to write sooner but in vain. I owe a number of letters to friends, and as usual, I am behind in my correspondence. For one thing, it has been very hot with plenty of moisture, making it hard to bear. In fact, I have suffered from headaches and nose-bleed. Besides, the general condition is such that it is [difficult?] for everybody to sit at a desk and write. In addition, I have many visitors seeking my advice on all sorts of matters: I get very tired, if not exhausted everyday. Nevertheless, I

am trying my best to help these helpless "residents," mostly ignorant rustics.

Whenever I attempt to write, I am tempted to write so much, I
often get lost in the midst of writing. This may happen in this letter
too; so do not expect to get anything brilliant. I am too perturbed
for that. However, I shall try to tell you a few matters that might
interest you. . . .

[In two paragraphs omitted here, Ichihashi repeats description of
camp life he gave Payson Treat in previous letters.]

If hell is a reality, our society is one; it is an awful punishment for
men and women of culture and refinement. There is an article, "Concentration Camp: U.S. Style," in the June 15th issue of the *The New
Republic*;[53] if you want a detailed description of another "center,"
read it for it presents a true picture without any exaggeration. . . .

Dr. Wilbur has probably told you what I am trying to do in the
field of "education" limited to those 16 and below. I am trying to
help "teachers" engaged in the work, of course without qualification. No "formal" education is allowed until September; it is estimated that there are 4,400 children in this school-age group. No
help from the management or outside is made; no equipment and no
material for the "school." Yet the "teachers" are doing remarkably
well, and my heart breaks when I think of the future of [these] wild
and undisciplined kiddies and the task facing the teachers. At my
suggestion an informal PTA was formed; I talked to the teachers and
the PTA. The first gathering brought about 600 persons. I am not
sure what I can accomplish, but I am persuaded to attempt what I
can do to alleviate, if possible, social and moral evils already manifest. We need help from the outside in every way to prevent the
breeding of [the] worst kind of humans. But alas no outsider is allowed inside the prison-gate! Reasons for this are too obvious. I
must end abruptly—too many callers.

Very sincerely,
Yamato

YAMATO ICHIHASHI TO PAYSON TREAT[54]

June 28, 1942.

Dear Chief:

As I wrote you that there was held an election of representatives
of the inmates to constitute the so-called "Self-Government," but it
has not yet been instituted, although three weeks have elapsed since.

The management is not interested to hear what the residents have to say. Sometime ago, you doubtless saw a dispatch relative to one of the "public incidents" which resulted in the arrest of six men because they used the Japanese language in violation of the army rule.[55] That is what the Associated Press reported. Let me tell you the truth about it as far as I have been able to discover.

The District VII (remember the camp is divided into seven political units) held an informal meeting, of course, with the permission of the American management represented by a chap named Wilkinson, the Personnel Director, under whose jurisdiction the government falls. Japanese was used in discussing matters of interest, as it had been the custom. A proposal was suggested that the Spanish Minister be invited to investigate the existing conditions in order to bring about a general improvement. A voice was raised against it by a notorious Japanese communist, named Matsui, commonly alleged to be a Korean.[56] (It is asserted that there are 15 Koreans in the camp, employed to do spying on behalf of the management.) He had been an "informer" in Los Angeles, and as a result, many innocent Japanese had been arrested and sent to concentration camps. There was and still is an intense feeling against Matsui, and when he raised his voice, the assembly became somewhat vehement. But the matter was settled. After the meeting was adjourned, several men attacked Matsui and another communist outside the assembly hall; they had to be taken to the hospital. The following morning 14 men, including the Mayor Sashihara who had presided over the meeting were arrested and sent out of the camp, but nobody knows where. When some of the officers asked of the management for an explanation, the answer was that it was the act of the F.B.I. (which is represented here), and it knew nothing, adding that the residents had no right to raise any question on the subject. When the said Sashihara was ordered out, his family was deprived of all the sleeping equipments. Whereupon two councilmen asked the management why this was done, and how or where the family was to sleep; the answer was [that] the officers had no business to telephone directly on such matters. To this day none of us knows why he was arrested and sent away; no justice seems possible. If any trouble occurs, the blame is always on the residents; such is the attitude of the Civilian Government as it operates here. No wonder then, the Japanese seek the army to manage the camps;* it is very unfortunate. Af-

---

*Some Japanese wished to be formally designated "prisoners of war" under the control of the United States Army, in the belief that their political status and living conditions

ter all, the Americans employed are here [supposedly] for the purpose of looking after [the] interests of the community, but they seem to be pre-occupied of their own affairs. They are trying their best to convert this camp into one of the relocation centers; they have to think of their own jobs. If that be their desire, it appears to me all the more important that they should conduct the community affairs more intelligently to make the residents more or less satisfied to remain here. As a matter of fact, many of the residents are already seeking means of being transferred to permanent camps. The management is completely ignorant of this and other "undercurrents" which pervade everywhere. Of the latter I have informed Chapman, and suggested that means be devised to prevent them from explosion. Nothing has come out of it so far. They only [want] to wield [an] iron hand, with intimidation as its sole weapon.[57]

Personally I am not interested in any agitation or trouble-making of any kind; my chief interest here is to render the unfortunate community life into a truly livable one. This can be done only when the management recognizes the existence of evil conditions and strives to remedy them as fast as possible. Many of the defects can be corrected without much effort and with no extra expense; we only need the ability to understand human nature. I am tackling, at the same time, the problem of improving the general behavior of the residents adult and youth; I am appealing to them and advising them that this is one phase we have to remedy in order to win the confidence and sympathy of the management. Co-operation is absolutely necessary between the two parties. I shall keep on doing this until I can see signs which I desire. Perhaps I will not succeed, perhaps I will fail; nevertheless I shall not give up.

There are many other matters I can specifically mention and detail, but as usual, there is no end to these. So I shall write you about one or two things at a time. We have had hot weather right along, the sun beating down on us; Kei and I are approaching the color of negroes; if you see us as we are, you would probably not recognize us. The food has been deteriorating again, and I am laughing at Kei who was so happy about the improved food; it lasted less than a week. With cordial greeting from this h'll.

Very sincerely,
Y.

---

would be clarified and improved because they would then come under provisions of the 1929 Geneva Convention.

YAMATO ICHIHASHI TO RAY LYMAN WILBUR [58]

July 3, 1942

Dear Dr. Wilbur:

Kei joins me in thanking you for the kind and sympathetic letters. I have vainly been trying to write you again. I have been kept very busy by many summons and numerous personal visits every day and every evening since my arrival here; the residents face a multitude of problems of all sorts, personal, community, social, moral, health, etc. It is indeed difficult to choose which of the problems to dwell upon, but I shall again attempt to write you about educational problems as they are faced here.

As stated before, no formal education is permitted until the fall, and what is being attempted is informal in character; this is confined to children 16 years and under. Nothing is being done for youth beyond that age group. This is exceedingly unfortunate socially and morally, but the management does not appreciate this fact and remains indifferent about these phases of life and others. I need not tell you about the danger of allowing youth to have nothing constructive to do and forced to loaf; youth are in the most dangerous period of life. Of course, I am more or less aware of the publicized plans and programs for evacuees, but these are, as you know, merely blue-print plans and programs at present, and nobody seems to know even when they are to be put in operation. We even do not know when or where we are to be relocated; this center is supposed to be a temporary one as we understand it, although it has been intimated to me by certain members of the management that it is doing everything to convert it into a permanent settlement, and for obvious reasons.

More specifically, the nursery department and the grade "school" at present are handling 1,774 pupils, mostly wild and undisciplined, due either to their background or the present environment. They are very difficult to manage. The "teachers" are inexperienced and unqualified youngsters who, nevertheless, are doing their best; under the circumstances they are doing remarkably well in my opinion. The "regular" (i.e., with *work card*, meaning that these receive wages, varying from $8 to $12 per month) teachers number 122; they have been assisted by some thirty-odd "volunteers" (i.e., without pay), but these were dismissed yesterday because the management refuses to grant them work cards. Thus the school work has been seriously damaged; I have been unable to discover reasons for the management stand. I only wonder whether it really is interested in its effort along educational lines; surely it should be able to see serious consequences of the inadequacy of educational facility.

Yesterday we had a meeting to discuss the problem of student evacuation (college and university students); two representatives of the National Council came and told us what they are trying to do [about] this problem.[59] We are going to register these and high school graduates of this year as the first step. The representatives could give us no definite information as regards the "movement." Thus we are forced to work blindly, and this fact made me embarrassed because the management asked me to advise registrants. How am I to function intelligently without necessary information as regards their possible opportunities?

The Council representatives made it clear that all of the students could not be given the opportunity of obtaining further education; they estimate the number of college and university students (formerly enrolled) to be about 2,400, exclusive of high school graduates. They talked about creating extension "schools" and correspondence "courses" for those who are forced to remain in different centers. They do not realize that these centers are altogether unfit for any intellectual pursuits; for example, at this center more than 18,000 humans dwell in an area less than a hundred acres, who are crowded in the crudest kind of living quarters which are very noisy and without any privacy. A number of young men and women have already approached me to negotiate on their behalf that the management find a quiet place for reading and study. I have investigated the entire center, but have failed to discover a spot which can be made a place for study. Such being the reality of this environment, educational attempt of any kind in this center is bound to fail; at least, it appears to me so. Moreover, our high "school" pupils will not do their homework daily assigned to them, due to the circumstances described above. Besides, most of the youngsters in or out of the school have succumbed to the idea that they are on a vacation or a perpetual picnic, and we have no means to control them. Even parents remain mostly helpless. In fact, the whole population has succumbed to this unfortunate environment and leads a life of primitives, almost approaching animal life.

Consequently, many moral problems have already arisen, especially among young girls and boys. Numerous cases of pregnancy have been reported to me, and if this be true, there will be born unfortunate children. I have warned parents of the existence of problems so that they realize their grave responsibility relative to their sons and daughters.*

I spoke of uncertainty under which we exist, especially as regards when and where we are to be removed since this center is an assembly center. Our son, Woodrow, is now relocated at the Tule Lake Center, and naturally we would like to join him where he is, and also I would like to be settled as soon as possible so that I can engage in my research work. I have been here a little over [one] month, but I have accomplished nothing. Will you be kind enough to find out, if possible, from the Military Headquarters at San Francisco, what should be done in order that we may be allowed to join our son when we are to be evacuated again? I understand that the American government promises not to separate families. It is needless to add that this request is not made for selfish reasons alone, I shall do whatever I am capable of doing for the well-being of the center to which we may be sent, but I would like [to] seek to go to Tule Lake to join [our] son, and incidentally to start my research as soon as possible. Please help us.

> Very sincerely yours,
> [Yamato Ichihashi]

DIARY [60]

[July] 3rd

The climate same.

The so-called Self-Government was dissolved without explanation or ceremony; in fact, it was [never?] formally instituted, though its members (assemblymen and councilmen) had duly been elected. No formal meeting was ever held. It is said that a substitute government will be formed by appointed men. At any rate, all this appears farcical in reality for nobody, aside [from] the residents themselves, is interested in [it]; and that for propaganda purposes. These have already been achieved from the standpoint of the military. The army

---

*One center report listed 200 unwed pregnant women at the end of July 1942, with an estimated 70 having become so in the center. The report also mentioned secret abortions and attempted suicides by the women, the spread of venereal disease and gangs. Tamie Tsuchiyama, "Preliminary Report on Japanese Evacuees at Santa Anita," July 31, 1942, JERS, B8.05.

did not like the idea of elections and hence the [order] for its dis-
solution.

It is also rumored that an "order" has been issued that all the issei
will be relieved from their present occupations in the center, but
why, it is not explained. Consequently, speculation and rumor run
rampant.

[July] 4th

This was decidedly the hottest day; a ceremony and festivity ruled
the day and the evening was devoted to entertainments. For residents, the day was made memorable by especially bad food three
times.

[July] 5th

The day started as the clearest one since our arrival here. The
mountains, which form the distant northern boundary, stand out
with their outlines very plain. At the foot of these mountains are
seen a number of attractive residences in the midst of luxuriant
vegetation.[61] It must be very pleasant there, whereas here it is a veritable hell. Proved to be the hottest day as yet—104 degrees.

[July] 6th

Started clear again, and proved to be another [hot] day. It continued
so till late at night. A letter came from Anne Bancroft Graham.* A
case of *jisatsu-misui* [failed suicide] issued as a result of gambling.
Cops informed me that the only problem at night now is that which
concerned the moral one of young girls and boys. There is no machinery to handle these cases. Japanese cops could chase them only,
while Caucasian cops are afraid to tackle them—fearing more reactions[?]. It is very sad to say the least. A woman came to see [me]
about a boy of 17 who refuses to repatriate with his parents. He was
turned[?] over to *Kitaji*[?] † as the first step.[62]

---

*Unidentified.
† The meaning of *Kitaji* is unclear.

[July] 7th

Another clear and hot day, but not as bad as the previous day. The old-age group [says?] management very unsatisfactory; *Kitaji* will resign their directorship, due to the faulty organization—the nisei who have no knowledge or appreciation of the problem. Yet these youngsters are allowed or authorized to act in an arbitrary manner and even over [*Kitaji?*]. There is breeding trouble in the school, partly due to the dismissal of volunteers. [I] am to meet teachers at 2 P.M., Wednesday (July 8th).

KEI ICHIHASHI TO JESSIE TREAT [63]

Arcadia
July 10 [1942]

Dear Mrs. Treat:

Thank you very much for the nice letter and box full of nice things. These pleased me more than I can express.

Lately the management began to allow the importation of some food articles, for instance 2 [pounds?] of cookies, 2 [pounds?] of candies, 1 cake, and 2 cans or bottles of fruit or fruit juice and so on. Then I heard a very funny story. Somebody imported a bottle of whiskey in a big cake, a few days ago. Yesterday one person received two fine watermelons, and the inspector cut them with a big knife, thinking that a bottle of whiskey was hidden inside. It is silly but true story.

The residents here are forced to lead a monotonous life, and most of the older people have nothing to do; so they play Japanese chess or read Japanese books. Even these books, any books which are written in Japanese, have been designated as contraband, and are to be delivered to the management by tomorrow (July 11th).

I miss gardening very much, and can't forget the well-cared gardens on the Stanford campus. In this center a few people are trying to grow radishes, green onions, tomatoes, cucumbers, etc., in wooden boxes; some are even trying to grow chrysanthemums or morning glories in M.J.B. coffee cans or big peach cans. Japanese are funny creatures, aren't they?

We have had very hot weather; the thermometer went up to 103 degrees in my room; it was just like living in an oven. Mr. Ichihashi got heat rashes and is suffering now. I stayed in the room, so he said "You have no nerves." Maybe so, but I am not sure about that.

Please give our best regards to Prof. Treat. Mr. Ichihashi asks to add that he is kept very busy by the presentation of many different problems. He spent all day yesterday registering relocation students and he has to continue this today also.

Sincerely yours,
Kei

YAMATO ICHIHASHI TO PAYSON TREAT [64]

July 13, 1942.

Dear Colleague:

As soon as the enclosed notice reached me, [65] I explained and asked the management to find out for me whether or not I could keep with me these research materials. The answer was to submit a written memorandum together with [Ray Lyman] Wilbur's note as regards my status at the university; this I did without delay.[66] But the man in charge told me today that no exception can be made; this meant either I have to place the books and monographs in care of the management or to ship them out. I took the liberty of sending the same to you so that they be kept safely until I am out of this camp, perhaps until the war is over. Please be kind enough to keep them for me. I am deprived of the privilege of carrying on a re-search project planned for the rest of my life. But who cares? Yet, I have been trying my best to help the management in every possible way; will it reciprocate? No, indeed. Well, there I am destined to die an intellectual death.

The self-government was recently dissolved but as usual without any explanation; later the authority asked the elected to submit an individual resignation. What do you think of that?

Today, the authority concerned launched what he calls a writers' project, with a view of writing a complete history of this center in an all-embracing manner. He asked me to supervise the work of some twenty-five youngsters who will be assigned the work. My promised salary per month is $16! [67] No Japanese employee has actually re-ceived pay except for April 3–15 so far; this state of affairs is creat-ing disturbances among the workers who number thousands. That is the way things are being attempted here, and of course we have to accept everything as an order. It is very hot and I have been and still am suffering from heat-rash just like a baby; so I shall abruptly end this but with a promise to write again.

> Very sincerely,
> Yamato

Please remember *us* to Madam. Please return the notice when you are good to write me again.

◻ President Wilbur and Edgar Robinson communicated Ichihashi's request to transfer from Santa Anita to Tule Lake directly to General John L. DeWitt in San Francisco, who quickly approved the move. Wilbur and Robinson immediately informed Ichihashi of the good news.[68] Ten permanent internment centers had been established: Amache (also known as Granada), Colorado; Gila, Arizona; Heart Mountain, Wyoming; Jerome, Arkansas; Manzanar, California; Minidoka, Idaho; Poston, Arizona; Rohwer, Arkansas; Topaz, Utah; and Tule Lake, California. ◗

KEI ICHIHASHI TO JESSIE TREAT [69]

> Arcadia
> July 17, 1942

Dear Mrs. Treat:

Thank you for such delicious cookies; we are enjoying them very much. The meal hours were shifted lately, and so we have to eat supper at 4:30 every day. That is a little too early. Very often we want something to eat later.

Mr. Ichihashi and I will move to Tule Lake some time next week, and so we are packing our baggages now; we are hoping to have a little better living quarters and better meals this time when we get there.

In this center foods are getting worse again. At breakfast, quite often we have grape fruits, but they are very small; so I measured them twice, and found that both of them were exactly 3 1/4 inches in diameter, then you know how small they are. One evening we ate apricots for dessert. Do you know how many we got? Only one apricot for dessert, very small one at that.

Today's dinner was:

Baked beans and green peas (canned)
Beets (salad)

Bread without butter (We have no butter here, except for toast) 1/4 cantaloupe for dessert and milk.

The lack of nourishment causes many troubles here, some young girls have eye trouble, others have some skin trouble, etc.

Lately the weather has been hot, but not very, very hot, and it cools down in the late afternoon. So we sit outside and enjoy cool evenings.

I have just heard of your accident. We are sorry for you. You are such a busy person, always, so that, I think, it might be a good chance for you to rest. We both are hoping you will recover very soon.

I am afraid that this will be the last letter from Arcadia; in the next one I shall write you about the [Tule Lake] relocation center.

> Sincerely yours,
> Kei

YAMATO ICHIHASHI TO RAY LYMAN WILBUR [70]

> [Santa Anita]
> July 25, 1942

Dear Dr. Wilbur:

Thank you very much; [71] we are leaving this center for Tule Lake Friday (the 26th). While here I tried my best to help both the administration and the Japanese residents in every way conceivable, but alas I have accomplished next to nothing partly due to my inability but largely due to many circumstances and reasons. [72]

However I am not entirely discouraged; when I get to the new center, I shall try to do the same for I know that any unnatural new community needs all the help it can get and that superior men should consider it an opportunity to serve. Please be kind enough to remember us to Mrs. Wilbur.

> Very respectfully,
> Yamato Ichihashi

We are busy packing.

◧ Along with the Ichihashis, approximately 25 other Stanford graduates and students were at Santa Anita. Their living conditions were in most cases considerably worse than those of the Ichihashis, such as the one odorous horse stall that two newly wed alumni couples had to share. Six students lived together in a common barrack and called it the "House," just as they had referred to the Japanese Student Clubhouse, where most of the Japanese students had resided while on campus. Graduates of the class of 1942 received their diplomas in the mail in June.[73]

The Ichihashis maintained some contact with the displaced Stanford community but were generally aloof. Still, during the two months of their stay, they had become prominent members of the Assembly Center's life. Yamato "was in great demand as a counselor," even though he had been "unaware of Japanese problems" since he had "not mingled" with them for the previous thirty years, according to a report written by a nisei for the Administration. Before the Ichihashis left Santa Anita, the Educational and Writers' Project gave a farewell tea for them, and the center newsletter announced their departure.[74]

Eager to see their son and hoping for better circumstances, Yamato and Kei Ichihashi set out for Tule Lake. Initially, their hopes did not seem to be misplaced. When they arrived at Newell, the train stop for Tule Lake camp, they were met personally by Samuel D. Friedman, the director of the camp housing office, and his wife and escorted to their new residence, removed from "the noise and dust of the crowd," according to the camp newsletter that reported their arrival. In the following days, Yamato responded to this special treatment with effusive public praise for the camp residents (they showed "all kinds of kindness") and administration (all their past statements, he concluded after an initial study of the camp's history, had exhibited "warm humanliness"). "This is as it should be," the *Daily Tulean Dispatch* quoted him as saying, "if [the administration] wants to have any sort of cooperative management in projects like this where the Japanese people are involved. The Japanese are a proud people. You cannot rule them with a club. When treated well, they know when and how to reciprocate." He encouraged his fellow residents, in turn, to avoid doing anything that would undermine the confidence of the administration in them. "Cooperate with the administration to make Tule Lake a better place to live in for themselves and for their children," the newsletter paraphrased Ichihashi's admonition to his fellow evacuees.[75]

Events quickly dashed the Ichihashis' positive feelings about Tule Lake. They soon found themselves in uncomfortable circumstances, as the following letter to Robinson describes. Just after sending the letter, however, Yamato was to suffer the most difficult event in his life, one that would make lost baggage trivial and his initial public praise of his new life at Tule Lake seem in retrospect terribly mistaken. ◼

YAMATO ICHIHASHI TO EDGAR ROBINSON [76]

W.R.A.* Tule Lake, Calif.
August 19, 1942

Dear Edgar:

Through your kind effort, we were transferred here from the Santa Anita Center; to be exact, we left the center on July 24 and arrived here about 11:30 P.M. on the following night. We were given Pullman accommodations for which [we] were extremely grateful as the trip proved to be very hot. The reason why I have not written to any one beyond the notification of my address, is because we have not received our luggage, though we have been here little short of 4 weeks. I hate to [override?] any authorities (bureaucratic) as I know their customary psychology, but now I am forced to do this: I must appeal to you to communicate the matter to the military authorities at San Francisco in order to expedite their dispatch to us.

Let me state the facts relative to our baggage: on the morning of our departure, at my request, a policeman named Cooper came to our living quarters in order to inspect the baggage. At that time, the said officer informed me that all the 15 pieces of our luggage would be checked with the train on which [we] were to travel; he was to accompany us as our guard. There were three tickets to check the baggage. But on our way from the Santa Anita Center to Los Angeles, the same Cooper told me that he had been called away on another assignment and that he had had no time to check the baggage. He, however, assured us that the baggage would be dispatched here by express and that we would get them on the following Tuesday (July 28th). Of course, we had to accept this, although we had with us only urgently needed articles—toilet articles, night gowns, etc.

The Tuesday came, but no sign of our belongings left behind. But still we waited until the end of the week but in vain. On Monday (August 3rd) I inquired at office here about the baggage. But they were found neither at Klamath Falls nor at the Center's warehouse.[77] Thereupon I requested the officer in charge here to make necessary inquiries concerning our luggage. At the same time I wrote to po-

---

*The War Relocation Authority (WRA) was created on March 18, 1942, as a civilian agency whose chief task became that of running the permanent relocation centers. Its first director was Milton S. Eisenhower, brother of the general and future president Dwight Eisenhower. Dillon S. Myer became director in mid-June 1942 and held that position until the close of the WRA in June 1946. The Army provided armed guards to control the perimeters of the camps.

liceman Cooper about the matter, but he has been completely silent about it.

Why the inquiry was delayed at this end, I do not know; it may have been assumed that the baggage will arrive in due course. This assumption proved to be wrong. So under the date of August 11th, a letter of inquiry relative to the matter was sent to Russell Amory, the Manager of the S.A.A.C. by Elmer Shirrell, the Director of this Center (called Project). No word has come from Amory to date. (On Monday 17th, a telegram was sent, but this too remains unanswered to date.)

Under the circumstances, the only recourse left for me, since the authorities here are helpless because they could not get "a rise" at Santa Anita, is to appeal to the highest authority concerned with the Japanese evacuees. Will you and Dr. Wilbur be kind enough to communicate the matter to General DeWitt and find out from him what should be done about it. Our baggage consists of 15 pieces, each of which was tagged, at the time of our departure, with our names, "Y" or "O" Ichihashi, with our original evacuation number "*31916*." The 15 pieces are made up as follows:

Six suit cases, one being very small,

One woman's hat case,

One valise,

Four carton boxes, two of which contain my research notes and materials,

and three bundles.

It is needless to mention inconveniences and embarrassments we had to put up with because we came here, as said above, only with the barest necessities. We have been living like savages, buying and borrowing what we could. It is getting rather cold and I have only a very light suit, etc.

Please help us as we are in the saddest plight.*

> Very cordially yours,
> Yamato

---

*Edgar Robinson, as Acting President of Stanford and also on behalf of Chancellor Ray Lyman Wilbur, wrote immediately to General DeWitt to request help in locating the Ichihashis' baggage. Robinson pressed DeWitt, stating "it is apparent that the case is quite desperate." The Army cooperated. Robinson also sent an "emergency package" to help the Ichihashis. Robinson to DeWitt, Aug. 21, 1942, and Sept. 9, 1942; Capt. Hugh Fullerton to Robinson, Sept. 9, 1942; all in EER, B15, F220.

Sharp Park-Tule Lake
August 20, 1942 –
April 1, 1943

t 2:00 P.M., August 25, 1942, Payson Treat received the following message from Woodrow Ichihashi:

> Dad asked me to write and notify you of his arrest by the F.B.I. He is in Tule Lake now but will leave today for San Francisco with a man from the Immigration and Naturalization Bureau. He would be very grateful if you could contact either this office (Immigration and Naturalization in San Francisco), or Army Headquarters there and find out what can be done to facilitate his investigation.
>
> Neither Mother nor Dad seems to know what the charges are so he is at loss. Please rest assured that both Mother and Dad are taking this mental blow very magnificently.[1]

Immediately after the United States declaration of war against Japan, the FBI arrested 1,500 issei suspected of being potential threats to domestic security. Ultimately, the Immigration and Naturalization Service (INS) held 2,000 Japanese at special detention centers for the duration of the war. Several thousand more "suspect enemy aliens" were temporarily detained, questioned, and eventually released, among them Yamato Ichihashi. He had no knowledge of the flurry of activity concerning him until the very day he was taken into custody by federal marshals.

According to the FBI file kept on Yamato Ichihashi, federal authorities reactivated his case in November 1941, but it was not until April 1942 that he came under active suspicion as a result of information received from a "confidential informant." The FBI had first monitored Ichihashi's activities in the early 1920's, because of his association with high-ranking Japanese visitors to the United States and his participation in international conferences, such as the 1922 Washington Disarmament Conference, which he attended as the personal secretary and interpreter for Japan's chief delegate, Baron Katō Tomosaburō. As early as 1921, FBI agents referred to Ichihashi as a "Japanese propagandist," although over the years they never alleged he had been involved in any illegal activity and his file lay quietly for two decades. Under wartime conditions, however, his past associations called attention to him.

The San Francisco FBI agent responsible for Ichihashi's case, N. J. L. Pieper, concluded in the spring of 1942 that he was a "potentially dangerous enemy alien." He was, however, unable to convince the local representative of the U.S. Justice Department to issue a warrant for Ichihashi's apprehension. Pieper continued to feel so strongly about Ichihashi that he filed a letter of protest to the Director of the FBI in Washington, J. Edgar Hoover. He argued that since the WRA was releasing some aliens to perform agricultural and other work, it was possible that Ichihashi might soon be freed from detention to "renew contacts and possibly engage in espionage activities." For this and other reasons, the agent believed Ichihashi should "be apprehended and placed in a concentration camp under the strict guidance of military authorities for the duration of the war."[2]

On July 3, Hoover forwarded a memorandum to Attorney General Francis Biddle, recommending Ichihashi's apprehension and special detention. "This individual," Hoover wrote, "has formerly served the Japanese Government, has indicated sympathies for Japan, and his freedom presents a potential source of danger to the internal security of this country." On August 19, Biddle signed a formal "presidential warrant," for the "arrest" of Dr. Yamato Ichihashi, "an alien enemy whom I deem dangerous to the public peace and safety of the United States." The FBI took Ichihashi into custody on August 22. His arrest was reported in the camp newspaper.[3]

Ichihashi spent six weeks in Sharp Park, an "internment camp" near San Francisco run by the INS, where despite having to wait on tables, a task he no doubt found humbling, he appears, surprisingly, to have found aspects of the experience moderately enjoyable. Sharp Park was located in what is now the town of Pacifica, about 15 miles south of San Francisco along the coast. Barbed wire, guard towers, and armed guards recruited from the Border Patrol surrounded the camp.[4] It assumed many of the functions that had been carried out at federal facilities on Angel Island in San Francisco Bay. (Ironically, the Angel Island immigration station, which burned down in 1940, had for decades been the main processing depot for tens of thousands of Chinese and Japanese immigrants.)

The center's idyllic setting pleased Ichihashi, who enjoyed the outdoors. He described his experiences in an essay that follows below, after several letters from Kei to Jessie Treat. Strangely, it does not seem that Yamato and Kei had any direct communication during his time under arrest. Although detainees were allowed to make phone calls and to send and receive mail at Sharp Park, no correspondence between Yamato on the one hand and Kei or Woodrow on the other has been located. Woodrow Ichihashi recalls having no communication at all with his father during his detention at Sharp Park.[5] ◼

KEI ICHIHASHI TO JESSIE TREAT[6]

Tule Lake
Sept. 5 [1942]

Dear Mrs. Treat:

I should have written to you sooner, but I couldn't get our belongings for a long time, and was unable to do anything. Finally I got our baggage and fixed up our living quarters to settle down.

This center is much better in every way—living quarters and food etc.—than the Santa Anita Assembly Center. Our living quarters are located at the quietest spot, and there are no little babies around here, so I am enjoying a quiet life.

The weather is still hot in the afternoon. The cold weather will come soon, and lasts for a long time. We already installed a big coal stove.

This center is located on the bottom of old Tule Lake; it was drained about 10 years ago, so I understand. The ground is sandy; when the wind blows, sand gets in the room and everything is so dusty, it is awful. The laundry and ironing room is very near, also the mess hall. It is very convenient.

In this center there are 4 community stores. They are carrying more things than the canteens at the Santa Anita Assembly Center, so that I got a few things and tried to fill our needs while we were waiting for our luggage. When I travel I always carry extra dresses, shoes and a few necessary articles, because I can't tell what may happen on the trip. Very fortunately I could manage for a month, anyhow. But on the contrary Mr. Ichihashi didn't bring any extra things, so consequently he suffered very much.

As you know Mr. Ichihashi went away two weeks ago so suddenly. I didn't know where he went exactly, but yesterday an old man came here to join his family from the immigration station, Sharp's Park, California, and he called on me and he said that "he met Mr. Ichihashi over there, he is in good health and he will write to you soon." This old man is deaf and not a well educated person, so when I tried to find out something about Mr. Ichihashi, I failed.

Sharp's Park is between Half Moon Bay and San Francisco, and a very nice place, so people say. I think the weather is cold over there, and he has no heavy clothes, just wearing a very light summer suit. So I am worrying about it.

I am very glad to hear that you are well and busy again. The other day I got a letter from Miss Fast,[7] and she said Stanford University had many freshmen this summer and they had a very busy quarter. Now it is September, the most quiet time on the campus. When we were at the Santa Anita Center we heard about Mrs. Bailey's accident[8] and we wrote to Mr. Bailey at once. I had thought that she was well already. I am sorry to hear that she has not recovered completely yet. I am hoping that she will be very well soon.

Please give my best regards to Dr. Treat.

> Very sincerely yours,
> Kei Ichihashi

P.S. I have to write to Miss Stoltenberg but I have so many things on my mind now, so please remember me to her when you see her.

I want to ask you another favour. Would you get me a pair of sport shoes? Shoes wear out very fast because of sandy ground here. I took my shoes to the repair shop yesterday, but they have too many shoes to repair, and they said "it will take more than 3 weeks to fix." I am wearing 7A sportshoes now, but send me 7 1/2 A or B shoes. Some company's shoes are sometimes a little smaller than other's.

Any color, any style will do, but if you can, get me rubber sole sport shoes, please.

◘ "It is a shocking thing," Edgar Robinson wrote in his diary on the day he learned the news of Ichihashi's arrest by the FBI. Immediately, his Stanford colleagues inquired about his status from the San Francisco office of the INS to learn how they might help their friend. Both Robinson and Stanford president Ray Lyman Wilbur personally wrote to Woodrow to assure him and his mother that they would do all they could to help. Wilbur sent a special delivery letter to the district chief of the INS to express in the most positive terms his support and respect for Ichihashi. "Here at Stanford," he wrote, "we have no reason to lack confidence in Professor Ichihashi. . . . He has devoted all of his time to scholarship, authorship and teaching."[9]

A few days after Ichihashi's arrival at Sharp Park, Payson and Jessie Treat paid him the first of several personal visits. They found their old friend "in good shape and spirits," and on September 2, Ichihashi telephoned Wilbur to inform him that his appearance before the Alien Enemy Hearing Board would be held the next day in San Francisco.[10] Treat attended as a character witness. He then reported to Wilbur that the INS had only been interested in Ichihashi's activities at the 1922 Washington Disarmament Conference, where he had served as an interpreter for the Japanese delegation. "They had absolutely nothing against him of any kind," Treat stated. Although the government interrogators, who included one of Ichihashi's former students, were apparently cordial, Ichihashi could not have legal counsel and was permitted to have only one friend present. Treat described the hearing as resembling "star chamber proceedings" and speculated that the Justice Department, as part of a "systematic investigation" of prominent aliens, had picked up Ichihashi simply because he was "one of the best known Japanese" in the country. Treat confidently predicted that Ichihashi would be cleared and returned to Tule Lake after a month. He was wrong.[11] ◘

KEI ICHIHASHI TO JESSIE TREAT [12]

Tule Lake
Sept. 10 [1942]

Dear Mrs. Treat:

Thank you for your letter dated the 4th of September.[13]
Since the incident [Yamato's arrest] occurred I was simply watch-

ing its development. [When] I received your kind letter I, was very much relieved.

I am very grateful for your kindness to visit Mr. Ichihashi at Sharp's Park. I am certain that he was much pleased to see both of you. I am waiting for a letter from him and am anxious to know about further developments.

I am very sorry to hear that Mr. Culver is very ill; [14] I am hoping that he will recover soon. Please remember me to Mrs. Culver when you see her.

I deeply appreciate Prof. Treat's kindness toward Mr. Ichihashi, so kindly extend my appreciation to him please.

> Affectionately yours,
> Kei Ichihashi

KEI ICHIHASHI TO PAYSON AND JESSIE TREAT [15]

> Tule Lake
> Sept. 16 [1942]

Dear Dr. and Mrs. Treat:

Thank you for your kind letter dated the 9th of September, [16] in which you explained about the hearing and all other things. I deeply appreciate your kindness towards my husband and your frequent visits to Sharp's Park. I have nothing to worry about now, and I am just waiting for his return.

I am so glad to hear that you planned to go to Lake Tahoe for a change before starting another year's work. I am certain that you enjoyed the trip.

As I look back it was a very eventful year, since last September. At the end of September I went to Oregon to live and the great December incident occurred. [17] I then was stranded in Eugene. Through many troubles I finally got permission to travel back to California and got home again. [18] Then I spent several uncertain months there, and moved to Southern California and was transferred to Tule Lake to settle down. And while I was waiting anxiously for a month for our mis-shipped luggage, the worst event in my life happened. Now I feel very serene and am enjoying a quiet life. It is a good chance to meditate and also to read. I am trying to read as much as I can.

Thank you for sending me the shoes so quickly. They are nice looking and very comfortable. I am sure I will enjoy wearing them through the winter.

With best wishes, very sincerely,
Kei Ichihashi

KEI ICHIHASHI TO JESSIE TREAT [19]

Tule Lake
Saturday
date of receipt, 13 Oct. 42 [20]

Dear Mrs. Treat:

Every Saturday afternoon radios are going loudly around here. Young people are listening to football games over the radios. The gay football season has come.

Stanford has already started, so the old campus must be getting busy again, I think. On the campus our old street trees must be beautiful with leaves beginning to fall down now. Around here we have no trees, even on the distant hills we can't see any. So I miss the beautiful campus trees very much.

I think you are enjoying fine autumn weather as usual. We had quite a strong wind yesterday and today. This morning I cleaned the room thoroughly, but in a couple of hours the table, lamp, books and everything was dusty with sand; it was awful. Generally the weather is fine. In the morning it is chilly sometimes, but in the afternoon it's very warm. We have had clear weather so far.

Tule Lake is a game reservation, so there are many kinds of birds around here. Every day hundreds of sea gulls come near our mess hall to get food. It is quite picturesque, when white sea gulls fly against the blue sky. In the early morning or after sunset, flocks of wild geese pass high up in the sky. I never saw so many wild geese in my life.

The Tule Lake farm, in which Japanese men and women are working, is producing many kinds of vegetables. They grow very nicely because of the rich soil. One day I saw a long turnip almost as big as a round gallon apple cider jar. Just imagine how big it was, and it was fine and solid. Radishes grow bigger than carrots. We have fine lettuce too. Thus we have plenty of fresh vegetables every day which is very fortunate. However meals are not good lately. Sometimes we have very poor menus.

Japanese who lived in Santa Clara County moved to the state of

Wyoming.[21] They are having a hard time, and the people who went to Arkansas have wind storms almost every day, so I understand.[22]

I think we were rather wise in deciding to come to Tule Lake, and I am very glad we are still living in California.

> With best wishes,
> Kei Ichihashi

◘ Not until late October was Yamato Ichihashi finally allowed to return to his family in Tule Lake, where he completed the following recollection of his move from Santa Anita and his eight-week ordeal after the FBI took him into custody and sent him to Sharp Park. ◘

RESEARCH ESSAY [23]

From Santa Anita to Tule Lake

We left the Santa Anita Center at 5:30 P.M. on Friday (July 24th) accompanied by cop Cooper as a guard who had promised to load our luggage on the train we were to take, but failed [to do so]; thus we had with us only things that were necessary on the journey. We took the 7:20 P.M. train at Los Angeles to which we had been transported on an army truck; the army authorized Pullman tickets for us but not for the guard, and so in order to avoid a ride on chairs, I bought his Pullman ticket as well as fed him on the train. The following day was hot and Kei was taken ill; the fellow passengers were friendly and kind. We arrived at Klamath Falls, Oregon at 10:20 P.M. Saturday (25th) and were met by Samuel D. Friedman and his wife from the Tule Lake WRA; we reached the camp a little before 12:00. We sought Woodrow everywhere and finally found him in the hospital, though not seriously ill. I had requested England, the Recreation Director at Santa Anita, to send him a telegram, but he failed to receive it; apparently it had not been dispatched. I had been mistaken for a medical doctor since the army in its communication had been referring to me as "Dr.;" I explained this, and consequently we were located at the present address of 7307-D instead of the previously arranged place in the midst of medic residences. This was fortunate since its location is good: quiet and good rustics as neighbors. Our family no. here is "15591."

Barracks are all constructed like those at Santa Anita, 20' x 100', but material being polished ship-laps instead of rough ones of Santa

Anita and covered externally with tar paper as in the case of Santa
Anita barracks. Each barrack is subdivided into 4, 5, or 6 "apartments"; our barrack is composed of 5, hence each measures 20′ ×
20′, with one window in front and 2 in back. As compared with our
8′ × 20′ quarters at Santa Anita, the present one is roomy; the lumber being white pine and still green, we could smell its freshness and
[it is] pleasant to look at. However, the camp ground, about 1,000
acres, is a sandy lake bottom drained about two decades ago, and so
when a strong wind blows, sands penetrate and dirty the interior.
Whirl-winds caused by south or south-east wind are indeed terrible.
Temperatures are high, 90–100 degrees, and thus neither the door
nor the windows could be kept closed; in fact, we found it impossible, on account of heat, to stay inside. The walls and the ceiling
were not covered until later in October, and that fact made the inside hot. Public institutions—showers, latrines, mess hall, laundry,
ironing room, and recreation hall attached to each block, made of 14
living barracks—are, on the whole, satisfactory (I thought) and food
served was good, certainly as compared with those of Santa Anita.
That was my first impression—from a hell to a heaven!

But our luggage failed to come and we were compelled to wear
dirty clothes and had to borrow sheets, pillow cases, chairs, blankets,
etc., and this [was the case] until [July] 28th when the luggage arrived due to the negotiation with the S.F. Army Headquarters. The
Santa Anita official indifference or inefficiency made us to suffer a
little worse than a month, despite the effort made from this side to
expedite the matter—with no responses of any kind from the other
end! Edgar [Robinson] having learned of this sad plight of ours, sent
us some apparels—very thoughtful of him.

On the afternoon Saturday [August] 22nd, I faced an unforget-
table incident: an F.B.I. agent named Robert Hart stationed at Red
Bluff accompanied by Tule Lake Police Chief Rhodes, a local cop
and Woodrow, came to the room at 2 : 30 and told me that I was
"under arrest." I asked [what] was the charge and he replied no
charge as far as he knew. I was told to pack things I wanted to take
with me, but as said before, I had no spare things with me. Hart
kindly advised me to take what I had and some money; we stopped
at the Administration Building, I suppose for the purpose of clearing. After riding about 7 miles, we reached the Tule Lake jail, having stopped at a local stationery [store] to buy a copy of the August
issue of "Readers' Digest" at Hart's suggestion; no other decent
publications were available.

The sight of the jail shocked me; it is a concrete building about

20′ × 20′; a part of the front is used as office and store-room; the
jail part was partitioned by iron-bars and walls into 2 rooms with a
small hallway where [there] was a sink and toilet; each room had two
simple beds. Rhodes handed me 1/2 doz. blankets, assuring me of
their cleanliness. But alas the jail was smelly and dirty and full of
buzzing flies. I have never seen the like in my life, and I think Hart
himself shared my feelings, though in silence; and Rhodes was
somewhat downcast, for the jail may be fit for the kind of humans he
handles such as drunks, speed violators, lumberjacks, etc. but quite
unfit for gentlemen. Here I arrived and [was] jailed at 3 : 30. Before
Hart departed, he assured me that I would be taken out of the jail
within 48 hours and so instructed Rhodes and to communicate with
the S.F. Immigration Service office, if necessary—this I learned afterward but not while in the jail. In fact, I only knew vaguely that I
was [to be] taken to S.F., and that was all since Hart told me nothing. I asked Hart whether he was coming to remove me; and he said
no, since his job had finished with the jailing; some one else was
coming to transport me, and he did not tell me that a U.S. marshall
had to do it.

Rhodes came frequently, and about 5 : 00 he took me to a hotel
restaurant for dinner; he said that the U.S. pays for my meals and it
has plenty of money and so I should eat anything I want. I had the
best meals while in the jail since my evacuation. I returned to the
jail, and I felt particularly the resounding noise that an iron-bar door
makes; I started to think of my fate and imagined all sorts of things
inevitable under the circumstances. Flies kept buzzing and mosquitoes began to visit and it was hot, smelly and disagreeable, though
Rhodes was kind enough to open all the windows there were. Night-
fall came and I tried to read and then put out the one light in the
room and tried to sleep but in vain. The experience was so novel and
the mind was in a state of agitation; I was alone in the jail that night,
but that was a Saturday night and the nearby residents were noisy,
singing and talking loudly—a drinking party. I must have slept a few
hours toward the morning, but was up and washed at 7 : 00. This my
first night in a jail; what a peculiar experience!

Sunday [August 23]

Rhodes, [whom] I expected, did not come until about 10 : 00. He explained that he was kept busy till late and said sorry to make you
wait for your breakfast; he brought the Sunday "San Francisco Ex-

aminer" and refused to take money for it, saying we have plenty of money in his office. Then we went to the same restaurant and [ate] a hearty breakfast. I read the paper and the magazine when I returned to the jail; my mind strayed in every imaginable direction since I did not know why I was in the jail. Thinking and meditation consumed most of the time until Rhodes appeared about 4:00 P.M. to take me for my dinner. I realized then that a jail-bird is fed only twice a day. I asked Rhodes whether I was permitted to write letters, he replied certainly; so I wrote a letter to Wilbur about my new experience and asked him to help.[24] Rhodes gave me a stamp and I mailed it when Rhodes took me for a short ride about the town. That night at 12:00 a drunk was jailed and his cell was locked and he was given a bucket[?]; he sang or yelled all night, creating disturbances but without knowing what he was doing. In the morning, he was quite sober and asked me to give him some water which I did—3 cupfuls.

That morning we went together to get our breakfast. The drunk was fined $10.00. Since he lost his registration (draft) card, without which he could [not find employment], Rhodes tried to get him a new one; for this purpose he wired to Fresno where he had registered. He could not get the card, but [did get] a slip explaining his status to enable him to find a job about 20 miles from Tule Lake; Rhodes suggested a place. He was freed. I was alone again. Rhodes began to worry about my removal since 48 hours expired at Monday (24th) 3:30, but the hoped for arrival of a marshall [had not materialized]. That day he spotted a U.S. marshall car and was positive that he came after me. He tried to contact him but in vain, until at midnight which he did by asking residents to help him. When he saw the marshall, the latter explained that he was here on other business (leave[?] cases in this region), but having learned of my case from Rhodes, he telephoned to the S.F. Headquarters and was told to remove me there as soon as possible. This I was told by Rhodes on Tuesday morning [who] stated that the Marshall would come and get me in the afternoon.

We had breakfast; and about 2:00 we went for lunch and there came the marshall and his nephew from Shasta. I joined them and left for S.F. about 3:00. We dropped off the nephew at Shasta—his home where he worked as a truck driver for Shell. We started southward and stopped at Redding for dinner; he invited me to eat all I cared. This marshall, named Hayden Saunders, an employee of the Justice Department for 20 years, proved to be very friendly and

talked freely to me on all the conceivable subjects, including the
war, against which he was bitterly opposed; he said about a dozen
ambitious men were responsible and told me his son, Jack Saunders,
a U.C. athlete (a swimmer) was killed a year ago as an aviation instructor because a defective plane had been given him; its wing fell
and down he came and [was] killed. He explained the internal organization of the Justice Department; he thought the F.B.I.'s Hoover
was ambitious and a self-boosting[?] politician, and as such he disliked him.[25] . . .

Hart [had] said that I was "under arrest," but Saunders said that I
was taken "into custody" since there was no charge against me.

Near Redding, Saunder's wife was born; here she and their
daughter were visiting her birthplace. Hayden took me there and
then decided that he himself would spend the night at the same
place since he had been driving more than 17 hours that day. He
took me [to] the Red Bluff Co. jail and requested its sheriff to give
me the best of accommodations. The jail was a typical one, barred
with a hall-way in the middle, the two sides subdivided into cells,
each having 2 iron bunks double-decked and a pot unclean but with
running water. I was allowed to take my bag with me, though ordi-
narily that is not permitted as I learned afterward. At the extreme
end of the hall, there was a shower but apparently not working, and
a large sink for face-washing. Of course, the interior was constructed
with iron and iron bars by means of which small cells were separated
from one another. There was no one else beside myself in the jail; it
was quiet and cool and I slept. In the morning I was introduced to
jail breakfast which [was] stuck thru a square-hole on the side of the
cell; it was contained in the old-fashioned bread-baking pan—4
pieces of bread but no butter, plenty of oatmeal, 2 fried eggs and a
tin-cup of coffee minus milk and sugar. This was a special treat, as I
learned afterward. I ate the eggs with a piece of bread and drank coffee; then inspected the cells and I found but very few *rakugaki* [graf-
fiti] among which a Japanese flag was found, whereas the walls of the
Tule Lake jail were covered with obscene pictures and inscriptions.

About 9:30 Saunders came and [we] walked out of the jail; I was
introduced to his wife and daughter and the latter's girl friend, who
were all going to Sacramento where the family resides, but we went
straight to S.F. via Vallejo where I saw "balloons" of every shape
floating above the navy yards as well as ships at anchor.[26] We
stopped at the S.F. Post Office building (7th and Mission Streets)
where the U.S. Attorney Frank J. Hennessy had his office (he is

U.S. Attorney of the Northern District of California). We reached
[there] at 2:00 PM Wednesday (26th), and I had a lunch at the office,
opposite of which was a cage where a dozen men were locked in.
The clerk in the office was a nice young man who offered me to-
bacco and ink to fill my pen. He smilingly said that it does not pay
to be a Japanese when he finger printed and recorded my name and
age. Saunders came out and said his boss[?] would send me back to
Stanford as a result of his conversation with Hennessy, but of course
I was not [so] naive as to believe it, though he might have been sincere. The school is in the military zone. He further said that he was
leaving for his Sacramento home, as this office will take me to the
Immigration Station Office at 801 Silver Avenue, and we parted.

About 3:30, 3 Germans and 3 Italians were called out of the cage
and I joined them. We were put on a covered truck with an iron-net
door on the back which was locked when we were in; we arrived at
the Immigration Office. Here our records of name and age, etc.
[were taken]; a repatriation form was signed [by others?]—no interest in my case. I was given a slip with the following items: "ICHI-
HASHI, Yamato 12044/1405." This is my identification numbers, the
former is the FBI case, the latter is my own number. I am to be referred to as "1405." I tried to find out [as to?] why I was brought but
in vain; the clerk suggested that I inquire of the Director of the
Sharp Park Detention Camp whither I will be taken soon. We were
then transferred to a bus and transported to the said Camp; I tried
here again but in vain since the Director was absent. The following
day we, the same group of 7, were returned to Silver Avenue and
were photographed twice: a front view and a side view; my photo
number is "#3529." In the [Sharp Park] Camp I was officially known
as "1405."

I was pleasantly surprised at the make-up of this camp, particularly [after] my experience at the crowded Santa Anita Center and
the spacious but monotonous Tule Lake Camp devoid of vegetation.
It is situated not far from Salada Beach in a beautiful valley which is
surrounded by hills covered with green trees and shrubs; on the
western side between low hills the Pacific Ocean is visible. The
ground is limited by tall iron net-fences and small in area; barracks
20' × 120' are well-built and painted outside and inside and are
regularly arranged; there are 10 of these for [?] inmates; each accommodating about 40, divided into 5 rooms for 8 persons each; if
double-decked (beds), 80 can be put in.[27] . . .

When I reached there, the flowers were in full bloom; the sight

was delightful to the eye. Thus I found my sojourn there of more
than 2 months strangely agreeable because of the beauty and the
kindly attitude of official personnel. Beside the climate, there was either warm or cool [air?] due to fog like that of San Francisco, but
never hot as in Santa Anita and Tule Lake and water is good. Consequently, I was able to keep clean and soon wore off my negro color
and regained my natural complexion. Treatment was satisfactory—
food abundant though often too greasy and powerfully seasoned
with garlic; supplies were freely given such as toothbrush and paste,
smokes, soaps, socks, underwears and lent shirts, shoes, overalls.
Sheets and pillow-case were changed every Monday, blankets were
clean. Here the Geneva Protocol as regards internees and prisoners
of war regulates, and hence, a better treatment all around as compared with assembly and relocation centers. Graft is doubtless practiced but not to the extent done elsewhere.

For one thing, the number of detainees never exceeded 500; there
are alien enemies—Japanese, German, and Italians, and "Interna-
tionals," mostly immigration cases. When I arrived there, the number was about 280, and when I left there on Oct. 26, there were only
(October 21st statistics) 145 men and 22 women or 167 in all, due to
release or internment. However, the increase and diminution are
not indicated by the number because new arrivals came during the
period.[28]. . .

In passing, there is another similar detention camp in Southern
California at Tuna Canyon where there were 17 Japanese, according
to one Takahashi who was taken at Santa Anita about a month ago
and then was removed from there to the Sharp Park—as he was a
resident at San Francisco.

On September 1st, a detailed record of my life in Japan and here
was registered by one Grover, an Immigration Service agent; this was
apparently used as the basis of questions at the hearing, which was
held on the 3rd at 3 : 30 P.M. at the Post Office Building. . . . An Immigration Service representative, a FBI agent, an U.S. attorney and
a recording secretary formed the investigation committee. Treat attended it as my witness. I was made to take an oath to tell nothing
but the truth. Then [U.S.] attorney Mercado (a former student of
Treat and mine) opened the hearing,[29] and said that the President
of the United States possessed the authority to intern alien enemies
without reason, adding in any case, if released, I will be sent back to
Tule Lake. The questions asked concerned my publications, my participation in international conferences diplomatic and scholarly, in

particular, the [1922] Washington Conference, my knowledge of
Ōmori and Yonai,* my property here and abroad, including bonds
and financial status, my scholarly status, armed services, propaganda
activities, etc. Asked by a Board member, I gave a brief report relative to my experiences since my evacuation, condemning the condition of life and the treatment at Santa Anita, the more satisfactory conditions and treatment at Tule Lake, and criticizing the procedures followed after my arrest (the jail at Tule Lake and at Red
Bluff). Everything was far more satisfactory at Sharp Park. Mercado
apologized about the jail and said that he was hoping for an early
rectification of the jail aspect.

Then Treat was sworn to, and asked questions very similar, except that whether he shared views of the journalistic war-mongers
and whether he ever discussed with me the possibility of war; the answers were in the negative. We were held for one hour and 20 minutes while the German was held ten minutes, Soki, three and Itagaki, 5. As soon as the formal hearing was over, Mercado came out
to the Waiting Room and led me away to a corner and talked to me
in a friendly manner—[he said] the office failed to intern 6 Japanese
who should have been since he was positive that they were agents of
the Japanese Government. I asked his advice in regard to getting extra clothes; he said, don't do it. Was this a hint of the board's recommendation for my release? He said that I would hear within three
weeks which is necessary for bureaucratic handling of the communication with the U.S. Attorney General [Francis] Biddle who decides.

In the 3rd week, Soki received the notice of his internment, and
on the following morning, he was sent to the Fort McDonald on
Angel Island, the former San Francisco Immigration Station. On the
4th week, Itagaki got the notice of his release, and a week later he
was sent to the Tule Lake Project, but notice came to me not until
the 13th of October (41 days after the date of hearings);[30] I was
asked to fill the form used to communicate [with Tule Lake?] and
determine the alleged truth of my former residence there, consid-

---

*Ōmori Takeo, a naval officer, attended Stanford before the war. According to the
report on Ichihashi's hearing, the FBI believed that Ōmori had been an active Japanese
spy in the United States before returning to Japan; Report of the Hearing on Yamato
Ichihashi, Sept. 3, 1942, Ichihashi SF INS File. Admiral Yonai Mitsumasa had been minister of the Imperial Navy and prime minister. Extremists in Japan actually considered
Yonai, who had opposed the Tripartite Pact with the Axis powers, a moderate and had him
replaced in July 1940. He later returned to the cabinet in 1944. He privately favored an
early end to the war and was a member of what was known as the "peace faction."

ered a necessary routine for which one week is consumed; I expected
to depart on the 19th or 20th [of October] from the Sharp Park, but
on the 16th (Saturday) at noon, I was told that the above form was
lost and requested to fill [out] another. This was done, but the notice of departure did not come until 3:30 PM. on the 26th (another
10 days were consumed).

Then I was told to pack up in haste since I had to leave the camp
a little after 4 o'clock in order to catch the 6:30 train which was due
at Klamath Falls at 6:30 A.M. of the 27th! [The three other Japanese]
were sent on the 9:05 A.M. train; but the officers were anxious to
dispatch me quickly after a long delay! I was given a dinner ticket
($1.00) on the train, which I kept having paid for it myself; it is
hereto attached. There is also attached the release note to the main
gate guard.[31]

◙ Yamato Ichihashi was thrilled to return to the Tule Lake Relocation
Camp, which was less restrictive than Sharp Park. "I am once more enjoying the freedom of space and at present the sky is thick with a multitude of flying wild geese; the atmosphere is poetic, but there are no flowers except those I brought with me," he wrote to Payson Treat from
Tule Lake upon his return. He repeatedly expressed his gratitude to the
Treats, Wilbur, and other colleagues for their help and support through
his recent ordeal.[32] He also found kind letters waiting for him from other
colleagues, such as Lynn White, Jr., and former Stanford students wishing him well which must have touched and sustained him.[33]

As government documents show, the federal authorities' opinion of
Yamato Ichihashi was decidedly different from what Treat and Ichihashi
had surmised from the special hearing. While Ichihashi had the impression that his San Francisco interrogation had gone well for him, the investigation board concluded that

> the associations and affiliations of the subject had been so close to promi-
> nent Japanese officials in Japan as well as in this country that it would be
> difficult for him to disassociate himself from their influence and that
> therefore he would be a potentially dangerous alien enemy to leave at
> large during the period of the war and they recommend his permanent
> internment.

The U.S. Attorney General ordered that Ichihashi be released on parole
in "the custody of a reputable United States citizen," and report to his
sponsor twice a month and a parole officer once a month. Ichihashi remained on probation until November 15, 1945, three months after Japan's surrender and seven months after his return to the Stanford campus in April 1945.[34]

At Tule Lake, a philosophical Yamato Ichihashi energetically returned to his research and writing on his relocation experiences. There
is no record of his reaction to the government's ruling on his status. ◗

YAMATO ICHIHASHI TO JESSIE TREAT [35]

Tule Lake, California
November 7, 1942

Dear Mrs. Treat:

It is for quite awhile since I had the pleasure of writing to you;
you are aware that I came back here safe and sound. Due to a sudden
change in climate I caught a cold at once, which subsequently developed into a worse case and forced me to stay in bed for several days.
However, I have now recovered from it more or less; I am up again.
But Kei is having her turn, although it is a mild case; I hope it will
stay that way and will be relieved from it soon. The shower and latrine are unheated and drafty, and there we seem to catch colds;
many people are suffering from such illness.

Evenings, nights and mornings are rather cold, in fact, freezing
and frosty; snows fall from time to time. But the living quarters can
be kept warm for we have good, coal stoves and thus far we have
found no shortage of fuel. Only we have to be very careful not to
over heat the rooms, which I am afraid many do. The smoke emitted
from stoves and chimneys makes the atmosphere gloomy, odorous
and disagreeable; it must be terrible in some places. We are fortunately situated in the extreme north-eastern corner of the camp,
but should a southwestern wind blow we too get the full benefit of
smokes and soots.

Nevertheless daytime has often been sunny and even delightful;
we sometimes have glorious and glowing sunsets. This natural
beauty is enhanced or rendered poetic by the visible presence of
wildlife; a multitude of wild geese fly about this region and fantastic
lines they form in their flights are indeed picturesque. I have never
seen in my life so great flocks of these wild birds; there must be millions of them. Seagulls are also quite numerous; they gather about
the mess-halls and enjoy a plenty of food. There are other kinds of
wild fowls. Besides, I brought with me house plants, flowers and cut-
tings; these have been carefully potted in tin cans by our old friend
and they are doing well. They comfort and delight us, but create
envy among our numerous visitors. At any rate, thus our monoto-

nous and unchanging life in this desolate place is made somewhat enjoyable, if we possess a responsive and sensitive nature to things of beauty, the moon, stars, birds, flowers.

My return here appears to be a source of satisfaction or relief among Americans and foreigners alike; many have already called on us to offer their congratulations and some of the Japanese callers, total strangers to me, have touched me deeply. Many do not know as yet of my return since the camp's daily made but a very inconspicuous mention of it. When they do discover this fact, they will probably stream into our humble tenement!

I must now come, without further unessentials, to the object of this writing; I wish to express my deep gratitude to you and Payson for what you two have done for us since our evacuation from our beloved campus and, in particular, during my sojourn, more strictly[?] my detention at the Sharp Park Camp. You made me happy in the midst of my extreme humiliation; this I shall never forget. As I now calmly review my sad experiences, I can truthfully say that they were very disagreeable but highly instructive (I learned many new things about war). I have no complaint against the American officials involved in the case, but I am still shocked about certain aspects in the procedure applied to the individuals unfortunate enough to have had similar experiences like those of mine. Consequently many suffered far more humiliating treatments, which I fortunately escaped.

You know that I have been an idealist all my life and as such I have been an admirer of American ideals. I am old enough to know better, but in the face of my recent experiences I have become more of a realist. The inefficiency and indifferences of bureaucracy everywhere shock me; in [my] case, seven weeks and five days were consumed between the hearing and the release. On October 13th I was notified of my release; I filled in a form at the official request; on the 16th I was told of the loss of that form and required a second form; that was at noon of Saturday and nothing was done about it until the following Monday. The officials needed one more week to check the truth of my "alleged" former residence at this Tule Lake project. At 3:30 o'clock PM (26th) I was told to pack up to be ready at 4:00; I had no time to say goodbye to a German baker who made a cake when he learned that the Japanese were holding a farewell party for me! But all this belongs to the past and I can veritably smile again; I am resettled with my family once more.

Lastly just a word about Woodrow. He has organized a *jazz* band, and since October 31st has been giving concerts in different wards (there are 7 wards in all; each ward is composed of 9 blocks, each of which represents an approximate population of 250 souls.)[36] He is getting "famous" in that kind of work while his parents stand askance; he is scheduled to play in our ward on November 16th and 17th. I am at loss of what I think of my son. Such is life alas, but I am in no way disheartened; maybe he was born that way![37]

Well, again thanking you, I remain

Very cordially yours,
Yamato

YAMATO ICHIHASHI TO PAYSON TREAT [38]

Tule Lake, California
November 20, 1942

Dear Payson:

The weather has continued to be miserable on the whole; wind-storms create sand-storms, it snows or rains, mornings and evenings are chilly with the ground being always frozen. I have been unable to get rid of my cold; I am still suffering from a sore throat, and the same is true of poor Kei. However, we have some sunshine during day-time, and I go out whenever it is possible. This explains why I have not been able to write you sooner, but fearful of further repri-mand, I am now determined to communicate with you by compos-ing the first report from this Project. But lest I forget, I wish to thank you for your nice letter;[39] you are free to write as often as you can. Also because of the meagerness and the poor quality of food served here, we have been enjoying the biscuits and the nuts you have given me while sojourning at the Sharp Park; for the gift we are extremely thankful. Other matters I shall not even touch because I wish to write a report on the Project.

According to available information, the "pioneer" group of colo-nists arrived here on May 27th; they were volunteers, 350 in num-ber. On that occasion, [Elmer D.] Shirrell, then Acting Project Di-rector, welcomed them with the following words: "The W.R.A. has provided for you the making of a fine colony at Tule Lake Project. This Valley has been compared to the Valley of the Nile in fertility. Within the last two decades this reclaimed lake bottom was opened to homesteaders and you saw as you travelled, the results of their ef-forts. You are pioneers in a great undertaking. Our country is at war and we must raise food. This is your assignment in the war effort.

This is your home. Please count on the staff to help make you comfortable. Welcome to Tule Lake."

I understand that there are some 21,000 acres of land in this
center that can be cultivated; the camp itself, however, occupies
about 1,000 acres incapable of cultivation and completely devoid of
vegetation. It is a spacious ground unlike the Santa Anita Assembly
Center where 18,500 humans were packed like sardines within less
than one hundred acres; it gives you the freedom of space, and that
is a distinct advantage, or at least I feel so having come from the
Stanford Campus. We miss greatly, however, trees, shrubs, flowers!
By July 27th, the population reached 14,993; the place is built for
about 15,000 as the maximum, though some 500 more can be
housed if necessary.

These colonists are housed in 896 barracks; each barrack is subdivided into 4, 5, or 6 apartments. Fourteen of these together with
a recreation hall, a mess hall, a laundry with an ironing room, and
a men's and women's showers and latrines, or 18 barracks in all, are
grouped as a block which is the administrative unit, containing about
250 persons. Nine of these blocks situated nearby are organized
into a ward, and there are seven wards in all (one ward contains
10 blocks). The number of non-living barracks varies somewhat
from block to block as well as in their arrangement. The example
given above represents the blocks in the VIIth ward where we happen to be quartered, and described as a "typical revised block." It is
superfluous to add that the population of blocks varies somewhat in
accordance with the subdivision of barracks, and consequently the
population of wards also. But the foregoing description is fairly accurate on the whole; it is hoped so even for historical purposes.

To each block, the administrative unit, is attached a Block Manager (must be a nisei), an appointee of the Administration. He is a
liaison officer between the Administration and the people. He represents the interest of the Administration and performs such duties as
follows: to inform the colonists of all rules, regulations, instructions,
information, and other forthcoming orders issued by the Administration. He is responsible for the collection and distribution of mail.
He is to check all changes in residence of colonists, and to oversee
that repairs, heating and sanitation are properly maintained. He handles household supplies and repairs. He is to act as a medium
between the mess hall and the people. He is a paid servant of the
Administration, and this fact often makes some of these block managers forget that they are serving the people. Consequently, there
exists a feeling of dissatisfaction on the part of the colonists, many

of whom are issei and aliens for whom nisei seem to have no respect. There has arisen a number of difficulties. Personally I think that the issei are not blameless; some of them are hard on nisei citizens, although these youngsters commit many blunders in their attitudes and speech. Linguistic difficulties are one great source of misunderstanding, and the oldsters do not like to be ruled by kids, especially their own sons and daughters!

On the other hand, each block elects a councilman to represent the interests of colonists; he is an unpaid agent of the block population; he too must be a nisei. He is assigned such duties as follows: To bring forth to the Council (composed of these block councilmen) complaints and suggestions pertaining to the welfare of the community. He is to inform the colonists of his block of all council regulations and policies, and to make reports to the Project Director concerning the functioning of the community services. Doubt generally exists as to the degree of weight these councilmen actually have with the Administration in carrying out their functions. His job is not an easy one. He is subjected to similar criticisms that are directed against the block managers. Besides, he often comes in conflict with the block manager; their jurisdictions are defined more or less clearly, but their applications create no end of trouble. It is hoped all around that they function in harmony to promote the general well-being of the community; but they are all young and inexperienced and not much should be expected of them.

The structure of this society is unnatural since it is composed of citizens and alien enemies; this distinction is made in every way since nisei alone can hold "political offices." Besides, these citizens are children of alien parents. Conflict between the two generations is normally bad enough; in this society it becomes intensified. Aliens have no voice; they have no channel of direct communication with the Administration. I have been hoping for rectification of this situation since the Santa Anita days, and [developments have] now convinced the Administration that something has to be done.

Under the name of *Planning Board*, it now proposes to create an advisory body to the Administration composed of seven issei; it is to give an organ to issei colonists through which they express their voice in regard to the management of the community welfare. These seven advisers are to be elected by the seven wards; they are issei twenty-five years and over, possessing some experience in personnel work and human relations, and must be social-minded, have good judgment, and command respect of colonists. They must be able to speak the Japanese and English languages fluently. I wonder how many possess such high qualifications! Be that as it may, the purpose and power of the Board are defined as follows:

a. An Advisory Board to the Administration and colonists on the formation and interpretation of basic policies.
b. Collect data and records for further study and research to determine causes of disputes and to take measures to prevent their future recurrences.
c. Guide complaints to appropriate departments.
d. Officers and research men who serve on the Planning Board shall have privileges to attend all hearings, meetings, and conferences relative to issues involving community welfare.
e. May request any person from any offices, boards, or departments to act in an advisory capacity to the Planning Board.

In respect to the research men mentioned above, it is provided that the Planning Board appoint three research men to serve as investigators for said Board. They shall devote full time to their work and shall be compensated by the W.R.A. One of these men is to be chosen by the Board to be their secretary and also to supervise the other two research men. Well, we shall see what the Board can do; it provides a safety-valve and as such it may serve useful purposes. Thus I shall conclude the present report, perhaps colorless and uninteresting; it is strictly legal and administrative.

At this point, I shall refer to my son's musical activities. His orchestra in conjunction with dancers, singers and other entertainers gave performances sixteen times, twice before the administrators and their families and fourteen times in different wards. They charged an admission of 10 cents; Kei and I attended the last performance. The patrons packed to the capacity of mess halls, and in fact, we could not get tickets, but were given complimentary tickets. Apparently, they were popular, but I am no judge of modern music. The dance-piece Woody has arranged made everybody sway to and fro; it must have appealed to the crowd. One thing I noticed: he seemed to have a perfect control over his musicians. Some of the dances were excellently performed and some of the songs were rendered remarkably. Well, well, what a confession by an old dog who cannot be taught new tricks!

Upon inquiry at the office, I am permitted to have my books and monographs in this camp, though the army may say that certain of these might be declared undesirable and [are] to be shipped back to you. I shall take a chance and ask you to be kind enough to send me the books in your care when convenient.[40]

With affection and gratitude, I am as ever,

Respectfully yours,
Yamato

Kei and Woodrow wish to send you and Madame their greetings.

KEI ICHIHASHI TO JESSIE TREAT [41]

Tule Lake
Dec. 5 [1942]

Dear Mrs. Treat:

We enjoyed rather mild weather for a while, but [during the] last three days it became quite cold. Yesterday morning the sky cleared up and I found the distant mountains covered with heavy snow. No wonder the air is very cold and crisp.

We, the residents of this project, are leading a very monotonous life as usual. However there are many different kinds of classes for the grown-ups, especially for women. For instance English class, flower arrangement class, sewing, flower making—with coloured paper—doll making, knitting and Japanese dancing (classical and modern). For youngsters there are classes teaching toe-dance, ballet dance, and other forms of dancing. Both these groups are very active.

Some ambitious women attend different classes day and night, so they are very busy, but seem to enjoy them all. Before they were evacuees they had to work very hard every day, so that most of them did not have enough time to learn anything, even English. Some women, middle age, just started this from abc. I feel awfully sorry for them. But they are attending the class regularly and are trying to learn English as much as they can.

The other day Mr. Ichihashi and I went to see an art exhibition. There were many beautiful wooden flower vases, artificial flowers, knitting wares, and other objects. Someday, they will have a general bazaar, I hope, and then I shall get some of the beautiful articles and will send them to you. In this project, wood works are very popular among men, while artificial flowers [are] among women. They are making many beautiful things.

Lately we are having very poor food every day, so that we must eat some things between meals. I used to get cookies and nuts at the canteen, but lately they don't carry these and candies. I should like to ask you to get us some sweets. There is no hurry about it. Please do it whenever it is convenient for you and send them to me. Our mess hall still does not supply silver wares except knives. Very fortunately we brought with us knives, forks and tea spoons, but not any soup spoons. We don't want expensive ones, as we have enough silver wares at home. Will you please buy 3 common soup spoons at the 5 and 10 cents store? Here is a list of articles that I would like to ask you to buy and send us:

3 soup spoons.

2 pairs of rubber gloves—if you can

1 small package of Vigoro[?]—or other fertilizer for potted plants. You can get them at the 5 and 10 cents store.

1 Cutex—oily cuticle remover.

1 scotch tape (transparent stickers) wide kind.

8 lbs. (about) cookies—the National Biscuit Company's common cookies are good enough, mix 3 or 4 different kinds, please.

6 cans Mrs. Bentsen's[?] home-made style Danish cookies.

2 two pound box of chocolate candies.

1 aluminum kettle—I put an old aluminum kettle on the gas range in our kitchen. If you can find it, please send it.

1 calendar, an advertising one such as you get from trade people, to be hung on the wall.

Please find enclosed a check for $15.00 to cover costs of the above purchases.

Very affectionately yours.
Kei Ichihashi

P.S. Mr. Ichihashi asks me to convey thanks to Mr. Treat for the books; he is very busy at present.

KEI ICHIHASHI TO JESSIE TREAT [42]

Tule Lake
Dec. 22 [1942]

Dear Mrs. Treat:

Thank you for your nice letter.[43] Yesterday we received two boxes of the parcels safely, and we were surprised to find so many nice

Christmas gifts from you, besides Miss Stoltenberg's. We are indeed very grateful. The calendar is attractive, and we appreciate it very much. Having lived on the campus so many years, I terribly missed the campus atmosphere since our evacuation in May. All the more therefore we will enjoy looking at the calendar during the coming year. Last night we used our old tea kettle and enjoyed tea. It was the first tea we had at home since we left the campus.

We are fast approaching the Christmas and New Year. One of our neighbors brought us a small xmas tree, and I fixed it with a few ornaments which I make myself, as I could not buy any here this year. Still another neighbor gave us Point-cetters [poinsettias] in a pot, artificial ones, of course, I put them in an appropriate corner. Therefore even our one-room tenement appears rather cheery and bright now. Yesterday morning another woman gave us an English holly and some other evergreens.

I am sure we will have a turkey dinner for Christmas and special rice cakes (a traditional New Year food for Japanese) for New Year's day.

I thank you again for your kindness in sending us many things and also your many thoughtful gifts.

I wish both of you a merry Christmas and a happy and most bright New Year.

Affectionately yours,
Kei Ichihashi

◻ During the closing weeks of 1942, Yamato Ichihashi completed several long essays chronicling his relocation experiences. This writing repeated virtually all the important information included in the material reproduced above and is therefore omitted here. Ichihashi also gave lectures on Japanese history to residents, including one on December 11 when he spoke for an hour and a half on the Hōryūji Temple, one of the most famous cultural sites in Japan. The reporter for the camp newspaper observed that Ichihashi's academic talk may have seemed as "dry as Tule Lake dust" to some and irrelevant in time of war, but as one who thirsted for something more than the mundane, the lecture "poured into my brain like pearls." He praised Ichihashi for helping him transcend the difficulties of the moment. The column ended: "The teacher from Nazareth said: 'Man Does Not Live By Bread Alone. . . .' And these lectures by the Stanford savant serve to remind us once again that we should not . . ."[44]

Ichihashi wrote his research essays in the blue books used by Stanford students for examinations, of which he had brought several to camp with him. Wanting something more permanent for systematic work, however, he asked Treat to send him a "diary book" for his daily record for 1943.[45] Treat sent him a leather-bound, gilt-edged personal chronicle for the new year. Ichihashi filled every page of this and 21 subsequent books with daily entries on his activities and on current events. He departed from this routine only in the last days before his death in 1963.

He used his diaries for multiple purposes: they served as personal calendars, listing future appointments and tasks; he recorded, in brief, his daily life, including people he met, meetings attended, and events personally witnessed; and he often listed references to current national or international events, making the diaries a personal almanac for himself. He frequently attached newspaper clippings from the *Palo Alto Times* or the camp newsletter to diary pages. Finally, Ichihashi also entered, usually in the extra pages for "Special Data" provided at the end of a calendar month, extended observations and analyses of important issues. He rarely, however, confided information of a strictly personal nature. References to his family life, for example, are infrequent and vague; references to his emotional state even more rare.

Ichihashi usually attended to his diary several times daily, which the marginalia, narrative, and different shades of blue pen ink make evident. Thus the reader often discovers how the weather and other important events unfolded during the day. (The weather was a very important matter, considering its capriciousness and the scant shelter the camps' primitive housing afforded.) His diary, however, is not a complete record; he omitted many encounters and activities. For example, he received many more requests for help from camp residents and solicitations from editors of periodicals for articles than his diary shows.

Ichihashi's idiosyncratic diary keeping makes deciphering his entries a challenge, since his verb tenses may change from future to present to past within one day's entries and some thoughts appear contradictory because actual events did not meet expectations. In addition, Ichihashi's handwriting was renowned for its illegibility (he joked about it himself with his correspondents), and his written English, especially in his personal diary where presumably he wrote in a more spontaneous way, reflects features of the Japanese language: frequent use of the passive tense, missing personal pronouns, and elliptical references. Moreover, Ichihashi's eyesight was deteriorating, and it appears he sometimes simply omitted words and punctuation or lost track of a phrase because he could not see clearly or was distracted. ◗

1943 DIARY [46]

Friday, January 1

The New Year welcomed and the Block gathered at the breakfast table and a talk was given to the gathering. The morning was cloudy and it snowed in the afternoon, but melted away as it turned out to be warm. The dinner was satisfactory with a chilled pompona [a type of fish] from L.A. For supper the chef invited us to a *tempura* party. Kuramotos [47] were the only other guests beside ourselves.

The day was quiet as most of the residents went to the carnival. But several persons made a new year call, mostly women; it was delightful despite the kind of life we are forced to continue in the camp.

For a summary of camp activities, refer to the *Dispatch*, [48] the new year's issue.

Nothing unpleasant happened today. Wild geese are to be seen no more (until next season); I miss them very much. Just as we were given a Xmas tree and hollies, we were presented with a *shōchikubai*,* a very well-made artificial one, and a vase with pines and daffodils by Kumasakas and Yokotas respectively. [49] We did not attend the carnival and spent a very quiet afternoon. The Recreation Hall is being taken advantage of in full by kids and youth. Good.

Saturday, January 2

The day started clear but remained cold till noon when it became sunny and warm—very delightful. But the snow on the ground melted, making it rather wet; still, it is sandy and not muddy. Since there will be no water from 8 P.M. [and] the shower has to close, I had my New Year bath at 5 P.M. Of course there was no facility yesterday.

Due to the alleged shortage of water, bath facilities were suspended today. The Rec. Hall flourishes. Research cont'd.

---

*A *bonsai* combination of pine, bamboo, and plum considered to be especially felicitous.

Sunday, January 3

Warnings were given that there will be no light because electric facilities had to be repaired; there was no light till about 11 A.M. The day turned out to be clear and crisp; rather cold but the ground was frozen and there was no slush. Pleasant feature. Juvenile delinquency is the prevailing topic; and many came and presented their ideas; none is based on knowledge or experiences. This is to be expected in this camp. We had to chase away invaders of the Rec. Hall from other Blocks; too bad. Research cont'd.

Monday, January 4

Prepared a talk to be given to the camp teachers. Research cont'd. The morning cloudy, but gradually clearing.

Coverley, the newly appointed Director took over duties on Dec. 30 when he arrived here.

The Recreation Dept. Japanese representative complained to our Block Manager in regard to the partition built by our men, and insisted that we should be satisfied with 1/3 of the Hall. They again came and protested, but Frank [Matsumoto] [50] could say nothing and asked them to refer to the Block as a whole. There it stands.

At 5 P.M. a note came from Coverley requesting me to come to the Administration at 11:00 A.M.; I asked Frank to see him and make a new appointment.

Tonight we were invited to a *sashimi* dinner by the chef. Kuramotos, Frank, Nakao and Terazaki were there. Afterward, we invited Mrs. Kuramoto to our home.

Nothing important occurred in the Camp.

Mrs. Yokota approached me in regard to *Fukuju-sō* [a plant popularly known as "pheasant's eye"] and I referred her to old Fukuhara, a bonsai expert, who had paid me a visit sometime ago.

Tuesday, January 5

The morning was cold and misty but toward noon it cleared up and became warm. The day was delightful.

I called on Coverley at 10:30 and found him to be one of my old students, who took all my courses, including the pro[seminar] and seminars. We discussed matters relative to the Project. He asked me to act as his personal adviser. But I refused to accept any official post, but promised to help him unofficially. It is rather fortunate that he should be the Director.[51]

I saw Jacoby[52] and discussed with him several matters, including the problem of juvenile delinquency. The fire chief was there and discussed with him the necessity of [naming?] some of the Americans who are to act as "guards" in their residential district in the same manner as Japanese guards in various blocks.

Ramey[53] came and invited us to a dinner before the lecture I am to give on the coming Thursday (7th); we served him tea.

Shirai[54] and Nakano called on us.

Woodrow came and I talked to him about a new job promised by Coverley.

Wednesday, January 6

Misty and very cold all day and all night.

Egusa[?] of the Rec. Dept. came to obtain my *vitae curriculae* for publicity purposes.

The customary lecture was given in the Ward V; poorest attendance so far.

Thursday, January 7

Again misty and cold all day and fog became rather dense at night.

In the morning, Isamu Iseri accompanied by his father came and told me that he was the foreman of the stove crew (14 isseis). In the beginning, he was promised that their jobs would be permanent (perhaps to make the jobs attractive); [when] the work was finished, the man in charge roughly told Iseri that there was no work for them. Arguments resulted and Laurentzen[?]* apparently lost [his] head and mishandled the foreman with the air of superiority clearly indicated in his notice of discharge: "Inefficiency and Insubordination." A hearing is to be held next evening. But on Friday Iseri reported that the hearing is postponed. We had dinner (the Caucasian

---

*Unidentified.

Mess Hall)* as Ramey's guests: Coverley and Topping[55] sat at the table. It was simple but good: steak, french-fried spuds, tomatoes, boiled onion, lettuce salad, pie, coffee and [?].

Spoke before the high school teachers at the Rec. Center, a barrack but well arranged with comfortable chairs and lounges. A billiard table, tables. The teachers got interested and kept me until after 10 PM. Many local problems were discussed.[56]

Friday, January 8

The morning was cloudy, misty and cold but from noon on it turned sunny and warm.

Iseri reported that the intended hearing on his case was postponed indefinitely.

Kuramoto told of a case of pregnant girl who had intercourse with two young men (definitely known); but by whom she has begotten it is difficult to determine since the situation as she tells, that one party's relationship began only in November, but the state of pregnancy according to K. appears to be 5 or 6 months. It is suspected that the 2nd party had a relationship for a longer period since they were once engaged, which was broken by the father's demand that he pay $1,000, which the boy rejected. But the boy and the girl made up at Pinedale Center[57] and apparently entered into a point of having had intercourse. The request to me to find out [more] by a physical examination by a doctor, and I consented to find out.

Tonight a Block meeting to be held at 7:00 to discuss juvenile delinquency problems in the Projects. . . .

. . . .

Saturday, January 9

Started very cold but later turned out to be nice and warm. Had a hair-cut and stopped by at Akamatsu[58] about the girl in trouble (to

---

*The camp administration used the term "Caucasian" to distinguish the staff from the Japanese residents. This created some bizarre circumstances, as when the term was used to refer to an African American staff member.

have the case determined as to the age of her baby). Early in afternoon he came, and together with Kuramoto arranged for an examination Sunday evening. Thus the day was consumed by visits and visitors. Kitagawa[59] came re: juvenile [problems], and I refused to accept the post on the Juvenile [Problem] Committee as an advisor.[60]

The toilet wall facing the trough where many obscene words and pictures were, was painted to cover them up.

Sunday, January 10

Started cold but turned out a regular spring day.

Two men called in re: *shimboku kai* ["get-together" society].

Three men called in re: Buddhists as to what they should do to maintain good conduct among themselves; they are dissatisfied with preaching which emphasizes [the] future and the priests fail to touch upon the life as the people are forced to lead and are losing all the good points they had outside.

A woman called in regard to flowers.

Monday, January 11

The day started cold as usual but turned [out] to be a nice afternoon. Kuramoto came and received Dr.'s report on the unfortunate pregnancy case; it was determined by Akamatsu that the baby was 3 months old. K. remained here for a long time.

Woodrow brought a chart of the Project, a book and laundry.

The Obanas paid us a visit in the afternoon.

The day was spent in discussing various social problems that are developing here. Adult schools were touched upon.

The rest was spent in writing and research.

Received a letter from Ralph[61] and a note of thanks from Ramey as regards the talk given before the high school teachers.

Tuesday, January 12

This day was a regular spring day, nice and delightful.

Kumasaka in the morning and Fukuhara in the afternoon took up most of my time.

However, I finished my lecture on the Taika Reform, [62] and also reviewed my lecture note on *Uji* and *Kabane*.*

Various problems, including the future of the Japanese were brought up and discussed. They all see a dark future, but nothing except spiritual determination on the part of individuals can help the situation.

I missed both [meals?], and am very tired.

◘ The steady stream of visitors who made their way to Ichihashi's residence every day deluged him with difficult questions large and small. What would be considered "personal" issues became "public" under the managed close quarters of the camp; tensions arising from conflicts between evacuees and between evacuees and the camp authorities mounted by the day. Constant rumormongering aggravated the situation. Despite Ichihashi's apparent unease in confronting these human issues, he seems to have given ample time to helping his fellow residents. He may have been genuinely concerned about their plight, or he may have simply found their stories part of the human drama he wished to understand and document. Whatever the case, his diary entries show that he was very busy. In addition to camp residents, he regularly met with camp administrators and visitors from the "outside," such as sociologists Dorothy Swain Thomas and W. I. Thomas and other researchers, who paid a visit to Ichihashi on January 14. Dorothy Thomas, a professor at the University of California, Berkeley, led a major study of the camps, the Japanese American Evacuation and Resettlement Study.[63]

At the same time, Ichihashi tried to pursue his own scholarly work. The vision of him attempting to read and think about eighth-century Japanese cultural history within the confines of the prison camp is anomalous indeed. On a warm day in mid-January, he complained to his block manager about the unpleasant habit of one of his neighbors of collecting and then dumping his urine in the open trough outside the living quarters. "I was ill all the afternoon because of its smell," Ichihashi recorded that day in his diary.[64]

Ichihashi faced other, more serious challenges. Not long after Tule Lake Camp Director Harvey M. Coverley and Ichihashi resumed their association, Coverley wrote a long, confidential letter to Stanford President Ray Lyman Wilbur asking for advice on a sensitive topic. Coverley wanted to know about Ichihashi's social and political views, since he was

---

* *Uji*, "clan" or "lineage-group," and *kabane*, aristocratic titles, were important features of feudal Japan.

being considered to help "promote our program of Americanization which includes, of course, an acceptance of the spirit as well as the form of democratic institutions." Coverley asked for Wilbur's estimate of Ichihashi's "fitness for such a task," especially since he had heard rumors that Ichihashi was "known to have certain Fascist tendencies and that he has little patience with or sympathy for that large group of evacuees which has had very limited economic advantages in the past and few opportunities for higher education." [65]

Wilbur's quick reply emphasized his faith in Ichihashi's intellect and values. It would be a "fine achievement" and "thoroughly worthwhile," Wilbur wrote, if Ichihashi were involved in the Americanization effort. At the same time, Wilbur also noted, that it was true that Ichihashi was known to possess an air of superiority which was probably a result of his upper-class background in Japan and his long professional standing in America. His manner may have accounted for "the impression that his ideas are Fascist." Wilbur, though, expressed no suspicion at all that Ichihashi may have been sympathetic to the belligerent powers. Indeed, Wilbur suggested, Ichihashi's recent experience as a detainee at Sharp Park, where he was required to do menial work, may have encouraged some humility in him. The Stanford president urged Coverley to give him a try.[66]

Coverley still had his doubts, however, and may have been responsible for the encounter described next in Ichihashi's diary. Ichihashi never became involved in an "Americanization program," probably because of his belief that his alien status made it inappropriate. ◾

DIARY

Monday, January 25

The day remained cold but not so as to keep the snow on ground to remain frozen; it melted making the ground very slushy and hard to walk on. Later a strong wind started to blow, and it is very disagreeable.

John D. Cook, Reports Officer, sent a woman to secure my ideas as to America's future "democracy," how American-Japanese [should] prepare themselves for the future; the degree of assimilation among them, etc. I refused to answer as I am legally an alien who has no business to advise the American government what it should do for the post-war America. It is proper for me to observe the Aristotelian injunction.[67] The woman herself became sensitive and asked whether she will be suspected as a stool-pigeon. [My] answer was: "I didn't think so." [Yet?] there may be suspicious individuals who could see nothing in any other way. Therefore one must be very tactful in dealing with them in regard to any matters official. The present [task is?] to gather opinions which will be made into a report for the Washington government.

Tuesday, January 26

It started cold but turned out warm, melting the snow as usual and making the ground slushy and flooded in spots; slippery or wet; therefore rather disagreeable.

Declined our repatriation.[68]

Advised Frank to keep his office free from loiterers who are often too many; official functions are difficult to perform because privacy is lacking. Spent spare time in reading monographs and "Life." Rickenbacker's story of his wrecked plane—the first 13 days, very thrilling but sad: one member passed away.[69]

Received a clipping in re: the new President of Stanford[70] from Payson.

Wednesday, January 27

Started as the previous day.

. . . .

This evening was devoted to the last of [series?] lectures at the Ward II; despite the snow and the flooded ground, the meeting was well attended by the young and old who were very attentive.[71] Whether appreciative or not the lectures from the attendance point of view have been successful and therefore worthwhile to have attempted. Everywhere I was received courteously, and the audience has been attentive. The Mess Halls seen were beautified and bareness of the construction was improved: curtains on the windows and empty spaces were filled with pictures, poems, artificial flowers, etc. The people are making the best of what they have.

. . . Tea was served after the lecture and a half-dozen men joined. Nakamura informed me that there was serious trouble in the Construction Department, which has the potentiality of developing into

a bad situation; wished to consult with me. Yasuda[72] composed a
sonnet inspired by my closing remark: it is the beauty of nature that
gives joy!

Thursday, January 28

Snow started early this morning and the ground is already covered
with snow; it is a gloomy day.

Fujioka, engineer, vs. Katayama, architect: the latter demands
that the former resign. A meeting of the Fujioka foremen to decide
what is to be done. The meeting of construction foremen was held
in the 73 Rec. Hall at which about 50 were present and Kitagawa
and I [attended] as observers. The conflict is between the two men:
Fujioka is accused of having overstepped his authority in checking
on [an] absent crew, but whose "time" was entered as if they worked
at the request of his Caucasian supervisor. He is accused by Katayama as having reported this fact as an *inu* [dog, or informer for the
Camp administration]; K's partisans are insistent to bring about the
resignation of F. The committee to negotiate failed because K's partisans are determined to oust F but the F partisans are equally determined to support their head, F. My advice was to appeal to the Planning Board to act as the intermediary to solve the problems as an
urgent matter since the K [partisans] threaten bodily harm if F refuses to step out. Patience is needed while the case is pending, and
[all] must avoid violence at any cost. The meeting lasted three hours.

Friday, January 29

It snowed last night, a few inches on the ground this morning. But it
cleared later, and it became warmer; consequently the snow began
to melt making the ground slushy again. It was said that Katayama is
a clever man and [has] a strong group to support him because he is
generous in treating his men: eats and smokes; clever advisers are
behind him, whereas Fujioka is a typical nisei as regards the Administration staff; while popular with his own crew so far, he is being
suspected as catering [to the Administration] and relies on his
authority.

The Planning Board, with some of the Councilmen[?], and religionists sat in session this morning to hear the Committee of the F
partisans; intends to do the same with the K partisans this afternoon;

also the Board of Directors of the Cooperatives was summoned to appear before it.

Fukuhara paid a visit with a gift of oranges; talked about drafting of nisei:[73] the answer inevitable since they must obey American laws.

It was miserable all day.

Sunday, January 31

Started clear but [became] very cold. Despite the bright sun-shine, the air remains cold though the snow on the ground melted some-what. This, I believe, is the coldest day so far.

. . . .

SPECIAL DATA[74]

Adult education program is not well considered, nor is it a very intelligent one: elementary English for aliens, mostly mothers of children and sewing and dress-making both for alien and nisei women and girls—these may prove of some value but interfere with domestic life: children and youngsters are neglected, a serious source of juvenile delinquency. There seems to be no justification (from the standpoint of the domestic situation) for such courses as artificial flower-making, flower-arranging and similar trivials, including *cha-noyu* [tea ceremony]. If the women belong to the leisure class [it would be one thing], but they are not, being mostly the wives of poor farmers and farm laborers. It seems that emphasis should be on practical matters such as domestic and individual sanitary measures, common medical and dental knowledge, elementary common education, etc., so as to make them better and intelligent mothers. Instead the courses offered tend to render them more vain—vanity should be discouraged and not encouraged, since it is a common weakness of the uneducated and uncultured. The woman in charge apparently knows nothing of the need of the women for whose general betterment she is assigned this task: their social, economic and cultural illiteracy. Of course, qualified teachers are lacking, and the language used is English—that means instructors have to be nisei; there may be some issei who are qualified, but they can use only Japanese which is forbidden. Teaching of the Japanese language is, of course, prohibited, though there are many nisei who would like to study it. The majority of issei are too old and beyond the range of any education, besides they have no foundation to continue any real useful education. Their intellectual plane is very low, being mostly of peasant origins in Japan and they have had no education in this country. That being the case, it is difficult to find intelligent leadership; the nisei are still too young and linguistically handicapped, though the population of the community varies between 14,000 and 15,000. Consequences due to the character of population will be discussed in the following month's [diary] end.

   Koto [Japanese harp] lessons are being taken by the wife of a former next door [neighbor]—a case in point—vanity.

◻ As hinted in Ichihashi's diary entry of January 29, one issue that dramatically elevated tensions within the camp was that of military service for the nisei. The question whether their son should serve in the U.S. armed services bedeviled the Ichihashi family, as it did thousands of others in the camps.

Before Pearl Harbor Japanese American young men, whether citizens or not, had regularly been drafted into the U.S. armed services. Many had served during World War I, and at the outbreak of World War II over 3,000 Japanese Americans, both drafted and enlisted, were in active service. After December 7, 1941, however, the Selective Service System increasingly discriminated against Japanese Americans and on March 30, 1942, ceased their induction altogether, contradicting its mandate of nondiscrimination. When he was first called up by his draft board in January 1942 in Oregon, Woodrow, a member of ROTC at the University, was told that he failed the physical; his slight weight and need to use eyeglasses supposedly made him unacceptable to the military. He says he would have gone if the military had taken him. It was not until January 1943 that Secretary of War Henry L. Stimson announced the organization of a special all-volunteer Japanese American fighting unit, later known as the 442nd Regimental Combat Team. (The army had already quietly begun to recruit Japanese Americans for military intelligence and linguistic work, and in early 1944 the government reinstated registration and the draft for nisei.) Woodrow recalls that after much thought, he decided to enlist because he felt it would help demonstrate his feeling for America. Yamato, however, "vehemently opposed" the idea on the grounds that the U.S. government had put him in camp solely because of his ancestry. The draft was one thing, he argued; if Woodrow had been drafted, Yamato would not have counseled breaking the law and resisting. But volunteering to serve and possibly die was another matter. Woodrow countered by pointing out that his father had brought him up to be a "good American." "Not to that extent!" was Yamato's reply. For "once in my life," Woodrow recalled many years later, he abided by his father's wishes and dropped the idea. Woodrow's recollection of the discussion does not necessarily differ from the following description in Yamato's diary. The question of the draft and military service arose again for the Ichihashis in 1944 and is discussed in Chapter 4.[75]

On top of the question of military service, camp residents had to endure what became known as the "registration crisis," which lasted from February to early April 1943. Ichihashi describes the crisis at Tule Lake in diary entries and other material reproduced below in this and the next chapter. Registration touched off similar crises at other camps, although Tule Lake experienced the greatest tension thanks to the poor planning of the Administration and its reaction to camp opposition. Forty-two percent of the residents either refused to register or answered "no" to two critical questions on the form. (These are described in note 81, below.)[76] ◼

DIARY

Wednesday, February 3

The day started bright and warm with usual results as far as the ground is concerned; some brought and laid extra soil in front of our house.

Woodrow came and expressed his desire to volunteer to enter the army and asked for my consent. I asked him to consider possible consequences on his parents in case the worst happens. . . .

. . . . .

We went to Ito's place for tea;[77] there were several people [there] and it turned out to be a very pleasant party. We left there at about 11:00 and it started to rain.

The mixed-up affair: Yamada and Iseri got married a few days [ago] having obtained their marriage license, although Kuramoto told me that the boy's mother is still unreconciled.

Thursday, February 4

It rained all night but due to the holes dug yesterday water did not accumulate although the ground is muddy.

A bank [of soil] was built in front of the barrack to make it possible to walk to and fro.

Shirai and his assistant called and reported about the construction trouble; the source of difficulty seems to lie in the fact of inefficiency [of] the white boss who knows nothing about the type of work assigned to him. Also he stated that the Planning Board is not functioning well, but this is to be expected since the members are interested in propagandizing their own achievements which in fact are non-existent. . . .

· · · ·

Friday, February 5

The day started and remained clear and warm all day. I was spared callers this day and was able to devote time to my research; finished the subject of Buddhism and government during the latter part of the Nara period [eighth century].

The statistics sent by Coverley were re-arranged [?]; discovered that the 14,599 [camp residents] was made up of 7,931 males and 6,668 females; 9,764 nisei composed of 5,002 males and 4762 females and 4,835 issei made up of 2,929 males and 1,906 females. As to age distribution, there are apparently certain margins of error. The concentration in certain age-groups makes the population rather abnormal; children are few. Minors, i.e., 17 years and below, number 4,629, leaving those 18 years and older as 9,970. There is a vast difference in the age distribution of nisei and issei, but this is [to be] expected because of the history of Japanese immigration.[78] Problems of the population are somewhat peculiar; certain ones appear in a more intensive form.

Read "Bambi" and found it delightful.

Monday, February 8

Snow continued to fall but lightly and intermittently it is, however, much colder but the snow on the ground is frozen and there are foot-long icicles from the eaves. It is naturally cloudy and gloomy. . . .

Kumasaka brought one Kurosawa [who] related about a case of divorce of a couple with a child; he told me that the husband wishes to divorce the wife if $100.00 [is] paid ostensibly in support of the child. The story is muddled as regards his threats. What has the wife done?

It is reported by Kuramotos that the case of Yamada and Iseri was settled by their marriage despite the boy's mother's opposition; Abe, the Block advisor, helped.

Ikeda's daughter's case is also settled by marriage which is to take place in the very near future.

The cases pending are two: the Inukai, Jr. and another couple both reaching the point of divorce—the blame is on the men according to the reports, but all the facts of the cases are not made clear to me. Hands off until such facts are given in full.

Tuesday, February 9

. . . .

It turned out warm in the afternoon. The weather is certainly changeable in a quick order.

Registration began.[79]

One of the soldier representatives at the Project made an address (read a prepared speech by some one higher up) which was an appeal to nisei boys to volunteer to form an exclusively Japanese combat team; this was to be trained in Mississippi and when ready will be sent where the government decides to send them. "However it will not be made to fight the Japanese enemy." Reasons so-called were clearly made in a fashion of *kodomo damashi* [hoodwinking children], as someone remarked. Not a word was said about the proposed registration of citizen women and aliens of both sexes. The form for these was to be "Application for Leave Clearance"; this fact created a good deal of anxiety and irritation among issei who felt that this would mean compulsory departures for all from the Project. It also [is] rumored that those at Manzanar refused to register.[80]

Wednesday, February 10

The day started [clear] but the ground remained frozen; later it turned out warm and the snow began to melt making the ground slushy. Called on Coverley in order to find out why the form for application for leave clearance was used for registration of alien and citizen women, 17 years and over. Frank Smith was called in and after a discussion it was decided that the caption Application for Leave Clearance be scratched out and the word Registration be substituted; the question 28 may be answered with qualification (if allowance to become a citizen of U.S.);[81] the registration is compulsory for all and the paragraph bearing on this subject be mimeographed and distributed in the Block Managers' offices to show the Washington authority. Orders and instructions will be issued in writing from the Director as regards the above changes by noon if possible. . . .

[The evening Block meeting] was well attended with numerous [representatives] from other Blocks; Kuramoto reported, and I explained the changes made and their significance together with questions that appear in the two forms to be answered.

Thursday, February 11

As the previous day it started clear and sunny; but the ground had been drained.

Fujii, a Planning Board member, and Miyake, the 31 Block Manager, came to obtain information and explanation as regards the registration forms. He stated that 80% of the Block Managers are nisei who are young and lack the art and mind to satisfy the residents.

One Kajiwara (71)[82] came and inquired how to renounce his U.S. citizenship, although possessed of real property and his brother is in the U.S. Army and parents (70 years) are in Japan. He will apply for repatriation.

One Horiuchi (11), a *kibei* [Japanese American educated in Japan] whose brother is in the U.S. Army and parents are here, wished to apply for repatriation.

. . . .

A nisei men's meeting to-night. They decided on the question 27 as "no" and 28 as "yes" but conditionally.

Yesterday Coverley said that he and his key men were glad to attend the "common folk's stag supper," except Thursdays and Sundays; these will be held by wards—about 15 men from each Block; no [other?] office holders may attend since they are to be informal and unofficial.

Saturday, February 13

It started cloudy but soon cleared up; rather cold but later warm. Mrs. Tanaka [visited] in re: two sons and a daughter.

Wrote invitation to a supper: Coverley and others; accepted it.

Tamiyasu brought a friend of his from the Ward VI, [asking] re:

registration; question 28 [and] issei and questions 27 and 28 [and] nisei.

Called on the Obanas in the evening. Somewhat cold but rather pleasant.

[Common folk's] suppers [with Coverley] must be looked after for they tend to become meaningless; i.e. the common folk may be ousted and their places be taken by the *yūshi* ["big shots"], which [defeats] the main object.

Sunday, February 14

Clear but very cold; the ground is frozen; later it became better.

Mrs. Yokota [came] in re: *geta* [wooden clogs].

Wild geese returned here after an absence of quite a while; at least they did not fly over the camp; some of these may live here permanently.

The movie show: T.B.[?] pictured Negroes and Indians. The main picture, the "Last of Mohicans." But very uncomfortable squatting on the floor.

A woman whose husband is in a concentration camp stopped and asked the same question in re: nisei registration; [she has] only one son in the family. . . .

Monday, February 15

The day started cloudy but not very cold; in fact it turned out to be a delightful day.

One Kanesaki, a *kibei*, but one who has expatriated by canceling his registration with a Japanese consulate;[83] he is with his mother while his brothers are in Japan and his father is deceased; he now wishes to apply for repatriation. It is technically doubtful; he is liable to arrest in Japan should he proceed there.

. . . .

Some of the nisei are said to have started a movement to organize the Civil Liberties Union in the Project.

The people are still in confusion, and apparently the Council and the Planning Board are either unable to reach [agreement about] what is to be discussed or else are procrastinating; Kuki of VII is being charged as a *inu* [dog—or informer], but this is nonsensical in my humble opinion. His attitude, however, is that of a dictator and hence he is apt to cause misunderstandings of all kind; he should learn to listen to others.

Coverley accepted the invitation of the VII to the supper of issei and will bring 5 or 6 of his men.

Tuesday, February 16

Already delightful almost at the dawn.

It is said that [WT], suspected as an *inu*, escaped to Chicago and his family is soon to follow: on his door was inscribed "Watch Your Steps" with a knife cut as a warning. He and Nakamura are the JACL leaders here, and the organization is said to be responsible for the present registration (volunteer for the Army).[84] The Block Manager of 70 is disliked by the people because of his dictatorial attitude. The man is [MI], from Kent, Washington.

This day a report came from the Planning Board and Council which presented . . . a series of questions relative to the registration to Coverley, asking for clarification; the questions and answers made by the latter were sent to the Block for its consideration.

A meeting was held in the evening and a report was made by K and I. Comments were made and further questions were asked. They seem to stand still where they were before. Clarification is still required both by the two groups.

. . . .

Wednesday, February 17

The day started bright and warm; it is indeed a delightful day.

The first caller was one Isozaki, a warden and a Hawaiian-born, 39 years of age.[85] He feels that he should not register because he will be denied full rights of citizenship. Birth certificates are not given to children born in this project and other projects but the reason why is not explained? [K] and [T] spotted as *inu*.

. . . .

One Tsubota and his mother 64 years old called. His brother is in the Army, now stationed in Mississippi. He would like to apply for repatriation for his family and his mother and unmarried sister. He is not in a position to volunteer or to serve.

Mr. Coverley supper is proceeding O.K. . . .

Suggested to Isozaki that older nisei help younger nisei as regards the registration. He asserted that jobs given do not pay at normal rates . . . he also stated that there are about 60 *inu* in the Project, several of whom are known to the wardens' office; some of these are females.

. . . The supper was attended by 102 [persons] and was very successful—received satisfaction. Flowers were given to the American guests and questions asked and answered. . . . Coverley said that he was informed that I was engaged in an organized movement against the "registration"; he himself did not believe it but warned me to be careful. What a nonsense! I have tried exactly the opposite, to calm the excited people to approach the matter coolly—time will do it.

Thursday, February 18

Today was delightful all day—balmy.

I wrote Coverley on behalf of Mrs. Yokota who presented him with her artificial flowers. In this note I asked Coverley to tell me the source of information as regards my alleged agitation; I shall call for it in person.[86]

I reported at the lunch time to the people of the Block about the above allegation and asked them to consider it by the Block as a whole since it [is] vital to my integrity.

One Tanabe (47) came [and] inquired about what will happen to his bank deposits if he should sign the repatriation [form?]. Answer: I don't know.

Fujii, the hospital janitor, was arrested and was told that he would be placed in the Klamath Falls jail because he, under the influence of drink, beat and injured another who has to stay at the hospital for 4 or 5 days, though his injury is not very serious. He was brought here at his request by Tsuda, the Investigation Chief. I pleaded for once to be lenient. He agreed that he should be jailed. . . .

. . . .

Sunday, February 21

Started gloomy but later cleared up for a while. . . .

Shirai, [and four others] came; his mother made *udon* [a type of noodle] and the chef made pies; we were enjoying these when at about 5:30 suddenly news reached [us] that about 10 soldiers equipped with machine guns and bayonetted rifles went to Block 42 and arrested 34 nisei who had been told to register on Friday but who had signed a statement that they (31 of these) would not register.[87] On Friday afternoon they were told by Jacoby to [re]consider and were given time until Monday when they were to register. The move on the part of the Administration on Sunday was a surprise. Two messengers came to this ward asking for three representatives to participate in a session to be held in their Block to discuss the situation. I [was] asked to notify Kuki and Kuramoto as to what should be done; no representatives were sent; asked Shirai, Watanabe and Nakamura to go to the Block to find out facts of the case. One Kawayoshi from 46 came and asked me to tell the boys of his Block to register because he himself had failed; my answer was [it was] too late and might worsen the situation. Before this time two mothers [came] with Mrs. N; they were told to decide first and then come. [Kenji] Ito came: The boys taken to Alturas, 60 miles from here; Iseri of 70 was quizzed by about 15 boys. The same night, the Council and the Planning Board held extraordinary sessions; the Council decided upon these proposals to present to the Administration: (1) [admit] its own mistake, (2) the arrested boys should be released, (3) a general strike if these demands are [not] met with. The sessions lasted until 1 A.M.

◻ Tensions rapidly mounted at Tule Lake after the arrest of the nisei, with authorities eventually taking into custody 140 persons. Many of these were subsequently sent to special concentration camps, and some were even convicted and jailed in regular prisons. "You can't imagine how close we came to machine-gunning the whole bunch of them," a camp official was quoted as saying. "The only thing that stopped us, I suppose, were the effects such a shooting would have had on the Japs holding our boys in Manila and China . . . and the fact that, in all these Tule Lake riots, a lot of Japs here got hurt fighting for us."[88]

For weeks, the camp at large was plagued by repeated threats of violence, rumormongering, and beatings. The tense atmosphere is reflected in the Ichihashis' diary entries and letters of the next few days. ◼

DIARY

Monday, February 22

Rain changed to snow but sun came, therefore it melted as it fell.
Called at the Administration at 11:00 and [was] rejected; came

back at noon; both the Council and the Planning Board resigned in body. A meeting is called for the evening to decide what is to be done: [the idea of a] strike left undecided by the resigned.

The meeting heard Kuramoto, the Planning Board representative's report on the incident and the resignation of the Council and the Board en masse; elected Tanabe as its new representative because Kuramoto who received a majority vote refused to serve.

Tuesday, February 23

The day started somewhat cloudy but snappy and crisp.

Sent Frank [Matsumoto] to the Administration to inform it that nisei girls are afraid to cover the distance because of possible violence on the way; come to get them or send the forms here for registration. The answer is o.k.: three registrants were sent and all except Mrs. Funai registered. The *Oregonian*, *Chronicle* and *Examiner* carried the story of 37 boys taken into custody; it is an accurate account, except the number accepted, without customary exaggeration.

Wakayama reported what had taken place last night in the Block among *kibei*; warned him to suppress it as it might develop into a *yabu-hebi* [stirring up a hornet's nest]. The arrested boys should not be made a part of any proposals.

Coverley warned fathers and mothers not to obstruct their sons' registration.

Major Marshall issued a statement relative to implications of possible answers to the questions 27 and 28.

Obana called and talked about helping to pacify the intense feeling; let it subside with time.

. . . .

KEI ICHIHASHI TO JESSIE TREAT [89]

Tule Lake
Feb. 24 [1943]

Dear Mrs. Treat:

Since the day of our evacuation the outside world must have changed in many ways. Food rationing, the shortage of meat: these things must create quite [big] problems for house wives. It is difficult to realize that in a place like Stanford University, there should have occurred so many changes. We are very grateful to you for the campus news.

It is nice to learn that the new president of the University was elected; it has solved one of the long-standing important problems of the University. Everybody interested must now feel quite satisfied.

The news of Mr. White's presidency of Mills College rather surprised us.[90] I have wished that he could become the president of a better college. It seems to me that he is progressing a little too fast. I am very sorry to hear that Mrs. Martin is ill.[91] I hope that she will recover completely in a short time.

We have been leading a monotonous life as usual, but Mr. Ichihashi has been very busy in helping the people in trouble. However during the last three weeks the people in this project have been excited so much that they have not done their own work earnestly; they have been and still are talking about the same thing day in day out; they are worrying themselves without an end. It is the problem of registration for both young and old people.

The very interesting thing is that young people are very serious this time, and do not yield very easily. I am not able to write in detail, but some thirty-seven young men were arrested and held in jails. I think you already know all about it through newspapers. Day and night so many anxious people young and old, fathers and mothers, all call on Mr. Ichihashi for consultation. We both are bothered so much that we can not do our own work. During the day time I cannot do anything, yet when evening comes I am very tired.

The people here all anticipated very cold weather at Tule Lake, but the climate is not so bad. Lately we enjoyed nice weather; in fact it was so warm that we did not need the fire in the afternoon in our apartment. Yesterday and today it snowed a little and the wind was rather cold, but the sun was quite warm. Our neighbors are mostly Oregonians and Washingtonians and are rather surprised because of the rather mild climate.

Very fortunately we both have been and are quite healthy despite the poor food we have been eating. I am not losing my weight much, but Mr. Ichihashi did, and is getting thinner. I hope you are all very well and are enjoying comfortable weather. Please give our best wishes to Prof. Treat.

Affectionately yours,
Kei Ichihashi

p.s. Mr. Ichihashi received a letter from Mr. Treat scolding him for his habitual weakness;[92] he asks me to say that he will reply as soon as he gets rid of his headache developed from over-work for a couple of months.

YAMATO ICHIHASHI TO PAYSON TREAT [93]

Tule Lake, California
February 26, 1943

Dear Payson:

Thanks for the kind letter; I don't blame you and lest I succumb to my disease, and I sit down [to] scribble, but three times I have been interrupted; [these] break up the thread of my thought each time and this is the fourth time I am starting; this time with the door blocked from the inside. It is difficult to count the number of days during which I failed to communicate. Well, thousands of apologies, especially for the failure to acknowledge the receipt of the nice diary which has been in use regularly since the beginning of the year. I hope it will prove valuable for future [reference?].

At the time of my evacuation, I decided on a plan to write letters to my friends, which would contain matters of historical interest in a serial form. But unfortunately this blue-print, like all others, has apparently turned out to be a mere blue-print and nothing more. For one thing, I was compelled to repeat and I despise repetition. These remarks are not made to explain my failure.

In my last note, I tried to give a description of the physical set up and the personnel of the Administration and the agencies together with a brief comment upon their relationships. Since then the so-called "self-government" was rendered permanent by reorganization. The City Council with 28 nisei members (4 from each ward); this is the organ of "self-government"; the members serve without pay. To meet the dissatisfaction of issei excluded from it, the so-called Planning Board was instituted; it has seven members. These seven were elected from among the Block Representatives, some 60 in number, elected from among issei by the public at large, always meaning those males and females 18 years old and over. This Board of Seven often summons the remaining Block representatives to sit in some of their sessions. The function of the Board is advisory, but from the beginning, the Board (its seven members) acted as if they were the *Genrō* [oligarchs] and so, they were soon labeled *Genri*, or "Elder Statesmen." They, however discovered that two of their number were running the show; when the people discovered this, they laughed at the five and began to criticize the manipulators. The institution thereafter seemed to have lost its prestige, if it had any. The *Genrō* became a joke, though perhaps they themselves remained unaware. *Another interruption for 4 hours, including the supper.* At any rate, whether the above assertion is true or not, politics is one of those things beyond my power of comprehension.

In the closing days of the last year, the Project Director named Shirrell resigned to accept another assignment, and his place was taken by Harvey M. Coverley, a Stanford '24, and one who did both the pro-seminar and seminar with me. I met him for the first time since his graduation. He is a likeable chap and I hope that he can escape from any trouble. The Project population is in an abnormal state of mind and requires a very skillful handling.

What has been happening at the University? Kei and I can learn only from you and your madam; others have been writing me but without giving me any specific information. I am sad to hear of a general disorganization of the Department, the building of which I too worked 30 years. Lynn [White] is apparently disappointed of this fact and this fact perhaps led him to his decision to accept the presidency of Mills College. Nevertheless, I feel his decision a mistake; his scholarly career will likely end and that will be a loss to himself and to the academic world. I only hope that he will return to his scholarly life before it is too late.

I have tried hard but fail to recall Dr. Tresidder and his wife. However Kei and I join you in the hope that our University will regain its true position under the wise guidance of the new President. I need not tell you how I love the institution as one of its sons.

I have been struggling to carry on my research under the circumstances most difficult yet encountered, despite the continued coming of poor, helpless people with many different problems, some of which are utterly unfamiliar to me: romances, domestic troubles, legal complications, but no intellectual problems. I try to help them, but alas. I have organized several essays (mostly in Japanese) on the topics that fall within the scope of my research.[94] I have used some of these as the basis of a series of lectures I gave throughout the camp (from ward to ward); these went well as far as I could tell. The people beg me to continue, but I am forced to quit for awhile because there are too many things that keep me very busy. And I am physically and mentally exhausted due to overwork and to the lack of necessary vitamins. But one cannot complain because the food situation in general, I understand, is unsatisfactory.

The weather has been unusual; we have had a veritable mixture of extremes—agreeable and disagreeable; one cannot be too careful for one is apt to be taken by a surprise. I have put winter underwears on again. Despite all Kei, Woodie and the old man have so far escaped any serious calamities; for this we are grateful because many are in the hospital.

Finally I shall mention the fact that we are having a little trouble in the camp just at present as you have doubtless seen in newspapers, but I hope that it will blow off soon. It is due to some misunderstandings which, I feel sure, time will solve, and when it is finished, I will tell you if it is worthwhile.

It is hoped that this note will find both you and your madam in the best of health. Please remember us to my colleagues and their families when you have opportunities.

> Affectionately yours
> Yamato Ichihashi

DIARY

Monday, March 1

The morning was snappy; mist shrouded the sky, though the sun appears red.

. . . .

Wild geese in large numbers seen; they fly low and show themselves big and fat; there are *hiyoko* [chicks, young geese] among flocks.

The day passed quietly around here. But during the last few days several were beaten, but only two seriously.

Received two notes from Wilbur: one stating that I am to be Professor Emeritus, effective September 1.[95] The other stating that the University pays me a pension. . . .

. . . .

Tuesday, March 2

The day started bright and clear, but a cold breeze blows.

B. Nakamura (48) came and stated that he has three sons, two of whom have already registered, but the 3rd has not; [he] should register regardless [of] what is being told, if that is his own desire. Four more boys were picked up for refusal [to register?] at Administration where it is being [carried out?]. This is the last day for nisei registration.

Male citizen registration extended until March 10th—Coverley notice in the *Dispatch*. Yasuda has been asked to convert the recalcitrants. The 73 [Block?] boys' registration went satisfactorily.

A number of boys and men were picked up today also: these and others including the original 37 are said to be kept in a Civilian Conservation Corp camp not very far from here, 7–16 miles according to [hearsay?].

Wardens are asked to watch males whom the Internal Security agents pick up between 12 and 5 A.M.

Wednesday, March 3

The day started snappy, but is clearing; later it became somewhat cloudy.

Today begins the registration of aliens.

Mrs. Hansen, a teacher, called; she is interested in tracing dragons as a symbol all over the world; its origin being in Egypt, according to her idea, whence it spread elsewhere, touching important parts of the world.

Yoshikawa (47) and Miko (42) called. The latter stated that the Block Manager took a positive stand and told nisei to register: the reaction [was] that 37 [nisei] revolted and 19 registered; the blame is that he did not leave choice for niseis' free will. Some laugh at the stupidity of the revolting nisei, many of whom are young. Their parents are worried over the 20 year sentences. Cars pass every night during the period between barracks almost every 5 minutes and no one can sleep. Four couples got separated on the stand of the husbands; the wives were picked up. Every day some ones are picked up. The extension means a further suffering. The 37 are separated into three groups. There still exists fear that the registration will result in compulsory departure from here.* It is doubted that issei there will register.

· · · ·

---

*The prospect of re-establishing life outside the camps and away from the West Coast, which the WRA had begun promoting, frightened many internees, especially the older ones, since no support was offered and there was much hostility toward persons of Japanese ancestry.

Thursday, March 4

Started hazy though cleared up later and turned out to be very delightful.

The situation seems to be subsiding, although the Administration is rather nervous about it yet. The *Dispatch* is made to carry a number of items relative to the registration; at this late date questions and answers relative to the male nisei still appear. The suspended social amenities started again as well as adult education and other recreational activities. The postponed movies held at the Mess Hall 74.

Sato gave us a folding chair.

Mrs. Kuramoto stopped by and had tea after the show.

"Steel Facts" reached me addressed here! [96]

Friday, March 5

Started hazy again but soon began clearing. Nevertheless it is colder than usual for [this] spring-like weather.

. . . .

Registration of issei is still [proceeding] with some difficulty; this is true of nisei; in fact, some 54 asked the Administration to [take] them to the C.C.C. where others picked up are now quartered. The matter is not handled intelligently.

Borrowed and read the report of Inter-Project Cooperatives Conference and found it interesting; it was held at Salt Lake City, Feb. 14–16. Six sessions in all and discussed various problems experienced and the proposed pool buying. [97] Those represented were Minidoka, Topaz, Heart Mountain, Tule Lake, with Americans representing the projects. . . .

Saturday, March 6

George Danzuka (1606-B) married to an Indian and has 4 children and is 53 years old. [98] Asked me to help him to get back to his Indian River home in central Oregon. Told him to bring a memo of his career.

Woodrow came as did Matsumoto. Found out the rumor to be baseless, [99] but advised the former to move here to avoid further complications. Sakuhara [100] asked him not to call on his girl and the girl was told to [do] the same. He will move in here when a truck is available. He is working in the slaughter house having quit the band.

There was a mixture of sun-shine and cloudy [weather], the latter dominating with showers. . . . Went with the K and saw the 22 Mess Hall exhibition of craft works; some are excellent.

Sunday, March 7

It rained early in the morning; but it stopped later. It continues cloudy. Advised Woodrow to move here immediately.

. . . .

Coal crew struck because they were told to work 8 hours instead [of] 4 which was in operation as a custom. Not much being said about the registration but which is by no means solved.

Rain falls off and on.

Monday, March 8

The rain stopped but it remains cloudy and warm.

One Mrs. Iseki, a nisei woman (46), with 2 sons and 2 daughters, came and stated that the sons would not register despite her pleas to do so. She was quite emotional and cried often. What would be their penalty; what could be done about it?

Abe, the barber, came and trimmed hair.

Informed that those in C.C.C. get only two meals; the living quarters are concrete floored and cold; Wakayamas asked for more clothes and blankets from here.

Ito came in re: calligraphy.

It rained toward the evening.

McEvoy's article on the "110,000 evacuees" has many points of interest (originally in the *Baltimore Sun*, condensed in the March issue of *Reader's Digest*).

Dispatch (3/9/43) reports that on the 5th, the Project population was 14,860; these changes are due to emigration to and immigration from other camps and elsewhere.

Tuesday, March 9

Somewhat cloudy but soon cleared up; snappy but crisp and delightful morning. Turned out to be a beautiful day.
    Prepared the Federal Income Tax Returns and mailed registered.
    The coal crew at present consists of 200 men with 5 foremen.
About 2 weeks ago, they were told to work 8 hours per day instead
of 4 hours, hitherto worked on the grounds of hardship; a few days
ago, the crew stopped working until the question is clarified. The
4 hour understanding? Was in effect for at least 6 [weeks?]? The new
demand is unreasonable according to the foreman (Motomachi,
1317-B, an old man and Yoshida, 5203-C, a young nisei) [they] came
to consult. Advised to form a negotiation committee to present the
matter to the Planning Board for seeking a solution. At present,
some high school boys are being employed to take the place of the
regular crew which has been declared to be "insubordinate" and discharged. The Administration's proposal is to reduce the crew of 200
to that of 100 with 8 hours of work. The present crew should be
controlled not to work until a solution is found; see to it that no new
crew is formed. The kids are a temporary measure, though under
Thompson, the new foreman. No violence under any circumstances.
                                   . . . .

Thursday, March 11

The day started bright but rather snappy: there was frost on the
ground and the barrack roofs.
    Fujii (1206-D) came and told me that he attempted to register at
8:15 last night but [S?] Tsukahara who was [there] registering others was told by Carroll not to register Fujii who was unable to answer immediately why [he] had not registered earlier. Nakaya
(1407-C) failed to register though he had wished to do so from the
beginning because his mother threatened him to *kandō suru* [disown]
if he did. Both hoped [there] would be another chance to do so.
    In the evening Fujii's mother with her daughter came and showed
[me] his petition to Coverley and Carroll that he be allowed to register. As to answers, I refused to advise and made a correction so as
not to involve anybody else, even indirectly.
    One of the Matsushima girls located near J[acoby?]'s office told
Frank that she spotted some F.B.I.s coming and going from that of-

fice. She is positive that an *inu* gets $50 if he has one get out of the Project for the usual destination. Interesting.

Frank was bothered about pushing the C.L.L. assembly;[101] he refused to be involved on the ground that the men behind this new organization are the same men who have been active in the J.A.C.L., which seems to have lost its popularity with the nisei at large.

Friday, March 12

The day started nice and clear, but it turned out cloudy in the afternoon; even rain fell though very lightly. Toward the evening it became cold and disagreeable.

One Morimura (46) came to ask for reference books on the history of Japan and Chinese: will recommend Sansom on Japan and Latourette on China.[102]

Ito brought 2 newspapers and stayed for a while. He discussed the newly proposed Civil Liberty League which will hold a second mass meeting tonight. Nothing concrete was reached at the first meeting. Asked him to inform me about the meet's outcome.

The situation appears to be quiet.

Kuramoto told me of one who is at (42) and finds himself uncomfortable where he [is] because his stand is not that of the Block residents. He would like to move out from his present residence; the situation is too hot.

It is asserted that there must be a few hundred in the C.C.C.; 200 more beds were recently sent there from this place. Since the cook left the camp due to too many daily changes, lunches are prepared at the 72 Mess Hall and sent there every day.

Saturday, March 13

It rained considerably during the last night, and the day started cloudy; it may rain again. Later a strong southerly wind, almost a gale started to blow; in the afternoon, some showers.

It was said that the object of the new Civil Liberty League was primarily to raise funds to aid Yasui in his trial case.*

---

*Minoru Yasui, a nisei graduate of the University of Oregon Law School and officer in the U.S. Army Reserve, was one of several Japanese Americans who challenged the consti-

Kei went and found Woodrow had changed his mind about moving here.

. . . .

Monday, March 15

The day started and remained cold all day.

This was the deadline for registration; the day's schedule was for the Ward VII and Kei and I went to #6608 to register and Mrs. Sodemann, Stanford '24, registered me and at her request I registered Kei. There were about 50 men and women when we reached there. The form used was amended as to the caption, namely from application for leave clearance to "registration" and [question] #28, to an oath to abide by the U.S. law and to act no wise against its war efforts.[103] Mrs. Sodemann promised to obtain income tax forms. In the afternoon (1–5) I helped the people in explaining the points they were not clear about as well as in registration: the nisei registrars [had] language difficulties. I registered Ikeda in person.

Called at the Kuramotos: he was still afraid of what others might say. It is hoped for no more trouble over this task, which was unfortunately bungled up in the beginning by [administration] mishandling. All the consequent troubles could have easily [been] avoided by a little more intelligence; of this I am quite sure.

Wednesday, March 17

It started a little warmer but cloudy; not particularly pleasant.

Danzuka came to check his memo; brought some nice oranges; asked him to keep an eye on Woodrow.

The situation relative to registration seems to be subsiding; the

---

tutionality of the evacuation order. In March 1942 in Portland, Oregon, Yasui deliberately violated the curfew restriction placed on persons of Japanese ancestry and had the police arrest him. One year later, the U.S. Court of Appeals for the Ninth Circuit referred his appeal of the conviction to the U.S. Supreme Court, which upheld the lower court's decision on his curfew violation. Through this and three other test cases, the Supreme Court upheld the constitutionality of relocation and internment. See Irons, *Justice at War*. (Two other challenges are described in the footnote on p. 371.) It is likely that Ichihashi had met Yasui in 1935 at the Second America-Japan Student Conference at Reed College, where Ichihashi was a featured speaker and Yasui a student delegate. The two were also involved in the 1937 Conference at Stanford. Caitlin James to author, March 28 and May 15, 1995.

soldier agents sent here from Washington, D.C. left the camp. [?]
according to serious allegations (rumors) from 400 to 500 nisei boys,
including those in the C.C. camp, have not registered.

. . . .

Thursday, March 18

The day started cloudy and very cold, but clouds began to disappear
from about 9:30; it remains rather cold.
　Mrs. Koga (7403-E), a widow, called to see what can be done
about changing the #27 and #28 answers *no* and *no* in [her son's]
registration; nothing [can be done, in] so far as it is known at present. Her son desires to change from no's to *no* and *yes*. She was told
to register herself.
　Ito brought "Time." . . .

. . . .

An invitation to [attend] an assembly of the Red Cross to be held
on next Sunday; wants money from aliens? About $2000.00 is said to
have been collected here thus far?

Friday, March 19

The day started clear but rather cold; later warm—cold wind.
　Danzuka brought his registration number, but not his family
number.
　The deadline for aliens and female citizen registration was set at
the 15th but extended till the 20th; but it is again [put back] until the
24th. It is generally said that 50% of the aliens and 25% of the male
and female citizens have not registered to date. Last night at the issei
conference, Coverley said that no definite action was decided as regards those aliens who fail to register, but the WRA has the authority to meet out some penalties. It is to be wondered.

Saturday, March 20

It started somewhat misty but later cleared up and turned to be
rather a warm day, like a spring day.
　Danzuka brought his family number and some cigars.
　Mrs. Nakatsuka came relative to a place where *ikebana* [flower ar-

ranging] lessons may be had in the Block and also for an exhibition; it depends on the number of persons interested since the monopoly of any place by a few is bound to create a hostile attitude in the Block.

. . . .

Woodrow did not come.

KEI ICHIHASHI TO JESSIE TREAT [104]

March 20 [1943]

Dear Mrs. Treat:

I am sending a box by parcel-post today. It contains artificial flowers: a tree-peony, some Easter lilies and some gardenias. When I packed them in the box, I bent the stems and fastened them on the bottom with wires. Please cut wires first and then take them out, and unbend the stems until they are straight. If you stick the Easter lilies in an earthen flower pot, they will be more effective I think.

The other day I went to see an art exhibition again. This time there were hundreds of flower vases there, some of which were just marvelous; but the artists did not sell their works. In our block too our people are planning to have an art exhibition in near future. Almost every man is making some artistic things to exhibit, even Mr. Ichihashi will exhibit a desk—he did not make it though—one of the neighbors made it for him the last fall. It is a beautifully-made desk, though an amateur's work. It is wonderful; some day he will show you the desk, as he is intending to take it with him to the campus.

The registration which I mentioned before has not been finished. Some of the people have been so disturbed by this registration, they are still worrying about it. The registrators are all the high school and grade school teachers, so that schools have been closed more than seven weeks now. It is just too bad.

The climate is very changeable here, one evening it was very cold and snow fell, then the following day it was nice and warm. The climate in high altitudes seems quite suitable to my health. The last few years, I had a flu every winter, but this time I did not have even a bad cold. I spent my childhood in a high altitude place in Japan, and its climate is very much like here. Since I came up here, I can enjoy this climate—atmosphere—very much.

At the campus it is about examination time and every body must be very busy. However, the real nice spring weather must be approaching at the same time.

I hope both of you are very well and enjoying the nice spring.

Affectionately yours,
Kei Ichihashi

P.S. Mr. Ichihashi is still preoccupied with many anxious people who continue to come to him for advice. He is very tired but is trying to help them.

DIARY

Tuesday, March 23

It started somewhat cloudy but soon cleared up and turned out warm and pleasant.

Mrs. Kuramoto brought one Yorozuya, already blind of one eye and is in danger of loosing the other; no doctor has been able to help him and therefore he would like to have the priority in [this] facility [to go to] Japan where he thinks he could find necessary care. He is alone here; his wife passed away recently and he has no relatives in this country. Advised [him] to obtain a doctor's certificate relative to his case as the first step.

Wednesday, March 24

It started and remained cloudy but no rain and warm.

. . . .

Five boys . . . desire to change their answer "no" to the question 28 to "yes" of their own accord. Write, as instructed, to Provo Marshall General, Munitions Building, Washington, D.C. for permission to do so with the reason or explanation. . . . Females write, for the same purpose, to WRA, Barr Building, Washington, D.C.

Saturday, March 27

The day started clear and beautiful from dawn.

Mrs. Kuramoto came and invited us to supper; stayed until 9:00 listening to records.

Ba Maw spoke over radio from Tokyo; [105] news as usual is quite the opposite [from] what one reads in newspapers and hears over radio here.

Sunday, March 28

It started slightly cloudy with rather a cold wind, a wind storm in fact.

It is asserted that about 53 mostly Hawaiians and [Northwesterners?] will volunteer from this Project to join the proposed combat team. This is a surprisingly small number on the basis of population here and in view of the prevalent sentiment among nisei [who] desire to leave for the outside for any kind of opportunity, including the armed services. . . .

Monday, March 29

The wind storm which had begun last night, continued into the dawn, kicking up sands as usual since this is a veritable desert and filling the living quarters with them and covering the floor thick with these dirty sands. In the morning, rain began to accompany [the wind] so that a real storm of wind, southerly, and rain began to prevail. Rain should help in keeping the sand from being blown skyward and then drop down toward the earth. This is decidedly a nasty day. The rain changed about 10:00AM into a rather heavy snow and almost simultaneously the gale ended.

The radio announced the sinking of two cruisers and 2 destroyers and 8,000 ton transport and a 5,000 ton vessel. The Nanking government declared war in the middle of January 1943 and is preparing the 3rd anniversary celebration of its re-entry in that city: Japan abrogated her extraterritorial rights and several others followed her example. Concessions are to be restored also.[106]

The gale started again about 3:00PM.

Mr. Tanabe informed [me] that an exhibition of *ikebana* (5 styles) are simultaneously beginning today for 4 days in different wards. At 4:00 both the snow and the gale stopped and then the sun began to shine, melting the snow on the ground. Crazy weather, if there is such [a thing]. This changed again: snow or a gale followed at 4:30—oh la la!—and continued into the night.

Tuesday, March 30

It started clear but with a strong cold southerly wind; thus the spring weather suddenly changed into a winter day and it is really cold.
Radio heard from 8 on till usual times.
Danzuka came, bringing apples.
Mrs. K and Kei went to see *ikebana* exhibitions.

. . . .

Wednesday, March 31

It started clear but with a cold wind; it is a wintry [day]. However, it later turned out to be a nice warm day, somewhat cloudy.

. . . .

The Red Cross drive is on with the goal of $1250 here; difficult for issei to enthusiastically respond to it under the circumstances in which they find themselves.

[Secretary of War Henry L.] Stimson: more than 1,000 volunteered (March 25) from the relocation centers; the combat team to be organized for European service of these and those already in the army and others (Camp Shelby, Mississippi is isolated from any town according to Sergeant Kuramoto and therefore no shopping is possible [he wrote] in a recent letter to his father). Washington seeks Buddhist chaplain for the team—Ha Ha!—233 volunteers from Poston, Colorado, the largest of all the projects.[107] . . .

Started to read Anna Seghers' "The Seventh Cross."[108]

KEI ICHIHASHI TO JESSIE TREAT [109]

Tule Lake
April 1 [1943]

Dear Mrs. Treat:

I imagine you had a very gay time attending at the launching ceremony of the "David Starr Jordan,"[110] and old Mrs. Jordan must have felt very much satisfied. It reminded me of the launching ceremony of a man of war at Yokosuka, the naval port near Tokyo.[111] I forgot the ship's name as it was long time ago. Anyhow it was a great occasion. Something happened, so that I could not go there, but my friends who attended the ceremony talked about its wonders for the following several days. It must have been very exciting.

I am sorry to hear of Mrs. Harris' death.[112] She was always so frail; one day she told me: "I can not live for [long?] after forty." It is so sad.

Thank you very much for the box of candies, they are so precious for me. Most of the people in the project have not tasted candies for a long time; even cookies are pretty hard to get here. So that many people are trying to make confections with breakfast foods such as corn flakes, puffed rice and wheat which they save instead of eating at the breakfast time. They harden these with honey or syrup (we can not get sugar of course) by heating the mixture on the stove and then cut it into small pieces. They sometimes add peanuts or walnuts into them; they taste pretty good and the people enjoy them very much with their tea.

We in the project are denied so many things; we have no freedom. As I do not expect anything, I do not suffer. But then those who live in free towns are also suffering in so many ways. I really feel sorry for them.

It is very nice of you to keep your mind on our house and garden. We mended our roof as much as we could before we left the campus last May, I hope it did not leak very badly.

When you see Misses Stoltenbergs please remember us to them, and if you don't mind, please give them one of the artificial flowers.

Now, I will tell you an interesting thing. If you have time try the radio between 9:30 and 11:00 a.m. every morning, you will get an Oriental broadcast.[113] They send quite interesting news as well as war prisoners' messages. Even a long-wave radio set can get them, if it is a good one. Set the radio about 170[?] on the dial, which is almost toward the end. The whole broadcast is rather amazing and entertaining.

I hope this note finds you and Prof. Treat in the best of health.

> Affectionately yours,
> Kei Ichihashi

◙ The Ichihashis' spirits remained high despite the turmoil around them in camp. Yamato, though busy with camp affairs and counseling fellow residents, still found time to develop his research material on his internment experience. He collected camp notices, completed a chronology of major camp events in 1942–43, and closely read issues of the *Dispatch* for news and anecdotes as well as statistical information on the camp and its residents, such as annual rainfall, gallons of water used daily, acreage under cultivation, and so forth.[114]

Kei, meanwhile found enjoyable activities to occupy her time. She attended craft classes and, like many other issei women, may have found an unusual degree of personal latitude in camp, with little cooking or other traditional domestic chores expected of her. The Christian minister Daisuke Kitagawa later wrote in a memoir that the issei women at Tule Lake "became unwittingly the happiest people in the relocation center." Probably exaggerating to emphasize the toll camp took on issei men who found themselves stripped of dignity and responsibility, he commented that the women "even began to look younger."[115] ◗

Tule Lake Relocation Center under construction, April 1942. (Record Group 210, National Archives)

Tule Lake Relocation Center. (Record Group 210, National Archives)

This page: Lunchtime for workers on the farm at Tule Lake. (Record Group 210, National Archives)

September 7, 1942, at Tule Lake. The WRA caption to this photo reads: "A fashion show was one of the many exhibits held at this relocation center on labor day. Great skill was shown in dressmaking and tailoring, and was thoroughly appreciated by the large audience which witnessed this display." (Record Group 210, National Archives)

September 7, 1942, at Tule Lake. The WRA caption reads: "A parade was held by evacuees to celebrate labor day. Great originality in costuming was shown." (Record Group 210, National Archives)

Print and film journalists and representatives of the Office of War Information at Tule Lake, May 1943. "Emperor of Tule Lake," the news article on Ichihashi, appeared after this visit. Milton Silverman is the eighth standing person from the left. (Record Group 210, National Archives)

A view of the Amache center, from the water tower. (Record Group 210, National Archives)

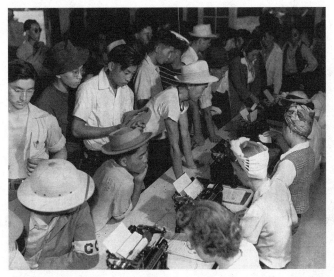

Early arrivals at Amache, August 1942. (Record Group 210, National Archives)

Summer carnival at Amache, no date. (Record Group 210, National Archives)

Amache, August 30, 1942. The WRA caption reads: "Two days after arrival and the first Sunday afternoon finds these volunteer workers of the first contingent have arranged their barracks as comfortably as possible and are spending an afternoon much in the manner of young folks anywhere else." (Record Group 210, National Archives)

Amache, December 10, 1942. The WRA caption reads: "An evening class in the adult education section who are taking up second-year German. Note that among the students of Japanese ancestry, there is also in regular attendance a caucasian grade school teacher." (Record Group 210, National Archives)

December 24, 1943. The WRA caption reads: "Christmas at the Granada Relocation Center didn't provide a Christmas tree for each barracks room home, but there was one at each mess hall, and it is the steward himself in a pair of red pajamas and a Santa Claus mask that makes the yuletide real for these children of Japanese ancestry who, along with their parents, were evacuated from the West coast." (Record Group 210, National Archives)

Block managers with supplies from the Japanese Red Cross, 1944(?). (Record Group 210, National Archives)

July 4, 1944, summer carnival at Amache. (Record Group 210, National Archives)

August 5, 1944, memorial service in the high school auditorium for six nisei from Amache who died in the fighting in Italy. (Record Group 210, National Archives)

This granite monument, erected in memory of the Amache residents who died in camp, was dedicated on September 6, 1945. Names of 148 persons, including 31 nisei who died in the war, are inscribed on the stone. (Record Group 210, National Archives)

The last of the residents of Amache leave for home; the camp closed on October 15, 1945. (Record Group 210, National Archives)

something exhilarating in living in these great hours, months and years of decision. I believe that if we place first things first, if we can have this human understanding, if we can have these essential charac-

teristics, then men and women can build a world of peace based upon righteousness, a world which will be fit for our children and our children's children and generations yet unborn.

JAPANESE AMERICAN RELATION

—Dr. Yamato Ichihashi

The Speaker's Table at the monthly luncheon meeting of the America-Japan Society on September 25, 1953 at the Industry Club of Japan, Marunouchi, Tokyo. Shown in the picture are, left to right: Dr. Yamato Ichihashi, Professor Emeritus of Stanford University, Mr. Takashi Komatsu, President of the Society, and Mrs. Margaret H. Williams, Cultural Attache of the American Embassy.

The following address by Dr. Yamato Ichihashi, Professor Emeritus of Stanford University, was delivered at the America-Japan Society's monthly luncheon meeting on September 25 at the Industry Club of Japan, Marunouchi, Tokyo.

Mr. Komatsu, Honored Guests, Ladies and Gentlemen:

With your permission, I would like to review the significant events in a century-old history of American-Japanese relations. The first half of the relationship was friendly, but the latter half was quite otherwise. Such a review may, therefore, provide, I hope, a perspective for more intelligent understanding of the current issues that confront our two countries. The subject is a touchy one, and my view on it may provoke misgivings from the mixed membership of the Society. So in order to avoid such a possibility, let me indulge your patience to preface this talk with a brief sketch of a peculiar life which the circumstances forced me to lead.

Exactly 50 years ago, I entered Stanford University as a freshman, specializing in economics. Between 1908 and 1910, I worked for the U.S. Congressional Immigration Commission and gathered information on Japanese immigrants residing in the Pacific Coast States. Then I went to Harvard to complete my graduate studies. In 1913 I joined the Stanford faculty. That year saw the enactment of California's first Alien Land Law. That was the culmination of 13-year-old anti-Japanism. As is well-known, it created a tension between the two peoples.

President Jordan of Stanford University, who was disturbed by the situation, felt the need of disseminating true knowledge about Japan, assigned me the task of teaching the domestic history of that country. But

it was a subject for which I had had no academic training. Therefore, for several years, I was allowed to straddle between the two departments of economics and history. I offered courses on "the principles of population" and "immigration problems in the United States" and also an elementary course on "Japanese history." Thereafter, however, I concentrated efforts on my main job. In such a way, a trained economist became camouflaged as a historian—a strange hybrid student, and I remained as such until my retirement.

While I was teaching, I was called upon to assist the Japanese Government as well as some private organizations in certain of their international conferences. Thus unwittingly I served two masters simultaneously. This fact proved, at times, to be rather embarrassing. For instance, during the war my wife and I with our son had to live in veritable concentration camps for three years.

At this same time, I am happily aware also of the fact that some 35 of my students were in Japan during the Occupation Period, and functioned intelligently and sympathetically because of their knowledge of Japan and her people. Moreover, some 30 of my students are now teaching history, economics, social sciences, international relations, etc., in American colleges and universities; while three are holding important diplomatic posts, including that of the Australian High Commissioner to India.

I am now an old man of 75, and a professor emeritus. That means I am an unemployed, free man, having no obligation to any master and subject to no pressure or restrictions, save to maintain a sense of decency toward fellow humans. I have no desire to deliberately offend anybody's feelings, but I will adhere to truth, even if it may hurt. My only ambition now is to

The first page of the text of Yamato Ichihashi's address to the America-Japan Society on September 25, 1953. With Ichihashi in the photo, taken at the Japan Industry Club, are Komatsu Takashi, president of the society, and Margaret H. Williams, cultural attache of the United States embassy. *The America-Japan Society Bulletin* 4 (1953). (Special Collections, Green Library, Stanford)

Tule Lake–Amache

April 1, 1943–
September 4, 1943

I chihashi enjoyed privileged status at Tule Lake. Camp residents bestowed on him respect and deferential treatment; he had the energetic support of influential friends and colleagues back at Stanford; former Stanford students, such as camp director Harvey Coverley, and the academics who populated the camp administration valued his opinion; and, on top of all else, he had an inside track to the highest levels of the WRA. Lisette Fast, the close companion of Edgar Robinson and Kei's good friend, was the sister-in-law of Ethel Barker Fast, personal secretary to Dillon S. Myer, the director of the WRA.[1] Ethel Fast's husband, Emery Fast, had attended Stanford graduate school and was a good friend of Ichihashi's. While there is no evidence that Ichihashi ever expected privileged treatment because of his former position or his personal connections, he always knew that he had special channels available to him. And though in actual practice, he often did enjoy exceptional considerations, these did not help him avoid the wearing grind of camp life that steadily took its toll on him and his family.

From the early days of internment, the federal government allowed some Japanese Americans to leave confinement on temporary furlough, usually for agricultural work in areas near their camp, or, in the case of nisei college students, to enroll in schools outside the restricted zone. In addition, the government also recruited internees for work in military language schools and then later into military service. But following the registration crisis, evacuees faced further challenges when the WRA increased pressure on all residents to "resettle" out of the camps to the Midwest or East Coast. Ichihashi recounts the questions posed by this new policy below, especially in his letter to Payson Treat on May 4, 1943. ◼

1943 DIARY [2]

Thursday, April 1

Actual Population, April 1, 1943 (Official)	
Central Utah (Topaz)	7,984
Colorado River [Poston], Arizona	17,386
Gila River, Arizona	13,244
Granada [Amache], Colorado	6,833
Heart Mountain, Wyoming	10,470
Jerome, Arkansas	8,399
Manzanar, California	9,497
Minidoka, Idaho	9,138
Rohwer, Arkansas	8,379
Tule Lake, California	14,534
Total	105,864

During the months of April and May, 4186 left the centers on "Indefinite Leave." The 105,864 was the number of aliens and citizens residing in the 10 centers on April 1, 1943.[3]

Tuesday, April 5

The day started clear but rather cold.

. . . .

The radio worked fine today; war news: April 1 – 5 in eastern India.

A meeting of the Block was held. K. reported about the damages done to the Recreation Hall and asked parents of kids (boys) 13 – 17 to advise their kids to refrain from further misdeeds and on the conduct of some boys and girls in the bathrooms. They stay there too long, wasting water and interfering with other bathers. He reminded them that some women take away washing-boards to the great inconvenience of others. Some are careless about ironing boards, leaving them unhung; kids play with them, breaking the hinges. . . .

. . . .

Monday, April 12

Another of the beautiful days. . . .

Dispatched the state tax returns.

. . . .

The April 17 issue of "Liberty"[4] presents a condensed version of Vanya Oakes' "White Man's Folly." Its editorial comment is "In Asia, our strongest ally against our most implacable enemy, is China—a country and people akin to us in many ways, who we should know better." The story is about the Sino-Japanese conflict which developed in the present world war. Vanya, of course, knows all about the Far East and in particular China (Shanghai journalist) and therefore Japan. The most [?] view is the acknowledgement of the existence of anti-British sentiment throughout the Far East: "They (the British) make me feel like an animal—like I ought to get down on the ground and thank them for a bit of meat—my money . . . I am not an animal," a Malay [is quoted as saying] in Singapore. The concluding words: "I believe our tendency is to date altogether too much from Pearl Harbor. If I learned anything in the Orient, it was that Pearl Harbor was merely one by-product of the dollar-chasing impulse which we permitted to blind us against the nature of the sphere in which we had long exerted a patronizing influence. For a long time to come we shall have to reap the unappetizing rewards of our misunderstanding and stupidity. But the sooner we comprehend that the Far East has forever ceased to be the happy hunting ground for predatory foreign interests that once it was, the sooner we shall be on the way to re-thinking the Far East in terms of our responsibilities to it." The West, i.e., U.S. and Britain [have] lost the resources of the Far East.

. . . .

Wednesday, April 14

Somewhat cooler but later turned out to be the hottest day so far. Toward late afternoon, it became cloudy; it looks stormy.

One Nakamura came and requested that I help him in his attempt to write a survey of the nisei in the Project, especially as regard the problem of their resettlement. An outline of topics was brought. I suggested to him to submit me his manuscript which is to be printed in the Tule Lake magazine. Needs guidance.

Tsurusaki took K., N and me on an inspection tour of the Project farms (5,000 or 6,000 acre tract); hog and chicken farms. Upon return, we stopped at the pickle factory. . . .

Thursday, April 15

Another nice summer day though cooler and more delightful.

. . . .

The much talked about conference between the issei representatives and Dillon Myer turned out to be a flop as expected.[5] Nothing came of it.

It is reported that the accepted repatriates are to be gathered from the various relocation centers to a special camp in Minnesota.[6]

[At] a congressional committee relative to the evacuated Japanese aliens and citizens, [General of the Western Defense Command, John] DeWitt presented his view: "The Jap is [a] Jap; he can't be changed."[7] They will not be permitted [back] to the West Coast; they had been chased out from it and will be kept there under a more strict surveillance. O.K. The axis declared that they will bomb the mainland; does this affect the treatment of the evacuees?

Friday, April 16

(#1308 at 7:30 P.M., the Stanford Reunion).[8]
    Another fine day so far as the morning is concerned; it continued so.
    Shirai came to inform me that [the Stanford reunion] was going to be a stag party. . . .
    The meeting was attended by the following: Akamatsu, Hashiba, Hara (who is to depart tomorrow for St. Louis), Obayashi, Obana, Shirai and myself.[9] The refreshments were prepared by Shirai aided by Nakamura.
    Obayashi accepted a teaching position at Colorado University, but [when] he found out that he was to teach in the Naval Japanese Language School, he canceled the appointment. . . .
    Nakamura went with the F.B.I. to the C.C.C. camp to investigate one of the 70 still there (c. 80% are kibei); they are there to complete their sentence. They have better camp equipments than here; they prepare their own meals and are guarded by soldiers. They don't seem to mind.
    Doctors versus Pedicord relations were detailed.[10]

Saturday, April 17

Another fine day but somewhat windy, consequently dusty.
    Today is officially designated as a general cleaning day; both inside and outside are to be cleaned . . . and for that purpose, the morning was declared a holiday as regards the customary labor. Each block was given 150 pine [trees] about 10 inches tall; they were planted around the barracks.
    Tin pails or buckets were distributed on the basis of one per family regardless of the size. No new news.

                    . . . .

Monday, April 19

It started to rain very early in the morning and continues; sometime it turned into *mizore* [sleet]. Later on became balmy.
    Received a note from Coverley last Saturday, requesting that I call on him at his office this morning at 11:00 A.M.
    This is my hair-cut day.
    Coverley showed me a letter from the Project Director [Ray

Johnston] of the Rohwer, Arkansas, Center which inquired [as to]
my pleasure in accepting his invitation for a period of six weeks to
six months in order that I instruct the young Japanese [there] as well
as those Americans who were [interested] on the subject of the Japanese people: anthropology, sociology, psychology and culture.

[My] answer was that I am not interested in handling anything
elementary because I have had no experience in handling such a
class of people.[11] I suggest to Coverley, why not try somewhat similar enterprise here, whereupon he called in [head of Community
Services Paul] Fleming. The latter doubted that there were enough
qualified nisei here in view of the fact that the more intelligent nisei
have departed and are departing. . . . I warned them that there will
be certain social trends which should be checked before they materi-
alize: delinquencies. . . .

Wednesday, April 21

During early morning it rained rather heavily, though it stopped toward the dawn; the world was cleaned of sand-dust and appears as a
delightful morning. Cloudy but nice.

Kei has been suffering from a cold and down in bed since
yesterday.

Nakatsuka-san made me a very nice tea-table.

. . . .

[Kenneth] Yasuda came over and stayed for a while; he asked me
what he should do. Answer: future is dark; no prospect to obtain the
opportunity for intellectual pursuits, since practically all the institutions of higher learning are preoccupied in training for the war;
many faculty men have been called away for the same purpose.

. . . .

It was broadcast from Tokyo that a colonist at Topaz was shot to
death by a guard in the watch-tower within the fence but on the alleged ground that he was out of the fence; but I understand that the
camp being now a free zone, one could go out even to town for shopping. At any rate, the residents struck in retaliation for the violent deed
for which they could find no valid reason according to a letter written
by a resident to his relative residing here. Thus Ito informed me.*

---

* On the evening of April 11, 1943, a sentry at the Topaz, Utah, camp shot to death
James Hatsuki Wakasa, a 63-year-old issei. After much controversy and investigation, the

Thursday, April 22

The day started delightful though the air is somewhat cool in spite of the bright sun. But a little later it became cloudy and a strong wind developed and keeps on blowing with the usual consequence of sand-dust.

Since the announcement of a detailed account of the Doolittle bombing of Tokyo on April 18, 1942,* true facts of the attack become impossible to hide here; so taking advantage of one aspect (severe punishment meted out to some who deliberately bombed a hospital and a school), Roosevelt sent a protest which appears to be for home consumption in order to camouflage the failure of the bombers to return except one plane and several men. Sixteen planes or 70 odd men were engaged in the attack which resulted only in slight damages to military objectives. The note as usual shows a brave tone for the purpose of satisfying the people, but it will have no effect otherwise.

Ito came bringing a cake and a hot-plate (loan).

A report of the Truman Commission [12] on the sinking of allied ships made public: 12,000,000 tons were sunk in 1942 or more than the tonnage built.

Friday, April 23

The day started clear but windy; later it became chilly and windy; still later there was a brief shower and then it turned out to be mild. Thus extreme changes in a rapid succession.

No particular news, but a continuation of the wrangling over the Doolittle bombing of Tokio last April 18, 1942; there was an elation over his alleged success which sacrificed 15 out of the 16 planes and

---

army held that the shooting was likely without just cause, although the sentry was acquitted of any wrongdoing. See Daniels, *Asian America*, pp. 228–31 and Ichihashi's diary entry for May 1, 1943, below.

*Lieutenant Colonel James H. Doolittle led a raid of 16 carrier-launched B-25s against Tokyo on April 18, 1942. The attack inflicted little material damage but was a major psychological blow against Japan and a boost for Allied morale. Eight of the 80 crew members involved, however, were captured when their planes landed in occupied China, and they were tried by the Japanese for war crimes in the bombing of civilian neighborhoods. In late April 1943, the White House denounced the trials and the death sentences handed down by the judges. The authorities in Tokyo ultimately commuted five of the sentences to life imprisonment, but three of the pilots were executed on October 10, 1943.

their crews. The Doolittle plane alone escaped with several men; it never got over Japan. Some of the captured were executed for their inhuman acts. Newspapers since yesterday have played up atrocities and continued today in a more elaborate manner.

Took a part of the cake to Kuramoto. . . . The Geneva Protocol in question is available?

Saturday, April 24

The day started more mild than it has been for a week; still it is somewhat cloudy.

One Oyama from 31 Block came and told me that he used to know me from 1903; he was a member of J.S.C. [Japanese Service Club?] of San Francisco.[13] Since then he lived in the mountain region and later went to the East where he learned photography. Returned to Sacramento where he was engaged in photo-studies for 20 years until he was evacuated. He wanted to know whether he could obtain a job in the Harvard University Press in order to learn the photolithographic process inspired by its reproductions of Japanese dictionaries.

Kuramotos sent us *katsuo-sashimi* [bonito] which we enjoyed. . . .

A notice from Nakamura to Block Managers relative to the coal crew strike caused allegedly by the discharge of a member. [Assistant project director Joe O.] Hayes threatened that unless coal is unloaded in time, it will be sold and the WRA will not be responsible for its shortage in the Project. But whose responsibility is supplying it to the residents? . . .

Monday, April 26

The morning started somewhat clear though clouds cover here and there; it is neither cold nor warm—like an early spring day.

Shirai came during my absence; paid him the [Stanford] reunion fee, 58 cents.

Announced that physical examinations of those who will volunteer for the Japanese combat team at the hospital at 1 : 00 P.M. and the clinic will be closed to the general public. There will be a meeting of the Ward to discuss the problem of the hospital. The departure of doctors and the shortage of nurse aides; 30 are needed right away. . . .

Tuesday, April 27

. . . .

The *Examiner* (4/26) carries "news" of the "Greatest Air-Sea Victory of the War" in the South-Pacific (3 days: April 15 on, or more recent?).[14] If the latter, not a word has come over the radio; if the earlier, a quite different story—which is which is not clear, but very confusing. . . .

Wednesday, April 28

It rained all night but stopped in the morning; it is cloudy and warm, though the surrounding hills and mountains are covered with snow. . . .

Mrs. [K] Yoshida (Oakland), whose husband, a nursery man was recently taken to S.F. for a hearing. He had been examined by the FBI in Oakland and also at Lincoln, between Sacramento and Marysville. He was arrested on March 10th because of the failure of his two sons 20 and 17 and daughter 21 [to register?] and suspicion that he was involved in the anti-registration agitation. He was taken to the Klamath Falls jail where he remained for three days; he was then taken to the C.C.C. On the 31st he was resummoned to the Project for an examination and as a result [the?] 2 boys were sent to the Utah isolation camp, but he was sent to the Klamath Falls jail again. Later he was taken to the Sharp Park Detention Center on April 6. He had his hearing on the 19th and is now awaiting decision. In the meantime [M] wrote to his wife, advising her to write through my aid to Frank Hennessy in order that he may be released on parole. My advice was time is inappropriate and such a note may prove superfluous—decision is pending and we don't know what it will be. According to her, 7 were arrested in the same manner.

We received a box of candies from Stoltenbergs.

Thursday, April 29

The morning started clear and warm and remained so till late in the afternoon when it became cloudy; but it remained fairly warm.

Ito brought the latest issue of "Time."

Yasuda called: he will quit his job. He was informed not to leave here for the outside because of anti-Japanese atmosphere intensified by the news of the captives' execution; Americans need no excuse for their hatred any way. Danzuka came while I was sleeping. I have been suffering from a cold for now three days—Kei for nearly a month.

Announced at lunch that there will be a movie show tomorrow evening.

Number of volunteers for the combat team still remains unannounced but why?

. . . .

Friday, April 30

It rained most of the night and continued into morning; we certainly have in this place very changeable weather which is bad for the sick, especially for the people with colds.

Further restrictions of hospital services due to the shortage of doctors were announced.

Ito informed me that 45 applied to volunteer (combat team) physical examinations and as a result, 25 were accepted while the rest were rejected. It is rumored that the atmosphere outside against Japanese has become worse to the point of being dangerous.

. . . .

Saturday, May 1

The rain stopped but it remains cloudy though somewhat warmer.

Block managers were assembled in the name of Coverley at 11:00 A.M., but Coverley failed to show up and when he was notified by telephone, he said that he was not responsible; half an hour [later] Hayes appeared saying that he was interviewing with the Council and the Planning Board and was delayed. He stated that coal remained unloaded from the train because of the strike of the coal crew which was caused by the termination of the Japanese foreman who had signed full-time (6 hours) for his men, who did not work full-time in reality. The WRA was responsible as far as bringing coal and other supplies as far as the Project and their distribution was up to the colonists who, if they did not wish to freeze, should get busy in bringing [the coal] to the residents.

Coverley's statement concluded thus: "Unloading coal is not a particularly desirable job, but there are infinitely more undesirable jobs being done throughout the world now—and without complaint." But why is there a coal crew paid by the Administration? Its failure to function is due to the mismanagement which is the responsibility of the man of the Administration in charge. How could the entire colonists be held responsible for this state of affairs. . . . It appears that none of the Administration men had any valid argument for their stand.

April 22 issue of [JACL newspaper] "Pacific Citizen": Wakasa killed at Topaz, Utah.

1) Hatsuki Wakasa, 62, was shot to death on April 11 by a military policeman at Topaz, Utah center; on the 21st an order [came] from Washington that all military police sentries except one will be withdrawn between 7 A.M. and 7 P.M. from gates and observation points adjacent to the inner boundaries of the project. The one exception will be a soldier stationed at the main gate to check incoming baggage and parties. 2) Washington sources declared that De-Witt was misquoted as to his testimony before the Congressional Hearing Comm., at S.F., relative to the Japanese evacuees: "A Jap is a Jap . . ." but in what respects, it is not stated. 3) April 18 DeWitt proclaimed that Japanese in uniform are free to enter and travel in military areas (nos. 1 and 2 zones) of the Western Defense Command.

◻ In a letter dated April 27, 1943, Payson Treat again affectionately scolded Ichihashi for not writing for more than a month and asked for even a postcard from his friend. If he could receive just a simple note, Treat told Ichihashi, "when your friends ask me (as they do very often) I can proudly reply, 'Oh, I just had a note from the Doctor and they are all feeling fine!'" Treat also brought Ichihashi up to date about developments on campus and mentioned that Kiyoshi K. Kawakami, a prominent Japanese American journalist on the East Coast and a mutual friend, had inquired of Ichihashi recently. Kawakami was the author of several books, including *The Real Japanese Question* (1921), and numerous articles on Japanese in America and Japanese-American relations. Ichihashi had assigned material from Kawakami's works in his classes.

The most important part of Treat's letter concerned repatriation, and Treat gingerly raised the issue with Ichihashi. He had heard a "report that was widespread" that "the Imperial Government had placed your name at the top of the list of nationals in this country who must be exchanged." Treat said he could not believe the rumor and had denied it publicly, "not on any knowledge of my own but on my belief." But now

Treat had heard a new rumor "from 'a well informed authority' " and wanted Ichihashi's authorization to refute it.

> It is said to the effect that you have stated that you intended to return to Japan at the close of the war; in fact, that you so indicated in some questionnaire. Now this is so contrary to the views which you have often expressed that I did not hesitate to say, "I don't believe it!" But I could do a better job if I could come out flatly and say, "There is absolutely no truth in that story!" There is so much ignorance, misunderstanding, misrepresentation, and confusion nowadays, that I rarely read anything or hear anything without being shocked.

Treat closed his letter by informing Ichihashi that Alfred Ehrman and Marshall Woodworth, two of the three men who had sat at his immigration hearing, had died, one in an automobile accident. Treat reflected, "How uncertain is life. What fools are those who could tell us what is going to happen in the future. How kind was the All Wise to deny us any knowledge of what lies ahead." [15] ◼

YAMATO ICHIHASHI TO PAYSON TREAT [16]

Tule Lake, Calif.
May 4, 1943

Dear Payson:

Thank you for the kind letter; instead of a card, I am going to write you a letter. In fact, I had been collecting information to compose a history of the recent registration debacle, but a little over two weeks ago I was knocked down with a nasty cold while I was looking after Kei who had developed a case of flu a couple weeks before. I am gradually getting over my cold, but Kei is still suffering; her case is nothing unique, since many people are suffering from the same illness. We have had and still have very changeable weather for the last 2 months: spring, summer, and winter have alternately occurred, together with rain, snow, hail, or terrific winds which mean sandstorms here. The people have not been able to re-adjust themselves quickly enough to meet the above weather condition. In addition, doctors and nurses having been diminishing due to the WRA policy of re-settlement, and consequently the hospital service has become utterly inadequate, and the food served us lacks necessary nourishments; thus they possess no power of resistance to illness, and when they become ill, they cannot easily recover. In short, life in this desolate camp devoid of vegetation is anything but a happy one, and the people without philosophic minds easily succumb to pessimism and become desperate, losing a sense of balance. However, do not worry about us since we have not as yet joined such a group and have been struggling to maintain somewhat a normal life despite all these circumstances; we are supposed to be educated and intelligent and capable of fighting against any evils, environmental or otherwise.

Your letter contains many interesting items of information. First of all, let me assure that my name was not even included in the list of nationals first to be exchanged, I am not apparently that important. While we were still at Santa Anita, there was issued an official notice that we might apply for repatriation, but we ignored it because we had no intention of going back to our native land; the same notice was given us here upon our arrival last July; we again ignored it. When I was arrested and taken to the S.F. Immigration Station, I was personally asked whether or not I intended to apply for repatriation; my answer was "not interested." While I was being detained at the Sharp Park, Kei received an inquiry about how we were getting along, via the International Red Cross; her answer was "we were faring O.K.," without mentioning what was actually happening to me at that time because she did not want our relatives and friends to worry about us. She was right. In January of this year, the State Department notified us that our names were included in the present list of nationals to be exchanged submitted by the Japanese government, adding that the negotiation for exchanges has not been completed; again we declined to accept the invitation or privilege for repatriation. Therefore you are absolutely right in denying, as you have done, the rumor even from "a well informed authoritative source," whatever that may be; I have stated our case in detail for your information. As to what we may do after the war, we have not made our decision one way or the other; who can tell whether this country will be an agreeable place for us to live, and if one were to believe what is being said at present, no Japanese are wanted here. Naturally we need not stay in a place we are not wanted; unlike Jews, we have our native-land, of which we are still citizens whose rights will be protected and respected. Old as I am, I am not as yet a helpless creature, and I will not be a beggar or even an object of charity, for I am certain of my ability to earn enough to support my family. I cannot and will not be content to exist in a place I am not wanted. More I need not say as you know me. So much for my stand on this question past, present and future.

I am indeed sorry to learn of the sad fate of two of the three "judges" who sat at my hearing; life is uncertain and transitory as

Buddha has taught. They are gone, but I am still here with the honor of being a "parolee," the meaning of which is unclear to me. Coverley tells me that he can free me to resettle in a free zone, if I were not a "parolee"; apparently I am still technically under the jurisdiction of the F.B.I., at least to the extent that I am not "a free man," unless they so decide again. In practice, such a status does not bother me in the least as I have no intention of leaving this camp until I am compelled to do so by an official "order," not because I like this hell, but because I am curious to find out what will be the fate of the poor people here as a whole. As I have written you before, the life here is anything but a desirable one from any standpoint: We are forced to live in the lowest order of a communistic cooperative life due to the combination of the administrative policy and the character of the residents—common mess halls, common showers, common latrines, common laundries and what not; the rates of compensation are fixed at $16 and $19 plus $2–3 for clothing for those who work (laborers and professionals); this ceiling on incomes together with the fact that all of us live in one-room "apartments," into which similarly constructed barracks are divided and furnished with wood or iron cots, mattresses, blankets, cast[-iron] coal heat stoves, but nothing else, not even chairs which I found even in one of the two jails I stayed. These facts have developed a sense of equality among the people and the value of [an] individual as an individual quality is completely ignored. Thus scavengers, called here "G-men," and Doctors stand on an equal footing, which must be a source of satisfaction to those of the lowest order of mankind. Such an artificial and unnatural society may be a noble experiment, but in my humble judgment nothing normal to human life can be expected in it; no progress in any direction can be hoped for; in fact, the residents have already become an abnormal people.

At this juncture, let me briefly write about the recent registration debacle. When Coverley assumed the post of the project Director in January of this year, he declared that his main object was to re-settle the residents outside (in non-military zones away from the three States where they had been residents) individually or in *small* groups. He expected appreciative reactions to this new policy, but in reality the people began to entertain doubt and even fears to be scattered in strange places in view of the prevailing hostile attitude against them throughout the country. Moreover, they soon learned that the nature of jobs available was limited—farm-labor and domestic service which will not enable them to support their families. Besides, the age composition of these residents clearly shows that the concentra-

tion in the issei population is around the 60–65 group, while that
of nisei is around 20 years of age; the former have no guts to adventure, the latter are too young to have a sense of perspective. Yes,
professionals: doctors, dentists, lawyers cannot practice in localities
where they cannot get Japanese clients. Such being the case, only a
few have applied for leave clearance whereas the Administration expected a wholesale application on the part of the residents. The local
officials were disappointed, disgusted, impatient, indignant; I bluntly
told Coverley that their expectation was unreasonable, but the inevitable reply of his and of his colleagues was that this was wartime and
the Japanese had no right to seek security economic, social or otherwise. (By the way, in my recent registration I was compelled to give
"references" and I included your name together with those of Edgar
[Robinson], Ralph [Lutz], Lynn [White] and [Ray Lyman] Wilbur.
I received letters from Edgar and Lynn that they were asked by the
WRA to write recommendations to it because I have applied for
leave for "employment, education or residence elsewhere," which in
fact I have not as I have stated on this particular point that I seek
"none." Doubtless you will get the same inquiry, if you have not already received it, please remember my stand on this as stated here;
I am not seeking even "residence elsewhere." Woodrow is anxious
to go to college where he can finish his training in architecture. If
you care, you can write a general recommendation as to my character, etc., even that will not be very important.[17]

To continue on the recent registration, it was in the midst of the
situation above stated, that Stimson announced in January that a
Japanese combat team will be organized and will call for volunteers
for it from among the nisei residing in the various concentration
camps, and at once a propaganda [campaign] was launched to encourage nisei to volunteer. On Feb. 3rd, it was officially announced
here that Stimson would send his military agents to call for volunteers for the team, and on the same day, the re-settlement officer
publicly complained that "not enough people are applying for their
clearance leaves." This practice of the local officials to handle the
volunteers and the leave clearances in general as if they were related
matters caused confusion among the residents as to what the government was trying to do, and became a source of misunderstanding
all around. A few days latter, it was announced: "a general registration at relocation centers of all evacuees who are 17 or more years
of age will start next week."

On the 9th, the Stimson military agents arrived here, and the
same evening, these delivered in each ward assembly a clever, po-

litico-legal "Army Induction Message," which climaxed with what a glorious opportunity the government was offering to nisei men 17–37 years old to join the combat team. Not a word was said on the proposed general registration of aliens and nisei women. Unfortunately, the message did not go over well even among the nisei who were directly involved; instead they began to grumble about the government's maltreatment accorded to them since their evacuation, denying their rights of citizenship, which the message justified on the ground of a military necessity. Personally I was somewhat surprised at this reaction of the nisei, but a number of issei sympathized with the discontented nisei. That was the situation prior to the general registration day.

The registration began on the 10th: nisei men, 17–37 with the "select[ive] service" form while the rest, 17-years and over with the ["application for leave clearance"] form, school-teachers being the registrars. The latter form had been a source of doubts and fears among the issei as already stated, and now they began to feel that if they should register in this form, they would be forced to leave the camp which was the last thing they wanted to do at the present, and consequently many became reluctant in registering. I have carefully examined the contents of the form; there were three objectionable features, (1) the caption ["application for leave clearance"], (2) one of the questions (#28) read: "Will you swear unqualified allegiance to the United States of America and forswear any form of allegiance or obedience to the Japanese emperor, or any other foreign government, power, or organization?" (3) state the desire for employment outside (hence application for leave clearance). In order to have these points clarified, I went to see Coverley and stated to him the above points, whereupon he showed the Washington instructions which, among other things, stated that "the registration was compulsory for all," but I found nowhere stated that the application for leave clearance was compulsory. I suggested that the caption of the form be changed to *Registration*, and he accepted it; that the question 28 be made so that aliens may answer it with qualifications, and this too was accepted by him. I did not press on the third point because if one did not desire, he can so formulate an answer to that effect indirectly. Coverley promised to issue a new order relative to the above changes by noon of the day, but it was delayed and delayed, causing a good deal of confusion among the people who naturally were ignorant of the changes proposed. The delay was due to the existence of the Council and the Planning Board, the official organs of *self-government*, which were unable to expedite the matters.

There developed agitators who opposed registration in general, which would not have arisen, had the matter been handled more judiciously and expeditiously. I was told one day by Coverley that he had received information (from some secret source) that I was leading an organized opposition to registration; he knew, however, that this was a charge without grounds and therefore he himself did not believe it. It is very plain that the Administration employs secret informers, though it denies it; the Japanese here call them "dogs," and they hurt the Japanese morale very badly and the dogs ought not to be employed. But police-minded bureaucrats can never see that way. You may be interested to know that these dogs are nisei and issei, both male and female; females are referred to as "cats," poor animals. At any rate, the situation became more tense as time went on, and finally reached a point of disturbance, because it became known definitely that many nisei men refused to register, and with the usual harangue and agitation.

By this time, the Administration lost its head; on Sunday evening, Feb. 21st, truck-loads of soldiers with bayonetted rifles, machine guns and tear-gas equipments appeared in one of the wards and arrested 31 nisei for the refusal to register. Afterward we learned that they were jailed at the Klamath Falls and Alturas prisons; its news spread throughout the camp like a wild fire. There then followed an excitement hitherto unknown in this place, and this was the worst of blunders yet committed by the Administration staff. In the end, a dozen issei "agitators" and 150 "disloyal" nisei were arrested and were detained in a nearby C.C.C. camp; these were eventually brought back to this camp and examined by "Judge" Coverley and suitable punishments were meted out to them; some of them were sent to an isolation camp in Utah, where the "agitators" and "disloyal" nisei from the Manzanar Camp are detained. Seven of the issei were sent to the Sharp Park, and at San Francisco they were brought before the Boards of Hearing. Their final fate is still unknown to me. About 70 of the nisei are still being held in the C.C.C. camp to complete their penalties which vary from 30 to 90 days and are being guarded by soldiers. In this procedure, Coverley acted "under the Presidential warrant": in judging and imposing punishments. I did not know that the President had the right of instituting a "court" in order to mete out punishments. There are many other angles to be considered, but enough has been said about the handling of the whole business in a stupid manner.

But what was the actual result? About 2,000 aliens and citizens refused to register; only 45 nisei men volunteered for the combat team, and of the number only 25 qualified and were accepted. It has left a bad taste in the residents' mouths; they still feel resentful toward the Administration, and therefore more trouble may be expected. This afternoon I attended a Project meeting at which I learned that the Chief of Internal Security, one Dr. Jacoby, a former professor at the College of the Pacific, had submitted his resignation. The Japanese here want him to continue in office, and I was elected as one of the five to constitute a committee which is to find out the best means to keep him here, if that be possible. All I can say at present is that those in charge of the evacuees, styling themselves as "Caucasians," are obsessed of a superiority complex and often indulge in threats and bluffs; they are the worst type of bureaucrats. Out of the seventy or so, there are only two who have had college education, and [the others?] are ignorant and incompetent. They can not understand or do not care to understand the peculiar psychology of the evacuee minds.

Well, I have to attend another meeting very soon, and so I have to end this note abruptly, but hoping that you and Madam continue to enjoy good health.[18]

> Very affectionately yours,
> Yamato Ichihashi

DIARY

Wednesday, May 5

Somewhat chill and cloudy but fairly good, though a little rain in the afternoon.

The case of the WRA versus [Kenji] Ito, Mikita[?], Taniguchi, Arima [came] before the court: Coverley as the judge and [WRA attorney Tony] O'Brien as the prosecutor. The Defendants were charged of riotous acts and disturbance of peace. The Plantiff was the eccentric Takano, a notorious character who complained that he had been beaten and otherwise threatened. The session began with a large audience; Ito acted as an attorney for himself and his three co-defendants [?] he and O'Brien soon developed a battle of wits. When Takano was called to the witness-stand, an interpreter became necessary. Coverley asked me to do that and I did. The court lasted from 9:30 to 11:45 and 1:30 to 5:45. Coverley declared: one hundred had been tried, but this was the longest one, though not very important. The case was "dismissed," but [Coverley?] "re-marked that Mikita could be punished technically with an assault, but he is not charged with it." The whole court was quite dramatic and Ito was the star. I was amused[?].

YAMATO ICHIHASHI TO EDGAR ROBINSON [19]

Tule Lake WRA, Newell, Cal.
May 6, 1943

Dear Edgar:

Thank you very much for the kind letter.[20] I am more or less familiar with bureaucratic ways, but I am somewhat surprised to learn of the WRA Director's inquiry. I have never applied for what is technically known here as "leave clearance" in order to seek "employment, education, or residence elsewhere." It is true, in the recent registration (compulsory) held here, the WRA employed for it the "Application for Leave Clearance" form and caused such an unnecessary debacle. As far as I am concerned, I filled it in as a mere registration and nothing more. However, in the same form was demanded that the registrant list five names as references and I took the privilege of including your name together with those of Dr. Wilbur, Payson, Ralph [Lutz], and Lynn [White].[21] Since I intend to remain here until I am restored to my home in the Campus, please write, if you care, a recommendation of a general nature. That might help the WRA.

Woodrow is anxious and so are we that [he] complete his college training in architecture in some institution, if that be possible. The life in this camp is anything but desirable, and if educational opportunity is not immediately available, he may desire to seek a job; he would like to work as a draftsman.

I am sorry to state that Kei has been suffering a very bad case of cold for over a month and that I also was down with a cold for nearly three weeks. I feel better now, and I am hoping for Kei's recovery soon.

Hoping, however, that you and Mrs. Robinson are enjoying the best of health, I remain,

Very respectfully yours,
Yamato Ichihashi

Please remember me kindly to the colleagues.

DIARY

Monday, May 10

The day [started] clear but cold with a strong wind.

. . . .

   Frank [Matsumoto]'s mother brought her 3rd son, a graduate
of the University of Washington, and a resident at the Utah center
who has volunteered for the combat team and is now visiting here
before going to Shelby, Mississippi.[22]
   The old Takaki came to say that his nephew also in the army has
been permitted to visit his wife and child and relatives.
   In passing, Jacoby told me that there was a soldier permitted to
visit here his dying father, but as soon as he arrived, he, Jacoby, was
instructed by the military headquarters to arrest him and hand him
over to the military authority. This he did against his wishes because
of [its] injustice and cruelty. Fortunately, the head in charge stated
that since there was no train to return the soldier, he might [stay]
here for 14 hours. The father died two days later. This sort of thing
made Jacoby sick: [thus] his resignation.
   Woodrow returned to draftsman job, quitting his slaughter-house
job.[23]

Tuesday, May 11

Like yesterday, it is clear but cold; there was alot of frost in the
morning; it is becoming warm as the day progressed.
   Sent a check ($1.50) to the bank to be placed in my commercial
account; it was the check from the National Geographic magazine.
   Takaki's nephew, Hayashi, stationed at Fort Harrison, Indiana-
polis, where about 90 [nisei] soldiers are (20 medical and 10 in headquarters). When called for combat team volunteers, about 20 applied. Why not order them? Discrimination as regards promotions
and other service duties obtains. Japanese are likely to be made into
labor battalion; Hayashi in the service since March, 1942, obtained
a furlough just now, though applied for it since January. Wrote to
DeWitt but received no answer, not even its acknowledgement.
Japanese soldiers became less enthusiastic when they heard DeWitt's
famous remarks; some officers are anti while others are more understanding.

Made a box-garden, a pretty good one, if it develops as I expect it to. It became quite warm in the afternoon.

KEI ICHIHASHI TO JESSIE TREAT [24]

Tule Lake
May 14 [1943]

Dear Mrs. Treat:

Thank you for your kind letter and the interesting newspaper clippings.[25]

I escaped from a bad cold during the winter, but in the early April we had a couple of very hot days—92 degrees in our room—and then I caught a cold. This is the sixth week since then, but I am still using gargling medicine which I brought with me from Palo Alto. The climate here is very changeable so that many people have bad colds at present. The sun is very hot because there are no shades here, as I wrote you before. We have no trees in this project, not even green grasses except some kind of reeds, 4 or 5 inches tall. There are no beautiful flowers, no song birds, so that we cannot see even the signs of the spring. The distant mountains are covered with snow and they are beautiful, but the wind is cold.

Thank you for the morning glory seeds. We will plant them for I think it will be a lot of fun. Mr. Ichihashi has already made boxes for them. I am just thinking how to sow the seeds and protect the young plants from frost, as we still have frost every morning.

People here are anxious to get green things. A person started to raise sweet potatoes—I do not mean to eat, but put them in glass jars and placed them in a warm spot. In a few weeks white roots began to come out and green shoots followed. Visitors seeing these, are much pleased. So in fact almost every house has them thus arranged. We have even three jars, which our kind neighbours brought to us. It may sound awfully silly, but we really enjoy them as we have no vegetation to speak of. About a month ago, we were given thousands of small pine trees about 3 or 4 inches tall. The people planted them in front of their apartments. When the bottom of Tule Lake becomes one of the greatest forests, the world will be a wonderful place, but [we] will not probably see the place so changed; we hope not.

I am sorry to hear that Mrs. Bailey still has some troubles. It is almost one year since she met with the accident. Mrs. Wilbur has not been well for the past few years, but I am so very sorry that she had a bad heart attack lately. I hope she will recover her strength very soon. Mrs. Green is one of our nice neighbors.[26] She used to be a frail looking lady, but she was quite an energetic woman for her age; when I was on the campus she and I talked of gardening quite often. I wish that she will recover soon and enjoy her gardening again. It is too bad that Mr. [George Bliss] Culver has been ill again and laid down so long. Mrs. Culver's anxiety must be very great. I hope that her husband is not very seriously ill when their son is in distant Africa. When you have a chance to see her please remember us to her.

Sincerely yours.
Kei Ichihashi

P.S. It was very nice of you to have refilled my moth ball bags. I am grateful indeed for your kindness. Please give my best wishes to Mr. Treat.

Your kind note relative to [a letter of] reference, Mr. Ichihashi has already written to Mr. Treat. In the recent compulsory registration, the authority used the form "application for leave clearance" which confused the residents as to its purpose and caused an unnecessary debacle. Mr. Ichihashi and I filled the form as a simple registration and not as an application for "employment, education or residence elsewhere" since we have no intention of moving out from this camp unless we are forced to do so, but the bureaucratic routine worker cannot apparently see or understand the specific answer we made in our cases. That being the case, please write a general recommendation on what I am; that will be quite sufficient. Among other things, we were asked to give as references five Americans who know me, so I took the liberty of naming you along with Miss Stoltenberg, Mrs. Wilbur, Mrs. Lutz, and Mrs. Robinson. Should they inquire, please tell them what I have written.[27]

◘ Throughout the month of May, Ichihashi worked to resolve the many conflicts that had arisen among the Tule Lake residents, as well as to improve relations between the residents and the disliked Administration. Requests for help came his way daily, and although he turned many down, he accepted the task of editing the *Tule Lake Interlude*, a special journal about relocation produced by young nisei at Tule Lake. As he had before the war, Ichihashi continued to have a special interest in the problems of the nisei and felt an obligation to inculcate in them what he believed to be the higher values of civilization that they lacked. "The course of ideas is creative intelligence which can be gained by severe intellectual discipline through schooling or otherwise," he once admonished a young audience in camp.[28] Ichihashi worked on the rough drafts of articles submitted to the *Interlude* to improve the language and sharpen opinions. He also wrote an introduction to the publication. The entire draft of his introduction is reproduced here because it conveys a sense of Ichihashi's public persona in camp.

The issue presents a series of articles written by young authors; they touch upon various aspects of the evacuee life as experienced by the *nisei* during the past year. The articles are descriptive, historical, sociological, philosophical, impressionistic and even flippant, and thus, because of their nature, they may appear somewhat disjointed. Nevertheless, they, as a whole, vividly portray and reveal the *nisei* minds as affected by what has happened to them since the outbreak of war. The writers speak simply and sincerely [of] that which they have felt and thought, and of the new environments in which they have been forced to live. To them it has been a drama, indeed, an intense one that has involved some 110,000 human souls; the drama has embodied many comedies and tragedies. How these comedies and tragedies strike the uninitiated can only be surmised, but to those who have actually participated in them, they are apt to stick for a long time. Ultimately, however, it is hoped that the more intelligent and courageous, at least, will emerge philosophically victorious.

At the same time, any human drama, and in particular, a tragic one, whether fleeting and limited in scope or no, should not escape serious attention of the thinking public since it too is involved if indirectly. After all, unless the public is willing to rectify its own mistakes (committed by whom does not matter), and then to help in restoring to a normal life, these unfortunate evacuees and more especially those of the young generation, this so human a problem will likely breed yet another far more tragic one that might drive them into a philosophy of despair. This must be avoided.

This writer is an old man and a long resident in the United States, whose mature years were devoted to teaching of American youths with the dream that their cultural life be rendered richer. Life is a serious business, and it should not be shattered by transitory misfortunes. It has to go on. Thinking men and women should read the articles in order to learn from them and to penetrate into the minds of their authors. Then they will understand the nature of their problems. With a necessary knowledge, they can help intelligently in solving them. If necessary, these few words may be interpreted as an appeal from a man who is not entirely ignorant of Americans and Japanese as well as their ideals, to those capable to view youth problems sympathetically and to strive for the general betterment of life.

Yamato Ichihashi[29] ▶

DIARY

Tuesday, May 18

Like yesterday's weather, only it is colder; it became warmer later, but with a breeze which kicks up some sands.

Nakamura brought me a list of repatriates dated May 1, 1943; the total number is 556, of which 73 withdrew, leaving 483 as the number which stood at that date.

The movie tonight: the WRA and Army propaganda on the evacuation of Japanese from the West Coast states to assembly centers and then to relocation centers.[30] The pictures centered on Los Angeles with Terminal Island, oil fields, etc. to justify the move on the ground of suspected deeds on the part of Japanese should invasion have occurred (its own fear and hysteria). Sorry to uproot them but a necessity. Alleged a considerate treatment to set "an example to the Axis." Bah. The Alaska pictures—a wild, snow-bound scene!

Wednesday, May 19

It is somewhat cold and cloudy; it was sulky and warm.

A number of newspapermen and photographers mostly [from] the Bay Region came here on Monday for a three-day visit to write up on the Center. Milton Silverman, a Stanford man and a chemist PHD came to interview and lunch with me.[31] Later a photographer [came] who took my picture. Hope nothing sensational comes out.

. . . .

Thursday, May 20

The day started clear but somewhat chilly; it remained so except rather a strong wind (north) kept blowing all day.

In the evening, we called on the Akamatsus and . . . [he] told us about all sorts of disagreeable situations at the hospital caused by Pedicord who seems to have a special liking for the show of his "authority" of his headship. Issues all kinds of stupid orders, many of which he immediately takes back when told so by the Japanese doctors. He does this via clerks and not directly with doctors. Today he ordered that hereafter only doctors, dentists, nurses and nurse-aides are to eat in the hospital mess hall. Others are excluded, but they deserve the same accommodation to save their time for one thing. Why this discrimination? Another cause of friction. Pedicord must suffer from the obsession of [a] superiority complex; but he is not strong enough to enforce his will. Maybe he became thus because he had been dealing with Negroes in the South . . .

Frank brought me the shoe-ration forms.[32]

Friday, May 21

The day started bright and quiet; a strong wind in the afternoon.

Accompanied one of the 10 trucks delivering mess supplies daily. Each truck gets from different warehouses about 8 in number, handling different items such as meats, vegetables, canned goods, rice, milk and eggs, etc., listed[?] articles for each mess hall. The loading and unloading are quickly and efficiently performed by 2 or 3 boys on the truck and aided by those in the warehouses. The hospital mess hall gets more balanced articles of better quality where such exist. After having delivered to several halls we got to the hospital hall where the boys were given a piece of pie each, and at the 68 mess hall all were invited to a cup of coffee and nice roast pork sandwiches. Returned home from there.

Heard Yamamoto was killed in an airplane in April, while he was leading a fleet of them (in action).[33]

Today all the block janitors were terminated by the Administration order. Some 64 in number according to a new policy of reducing the number of workers here from about 6,500 to 5,000 or so.

. . . .

Saturday, May 22

It is again nice and warm in the morning; it develop[s] a strong wind.

Yasuda brought a note from Myer to Coverley concerning an attempt being made at Yale under Holland's directorship to develop young instructors of the Japanese language for the benefit of Army men.[34] These are to be trained as instructor-assistants with a monthly allowance of $150.00 during training periods. But later they are to teach soldiers, adding the possibility of doing independent research. Yasuda is hesitant to become a language teacher.

Noguchi informed me that Namba's crippled and helpless sister

27 or 28 is being prevented by her relatives from social welfare grants; they are inhuman beasts. Appealed to me to find out about securing it.

Sunday, May 23

It turned out again a beautiful [day] but hot with a gentle breeze.

. . . the five man committee of the hospital *kōenkai* [support society] came and requested me to aid in solving the conflict between Pedicord and Japanese doctors, the latter saying that either the former is discharged or else they will quit in body—the reason is his incompatible personality—dictatorial—changes are made arbitrarily and frequently without consultation. . . .

Monday, May 24

It was rather warm last night and this morning started clear and summer-like; it so remained all day.

The *Chronicle* advertises that a series of articles on the Project by Milton Silverman starts tomorrow (Tues).

The movie: "Invisible Agent," American-British propaganda picture, a take-off on Germany and Japan but not clever enough to go over—Gestapo cruelty and mutual hatred between Germans and Japanese. Things repeated so often already. At its best it is infantile and amusing to children perhaps.

Hospital case continued: *Byōin Kōenkai* [hospital support society] Committee called a block meeting throughout the Project to decide the best ways and means to aid the doctors in their fight against Pedicord—resignation of Pedicord or of Doctors.

Yamato wrote from Topaz, Utah project: Chiura was beaten a month ago but no culprit arrested as yet; a *bokushi* [minister] was hit with a stone, but no serious damage. The most serious case is the fight between two doctors, Harada, formerly of Tule Lake and Ito, rather popular with the people. Professional jealousy.

Tuesday, May 25

Another delightful morning; it is likely to develop into another day like that of yesterday.

Ito brought new magazines and stayed for a while going over a number of things as usual.

Received a letter from [Kiyoshi K.] Kawakami, the content of which surprised me somewhat if he is sincere.[35] The interesting item related to the relocation centers: the government will discontinue them, but what will be the fate of the issei and their minor children? What can they do in the majority of cases, as they have lost everything they ever possessed.

. . . .

Wednesday, May 26

It is another delightful morning; it remained so and rather hot.

Exactly one year ago this day (Tuesday), we were evacuated from our home about 10:00 A.M. . . . that was the beginning of our unhappy life to date.

Yoshioka, steward[?], Kajiwara, an advisor with a young chap named Nakao from the same block came and informed [me] that these and 7 others were accused of stealing and concealing $140 worth of supplies from the mess hall and placing the same in the boiler-room. In reality, this was done with the understanding of the entire block, but the Administration was informed of this by an *inu*, and [mess manager Ralph C.] Peck and 4 others came and confiscated [the goods] from the said room. Yesterday these men were arraigned before the "court" with O'Brien, prosecutor, and Fleming, judge, and were told [to plead] guilty or not guilty. They all said not guilty. The 2nd court will be held next Friday; what should they do? Advised that all the block residents attend the court as the witness to testify.

Nakao asked about Umezu[?], a T.B. victim, now at Leupp, Arizona;[36] his condition is worse, but no doctor and medical care—isolated. Can arrangements be made so that he be brought back here, his original residences, to receive proper treatment? But [he was] sent to the C.C.C. camp and received a 90 days sentence in connection with his refusal to register. [I advised, get a] doctor's certificate first, and then appeal to Leupp's Director to arrange with Coverley. Similar cases developed after the 47 case, in the blocks 40 and 41, according to the men from 47.

Thursday, May 27

Another nice morning somewhat cooler than yesterday.

At 12:00 just a year ago, we arrived at Santa Anita after a bad train ride . . . that was the beginning of life in a hell.

Danzuka came and said since his appeal has been turned down, he might as well make his mind to rest here; [leave officer Lorne] Huycke told him to go outside and work, but Danzuka thought he would not do it, being too old.

The cook invited us to dinner (*maguro sashimi* [raw tuna]).

We had a sprinkling shower and a thunder storm for a brief moment.

A call for volunteers for unloading and transporting coal to respective blocks. The order came from Sakahara to the Block Manager.

❏ On the front page for May 25, 1943, the *San Francisco Chronicle* began a five-part report on life at the Tule Lake Relocation Center. Milton Silverman, who had worked as a researcher for the army and WRA for a short while before writing his articles for the *Chronicle*, drew from his recent visit with other journalists to Tule Lake. The first four installments described camp life and the attitudes of residents and administrators based on a number of interviews, and the moderately sympathetic tone of the writing was captured in the headline of the first article: "The Inside Story—It's an Unhealthy Situation for All." The last article, however, focused entirely on Ichihashi. It was entitled, "'The Emperor of Tulelake': Japanese Professor (Formerly of Stanford) Wields Great Power Inside the Camp."

Silverman, purporting to present simply a "factual report," began his long report:

> A little Japanese professor who once was kidded and ridiculed by thousands of his American college students is today called the 'Emperor of Tulelake.'
>
> He is this colony's man of mystery.
>
> He is accepted by some high intelligence officers as a helpful, pro-American alien, suspected by others as a sinister, dangerous fifth columnist.

Silverman did not try to solve the mystery in the remainder of his article, but reviewed Ichihashi's life and career at Stanford (where he was known to some, Silverman alleged, as "Doc Itchy-Scratchy"). The reporter included lengthy quotes from an interview with Ichihashi and a description of his residence, which was described as suspiciously more posh than others at Tule Lake. "Ichihashi and his room, his family, his ideas and his problems are probably the keynote to this entire project." Even if one could figure out the enigma of Ichihashi and the whole relocation policy, Silverman offered, and if you "can get anybody to agree with you, you can have [the whole mess]."[37]

The *Daily Tulean Dispatch* reported record sales of the *Chronicle* in camp, but made no comment on the articles. ◗

YAMATO ICHIHASHI TO PAYSON TREAT [38]

May 29, 1943

Dear Payson:

I have been planning to write you for a week with 5 selected items of interest, but instead I write you on the articles by Milton Silverman, appearing in the San Francisco *Chronicle* since the 26th.

One day he dropped in at my room and presented himself as an A.B. and a Ph.D. in Chemistry, Stanford, and an A.M., [University of] California. I treated him as a gentleman. Now he proves himself utterly unworthy of such a consideration; he turns out to be a stupid ass who should never have been "honored" with such an array of college degrees.

Many of his statements are in quotation marks and are attributed to officials here; but they are unbelievable. One named A. E. O. O'Brien, the Project Attorney, sent to the *Chronicle* Editor a telegram charging him with libel. Others may follow suit.

Today's article makes me the theme with a ridiculous title. The "Statements" alleged to have been made by me contain a few truths, a pack of half-truths, and a superabundance of lies. No intelligent persons will be taken in by these, but unfortunately there are many ignorant individuals who are happy to swallow even the most ridiculous, if suitable to their prejudiced minds. That is a misfortune.

Of course, I am helpless [regarding] how much I am abused at this particular time. In a normal time, I may write to tell him what I think of his dirty work, even if he possesses a Ph.D. from Stanford or because of it. Note that he is clever enough to use his education to mix things in such a manner so that the whole may appear quite plausible. He is unscrupulous, perhaps called for by his present occupation. As you know, I don't get emotional over newspaper stories even if they are personal. But coming as it does from another Stanford man, I at least detest it. Besides, this kind of writing cheapens the dignity of Americans.

Please inform my friends how I feel about the article, if necessary.[39] My philosophy of life does not change despite what fools may do to me or say about me.

Very affectionately,
Yamato Ichihashi

p.s. Kei has recovered and is normal again; She has to be careful, however, because the climate is still very variable. Please remember us to Mrs. Treat.

DIARY

Monday, May 31

Rained continued from last night and it is somewhat chilly this morning; it rained all day. . . .

Tsuda informed me about the Japanese gambling which inevitably [results] in their losses. Even here, capitalists invest in the establishments, 4 in number; most of them gamble so that even they lose in the end. A week from last Saturday O.I.S. [Office of Internal Security] accompanied by Tsuda raided 3 of the 4 places, but found only one was actually gambling where about $600 was taken. Their (about 11 persons) trial will be held soon. The question is can the WRA confiscate or fine them other than jail sentences (maximum of 90 days?) They may be taken to a regular court. . . . Also, the recent Minidoka paper announced that its colonists are getting shoes in a much more liberal way. . . . Coal volunteers are called out again.

Kuramoto said: the Coop Board rejected Alberson's [community enterprises director Irving D. Elberson] proposal that it take over the *Dispatch* and publish it in a printed form. This was done for one [named] Davis, a printer at Klamath Falls. This is nothing [more] than an attempted graft, since it was to find a new job for Davis [when] he will be discharged from his present job he holds under the WRA. The *Dispatch* is not worth the improvement in form; it is no better than a high school paper. Besides, a free press will not be allowed [here]. . . .

A chap, translator into Japanese, came here late at night and inquired about the recent *Chronicle* articles on the Tule Lake, espe-

cially centering about me. [He asked] any pressure [on me]? Kei stu-
pidly said none. I told [her] what I thought of the stupidity, for I was
mad. She called on Obana to request that no notice, certainly no
translation of the last article be published, even in the *Dispatch.*

Tuesday, June 1

This is the 3rd consecutive rain we have had accompanied by a
rather strong southerly (mostly) wind; but this morning, it is blowing harder than the previous days. Later it became intermittent
mixed with sunshine. It snowed for about an hour—3 P.M. This day
was the craziest one as regards weather since we had everything—
rain, sunshine, snow.

Volunteers for coal unloading were called again on the grounds
[that] there are 20 carloads; the blocks 71, 73 and 74 were assigned
tomorrow; it was decided at a meeting of the block sometime ago
that either all (one per family) volunteer or none. This was again so
decided though the Administration wishes to limit the number to 25
per block; workers will get credit, if they volunteer.

. . . .

KEI ICHIHASHI TO JESSIE TREAT [40]

Tule Lake
June 15 [1943]

Dear Mrs. Treat:

Thank you for the box of candies. I greatly appreciate your kindness. When I was on the campus, I did not miss candies, but at present, it is very hard to get anything satisfying here, so that I enjoy
them so much more.

The people in this project are trying to get things by mail order
very often, but it is a time consuming way. The other day I ordered
certain things from Sear's Roebuck Company, and three or four
weeks later I received an answer saying that they did not have what I
ordered in their stock. This time I made a similar order from Mont-
gomery Ward Company; I am still hoping that I may be able to get
the things.

We are having very changeable weather here as usual, but life is
monotonous. It seems that the people are getting tired of this life,

and many troubles have occurred lately. Just a few days ago, a woman hanged herself. At first her husband (a gambler, people say) was arrested. But as there was discovered a note written by her, he was released in a couple of days. I heard that the woman attended the flower arrangement class the previous night as usual, and she was chatting with friends very happily because she had become a grandmother. But nine or ten hours later in the following morning she was found dead. The people who knew her could not believe that she had committed a suicide and all kinds of rumors spread all over the project. Anyhow this is the first case of suicide in this project.

Many women are still doing flower arrangement and paper flower-making, beside these they are making some ornaments with little shells. There are several different kinds of little shells that are found here, as the ground is the bottom of an old lake. Some kinds of shells are as small as rice grains. They bleach these shells with some chemicals at first, and then color them, using very often finger nail polish. This work is very popular among women at present. The other day I went to see an art exhibition and saw beautifully made flowers with these little shells. They were just marvelous, shinning like precious jewels.

Well, it is already the middle of June, and you have doubtless nice summer days on the campus, I think, but we had a little of snow and hail just two weeks ago. However in spite of the changeable weather we both are quite well, so please do not worry about us.

I hope this note finds you and Mr. Treat in the best of health.

Affectionately yours,
Kei Ichihashi

◘ In early June, Ichihashi learned that the Committee on Emeritus Professors wished to honor him at a party at the Stanford campus. It was bittersweet news: the invitation, he wrote in his diary, was a "mere formality so far as we are concerned, since we are confined here without the liberty of movement anywhere." He tried to devote more of his time to his historical research, including translating some Japanese texts, but camp politics and events disrupted his life constantly. An elderly evacuee sought Ichihashi's help in trying to reunite with his Caucasian wife, who remained at their home in Sacramento because she had serious heart trouble. (Some Caucasian wives voluntarily went to camp with their Japanese husbands; government policy exempted Japanese wives of Caucasian men from the requirement of going to camp.)[41] Ichihashi was pessimistic that anything could be done for the man. Conflict at the hospital continued, too, and Ichihashi saw no solution in sight. At the end of June, residents handed Coverley a petition with hundreds of signatures demanding that something be done about Pedicord at the camp hospital.[42] It produced nothing. At the same time, Ichihashi became increasingly impatient with the behavior of his fellow internees, whom he judged to be selfish and unintelligent. In general, Ichihashi's cynicism about almost everything appeared to mount. On the other hand, the "high points" of his days were when friends brought treats, such as fresh cherries, flowers, cigars, or "real ice cream." The occasional greetings from friends and acquaintances elsewhere, as from another former student of his who had become the librarian at the Poston Relocation camp, also brightened his day.

In June, the Ichihashis also began to develop a friendship with Marvin Opler and his family. Opler worked as one of the WRA's community analysts, who conducted close study of the lives of the residents in the camps. Many of these researchers were from academic backgrounds, Opler himself being an anthropologist from Reed College. After meeting him for the first time, Ichihashi wrote in his diary that he hoped Opler would turn out to be "a scholar interested in culture, as he says." Opler went on to write several essays and coauthor a book on relocation.[43]

Payson and Jessie Treat regularly informed the Ichihashis about the many changes the war brought to the erstwhile leisurely existence at Stanford. They told of rationing, administration efforts to simplify the university's structure, the influx of "student-soldiers" on the campus, and the not-all-to-the-good changes in the intellectual life of the school. Among the newcomers to campus were Japanese American GIs learning Japanese for use in the Pacific War. In early May, the university sponsored a two-day conference on the "Humanities and the War and the Postwar World" and announced its plans to establish a "school for a military government" for postwar Japan, the Malay Peninsula, and Indonesia. They learned too of war deaths in the Stanford family. "The gold stars on the Stanford flag are steadily growing in number, and I fear there will be painfully many of them before the last salvo," Payson Treat sadly wrote Ichihashi. At the June commencement, the university listed the absent Ichihashi in the roster of five new emeritus professors, normally a status of great honor. Treat told Ichihashi that he was the first and "only man who taught many years [in the History Department] who lived to become emeritus." One wonders if Treat's comment helped to console Ichihashi, as Treat intended, or whether it only served to stir more bitterness within his colleague by underscoring the incarceration that prevented enjoyment of the honor.[44] ◾

DIARY

Saturday, July 3

It is essentially clear and warm, though there are a few clouds scattered over the sky. It became a windy day, though not very strong.

July 4th festivity began today with *sumō* at 2:00 P.M. followed by soft-ball games; in the evening *ondo* [a musical performance with dancing and hand-clapping]. But why this enthusiastic celebration? Perhaps it is explained by the monotony of life, but to this must be added the character of the people who find no other avenue for emotional outlet; they lack any serious interest, perhaps not intelligent enough, rather pathetic. It is to be wondered [whether] they ever think of their future—very doubtful—no signs of this kind. Saw the "*ondo*."

Sunday, July 4

It is again a delightful day and remained so throughout. In the evening we went to see the show which consisted of the usual dances with a few songs. The dramatic performance was postponed on account of the illness of an actor. The most surprising feature was the attendance; perhaps 10,000 watched either sitting on the ground or standing on the side, very few on folding chairs. The monotony of life imposed and the cultural level largely explain the phenomenon.

Monday, July 5

This is a real 4th of July weather—hot but clear; a gentle breeze started in the afternoon. Remained hot, the thermometer stayed at 91 degrees or so.

Kuramoto Mrs. brought us two delicious peaches in the afternoon. Kumagai whom we have not seen for quite a spell, came this afternoon; he is suffering from con[stipation?]. He brought us 1/2 doz of the same kind of peaches.

Nothing disagreeable occurred so far today alas!

A barrack (chicken house) was destroyed by a fire early this morning and c. 6000 chicks were burnt to death; as to the cause of the fire, it remains unknown but is said to have been the carelessness of a worker (threw a burning match which caught on an oil tank and caused it to ignite, thus starting the fire). But this is a mere assertion.

Wednesday, July 7

It is another fine day and much cooler due to a gentle breeze. Later strong southerly wind—short gales with flying sand and dust. . . .

Woodrow came and informed [us] that he had arranged to depart from the Project on a permanent leave (of course consulting us) and we were rather disappointed. Kei pleaded with him to change it into a temporary leave but in vain. I advised him to make education his goal and not work and making money (I doubt his ability to save[?] what he earns); finish school as soon as possible. He stayed with us tonight, coming back from a farewell party at 1:00 A.M. Kei talked to him for a while. His present job is with *Johnson Milk Company,* 3300 Caniff Avenue, Detroit, Michigan.

The WRA gave him $122.00 as a grant in reaching his destination; of this amount: $50.00 in cash, 11 $1.00 meal slips and the remainder for the transportation: the bus fare to Reno, from there to Chicago and from there to Detroit (10 hours on a train.) He's expected to stop off at Denver, Colorado at his own expense.[45]

Thursday, July 8

It started somewhat cloudy and therefore humid, making the atmosphere rather sultry.

We went to see Woodrow off; the bus left for Reno at about 8:30 and is due at Reno about 4:30. About 25, mostly nisei, were on the bus for Reno; but more than 200 were there to bid them goodbyes. The Japanese still retain and show their *sō-gei* [welcome and farewell] habits as well as their gift-giving. Woodrow had apparently made many friends here for there were quite a number of boys and a few girls to see him off (their callings "Woodie" indicated); many brought him parting gifts; he had an armful of such. By the time we started for our barrack, it became rather warm—sultry.

. . . Fixed the window screens because mosquitoes began to bother.

San Francisco *Examiner* reports on the Sharp Park "Sino-Jap riot."[46]

Monday, July 12

It is another nice morning but rather chilly. Hot later.

My attention has been called [to the fact] that moonshine is being brewed in many blocks throughout the project, including the 73 [the Ichihashis' block]. Kids are talking about it here—bad, extremely bad but what [can] be done about it as prohibition is enforced here. In one block drinking and gambling resulted in one fellow [being] stabbed and now being investigated: too bad.

The *Dispatch* carries news that segregation of those who are disloyal to the U.S. from those who are loyal will be effected within a few months. This will be a third headache following those of disqualifications for the city council and the reduction of employment.

Another Dr. [?] left the project to serve as an Army surgeon.

Had *tōfu* at K's in the evening.

Ito dropped in and brought the Examiner mis-sent to his office.

Frank was told by Kumagai, the housing supervisor, that small families living on this side of the block will be moved to the other side where barracks are arranged into 6 rooms each, while here there are only five rooms and that larger families will be placed. This will be done in September—another headache and this will make a 4th one.

◘ Ichihashi, along with most other camp residents, became preoccupied with the "segregation" issue. Beginning in the summer of 1943, the WRA began to define certain evacuees as "disloyal to the United States," using responses to question 28 in the registration form and other evidence as the basis for their decisions. The WRA also decided to transform Tule Lake from a "relocation camp" into a "segregation center," where those declared disloyal were to be kept. Eventually more than 18,000 Japanese Americans were incarcerated in the segregation center. About one-third of them had been designated as disloyal; the rest were their family members or residents who did not want to move to another center. By war's end, 7,222 people at Tule Lake had made formal application to go to Japan; almost 65 percent of these were nisei who renounced their American citizenship.[47]

As the atmosphere became increasingly tense at Tule Lake, Ichihashi again found himself at the center of controversy. Just a few months earlier he had been branded an "emperor" and the alleged leader of anti-American activity at the camp, but in the summer of 1943 he discovered that because of his community activities and efforts to engage Coverley in improving living conditions, some Japanese in the camp began to accuse him with being allied with Coverley and, as he wrote in his diary, "actually working against the Japanese here!" He later even heard that some residents were spreading the rumor that he had been duped by alleged FBI agents planted among the camp personnel and had collaborated with them.[48] As Ichihashi had noted previously on numerous occasions, having the reputation of being a "collaborator" could be truly dangerous.

In the following lengthy letters to Treat, Ichihashi discusses the segregation decision and its implications. While Ichihashi's diary entries for this period contain much detail about the residents' reaction and to the implementing of segregation, these are not reproduced here since his letters to Treat well describe the main features of the segregation debacle. ◼

YAMATO ICHIHASHI TO PAYSON TREAT [49]

Newell, California
July 18, 1943

Dear Payson:

As usual my intention of writing to you has failed until today; first of all, I am going to list the topics about which I have been wanting to inform you: the "court" in the project as it actually functions in dealing with evacuee offenders, combining comedies and tragedies which are often very entertaining; the famous case of Dr. Jacoby's resignation which I was able to have rescinded because the residents like him very much; an interesting case of extortion involving several men and women, which was finally settled out of the court; the changed WRA policy in regard to the composition of the City Council, making both nisei and issei eligible; more or less organized agitations against the hospital chief with whom the Japanese doctors could not work in harness and who is equally unpopular with the Japanese residents and American employees, a southerner with deep-rooted racial prejudice, etc. But more recently there have arisen three problems that are vital to the interest of the evacuees: (1) the announced disqualifications for council membership; (2) a drastic cut proposed in regard to the number of Japanese laborers skilled and unskilled; and finally the proposed segregation of loyal and disloyal citizens and aliens. I shall briefly state facts relating to the last-mentioned three problems for your information.

The idea of reviving the city council (erroneously called self-government) with nisei and issei councilmen met with general favor, and a group of men was chosen to amend the charter. While this was being done, the WRA announced the new disqualifications for council participants: accordingly, those who fall within the following categories cannot participate in the council—(1) repatriates and expatriates; (2) men and women who did not register in February and March; (3) men and women who did not swear an unqualified allegiance to the United States at the time of their registration; and (4) those who have been denied leave clearance (for resettlement outside). These disqualifications affect about 4,500 persons among whom are found those who would like to pose as political "leaders." Consequently, there has arisen a series of agitations against the entire disqualifications. Personally, however, I think that the elimination of the so-called leaders rather tends to help the residents as a whole. But politics is politics, and I am afraid that there will be no council which no one will miss except politicians.

As to the policy of the WRA of reducing the number of laborers from the present 5,900 to about 4,300 by September 1st in three monthly installments, there has already followed many a headache. Though the laborers are paid at the rates of $12, 16 and 19 per capita, per month, these individual incomes help in meeting the financial distress of poor families. Therefore, so large a cut in the number of laborers at once creates family budgetary havocs and thereby cause innumerable social problems. I suggested that a joint committee of Americans and Japanese be formed to make a careful study of the individual family situation in order to reduce to a minimum probable hardships attending the reduction. The proposal was unanimously adopted, but to this day no Japanese has been found to serve on the committee; politicians are always clever in not facing any hard problems. It has to be faced, but how I do not know as yet.

The segregation on the grounds exactly similar to the disqualifications stated above, is a bomb-shell, to put it mildly. No one seems to like the idea of joining the black-sheep camp, even if one is a black-sheep; this is quite understandable. For that matter, the WRA administrators themselves are not particularly enthusiastic about the whole business. But the order came from Washington, and they have to execute it, and are seeking assistance from some of the evacuees in this connection. About 4,500 are affected on the basis of careful checking; it is thus a big and nasty problem. The saddest aspect of it is the necessity of separating members of the same family. Expatriates and repatriates are the first to be shipped to the black-sheep camp (still undesignated) without further ado from September 1st on. But others are to have hearings before their final fate is decided. We do not know the procedure to be followed in this connection as yet. In the meantime, I suggested that every means of publicity be employed such as newspaper, public assembly, etc., in order to disseminate necessary and true information to prepare the people for the inevitable and to prevent foolish rumors from spreading. Agitations by those who are affected are bound to arise, but we must prevent what happened at the time of registration in the spring.

You can imagine how busy I have been and am being kept, from the above statement. Of course, I still refuse to mix up publicly with other political leaders. Such contributions that I can make are being made in a private capacity. At any rate, both Kei and I are well despite these difficult times intensified by hot weather during the last few weeks. By the way, Woodrow left recently for Detroit to work for a while in order to find a school where he can finish his study as soon as possible. Yes, *Tule Lake Interlude* was sent to you and others at my request. Please be kind enough to inform the secretary of the [History] Department that the magazines mailed reached me, and also request her to have the University send me a copy of the latest *Register*.

Hoping that this note will find you and your madam well and happy despite many hardships you are encountering, I am

> Very affectionately yours,
> Yamato Ichihashi

YAMATO ICHIHASHI TO PAYSON TREAT [50]

July 25, 1943

Dear Payson:

A mention has been made, in a previous report, of the newly adopted WRA policy of segregation between those who are "loyal" and "disloyal" to the United States among the Japanese who are now residing in the various WRA projects. This note is a continuation of the same report on what has followed since then, but let me repeat briefly as a preliminary what has already taken place. On July 15th, seven of the Japanese "leaders" were called in by Coverley to meet in a conference with him and three of his colleagues who hold the key positions. It was stated by Coverley that about 4,500 were directly affected by the definition of the "disloyal," or roughly one-third of the entire population of this project. Thus numerically alone it is a big problem.

On the following Monday, July 19th, Coverley was informed by the chief director of the WRA, Dillon Myer, that the Tule Lake Project was designated as the camp for the segregates or black-sheep; this was more or less anticipated by some of us, but nonetheless it proved to be a bomb shell to the majority, especially to those who are "loyal" and who are compelled to move again. On the 22nd, a second conference was held between the same groups already indicated, to inform one another concerning reactions of the residents at large and to discover the best method of meeting the situation, which will likely lead to the development of a series of troubles.

At this conference the following facts, observations, opinions, etc., were revealed:

(1) Why was it that the changes made so far in the WRA policy always resulted in imposing beatings on the loyal ones, the present case being no exception? These loyal ones constitute two-thirds of the population, and will be forced to move again. These are indignant because the disloyal ones not only escape inconveniences and hardships attending a mass movement, but also suffer no real restrictions, the declared restriction being that they will not be allowed to re-settle outside for the duration. Herein is found the source of dissatisfaction on the part of loyal ones; let me make this point clear.

(2) The restriction to be imposed on the disloyal ones is interpreted by the WRA as a stigma of the worst kind, but the Japanese do not see it in that light. By far the great majority of the issei are now too old to adventure again; they had worked hard from 30 to 45 years to build up such foundations which they had been capable of; but they were mercilessly and completely uprooted from these foundations. They have no hope, are afraid of strange and hostile environments, and they are now physically and mentally incapable to repeat what they were able to do in the prime of their life. These are the reasons why they do not wish to re-settle outside, and therefore the so-called stigma is no stigma at all to such people. Such being the case, the issei whether loyal or disloyal are united in disagreeing with the WRA interpretation.

(3) Moreover, the people have lived in this project for a year or more, striving to re-adjust themselves, and have succeeded remarkably well in this respect. The surrounding nature and the prevailing climatic condition have previously been described: barren, monotonous, desolate and without vegetation to speak of, and yet many have created "gardens" with such available rocks, weeds, sage-brush, etc.; they have converted their bare and furnitureless one-room tenements into somewhat decent and habitable "homes" by improvis-

ing all sorts of household articles out of scrap-wood. They have developed new friendships. They have even adjusted themselves to an unnatural, communistic, community life, and have created a more or less tolerant human society. Consequently they have become attached and devoted to their own created "city," and they do not want to be broken up again and scattered in small numbers among the nine remaining projects which are to them strange lands; wherever they go, they will be treated as green-horns, and they do not like it. Sentiments? Maybe, but their feeling is intense.

(4) From the foregoing observations, you may easily surmise that the proposed policy as it affects this project is apt to cause a general rebellion on the part of the loyal people even to the point of deliberately making themselves disloyal because of their intense desire to remain here or of avoiding the necessity of going elsewhere. The local administration has emphatically been told of such a possibility, and this time it appears that the administration appears to be sympathetic with the Japanese stand. In fact, its personnel seem to dislike to see this project made into the segregation camp, but of course because of their own selfish interests. Black-sheep will not be easy to manage.

(5) So they asked for our advice in order to present effectively their/our case at the conference to be held at Denver on the coming Monday–Tuesday, at which will gather delegates from the ten projects to thresh out various problems attendant on the policy. Therefore our delegates, all the administration men, may work for some modifications of the policy, but my own personal feeling is that they will not succeed in modifying the policy so as to make this project other than the black-sheep camp.

(6) But to me by far the worst implication of the segregation policy, which was no doubt adopted because of the pressure brought about by cheap politicians and interested parties, appears as follows:

a) The wholesale evacuation of the Japanese as a people was carried out by a military necessity, and because there was no time for the differentiation of individuals. At the same time, those who were suspected of being hostile or dangerous to the interests of this country, were thrown into concentration camps. These are called internees, but the meaning of which has never been clearly defined except in a negative sense. For that matter, the status of evacuees, Japanese citizens and aliens, remains undefined to this day, resulting in technical confusion between municipal and international law. Citizens are denied their constitutional rights and aliens of their international legal protection. In this respect, prisoners of war and internees are better off because they are being governed according to the provisions of the Geneva Protocol.

b) When the segregation is effected, how could the American government continue to justify the present policy of keeping the loyal citizens and aliens in the relocation centers? It conflicts with the fundamental reason given for the wholesale evacuation. Why are those who have proved themselves to be loyal to the American interests to be denied their right of returning to their respective homes wherever they may be, and be allowed to resume their legitimate trades, businesses or professions? Such desire and aspiration are quite natural with any people, and thus they can make contributions to America; the gains resulting from such treatment are mutual and avoid the necessity of wasting public money which should not be wasted in a meaningless enterprise. What rational reasons are there of further subjecting the poor devils to an unnatural communistic life, the life [abhorrent] to Americans and to any normal peoples?

c) If the policy is continued, there can be [but] one explanation, but which, in principle, has been denied and is now being denied everyday, namely, [there is] no discrimination because of color, race or religious belief. Why [then] are Italians and Germans (aliens) given such freedom and rights or privileges, and why are loyal Japanese citizens and aliens denied the same freedom, etc.? Obviously, as individuals, Japanese are no different from Italians or Germans. Surely the American government cannot afford to be so glaringly inconsistent; a few days ago, an appeal came from the Army to Japanese citizens and their parents that the former join the Army Language School, denying racial discrimination as an established principle. What are the Japanese people to do in such circumstances? Besides, the present treatment of the Japanese on racial grounds carries bad implications for all the colored peoples of the world, including Chinese and Indians.

The foregoing statement is superfluous as far as you are concerned, but I wanted to inform you of the facts relative to the newly adopted segregation policy and its implications. Let me add that in the midst of this grave situation Coverley has resigned and left the project yesterday; he told us that he will enter the Military Administrators School in Virginia. There are many other things I might have mentioned, but I am afraid to make the present report too long.

With best wishes to you and your Madam, I remain,

Very affectionately yours,
Yamato Ichihashi [51]

KEI ICHIHASHI TO JESSIE TREAT [52]

Tule Lake
August 1 [1943]

Dear Mrs. Treat:

Yesterday I received your letter and two boxes of the parcels safely. I am glad that you are well and very busy as usual. I thank you for your kindness in buying so many things and sending them to me. Everything is fine. The umbrella is so beautiful, and I like it very much. The under-wears are so nice that I should like to get several of them, but please do not send them to me, until I will ask you for them again.

About three weeks ago we were announced that a segregation program will be undertaken on September 1st so that people have been much disturbed. The other day this project director, Mr. Coverley, got a long distance telephone call from Dillon Myer of the War Relocation Authority, and it [is] said that the Tule Lake Project has been designated as the center for evacuees who are considered disloyal to the United States. Well!! I have to move to some other center! It is the fate! I suppose. But many people are discontented with this announcement, and protest it. They say that disloyal ones should move out. I don't blame them, but I fear their protest will not succeed: for a while I will watch its development.

I am going to send you a box by parcel-post. It contains shell works: a few corsages and two bunches of flowers; I have tried to plant these flowers in a pot, but I am not able to get a suitable thing here. If you get a little pot, green or pink, and stick these flowers in, and cover a wooden flower-holder with clean sand, and then put those little shells, which I put in a small paper bag, on the top, they will be more effective, I think. As I thought I would not stay here very long, I picked up those little shells near our barrack yesterday. They are not very good, but unless we dig the ground 5 or 6 feet deep we can not get good ones.

The shell works are all made by our neighbours, not my work. Many women are doing shell works, but it takes much time and needs effort. In the first place it is very hard to get good shells: one of the women in our block was bitten by a scorpion the other day while she was picking shells, and another was injured. Last fall some woman was badly injured, so that shell hunting was once banned by the authority, so I understand.

I hope you like them, and if you don't mind, please give one of them to Misses Stoltenberg.

I thank you again for your kindness in sending many things and also your thoughtful precious gifts.

Affectionately yours,
Kei Ichihashi

YAMATO ICHIHASHI TO PAYSON TREAT[53]

Tule Lake WRA, Newell, CA.
August 11, 1943.

Dear Payson:

Here is a third report on segregation. Just as I anticipated, no fundamental changes have been made in the announced WRA policy of segregation. This place remains the segregation camp. Recently Dillon Myer offered the following explanations for the choice: 1) "Tule Lake is one of the largest centers in the country, accommodating more than 15,000 Japanese," 2) "here agricultural land is available for subsistence of the Japanese and work opportunities," 3) "there are . . . a larger number of evacuees at Tule Lake who normally would be segregated than at any other center," and 4) "because the center lies at the edge of an evacuated area." The meaning of the last explanation is not clear to me; as I see it, the camp is on an isolated spot, its only nearby town being that of Tule Lake with a population of less than 1,000. At any rate, because of the decision, so-called loyal residents of this camp are to be removed to other camps except Manzanar, Gila and Poston which are closed to them.

At one of the three conferences between the staff and several "representative" Japanese, we were told that the idea of segregating *kibei*[54] and others had been suggested by a naval officer as early as May, 1942 but rejected by the WRA at that time. However, the WRA started at once to gather information for the same purpose. Following the Senate resolution requesting the President that such segregation be put in force,[55] a conference of the project directors was held in Washington in June–July of this year. But nothing was told us about what had transpired then; the segregation policy was made public late in July, and the Denver conference took place on July 26–27.

The segregates have already been described by categories, but in reply to your request let me explain the terms repatriates and expatriates. The former are alien Japanese who have applied for return

to Japan, while the latter are Japanese-American citizens, mostly minors, who have also applied through their parents for return or accompany their parents to Japan. To me the definitions are somewhat
technically or legally wrong, but that is what the American government gives; likewise I am described as a parolee. Moreover, a few
days ago, there was added another category of disloyal alien Japanese and Japanese-American citizens, namely, "persons for whom
the Japanese-American Joint Board established in the Provost Marshal General's office does not affirmatively recommend leave clearance, and persons about whom there is other information indicating
loyalty to Japan." Nothing is clear as to who constitute this Board or
what information it possesses as regards various individuals; it may
be the American equivalent of the Gestapo.[56] I hope that the categories of segregates are made clear with the aid of the information at
your hand.

Those who do not fall within the foregoing categories are considered loyal and free; they are to be removed to other camps
whence, if they so desire, they will be assisted to re-settle outside.
This sounds simple, but in reality it is not so simple, because of the
so-called disloyal ones [who] will be first removed to other camps
where they will be examined in order to determine their exact status.
Why this complicated method is used I do not know; perhaps that is
the bureaucratic way of doing things. Be that as it may, as stated before, this freedom of re-settlement outside is still unwelcome to the
majority of issei for the reasons already explained. Despite our repeated warnings on this point, the WRA agents seem still to persist
in thinking optimistically that the issei are happy of the proffered
opportunity of re-settlement; bureaucratic minds are incapable of
learning anything other than what they themselves can figure out.

In this connection, you may be interested to know that many
agents or propagandists from the WRA and elsewhere are now in
this camp in order to encourage the free people, in particular, nisei
to re-settle in the Mid-West and East by drawing glowing pictures
of the marvelous conditions in those regions for work opportunities.
These are of course high-pressure salesmen and as such they naturally indulge in falsehoods and deliberate lies; they have been told
by some of the maturer and thinking nisei why not tell them truths
once in a while. These nisei have been getting letters from their
friends who have left the camp, trying to find ways and means to resettle but in vain. The people ask me why the government is em-
ploying these agents, and of course my answer is, I do not know; privately, however, I think that the government, probably advised by

the judiciary, is trying to make the nisei get out of the camps in order to avoid the constitutional question, which is necessarily involved in evacuating them into camps without the due process of law. This is a pure guess on my part and it is not to be taken seriously for the time being.

But the administration here seems to sense the tension quite prevalent, and is proceeding very cautiously unlike at the time of registration. The new director,[57] far more politic than his predecessor, is quietly seeking help from representative residents as already hinted. This fact he is carefully concealing from the people at large, and in response, our politicians are trying to organize a committee on segregation. For this purpose they have again utilized the practically defunct Planning Board, and asked each block to elect one issei and one nisei to represent their respective wards, and 14 men together to constitute the said committee. Some blocks and some wards have refused to respond to this call, but others have. I am the issei representative of my block, but am quite dubious of the committee to be, and if organized, its work. That is yet to be seen.

In the meantime, the director has named ten of his staff as speakers whose task is to clarify to the people everything relating to segregation. Already they have bungled up to a considerable degree because they have been talking without careful plans; their interpretations, for instance, often contradict one another. The residents are, as a result, left more confused. The Administration has promised to distribute a manual detailing the procedure of the movements, but they have [not] come as yet. Nothing definitive is known as regards treatments to be accorded to the loyal or disloyal. The Okies removed twice or thrice already are awaiting their fate either for another movement or segregation into this concentration camp. They see nothing but the darkness before them. Would you blame them under the circumstances?

In the midst of this sad situation news or rumor reaches from Japan that the Japanese government has entered into negotiations with the American government that it be allowed to send money to be distributed among those unfortunate evacuees who have not so far received monetary aid (pocket money) from the WRA and who have no prospect of doing so in the future. This is true of all those who have not accepted jobs paying from $12 to $19 per month plus clothing allowances of about $3 person. There are a great many who did not care to have jobs or could not get jobs because there are not enough jobs to go around. Moreover, recently the WRA effected a drastic cut in employment. Some of these, if proved penniless, have been receiving charities, $4.75 per male per month and $4.25 per fe-

male. Apparently these facts have become known to the Japanese authorities, hence the negotiation. This is bad from the standpoint of
America, for it will leave a nasty record; after all no war can last forever. If the American government is unwilling to spend a necessary
amount of money to properly take care of the people whom they
forced to lead a helpless life, it has to rectify in some other ways.
The Japanese, as you know well, are not charity seekers.

It is needless to say that I am bothered everyday again by the
poor, ignorant people, and yet thus far I have been fairly well and
functioning. I am very sorry to learn of Ralph's condition, and I
hope for his speedy recovery.[58] When you see him, will you please
remember us to him and Margaret?

Finally, I must ask of you another favor. Perhaps I did mention to
you that I have not drawn a single cent from the university since my
evacuation, and have asked Mr. Walker [Stanford's financial officer]
to keep my salary with the university, out of which he is to take
whatever I owe the institution. I need not explain why I made such
an arrangement. From September [1943], I receive no salary, but a
pension. Will you be kind enough to find out for me whether or not
my pension is subject to income tax, federal or state? I understood
from Miss Stoltenberg that a pension is not subject to such taxes. I
am anxious to know definitely one way or the other. Please help me
for somehow I do not like to inquire of Mr. Walker whom I do not
know intimately.[59]

More reports will follow on segregation and its related problems
when I find time to write such. Once more, wishing you and Madam
the very best of health in spite of many hardships.

> Yours very affectionately,
> Yamato Ichihashi

KEI ICHIHASHI TO JESSIE TREAT [60]

> Tule Lake
> August 17 [1943]

Dear Mrs. Treat:

I am glad to know that you went to Carmel to get a chance to rest
again. It was very nice. Nobody grows younger, so that we must be
very careful in every way. I rather worked hard for many years, but
lately I consider my health and reduce my work, and also I am trying
not to worry about anything.

In our block there was a funeral for a woman, just a few days ago.

250

She died of hemorrhage, and people say she worked too hard. Our block sent a beautiful wreath, of course, but we, women, spent a whole day and made an artificial flower wreath with many calalilies, pink roses and carnations, etc. It was large and beautiful, and her soul was deeply consoled, I think.

Since the segregation problem was announced many young people are going out. When they go out some people have definite jobs outside, but some ones haven't, however, they are still trying to go out. I do not know if it is true or not, but I have heard that Japanese are paid the lowest wages, and some young people can not get enough money to live, because a cost of living is very high and they are having hard time.[61]

I do not know yet when we are moved into the other center. Some families, however, start packing already. The first group will move about Sept. 10th, so I understand. As soon as we are announced where and when we are moved to, I will write and inform to you. I do not worry anything about it at all. I will move as many times as the authorities want to. Before I move I should like to ask you to send me a few more things with underwears.

A. 1 tie, 2 or 3 dollars one. This is a gift for an old gentleman. A blue tie (or brown) not much red colour in it, if it will be possible, because old men (Japanese) do not wear gay things.
B. 1 bottle of oily cuticle remover, (not polish remover).
C. 1 kitchen knife.
D. 1 larger saucepan and its lid.

I think both C. and D. you can find in our old kitchen. For a long time I tried to buy a kitchen knife and an aluminum pan, but I could not. So that I ask you to send me our old ones. I enclose a cheque for $10 in this letter; please get me 4 vests and 4 bloomers, too, if you can.

> Sincerely yours
> Kei Ichihashi

P.S. We both are sorry to know that Mr. Lutz is ill. His wife's anxiety must be great. When you have a chance to see Mrs. Lutz, please remember us to her.

▢ Events moved quickly toward the impending segregation, and camp residents remained confused, agitated, and angry about the new policy. Ichihashi tried to help clarify the situation and was elected by his block as a representative to a camp committee, named the Community Representatives, organized to contend with questions raised by the segregation order. In announcing its formation to the camp administration, the committee described itself as "an official Body" that "will undertake all communications and negotiations with the administration" on segregation. Ichihashi and two others became the committee's principal leaders. At the same time, he and Kei tried to determine their own future, including where they themselves would transfer. At first, they inquired whether they could simply remain at Tule Lake, but then later they thought about moving to Minidoka in Idaho. Finally they decided on moving to Amache (also known as Granada) in Colorado.[62] The development that most disrupted their emotional lives was not segregation, however, but the startling news that came to them from their son Woodrow on August 25. ◼

DIARY

Tuesday, August 24

Remained cloudy but warmer than yesterday.

Started to clip newspapers.

Decided to go to Granada, and informed Opler who called again for the same purpose; he promised to do his best with Best who is a bureaucrat; [thus?] will his conduct [be] according to the rules and regulations. But Best did promise to consider my case because of my status.[63]

Fujii, the hospital janitor, got a nice job at the hospital at the University of Nebraska, where about 2,000 wounded soldiers are hospitalized. Incidentally, [I was] informed that 146 died here [at Tule Lake] since the beginning to date; of these 94 had post-mortem operations. The WRA pays $75 per each, the funeral expenses, but in fact it is the price paid for the body. It is sent to Portland from where a couple of tea-spoons of ashes are sent here, but nobody knows how the body is disposed. Such is the fate of those who die here.[64]

. . . .

August 25

Started clear and much warmer and continued to be warm.

. . . .

When wild geese returned here, I don't know, but yesterday I saw a small flock of them. Spent the evening in clipping newspapers.

Attended the meeting of the Community Representatives and received copies of the Japanese government message to be distributed among the blocks of this ward. A number of requests were presented to the meeting by various members but none of which were of general interest to the people as a whole. . . .

A couple named Tanino, repatriates, came to consult about their son, [R?], a student, about to be taken into the Army. He is a dual citizen. But nothing can be done was my advice.

Woodrow's shocking letter was received; Kei is very much upset.*

. . . .

August 26

Started clear but cloudy and still later warmer.

Spent the morning and early afternoon in clipping the papers. Finished but rather tired.

Kei continues to be upset over Woodrow's affair.

Ito came and I consulted him about a will to be made.†

. . . .

---

*Woodrow's letter informed his parents of his marriage to Alyce Sakumura of Sacramento. The two had met at Tule Lake, and their secret romance was one of the reasons they had decided to leave the camp. They were married in Chicago and then went to Detroit. Woodrow was drafted into the army in August 1944 and sent to Europe in early 1945. He returned to civilian life in July 1946.

Ichihashi's fury over his only child's marriage apparently had much to do with his notions of social class and proper filial behavior. He refused to have anything to do with Woodrow for almost twenty years; only in 1962, while Woodrow was recuperating from an eye operation did he consent to have his son visit for a few weeks. Yamato died a few months later, without ever meeting his four grandchildren. His uncompromising attitude and anger divided Yamato and Kei for their remaining months at Tule Lake and estranged them for the rest of their lives. The alienation from Woodrow and his family was the source of profound unhappiness for Kei. Despite Yamato's opposition, she continued to try to maintain a relationship with Woodrow and his family. In the fall of 1958, she visited them in Chicago. Although even family friends were not familiar with the estrangement between Yamato and Woodrow, the FBI had reports about their troubles. As of this writing, Woodrow and Alyce have been married for over 50 years. Author's interviews with W. Ichihashi, April 5, Oct. 29, 1992, and Feb. 22, 1995; FBI report, Dec. 17, 1943, Ichihashi FBI File.

†Kenji Ito worked with Ichihashi over several days to complete Ichihashi's last will and testament. He left all but a few dollars to Kei, with Woodrow virtually read out of the will; this, along with Yamato's subsequent behavior, confirms that it was Yamato, not Kei, who was most disturbed by Woodrow's marriage. Ichihashi never revised the document before his death in 1963. Yamato Ichihashi probate file, #59701, Santa Clara County Municipal Records.

One Kasai, a Bay Region resident now at Topaz but here on a visit. The natural condition [at Topaz] is comparable to this camp, but somewhat worse as regards the soil, climate, sand storms. Very changeable. He estimates that about 1,500 can be taken [there], but otherwise it will be crowded. Barracks are arranged slightly differently, but similar. He talked about a *shazai-kai* [apology meeting] at which the officers were made to apologize relative to the visit of the Spanish Consul, in re: repatriation.[65] He talked about men, [I.& M], the woman I saw at the Sharp Park, died or killed herself, [C] was injured for his *deshabari* [presumption], [Y], etc. Asked me why the people are not united in thought. Answer: local jealousies as they are from California, Washington, and Oregon; the differences of their back-ground history. California is famous for anti-Japanism and the people are very bitter; not so with those from the Northwest; this is a matter of degree. I failed to see any fundamental differences; they are all "Japs" in these states and now elsewhere generally.

YAMATO ICHIHASHI TO JESSIE TREAT [66]

Tule Lake WRA
Newell, California
Aug. 27. 1943

Dear Mrs. Treat:

It has been my intention to drop you a line from time to time, but as usual I have failed miserably. This time I must. First of all let me inform you that Kei just received the package and letter and is very happy. The necktie is fine and the old man to get it will be glad, we are sure. Thank you for the things, and in particular for your kind gifts.

One Dr. Opler, a professor at Reed College, is now in this camp as the analyst. What it means: he and his wife, from New York and Columbia graduates, are the only decent Americans we know here. We exchanged calls and had tea. Opler is now negotiating with the new director on our behalf so that we may escape the trials and hardships of the mass movements; of course he is doing this on his own initiative as you know us, we would not ask for favors from American officials. If he succeeds, we will be leaving here for Granada, Colorado, the best place for us, before September 10th to avoid technicalities, when the mass movement [of other evacuees] is to begin.

In connection with the segregation, I have permitted myself to

work publicly for the 1st time on behalf of the poor people so as to
minimize inevitable troubles—already there are signs of trouble due
to the usual mishandling—the administrators make promises which
they do not fulfill. Lies are indulged in and/or soft-peddled—very
stupid. We are now in the midst of terrible confusion with dark
clouds overhanging. More of this when I get time (perhaps after our
departure from here).

What follows is "musts." I recall that my car's tank is full of gas
when we left; please use it. The garage key is with Miss Stoltenberg.
You have to break the other door to reach the tank. Do anything,
but please use it.[67]

Secondly, I am very sorry about Ralph [Lutz] and Margaret—the
latter's recent car accident is most unfortunate. I propose that she
use my car. Of course, it is not insured and without license, but otherwise it can be made usable without huge work—it was in a very
[good] condition as it was fixed just before we left, and the tires are
new. If they feel like to buy it to satisfy themselves, that is OK with
me; we can arrange it later, but let Margaret use it. One thing is that
we don't remember where we put the key to the car; she has to have
it made. (Authorized by the owner, Yamato Ichihashi.)

In haste, I am (Kei will write you soon),

> Very affectionately,
> Yamato

◻ The Ichihashis believed that they had received special treatment in
being allowed to leave early for Granada, and while true, it was not for
the reasons they had assumed. Yamato thought his status and reputation
were responsible for his departure by Pullman train, a belief encouraged
by the camp administrators. They, however, were eager to have Ichihashi leave Tule Lake because they became convinced *he* was leading the
opposition to the effort to segregate the evacuees. Raymond Best, who
succeeded Coverley as Director of Tule Lake, sent a confidential memorandum to James Lindley, the Granada camp director, to inform him
that Ichihashi's move was an "administrative" decision since it was felt
Ichihashi was "the focal point for anti-segregation feeling." Best reported, Ichihashi's "activities seem to have been prompted by his pro-
Japanese proclivities in any crisis which arises on the project, and his
ego-mania."

Best provided some circumstantial evidence to support his allegation,
including Ichihashi's involvement with the camp committee on segregation, but because authorities had "very little written evidence" against
Ichihashi and had to rely principally on verbal evidence, including

"statements of others," there were no grounds for keeping Ichihashi with the "disloyals" at Tule Lake. Best wanted Ichihashi to go as quickly as possible "before any additional resistance to the segregation movement can crystallize." The entries in Ichihashi's diary do not substantiate the administration's suspicions that he actively resisted the segregation.[68] ◧

DIARY

Tuesday, August 31

Clear and cool as yesterday, but developing warm.

Spent the morning in preparing the report to be presented to the first assembly of the block representatives to be held either on Wednesday or Thursday.

[H?] and her sister called.

Nagai came to inform about dissatisfaction felt throughout the Ward VII and expressed the desirability of a ward assembly at an early date.

Ito came in re: will writing.

Due to the inability to coordinate the work of the administration staff, the people are more confused than ever; some threaten to go on sit-down strikes for various reasons.

SPECIAL DATA

In preparation to convert this camp, Tule Lake, into the segregation one, the original barbed-wire fence has been torn down; there is being built a more substantial metal fence (iron-pipe bolted with substantial mesh-wire) like the kind I saw at the Sharp Park Detention Camp. Immediately beyond this fence which encloses the whole area, is built a wide automobile road, the only decent one ever attempted. More watch-towers are also being built. Since the announcement of the first 2 batches of departees, the whole atmosphere has become somewhat tense.

About 20 feet inward from the outer fence, wooden pillars are erected probably to form the inner barbed wire fence. Between this and the outer fence is another wide dirt road.

KEI ICHIHASHI TO JESSIE TREAT [69]

Tule Lake
Sept. 1 [1943]

Dear Mrs. Treat:

I received your package safely, as Mr. Ichihashi had written to you. I am very grateful for your kindness.

The tie is just fine, I like it very much, and the old man will enjoy to wear it, I am sure. After I [have] moved into the other center, I think I can buy things at near town, so that if you do not get the underwears yet, please do not buy them. I thought I put a large knife in a kitchen drawer, as I bought a new one before I left, maybe I put it in some different place.

I have been enjoying to see morning glories every morning, they are really beautiful. I planted them in cans and put cans in shallow wooden boxes, thus I can take them in the room every night. It is too cold for the plants in the evening here, a couple days ago we had quite heavy frost.

We have been informed [we are] to go to Granada, Colorado on the 13th of September with other evacuees, so that we will be there on the 16th.[70] Granada Center is a little better in every way than Tule Lake according to our friends' reports. When I [have] moved there I will write you all about a new center. I think I shall be very busy the next several days to wash a few things and pack our belongings.

I thank you again for your kindness in sending me many things, and also your many nice gifts.

I hope you and Mr. Treat will enjoy a real nice vacation.

Sincerely yours,
Kei Ichihashi

DIARY

Friday, September 3

The same weather as the previous several days.

Busy packing. . . .

Our intended coffee party this evening flopped, so we distributed things—chickens to Ito, Kuramoto, Nakatsuka. Many people from the block and other places came to bid us good-byes.

Got the wills completed. . . . Kenji left at 11:30.

Saturday, September 4

. . . .

The bus came at 9:50 AM and left at 9:55. Most of the block people and others were there to see us off. Two of the checkable baggage pieces were put on the bus, and [evacuee property officer J. Sheldon] Lowry promised to express at once the remaining three pieces. One Mrs. Powell [accompanied us] as our escort. Pleasant trip as far as Alturas; good road and steady bus, but thence bad and snaky roads and hot; rather disagreeable. Had our lunch at Alturas. $2.00 for three; $3.50 for a room with bath (Hotel Menlo) per night. Had dinner at "Oakland," $1.50 and 15 cent tip.

Found [it] noisy all night, but bath was good.

◘ The Ichihashis spent two nights in Reno, Nevada, before leaving by train for Colorado, with 85 percent of their train mates being soldiers and sailors. "All courteous," as Ichihashi noted on his way to a new internment camp.[71] ◘

Amache

September 5, 1943– February 29, 1944

I t took the Ichihashis several weeks to get settled in their new home at Amache (also called Granada for the name of a nearby town), but by mid-October 1943, Yamato Ichihashi returned to his effort to document his relocation experience. On or about October 23, he completed the following essay, which described the move to Colorado and his impressions of the new camp. ◗

RESEARCH ESSAY [1]

Relocation From Tule Lake to Granada

Due to the newly adopted policy of the WRA, the segregation between so-called "loyal" and "disloyal" or pro-American and pro-
Japanese Japanese aliens and their American-citizen offspring became necessary. There soon followed the announcement that the
Tule Lake Center was selected as the camp for pro-Japanese elements, and its residents, especially "loyal" ones were much dismayed
since they had to be removed from there to other centers en masse.
Approximate numbers involved in these mass movements to and fro
have already been indicated;[2] from [them] alone one can easily surmise the stupendous character of the task in effecting the removals.

Realizing inevitable hardships of such mass movements, an
American friend, and a former professor at Reed College, Marvin
Opler, inquired whether or not we would like to avoid possible
hardships by being "transferred" to Granada under a normal condition. He added that in order to avoid technicality, such a transfer
must be effected before September 10th when mass movements
were to begin. We were more than glad to accept his suggestion.

Thus by special arrangements between the project directors of
Tule Lake and Granada, we departed from the former center on
September 4th (within 24 hours after the notice) for Reno by a bus.
This trip consumed 9 hours and was anything but pleasant most of
the way. At the world's "Biggest Little City" we spent two nights;
after our first baths and nice dinner at a moderate price, we recovered somewhat from our exhaustion, and tried to retire but in vain
because of the noise of civilization. This was a Saturday night, and
the city is full of drinking places and gambling dens. The following
Sunday was quiet and we were able to rest.

At 5:40 A.M. on the morning of the 6th, we got on a train, and the
trip was entirely new to Kei, but it proved to be rather monotonous
even to her until she saw the amazing Salt Lake. The Lake left a
deep impression on her, but the trip from Ogden to Cheyenne and
Denver was again monotonous. At Denver we transferred to a Santa
Fe train, and the scenery from Denver on became interesting—
some fantastically shaped hills and rocks upon some of them were
particularly attractive. The train runs in a southerly direction as far
as Pueblo and then it turns eastward until we reached our destination, Lamar, a town of several thousand inhabitants. Ten miles be-

yond is found a small town of Granada (several hundred inhabitants); it is situated at a south-eastern corner of the State. We were
met at Lamar by a representative of the WRA, and by him we were
brought to the camp at about 10:00 P.M. on the 7th.

The camp bears the name of Amache, named after Amache,
"beautiful daughter of Ochi-nee chief of the Cheyenne Indian tribe
which roamed these wind-swept prairies and pitched their tepees
amongst the cottonwoods along the Arkansas River."[3] The camp is
situated about 1 1/2 miles south-west of Granada; it is popularly
known as the "Sand Hill." It embraces an area of one square mile
and stands in the midst of a vast plain stretching in four directions,
and thus it overlooks the bottom land of the Arkansas River. The
camp "literally sprang [up] overnight on a desolate prairie where . . .
only sagebrush, cactus and Russian thistles survive the winter snow
and the hot summer sun. The only creatures which seem to feel at
home here are jackrabbits, rattlesnakes and turtle." Whether named
Amache or Sand Hill, the spot is famous, besides the afore-men-
tioned flora and fauna, for its variable climate richly interspersed
with heat and cold, gales and sand-storms, lightning and cloud-
bursts, etc., most of which we have already experienced. Nevertheless, it is not an intolerable place to live; in fact, Kei and I have become very much attached to our new "home." There exists a
number of pleasant phases which were conspicuously absent at Tule
Lake: the camp is smaller and more compact, and yet spacious because of the skillful arrangement of barracks; the inhabitants are
quiet and sensible: only 125 persons were removed to Tule Lake; the
administrative personnel is decidedly more understanding and sympathetic towards the residents, the director himself setting an excellent example in his everyday conduct. Of course there is plenty of
room for improvement; no human community can escape this fact.

Before attempting at a more detailed description of the above
phases, let me pause and tell of a number of unexpected complications we encountered before we were able to settle permanently in
the present quarters which we occupy. Upon our arrival here we
were taken in by our friends until our assigned apartment could be
made habitable; we stayed with these friends for a week. The apartment was ready and we occupied it (6-E 7-C), having arranged the de
lux furniture sent by our newly discovered relatives (of whom more
information later), together with what we have brought with us. The
barrack in question is situated near the ponds of waste-water, mistakenly described by one journalist as de lux swimming tanks; when
wind blows in the direction of the barrack, we get the benefit of

their unpleasant odor, but for this we were prepared. But the first night we slept in the room, we discovered that the room itself had been polluted by its former occupant, an aged reverend, who had lost the control over his body. Of this fact nobody was aware, but before we occupied it, we had cleaned it thoroughly with plenty of water which brought to the surface what had soaked beneath the brick floor and made the room intolerably odorous. This unsanitary condition forced us to apply for another room, but the response was slow in coming because in the meantime the batch of removals from Tule Lake had reached the camp, which was suffering from a short-age of rooms to accommodate the newcomers! Thus for several days we were made to suffer. Finally, at the end of a week, we were given another room by the Housing Supervisor, and we proceeded to clean this room (6-G 2-D), expecting to occupy it as soon as possible. But this time, a hitch arose over the room because of the opposition of the block manager who was having trouble in getting the coop-eration of the block residents in making room for Tule Lake arri-vals. The room in question had been assigned to a family already re-fjsiding in the block, but which refused to move into it and [the block manager] insisted that the family move into it. Of these com-plications we knew nothing, but in the end we were victimized and were told that we could not occupy it. That was the second room we had to clean but failed to get it; we were left stranded once again. The room we had cleaned was occupied by another family from Tule Lake; it was a joke, a very mean one as far as we were con-cerned. The only satisfaction in this connection was the discharge of the obnoxious block manager by the administration which became dissatisfied with his failure to keep the block residents in harmony and peace. Our housing trouble finally reached the ear of Lindley;[4] he demanded of Walker, the Housing Supervisor, why we were not settled and ordered him to allot us a room disregarding other situa-tions: "they have had enough trouble already." Whereupon he gave me the right to choose one. Of the four suggested, I chose the one which we now occupy, namely, 10-H 12D, though I found it in a ter-rible condition: the walls are scratched all over, and the ceiling too for no apparent reasons; dust and junk were so piled up on the floor so as to fill five wheel-barrow fulls; the windows were so dirty that their transparency was gone. We were obliged again to engage in house-cleaning for a third time; but we were able to move into this apartment on the 19th (Sunday). Since then until a day or two ago, we [were] forced to spend most of the time in fixing up the room, and only then did we feel that we were more or less finally settled.

In making the room habitable, we needed a number of things, including lumber which was promised us but never supplied to this day. Our friends came to our rescue, in particular, Yuhora whom I used to know when I was young; he secured necessary materials and fixed the room with the aid of his friend, Takahashi.[5] Still, we needed some other objects which we intended to purchase at Lamar, but the development of infantile paralysis [polio] outside made the project adopt a policy to prevent the coming into, and going out, of the project. Nevertheless, there have developed four cases, not counting one who contracted it and went out, and died. This rule has been in operation a week after our arrival here to date; the Sakai family paid a visit on the 8th,[6] and his boy brought the furniture on the 9th; the family came again, but was unable to come into the camp and so they left with a cop some melons and vegetables to be delivered to us. Of course, we have never been able to go out to date; thus one freedom of going out granted to the residents has not been available; consequently we are without a number of things very much needed for the room and for our comfort. Such has been our plight, but it is useless to feel blue about it; we have to make the best of the worst situation.

Physical-Setup.

The camp itself "is located within the southern boundary of the mile-square overlooking the rich bottom land of the Arkansas River. This location is bordered on the west by a cemetery, dump pile, and sewer farm, and on the east by a rolling prairie that stretches away into the state of Kansas. The northern limit is occupied by rows of warehouses, appointed personnel living quarters, administration buildings, and by the Military Police compound. Isolated in the northeastern corner is the center's . . . hospital, gleaming white against the dusty background with its three black smoke stacks reaching into the empty sky." "(The one distinguishing landmark, visible ten miles away, is the project's water tank whose orange and white checkered wall rises seventy-two feet above the highest point of the center ground)."

The remaining section, a major portion of the camp area, south of the ground devoted to the aforesaid buildings, is given to the evacuee residences consisting of 360 barracks. These 360 barracks are grouped into thirty blocks; each block consists of 12 of these living barracks plus its own community mess hall, laundry, toilet and

shower, and recreation hall. Each block is placed under the management of a "block manager who is aided by a runner," both being the
appointees of the administration. Again, these 30 blocks are grouped
into five "districts," which are the largest political units in the general organization of the camp. These blocks are arranged in five
rows, running north and south and beginning at the west, and
named 6E, 7E, 8E, 9E, 10E, 11E and 12E, seven blocks in all; immediately to the east of this first row is the F unit, followed by the G, H,
and K units. The F, G, and K have only five blocks each; in addition
there is one block, 9L, which stands alone at the eastern extremity,
but in the line of 9's. The unoccupied block areas are given over to
schools or left empty; one of the residential blocks is still being used
to house an elementary school. The accompanying chart will make
the arrangement of blocks more vivid.*

The barracks are identical in size and shape, they being 120 by 20
feet with the height of   feet;† they are built of wood on concrete
foundations; their exterior walls are covered mostly with sanded
boards made of sugar cane pulps, while some are covered with tar
papers as in the case of roofs. These walls are of three different col-
ors: dark blue, green and very light brown which break monotony,
but the roof is covered with black or green tar paper. As compared
with the external appearance of Tule Lake barracks uniformly covered with black tar paper, the barracks here are pleasanter to look at.
Another pleasant feature is rendered by the planting of cotton-wood
around the barracks by the Japanese residents at their own expense
as well as by flower gardens also created by the Japanese. Vegetable
gardens, however, often appear unsightly because their plots have
not been carefully chosen or the lack of proper care.

Finally, each barrack is divided into 6 rooms: two of 16 × 20, two
of 20 × 20 and two of 24 × 20; these are allocated to families according to their size or groups of single individuals. Some of these
rooms have been rendered into quite habitable living quarters while
others are left barren and disorderly. Here human nature manifests
itself most vividly, destroying uniformity by applying its ingenuity in
beautification or by remaining utterly indifferent in this regard. Man
may be born equal, and may be treated equally, but he will not remain the same; humans are fundamentally different in their nature,

---

*The chart is not reproduced in this book, but the camp is shown in a photograph
following p. 202.

†Ichihashi apparently intended to insert the height measurement in the space he provided, but it remains blank.

and therefore in their habit and thought. Even the floors which are built of unsightly bricks or cold concrete are rendered pleasant in some, while others are left as they are which are prehistorically primitive. Some prehistorical men would have done better than some civilized men in making their simple habitats more pleasing to the eye as prehistoric relics clearly prove. I am somewhat surprised at some of my fellow-countrymen who are supposedly all lovers of nature and things beautiful.

The People.

The Granada Relocation Center was officially opened on August 29, 1942, with the arrival of the first contingent from the Merced Assembly Center. Subsequently on September 15,[7] groups from the Santa Anita Assembly Center began to arrive, completing the project's occupation by the 30th. The population was half urban from Los Angeles and half rural from Merced, to which had been assembled the people from the rural sections of the central valleys and the San Francisco Bay area. The total population was 7,620 of which number two-thirds (5,497) were American citizens and one-third, Japanese aliens. Occupationally the urban element was composed of merchants, hotel and restaurant operators, gardeners and landscape artists, salesmen and clerks as well as of a small number of doctors, dentists, lawyers, scientists, optometrists, jewelers, etc. The rural element was made up of farmers and their families and farm laborers and their families. The population as a whole contained its quota of others such as artisans and laymen, architects, craftsmen, musicians, school children and college students, mechanics, truck drivers, common laborers, as well as teachers and priests, Christian and Buddhist. In other words, the population of Amache does not occupationally differ very much from that of any community of a comparable size despite the fact of its abnormal age-composition and sex-distribution. The last fact is true of the population at all the centers, in fact; this was true of the Japanese population in the United States before the outbreak of the war and therefore before its evacuation.

However, the Amache population, like all the other center populations, has not remained static for various reasons, in particular, for the reason of the WRA policy of relocation (re-settlement) which encourages the people to move outside and settle in the Middle West and East. This policy was put in effect about a year ago. Recently (October 13, 1943) the *Pioneer* [the camp newspaper] published the following interesting facts relative to the population movements:

1) Since the establishment of the project, more than 1,300 evacuees have obtained permission to leave for permanent outside employment (and settlement);

2) In addition, 945 other residents are now on temporary seasonal leave, mostly for farm-harvest work in Colorado and Nebraska; there are about 125 seasonal workers in Kansas working on railroads;

3) The Amache population stands at slightly over 6,400. In connection with the above facts, the following should be remembered: On September 15 and 22, 1943, there arrived from Tule Lake 513[?] and 478, whereas 125 Amache residents were removed to the Segregation Camp; 135 more were to come here from Tule Lake, but due to the lack of accommodation, they were directed elsewhere.

These movements above noted have not affected the general character of the population, and yet as compared with the population of Tule Lake, for example, the people appear, on the whole, to be quiet and sensible. But on the other hand, passivity in general seems to be their conspicuous mark; they are not active in work, play, hobbies, intellectual pursuits. The following may explain:

1) This center is in a free zone,[8] and the people are allowed a larger degree of freedom of movement; they can go outside for pleasure or for shopping without restrictions. Prohibition is not strictly enforced, and there is no necessity of fabricating moon-shine drinks.

2) The character of age-composition and sex-distribution appears to be quite different (no statistics are available as yet), but many old men and women are present. There are many young nisei women, but they are mostly mothers of small children; their husbands in many cases are working outside or soldiering. Youngsters are mostly of high school and grammar school age; others are mere infants. Adult men, such as there are, seem to lack the guts, and they would not adventure, and prefer to lead a quiet, passive life in the camp. There is not much room for politicians and there are very few of them, if any. True intellectuals are conspicuous by their absence, and their place is made up [for] by "know-alls," who do not, however, find opportunities for playing leading roles of any kind. In fact, they are [not?] wanted by anybody. Even professional entertainers and amateur entertainers are few in number, and they are not popular and have no opportunities to appear in public. Musicians are also conspicuous by their absence, and talents of any kind are absent.

3) The people are not pleasure seekers, and do not hunger for entertainment of any kind. Some issei play *goh* and *shōgi* [Japanese board games], others engage in group-gossiping; they do not even discuss the war. They may be philosophers or just plain dumbs. In either case, they make no noise, and retire very early. The whole camp is dark, as outside lights are few and dim and far between; there is no night life in the camp, and it is a paradise for old people who love quietude.

4) Youngsters are too small [to cause trouble] beyond making a lot of noise in the day time, but are made to sleep early. Most of the women whether young or old are too busy in their household duties; apparently they are satisfied with family drudgeries. It is good for infants. But they may lack ambitions to become ladies like those found among the Tule Lake women.

5) Besides, the climate here strikes me as energy-sapping; I feel tired all the time; I sleep as I have never slept before. It requires a good of deal of effort to work hard, at least mentally, in spite of a general favorable condition for study and meditation. There is no noise created by man, though there is a plenty of what nature makes: thunder and gale. I hope never to succumb to an inactive life; I must strive to stir my mental efforts against all odds.

There may be other reasons for human passivity in general at this camp, but the foregoing appear to be more important ones as far as I can see and feel. In a sense, it is too bad that we should be forced to lead such a life; it is particularly bad for those who have to prepare themselves for the future. Young people need strong stimuli in order to prevent [themselves] from succumbing to inactivity; how such needed stimuli can be created requires hard thinking on the part of those who are endowed with active brains.

The Administration.

The administration of the project is organized as elsewhere, but it is housed in three modest buildings, in which offices very unpretentious in character are arranged for the various officers. They are located not far from the entrance gate of the camp, i.e., at the northern end. The offices are easily accessible to the residents, and formality is absent; the director himself occupies a simple office, and meets every caller very informally. His example seems to be followed by all the other members of the administration. Thus the relationship between the administration and the residents is not only informal, but even intimate, reducing to a minimum any irritation, if any. It has been remarked elsewhere that the administrative personnel is decidedly more understanding and sympathetic; it is free from the California-type of anti-Japanese prejudice. This fact largely influences the behavior of the Japanese evacuee residents; it helps in rendering the latter content with the life enforced on them, as they are appreciative of the sympathy shown them. The net result is mutual satisfaction.

The above observation is not a mere guess, but based on my own experiences with several members of the personnel, including the director. I was impressed with the sympathetic attitude of Adams, assistant director of the Internal Security, who met us at Lamar; the conversation during the trip to the camp proved it. Next day, I met Lindley and was treated courteously; he struck me as a sincere man, even if he is politic. He does not depend on his subordinates, but performs whatever one asks of him. For example, concerning my luggage sent here from Tule Lake COD, he himself went and called in Holiday[9] who has charge over such matters, and instructed him to make necessary arrangements; the luggage came to me without any more trouble. I applied to him for permission to meet the first batch [of transferees] from Tule Lake, at Granada, and was granted it, although no one else was permitted [to do so] to avoid unnecessary confusion; he knew why I wanted to meet the transferees. At the station, I saw him helping the people alighting from the train with comforting words; he certainly shows his interest in the people whom he has to govern. I met [Donald T.] Horn, the project attorney, relative to the income tax declaration; he too was courteously helpful. This was the same man who brought back from Granada Kiyohara[10] and myself to the camp; with him was his wife on this occasion, and she too was very courteous.

It should [not?] be understood that the administration coddles the people, far from it; it insists that the people must be obedient to and observant of the rules and regulations as well as cooperative in performing necessary functions and tasks. They are responsive to such desires and requests. Voluntary labor is common when emergencies arise. Those who do not, as well as trouble-makers, are few and inconspicuous; recall that only 125 had to be transferred to Tule Lake, and not all of them belonged to the category of undesirables (repatriates and expatriates). The administration must therefore be credited of having been rather successful; certainly there is no comparison between it and that of Tule Lake. I have heard no loud complaints from either side.

Community Government.

The central executive and legislative body of the residents is the community council composed of one representative from each of the twenty-nine blocks into which units the residents are grouped. These representatives are elected by popular vote, from among their respective block residents, who are 18 years of age or over, both male and female as elsewhere. These twenty-nine blocks are grouped into five districts; five councilmen resident in each of these five districts are chosen or elected to constitute the council's executive committee. At present, three nisei and two issei form that committee. The council is charged with the prescription[?] of ordinances, regulations, and laws which govern community life in the project. It is aided by a judicial commission of 8 members appointed by the council; the eight members are as follows: three members of the administrative personnel and five evacuee residents. The commission hears and tries cases of violation of community regulations. It is also aided by an arbitration commission composed of 15 appointed from among the evacuee residents. It arbitrates civil disputes among the residents of the project.

As mentioned already, there exist other public functionaries called block managers, twenty-nine in number, who are aided by an equal number of "runners." It so happens that the council membership is dominated by nisei, there being only five issei members, whereas the block managers and runners are chosen by the administration from among the issei residents. Since the council is made up of young, inexperienced nisei, and mostly incapable and indifferent, it inevitably developed the domination of politics by the issei block managers; this may be fortunate or unfortunate depending upon one's view. How much politics the latter indulge in is yet to be discovered as far as I am concerned, yet some of them form cliques of their own in order to maintain their positions or to attempt to dominate their respective block residents. I had an experience with one of these domineering type of block managers, relative to the allocation of a living quarters (6-G). Democracy is not working, but the chief reason for this may lie in the fact of a general indifference of the residents themselves, whether nisei or issei. Politics is not apparently popular in this project; "the least governed, the better," seems to be the motto. There naturally exist a few pseudo-intellectuals who attempt to formulate various lines of public activities; I am familiar with one of such a group, but [he] lacks real intellectual powers, and even general intelligence. They are not likely to get away with their efforts.

Education and Religion.

The information pamphlet gives the following facts on public education: there were organized [schools] for the benefit of evacuee children and youths elementary, junior- and senior-high schools, which together used to occupy the whole of 8-н block, but lately the high (senior) school was removed into the newly constructed building, which can accommodate 600 pupils. "The educational program is conducted in cooperation with the Colorado State Department of Education and offers curriculums not unlike those of any comparable institution outside the center." The school enrollment as of April 1, 1943 is as follows: nursery, 152; kindergarten, 95; elementary, 681; junior high, 433; senior high, 550. That gives a total of 1,911 pupils.

"On the regular staff are 50 Caucasian teachers, 4 principals and a superintendent. Augmenting this staff are eleven accredited evacuee instructors, thirty-seven assistant teachers and twenty-eight specialists." The quality of education offered is yet to be evaluated for which there is no information available.

"Special adult classes are held nightly to teach typing, shorthand, English, dress-making, drafting, handicraft and fine arts." The *Pioneer* under the date of Oct. 9, 1943, reports that "961 persons are enrolled in the various classes, according to Samuel Gordon, night school director. This total does not indicate that there are actually 961 different persons enrolled, as one person may be attending three or four classes. As expected, the women outnumber men, 876 to only 85. There are 57 classes with 25 instructors, and a total of 36 paid workers which include teachers, janitors, secretaries, runners, and part-time appointed personnel instructors."

On *religion*, the pamphlet states: "The religion of Amache is predominantly Protestant with representatives from the following denominational groups: Methodist, Baptist, Presbyterian, Holiness, and Seventh-Day-Adventists. Their total membership approximates

2,000 (this must be an exaggeration) with 15 ordained ministers who take turn conducting services each Sunday in both English and Japanese."

"The next largest group are those of the Buddhist faith. They number about 600 (this must be an underestimate) and conduct their services in a typical oriental pattern. However, English services are also conducted for the nisei. . . ."

"Another group are the Catholics who hold their mass on Saturday mornings, officiated by a Father who resides in a neighboring community and visits the center every week for this purpose."

Since all these services have been suspended since my arrival here on account of the polio situation, there is no way of finding out how well they are attended. Neither is there means of discovering the character or quality of services offered by the religious leaders. These are far more important than the mere existence of religious institutions. There prevails a good deal of criticism on those points by residents in general; how well such criticisms are grounded, it is difficult to know. But no observer can escape the general fact that religious influences in these camps are extremely meager; what is the reason for this? Does it differ very much from what prevails in normal society?

Communal Institutions.

Living quarters provided in rectangular army-style barracks for the residents have already been described in detail elsewhere. Here attention will be confined to mess halls, latrines, wash-rooms, showers, and laundries which are provided in each block and used in common by its residents.

The mess hall here does not differ in character and equipment from that which is provided in the other centers; it is a plain barrack 100 × 40 feet with a seating capacity of 200 to 250 persons with roughly constructed plain tables and benches for seats. The last are very uncomfortable to say the least of it. "The functional activity of the block is centered around the mess hall where the evacuees go not only to eat their three meals a day but hold their talent shows, block meetings, movies and dances." I have been here a month and a half, but have not encountered any of the above activity save three meals a day. Meals are prepared and served entirely by evacuee workers.

The kitchen is equipped "with an up-to-date refrigerator, two galvanized sinks, water heater, steam sterilizer, and three coal stoves." Sanitation should be perfect, but the kitchen personnel appears to be untidy due to the lack of uniform clothing which is usually provided by the WRA in other centers. Thus instead of white apparels and white caps, the workers wear dark shirts and overalls over which they wear unclean aprons; women's apparels are no better. This is true of cooks, servers, and dish-washers.

The meals are served cafeteria style, each individual lining up at the kitchen counter to receive his plate and then sitting at a table on a bench. "Coffee is served in the mornings, while tea, water or milk is provided at other meals. The menus are prepared by the WRA mess division and adhere strictly to the ration regulations governing any institution outside the center." Formerly, 46 cents per day per capita was allotted for meals, but from the month of September of this year, the allotment has been reduced to 32 cents. Consequently, meals have been extremely poor in quality; too much of starchy food consisting of rice, noodles, beans, etc., is served too frequently; meats in any form are conspicuous by their absence. Menu-makers and cooks are helpless since they do [not] get proper food supplies; the people are given bulks, but not balanced meals to provide necessary nutrition. They have lost their power of resistance to illness and become ill very easily; their general state of lethargy may be explained by this fact.

The remaining communal institutions: latrines, wash-rooms, showers, and laundries are relatively well-equipped and kept clean by the janitors. The residents too seem to cooperate in maintaining these places clean and therefore sanitary. As compared with those of Tule Lake, these show a distinct improvement and are superior. Individual porcelain wash-basins and urinating pots are particularly nice, as compared with the troughs (galvanized) of Tule Lake. Moreover, these rooms are well lighted by the sunshine or by electric lamps. All in all these places are satisfactory, and tend to prevent spreading of contagious diseases.

Hospital. The center maintains a hospital to maintain the health of the residents. It is the seventeen-winged structure built identical to an Army-post unit, and has approximately 150 beds. It is staffed by a chief medical officer, a member of the WRA, and five evacuee doctors. An American registered nurse supervises registered student nurse and nurse-aids picked from among the evacuee residents, numbering one, three and twenty-one respectively. These form but a small fraction of the total of 219 hospital employees. The hospital is [said] to be comparable to any first class institution of similar size, having complete equipment to care for almost any kind of ailment.

"Among the many divisions of the medical units are the outpatient clinic, pharmacy, optometry, laboratory, X-ray department, all located in the out-patient building, and the dental clinic. The outpatient clinic is the busiest section of the unit. Approximately 800 patients are treated here in one week alone. The surgery ward is a special unit for minor and major operations. The dental clinic, staffed by seven evacuee dentists, treats 125 patients daily.... Service is limited to emergency cases."

Externally, the hospital isolated in the northeastern corner of the camp, gleams "white against the dusty background with its three black smoke stacks reaching the empty sky."

Police Department. The duty of preserving law and order within the center lies in the hands of the police department. The force, headed by an internal security officer, a member of the WRA, consists of 60 evacuee police men trained in police tactics. "Their efficiency is attested by the fact that no serious crime has occurred within the center to date." The force is organized as follows: evacuee chief-of-police, 3 captains, 3 desk sergeants, 3 field sergeants, one release sergeant, one transportation sergeant and 48 patrolmen. The last-mentioned are assigned beats in 8-hour shifts. The headquarter and barrack are located in block 8-F, while the office is located in the south administration building.

It may be noted that the function of the military police is restricted to the patrolling of areas outside the center and has no jurisdiction within it.

Fire Department. The fire department is located on the main street between the residential and administration areas. It houses two modern Ford trucks equipped with a triple combination pumper capable of throwing 500 gallons of water per minute. The equipment is manned twenty-four [hours] a day by three shifts of platoons comprising eight to ten men each. The responsibility rests with a fire-protection chief, his assistant, and an evacuee chief. Living accommodations are provided for the firemen who are on night duty. In addition to these members, are volunteer and auxiliary foremen from each block who receive periodic training in fire combat. A fire is reported through emergency telephones located throughout the camp.

Water and Power. The water for the project is supplied by four wells approximately 800 feet deep. They are equipped with pumps driven by a forty-horse-power electric motor which discharges 350 gallons per minute into a 200,000 gallon storage tank. Here it is chlorinated to safeguard against pollution. From the tank two 750 gallon per minute centrifugal pumps driven by forty-horse-power motors force the water into an elevated 25,000 gallon tank seventy-two feet high constructed on the southern boundary of the camp. Gasoline-driven standby pumps are installed in Cell No. 3 and the storage tank to take care of any emergency arising out of power failure.

The large amount of water used by the evacuees for normal living purposes can be seen when it is noted that the 25,000 gallon tank cannot be kept full for more than thirty minutes if the supply is shut off from the main storage tank.

Electric power is supplied by the Lamar Branch of the Rural Electrification Administration. Approximately 234,000 kilowatt hours are consumed per month in the center.

Warehouses. Fourteen standard warehouses 40 × 100 feet occupy the northwest corner on the project site. They are used for storing mess-division supplies, furnitures, motor-pool equipment, community enterprise stocks, public-service supplies, and many other miscellaneous items.

In this area also are located two walk-in refrigeration plants 20 × 100 feet, a meat house and a carpenter shop.

Employment. The relocation centers are organized in a manner that requires dependency upon the performance of necessary labor on the part of evacuee residents to a very large extent. Only responsible administrative duties, supervisory, and managerial tasks are performed by the appointed WRA personnel, exclusively Caucasian; the rest is performed by evacuees who are paid $12, 16, or 19 [per month] according to the skill required in performing assigned tasks, covering a wide range of skilled and unskilled labor. They receive, in addition, a clothing allowance, and of course board and room, the last of which is provided for all evacuee residents. These are all employees of the government, i.e., the WRA, as no private enterprise is permitted in the centers.

In this center, according to the pamphlet, "there is a total of [3,476?] evacuees employed in approximately [25?] different departments, each supervised by Caucasians who are termed the appointed personnel. Sections under the departments are usually headed by evacuees who have had previous experience in the particular work.

"As an example, the numerous functions of the public-works division, which employs 56 people, may be cited. Its responsibilities include the planning and beautification of the center, maintenances of sewage, plumbing, power and sanitation, construction of roads and houses and the control of soil erosion."

WRA Farm. The main industry of the center is agriculture. Its object is to produce enough vegetables and meat so that it will be, to a great extent, self-sufficient.

"The actual land under the farm section embraces 4,095 acres known as the X-Y Ranch and 5,688 acres known as the Koen Ranch formerly operated by the American Crystal Sugar Company. Of this acreage, almost 6,000 is under irrigation. The water is supplied by the Lamar Canal and Manvel Ditch of which 40% and 67% respectively of the capital stock is held by the WRA. The water rights of the X-Y Ditch is entirely owned by the WRA.

"Equipment used in farming includes a number of large track-type tractors and twenty Fords. There is also a completely equipped blacksmith-shop for general repair, electric and gas welding, forge work, drilling and cutting.

"The present plan calls for 500 acres of vegetables some of which are: onions, beans, corn, potatoes, carrots, lettuce, tomatoes, cauliflowers, cabbage, cantaloupe, and watermelons. Other seedings include 800 acres of alfalfa, with several hundred acres in corn, grain, and sorghum.

"Another important farm program is livestock production. At present there are 1,000 chickens and 525 hogs which will be increased to 20,000 and 1,000 respectively. The hogs are fattened on garbage accumulated within the center. Further plans in this department call for a possible start in beef production." The last-mentioned has been started with a small number of cattle.

The foregoing presents a brief historical survey of the main facts, beginning with the segregation as we experienced in being transferred from Tule Lake to this center (September 4th–October 22nd), with the exception of resettlement which will be treated separately elsewhere.[11]

KEI ICHIHASHI TO JESSIE TREAT [12]

Amache, Colorado
Oct. 8 [1943]

Dear Mrs. Treat:

Thank you for delicious candies. I thought I could not eat California candies any more; it is too good to eat delicious California candies here. It was rather surprising to receive a knife; I do not know how it was in the kitchen drawer; it is one of the oldest knives I have, and I did not use it for many years. At the evacuation time every thing was mixed up, I think. However it is very handy, I used it this morning already. As I wrote you before,[13] we found many old acquaintances here, and some of them brought us big watermelons and honey dews, but we didn't have any big knives yet, so that it was quite a problem how to cut [them]; however, on the second day we tasted the sweetest watermelon in our life, and everybody who ate it, fully praised it. Since we came here we were planning to go out to buy some necessary things at Lamar, the nearby town, but we have been banned to go out because of infantile paralysis. There are 169 cases in this state at present. We do not know when we shall be able to go out for shopping, so we are very glad to have had the knife, and are very grateful for your kindness indeed.

Last night I saw a map and found the situation of Granada. It is situated in the south-eastern corner of the state of Colorado, and very close to the border. Granada is too small to find on the map, but you can find Lamar, and Granada is nine miles east of Lamar.

The project is on the sand hill, and when the wind blows, sand gets in the room, but it is very clean sand, so that we do not suffer so badly as at Tule Lake. Very fortunately we have soft water here, and it is very good for washing. Last spring's people planted trees around the barracks, and flowers and vegetables grow very nicely between the barracks; some families even have beautiful lawns. It seems to me [that the] people who come here from Tule Lake are very much satisfied. From our block at Tule Lake, five families came here so far. A few days ago our all belongings arrived safely, and we are fixing our new living quarters, but [it is] not quite finished yet.

As you know I am worrying about the vacant [Stanford] house, if some careful people could use the house it would be much better on the whole, I think. I have not received a letter from her which you mentioned.[14]

Please give my best wishes to Mr. Treat.

Sincerely yours,
Kei Ichihashi

1943 DIARY [15]

Monday, October 18

Again it started clear and chilly as yesterday, but later it turned out to be rather hot which was, however, soon moderated by a breeze gentle, until later in the evening when it became somewhat strong. It certainly is variable.

Spent most of the morning in writing a history of the relocation from Tule Lake to this project, but still it is unfinished as I began to feel rather tired toward the noon. The food today was very poor and I could not eat enough of it. Received a letter from Payson and also articles from *Time* and *Life* asking for my view of them; of course I shall not attempt to meet the request.*

After the dinner I felt a little better but not well. The wind turned into a gale but not very strong; no doubt sands will be blown as usual.

Tuesday, October 19

Started cloudy and rather warm (65 degrees) and sultry; it is not pleasant as a breeze blows sands in all directions, and as the wind becomes a strong gale; sand storms become worse—stormy day. A southwest gale from 10:00 on; this is yet the worst sand-storm we have encountered since our arrival; nothing is visible in short distances despite the bright sunshine. Finer sands penetrated through

---

*The letter from Treat has not been located. Ichihashi received a letter from an editorial vice president of Time, Inc. asking for his opinion about articles that had appeared in *Time* and *Life* speculating on the political and economic situation of the future postwar world. "All of us here are interested in what you have to say about the job our magazines are doing," the friendly inquiry offered (Hodgins to Ichihashi, Sept. 10, 1943, IP, B5, F8).

windows and not covered everything in the room, but piled on the
floor quite deeply; it is quite disagreeable to live in a sand-filled
room. It is worse outside where sands fly about with terrific gale
[force], hitting the face and filling every orifice, the mouth becoming gritty. This state continued all day, but toward the night-fall the
storm subsided, leaving finer sands piled up on certain spots. To
walk over these sand-covered places, one felt like walking over
freshly fallen snow-bound grounds, soft and sinking; it is rather a
novel experience for me. I wonder if the situation resembles that
of deserts!

The history of the relocation was continued.

YAMATO ICHIHASHI TO
PAYSON AND JESSIE TREAT [16]

IO-H I2-D
Amache, Colorado
October 21, 1943

Dear Friends:

Needless to say that I have been trying to write you sooner but in
vain; for one thing we were unable to settle permanently for over
two weeks though we cleaned three "apartments." Even the one
we now occupy has not been rendered habitable till a few days ago,
and this we had to do with many interruptions: the lack of necessary
materials and frequent visits of "friends." What Kei reported has
proved to be premature in many respects: the weather has been mar-
velously pleasant for many days, though it is energy-sapping, all of
us sleep long hours and still feel lazy; the remaining days have been
terrible: thunder and lightning, hot and cold, gales and sand-storms
climaxed with cloud bursts. Nevertheless, we have become attached
to the place for other reasons which are many, and these will be
reported in full when my typewriter is fixed as Payson hates my
hand[writing], comparable with that of Edgar's.[17] I am writing this
note to avoid the boss's scolding.

The camp was named after Amache, "beautiful daughter of Ochi-
nee chief of the Cheyenne Tribe which used to roam these wind-
swept prairies . . . ," but popularly the spot is known as "Sand Hill"
which is less romantic, but truer to its nature. Dear Madam, the
camp is situated in a southeastern corner of the state, near the small
farming village of Granada, in the midst of a vast plain, monoto-

nously unbeautiful. Its flora are confined to sagebrush, cactus and Russian thistles and cotton-woods planted by man here and there; its fauna are jackrabbits, rattle-snakes and turtle.

The people both Japanese and American are nice, quiet and more sensible; this fact makes this camp a paradise for gentlemen and scholars who love quietude and meditation. Yes, our newly discovered relatives [are] named Sakai; the head of the family is a cousin of George Mizota who is married to a sister of Kei;[18] through the latter they have known me too for years. Sakai is the pioneer in this region and a rich farmer quite capable of sending us de lux furniture; he is a likable chap. We have seen him and his family but once so far; they could not visit since on account of the polio situation—there are four cases in the camp. But they have been sending us vegetables and flowers. Of course, we have never been able to go outside, which is permitted under the normal condition.

It is hoped that this note will find both of you happy and in good health.

Very affectionately
Yamato

DIARY

Monday, October 25

Started clear and soon became warm, and remained so.
Wrote to Frank Matsumoto, Chicago and Kenji Ito, Hunt, Idaho.[19] Sakai came to get men to work for him and called on us; it is a very busy season in sugar beets, onions, etc. At the time of evacuation, the Japanese residents in this state were threatened to be included [in relocation] and the F.B.I. visited them a number of times. However, in the end this was [not] done; in fact, not a single person in the state was interned, though [Japanese in] Wyoming, Nebraska, etc. did not escape in entirety. Though there has been a manifest anti-Japanese sentiment, still there does [not] exist a feeling of hostility since the outbreak of the war. Denver is free [of it?].

Tuesday, October 26

Clear and snappy; a plenty of frost, but later became warm as in the spring. In the afternoon, a breeze developed kicking up some sands.

Mrs. Kuramoto[20] brought a chicken and tofu, and borrowed our *sukiyaki nabe* [a pan for cooking *sukiyaki*, a dish with meat and vegetables].

Yokozeki, the newly appointed block director came to take partial census: name, age, family head and the family number (31,916, original one.) Later he is to check families by their numbers, by sexes, and by occupations. The purpose is to check movements in and out of the residents weekly; he is to make such weekly reports to the director. I need such information.

Wrote Lisette.[21]

Spent the rest of the time in reading.

The Philippines made independent on the 14th [?] and Jose P. Laurel became its first president.[22]

Wednesday, October 27

Chilly with thick frost, but it cleared and became warm and remained so throughout the day.

In the afternoon, K. Ono, formerly of Sacramento but a resident-farmer [for] 17 years at . . . Alamosa, Colorado; he was the leader of the Sacramento Aichi Club and used to know me.[23] He came to the center to visit his friends . . . and had an extended visit with me. Yuhora cut my hair. We had chicken sukiyaki dinner together.

Ono told me of a conference held by the [Japanese] residents of Nebraska, Utah and Colorado at which Rev. Kanno proposed that they publicly swear their allegiance to the U.S. but [the proposal] did not pass. They were ready to abide by the laws, but non-citizens could not [do] what Kanno demanded. The irony was that he was arrested and interned while none [of the] others residing in the three states encountered such a fate. Why was he interned remains a question. Farmers in these states have made money though most of it has been paid as taxes.

Spent the rest of [the] time in research.

Kiyo [Kiyohara?] came and collected 30 cents for October-December. 10 cents per family [per month] to provide a fund to help sick, death and marriages.

Thursday, October 28

Started clear and warmer than yesterday, and gradually hot reaching 86 degrees inside and remained so all day.

Spent the morning in typing research material (China) in connection with Korean history.

. . . .

The "Pioneer" of yesterday published [a notice on] the removal of the ban on the ingress and egress from and to the camp on account of polio on Monday past (25th). But hitherto available mail truck for transportation to Lamar is made unavailable. Instead, those going to the town must use the regular bus which started at the gate at 11:15 A.M.

It also announced that chicken would be served on Halloween.

Resettlement propaganda movies shown to the public along with talks by "experts."

Friday, October 29

The day started clear and actually warm. A gentle breeze in the morning became a strong gale and sand-storm. Thunder.

Maruse* said that he learned indirectly [that] those on "parole" outside the relocation centers must make weekly reports to those authorities in charge; if this be true, they are treated as if they are legally on parole which is incomprehensible. Check this so as to be sure.

. . . .

Saturday, October 30

Started clear but with a stormy atmosphere, but turned out nice.

Sakai sent 2 chickens and some 30 eggs by a woman named Koga.

The "Pioneer" states: 60 more will come from Tule Lake, 12 families and 12 single persons.

25 are daily allowed to go to Lamar.

17 nisei girls arrested at Denver for prostitution; 5 more as spies because of a photo taken from an escaped German prisoner of war—picture of embracing between these girls and some German prisoners while working on a farm.

The strike of 15,000 at Tule Lake.[24]

---

*Unidentified. The Amache directory lists no one with the surname Maruse.

A Halloween party for youth and kids in the mess hall.
Supper is announced at 5:00.

Sunday, October 31

Overcast and cold in the morning; rain fell—hail—again rain; this is
really wintery weather cold and damp; cleared up toward the
evening.

Learned that Domoto Kanejiro had passed away Saturday morning;[25] he was 77; artificial flowers are to be sent and we joined the
group.

It is said that all the Japanese doctors have left or are leaving Tule
Lake and that Negress nurses are being substituted in the hospital.

Tanji brought a pot of chrysanthemums and some sweet potatoes
of Kayashima who had been out working on a bean field.[26]

YAMATO ICHIHASHI TO PAYSON TREAT [27]

10-H 12-D
Amache, Colo.
Oct. 31, 1943

Dear Payson:

The typewriter has been repaired, and there is no more excuse
for not writing, so here goes a partial report of this new relocation
center. As has been intimated before, this center is so quiet due to
the passive character of its residents; there have been no exciting
events since our arrival here, and for that matter, no interesting occurrences. This is an impressive fact for one who has come from
Tule Lake, although I do not wish to convey the idea that the residents of Tule Lake are a bad lot, even if they are characterized "disloyal"; for their behavior, the administration is largely responsible,
or perhaps the policy of the WRA is, in that the people are forced to
develop an abnormal psychology to an unfortunate degree. Perhaps
they are foolish not to realize that the world finds itself in an abnormal state and that no one is sensible. But enough on reflection.

The camp is situated in the midst of a vast prairie, and bears a
romantic name of Amache, but is more popularly known as the
"Sand Hill" which is more appropriate to its natural characteristics.
It is subject to famous, "unusual" weather: gales and sandstorms,

thunder and lightning, cloud-bursts, hot and cold; just now hails are dropping, which might change into rain at any moment. One does not know what to wear to protect himself, and consequently illness prevails, keeping doctors very busy. However, Kei and I have been very fortunate in having escaped any illness; the only incident along this line was that one day Kei bit a small pebble mixed in rice she was eating and one of the fillings was broken; but the dentist is not supplied with necessary materials to refill it, cement alone being available. This has been our only misfortune [so] far.

The barracks here are like those of all the centers, although as compared with those of Tule Lake, they have a slightly better external appearance. They are 120 × 20 feet, and are subdivided into six "apartments" of three different sizes: 16, 20 and 24, and these are assigned to families according to their size. The windows are larger in size and allow more light into the interior; the floor is either of concrete or bricks. Apparently the insulation is poor, and conversations on either side can be heard too distinctly to our discomfort. We occupy one of the middle rooms and have for one of our neighbors, a young mother with three little children who cry and make noise aplenty for our benefit day and night. I have just secured statistical information on the residents of this block: the total population is 196 made up of 100 males and 96 females; their distribution by age are as follows: [28]

0–17	18–24	25–34	35–44	45–54	55–64	65–Over
75	22	19	20	19	24	18

The first group is largely made of small children while most of the last age-groups are those of 60 or over, and these together number over one hundred out of the total of 196. This distribution is more or less typical of the entire population of the camp, and largely explains the passive character of the people. They seem to lack aspirations of any kind; adults resemble retired people, while the majority of youngsters are in the crying stage.

This center was opened on August 27, 1942, with the arrival of the first contingent from the Merced Assembly Center, the people from the central valley, and subsequently, the residents of the Santa Anita Assembly Center joined between September 19–30. Some of the first group informed me that the camp was not quite ready for human habitation; for instance, latrines did not exist at the time of their arrival, and they suffered a good deal of physical discomforts. I can well imagine that, because the similar situation obtained when the first contingents reached the Santa Anita Assembly Center. The meals served at both places were extremely bad, causing illness of all sorts. At any rate, when the occupation of the camp was completed, the population stood at about 7,600, of which number two-thirds were nisei and one-third, issei aliens. Occupationally, one half was rural and one half was urban, with the customary distribution in respective districts; the former was composed of farmers and farmhands from the valley, while the latter was from the city of Los Angeles. In other words, the character of the Amache population was similar to that of the other centers.

However, since the WRA adopted its policy of re-settlement, a larger number moved outside; according to a published account, more than 1,300 left the camp by October 13, 1943 to work outside permanently, i.e., these are not permitted to return to the camp. And on the same date, nearly 1,000 more were working on temporary leave; these can come back, if they so desire. The majority of these was composed of men in more vigorous age-groups, with some adventurers, young boys and girls. At the present, the population stands at about 6,400, including 1,000 recently arrived from Tule Lake; the latter is made up of "loyal" citizens and aliens, old men and women, young mothers and children, all lacking "guts."

The polio situation has subsided as the weather has become cold, and the ban on outside shopping has been removed since last Monday. We are hoping to take a trip to our nearest town, Lamar, about 10 miles to the west, where, we are informed, we can shop. At present, we confront the problem of transportation, and only 25 are daily permitted to leave the camp, and the competition is very keen. In the meantime, we are more fortunate than most of the residents because of our discovery of new relatives who have been helping us in many ways. This week an Aichi man whom we used to know at Sacramento, but a resident of Colorado for the [last] 17 years, paid us a visit; we were mutually surprised at our grey hair: mine has grown quite white due to the lack of necessary vitamins. The food served here is particularly poor; it could not be otherwise, since the WRA spends only 32 cents per capita per day. Yet Kei and I have done fairly well so far, and you must not worry about us; somehow we will continue to manage to keep up our pep.

Hoping that this note will find you, despite your hard work in the garden, in the best of health, and your Madam in the same state, [I] remain,

> Very affectionately yours,
> Yamato[29]

DIARY

Monday, November 1

Overcast but mild, but it started snowing at 7:45 A.M. This is the first snow here this year; later it turned out clear but chilly.

Wrote to Treat (mailed it) and to Opler.[30]

Yuhora paid a long visit in the morning.

So did Mrs. Yoshihara,[31] bringing a bowl of *udon*.

The former talked of his future; the latter about her oldest son and his family trouble.

Invited to a chicken dinner at the Kuramotos.

Kei received a letter from Jessie.[32]

This is Nov. 1, but the weather is far from that of the winter, though [it] started with a little snow in the morning.

I dropped my tube of tooth-paste on the way from the washroom, but somebody picked it up and kept it only within a minute, a very bad habit.

[Satoru] Kuramoto, block manager, is convinced that the 29[?] managers dominate the camp politics much resembling the Tule Lake Planning Board, with a similar attitude of hirings toward the administration and with dictatorial contempt on the residents; the Council here does not count on practical politics. Moreover, he anticipates conflicts between managers and directors of the blocks— rivalries for power.

The "pronouncement" of the tripartite conference at Moscow[33]—see *Palo Alto Times*, [discussion was] confined to Europe. Russia would not agree to anything involving Japan.

Tuesday, November 2

Clear but cold with a plenty of frost; soon the sun began to shine but the wind is still chilly.

Jessie wrote Kei telling, among other things, that the house was struck with moths and had [to have] an expert attend to them.[34] . . .

. . . .

Finished the typing of three notes based on Fujita, [?] and Suematsu on Korean-Japanese relations down to about the 5th century, A.D.[35]

Learned that Tom Storey had passed away on October 25th.[36]

Obviously the above news [in the attached clipping about Tule Lake] is an exaggeration, if not a deliberate falsehood;[37] for instance the claim that 300–500 men volunteers from the WRA centers.

Wednesday, November 3

Clear and cold with frost; the sun shines but the air is chilly with a western wind.

Wrote to Jessie thanking her for demothing the house; sent her a check for $20 and Kei's room key for further repair and explained why I refuse to rent the house: [our] possible release.

The "Pioneer" reports:

1) WRA confab at Denver on Dec. 6th to discuss 1945 budgets.

2) Quotes a report from S.F. under Oct. 29: "Close to 400 from other relocation centers were enroute to Tule Lake Segregation Center[38] to harvest root crops which disloyal Japanese had refused to gather." The crops: potatoes, carrots, beets, etc. "A strong guard is being maintained over the 14,000 Japanese in the segregation center. . . . There has been no violence." But today, I was told that Best had been attacked—a rumor?

3) During October, 176 relocated (indefinitely); this brings the number of re-settles to 1,411 since the beginning of the year from this center. However, during the same month, 245 went out on seasonal work leave, and the total 1,428 since Jan. 1 or 17 more than the indefinites.

Received a letter and a box of candies from Frank Matsumoto, Chicago.

YAMATO ICHIHASHI TO JESSIE TREAT [39]

10-H 12-D
Amache, Colorado
Nov. 3rd, 1943

Dear Mrs. Treat:

Yesterday afternoon Kei received your kind letter and she asked me to write an answer relative to the house-matters which you were so kind enough to attend. She herself will write you on other matters. But after all, what can I say except to thank you sincerely for what you have been doing on our behalf, in particular, since our sad "evacuation" and beg you to continue to do so; please have the roof repaired and the necessary key or keys made; I have enclosed a check to cover their possible cost, if it proves insufficient, let me know. Thank you.

I am naturally touched by the sad nature of events relative to institutions and persons. Though completely isolated from the rest of the world now for a year and half, we have never been free from the sad aspects of human [existence], even apart from the world at large rendered so tragic. I am too appalled to permit myself to think, for instance, of what has happened or is happening to my relatives and friends in distant Japan; no word has reached me for two years. At Santa Anita, Tule Lake, Sharp Park, and here at Amache I have been forced to witness sad aspects of human life without relief; almost daily I have been encountering the death of men and women whose life history of struggle for thirty, forty, fifty years had been known to me. I have attended more funerals during this short period than I had had in my lifetime; I am going to attend another today of a man who had died at 77 years of age. But it is not death alone that saddens my heart, but the stupid behavior of young and old, resulting in the shattering of families and of controlled domestic relations, in the breaking up of true friendships. Individuals have become selfish, self-centered or egoistic or else so apathetic as to lose a balanced view of life. In brief, men and women have been washed out [of] whatsoever culture and refinement they once had possessed; they have reverted to savages and in many cases to beasts. This is the fruit of a forced communistic life as I see it. But enough of this.

Hard as it is, the strong cannot afford to become pessimistic but must strive to remain optimistic despite all; I am trying to save myself by remaining an intellectual man working hard on research. It may be a wishful thinking, but information reaches me that we may be released to our homes not in [the not too] distant future; that is the reason why I did not think it wise to rent the house for the time being. By the way, when the repairer comes, please let him examine the sky light over the attic in the back part of the house and fix it, if necessary. That necessitates an examination of Kei's room and so the key is enclosed, which we ask you to keep so long as we are out.

Sincerely appreciate of your kindness, I remain

Very affectionately
Yamato

KEI ICHIHASHI TO JESSIE TREAT [40]

Amache
November 4 [1943]

Dear Mrs. Treat:

Thank you for your kind letter. It is very nice of you to keep your mind on our house, and have done so much for it. We are appreciat[ing it] very much, indeed. Yesterday morning I told Mr. I. to write a letter to you at once, (he is such a poor business man, so that I let him do that, he has to learn something) and I took the letter to the post office to mail myself. In this project, the post office is not far away from our apartment; it takes ten minutes to walk. But at Tule Lake it was very far away, therefore in the winter it was very inconvenient to go to the post office. This morning when I went out, the sun was shining brightly but the west wind was cold, as we had heavy frost in the morning. (A couple days ago the first snow fell, just a little). The cold wind ceased and [it is] getting warmer in the afternoon; the temperature was 80 degrees in the room without the fire. Fortunately we still have a very nice weather around here this year.

Lately the food is not good, and I have heard that they are spending 32 cents a day per person, no wonder we can not get sufficient meals. Since you sent us the kitchen knife we had chicken sukiyaki several times in the room; they were not so bad. A Japanese merchant in Granada (he was in this center till last spring, and before the evacuation he had a big fish market in Los Angeles) delivers fresh fish and chickens every other day, so that we can buy fresh fish and chickens at any time and we are trying to get enough nourishment. At present we are quite healthy, so please do not worry about us.

The other day one of my acquaintances brought me a pot of chrysanthemums, and about three weeks ago my "new cousins" sent me a box full of chrysanthemums by the express. They were not as good as I had in our home garden—I think you remember that every autumn I had several kinds of chrysanthemums in the back yard—but I appreciate them very much, because I could not get any at Tule Lake last year, and I missed them so much. Now I have a pot of beautiful chrysanthemums and I am very much pleased. How about your garden this year? I imagine Mr. Treat [is] working very hard in your beautiful large garden. The campus seems to be very active and everybody is busy; that is very nice.

It is so sad to hear of Dr. Storey's death. He and his wife spent the summertime on the campus very happily, so I understand, and he has gone so suddenly, nobody can believe it. I am glad that Mr. Lutz is back teaching, but I hope he'll not do too many things. Poor Mrs. Lutz, she has had so many troubles one after another. I am hoping that her daughter will recover soon. Please remember me to her when you have a chance to see her.

Sincerely yours,
Kei Ichihashi

DIARY

Thursday, November 4

Overcast and chilly, but it soon turned out to be a nice day. Felt unwell with a pain on the chest and slept most of the morning and then felt better. Did some translating.

The afternoon (1:30–3:30), attended the funeral of Domoto Kanejiro, a resident in the U.S. for 60 [years] and died at 77. Among others, Lindley spoke.

It is said that the situation in Tule Lake worsened; it is too bad. It would be wiser to be honest: the WRA should give up the handling of its residents, but recognize them as internees and treat them as such since they are that in reality. It is absurd to continue the present illogical treatment as a special class of evacuees; separate, if necessary, citizens from aliens and deal with them according to right legal procedures, i.e., citizens according to domestic laws, aliens (enemy aliens) according to the Geneva Protocol. There is no justice in mixing the two legally and otherwise.

Kayashima brought one Tanabe whom I thought had seen the outside, and soon Kiyohara joined; they stayed until 11:15. They discussed all sorts of things.

◙ Throughout November and into the winter, Tule Lake was the scene of continual disturbances. WRA officials became so worried that they called in the army to control the center. Martial law was declared at the camp for two weeks after a protest on November 1. All the while, newspapers around the country painted a sensationalized picture of events, suggesting that traitorous and violent Japanese threatened open rebellion. Indeed, several serious beatings, hunger strikes, a murder, and a killing of an evacuee by a sentry occurred during this time. Ichihashi tried to follow the events by reading copies of the Tule Lake newspaper and the *Palo Alto Times* (to which he subscribed from camp) and through his correspondence and the evacuee grapevine.[41] While tensions like these at Tule Lake did not plague Amache, camp life there too was full of anxiety. Suspicion, envy, petty competition, and personal animosities seemed ubiquitous. It was not the benign place Ichihashi first thought it was upon his arrival. ◗

DIARY

Wednesday, November 10, 1943

Clear and rather cold, but later turned [out] to be a nice day.

Attended the meeting [on "Evacuee Future in California"] which lasted from 9:00–12:00; [Relocation Supervisor Vernon] Kennedy spoke. See the notes attached.

.   .   .   .

[Notes from the meeting:]

1) An evacuee relocation committee is desired, but this has [to have] the full confidence of the WRA and the residents at large; [otherwise] it can't function in a useful way.

2) Japanese future outlook in California: with the possible exception of land-owning farmers, the former industrial and professional set up (urban activities) are washed up and impossible to restore. The reason is the local public sentiment and the military necessity; if such an attempt be made, laws will be enacted against it, though such laws may be unconstitutional.

3) Consequently the people must "sit in the centers" or relocate elsewhere (Midwest). The prevalent confusion over these issues must be cleared away and a new type of thinking must be made by individuals.

4) Men should accept available jobs as they come and be willing to work as laborers until they win local confidence and friendship for better employment, business, farming, etc. No choice in the initial stage. Necessary knowledge relative to Japanese must be spread through crusade and "contacts." Must start all over again in pioneering. This is all right for nisei, but not issei who are now too old and have no "guts" to adventure; for the latter, a different approach must be formulated. Agreed, but let the nisei spearhead for the issei.

5) The WRA is not prepared to offer financial aids of any kind in connection with the resettlement of issei or nisei.

6) All the foregoing may not fit the facts of circumstances surrounding the people. Therefore the first step in deciding to relocate or not [is that] true information must be had and this can be obtained by thorough and intelligent surveys by "experts." That should be the first task of the proposed committee (not a mere advisory committee for those who have decided to resettle).[42]

Thursday, November 11

Clear but not so cold as yesterday, but soon a cold breeze developed and for a while caused a slight sand storm. Overcast for some time.

Yuhora cut my hair.

... [Kuramoto] informed [me] that there is a call (by the government) for 15 Japanese who can listen to the Japanese broadcast via the medium of phonograph records and translate into English at a salary of $200 per month, but with the prospect of raises. Educated Japanese in both their native tongue and in English; it is wondered how many such individuals are available among the residents in not only the centers but in the U.S. at large; hardly any, if so, how about the compensation? At any rate, the applicants are to be tested by the Colorado Japanese Language School "authorities." If they qualify, they are to be trained there for two weeks! Ha-ha!

A welcome reception for the Tuleans in the evening. . . . School children to provide entertainments.

Friday, November 12

Started clear and cold, but later turned out rather a nice day.

[N] came and asked me how marriages among the nisei here should be facilitated "to prevent the inevitable growth of old maids." Answer: [I] don't believe in the encouragement of such marriages under the existing circumstances and because of the uncertainty of young men's future prospect of earning steady livelihood. He started to argue and I put him off. He is one of the Mr. Know-alls. . . .

Kono who was recently released from Santa Fe told me that there were about 1,300 still there.[43] About two months ago, there were about 2,300; therefore about 1,000 must have been released during those months. . . .

Saturday, November 13

Clear and wintry but not very cold. Soon overcast and a cold breeze.
. . . .

Spoke before the Block 9-K; good attendance; many old acquaintances, including those whom I used to know in *Fukuin-Kai*[44] [and]
the artist who gave [me] a charcoal sketch of Santa Anita. The block
residents are from L.A. The neighboring block residents invited to
the lecture. Refreshments were served—about 20 remained at
coffee.

Sunday, November 14

Rather a nice morning, and remained so throughout the day.
Invited by Yoshihara for breakfast.
Saw the artificial flower exhibit, including a large number of *bon-
kei* [miniature garden landscapes]. Some of them, in particular the
latter, showed skill. What interested me most were *senryū* [short,
humorous verse] and *dodoitsu* [limericks] on the old women and artistic efforts.
About 50 more arrived from Tule Lake; 250 more went to Minidoka and Rohwer. These were hastily removed on account of the recent trouble in the camp.

Monday, November 15

Clear and chilly, but developed into a nice day without any breeze.
[I gave] a talk before the Blue Star Mothers' Club at 7:00 P.M., 6-E
Rec. Hall.[45] This organization has more than 100 members (mothers
and immediate relatives) and is financially supported by the WRA,
which interprets its functions as those of loyal citizens, like their soldier sons. Hence no membership fee is collected. Its main purpose
is, of course, to promote the interests of their sons in an organized
form. After my talk, the chair woman enumerated a number of
points to justify their position as mothers of the soldiers (American
citizens while they themselves are Japanese subjects) with a conclusion of *gaden-insui teki* [seeking to promote one's own interests?].
[My] advice: don't try to think too deeply because in reality these
conflicts are incapable of being logically explained *ad infinitum*. Accept it as an inevitable incident in the world of conflict.

Received letters from Jessie and Opler and an estimate on roof repairs from R. L. Reaves Roofing Co.

Thursday, November 25

Cloudy but warm with the sprinkling of rain off and on and remained so until 5 P.M., when it changed to snow until about midnight.

We are going to Sakais for Thanksgiving dinner. Sakai came and we picked up Kiyohara and Kayashima and left the camp about 10:00 A.M. on the temporary leave cards which are required for distances more than 20 miles. Sakai's farm is a big one, growing melons, vegetables, such as beets, corn, onions, etc. and has some horses and cattle, turkeys, chickens, ducks, sheep (800 head to be sold as lamb—a year old). . . .

We had a fine dinner (turkey and usual items). We also had a supper—*udon, sashimi, tempura, tamagoyaki* [fried egg], *takuwan* [pickled radish]. Since the weather was bad, we stayed in the house most of the time. This was the first farm Kei saw. We left the house at 8:30; it snowed rather heavily but reached the camp at 10:00 in safety, and got to the room about 10:30 since Sakai had to visit the police station about his employees, 4 in number and the pass to return. It was the first visit outside of the camps since our evacuation May 26, 1942; myself as a "free" individual, while Kei was out for the first having never been out except from our home to Santa Anita, from Santa Anita to Tule Lake, and from Tule Lake to Lamar and Amache.

◻ During these winter weeks, Ichihashi found that his attention was occupied by a variety of matters, some of which he was sure had historical significance and others, presumably, none. He attended to the rental of his Stanford house, eventually agreeing to rent to a young staff member named Alice Westbrook and her mother. He also discovered that a number of Amache residents were originally from his home area in Japan, and he was kept busy getting acquainted with them. At the same time, he tried to keep abreast of the developments at Tule Lake, which was in the national news constantly, as well as the progress of the war in the Pacific and local affairs at Amache. All the while, he made efforts to continue with his scholarly research into Japanese historical materials. (It is an ironic twist of events that the work he most valued as a historian has little worth to us today, while the mundane matters of his own daily existence in camp now intrigue us.) As he commented to Jessie Treat in one letter, he and Kei were trying hard to be "philosophic" about life, despite all the sad events in the world and their difficult circumstances. Camp life, though, was slowly grinding down the Ichihashis. As one Stanford alumnus observed to Payson Treat after he had left relocation camp, he had experienced a real "mental concentration camp," where a "barbed wire neurosis" prevailed.[46]

Unknown to the Treats, and to perhaps anyone else in the world, the Ichihashis were enduring agonizing emotional torment. They had developed deep differences over Woodrow's marriage, so deep that they ceased even talking to each other beginning sometime just after Thanksgiving 1943 and began to lead virtually separate lives. Life within their barrack room became a form of solitary confinement for them. One wonders about Ichihashi's state of mind in reading the following diary entries, since he does not even mention the estrangement in his journal until January 1, 1944. ◨

DIARY

Tuesday, December 7

Starts overcast and cold as usual, but it turned out rather a nice, warm day.

The second anniversary [of Pearl Harbor], but still everything remains uncertain. Nothing can be envisaged even for the immediate future.

Yuhora helped in bringing two wheel-barrowfuls of coal and putting it in the coal bin.

Received a Christmas card from Kazu Takahashi with a note, telling among other things, what Stanford "kids" are doing; most of them have relocated.[47]

A year ago today no Japanese was allowed to go even to Granada, but there is no such restriction on this second anniversary. Does this signify anything?

Of the 220 odd residents in the block, more than 50 are down with colds which are prevalent not only in the camp but throughout the U.S. Miura is troubled because among the sick are many who work—these create the necessity of substitutes. One has to be very careful of his health. Has this illness got anything to do with the war? If so, what will it be later? Terrible to think.

Wednesday, December 8

Starts overcast and gloomy but not as cold as yesterday; it remained gloomy all day with a faint sunshine now and then.

Buddy Iwata returned from the University of Colorado,[48] Boulder, where he teaches Japanese (now nearly a year) informed me that there are 100 teachers in the Naval Language School, of whom, 10 are Americans and 90 are Japanese, issei about 1/3, the rest being nisei and kibei. They are both men and women. There are in attendance 500–600 students made up of *shōi* [a junior officer]. The Japanese teachers are paid $200 per month at the start, raised to $350 in rare instances; the time spent in teaching is from 18 to 21 hrs a week. The work appears to be successful: reading, conversation and calligraphy, including *sōsho* [a very cursive style of calligraphy]. . . .

Future of the issei and nisei here and outside discussed; his opinion was that most of the relocatees are facing hardships. But nisei should relocate as the life in the centers is demoralizing for most of them. Yuhora added: what will they do when they are free? Many will find difficulty earning their livelihood and have no money of their own. The only exception is farmers who were wise enough to make suitable arrangements at the time of their evacuation. Professionals and tradesmen without funds are the most difficult case.

YAMATO ICHIHASHI TO JESSIE TREAT [49]

10-H 12-D
Amache, Colorado
December 14, 1943

My dear Mrs. Treat:

. . . .

I am sorry to learn that Payson has been ill, but hope that he will recover soon. Speaking of illness, this camp has been suffering from influenza in a disproportionate manner; in our block with 220 residents, are more than 50 of these persons are confined in bed—this list includes Kei as well. I was down for a week with a headache and a sore throat. What is true of our block is generally true of all the other blocks, and the working men and women are being affected. There is some disarrangement in every department of labor division; all we can hope is that it will not worsen. Otherwise, the life here is monotonous or dead intellectually and even emotionally.

Please tell Payson (he does not like my beautiful illegible hand writing)[50] that I am tired of reporting on the center life all the time and that I have been trying to compose an history report on Sino-Korean-Japanese relations within the Japanese prehistoric period (1st and 2nd centuries B.C.)–the 3rd century A.D. The sources are archaeological relics, fragments of ancient Korean records, the Japanese *Kojiki, Nihongi* and *Fūdoki* (local histories and geographies),[51] and the Chinese histories (official), the *Shanghai-King*, (a geography of fauna and flora with miscellaneous geographic features), the Early Han Record (*Chien Han Shu*), the Late Han Records (*Hou Han Shu*), and the Wei Record (*Wei-Chih*) based on contemporary Wei records, *Giryaku* (this is [transliterated] into Japanese, [since] I don't know its pronunciation in Chinese (*Wei-ryaku*?). Many Japanese and most Western scholars, including our learned [George B.] Sansom, have failed to use "historically" the Chinese sources in particular. I shall try to justify this wholesale criticism.

All who have returned from the Far East must be happy just as the Japanese who have reached Japan must feel happy;[52] I know several and asked [them] to carry messages (oral, no written ones permitted), but I am not sure whether they were delivered to my relatives and friends who are doubtless anxious about us. I will get the issue of *Life*—Thanks.

> Very affectionately,
> Yamato Ichihashi

SPECIAL DATA[53]

Sunday, Dec. 19

Regarding Amache Camp Politics: As noted very often as regards various matters relating to this camp, the life here is conspicuous for its passivity and serenity. The politics are monopolized by the block managers whose group much resembles that of the defunct Tule Lake Planning Board—all-knowing and bureaucratic. The city council is completely dominated or ignored; it in reality has nothing to do with the civic life. They say the councilmen are unpaid and therefore indifferent—this seems to be the prevailing public opinion—and accept the situation as if inevitable; recently so-called nominations for council were made in this block (in a meeting attended by some 15 men, mostly issei); that meant the selection of one of them as its councilman. No election was held; the only election ever held was that of the co-op board officer. No wonder then that any chap with guts refuses to serve in that capacity or perhaps there are no youths with political ambition. Money seems to be the most decisive factor in the life of young and old alike. With pay, yes; with no pay, no. Under the circumstances, any group interested to run the show could do so without encountering any obstacles, to wit: the block managers; the relocation committee, self-named, and yet pretending to have been chosen by the public because the council and the block-managers endorsed it.

It was the block managers who decided to present Xmas gifts in money to the hospital staff and collected $1200 from the residents without a previous consultation. If this is not a dictatorship, what is it?

A Spanish consul is to visit here about Dec. 27–28 for the purpose of finding out the existing conditions in the WRA centers and report on them to the Japanese government. He will be accompanied by H. M. Banninghoff of the State Department and one Miss Augusta Wagner, a former teacher at Peiping recently repatriated from Weishien, China. The "Pioneer" says, "the consul will confer with the block managers and with members of the appointed personnel" (WRA officials). . . . "He will be escorted on an inspection tour through the hospital, mess halls and to other divisions of the center." The escorts are likely to be some WRA officials. Thus the consul will get a distorted picture instead of an accurate one, even if he is trained to do this kind of job; he will be given a picture the WRA wishes to give. Anyhow, the people will not be consulted, though their government doubtless desires to know what they are experiencing and feeling about their treatment. This evidenced by Japan's refusal to proceed further in the exchange negotiations until it learns more accurately about the American treatments of Japanese nationals in internment, detention and relocation camps and in the Tule Lake camp for "disloyal" (see *Palo Alto Times*, 12/13). All the more it is important to obtain true information to do justice all around. But alas, it is impossible for the Spanish consul to do so. Once more, the illogical lumping of issei and nisei assumes importance. Japan can interest herself over issei alone; Biddle [has declared]: nisei can't be kept in such camps constitutionally.[54] It is an anomaly.

◻ During December, the Ichihashis received Christmas cards from friends in other relocation camps, from those who had resettled, and from Stanfordites, as they were called. They also received a note from Woodrow that told them about his living situation and, what should have been very happy news, that a grandchild was expected in the spring. Ichihashi noted the information in his diary entry of December 21 without comment. The news undoubtedly further aggravated the already tortured relationship between Yamato and Kei, who wanted to reconcile with Woodrow. Kei probably hoped to rejoice in her son's joy, but Yamato remained obdurate and bitter. In early January, he is almost gleeful that a Christmas card Kei sent Woodrow is returned undelivered because it was misaddressed. ◾

DIARY

Sunday, December 25

The most beautiful morning with the crescent moon with its rim plainly visible with some of the brilliant stars shining in the blue sky. A truly wonderful Christmas morning. It is not even cold. Received [Christmas cards and some gifts]. Kurahashi[55] brought some *udon*. Kiyohara came to greet. Okubos[56] were down and Kayashima is in the hospital where he was operated for *ji* [hemorrhoids].

Sunday, December 26

Somewhat overcast with frost as yesterday; overcast and gloomy with a strong wind in late afternoon.

Ando came to consult about his proposed resettlement in Boston; Kurahashi brought *tsuke-mono* [pickled vegetables].

Received from Shizuko [Ichihashi's younger sister, in Tokyo] a message and inquiry via Red Cross. . . . 昨今如何御暮シカト御案ジ致シテ居リマス御身体大切ニ近況御知ラセ願ヒマス ["I have been wondering how you have been recently. Take care of yourself and let me know your situation."] This is the second of the messages, the first having come late August, 1942 in the name of the Red Cross; Kei replied. This time it was replied: "Thank you for your kind message and inquiry. We are all well. Do not worry. Hoping this will find you and others in best health."

Monday, December 27

Overcast, gloomy and cold; snow began to fall about 11:30, but soon stopped.

Received a Xmas card and a box of candies from Frank Matsumoto [in Chicago]. The neighborhood boys put coal in the bin.

Tuesday, December 28

Started overcast and nippy with frost, but cleared up and warm but with a cold breeze.

Received a Xmas card from Hattie Wakabayashi.*

Wrote to Payson the first report on the research.[57]

Called on K and K. The latter while in the hospital learned that each nurse aide received $15 as the Xmas gift; Drs. and technicians, $50 each, but this will not be reported publicly. The total donation amounted to over $1200.

. . . .

Wednesday, December 29

Overcast and nippy with frost, but later cleared up and became warm.

Yuhora brought Kuramatsu[58] who brought a box of candies; talked about art and general problems of the block. Showers are out of order for the second [time]; the first [breakdown was] for 5 days.

Kenji sent us a carton of cigarettes.

The rice washed for *mochi tsuki* tomorrow.†

Volunteers were called to dress the chickens to be served [on the] New Year.

Thursday, December 30

Started clear but nippy with frost, but soon the sun shone and was warm.

---

*Unidentified.

†*Mochi* is a sweet treat made from rice for the New Year's celebration. *Mochi tsuki* is the process of pounding the rice.

Mochi tsuki in the block.

Learned from elder Yuhora who resided there one year that the Poston Camp [in Arizona] though hot in summer (120 degrees for a day), but there is plenty of water: between the barracks are dug ponds [with] carps in [them] and beautiful with an abundance of trees. The camp is very attractive. There is no winter. March–April are most agreeable, and excellent for the cultivation of agricultural produce, especially mellons. It consists of 3 separate camps; the number I, largest; the other two are half this size; about 3 miles apart from one another. The maximum population was 15,000–16,000. It is a good place except in summer heat.

. . . .

Friday, December 31

Milder as compared with the few preceding days, though overcast and frost on the roofs and grounds. Remained mild all day.

This is the last day of the year, and many, many thoughts come to mind, covering happenings since the outbreak of the war Dec. 7, 1941 (Nov. 26–27),[59] especially since the forced evacuation en masse from our homes in the West Coast.

[Here, for several paragraphs, Ichihashi reviews the sequence of difficult and unhappy events in relocation, which has been presented in previous documents.]

Water is shut off completely; this is a nice ending of the year.

◪ The New Year, a very special time among Japanese, did not begin auspiciously for the Ichihashis. The strains in their relationship continued to divide them. Their mutual silence, which began in late November, continued into 1944. Compounding the marital problems was the poor health both suffered, the harsh weather—the temperature hovered around zero degrees in winter—and most of all, of course, the grinding wear of internment. Yamato increasingly retreated into his own research work on esoteric historical issues, wrote fewer letters and briefer diary entries and, in his cantankerous criticism of almost all around him and in the sarcasm of his observations, seemed to grow increasingly embittered. Japanese phrases occurred more frequently in his writing. Kei, on the other hand, handled the crisis in her own way by becoming reflective, even philosophical, and befriending her camp neighbors. She stepped up her correspondence with Jessie Treat, and though she avoided any mention of the problems in her personal life, she began referring to her husband simply as "Ichihashi." ◪

1944 DIARY [60]

Saturday, January 1

Clear but snippy with plenty of frost, turned out to be a delightful day.

This is the quietest New Year experienced if my memory serves
me right; it is almost deathly and normal signs of life are conspicuous by their absence. Cooked my own breakfast of bacon and eggs
and tea and toast. Over a month now no words exchanged since
prior of the illness. Still pretending to be unwell (3 weeks), but
spending most of the time in eating and toileting—truly marvelous.
What a New Year for me; may be it is a bad beginning or may be
not; who can tell?

. . . .

Sunday, January 2

Clear but snippy with frost.

Takahashi [61] raised the question: his eldest son's case—no application for *kokuseki ridatsu* [renunciation of U.S. citizenship?] therefore:
nijūkokuseki [dual citizenship]. The answer: the rights and duties are
determined in what territory he resides. Anxious to avoid drafting;
he is 21 now. Recently a form was brought [asking?] where he is to
reside legally, but [he] is going to Chicago to attend a school. Will
he be free from drafting? No; it will depend on the interpretations
given the rules governing. At present, those who are working on
farms are free, but that may be changed.

Okubos and Kiyohara made new year calls. So did Kurahashi.
The shower is still out of order. . . .

Monday, January 3

Bright and delightful though cold (wintry); it proved to be a
beautiful day.

[A number of friends] came to pay New Year calls. . . .

The block shower repaired temporarily and had one, [first] since
Dec. 31, 1943. A cop brought a telegram addressed here but for

Hamaguchi and told me that he is having difficulty in identifying the people to whom such messages are sent due to wrong addresses; he had another addressed to 10-K which is nonexistent. Why does not an office keep a directory kept up-to-date [to] avoid just such difficulties? The administration is stupid or inefficient. A directory is easy enough to compile, but [there is] no organizing head; consequences may be serious. The demand of WRA at this time for notification of bases of cancellation of repatriation applications clearly indicates their failure to keep records in file or if kept, in nonusable manner.[62]

Tuesday, January 4

Cloudy and colder than yesterday, with more frost; a breeze developed making [it] more nippy; little sun shine in the afternoon.

Nothing worthy to be recorded; all the day long, it was *heibon* [ordinary, banal].

Devoted to research: reading and translating.

Received a large box of Wilson candies from Misses Stoltenbergs.

KEI ICHIHASHI TO JESSIE TREAT [63]

Amache
January 5 [1944]

Dear Mrs. Treat:

Happy New Year!! I thank you for your kindness showed us during the year of 1943. 1944 will be very eventful for me, I don't know why, but I just feel so. Just before Christmas I had a bad cold for two weeks, and this is the fourth week, but I am still very weak and cannot do anything else so that I have been writing letters to friends since new year's day. This is a good chance for me to write.

Since I came to Granada I had sand storms several times, and one of them was just terrible. After Thanksgiving day, snow fell three or four times and the weather is quite cold and no strong wind, and I shall not be suffered by sand storms till the warm spring comes again. If I have no sand storm, this center is a nice place to live. As you know I found "new cousins" at Las Animas, 50 miles away from here. They are trying to be nice for us. In September when we came here they sent us a few furnitures to let us have a little comfort.

Thanksgiving day we were invited [to their home] and we had nice time with them all day over there. For Xmas they saved their ration points and sent us a very big piece of beef besides a nice Xmas basket; between these occasions they sent us many nice things. I feel rather sorry for them to do so much for us. Do you know how I keep these things in my one room tenement? I converted one of the screened windows into a nice cooler; one of my neighbours fixed it the other day, and he is also planning to make a small sink for me. In my apartment, there is a Japanese style closet which also he built when I moved in. He lives near my apartment. He is short and thin, and has a wrinkled brown face. Naturally I thought he would be an old man, before I knew him, but I was told that he was [only] 57, so I named him "Oshi shian" [*oji san*], it means an uncle. He is a farmer, and was at many places in California, before he came to the Center. He was brought up in a nice family in Japan, and when 13 years old he came to this country; now he is anxious to go to the South Pacific when the war is over; he is a very interesting man. He used to live with Ichihashi at the same house (a club house or something) in San Francisco about 45 years ago, though Ichihashi does not remember it at all.

Since we came here Ichihashi met several old friends of his school boy days. It was rather surprising for him. One day he met an old man in the mess hall; an old man said that "I lived with you at the same place in San Francisco almost 50 years ago, etc., etc." Finally Ichihashi asked him his name, but he did not tell it and went away. Forty or fifty years ago many ambitious young men came to this country, but most of them failed; they even didn't make enough money to live, and now they are staying in the Centers without desires, without hopes. They are too old to have any hope. It is tragedy.

I hope this note finds you in the best of health.

> Affectionately,
> Kei I.

p.s. Thank you for nice cookies. We Japanese are tea drinking people; whenever I have visitors I brew tea, so I must always keep some cakes and cookies.

DIARY

Sunday, January 9

Clear but rather cold since yesterday.

The sore throat developed worse and [is] painful; so I stayed in bed all day. Sakai visited, bringing many eggs and two large beef steaks. Yoshihara inquired whether I need some things. Kei replied that she would go and get what is needed: [then?] she did go and got what she wanted. Prepared her own meal (with steak), ate it without saying a word! What a marvelous conduct! A damned stupid fool; she thinks she can get away with it.

Yuhora called and stayed till 9:30. I had my rice and eggs.

Friday, January 14

Clear but rather nippy; bright with sunshine; still cold.

Yoshihara told me how *udon* was made for the mess crew yesterday and for the residents today with a simple machine which costs only $7.50.

Akahashi called and talked about the conditions in the camp and the war situation.

. . . .

Kei sent a Xmas card to Woodrow but [it] was returned because of his old address—Johnson Milk Company, which he left without her knowledge as early as last August. Curious is woman's psychology.

Saturday, January 15

Started overcast and remained so all day but not nippy as it has been.

. . . .

Kujo[64] reported that a group of boys, "gangsters," disturbed the residents by making loud noises in the latrine and shower room and broke the heat adjuster so that from tonight on the shower room would be closed at 10:00 P.M. Why don't they see to it that they be thrown out from the Block as they do not belong here? Why hesitate? Afraid? In fact, they hang around in this Block and eat regularly as if they are residents, clearly showing that they know the people are spineless and "gangsters'" instincts make them take advantage of the block and behave as they do. Why not report them to the police?

YAMATO ICHIHASHI TO NOBORU SHIRAI [65]

10-H 12-D
Amache, Colorado.
January 15, 1944

Dear Shirai Kun [66]

First of all, let me wish you and your family A Happy New Year, though much belated.

I was naturally very happy to hear from you [67] and to learn that you had escaped a worse fate during the recent trouble [at Tule Lake]; I was much worried because I only knew what the newspapers said about the incidents. I still feel better if you and your family were out of the center and settled elsewhere. I am still hoping that such a removal can be effected soon. In the meantime what you have outlined relative to the whole incident gives me a new light, and [I] feel very much relieved. Please be kind enough to send me a full and detailed report on the same subject when you can; I am exceedingly anxious to obtain facts and truths about it for my future reference.

A few days ago, a letter with an enclosure came from Kenji [Ito], [68] which together reveal the fact that all is not well in Minidoka, allegedly a "model center," for not only did they have a janitors' strike which left the residents there without hot water for several days, but the residents submitted a ten page report to the Spanish Consul, detailing facts and reasons for their dissatisfaction and asking him to communicate it to the Japanese government as well as to negotiate with the American government. They apparently have no confidence in the WRA staff of the center. In passing, he mentioned Emerson, the truck driver, with stolen meats and other items, was killed as the result of a collision with a train; the arrest, in Sacramento, of Peck trying to dispose stolen canned goods, and Slim Tsuda having been picked up by the Army for engaging in black-market deals. Can you confirm these as true?

My wife was forced to bed with flu early in December and was unable to leave it until a few days ago; she is still weak and nervous. During the night of January 6th, snow fell and the following morning the ground was frozen and slippery, and in the same afternoon, I had a magnificent fall, but fortunately without any injury (some thirty persons were injured during the same day) and how many fell I cannot tell. At any rate, the same day I was forced to bed with a suddenly developed sore throat and aching bones due to the fall. I got up today, but still feel rather weak. This explains why I failed to write you sooner.

This camp is quiet and peaceful because the residents here have no guts and they are willing to put up with the WRA no matter how it treats them without complaints. They are under the thumb of the block managers, all issei, who conduct themselves very much after the manner of the Planning Boarders of Tule Lake. They represent the WRA like faithful "dogs" and find no fault whatsoever, and they force the people to swallow that as a fact. What is the matter with the Council? It is largely composed of nisei boys and girls incapable and inarticulate, and thus they are a helpless lot, to say the least of it. They are dominated by the block managers! The residents except the Tuleans are made up of townspeople of Los Angeles and farmers from Central California drawn from Santa Anita and Merced assembly centers. They are so conspicuously *gari-gari* [beggarly, needy] that they do not care or think about anything. They are content with the lowly standard of living imposed on them with such miserable meals and such primitive shelters and such heartless treatment by the authorities. For instance, we thus far received wooden cots, comforters (not blankets), and a broom only. They are being handled like a bunch of *buta* [pigs] and they behave like those dispeakable [despicable?] animals. Either they have lost or have no aspiration or ambition; thus they have been rendered or are passive beyond imagination and in fact dead except physically. And if there are those who are capable of thinking, they remain completely in hiding. These are some of the reasons why the block managers get away with their autocracy.

The New Year was conventionally observed in this camp as elsewhere; the director allowed each block to buy and drink two gallons of sake on the occasion. Our block must be an exception even in this respect for we did not have even *ozōni* [traditional New Year's soup, made with pounded rice cakes], for its residents were more than anxious that they should receive an equal number of *omochi* [pounded rice cakes]; they were fearful that some might eat more *ozōni*. This sort of attitude leads me to characterize them as ego-centric *buta*, hardly humans. In other words, we passed the new year night and new year day like ghosts in a graveyard! I prefer quietude born of philosophy, but this is a dead town which I do not like. Yet it is inhabited by *Dai Nippon Teikoku Shin-min* [subjects of the Greater Japanese Empire]! What do you think of such a group, if you should be obliged to share such a life with such a people?

> Very sincerely yours,
> [Yamato Ichihashi]

YAMATO ICHIHASHI TO PAYSON TREAT [69]

> 10-H 12-D
> Amache, Colorado.
> Jan. 19, 1944

Dear Payson:

Thank you for the kind letter.[70] I am glad to learn that you were able to pass the Christmas and the New Year happily and that you are to enjoy your last Sabbatical leave even if it is a partial one. Unfortunately ours has been otherwise: Kei was forced to bed early in December and thus remained in bed for nearly five weeks with flu. Although she has been up for more than ten days she still coughs and [is] weak and nervous. During the night of Jan. 6th, snow fell rather heavily and the following day the ground was frozen and slippery, and in the same afternoon, I had a magnificent fall, but fortunately without any injury (some thirty persons fell and were injured). The same evening, I was forced to bed with a suddenly developed sore throat and aching old bones due to the fall. I got up five days ago, but still feel rather groggy. On the New Year Eve, Kei was still in bed and I alone sat in our apartment; the world was quiet and lifeless, an unusual situation in a Japanese community. In short, we passed the new year eve and day like ghosts in a graveyard! But no more about this camp. Below follows a continuation of the "report."

[The next two pages of Ichihashi's letter report on his research and thoughts about the Chinese classic *Qian Han Shu*, a history of the early Han dynasty (206 B.C.–A.D. 25) and neolithic Japan.]

Wishing you and Madam continued happiness and good health, I remain,

> Very affectionately yours,
> [Yamato Ichihashi]

DIARY

Monday, January 31

Somewhat overcast and cold with frost; later it became milder.

The people are agitated over the draft.*

Kujo announced that *imonhin* [relief goods from Japan] consisting of *shōyu* [soy sauce], *miso* [bean paste], *kusuri* [medicine], *gakki* [musical instruments] will reach here in a few days; he made a speech which was greeted with hand-clapping by some.

A letter came from Jessie to both [of us]; later came a box of candies from her. The tax report from the University; and from the Block the monthly [register?].

SPECIAL DATA

Observations: That it has been noted of the passive (dead) character of the residents was interestingly demonstrated in their attitude in connection with the New Year, considered as the most important festivity by the Japanese people. It was so indifferent to a degree of complete absence of a festive spirit that nothing happened. It was a welcome of the New Year by "ghosts in a grave yard."

A new council was elected and the names of its membership were published. The majority of them were re-elected, while the new ones turned out to be Tuleans; again the majority is made up of nisei. Thus the previous nonfunctioning body was recreated. However, the minority new blood may modify its character, but rather doubtful. In either case, it will very likely be dominated by the block managers who are apparently more experienced in local politics and

---

*As noted above, the Selective Service System had decided in March 1942 to exclude persons of Japanese ancestry from army induction. Then, in January 1943, the army organized the Japanese American volunteer unit, the 442nd Regimental Combat Team. By early January 1944, the government changed its policy again and reinstituted the draft for Japanese Americans. By November 1944 even Japanese aliens were allowed to volunteer for the army. Altogether, some 23,000 nisei served in the armed forces during World War II, in combat, in military intelligence, and in other capacities in both the European and Pacific theaters. The reinstitution of the draft provoked another major crisis among internees, which is documented by Ichihashi below. On the evacuees and the draft, see Daniels, *Asian America*, pp. 247–58.

possess more of the WRA "authority." The residents are unaware that the latter could not legally and logically represent the residents' interests since the block managers are hirings of the W.R.A. They are stupid enough to justify the inactivity on account of the councilmen's "honorary" position, i.e., they are [not?] paid for their job! In fact, no one appears to be enthusiastic about the body or its membership. Yet they grumble enough individually.

It is interesting to observe that females are more aggressive about public affairs than males; for one thing, they are organized: the Christian women, the Buddhist women, the Blue [Star] Mothers, the Red Cross, the Women's Federation (*Renmei*). Whether due to their vanity or not, they make an organized voice, often stupid, in the world where males are inarticulate. A rather curious phenomenon.

The main problems faced by the residents since the New Year are 1) the WRA high-pressure campaign of re-settlement; 2) the proposed reduction of camp employment; 3) the new draft which will induct nisei; 4) the distribution of the *imonhin*.

[Re:] 1) Many nisei have responded, but issei are immobile who still fear that they could not make a go of it, and beside it is now commonly charged that they have lost ambition, guts and have developed "a bread-line complex."[71]

2) the second proposal seems to have subsided because the actual cut appears to have been postponed by the staff. The residents' minds are incapable of seeing anything ahead beyond what takes place immediately. They pay no attention to anything unless it confronts them "now."

3) Parents are more worried about this problem than nisei themselves and try or formulate excuses not to submit—these are senseless and unreasoning. The latters' attitude is due to their ignorance; they too lack guts and therefore determination one way or another. They appear a helpless lot. Nothing can be done for them, though they would desire it. A general confusion seems to prevail as regards the citizen status of nisei and issei caused by the mass evacuation policy and other U.S. policies applied to the Japanese aliens and citizens alike. Whose fault is it?

4) [Observations] later since it is yet to be executed.

DIARY

Tuesday, February 1

Overcast and cold, but later cleared up with a warm sun-shine.

. . . .

Payson sent many varieties of sweet pea seeds.

Visited Kuramatsu's "studio" and [saw] a number of oil paintings—all of them Monterey and its vicinity—beaches and waves. Some are striking.

Mrs. Uratsu[72] informed me that mothers of boys to be drafted had discussed [the issue] in order to find ways [to escape] from it; thought of appealing to Roosevelt on the ground that these boys have been and still are being treated as "enemy-aliens." This is the height of stupidity. . . . [There is] no one to guide or think for them or perhaps no one is willing because of the prevalent ego-centrism of the people who are passive and complacent (have been) in their everyday life, but become agitated and get excited whenever anything directly touching their own selfish interest. Natural? Even so, they manifest no intelligence, no reasoning power.

DRAFT, YAMATO ICHIHASHI TO JESSIE TREAT[73]

[early February 1944]

[Dear Mrs. Treat:]

Thank you for the kind letter, candies and sweet-pea seeds, and also for your affectionate interest in us and our house. This is all I can say at present because I find no words to adequately express our real gratitude to you. When I can see you and Payson again, I may be able to do better, though I do know that I can never repay you. Meanwhile I shall try, with aid of a flora-culturist, to get the best results from the seeds when season arrives; we are still in the midst of winter. The weather, here since the dawn of the year, has been a mixture of every variable condition imaginable and mostly composed of gloomy, cold and windy days with frost regularly and infrequent snow or rain, but with some rather surprisingly warm days with bright sunshine, like spring days. These changes take place suddenly and without warnings; we may expect changes hourly. One has to be very alert in order to escape the effect of such conditions.

Though completely isolated in this desert, I know more or less
life in general in the outside world is as full of sad occurrences; it is
difficult even for a habitual optimist to remain optimistic. I suppose
that such a state of affairs is inevitable in war time and in belligerent
countries. The sudden death of Mrs. Hoover shocked me,[74] though
I am hardened about the phenomenon. In the camps, including [this]
one, the death-rate is very high due to many reasons. I have attended more funerals in the camps than I have in [the rest of my]
life time. Even death has its redeeming feature; the deceased will
not know sadness any more. Those of us blessed with life continue
to [be] confronted with sad events and must bear the burden of
spiritual suffering in cumulative form as time progresses.

(U.S. casualties reported by the Associated Press on February 2)

2/2 [Total]	Dead	Wounded	Missing	Prisoners
146,186	33,153	49,518	33,617	29,898

DIARY

Saturday, February 5

Overcast but mild, soon cleared up and warm and bright.

A general confusion among nisei concerning the notification
[which] came relative to the selective board. Classification or reclas-
sification [is] "1-A"; it is a mere notice that the recipient will be
called at any time for physical and mental examinations for the military service. If qualified, one will be inducted within from 10 to 90
days. "Appeal" must be made within 10 days after the receipt of the
card. Family financial conditions are not valid for deferment, as such
need will be provided by the government. Deferred occupations:
railroad, agriculture and war industries if proved important on the
basis [of] individual workers.

. . . .

Sunday, February 6

Gloomy all day.

Yuhora came with telegrams from Hiro relative to his return;
confusing but finally cleared up. Kuramatsu and Yuhora had tea.
Had [it?] out with Kei; she is very unreasonable.

. . . .

Monday, February 7

The sun penetrates thin clouds, scattered and warm. Gloomy and sultry.

Hattori[75] and some youngsters came but told them not to bother me in the morning.

Takahashi finally settled his farm propositions with Konno, etc.[76] Yuhora's son will return here tonight.

Kurahashi came to get inscriptions for *hyōsatsu* [nameplates]; nothing doing. One Iijima (6F), a nisei and a number of nisei groups [are] opposed to service; they have been discussing in meetings and wish advice how they should do this as a group. Advised: whatever they intend to do should be [done] individually instead of group actions. Each must be responsible for his own conduct but not in partnership.

. . . .

Tuesday, February 8

Clear and warm, but little later became overcast and cold. Rather a nasty day.

Kujo reported that it had been decided at the meeting held last night to distribute the *imonhin* on the basis of apartment units, but if occupied by one person, such will get 50% of the unit share and if more than five, additional shares will be given. But before this decision was arrived at, there was the demand for per capita distribution; this was turned down on the ground that contributions have been collected on the basis of apartment units. Actually, *shōyu* and tea were thus distributed; *miso* is to be kept in the mess hall, while drugs [will be] in the manager's hands, as there are not enough to go around to be given to the needy. What is left over will be given to large families.

The *imonhin* were distributed as follows per apartments: 3/4 gallon of *shōyu*, 1 1/2 *kin* [measure of weight equaling 1.32 pounds] of tea and a small amount of *miso*. This meant that both the Japanese subjects and American citizens received an equal share of the three items thus at hand. It is really funny that even the families of American soldiers were included among the recipients. Was this a generosity on the part of issei or was it due to their *gari-gari* anxiety on the part of parents with many kids who would have received larger shares whether on per capita or family or apartment basis. . . . What are they going to do with books and *gakki*? I wonder.

KEI ICHIHASHI TO JESSIE TREAT [77]

Amache, Colo.
February 8 [1944]

Dear Mrs. Treat:

January passed so rapidly. We had a very mild weather here, in spite of snow fall twice in a month. The first one fell on the 6th, and the hospital got busy, as many people fell on the iced ground and were injured.

About three weeks ago we had a beautiful day so warm and nice that I thought it would be perfectly safe to go out to see a doctor and get some medicines. So I went to the hospital [for the] first time since I had the flu last Xmas; it sounds awfully silly, but there is no taxi service here. No doctors come to our apartments to see patients. This is the rule in the Center. They send us a hospital car, if patients request, of course. Just before Christmas a young girl, 21 years old, got a heart attack, so her parents telephoned to the hospital and asked them for a doctor. But they sent them a car instead of a doctor, and the girl died in the car on the way to the hospital. It was very sad. Well, I have taken medicines and I am well now; this is a thing to be thankful for.

Thank you very much for dee–licious candies and the seeds of sweet peas. Such nice candies are too luxurious for the life in this tenement house. And I have another luxury—carnations which my "new cousins" brought us last Sunday. One of our visitors criticized that these beautiful carnations and high toned candies do not fit to the barracks. Well, it is true, but I am enjoying sweet candies and beautiful flowers and a few real pictures which an artist gave to us, and I am quite contented with these things. Since the New Year's Day I feel serene unusually, and on sunny days I sit in the sun quietly, and try to cling [to] my philosophy. I should have written sooner, but I was very busy to do so many things after the confinement of several weeks.

I have heard from Mildred Clyde;[78] she wrote that she got our address from you, and "it is queer to write after so long a silence," she said. I asked "Oshishian," one of our neighbors, to get me some fertilizer for the sweet peas. He knows the best kind for them and also where to get it; and he has promised to bring it to me very soon, so I will sow them nicely at the proper season.

I think Prof. Treat is teaching this quarter and [is] busy again; I hope he will not work too hard.

Sincerely yours,
Kei Ichihashi

DIARY

February 9

Started overcast with rather a strong and cold wind; very gloomy
and cold—the wind grows stronger. They day was nasty with wind
and stand storm.

. . . .

Called on Kuramatsu and saw the paintings; they are very attractive and beautiful. Yuhora informed me that I can have three pictures when he makes frames for them.

"Pioneer": nothing important.

Silence prevails at home; I had supper alone at home, which is
the rule now; what will develop I don't know and it does not matter;
only I feel sorry for the fool.

Saturday, February 12

Started overcast and cold with frost—very gloomy, the very opposite of yesterday. The cold became somewhat modified when the sun
was out, but gloomy on the whole.

Yuhora and Takahashi started to make frames for the paintings;
the work is better than anticipated.

Yoshihara brought a can.

Worked on the tax return.

Yuhora brought the first painting (the Colorado scene.)

Speaking of the rate [of death] among the prisoners of war, I am
reminded of the very high death-rate among the evacuees in the
various relocation camps. The causes: age-composition, inadequate
medical care, food—insufficient nourishment, the lack of vitamins;
result: no resistance power to illness and easily succumb to it.

Sunday, February 13

Continues gloomy and cold. Snow began to fall in the afternoon,
but for a very short while. However it remained cold all day.

Kayashima called in the afternoon; so did Yoshihara.

Called on the Okubos in the evening and he talked on draft, *im-
onbin* distribution and the mess hall situation—the preparation of
food is generally poor because those who work here have had no

experience as cooks. I suggested the only way to improve it is to establish a *kōshūkai* [short training course] and compel the cooks to attend these demonstrated lectures by experts. The food served is terrible, partly due to the above fact; the supplies should be improved.

Monday, February 14

Somewhat overcast but much warmer than previous days, later it became more cloudy and windy making it cold again.

Learned there is an "*inu*" in the block; among others, he is recording the names of callers here and at Takahashi. He is that notorious guy opposite [here?]. What is the purpose is not of course [important], but one has to be on the alert whether he is innocent.

Suffered a mild case of *geri* [diarrhea] caused by what I must have eaten yesterday.

The food seems to get worse; breakfast alone is tolerable; too much starch: rice and noodles, rice and beans very regularly, [served] at least twice a week; fish served always salted or chilled but tasteless in either case or else old and smelly, often on the edge of being spoiled. However, most of the residents being farmers or laborers, appear to be insensitive to all these and hence remain silent.

Due to the "eats," quite a large number of persons suffered cases of diarrhoea in this block and throughout the center; spoiled fish Friday and the mince-pie served on Sunday.

Informed that the girl ([?]) is acting as a cat [female "*inu*"].

Tuesday, February 15

Overcast and cold. *Kona-yuki* [powdery snow] started to fall in the morning; lessened but still a little continues to fall—very gloomy though not very cold.

Oki called and informed me that quite a number of the draft-age group are worked up and are discussing possible methods of protest; it is up to the maturer ones of nisei to guide and lead the younger ones so that they will not do anything foolish. Avoid emotion and keep calm and think hard before any positive action is taken to minimize unnecessary troubles.

Mrs. Yoshihara came. Yuhora informed me that the main sewer pipes got out of order and, for instance, the 9H latrine was flooded

with waste-water—a terrible state. But they were finally fixed.
The people were forced to use the 10-H latrine in the meantime.
The pipes are only 8 inches in diameter. We escaped because of the
elevation.

The diarrhea continues to prevail—the fish served at the Monday
supper.

The sewer main in 9H was filled with broken pipes and chunks of
coal to stop the flow of water; this was also true in another block.
This must have been the work of big boys—was it a prank or with
deliberate purpose? In either case it was bad because it caused the
suffering of residents, beside the damage to property.*

Boys in the [induction] age-group held a meeting this evening to
discuss the draft problem. Y joined us to enjoy *ohagi* [rice dumplings
covered with bean jam] brought by Mrs. Yoshihara.

Wednesday, February 16

Clear and cold with frost even [canopying?] trees; in the afternoon it
cleared up and the sun shone, making it warm though with a slightly
cold breeze.

It seems that nisei are still confused as to the exact meanings of
"A-1"; tried to tell them what [it] means, as there are some who received c-4.[79] Discussions in small groups continue; there was an
assembly in the evening: pros and cons on the subject of group
protest.[80]

Called on Kuramatsu and got *three pictures*: the Rocky [Moun-
tain] scenery, a scenery in Wyoming-Colorado border and the "17
miles shore."[81]

Thursday, February 17

Overcast and cold; snow keeps on falling but in such a manner that
it does not remain on the ground—small quantity and dry. Gloomy
and miserable.

Yoshihara and Kurahashi called.

---

*This paragraph was a late addition to the entry, keyed to the comments on the broken
sewer by an asterisk. The following paragraph was also apparently added at the same time.

Caught a cold? Coughing since last night.

Rademaker and Okubo called; the former brought some statistics of the center population and three samples of the questions and requests made by blocks relative to the selective service of the nisei draft-agers.[82] Informed that at the meeting held last night some kibei made speeches to oppose the idea of military service. It was finally resolved to ask each block draft-agers now they were able to go in support and asked the council to formulate coordinated questions and requests to be sent to the President, Army Secretary and Navy Secretary and also Dillon Myer. A continuation meeting was held this evening which heard the reports from the blocks. The result: no group action but individual, though four blocks supported the former. Thus the idea petered out. Kibei failed.[83]

[Internal security chief Harlow W.] Tomlinson came [to the meeting] at the instruction of Lindley and made a brief speech: 1) meetings [have been] held without permit; 2) tonight's meeting was the last one tolerated; 3) more may be held if permit is secured; agitation against the draft law liable to penalties; asked agitators whether they have applied for expatriation and are going to Tule Lake; do not succumb to them; be mindful of penalties. Disgruntled appeared very few. No more agitation meetings to be held except to examine the report of the Council. No action or speech from the floor at tonight's meeting; many issei and some women were present. . . .

John R[ademaker]: one or both centers in Arizona will be closed, but not Manzanar because the latter is in California and is inhabited by "loyal" ones. They are "there" and have been "there"; they can't be kicked out now or in the future, before, during or after the war is over. The "coming of 500 from Manzanar" is a mere rumor—has never been more than that.

Friday, February 18

Overcast and cold.

Met the boys and told them that they had no guts; they ought to conduct their meetings better or else they should refrain from their critical attitude toward issei meetings. Saw no difference between the two.

Told Sakai about the alleged *inu*; the Council should investigate because they are bad for the morale of the evacuee life. Let us have a showdown.

Received a letter from Payson; three notices.[84] My cold grew worse and stayed in the room.

Wednesday, February 23

Started cloudy but cleared up; it became warm.
  Got out of bed, though somewhat weak.
  Mori and Kuramoto [came] with oranges.
  Had Yuhora for chicken sukiyaki.
  48 Amacheans summoned for physical exams: of the number, 25 are residents in Amache . . . 7 were former center residents; 16 were called by draft-boards in California and elsewhere.

· · · ·

Thursday, February 24

A beautiful spring-like day.
  Consulted the federal agent respecting tax return.
  Had an extended talk with [Center attorney Donald] Horn—future of the nisei.
  Kiyohara suggested a trip to Granada for lunch and walked there only to find the "chop suey" [house] closed for repairs; but Kay* was there and we were rescued. He told the man to prepare our meals: sashimi, soup and pickles, rice boiled. It was good. It was Kay's treat. Stopped at the bank, and on the way back we were picked up by a local farmer driving an old fashioned wagon driven by a team of horses—the man had a colt 3 months old. It was an experience which I had not had for 30 or 40 years.

· · · ·

Friday, February 25

Clear but a strong breeze—sand storm. It started to blow last night and continues thus all the day. Very disagreeable.
  Had the first breakfast since [I took] ill on the 19th, and [had] lunch too, and supper too.

---

* Unidentified.

Nothing important happened, but a terrific gale continued to rage all day, kicking sand, both fine and coarse which pained when for instance [it] hit [my] face. It was impossible to be out and no one except those who had to do, was out. The camp was deserted.

Saturday, February 26

The gale subsided completely and the morning started partially overcast with frost, but not particularly cold. Turned out a nice and warm day.

. . . .

. . . Abe Shiro, chairman of the Council and Kawashima, a kibei, who presided over the meetings on draft questions were quizzed by a F.B.I. [agent] (Tomlinson present) relative to the meetings [according to rumors]. The WRA is not truly sympathetic to the evacuees since it is willing to do things hurtful to their interests; [but] who assumed that they were to begin with? The Amacheans are too dumb to know anything. Johnson[85] asked the Council to take a positive stand on the draft issue and persuade nisei to respond to it; the Council could not since their citizenship rights are still denied them. Besides, the draft is an individual matter. Lindley and Horn agreed with the Council position.

K: the JACL never endorsed evacuation as such; it was forced upon the nisei by military order? At the Salt Lake Conference, it asked for the restitution of citizenship rights, but was responded [to] by the proposal for a "combat team." One year elapsed since, but still no restoration of their rights and on the top of that, the gov't imposed [the] "draft" on them. Therefore, nisei held meetings in order to study ways and means of regaining their rights of citizenship simultaneously with their willing response to draft call and not for the purpose of evading or opposing the draft. Some members of the WRA concluded that the latter was the purpose; Tomlinson's talk at the 2nd meeting more than implied that. "Police mind": he regards everybody as a criminal or potential one.

Monday, February 28

Snow piled up 2 inches with icicles from eaves. Continues to be overcast. Remained gloomy but rather warm all the day.

The residents suffered diarrhoea generally on account of the food eaten at Sunday supper. Told Miura to find out whether it was the meat supplied or the keeping and preparation in the kitchen; added that spoiled things should not be served—fish has often been in such a condition. Simply because of the dumbness [of the residents], they should not be taken advantage in this or in any other way; those who are responsible should function on behalf of those whom they serve: block managers, stewards, etc. i.e. "public servants"....

． ． ． ．

Tuesday, February 29

Overcast, damp and cold; remained miserable and gloomy.
    Kurahashi called.
    Yuhora brought another painting; an excellent work—the 17 mile shore with waves dashing on rocks—colors rather attractive. He massaged me all over and [I] felt relieved from the stiffness; the eye trouble is apparently [of] the same cause.
    Kujo asked for individual [evacuee] reports on the properties damaged where they were stored, such [as] churches, temples, private houses; these reports were asked for [by] the Spanish Consulate at S.F. at the request of the Japanese government.

． ． ． ．

SPECIAL DATA

Observations on the *imonhin* and their distribution:
    On January 31st, Kujo announced the arrival of *imonhin*. . . . Each [block] was to decide how to distribute [them]. Some blocks have already distributed on the basis of per capita, family, apartment; one excluded kids 12 and below. The best method is for issei to receive and share with nisei and sansei [third-generation Japanese Americans] (with explanation as to the nature of gifts to which they have no claim), who are to receive them because the issei wish. Kiyohara informed [me] on the 6th that the *imonhin* came to prisoners of war and internees-detainees; for instance, each keg of shoyu had names and addresses, 3,200 or 3,400 in number; but many have been released on parole. At Santa Fe, a committee of three suggested that after having distributed a keg to each, what is left over, because railroads refused to distribute to those who have been released, be distributed among the 10 relocation centers.

The committee did this without consulting the internees who kicked up a rumpus. Anyhow, thus this center received as itemized on February 2nd. In some blocks, parents of kids demanded per capita distribution—a "bread-line complex"; differences are only a matter of degree. They are all *kojiki* [beggars]. *Amerika heitai* [American soldiers'] families included. How could they ask, as they are enemy aliens, for *imonhin* from Japan, public or private? If they did or do, they have no pride of their status. A mere fact that they are *nihonjin* [of Japanese ancestry] is meaningless except on the basis of status. Always wiling to stick out their hands like beggars. Very *asamashii* [pathetic].

5

Amache
March 1, 1944–
December 31, 1944

By March 1944, the Ichihashis had settled into a tense but stable routine at Amache. Every day Yamato received friends and visitors with whom he discussed camp affairs and particular individual problems. The principal worry was the draft, as families wrestled with the emotional, political, and legal ramifications of the prospect of sons entering the military to fight in the war. As a "representative from the community at large," Yamato participated on a special camp committee that helped provide information to draft-age nisei. But his participation in formal camp affairs was minimal. One reason for this, he later confessed to James Lindley, the camp director, was that when he assumed a leading role at Tule Lake, his motives had come under suspicion and were misinterpreted. He therefore resolved that at Amache he would "lead a quiet and self-contained life." [1]

While Yamato's diary indicates he frequently discussed the progress of the war with friends, his entries contain only sporadic comments about the international situation. From these, and the many newspaper clippings about the war from the daily *Palo Alto Times* that he pasted in his diary, though, one has the impression that he was sickened by the savagery of war and felt particular sympathy with the suffering of civilians in Japan. He took special notice of articles that reported on Japanese allegations of American atrocities against them and on the continuing mistreatment of persons of Japanese ancestry in America.

Relations between Yamato and Kei continued to be tense, with the two seemingly living separate lives within their constrained circumstances. Kei's correspondence with Jessie Treat and Yamato's correspondence and diary contain only a few references to shared activities or experiences. Still, the mundane chores of life constantly intruded to keep them busy: income tax had to be paid, even from within the camp; the maintenance and rental of their Stanford home demanded attention; and nagging health problems plagued them, especially Yamato's increasingly severe eye troubles, which were diagnosed as early cataracts. In addition to burying himself in the study of early Japanese cultural history, Yamato was frequently asked to serve community needs, including teaching an adult education course on Japanese cultural history and advising various governing bodies.

Kei, on the other hand, expresses a deepening philosophical, almost spiritual outlook that seemed to provide solace for the physical hardships and personal unhappiness she suffered in Amache. Her thoughtfulness and caring for others within and without the camp stands in contrast to her husband's heightened crankiness and arrogance. Her letters to Jessie Treat virtually cease making any explicit reference to Yamato.

Despite the tedium of prison camp existence, unsettling developments kept the Amache inhabitants uneasy and anxious. Young men were drafted to go to war; other individuals departed for school or jobs and unknown futures in the Midwest; bickering, jealousies, and suspicion among those remaining in Amache became a part of daily life; and there was always the presence of death, of those in war, of the ill in camp, and of the elderly. ◾

1944 DIARY[2]

Wednesday, March 1

Cloudy but rather mild; soon a cold breeze began to blow rendering the day miserable. In the afternoon, it cleared in part and the sun shone and was warm.

Mrs. Ishizu [visited] in re: her son's draft: 1-A card from Merced, California where he was registered; [he is] now 22 and working in Middletown, Connecticut. . . . [She wants to] find out whether he could take his physical test where he now resides. The family at 9-H 1-B came from Livingston, California. The old man, 62, is invalid and his wife is 52 and is working in the 10-H mess. The boy is their only son.

Sakai called bringing [linoleum] floor covering and chicken for frying; we had lunch. We had unusual menu (liver fried); first since our arrival and Yuhora said the first since his arrival. The outside is often disagreeable whenever anti-Japanese propaganda runs rampant. The [war] bond sale did not [go] well in his town which is financially well-to-do. House to house canvassing was done twice.

Y. massaged me; later called on Kuramatsu and he gave me three more paintings—small in size.

The night was clear with the moon and stars.

. . . .

Thursday, March 2

Clear and delightful as anticipated; but soon mist appeared and became cold. What a quick change! A strong wind following, kicking up some sands.

Akahashi called.

An official notice came to Hiro [Yuhora], "Physically fit; acceptable for general military service." Sent to him at his present address. . . .

No particular happening during the day.

Meals slightly better prepared.

Clothing allowance is not being made here monthly; Tuleans since October have not received any so far.

Friday, March 3

It started to rain early in the morning, and it is rather cold—miserable. Changed to snow which was anticipated yesterday. Snow stopped in the evening.

                    . . . .

Today is *Sangatsu-sekku* [Girls' Day or Doll Festival] and the mess served *ohagi* [rice dumplings covered with bean jam] in addition to the usual fish supper, but we had fried chicken in the room.

Nothing worthy to be noted happened today, except anxiety over the draft on the part of many parents. Those registered in the West Coast states—California, Oregon and Washington—are being notified by the local selective boards which are apparently anxious to swell their numbers to meet their quota advantageously to Caucasian inductees! Yet they were and are still agitating against the return of nisei to their former residences; a clear evidence of their selfishness.

KEI ICHIHASHI TO JESSIE TREAT [3]

Amache, Colorado
March 3 [1944]

Dear Mrs. Treat:

It ought to be the doll festival day, today, and this is the flower festival month; it sounds all very gay. The people in California have beautiful flowers, hyacinth, tulips, irises and many other flowers in their gardens, and pretty soon wisterias will bloom. I have heard that you had bad snowstorms at some parts of California lately. I hope you haven't suffered very much from the recent bad weather.

We have had rather pleasant weather here, but we haven't any flowers or any green grasses yet. The ground is still bare. When we go out, we can see a wide country stretched out to the horizon to meet the pale blue sky, but we do not see any sign of the spring.

I have heard from Miss Stoltenberg, and she said "We are very glad to have good neighbours." I am glad, too, that the decent people use my house. Many people were saddened by Mrs. Hoover's death. When I read the news of her sudden death, I was very much shocked, and could not believe it, and I had been wondering about her sudden death till you wrote us. She was such a wonderful lady. I do not read much of the war news lately. I am simply waiting for the war to come to the end. People are suffering everywhere, at the war front also the home front. It is the most dreadful nightmare.

I should like to ask you a favour. As I enclose a doctor's prescription, which is for vitamins, so I understand, would you please get them and send them for me? There is no hurry about it, please do it whenever it is convenient for you. I have just recalled that I was one of the good customers of the University Pharmacy at Palo Alto before the evacuation. If an owner of the store is the same person, Mr. Robinson?—I have forgotten his name—he will be glad to send any medicines to me. So if it is more convenient for you to order, please do it at the University Pharmacy.

The other day I went to see an eye doctor, and he advised me to take some vitamins. If I go to a near-by town, Lamar, I think I shall be able to get the medicine there. Lamar is just 15 miles away from here, but it is very inconvenient to go, as a connection of the transportation is very bad. I tried to get a good chance to go there for a month, and I have failed.

Please give my best wishes to Prof. Treat, and I hope you do not work too hard.

> Sincerely yours,
> Kei Ichihashi

DIARY

Wednesday, March 8

Clear and not very nippy; no frost, though a cold breeze. The sun shines brightly. Remained nice and warm without violent wind, though overcast.

. . . .

"Pioneer": 1) Pre-induction physical calls: 8th, 15th and 22nd; 2) Ickes[4] reports that 402 took exams in the first call, but 7 refused, 5 from Amache and 2 Minidoka; 3) California [Draft] Boards call [up] 42 in Amache, but [only] 34 are residing here while others have "relocated;" 4) the Blue Star Mothers and the Women Federation are to present a joint resolution—the restoration of the rights of citizenship. . . . 5) Additional hearings on loyalty vs. disloyalty at Tule Lake. . . . 6) 2,500 nisei students are enrolled in 450 institutions in 46 different states, reported by National Director C. V. Hibbard of Japanese-American Student Relocation Council.[5]

Called on Kuramatsu and found many paintings on new subjects, including water-falls.

Thursday, March 9

Partly cloudy and somewhat chilly, though no frost; a strong wind with some sands kicked up, but the sun shines through clouds which partly cover the sky.

The people are excited over the rumors of the complete destruction of the fleet transports.[6] [Admiral Nimitz?] is in Washington. Rumors started since yesterday and still persist: the *Daihon'ei happyō* "Amache" D, etc.[7]

Also alleged that nisei working in airplane plants had been discharged and were inducted or summoned to the pre-induction physicals whereas the *ketō* [pejorative for whites, Westerner] workers in the same plants had been granted deferments.

One George Oki,[8] 9-E 3-B was brought by one *Aichi-jin* [a person from Aichi, Ichihashi's home prefecture]; the boy will be 20 next July. He was recently examined in Denver and passed the test, and is to be inducted soon. His mother prefers to have him to disobey his induction call despite the inevitable penalty of 20 years imprisonment, but the boy prefers to go into the Army. What advice if any? None except to follow his own decision. He told me that there was another case like his; at present this boy agrees with his mother, though what he will do actually was unknown. Tragic cases to say the least, but inevitable!

Called on Kuramatsu with Yuhora and he gave Kei 2 small paintings.

Kura sent news (2/26 *Daihon'ei*) of the *daishōri* [sweeping victory] following Truk,[9] which allowed the enemy to attack. The Anglo-American fleet—the fight continuing.

Friday, March 10

Somewhat overcast but the sun shone and it was not only warm, [but was] even hot as a summer day throughout.

Learned that Emi, a man of 69 passed away last night at 9—a

heart attack. This is the second death in this block since our arrival here.

Yuhora and I made frames for pictures.

Yoshimas called bringing a pie.

No other event noteworthy occurred during the day.

Kujo announced that tomorrow an agent to assist income tax return would be in Horn's office all day.

Tuesday, March 21

A strong wind with rain; dark and cold—very disagreeable. Rain and then hails and snow with a gale; another blizzard? A very miserable day.

. . . .

Miyama Masao (6-н 1-c) [10] who leads the Adult Education since [Samuel] Gordon's departure called; he is a kibei who finished *chūgaku* [junior high school] attended Sacramento Junior College and served as the *kanji* [chief secretary] of Lodi [California] Nihonjinkai [Japanese Association]. For the latter reason, he was quizzed by the F.B.I. a number of times; married with 2 kids. Summoned to a hearing here tomorrow to determine his loyalty. He came to inquire whether or not I would participate in Adult Education. The answer, as it is organized, no, since there is nothing I can do. Asked whether I could give him private lessons, again the answer was no since others will apply. Find out whether there is a sufficient number [of persons] desirous of intellectual pursuits—stimuli so as to remain awake. [?] has a bad reputation among the Japanese in Sacramento and Lodi. When the war started, he worked for the F.B.I.; [he was] an insurance agent—must have played bad tricks on his clients. Intelligent but abuses his intelligence. Kujo and Iko agreed.

Wednesday, March 22

Started clear but cold; it remained so despite the bright sunshine. Nothing in particular as far as the camp is concerned.

. . . .

"*Pioneer*" carried the following items of news: 1) 17 draftees in Amache received March 27 induction orders; 2) 3 taken into custody by U.S. marshall because they failed to respond to physicals March 15—handcuffed and taken to the Federal Institution of Correction; 3) transfer of draft (California boards) impossible, [says?] Pasadena; 4) Ickes: resettlers: Chicago leads with 3,500, Denver with 1,083 follows; more than 19,000 have been granted indefinite leave while seasonal leave counts between 2,000 and 3,000. Two-thirds are American citizens of whom 72% have never seen Japan, including kids, nisei and sansei; 5) the last of the [San Francisco] *Chronicle* articles on the evacuees and their resettlement by Flynn—they are not likely to return to the West Coast states.

Rademaker and [Masao] Miyama, with a bag of sugar and a piece of meat as gifts, called relative to the subject on a course of "cultural evolution." Rademaker advised me [about American] nationalistic and patriotic sentiments that dominate the Administration staff, and that being the case, it is injudicious to attempt [a course] at "current topics," "post-war plans," "international organization." No matter how objective one tries to be, unless it is rendered "Americanistic," he will be misunderstood or misinterpreted and made to suffer. Hence "cultural" is the way out. Some members of the staff will join the class with qualified evacuees.

KEI ICHIHASHI TO JESSIE TREAT[11]

Amache
March 29 [1944]

Dear Mrs. Treat:

Thank you for two nice letters[12] and very interesting newspaper clippings. I have never seen the pictures of "Historic scene of Leland Stanford laying the corner-stone, May 14, 1887" before, and it is very interesting; so I will keep it for a souvenir.

The parcel post has just arrived, I thank you for sending me vitamins. But I didn't dream it would make you so much trouble. When the doctor gave me the prescription, he said that [they would be] 100 for $5.00, and take one every day. It seemed very simple so that I thought these vitamins were ready made, packed in a bottle and sold, something like the one I got a long time ago. I am very sorry for you. Thank you very much for sweet extra vitamins, only I warn you that if you send me sweet vitamins so often I may become a fat woman like somebody else, and you will not recognize me when I get back to the campus.

Speaking of poison oak, I feel the slap of the warm spring breeze in my face. When I think of the full water of the beautiful Lagunita Lake, and swimming and canoeing, also the picturesque boat house, they are all so attractive that I should like to go back to the campus and enjoy the spring. On the contrary, we had a very cold, windy day yesterday, and it snowed last night. We have a very changeable weather lately, people say it is worse than last year.

As I have been thinking of Lutz's family, I am glad to know that Mrs. Lutz went south with her daughters and they are quite well. Before I left the campus I noticed Mr. Lutz's gray hair. It seems to me as if he attempted to do so many things and consequently he worked a little too hard. I always think of our old friend on the campus also Palo Alto. If you have a chance to see old ladies Mrs. Branner and Mrs. [Lyon?],[13] please remember us to them. I think Mrs. Lyon is still living in the same house at Palo Alto. A Japanese boy, Yoshida, used to work for her for years. But he is in one of the camps now, so I wonder how she is managing to keep her house, as it is very hard to get any helpers now a days.

I am glad to know that Mr. and Mrs. Culver[14] got the letter from their son in Europe. Please give our best wishes to them when you see them. I have heard many Japanese boys left for certain places lately, but I didn't know that Dr. Kitagawa's son[15] went to the Pacific. Just a couple days ago 18 boys were inducted from this project, and I think another group will follow them very soon.

Last Xmas we got nice Wilson's candies from our good neighbour, which were specially good ones, and we enjoyed them very much. Right after we received candies, Ichihashi was writing a letter, so that I thought he sent a letter to Misses Stoltenberg to express our thanks. He wrote a letter, but maybe he didn't mention anything about the candies. I don't know, I can't understand. Anyhow I told him to write again and so he did, I think. As a rule in my family I write all Japanese letters to respond and he does to American friends.

I thank you again for sending me vitamins and specially for sweet candies, I deeply appreciate your kindness.

> With best wishes, sincerely,
> Kei Ichihashi

◘ Dreadful weather plagued Amache in late March and April—biting sandstorms swept the camp for days at a time and often kept the Ichihashis, who were frequently sick, indoors. Yamato made use of the time to prepare his course on the cultural history of Japan for camp residents.[16] He enjoyed the many visits from friends and himself spent many hours with the painter Kuramatsu and Yuhora, as they reviewed paintings and helped make frames together.

Much of Ichihashi's diary was devoted to recording the daily activities of its keeper: the many visitors and their incessant gifts of foods, plants and flowers, and other sundry items, summaries of detailed discussions about camp affairs and evacuee problems, his attendance at meetings, requests to serve on various committees, and his delivery of occasional lectures.[17] The diary continued to contain virtually nothing about Kei or Woodrow, but it appears that Yamato and Kei had resumed speaking to one another. On April 25, he jotted this cryptic diary note, "Promised Kei a new broom. 'Two cots, 2 mattresses, 4 comforters and no bucket.'" ◗

DIARY

Friday, April 28

Another cloudy, gloomy morning. Soon a wind and light rain started to fall, making the day a miserable one, cold and wet. Rain continued heavily.

. . . .

The case of a family relocated: if the man is inducted into the Army, could his wife and child live in a relocation center as evacuees? They will receive the customary allowances. Is there a precedent which makes their case *yes* or *no*? The common sense seems to answer it, no? Wards of the government in a double sense; yet there actually exist such cases in this center and doubtless in other centers, though their status appears somewhat different [since] they were here or in other centers when their husbands entered the Army.

Tuesday, May 2

Overcast and disagreeable; it looks like a rainy day. Late in the afternoon, it became stormy and rather violent.

My cold is slightly better this morning, but it turned out worse as the day progressed and rather bad in late afternoon. Consequently I was unable to attend the first session of my class; bad weather and bad cold. . . .

. . . .

Wednesday, May 3

Started cold but windy and remained so all day; later it became cloudy and gloomy.

. . . .

My cold hangs on with a headache and a sore throat.

"Pioneer": 1) no Pacific fighting for nisei; 2) school kids forbidden to get gate-passes; 3) 1,300 Jeromites[18] applied here though only 500 can be accommodated; 4) Tule Lake "agitators" about 100 in number to be interned at Leupp Camp, near Winslow, Arizona.[19] This place will be reopened for the purpose; 5) [New York City Mayor F. H.] LaGuardia, Governor [Walter Evans] Edge of New Jersey and Governor [John William] Bricker of Ohio—all [are] against relocation of Japanese [in their areas]; 6) Letters attack on these three—a fight is on.

Thursday, May 4

Started clear and cold; a cold wind continues and customary sandstorms following. Cloudy in the afternoon and also windy.

. . . .

Miyama called and said that 38 are enrolled [in my cultural history class]. Kato wanted credit—nothing doing at present as far as I am concerned! Negotiating for a room in the high school.

Received the May [house rent] check from Westbrook.

Kurahashi came to invite me to *udon*—accepted.

A block meeting was called but [I am] unable to attend it.

M brought 5 pieces rag-rugs.

Friday, May 5

Started clear and sunny with no wind. Remained a nice, warm day.

Fixed the coat-hanger so that it stands steadily.

[Reports Officer Joseph H.] McClelland informed me that the rumor is current that those on "parole" are forbidden to relocate and he, having received a list of such parolees in order to correct it for their information, [clarifies] that the rumor is absolutely baseless. In fact, they can relocate if they desire; there are individuals whether

parolees or not who are not permitted to do so due to the order of
the Dept. of Justice (F.B.I.)

Paul Yamamoto[20] came with his father and a box of candies and
said that he had passed the tests and would be inducted on the 9th,
the immediate destination being Fort Logan, Denver.

Mrs. Yoshihara invited us to supper to be served at 5:30.

Received a note from Payson, giving me, among others, sad news
about Stanford; he damns Tresidder as ignorant of academic affairs.
[Treat] will retire, if possible, when he reaches the age at the end of
this year.[21]

. . . .

Saturday, May 6

Started clear and sunny and it so remained thru the day;
rather warm.

Finished the [window] screen, except hinges.

Nothing of importance. "Pioneer": 1) 158 will graduate [from]
high school in May (18);[22] 2) a community affairs office burglarized
of $166.00 but $135.15 worth of coins untouched; why such large
sums of money be kept in an unprotected place, especially "public"
funds?; 3) [Governor] Bricker attacks Ickes and WRA "New Deal-
ers"; 4) increase of clothing allowances and social grants discussed in
Washington at a conference of center delegates. . . . 5) LaGuardia's
stand criticized; 6) my class to be held in high school room 24. . . .

. . . .

Sunday, May 7

Cloudy but mild; in the afternoon sunny and warm and then at 4:30
cloudy and windy with sands. Rain storm at 6:00; it continued
through the night.

Saw 2 baseball games in the morning and in the afternoon;
crowds out were rather small, but the games were interesting. Nothing unusual happened. Yuhora called and talked until 10:30.

KEI ICHIHASHI TO JESSIE TREAT[23]

Amache
May 7 [1944]

Dear Mrs. Treat:

It is Sunday today, and I am enjoying the Sunday quiet. The sky is gray and it rained a bit this morning, and I have made a fire and am staying in the room. On the contrary, it was very warm all day yesterday, so that everybody was staying out in the shade. Even in the evening we had a warm breeze and the beautiful moon. It was a sort of a tropical night and too beautiful to sleep.

We are planning to make a nice garden in front of our apartment. A few days ago one of the professional gardeners came and planted Xmas berries for us, and he promised to bring some chrysanthemums to plant, and some other plants, which suit to this soil. He used to live at Redwood City and was one of the chrysanthemum growers there.[24] Last fall we enjoyed a pot of white chrysanthemums which he brought for us, but this year we are expecting to enjoy our own flowers in autumn. He is also planning to sow morning glories seeds which we call "sky blue." They are beautiful blue flowers very much like ones which you sent us last year at Tule Lake. Morning glories grow very nicely here. When we came to this project last September "sky blue" were blooming beautifully at one of our friend's place; they were just gorgeous. In Colorado it seems to me the spring approaches very slowly. There are two Japanese elm trees in front of our tenement, which we planted last Xmastime, and the leaves are just coming out and they are so delicate and pretty. Lawns are getting green now. People say the weather is hot in June here, but at present we are making a fire every morning.

The time has passed almost two years since we retreated. I am leading a sort of a cloistered life after I came to this center last September. I do not see any movies and do not attend any gatherings; I even don't listen to the radio lately. When people come I always welcome them but I never call on them, unless it is very necessary. There is no color, no glow in the every day life especially since last Xmas. At that time I had a bad cold and stayed in bed for two weeks and I had an opportunity to meditate deeply day and night.[25] Since then I feel quite serene and my soul is not disturbed much, so that I am able to see the things clearly and think straight. When I look back, I was worrying for many years—I may tell you all about it some day—but nothing bothers me now, at least for a while. I am reading every day and think quietly. I am so far away from civilization, but the queer part of it is that I am able to accept this strange life as a cloistered life and I feel serene. Some day I have to step into the civilized world, but I don't know how I feel about it. I do not regret at all that once in my life I had the retreat.

Yesterday I received [your] box of a precious gift. They are very delicious but are too luxurious for the cloistered life; I lick the luxurious prunes and for a moment I peep into the civilized world which I left far behind, and enjoy it, and also I am very grateful for your kindness.

I hope this note finds you in best health.

> Affectionately yours,
> Kei Ichihashi

YAMATO ICHIHASHI TO PAYSON TREAT[26]

> 10-H 12-D
> Amache, Colorado
> May 7, 1944

Dear Payson:

I am quite sure that none of your letters has gone astray though the postal delivery is very slow and irregular, and thus the failure of acknowledging them is entirely my own responsibility. Before I forget, I wish to thank you for the box of delicious fruits. Since the beginning of the year, I have had four nasty colds; the 4th one is still hanging on; Kei seems to have a perpetual cold though mild most of the time. In addition, as Ralph [Lutz] informed you, I have been and still am suffering from an eye trouble which has forced me to refrain from using them or rather it, the diseased right eye. Be that as it may, I should have managed to write you and Madam. The only thing I can do is to apologize and this I wish to do sincerely.

You raised a question in regard to the duration of Loyang as a Chinese Colony. First of all, I am afraid that practically all the earlier works, including that of Hulbert[27] require thorough re-investigations. I do not know of historical researches of Chinese scholars, but Japanese historians during the past thirty years or so, have practically re-written the history of ancient Sino-Korean-Japanese international relations (in the form of monographs) on the basis of their painstaking researches. I am following these modern research scholars, but I am not completely satisfied and therefore whatsoever I say or write is "tentative." I shall not publish anything until I shall have had an opportunity "to check" everything.

Your late news concerning the new developments at Stanford both disappoint and shock me; I have been hoping for a better turn under the new President. The life-blood of a university is scholarship, and no real university is possible without true scholars; administrators are a secondary subsidiary in my humble opinion, but unfortunately these often decide the destiny of universities at the expense of true scholarship. Having had more than forty years of connection with Stanford as a student and as a teacher with an ideal as regards its future, I look upon such trends as you state as a tragedy. I have always taken for granted that the academic world remains unaffected by any temporary situations in the pursuit of its destiny. But apparently I am mistaken. Under the circumstances, I do not blame you in the least, though Stanford needs men like you, in not wishing to remain active in our beloved institution longer than it is necessary. May I still [see] that some scholarly Stanfordites arise and guide the destiny of our Stanford?

Thank you for the news concerning the activities of "our" boys [in the military]; they touch me in this sad moment. I am so completely isolated and lonely because I am forced to live a life so abnormal in a community devoid of intellectuality. It is really amazing that mankind can exist as it does at this center. I have always damned war and shall continue to do so more vigorously the rest of my life for I have learned enough of the evils that accompany war. A dangerous thought! Best regards to you and Madam.

> Very affectionately yours,
> Yamato Ichihashi

With apologies for my beautiful handwriting.

DIARY

Saturday, May 20

Started clear but with rather a strong breeze which later subsided and [became] warm.

Went to the office and asked and got the permit to Las Animas.

Mrs. Kuramoto came and told me that [daughter] June had run

away and got married without telling her parents who are consequently mad—in particular [Mr.] Kuramoto.[28] The boy she married
is only a high school graduate and not steady. Asked me to tell [Mr.]
Kuramoto not to be too severe with her.

"Pioneer": 1) 93 went to Tule Lake from here Thursday night;
2) 13 came from Jerome (Pullman cases) on Thursday; 3) farm asks
for 100 workers; 4) there are 409 who are 65 and over; of the number, 334 are males and 75 are females. . . .

Sunday, May 21

Thunder and rain all night but cleared up in the morning—delightful without a breeze and became warm.

Sakais and the baby and his cousin in two cars came at 11:00. One
Animatsu, his friend, came to get us, Kiyohara and Kayashima, Mrs.
Animatsu, a cop named Matsuoka, his wife and daughter and Yama-
gas and his mother and Higakis joined. We went to the bank of the
Arkansas River, passing the X-Y farm where cattle are kept.[29] We
had a delightful day and a delicious lunch all made by Mrs. Sakai;
everybody enjoyed the picnic. We left there at 4:00. Just as we
reached the camp, a terrific sand-storm came on followed by a heavy
shower—thunder and lightning. Sakai left cigars left over with me.

Monday, May 22

Thin clouds cover the sky with a cold breeze; later turned out warm
and remained so throughout the day.

Fixed the celotex[30] to shade the stove and its ugly pipe.

Kurahashi came to invite me to *udon*; Kuramatsu also went.

In the evening, Mrs. Nakata called, bringing some asparagus sent
from Washington. Talked about the case of June's marriage without
telling her parents about it. But there was a warning because sometime ago, she went with the boy to have lunch at Granada, but in
reality tried to go to Denver; but she had no permit to do so. She
stayed out two nights. Both parents should have been suspicious or
[taken] precautions when she went out for the 2nd time. Kuramoto
signed the application for permit to Denver. She then got married
and then sent to the parents a telegraphic notice. She was to pay a
visit here today or tonight. Kuramoto probably knew nothing of the

kind. But his wife had been warned sufficiently by Mrs. Nakata and yet she did not believe it. It came to pass. What can they do about it? What can be done? It is another bad case; that is all as far as I can see. A nisei stupidity.

Tuesday, May 23

Started clear and warm—delightful; in the afternoon a strong wind developed but no sand-storm as yet.

The promised roof-repairing [of our home] was not done in the morning and so [George] Oki went to the office at least to get the treated[?] tar-paper so that we can fix it temporarily. The WRA inefficiency is again demonstrated. It had been informed more than 2 months ago that many barracks had leaky roofs, largely due to rotting of the tar papers where they are nailed with small wooden slats (lathes).

Finished the discussion of pristine Buddhism in India. Many were absent from the class, a bad habit.

Wednesday, May 24

Started clear and warm without a wind to speak of.

As requested by Oki, men are cleaning the coal piles; in this section of barracks, Sano and Yuhora cleaned it already. Spent some time in reading *Civilization: Past and Present* by T[homas] Walter Wallbank and Alastair M. Taylor in 2 volumes, 1942—a superficial survey outline; it could not be otherwise as it is based on English text-books only.

Mrs. Yoshihara called in the evening and brought a piece of sponge cake she had made.

.   .   .   .

A number of evacuees leaving for the [agricultural] season were detained because they had with [them] blankets, mattresses, etc., [according to] Kurahashi.

Kuramatsu reported that there is a number who, having relocated on indefinite leave, sneaked back and lived here without paying their board and room; these will be forced to go out as penalty regardless of their family connections or other circumstances. Some tried to leave here on the seasonal leave and were caught.

Wednesday, May 31

Started clear and delightful; but later turned out rather hot. Late in the afternoon there was a light shower but cleared up and became cooler.

Yuhora and I got weeds (natural lawn-grass) and planted them in the garden.

Ono came to invite me to *udon* lunch at Kurahashi's.

In the evening went to the field beyond 9L and got some flowering wild plants and put them also in front.

Miyama brought a copy of Sansom's new edition of his history of Japan.[31]

. . . .

"Pioneer" 1) Myer: no plan to maintain any of the centers in the post-war period; they will be closed as soon as the military necessity is over; 2)) the same favors the return of the evacuees to the West Coast; 3) 25 depart for physical examination (left on Monday); 4) 16 [who] enlisted [in the] reserves [are to] report to [Camp] Shelby for active service; 5) American League is formed in Colorado to bar Japanese aliens from the U.S.; 6) Shoichi James Okamoto, a nisei, was shot to death by a soldier (sentry) at Tule Lake;* 7) two local boys were arrested for violation of the Federal postal laws; [sent] "obscene and vulgar" letters to a prisoner in the Denver County jail.

Sunday, June 4

Clear with a cool breeze; a violent wind blew briefly. Hattori came and put three posts to protect the morning glories which he planted. Soon after, a terrific gale came (noon) but lasted briefly.

Last night [at a dinner in his honor] Rademaker stated that the Japanese who so wish, will be returned to the West Coast states but not all at once but gradually; first those related to the men serving in the Army, "before the end of the present year."

. . . .

---

*On May 24, 1944, a sentry shot Okamoto, who died the following day. The sentry was acquitted in a court martial and was fined $1.00 for "unauthorized use of government property" (a bullet). See Weglyn, *Years of Infamy*, p. 312, n. 3.

Monday, June 5

Started clear with a cool breeze; it became stronger toward the evening and kicked up some sands as usual.

. . . .

Sakai called and brought a chicken and some strawberries raised in his place; he came to get laborers, but permission from Denver office had to be secured before they could be released from the center since the rule is that men [can] be made available only for the essential agricultural produce.

Received a check from Westbrook.

The first strawberries we tasted since the evacuation; somewhat green and sour but tasted good. We shared them with Yoshiharas and Yuhoras, though not many.

Dropped in the Adult Education Office to find books on Colorado, but found none; [elementary principal Enoch] Dumas promised to gather such that he happens to have in his school library. "Rather elementary," he said. A nice chap.

Thursday, June 8

Started partly overcast with a sprinkling of rain but no wind to speak of; but a strong wind blew with some rain.

Yonemura[32] came this morning with a chicken, but I was in bed as I was unable to sleep all through the night; had a *sukiyaki* supper and invited Yuhora.

Oki brought Tom Bodine's National Japanese-American Student Relocation Council report on Tule Lake under the date of April 20, 1944.[33] Its population is [now] about 20,000 which live in barracks grouped into 85 "blocks."

Education [at Tule Lake]: The school has only just reopened at Tule and about 2,400 kids are enrolled in it, while some 4,000 are in the Japanese Language School; neither is compulsory. None desires to seek college education (through relocation), as they think [they are] unwanted Japs. No adult education yet organized.

The camp: the huge manproof fences spiked with barbed wire— the four gates to pass in and out—create a corresponding psychology. Young nisei (still American at heart), versus older nisei (who are now in heart and soul Japanese because of their appreciation of what the parents have done for them and they wish to satisfy their old parents; the former unconscious of the bitterness of evacuation).

The soldiers: they are everywhere with rifles on their shoulders.

The "stockade": a tragic place where are confined men for political reasons; these men and their wives and children beyond 100 feet.

The result: "The air breathes mistrust and suspicion. Neighbors don't dare speak of their problems to other neighbors. Everybody seems to suspect everybody else of this, that, or the other. But as I say, that seems to be slowly wearing off."

"I am very sorry the Christian Churches of this country have turned their backs on Tule Lake. True, there are only 550 Christians here and 14,000 Buddhists, but that's no reason to desert them!"

No recreational equipment—the government is indifferent toward these disloyal ones; nor outside organized agencies to help—worse than the internment camps.

Friday, June 9

Overcast and cool though no breeze, but soon a strong wind with a sand storm developed and continued toward the evening when it subsided somewhat, though a less terrific wind is still blowing.

Yuhora brought some asparagus.

Okubo called with a note from Rademaker who also [is] having sent a copy of his thesis via the same and asked me to glance it over. Okubo told me, among other things, that the "Pioneer" had failed to appear due to the refusal of its staff to translate the brief report on Tsuchiya and [W. Ray] Johnson in a derogatory manner though requested or demanded by Johnson.*

Hattori brought the same report (clipping) to show me; he consulted me about his desire to have Tsuchiya removed from the position of the block representative, which he holds to this day despite the fact that he has been kicked out of his block manager's job long ago. He took his indefinite leave in order to farm in the vicinity (400 acres) in partnership with [Harlow W.] Tomlinson and Johnson it is alleged. Tsuchiya commutes from the camp. Recently he was discovered to have taken from the center some cots, mattresses and comforters to provide for his laborers also drawn from here. These sneak

---

*See Ichihashi's diary entry for June 15, 1944, below.

back every Saturday. There is fishy doing on the part of Tsuchiya, who seems to enjoy special "protection." He has the reputation of being a cheat before the evacuation and also in the center.

Sunday, June 11

Clear with a strong wind and sand storms. A terrific short shower in the evening.

Heard the *Nichiren-shū* service with the customary drum-beating this morning; there must be a large number of its faithful by the noise heard.[34]

Marvelous lightning and thundering in distances in all directions. Due to the shower, the temperature cooled off and delightful after a disagreeable warm, heavy weather; continued into the mid-night with a light shower.

. . . .

Monday, June 12

Overcast in spots—the warmth modified by a cool breeze which later developed into rather strong [wind] but no sandstorm; the sand having been wet by the shower of the previous night; it subsided toward the evening. It turned cool.

Yuhora, I, and Takahashi cleaned up the back-yard.

Oki informed me that a family of three from Jerome, originally from Tule Lake, will occupy the next room and also 19 were caught going on seasonal leave with government property (comforters, mattresses, cots, etc.). He will get their names for me. Kuramoto had previously told me that Johnson had offered to loan these articles if the employer would make an appropriate deposit, promising to return it when the goods are returned.

Read Warner's book (*Sculpture in the Suiko Period*) (i.e. notes).[35]

Watched a base-ball game after the supper.

Tuesday, June 13

Started clear and delightful without a breeze; became rather warm; a little shower at 6:30PM.

Dispatched the balance of the Federal Income and Victory Tax . . . for the year. . . .

Sakai came [for] his men and brought flowers, including some *shakuyaku* [peonies]—beautiful-colored, raised in his place.

The [class] session was devoted to a discussion of "origins of the Japanese." . . .

Wednesday, June 14

Started clear and warm. Toward the noon a strong wind with sand storm developed; terrible as usual; subsided somewhat at 7:00; warm.

Fixed the garden; Yuhora and I potted morning-glories from the Sano plot.

. . . .

The "Pioneer" has discontinued the Japanese section for the time being due to the expert-labor shortage: 1) 21 answer Army [examination?] but 4 failed to report; 2) 5th war loan drive is under way; 3) this is a general cleaning [day] in the center; 4) hospital reports 68 births as of June 13 since the beginning of the year; 5) Methodist convention (June 6): majority of issei and nisei [are] loyal [and] should be treated like others; 6) the case of 14 Amache boys will be tried on June 27, the charge being their failure to report for the Army examination; 7) candidates for Council are listed of whom 12 are re-nominees. . . .

Thursday, June 15

Started clear and warm with a gentle breeze; it has remained so and rather warm all day though a breeze relieved somewhat.

Yoshihara called and brought a small chunk of ice.

Oki informed me re: the "Pioneer" vs. Johnson; he forced one of the Japanese section staff to resign on account of the press report (in the *Utah Nippō*)[36] concerning Tsuchiya's bad practices and his protection of the man despite Tsuchiya's obvious wrong. Because this man refused to translate the news into English. His practical dismissal caused the three other members of the staff to quit in sympathy. Hence no Japanese section since the last Wednesday, together with the failure of one previous issue from appearing. In this case the English staff members have remained as if nothing has happened! What kind of organization is the "Pioneer"? McClelland announces that there will be no Japanese section "for the time being" until a new staff is recruited!!! The case proves once again that the camp leadership, including the co-op which is involved, lacks the guts; it is ready to compromise with the WRA regardless of the principles involved. Each for himself seems to be the guiding principle; it is hopeless to expect to see the guarding of general welfare unless it coincides with the interests of the personnel.

Wednesday, June 21

Overcast and very warm with a very slight breeze. A brief but violent wind-sand storm and preceded by a very slight shower.

The Jeromites arrived here at 8:30–9:30.

Akahashi dropped in; later Arakawa (Hawaii) came; he had come from Jerome.

Kuniyoshi brought for introduction a fellow Ryukyu man; the others are mostly Hiroshima *hyakushō* [bumpkins].

The "Pioneer": 1) Greetings by Lindley to the Jeromites, (550); 2) a nisei girl at Pueblo committed suicide, a 16 year old married to a Chinese soldier; 3) 5,500 at Jerome to be removed by July 1st as follows: 2,500 to Rohwer, 500 each to Heart Mountain, Gila and Amache; the rest?; 4) 16 councilmen re-elected.

Thursday, June 22

Started with thin scattering [of rain] and with a gentle breeze. Turned out another rather hot day though not as hot as yesterday (hottest so far about 100 degrees). But it cooled off beautifully after the sunset.

Oki brought Myer's notice relative to the alien land laws of the three west coast states where escheat proceeding may develop for violations of the laws.

Kurahashi came.

The Watanabe family, [which] moved to the next door, behave in a peculiar manner. The mother visits, leaving the little girl behind since their arrival; while her 17 year old boy never stays at home. The girl is very forward. The woman's former husband named Tanaka committed suicide and [she is] now married to a fellow named Watanabe who is working outside. The kids are his step-children. . . .

Friday, June 23

Started clear and delightful; remained so with a wind in the morning but at the noon it became rather hot though the wind continued to blow. Somewhat overcast.

A Jeromite: The Jerome center [was] hot and damp; [it was] full of bugs, including mosquitoes and wood ticks. When the segregation took place, some 1,500 went to Tule Lake; later 750 more went, out of the total population of more than 8,000. The segregation situation in the Rohwer Center was similar to that of Jerome.

The transferees were mainly from California, mostly from Sacramento and its vicinity via Tule Lake; farmers mostly. . . .

KEI ICHIHASHI TO JESSIE TREAT [37]

Amache
June 29 [1944]

Dear Mrs. Treat:

It is almost the commencement time so that people on the Stanford campus must be very busy now. I have been thinking of you lately but I could not write a letter. I have been busy to do some sewing as I have borrowed a sewing machine and it is the first time to use a machine since I left the campus. The weather is getting hot so suddenly and I need some light dresses very badly. Last summer at Tule Lake I got some summer dresses by mail order but they did not fit me well, so I have decided to make a few dresses by myself, but it is pretty hard to get suitable materials here.

It seems to me the summer weather in this center is worse than Tule Lake. The temperature is higher than Tule Lake in day time, and the heat does not cool down in the evening as at Tule Lake Center, so it is pretty hard to sleep for us sometime. But I am able to resist the summer heat and do not mind the hot weather very much, so please do not worry about it. Wild flowers are still pretty here and even cactus is blooming in pale yellow and red. Rattle snakes are nesting in the fields, and the other day in our block some person caught a small one right on the front lawn of his apartment; and it had two bells(?) on the tail. Sometimes snakes get into the laundry room. It also happened in our block that when some invalid was taking his meal in the room a snake was creeping right above the table, which was placed against the wall. We have a lot of crickets around here, and it is very interesting to listen to the singing insects in the evening; but people say that pretty soon these crickets will get into rooms and eat woolen clothes, so we watch them carefully.

A few days ago about 530 Japanese people came from Jerome Center, as you know Jerome project will be closed on July 1st. Jerome must be one of the hot centers, the [former residents'] complexions are very dark and I never saw such dark brown Japanese before. When they arrived it was the hottest day we had ever had here and we were all very much surprised to hear the newcomers saying "Amache is a nice and cool place." Those newcomers mostly were at Tule Lake before and were transferred to Jerome last September when we came here. To our block five new families came, and one of the families used to live at Mountain View [38] (parents and three children) and they moved five times since the evacuation problem started. Wasn't it awful packing everything and moved five times in about two years? We have heard that Minidoka Center in Idaho will be closed next. Maybe we shall be moved to some other center, too, but we don't know what will happen to us at all, we are just "Okies" or "Arkies," so we must prepare to move at any time.

I hope you will have a nice summer vacation and get a good rest. Please give my best regards to Prof. Treat.

Affectionately yours,
Kei Ichihashi

DIARY

Monday, July 3

Clear though with scatter clouds in spots. Became warm and then at 5:00 P.M. a terrific wind accompanied by a sand storm which is still continuing and with lightning and thunder and a little shower. Lightning and thunder continue and shower came at 7:45.

Miyama brought some artificial flowers; asked me whether I am willing to take a vacation [from teaching the Japanese culture class] until the fall—ok'd the suggestion.

Oki informed me that the chap in jail charged with stealing some supplies, [when] his room was checked were found there. It is a disgrace since the things found were such that [he] could have asked and obtained: baby-food, peanut butter, etc., taken in cases!

It is said that yesterday the [Independence Day] carnival took in more than $2,000.00. It is continuing [today] but due to a threat-ened shower, the "talent show" was postponed. Shower came at 7:45 as expected. Nonetheless a lot of people turned out and were doubt-less soaked.

. . . .

Tuesday, July 4

Overcast and cool—wholly unexpected and remained so till 6:45 when it began to rain in the manner of the last evening, i.e., without lightning and thundering. Good for the garden but bad for the carnival!

Kurahashi brought some zinnia[?] and later a pot of *matsuba-botan* [portulaca?] and of petunia. Hattori followed and the two fixed the garden with string climbers for morning glories and gourd vines. Hattori planted *matsuba-botan* along its borders.

. . . .

Went to see the baseball game and there I was informed by Take-sue that a wire was received here saying that Hitomi of Sacramento was killed.* He was the chap who had attempted to buy up the co-op at Tule Lake at the time of "segregation." He added that his elder brother had been sand-bagged and hit with a baseball bat and he lost his sight and hearing. It is tragic whether they deserved such treat-ments or not; Japanese fighting Japanese in a center, even in the Tule Lake center.

Wednesday, July 5

Started clear with a strong wind but the sand is still wet, alas; but [later] the wind became stronger and sands flew as usual all day long.

Yonemura called and brought some cans of ham. He talked about Kuramoto who is creating a scandal over the runner [internee assis-tant to a block manager] whom Yonemura knows [to be] a *morazumo* [pimp or gangster], and the whole block came to know about [it], especially after he and his wife had arguments in voices that could be heard all over. He has created a bad impression in the block.

. . . .

---

*In the evening of July 2, Yaozo Hitomi, the reportedly proadministration manager of the cooperative store at Tule Lake, had his throat cut.

The "Pioneer": 1) Spanish Vice-Consul Martin accompanied by Ch[arles] C. Eberhardt [a Department of State officer] is to visit here on the 7th; he will see issei in groups or individuals who care to meet him; 2) evacuees may relocate outside the continental U.S.; what does this mean is not made clear; 3) the carnival took in $2,582.20 the final day! 4) Amache co-op bought $10,000 worth of U.S. bonds, but out of what funds? They bear 2% interest; 5) Amache draft evaders got from 10 to 18 months imprisonment, i.e. 11 out of the 14 (18 to 29 years old) 6) one Sadao Nakao, 19 years old, committed suicide at Jerome by hanging; nervous break-down was the cause; 7) bill in the house to allow the naturalization of alien Koreans like Chinese;[39] 8) 19 Japanese in Tule Lake were sent (June 29) to an internment camp: 15 on presidential warrants and 4 former internees for violation of parole; 9) 12 nisei in Mini-doka face draft evasion charge; 10) 63 Heart Mountain nisei ap-pealed to U.S. District Court[?].

Thursday, July 6

Starts with scattered clouds here and there and with a gentle breeze. Became rather warm and remained so till late evening. Clear mostly.

The "Pioneer" (7/5): 1) as of May 31, 1,093 nisei taken into the Army out of 3,312 called; 669 rejected and 139 failed to report for pre-induction examinations.

Mrs. Yoshihara called and I called on them in the evening and had crushed ice.

Oki announced: the carnival took in more than $6,500 or about $1.00 per capita of the residents! I wonder what the people think about such expenditure. [Spanish Vice-Consul] Martin is willing to meet issei.

. . . .

The people are talking about the killing of Hitomi; opinion is di-vided; the alleged cause was that he was an *inu* and his brother, who had been beaten prior to the murder, was probably mistaken for his young brother. It is a double tragedy!

Friday, July 7

Started with scattered clouds here and there but clearing up with a gentle breeze. Remained warm till the sunset; then a cool wind.

Sp. Consul Martin came and met the block managers. The following questions were asked: 1) The exact status of dual citizenship—one's obligations to U.S. and Japan—military service, etc. A very foolish question. 2) Repatriation: a third exchange boat? Requests? 3) Clothing allowances and cash advances: double the former; 4) Evacuee property status in California; 5) Have the floor covered with wood or linoleum.

He asked in behalf of the Japanese government that a complete report be submitted to him by the center in regard to deaths with the following details: 1. Names, 2. Place of civil register or birth in Japan, 3. Date of birth, 4. Civil status, 5. Occupations or professions (pre-evacuation), 6. Date of death, 7. Place of death, 8. Circumstances of death, violent or other details as far as possible, 9. Names of the nearest kin, 10. Have the nearest kin been immediately notified of such deaths, 11. Details of the burial, 12. Copies of death certificates, 13. Wills (if any), 14. Intestate death. This should have been done in the beginning as soon as the evacuation was put in force. It is hoped that such records are kept and made available. Ministers (Christians) and priests (Buddhist) ought to know.

YAMATO ICHIHASHI TO JESSIE TREAT[40]

10-H 12-D
Amache, Colorado
July 11, 1944

Dear Mrs. Treat:

Thank you for the kind suggestion as regards the ceilings and walls; I asked Miss Westbrook to have them repaired.

I should have written to you sooner and oftener thanking you for your many kind deeds, but due to an eye trouble which had forced me from using them; the cause has not as yet been determined. Very likely an operation has to be performed. At any rate, I have never forgotten for a moment what you and Payson have been doing for us—we are very grateful. I have already tried three times to make the sweet peas which you so thoughtfully sent us now sometime ago [grow], but completely failed twice. The third time, I planted some in a box, paying the greatest care I am capable of; this time they are growing though not in a healthy condition and are now about 5 inches in height; I am [not] sure as yet whether I [will] succeed in making them bloom. The poor soil, the peculiar climate and harmful gales make it unfit for any tender vegetation.

Since the beginning of the month, we have had cloudy and rather cool weather with intermittent showers; last night there was a terrific storm—shower, thunder-lightning, and a gale and such plants as we had in front of our room were beaten down, a tragic sight!

Payson informs me of the sad events and phenomena that crowd the once happy campus and its vicinity. The life here is also crowded with similar happenings; the people appear no longer to be able to think seriously about anything. Two years of the unnatural life enforced on them seems to have killed their guts and they don't seem to care. Of course, the issei are all old, with relatively a few in their 50's; in this camp there are 130 men and women who are 70 years and over; most of them are in [their] mid-60's. Nisei boys are out in the Army or working; nisei women are mostly young mothers but with children (3rd generation) and school kids. They are helpless wards of the U.S. government.

Of course, high-pressure propaganda is being conducted for relocation in the Mid-West and East. I often wonder what these propagandists expect the aged and heavily burdened young females to do outside. You may be interested to know that these propagandists include many professional religionists, American and Japanese. They all paint a sad picture of California—organized anti-Japanism, the invasion of Negroes and other lowly elements—hopeless for the Japanese to regain their "homes."

My eyes begin to cloud and I had better [end] here. But please tell Payson that I shall continue "reporting" on my research as soon as I gain something worthwhile.

> Affectionately yours
> Yamato Ichihashi

DIARY

Sunday, July 16

Overcast with a cool breeze; cleared up and hot and sultry.

Oki came to consult on the advisability of holding a memorial service in behalf of Yamaji's son, who was killed while serving in the U.S. Army in Italy: "public" or private [service] must be decided first; if the former, the block managers and the council should sponsor it according to the center practice; if the latter, the block if it so desires, may sponsor it.

. . . .

Monday, July 17

Started clear with the sun quite hot despite a breeze. Turned out to be one of the hottest days, though about 9:00 P.M. became cool.

Kawasaki: He was asked by Gillet, Executive Secretary of the Congregation (Relocation Committee) who was accompanied by Kitagawa,[41] an opportunist as I saw at Tule Lake, to prepare a blueprint with a view of creating an efficient organization at Chicago—a hostel?—to help Japanese evacuees whether Buddhists or non-Christian groups in relocating.[42] . . .

He asked my advice which was given as follows: issei are enemy aliens who should always be distinguished from nisei when any public or legal issues are up, though [this issue is] confused by the ignorant issei and nisei, especially when they become emotional. I seek no charity, religious or otherwise, as I am a subject of Japan (this fact too is forgotten whenever expedient). Inexperienced young people should not pretend to create any plans of rescue or help [for] those whom they do not know and understand; that is presumptuous. The question of relocating rests with individuals and the initiative must come from them and not pressure groups even if supported by a public policy. In Chicago relocatees face housing problems, Gillet admits. Kawasaki not in a position to undertake the requested blueprint.

I know the purpose of this [and of] rather like groups: the future of missions. These boards-of-missions supported organizations must be mindful of this fundamental fact: they are guided in the present conduct by this fact, except the Friend's Society which has no proselytizing aims. In the beginning of evacuation movements, they all remained indifferent and some individual workers indeed used their relationships to add to the prosecution [of some]. Many were interned at their suggestions. One is known as a head *inu* of the F.B.I. and has had Japanese *inu* under him—hard on Buddhist priests, etc. At any rate, at this belated time, their conferences pass resolutions on the wrongs committed, but which they did not see earlier and insist on restoring to them [the right] to return to their houses or relocate from the 9 camps!

Tuesday, July 18

Started clear with a cool breeze. Then it turned out rather hot, but in the afternoon it became cloudy and the breeze became stronger.

The clouds became thick towards the evening. Lightning, thunder, rain at 3 A.M.

Yamagi's (originally from Mountain View farm) son was killed in Italy on June 15th and this evening Muranaga, a cook, was notified of his son's death, also in Italy on the 26th; both were volunteers. These were the first cases of nisei soldiers killed from this center [where] their parents now live. . . .

· · · ·

Wednesday, July 19

Started with scattered clouds and a cool breeze. Became hot but somewhat modified by a breeze strong enough to kick up some sands and sultry. Heavy lightning; thunder-shower commenced about 7:40 P.M.

The "Pioneer": 1) citizenship renouncing bill signed July 1st by Roosevelt and the "Washington Post's" explanation (10th) of its real meaning;[43] 2) alien Japanese may be named beneficiaries of insurance bought by nisei U.S. servicemen; 3) Ickes: 26 alien Japanese removed from Tule Lake to internment camps under the Department of Justice during the past 3 months, who had been arrested and confined in a fenced-off stockade at the Center as a result of last November 1943's disturbance; at the time 111 aliens and 229 citizens, suspected of complicity, were placed in the stockade. Since then these cases were reviewed and aliens whose records made them eligible for internment camps were transferred to the Department of Justice and citizens with records as chronic trouble-makers were retained while others were released after confinement from 2 to 8 months; no aliens in the stockade at present, but 25 citizens still remain there; 4) Laurence E. Davies:[44] evacuees may be returned to the West Coast before the war ends. . . .

Thursday, July 20

Cloudy with *kirisame* [drizzle, misty rain] and rather cool; somewhat cleared up and hot. Later became cloudy, but again cleared up somewhat.

The Tōjō cabinet resigned and Koiso-Yonai[45] ordered to form a coalition cabinet (broadcast this morning). The Tōjō era [lasted] since 1941, or 3 years duration.

Young Hamatani called with a box of candies: among other things, he said that nisei should not remain in the camp for they gain nothing good; but boys and girls in teens relocating by themselves without their parents to look after them are morally degenerating. The money they earn is being spent in a manner that will not help in developing themselves and thus the parents are not only gaining nothing but they must [contend with] the consequence of their children's moral degeneration. Spokane, Washington and Ontario, Oregon offer splendid opportunities for farming (about 6,000 evacuees are [resettled?]), all Americanized to a degree surprising. No Japanese is spoken even among these Issei. Many, however, lack proper manner and etiquette; minor matters but important to correct them. Big cities are no place for young nisei to relocate; even camps, especially big ones [with] Japanese workers (issei and nisei) are bad because of the prevalence of gambling. There are professionals to milk them—issei usually quit at 10:00 or 11:00 but nisei keep on gambling until the morning. Some control must be exercised otherwise they are heading to the hell. This sort of information is needed for those who relocate, instead of meaningless platitudes.

KEI ICHIHASHI TO JESSIE TREAT[46]

Amache, Colo.
July 20 [1944]

Dear Mrs. Treat:

Thank you for a box of delicious candies. We are not able to get any fancy chocolate candies here, just a cheap kind for kiddies, so I shall appreciate them very much.

We are leading a monotonous life as usual. At present the residents of this project are mostly old people and little children and their young mothers. Young men are very few, and the population is about 7,000. We had 4-Days Midsummer Carnival shows on the Independence Day and the weekend. About 15[?] organizations (Y.M.C.A., Boyscouts, Blue Star Mothers, Y.W.C.A., etc.) managed many booths (for sandwiches, hamburgers, shaved ice, bingo, duck ring, etc.) and they got a gross income of $6,562. The shows started at 5 o'clock every evening except Sunday. All the offices were not closed on the holiday this year, and everybody worked all day, and it is said that this is President Roosevelt's order. But outside of the center many stores were closed on the Independence Day, so I un-

derstood. In this small community, these 7,000 people spent about
$6,500 for the carnival shows. I just wonder how people can spend
so much money for such things. They have no income, just working
people (cooks, janitors, office boys and girls, etc.) get $16 per month,
so I can not understand their attitude.

Paul Clyde[47] is teaching at Stanford this summer, so I understand. Last time I went to Japan, he was in Tokyo, so that I have not
seen him in more than ten years. How is he? Is he very happy? I
know he remarried and I have heard his wife is a southerner. Please
let me know all about them. Paul's children are quite big now and
they visited him in June before he left for California. Mildred Clyde
seems very unhappy and is worrying about the children. I have
heard about many divorce cases, but for children's sake I don't know
if it is a wise thing to do or not. A few weeks ago we got the announcement of Max Savelle's marriage and I am wondering what
Carmen is doing now.[48] Mr. Luntz (Russian professor) also remarried sometime ago. The first Mrs. Luntz died or divorced, I do not
know. I often think of her and their son who used to belong to the
same group of boy scouts with Woodrow on the campus.[49] If you
would let me know about her in the next letter, I should appreciate
it very much. [In the] last two years, since I was evacuated, so many
things have happened for the campus people, [and] also the friends
at Palo Alto, but I am not able to know [about] every one of them.
It is so sad to hear Mrs. Storey's death. She had written a letter to us
last November right after Dr. Storey's death,[50] and it was such a nice
friendly letter, and I did not dream that she would follow her husband so soon.

We have had a hot weather as I wrote you before, and it is rather
a sticky weather, not like in California; it reminds me of the hot
summer days in Tokyo. We had lightnings and thunderstorms several times lately. There are no mountains around here, so that the
sky is vast and at the same time four or five lightnings appear in the
black velvety sky, and it is just a gorgeous sight, and I often watch
them in the evening.

I hope you will have fine summer weather on the campus and enjoy the very nice summer vacation.

        Affectionately yours,
        Kei Ichihashi

DIARY

Thursday, July 27

Started clear with a breeze—rather a delightful morning. But it soon
turned out very hot and remained till late evening when a cool
breeze developed.

It is reported that some [Amache nisei] were wounded in Italy
and their cases were reported to their respective parents residing in
the Center. These were in addition to the five who had been [killed].
About 100 men had volunteered from here when first called for, and
the above casualties were exclusively among these volunteers. Expected but sad news.

No important news otherwise.

Did some research and some re-writing of the essays in Japanese.

Friday, July 28

A clear, delightful morning, but soon changing into a hot day. In
the afternoon rather a strong breeze developed, modifying the heat
somewhat. Thus it remained till late evening.

Oki's father died late in the afternoon.

So far, seven cases of death among those who had volunteered
from this Center, whose memorial services will be held next
Saturday.

Saturday, July 29

Somewhat cloudy but clear in spots and cool, but it turned out
warm, however with a strong breeze. At 5:00 lightning, thunder-
shower with a gale from all directions came. Rain not heavy, but
the weather cooled off.

Sakai came bringing with him old Mizota, George's uncle, and
also with cucumbers, peaches and grapes.

Yoshihara came with a half of a cantaloupe.

The "Pioneer": 1) 25 more to be inducted tomorrow morning
2) Tule Lake draft evasion cases (27 nisei) were dismissed on the
ground of their declared disloyalty to U.S.; 3) 2 more Amache nisei
are charged as draft evaders; 4) "Labor shortage severe!"

Sunday, July 30

Clear with a cool breeze; delightful; later became warm though the breeze continued.

In the afternoon we were invited to a water-melon party at the Okubos; it was a hot trip; the melon was ice-cold and satisfying.

The boys scheduled to leave this morning for Ft. Logan were told that the date was indefinitely postponed.

Okubo reported that every day 4 to 5 persons come for consultation as regards indefinite leave.

Monday, July 31

Started clear with a slight breeze; soon turned out to be one of the hottest days—113 degrees in temperature with a good deal of moisture. Very uncomfortable till late in the night.

No news of importance.

Tuesday, August 1

Started clear with plenty of moisture due to dew during the night; but soon became very hot and remained so till evening.

Received from the Harvard Peabody Museum a copy of the Dixon Memorial Essays on the anthropology of Oceania and Asia sent by Hulse who wrote on the physical characteristics of the Japanese.[51]

Wednesday, August 2

Clear with a cool breeze, but soon became very hot as yesterday and remained so till the sunset, when a cool breeze started although the room remained very warm and uncomfortable.

A Japanese cop came here at 1:30 and asked me to accompany him to an office where a young American wanted to see me; I was taken to Tomlinson's office and the man was a F.B.I. [agent who asked] whether I knew [Kanzō] Shiozaki, Consul General at San Francisco. The inquiry centered about an alleged dealing with him (in 1937). He said that he had information that I got money from him to cover the expense of my trip to the Far East; of course it was flatly denied, because it was a pure fabrication. Alleged further that I was arranging for an America-Japan student conference which is another fabrication.[52] Another point was whether or not I was connected with the Japanese Navy; whether I ever applied to its Academy, etc. I was too young. I came here in 1894 when I was 16 years old. Some heat developed over the implications of this groundless and suspicious "information" or rather misinformation he alleged to possess. *Inu* must have been the source.[53]

. . . .

Thursday, August 3

Clear with a cool breeze, but soon became very hot (sultry) and re-mained till late evening. Cloudy somewhat in afternoon.

Received a letter from Hiro.

Attended the Oki *otsuya* [wake]. Yonemura preached and Okubo presided and spoke briefly on the deceased.

Friday, August 4

Clear with rather a strong breeze—warm; it remained so all day.

. . . .

Attended the Oki funeral 2–4:00 in the afternoon; the temple was nearly filled. "All is suffering" was the theme of Yonemura's ser-mon. Too long.

. . . .

Saturday, August 5

Started cloudy and rain, but soon stopped though remained cloudy. A gale started at 7:40 P.M.; soon followed by lightning—thunder—shower.

Attended the memorial service for the 6 soldiers from here killed in Italy; its program [by] the end, the High School auditorium was filled and many standing.

Brought *udon* home and had it for supper.

Palo Alto Times of August 1 came.

The "Pioneer": 1) "comfort bag" movement by one Mrs. Miyake (nisei) from Jerome; 2) kids' vandalism—cutting of unripe watermelons reported; 3) help to keep polio out—dangerous season; 4) Chicago: 59 nisei discharged to comply with union ultimatum; 5) 30 seniors [in] high school to get diplomas; 6) relocation in Georgia and Louisiana hopeful—the committee reports and further details to be investigated (in Japanese section); 7) men 26–29 face draft unless in essential jobs.

Friday, August 11

Clear and cool early in the morning. The breeze kept up, but it remained hot though not as hot as yesterday.

McClelland called and asked for suggestions for a method to be used to gather necessary information to bring about changes in the present WRA relocation policy which is not succeeding. He is interested in the case method: individual families studied in details to secure types that dominate the family composition in the center; with this information he wishes to approach the Washington head-office for a change. "A widow with five small kids" cannot relocate without financial aid as she has no money; transportation plus $25.00 will not do it. A boy of 16 applied for indefinite leave for Colorado Springs, lying that his parents were in Chicago but their address unknown and that his brother was in Colorado Springs, whose address too was unknown. A case showing the prevailing parents-children relationship: no parental control in the present camp life which will worsen as time is prolonged.

Sakai sent us a crate of cantaloupe.

Attended the Louisiana relocation meeting. About 100 were present, mostly men. Miyamoto reported on the basis of the propaganda material sent here by the interested party. Tajima, a former produce shipper and Takata, also a shipper—all from L.A. spoke favorably as regards the Louisiana delta land not far from New Orleans. About 5 men are to be sent for investigation (paid by the WRA and $2,500.00 given [by] the Congregation aid group.) If found suitable, Takata would like to approach the U.S. government for a loan big enough to create a mass settlement in Louisiana, but not Georgia, which is less suitable, of farmers to raise crops for local consumption and for Chicago, New York, and Montreal, etc. and thus all the related enterprises involved to be created and managed by the settlers—farmers and produce-handlers. The picture drawn was glowing but admittedly propaganda due to the source of information. The most actively interested men mentioned are all from L.A.: 2 shippers and 1 *yūshi* [supporter], without knowledge or experience. . . .

Thursday, August 17

Started cloudy and cool. Remained thus all day and after the sunset it became rather cool.

. . . .

Kurahashi brought *udon* which I had for supper. He came again after the supper time and inquired on behalf of a family from Walnut Grove who had applied for repatriation directly to the Spanish Embassy. They were summoned [to the] office and advised to cancel it. They have a house but also a son who will be 18 in a year or two. What they should do? Advice: cancellation as there is no possibility of their being included in the [official repatriation] list, even if a third exchange boat materializes soon. There appears to [be] no advantage in being repatriates and expatriates according to the information given.

Friday, August 18

Starts with thin scattered clouds here and there and with rather a strong breeze which grew stronger in the afternoon, kicking up sands as usual in the evening as well. Very bad.

. . . .

Kids (female) are getting worse with time; their parents are absolutely indifferent toward their evil behavior and speech.

Yuhora discovered bed bugs which he says came from the next room, but Sano two weeks ago found some in his corner room. We have to be on look-out for their invasion.

. . . .

KEI ICHIHASHI TO JESSIE TREAT[54]

Amache
August 18 [1944]

Dear Mrs. Treat:

It gave me great pleasure to read your interesting letter dated the 8th of August.[55] I thank you for a box of candies. They are my favorite ones, but I could not taste them for a long time, so I am very much pleased.

I am glad to know that you are enjoying a nice and cool summer weather at Stanford. I am quite envious of it, as I have had a very hot weather the last few weeks. Besides I have a hay fever and am obliged to stay in the room, because I feel my fever gets worse after I sat in a breeze or walked in a wind. At the present in this center many people are suffering from hay fever. Doctors are handling many cases in the hospital every day, and more than 60 percent of them are cases of a hay fever. It rained often last spring, so that many kinds of wild flowers are growing around here this year, and especially wild sun flowers are thick. People say that these sun flowers are very bad for a hay fever, and they are trying to uproot the plants around their barracks, but there are still many flowers in the fields. I have never had a hay fever in California, therefore this is my first experience and the slightest case, I think, but it is still not a pleasant feeling at all.

About two weeks ago, at the high school auditorium, a memorial service was held for the seven soldiers who died in action on the Italian front recently. They volunteered for service from this center last year, and one of them was a mere kid, just 18 years old. We feel so sorry for them, also their families, and two of the families live in our block. I have heard that about forty young boys were wounded in the same action in Italy.

The *Bon*-service, the festival of the dead (a Buddhist two-days memorial service in this season) was held last week end. And the same evening we had *Bon*-dances. You know what they are. I think you saw them in Japan some time ago. Nowadays the *Bon*-dances are modernized and are a little fancier. In these evenings, many young girls [appeared] clad in gay, multi-coloured kimonos and danced. There were no tum tum drums, but some modern Japanese music by records was provided, and it was a quite picturesque prospect.

I am very glad to hear that Paul [Clyde] is happy now, I hope it will last forever. Mary seems to be an intelligent and also polished woman. I hope she will be kind to the children. A long time ago Mildred told me that her mother didn't like her marriage from the very beginning, because Clyde's first name was Paul. Mildred's eldest sister was married to a Mr. Paul, and their married life was not very happy. After she died Mr. Paul married again, but he didn't take care of the children well enough, (two girls 5 and 3 at that time if I remember rightly). So Mildred's mother took care of them, and one of them married already. I understand Mildred's mother does not know about her divorce yet.

I was wondering about the Luntzs' affair so long. But Mr. Luntz divorced and remarried. Well, queer world! But this is the Life, may be! I am so sorry that both Dr. and Mrs. Wilbur had heart attacks, and they are not very well yet. Dr. Wilbur worked very hard as the president of the University for more than 20 years, so that it is about time to take a good rest for a while. I sincerely hope he will regain his health again very soon.

I am going to send you some flowers by parcel post. If you arrange the water lilies in a shallow vase and cover the bottom with white sands, I think it will be more effective. I hope you will like the flowers.

Affectionately yours,
Kei Ichihashi

DIARY

Saturday, August 19

Started with scattered clouds and a strong breeze; sands flying; sultry. The breeze continues and clouds thicken and little rain falls, and more of the same later at night.

Terami brought Jackson, a young woman (Babette Samuelson) working on the national opinion and one Hayakawa born in Canada and teaching English in Denver University. They visited the camp. (Hayakawa's *Language in Action*).[56]

. . . .

Sunday, August 20

. . . .

Learned that the Jerome [Camp] recently vacated by the Japanese evacuees was soon occupied by wounded soldiers despite the rumor that it would be turned into a camp for refugees from Europe (mostly Jews). These have been located elsewhere.

. . . .

KEI ICHIHASHI TO JESSIE TREAT [57]

Amache
August 25 [1944]

Dear Mrs. Treat:

I received a package of cookies. I think I am one of the most lucky persons to get such nice things so often. It was a box of candies last week, and a package of delicious cookies this week. I am very grateful for your kindness, and I shall enjoy them with my cup of tea.

At the present I have enough tea both black and green. Green tea which came from the Japanese Red Cross last January, and black Lipton tea which one of my friends gave to me last September, when she had a chance to go back to Japan with her husband and baby boy by the exchange boat. So I still have enough supply of tea now. Since I am accustomed to this strange life I miss hardly anything, but once in a while I want to take a cup of green tea, a really good one; also a well-made cup of coffee with rich fresh cream. In the center they serve a cup of coffee for breakfast every morning. But cooks don't know how to make good coffee, besides there is no fresh cream, just canned milk, and it does not taste good, so that I often want to take a glass of milk instead of coffee.

Manpower shortage is a great menace for housewives. Nowadays even ladies are obliged to do their own house cleanings. House cleaning is not an easy job, especially a nice house like yours. I imagine Professor Treat is working in the large garden to keep it beautifully this summer. It seems to me every professor needs some physical exercise, so gardening will be good for him.

I am glad to hear that Fusako [58] finally went east and is leading a normal life again. In every center most young girls and boys went out and got some jobs, and only old people and little children are left. Therefore we haven't enough working men in the project. Yesterday a woman about fifty years old who lives next room volunteered for the farm work, and went out with her seven year old girl, for there was nobody [to take] care of this little girl at home. Her husband found some job and took a seasonal leave sometime ago and he lives outside now. Thus even we have to discuss the problem of manpower shortage in the center.

I thank you again—our delicious cookies. I shall enjoy them with my tea.

Sincerely yours,
Kei Ichihashi

DIARY

Wednesday, August 30

Clear and actually cold with a strong wind soon developing and some sands flying. The wind subsided in afternoon and the evening was calm.

The "Pioneer": 1) two of the three nisei involved in the exclusion suit before the California Superior Court were granted permits by the military to remain in that State. The 3rd?; 2) Service for 120 nisei dead in Italy; 3) The Pacific Coast Association of Friends (Quakers) held its annual meeting at Palo Alto pledged to help the return of the nisei to their original houses in the West Coast states; 4) Teamsters oppose nisei employment in the Western states; 5) "To date, about 2,500 nisei students entered more than 500 colleges and universities in 46 states;" 6) "The council (National Japanese American Relocation Council), the churches and other friendly organizations have aided approximately 535 nisei students to the extent of $133,000 up to this time."

Called on Okubos in the evening.

Thursday, August 31

Clear and cold in the morning; it turned out another warm [day] and remained till the sunset when it became delightful with a breeze.

No news of importance but rumors run rampant that this center will be closed to its residents who will be removed shortly, pos-

sibly in October to the Poston Center while this center will house
wounded soldiers. Such rumors arise because the government has no
fixed policy relative the evacuees as regards their final settlement.

Received a note from Mrs. Sakai inviting us to come next Sunday
and stay overnight; replied that we would spend Sunday only with
them as we do not wish to bother them too much since they are still
busy in disposing their cantaloupes.

Thursday, September 7

Clear and cool with a fairly strong breeze. Warm in the afternoon,
but cooled off later. A beautiful evening.

We came here a year ago this night about 10:30 P.M.

Kurahashi came and invited me to go with him to his room to get
udon which I had for supper.

Oki brought a slip to be filled; relatives in Japan to be notified in
case of emergency. I said that I would not do it as I saw no advantage
in so doing. The government has this information in the original
alien registration, and its objective was not made [clear?].

A note was received stating that Woodrow was inducted into
the Army August 8th and his whereabouts are not known; it was an
item impudent in nature—quite insulting. No answer will be
written.[59]

. . . .

Friday, September 15

Started with clouds covering the sky and cold, but soon began to
disappear little by little and warming. Became cloudy again at noon
and was soon followed by a strong wind-sand storm and lasted most
of the night.

. . . .

The Poston paper under the date of September 5th reported the
overall population by centers as follows:

Manzanar	5,448	checked Sept. 20 as 5,415
Topaz	5,899	=
Granada	5,900	?
Rohwer	6,626	=
Minidoka	6,899	=

Heart Mountain	8,726	8,721
Gila	9,887	9,478
Poston	11,401	=
Tule Lake	18,698	=
Total	79,484	

It has been estimated that 20,000 can resettle when the West Coast states are open to the evacuees, leaving a balance of 59,484 who see no prospect of resettling in any place?

YAMATO ICHIHASHI TO PAYSON TREAT[60]

10-H 12-D
Amache, Colorado
September 22, 1944

Dear Payson:

Thank you very much for the kind letter full of interesting and instructive information,[61] and with many apologies for my usual failure. Let me say that I cannot state whether my eyes are better or worse as they are about the same as far as I can feel; even the doctor was not certain as all he could say was my trouble is caused by the lack of necessary vitamins, the nervous trouble or the old age or the combination of all the three. He asked me to wait patiently for a while, and if the worst developed, he would perform an operation and then see what might happen. I have had to put up with such uncertainties. Then recently this doctor left the camp and relocated outside; and there is no other doctor who knows anything about eye troubles. Such is the plight in which I now find myself, and it is still painful to read or write for any length of time.

In the meantime, the conditions in the camp have grown from bad to worse as the people have [been] confronted with difficulties one after another. To meet the situation, the incapable administrative staff has used intimidations and threats as their only weapon in dealing with the evacuees, and consequently the people have become apprehensive, fearful, and suspicious. It is a tragic situation to say the least. For example, for more than a month, the camp has faced an acute labor-shortage situation caused by the WRA relocation policy, which has caused the departure of men in vigorous age-groups from the camp, leaving behind a residual population composed of old men and women, and young mothers and a multitude of children, who cannot perform heavy manual labor.

Normally, there have been employed about 2,500 workers in this camp, but their number has gradually diminished so that there are only 2,000 who are working at present, a shortage of 500. In the face of this situation, the administration applies pressure (intimidations and threats) to the evacuees so that they themselves solve the problem as if the Japanese were solely responsible for it. The situation is somewhat aggravated by the incapable and unintelligent evacuees holding the positions of block managers and councilmen. At any rate, under the circumstances, it is inevitable that the relations between the administration and the evacuees should have become worse and worse.

Whenever the people face difficulties, they make the practice (this includes the block managers and councilmen) of calling on me for help. Thus for the past six months or so, despite my own trouble, I have been forced to exert myself in helping them, and am still trying. But I am not very successful in handling such delicate, complicated, all-embracing human problems, political, social, economic, psychological, etc. Such is the state of affairs here.

Of course, the fundamental problem of the evacuees is that of resettlement (called "relocation" officially) to a normal life. About six months ago, I learned as a rumor that the western states would be open to the evacuees. At once, I began to inquire into probable percentages of the evacuees in the various camps, who would be able to take advantage of such a policy when put in operation. Due to many and varied reasons, it is generally agreed that only from 10% to 15% could immediately return to their "homes" in the western states. There are still living more than 80,000 Japanese in the nine centers, including Tule Lake; 10% of this population is 8,000; and 15%, 12,000, which leaves in the centers a residual population of from 72,000 to 68,000, the numbers which cannot return to the west coast states. As already stated before, this residual population is made up of aged issei men and women and their minor children; their adult sons, including a few daughters, are serving in armed forces or are already resettled outside; and of young nisei mothers and their small children, whose husbands and fathers are either in the armed forces or are trying to establish themselves in various localities in the midwest and in the east. Moreover, as you well know, most of the evacuees whether issei or nisei have lost most of their possessions at the time of evacuation. Some had no funds; others who had savings, consumed such during the past two and a half years of their living in the camps. They have no home to return to, and have no money to start a normal life again, and most of the issei are over 60 years of age. They are in a tragic plight.

I feel duty-bound to assist in finding some ways and means to help the helpless people before I can think of my own relatively, simple problem of resettlement. Nonetheless, I am appreciative of your kind suggestions; I need not tell you again that there is nothing agreeable in a miserable, lowest-plane communistic life enforced on us. But alas I cannot abandon the poor people in their plight, and I am determined to do what I can for them. More than that I cannot now write as it hurts my eyes and my bleeding-heart, but will write you again very soon.

Very affectionately yours,
Yamato Ichihashi

P.S. Just as I finished this note, Mrs. Emery Fast,[62] secretary to Dillon Myer, paid us a visit, accompanied by the local relocation officer. She has been in touch with Lisette Fast about possibilities of our being returned to the campus home, and told me that I was being wanted by the university to resume teaching as there was no one to replace me (Edgar's desire). Therefore she asked me to make necessary applications for the purpose, saying that Myer would do everything within his power. My reply was that I had had no official communication of any kind from the university, and repeated what I have stated above about my determination. She asked me to weigh the relative merits of the two tasks before me and arrive at a decision. I promised her to do this. In the meantime, she will communicate further with Lisette, concerning this matter, and our interviews. I thought that you might be interested in hearing about this incident.[63]

With best wishes to you and your Madame, I am as ever.

Y.I.

DIARY

Sunday, September 24

Overcast and cold and remained so.

Christian ministers and local ones are to meet in a conference at 7-H church on Monday morning; Haratani[64] came to ask me to attend it. I accepted the invitation.

Mrs. Ishizu died this morning; this is the 41th death exclusive of the soldiers killed since our arrival here.

No news of importance.

Wrote to Payson.[65]

Monday, September 25

Overcast and cool, a strong breeze developed in the afternoon and more cloudy.

The party of 4 American religious workers, including a woman, which was received by the Japanese Christian ministers, [met]; I was the only layman. The visitors all talked and then I was called upon for a remark, which interested McCracken. He talked to me alone after the others went on an inspection tour. He asked me about the work of ministers: [I said] they seem to be concerned most of [all about] their ministerial insignia—black ties, white shirts and dark suits which set them apart from the rest; obsessed of their status-dignity. If they learn to be a part of the people among whom they work, they might be able to obtain [a] following. They are not doing anything (they may be incapable) for the general good of the people. They are indifferent to the realities of the situation under which they live. The evacuees have no freedom of expression and the WRA appears to be willing to intimidate and threaten, and they are unhappy. . . .

Thursday, September 28

Overcast and actually cold; it turned out hot in the afternoon. But cooled off later and became cold near the sunset.

. . . .

Oki was summoned tomorrow afternoon for an interview and hearing on his leave clearance. He has to attend the Ishizu funeral, a good excuse as he has written to the C.L.U.[66] for advice on this stoppage on a very thin basis: he wishes to have a showdown. The WRA takes this method of making him another of its "obedient servants"; in the past, he questioned some of the WRA "orders." He thinks the WRA has no authority when it stopped him from going to Denver to transact an important personal business [matter], especially in view of the fact that he had been permitted twice before to go to the same city.

. . . .

Friday, September 29

Started very clear and somewhat cool, a typical autumnal morning. It turned fairly warm and remained so until the evening. A clear stormy night.

Okubo loaned me the Sept. 21 issue of "The Newell Star."[67]

The Ishizu funeral was held at 16-H church at 1:30–3:00PM; it was attended to the capacity. Some *monchaku* [dispute] among those who arranged it.

No news of importance.

Saturday, September 30

Clear with a warm sun and cool breeze—delightful. Remained so all day and the evening is mild.

Two pairs of pants @ $23.73 plus tax 47 cents = $24.22 ordered at co-op. To be ready in 2 weeks. Gave Kei $100.00 for daily use.

The "Pioneer": 1) another census to be taken tomorrow morning after breakfast and everybody is asked to remain in his room. 2) Myer said: 1/4 of the evacuees will not return to their "home" in the West; about 20,000 will be scattered all over the country; the opening of the West is up to the Army; 31,000 have been relocated; 3) the recent conference of the Project Directors focused their attention on liquidation of the centers, reported Lindley. Japanese section: An appeal to women residents from the Hospital.

A talent show is being held at the open-door stage.

Went to Kurahashi with Kuramatsu for *udon* lunch; Ono is again visiting.

Received the August statement from Bank of America; must write demanding the similar statement for June and July and to make correction of our names and our address.

The block meeting decided to request each unit to send a volunteer to transport food provisions during the labor shortage emergency.

SPECIAL DATA

The Tule Lake "Center" publishes under the name of "The Newell Star" and 鶴嶺湖新報. The copy dated September 21, 1944, Vol. I No. 30 contains the following items: 1) the center residents decided to send gifts to the Japanese prisoners-of-war in the U.S., 750 in number; this is permitted by the Geneva Protocol, Article 30; 2) a year ago, on September 18, 1943, the first group of transferees reached the Center from Amache, numbering 125 and 433 from Rohwer in the same afternoon; 3) the Department of Justice recently announced that the alien population in the U.S. stands at about 3,400,000 as compared with about 5,000,000 at the time of the alien registration in 1940; 4) frozen bank funds (accounts) may be withdrawn for family needs; 5) religious services in the center are mostly Buddhistic, though Catholic and 7th Day Adventist are mentioned in the church service announcement. Japanese section in the main presents the same items as the English section.

DIARY

Sunday, October 1

A heavy fog (the ground is wet and very cold). Cold *all* day.

A number of rooms started their heating stoves.

Mrs. Kuramoto came with *senbei* [rice crackers] and stayed for a couple of hours.

Oki raised a question about the 4 categories into which the U.S. residents are divided: citizens, nationals without franchise (Indians and Filipinos), aliens, and enemy aliens: right. Military duty for all in emergency situation: yes.

The block meeting of women was held to request that one woman volunteer a day to pick and can tomatoes; the first woman agreed was Mrs. Matsumoto.

Wednesday, October 4

Overcast but mild as compared with the previous few days; about 8:30 it started to rain and continued all day.

Washino called, having returned from Walla Walla, Washington where he had earned about $500.00; anti-Japanism was very strong and therefore very uncomfortable. Restaurants, including Chinese ones, and barber shops refused services to Japanese customers.

Yoshihara came and stayed for a while; asked for the monthly hospital contribution of 5 cents per capita.

.   .   .   .

Thursday, October 5

The morning started very clear but with a cold wind, but it turned out to be a nice, warm day and remained so till the sunset.

No news of importance.

Miyamoto as chairman of *Ishi Kōenkai* [medical support society] issued an appeal, through the block managers, to issei women to help at the hospital; but why issei women alone? There are many nisei women who are not doing anything.

· · · ·

Sunday, October 15

Started clear and warm but soon became overcast and misty and cold. Cleared off and the sun shines; later a strong breeze developed though warm.

Mrs. Kuramoto brought a piece of *maguro* [tuna for sashimi] and stayed until 11:00 A.M. talking, as usual, about the block managers versus councilmen and women in public. . . . Informed that the council was thrown out from office by Lindley who stated that the WRA cannot cooperate with it so long as Ed [68] remained its chairman! He must have a very bad opinion of the man due to *inu's* information. Hoshimiya in [community analyst J. Ralph] McFarling's office came to Oki and said: Ed should be advised by an influential man to resign from the chairmanship—did he mean me? A funny business to say the least. Did McFarling make Hoshimiya undertake the job? It is now plain that the personnel is united on this affair. If so, why do they hesitate to take a positive measure to remove him, if they find legitimate reasons for such an action?

Monday, October 16

It rained late the last night after a heavy shower and this morning is still overcast but warm. Cleared up in some part but rather a strong wind developed; still, fortunately, the ground is wet and no sands are flying.

Received a letter on his recent trip to California, Sacramento and Placer County from Hamatani; anti-Japanese atmosphere is bad due to the presence of Filipinos and Chinamen who dominate in farms and farm-hands. It is instructive information.

Oki reported that he advised Hoshimiya to see me relative to the Council rumpus but he did not show up. It is futile to do anything about it; Ed is likely to be made the scapegoat in the final [show]down.

Mitani registered three blocks relative to relocation; a majority replied that they would resettle only if and when the West is open; a mere camouflage as they would really [prefer] to stay here as long as possible as compared with hardships they have to face outside. But the WRA will fix a deadline as regards the closing all the centers except the Tule Lake Center and will take care of the aged and the helpless by the U.S. Social Security Office as "public charges." That will be cheaper financially.

Saturday, October 21

Frost but clear and nippy, but even turned [out] to be a nice warm day even without a breeze to speak of, cooling after the sunset.
. . . .

The "Pioneer": 1) start center-wide volunteer harvest; 2) the Korematsu and Endo cases;* 3) Myer rebukes group opposing coast return at Seattle; [news about] the New Orleans agricultural and fishery plans. . . .

Sunday, October 22

Clear but cool, but turned out a nice warm day without a breeze to speak of.
In the morning, saw Hattori's chrysanthemums in partial bloom; they will be in full bloom in 1 or 2 weeks; the variety is limited but they are unusually excellent for the locality. . . .

---

*Fred Korematsu was a resident of the Oakland area when the war broke out. He was arrested for violating curfew regulations and failing to leave a restricted area. The Northern California chapter of the American Civil Liberties Union accepted his case and took it all the way to the Supreme Court to challenge the constitutionality of the evacuation order. Mitsuye Endo was a young nisei woman who worked for the California State Highway Commission at the time of evacuation. After she went to camp, she filed a *habeas corpus* petition and challenged her detention. Her case, too, went to the Supreme Court. In December 1944, the court upheld the government's power to evacuate during time of military emergency and rejected Korematsu's appeal. In the Endo case, the court ruled that citizens who were deemed loyal could not be kept indefinitely in detention; the ruling had little effect on the WRA, though, which was already releasing evacuees through the resettlement program. For more on the Supreme Court cases, see Irons, *Justice at War*.

Friday, October 27

The same as yesterday; clear with thin, filmy clouds. Clouds spread in the afternoon and a strong wind developed and blowing into the evening.

Hattori came and said that he would cut some of his chrysanthemums and invited us to see them before; I took Kei and two neighbors to see them.

The "Pioneer": 1) 12 more inducted last Monday; 2) more than 800 volunteers for farm work; 3) up to October 1 since draft act was put in force, F.B.I. had handled and closed 417,677 cases; 10,490 convicted: with a total imprisonment of 26,780 years, 1 month and 13 days and fines of $992,859. The bureau has 23,816 cases pending.

Oki came and asked me to advise on the matter of collecting monetary donations from the center residents here for Japanese prisoners of war in the U.S., with the "International Red Cross" as an agent; this was cooked up by the "block heads" as usual.[69] Each was asked to announce it in his own block but this was called off; instead, each is to get donations quietly!!! Illogical enterprise: why involve the International Red Cross nominally? It is the American Red Cross which handles it in reality. This collection should be confined to issei who should take the initiative as was done at the Tule Lake center whose inmates are all pro-Japan, whether issei or nisei; but here citizens and aliens are distinguished whenever the WRA finds it expedient. Citizens should refrain from doing anything which might appear pro-Japanese to newspapers and hostile public to avoid hurting themselves, I think.

Saturday, October 28

The same as yesterday but cold with a strong breeze; but remained the same.

Went to Kurahashi and found Ono still there; had *udon* lunch.

Mrs. Kuramoto came with ice cream and showed a letter from her son, Tom, which said that Woodrow is in the Camp Shelby, since when it is not known; [they have] not met as yet. 勉 [Tsutoma, Woodrow's middle name] at Shelby.

Received a card from the tailor, brought by Nakawatase saying that the pants ordered were at the co-op.

Yoshihara came in the evening and had tea with us. *Life* brought.
No other news of importance.
Research on the constitution of Prince Shōtoku.[70]

KEI ICHIHASHI TO JESSIE TREAT[71]

Amache
Oct. 28 [1944]

Dear Mrs. Treat:

I am glad to hear that Stanford University has returned to the normal schedule this year once more, and less uniformed men are on the campus. It is almost November, so the bright warm sun is shining on the campus and the leaves of elm trees have turned into beautiful colours and are falling every morning. At present, far away in Colorado, I am just thinking how beautiful the old elm trees on Salvatierra Street are! But some day I may be able to go back to California. It will be very nice.

I don't know exactly when we Japanese evacuees shall be able to go back to the home town. But several weeks ago Mr. Dillon Myer, the director of the W.R.A., said that all Japanese evacuees would be permitted to go back to the West Coast before the war is over, so that the evacuees will be able to go home sooner than they expected. However some people hesitate to go back to their old home right away. And some ones don't know what to do, because they sold their property, furnitures, automobiles, etc., even their farm land and they have no places to go back now. The other day one of my neighbours told me "I don't want to take a risk, so I shall stay in this unpleasant camp till the war is over." He is an old farmer and owns a house and farm land in California. And his home town is a small place, but even in this small community forty-five young Americans were killed in the Pacific some time ago, and more soldiers and sailors will be killed and wounded before the war is over. This old farmer doesn't want to go back to live in such a community where so many unhappy mothers, fathers and all relatives live, therefore he has decided to stay in the center till the end of the war.

I am just wondering how many evacuees will really be able to go back to their home town without fear at the present. It seems to me that W.R.A. is trying to push all the evacuees out of the centers, but this won't be a easy task.

I spent more than two years in the centers and have led a queer life. But I do not regret it, as I had many quiet and undisturbing days in the camp and I had chances to think about many problems quietly, for the first time in my life. I don't know yet when I shall be able to go back to sunny California, although I am mentally preparing to start a new life again when the time comes.

I received a box full of nice things. My favorite almond cookies, tasty cinnamon candies, famous Mrs. Bentsen's Danish cookies and Santa Clara prunes; they are all very delicious. I thank you for your kindness in sending me such nice things. I shall enjoy them very much.

I am very glad to know that Prof. Treat is teaching happily for his last year now. I hope he will not work too hard. Will you please give my best wishes to him?

> Affectionately yours,
> Kei Ichihashi

DIARY

Monday, October 30

The weather continues about the same as the previous day; later somewhat cloudy but rather warm.

. . . .

Kishi came and asked me to attend the late Domoto's one year memorial gathering. From 7:00–8:30 the service lasted; about 20 men and women packed the [church?] rooms with 2 *bokushi* [ministers], Haratani and Yoshioka. Hymns, prayers and remarks on the late Domoto.

Thursday, November 2

A regular, autumnal weather with scattered clouds and a strong breeze; cleared up and became warm. Then overcast with a cold wind.

Mrs. Yoshihara brought a piece of apple pie and stayed on and talked about the diarrhoea suffered by the block residents caused by the supper eaten Tuesday.

. . . .

Sano came and said that it was decided that 50 cents per family would be collected for *imonhin* for the *horyo* [Japanese prisoners of war]. Not being clear, [I] inquired of Yoshihara and found out that at a block meeting this business had been turned over to Oki and [S?], block managers. After the lunch, however, they told block-heads to collect 50 cents, per [unit?], including nisei families when willing. No names will be mentioned. Still illogical but left to individual judgment. Sneaky!

Friday, November 3

Clear and cold. Became somewhat cloudy and cold after late afternoon. Though warm during the day.

Research in the morning.

Sakai brought an invitation (in the form of a letter) to the talent show tomorrow evening. The purpose is to get a donation to the War Fund—admission 5 cents for kids and 10 cents for adults. This is interesting in view of the *imon* collection of yesterday!

. . . .

Monday, November 6

Somewhat overcast with a cold wind—wintry; it began to rain at 10:45, thunder and lightning following later in the afternoon. Rain continued into the night.

Oki came relative to the classes in the Japanese language in the center; discussion is on whether it should be permitted or not. Those who oppose must be ignorant of the new trend in the educational world which is, though belated, beginning to realize the importance of Far Eastern Studies: history, culture, language, etc. The School of Humanities wherever organized is leading the movement in the institutions which have paid no attention to that part of the world. Of course, the WRA is only interested in education as an incident in the management of the Japanese evacuees. . . .

. . . .

YAMATO ICHIHASHI TO PAYSON TREAT[72]

10-H 12-D
Amache, Colorado
November 5, 1944

Dear Payson:

Thank you very much for the interesting news and the clippings.[73] You and I have the right to be amused at the audacious advertisement of the School of Humanities not only at Stanford, but elsewhere concerning the importance of understanding Far Eastern history, etc. Still more amusing is the pontifical attitude assumed by these overnight experts; no real scholar could afford to be boastful, they should be modest and even humble. I also learn, from other sources, of the appointment of Oriental language experts at Stanford and elsewhere to teach these important languages! The present group of experts at Stanford mentioned by you somehow fails to impress me except in a negative sense.[74] Yet you comfort me when you state that the new president is trying to restore academic integrity at the institution. An institution of learning mainly depends on its faculty for its reputation. Some of us have contributed to the establishment of a sound foundation so that a younger group should be able to build on it a worthy structure, if it is properly equipped.

I am rather sorry to learn that the elders of the department are not so well as they should be, but if otherwise, perhaps they would not enjoy such a title. All of us grow old as time goes on, and inevitably feel consequences of the age. Though still suffering more or less, I have not been loafing on my job. As I promised you, I shall be able to report soon on the result of my research on the *Wei Chih*;[75] that might prove to be disturbing to those who have written on the subject in an authoritative manner. I am also investigating available literature on Prince Shōtoku, and am already discovering a number of things relating to him historically misinterpreted: Buddhism as the Prince understood it and as it was practiced by ordinary people of the time; his "constitution" appears to be so generally misunderstood because of the failure to see the history in its proper perspective; his remarkable ability to utilize his knowledge, though limited in its scope, in dealing with contemporary politics, especially domestic politics, etc. All this will be reported when ready.

My diary tells me that during the month of October we enjoyed, except the first four days, remarkable weather, a warm and delightful Indian summer devoid of storms of any kind. This is rather unusual for this region. However, since the dawn of November, mornings have been cloudy and chilly, but the sun has been shining brightly during the day until near the sun-set. We have thus far escaped from the famous sand-storms. In fact, the flowers in my "garden" are still blooming, including morning-glories! The sweet-pea seeds you thoughtfully sent me were planted in the spring, and since then I have carefully tended them against all the expert advice that they would not bloom in this place. I think that the local summer was too hot for them and the beating they got from the sand-storms was too much for them; consequently many died. But a few surviving ones are now blossoming to a great surprise of every expert!

Please don't worry about my obsession of [my] "indispensability" for I am positive that I am quite free from such a foolish notion. But I am curious to find out how the ignorant people face and solve the inevitable; this is a marvelous opportunity for me to satisfy my curiosity, if I assist them a little. My main interest is philosophic and my desire to help them is perhaps incidental. I am not motivated by noble ideals as politicians so often are; I am curious to learn, as much as is possible, how human nature acts and reacts. At the same time, it is impossible in the environment like this, to completely suppress one's feelings of compassion for the poor and ignorant who are utterly incapable to see the nature of their own troubles, and still less to discover ways and means of solving them. Since the evacuation, one discovery I have made is that my fellow countrymen in America, are not intelligent as I have credited them before. In saying this, I hope that I am not a victim of a superiority complex.

> Very affectionately yours,
> Yamato Ichihashi

Please excuse the poor composition and the abrupt ending; it is partly due to some callers alas!

DIARY

Tuesday, November 7, 1944

Rained a good deal during the night, but cleared by the morning with rather a strong wind; it is chilly. Later it became warm with a bright sunshine, the wind having died out completely.

. . . .

... [Henry] Tani and [Kazuyuki] Takahashi sent a list of Japanese Stanford alumni with a questionnaire to be filled in; Tani is still the same monkey that he has been; Kazu ought to be ashamed of himself; the mail is also sent to Woodrow!

. . . .

◘ The November 8 issue of the camp newspaper announced that in the national election on the previous day Franklin D. Roosevelt had been elected to his fourth presidential term, but politics and the war seemed to interest Ichihashi less than before. The fortunes of war had turned decisively against Tokyo: Allied forces steadily inflicted defeats on the Japanese. In July and August, they lost control of strategic islands like Saipan and Guam in the central Pacific. In late October, U.S. forces successfully landed on Leyte in the southern Philippines and shattered the Japanese navy in one of the greatest naval battles in history, in the Leyte Gulf. Ichihashi did not even note the events in his diary: "no news of importance" is what he wrote during the days of the battle. He retreated into his study of ancient Japan. ◼

DIARY

Saturday, November 11

As usual for these days, started clear and cold then warming; rather warm till the sunset when it became cool but not cold. Mild.

Kei is still in bed [because of diarrhoea].

Yonemura brought a Buddhist priest, Kubose, a young nisei who is working in Chicago where he informed me that about 11,000 Japanese, mostly nisei, many of whom directly relocated, but some from nearby cities like Cleveland, Detroit, St. Louis, etc. [now live]. They are scattered throughout the city though there are two concentrated groups; there have sprung a number of trades catering to these Japanese, eating places like *udon'ya*, *sushi'ya* [sellers of *udon* and *sushi*], Japanese food supplies and others to meet needed services. He is in favor in the relocation of those who are in a position to do so in localities other than the West. Kuramatsu and I went to K for *udon*.

Sunday, November 12

With some thin scattered clouds but mild, but later became overcast with thin clouds and cold, though the sun peeps thru the clouds. Then at 5:30 came a rather strong wind and a sand-storm.

Oseiyei[?]* passed away in the Nagoya hospital S. told us.

Hattori came with three cut chrysanthemums, white, red, and yellow and told me [of] his son's death in action in south France where the Japanese combat team had been transferred from Italy recently. Extended him my sympathies.

No other news of importance.

Monday, November 13

A strong gale during the night; a strong, cold wind in the clear morning, kicking up some sands. The wind continued and sands keep flying.

McFarling with Hoshimiya called and asked me about teaching the Japanese [language]; [I] said it would provide a common medium of expression now lacking between parents and children, which causes many tragic situations unknown generally. The learning of language has merits but no demerits; it enhances one's vocabulary and opens up a new vista to human achievements.

George Miyama called with a carton of "Chesterfields"; he had spent some time at Laramie, Wyoming. Those outside are not happy. He also brought some maps.

Tuesday, November 14

Clear and cold with a slight breeze. Turned out a nice, sunny day though a cool wind continued to blow.

Had a hair cut.

Announced: a meeting of the Blue Star Club; a meeting at [T?] Hall to give information relative to family relocation in Nebraska where they can work at the Army ordinance plant: 300 families are

---

*Unidentified.

wanted from this center. A similar effort to recruit workers from evacuees in the other centers. Both issei and nisei are wanted!

. . . .

◻ Officials in the Department of Justice in Washington continued to be interested in Yamato Ichihashi and asked the Amache administration for a report on his "activities, attitude, and conduct"; there was also a request that interviews be conducted with "his neighbors, supervisor, or anyone having personal contact" with him. James Lindley, camp director, did not have much to say in his confidential reply of November 14. His comments, though, provide another vantage point on Ichihashi's life in camp. The report read in part:

> I have talked with Dr. Ichihashi only three or four times and have seldom heard him discussed by others. I have talked to some of his evacuee neighbors and to individuals on the staff who all state that they have only a slight acquaintance with him. To people in general he seems to be enigmatic. He is respected by the residents because of his position as a scholar and University professor and partly because of his knowledge of Japanese culture. Most people do not seem to know just how to take him, and he in turn having had little contact with Japanese during his forty years at Stanford University seems to have difficulty in relating to them, and has a tendency to hold himself aloof. He takes, and has taken, no responsible part in center organization.
>
> He appears to be an impersonal observer of the passing scene rather than a participant.

Lindley ended his letter apologizing for the much delayed response; as he tried to explain, echoing many others who had encountered Ichihashi before, "it has been rather difficult to obtain information regarding Dr. Ichihashi." [76] ◼

DIARY

Sunday, November 19

> Cloudy and misty but mild, a few drops of rain. When the clouds scattered, a warm sun peeped for a short while, but overcast and cold—gloomy on the whole.
>
> Notices to date make it 7 killed in action in France for the Center; it is feared that the number is likely to increase because of the report that many had been killed and wounded in the campaign in France.
>
> No other news of importance.
>
> Research on the Taika Reform. [77]

Monday, November 20

Clear and cold with a lot of frost, but later turned out to be a nice warm day without any wind.

Sakais came to visit; they came to console [M?], whose son was killed in action in France, one of the 7 soldiers. Talked about general matters.

Paul Yamamoto, now a student at the Snelling Army Japanese Language School since August; will be there for 9 months. Informed me Buddy Iwata had resigned or had been discharged from the Navy Japanese Language School at Boulder and is now working as a radio monitor at Denver (to translate Japanese broadcasts). The school [has had] Japanese discharged or reduced in number; the Navy has now enough of officers thus trained—a mere guess.

Wednesday, November 22

Clear and cold though no frost; turned out [to be] another sun-shiny day, though with filmy, scattered clouds and a breeze.

Kay Hamatani visited with some apples. [Japanese?] farmers in Idaho are not doing well and some lost what they had invested, mostly in one-crop industries; they fail to realize the value of diversified agriculture. They are mostly from the Northwest and small scale truck gardeners. In California, the Filipinos and Chinamen will be the biggest and most dangerous enemies that the Japanese will encounter; the Caucasians are not hostile though they interfere with Japanese farming or their produce.

A second memorial service was held in the afternoon in honor of the 7 men killed in France. A long, long service as I expected.

Oki brought a chap named Shibata who is here to recruit laborers for the hemp factory situated about 60 miles from Chicago; men only. He hopes to get 60 from this center; it is a war industry which will close with the end of the war and a temporary affair. What interested me most was his statement that nisei are not stable and he prefers to get issei to work for they are likely to be more stable. There are 3 Buddhist churches in Chicago where he is stationed. Each has about 500 attendants!

. . . .

Thursday, November 23

Clear and cold but no frost; but soon turned out [to be] a bright, sunny day with a strong wind which kicked up sands for a while, but the wind subsided toward the evening. Later a howling wind developed. What weather!

Research on the ancient codes [of Japan].

Chicken and not turkey was served for dinner; this day was declared the Thanksgiving Day! Was this due to the scarcity of the latter birds?

No news of importance. . . .

Read stories.

YAMATO ICHIHASHI TO PAYSON TREAT[78]

10-H 12-D
Amache, Colorado
Nov. 26, 1944

Dear Payson:

On Wednesday last, 22nd, a second memorial service was held in honor of the seven nisei soldiers killed in France. Nearly 700 boys, who were residents, or whose parents are residing here, are now serving in the U.S. Army. At present, the total camp population is no more than 5,500: 3,346 citizens and 2,200 aliens. Practically all the issei families have from one to four boys serving as soldiers. Thus the percentage is rather high, and consequently, official casualty notices have been coming quite regularly. We are reminded of the sadness of war with the who-will-be-next anxiety.

On Saturday there was to be a party in honor of the aged residents, 65 and over, but a terrible blizzard throughout the day made it impossible to be held. Instead, its intended mementos were distributed among the guests to have been, who numbered 477! The number is made up of 383 men and only 94 women, showing the interesting fact that the once famous "picture brides" were much younger than the men they married, and that many men were obliged to remain single. Be that as it may, those 65 and over form a little more than 21 percent of the total issei population. Moreover, according to my own study, the issei in the age-group of 60–64 is over 400, or the total number of those of 60 and over is nearly 900 in the population of 2,500. The rest is made up of those mostly in their 50's with some in their 40's. Thus the age-composition of the issei population graphically forms a lopsided top whereas a normal population forms a pyramid.

Nisei or their offspring number some 3,000 strong, and concentrate in the age-group of 20's, while the older ones are married and are blessed or cursed with a multitude of minor kids. These facts reveal many abnormal results, among which the following may be noted:

1) The majority of issei are no longer enjoying the period of vigorous activity and are not consequently ambitious as they used to be. Their future is uncertain and even looms dark. If [the adage] "the old must and the young may" holds true, they will be gone, most of them in a comparatively short time. Therefore it seems that even anti-Japanists should be relieved of their anxiety.

2) The high percentage of nisei in the armed services is doubtlessly due to their age-distribution and to their relatively good physical conditions. Most of them have been reared on the farm. But to their aged parents who rely, because of their old habit, on their grown-up sons for support, and for this reason, the old folk have made unusual sacrifices in the up-bringing of nisei, for instance, in their education, their going to unknown destiny results in intensifying their hopelessness. They are patriotic, but they cannot forget the consequent problems created by the situation.

3) Those who are left behind, are their female offspring who are either still young and require their care, education, etc. or mature and married ones who have many children. They may be a source of consolation, but at the same time they constitute an economic burden which is now hard for the old to bear because of the loss they had incurred at the time of evacuation or their old age or both.

4) Because they are thus conditioned, they get more and more pessimistic in their outlook. They are losing their power of thinking. They are becoming irresponsible and vegetate because they have plenty of leisure. They do not gaze at stars and enjoy their beauty, but they seek moonshines of all sorts to satisfy their fleeting joys. Sad is the picture, but which one cannot escape observing. It is in such an environment in which I have now lived for two and a half years.

The weather has been remarkable. Until yesterday we have enjoyed a long-continued Indian summer from the mid-October which according to old timers, marks the beginning of winter here. Then all of a sudden it changed yesterday. A howling wind started during the night of Friday rattling and shaking our palatial barracks.

At the dawn of Saturday, a terrific blizzard commenced, whirling powdery snow and sands together in all directions. Never have I encountered such a storm in my 66 years! But to-day the sun is shining brightly again though its warmth is killed by a chilly wind. Despite it all, we are fairly well, though Kei has a slight cold as usual.

Hoping that you and Madam are in the best of health, I am,

> Very affectionately yours,
> Yamato Ichihashi

P.S. My research report is not ready as yet; too many interruptions.

KEI ICHIHASHI TO JESSIE TREAT [79]

> Amache, Cal.
> December 11 [1944]

Dear Mrs. Treat:

I should have written sooner, but I have not been very well since last September, and I caught cold in the beginning of November and also I had stomach trouble, which was a sort of epidemic in the camp, and many children and grown-ups suffered from it. So I had a sort of vacation lately and I am still not able to get rid of a bad cold, but I have started to work again, so please do not worry about me.

It doesn't seem possible time can fly so fast. Now we must celebrate Christmas very soon again, and I am going to send you a small box by parcel post, it is just a trifling gift. Postmasters warned that all Christmas packages should be sent out early this year, so that I follow their advice and send it out today; if it reaches you too soon, please do not open it till Xmas morning.

In California there was much rain in this fall, so I understood. But here we had no rain at all, the weather was just fine and it was such a beautiful autumn, bright and crisp every day, and Colorado farmers said "such a fine autumn comes only once in ten years." We had, however, a snowfall yesterday, and it was the fourth time. But today the sun is so warm and the sky is very bright. It is rather too good for winter.

In the outside world people, especially housewives, are busy for the preparation of the holiday—Xmas shopping and for everything. But in the center we have no Xmas shoppings, no excitement for the season, and I am still enjoying an uneventful, quiet life. Last year I went to my "new cousins" home, about 50 miles away from here, on

Thanksgiving Day, but I have been invited to Christmas dinner this year. I don't mind much about a turkey dinner, but a 50 miles country drive is something to me. I have been cooped up in the camp so long, and I went out of the camp only 3 times since I came here—3 times in 16 months. So I am quite anticipating to enjoy a nice countryside drive on Christmas day.

I sincerely hope for you, for me, for everybody [that the] New Year will be brighter. Please present my kind respects to Prof. Treat. I hope this note finds you in the best health.

> Affectionately yours,
> Kei Ichihashi

KEI ICHIHASHI TO JESSIE TREAT[80]

> Amache, Colo.
> December 17 [1944]

Dear Mrs. Treat:

I received two packages by parcel post safely. I do not know how to thank both of you for your kindness, and I have decided not to open the presents till Christmas morning. I have no Xmas tree this year, even a miniature one I cannot get yet, so I have fixed a table with some red cyclamens and white fresias, both flowers are artificial ones of course, to get a bit of holiday atmosphere and put Xmas packages also cards beside the flowers. Today, very fortunately I have got a pot of beautiful azaleas, so my Xmas table is very attractive.

Two years ago about this time at Tule Lake, a friend of mine made me some artificial poinsettias so that I put them in an appropriate corner in my room. And on Xmas Day, a friend, who used to live in San Francisco, called on me and she thought I got the beautiful poinsettias from a flower shop at a nearby town, they were so attractive and real. This morning I went to the mess hall and saw a pot of poinsettia on the table. And its pot was not much larger than a tea cup, and a stem was about a foot long, and [it was] rather a thick stem and not attractive at all. Then I thought some woman displayed her own work on the table—many persons do—as it was the season of poinsettias. But I was rather surprised as it was a real flower, and some one said that the flower came from Colorado Springs. The famous hotel at Colorado Springs has a large nursery and there are all kinds of flowers, and they are growing many poinsettias too, but those flowers are not as pretty as the poinsettias in California, so a friend of mine explained, and he was there a couple weeks ago.

In Colorado flowers are so expensive that California people cannot imagine. From time to time I get some carnations and red buds of roses; they are very common in California but my friends think I am very luxurious to get such things. One day a friend of mine ordered a certain amount of flowers to use for a funeral service, and afterwards he received a bill of $35.00 for them; and he was very much surprised and told me that the amount of the ordered flowers was about $5.00 worth of things in California. He was formerly a nursery man so he knows more about flowers and plants than average persons.

Well! The year-end is close at hand; as I look back I was always very busy about this time of year, but on the contrary I have nothing to do for the season, nothing to worry about shopping or preparations now. I am doing queer living in the queer quarters, as you imagine, but I have very attractive flowers on the table and I can look at the beautiful sunset through the queer windows, and I am steeping in this wonderfully serene atmosphere. And I have been longing to have this atmosphere for many years, so that my soul is quite contented now. But next year I shall go back and start busy life again—new life.

> Yours truly,
> Kei Ichihashi

DIARY

Sunday, December 17

Somewhat overcast but relatively mild in the morning; the clouds are vanishing gradually and the sun is getting warmer. Became overcast again accompanied with a cold wind. It began to snow at 5:30 P.M.

. . . .

Miura informed [me] that the WRA would announce publicly relative to the West Coast return soon; it had informed the block managers this afternoon. The time: January to June. The "Pioneer" "Extra" announcing the removal of [the] exclusion [order] from the West Coast area effective on January 2, 1945; free for all evacuees to return to the West Coast states from that date!

Monday, December 18

Clear and cold with frost aplenty, but soon the sun began to shine. Remained cold all day, the evening being mild somewhat.

The whole camp is pervaded with reactions as regards the announced policy permitting the return of evacuees to the West Coast states; all tend toward the idea or feeling of putting the inevitable to the last day and thus showing the lack of courage; [they] are afraid to face it like a necessary but painful surgical operation.

. . . .

Called on Okubos in the evening; the old man is just [like?] another as regards the new policy; he thinks that either financial aid is forthcoming or ought to come. The WRA ought [to be able to] save funds by shortening the period of maintenance, which should be given to evacuees. All sorts of such foolish ideas are being hatched due to their wishful thinking.

The "Pioneer" (Extra) Japanese translation of the announcement distributed.

Tuesday, December 19

Clear and cold though not very and with frost; then became thinly overcast and in the afternoon the sun shines and warm as there is no wind.

Dispatched letters to Jessie and Payson.

. . . .

A notice from Washington, D.C. in regard to the return: three categories: 1) those who are free; 2) those who are not free and 3) those whose status remains undetermined; the vast majority are free.

Received four Christmas cards.

The gardener in the school named Frank Fujii of 9-s 4-c called and asked me to help the helpless men and women and their families as regards the announced policy, who are financially hard up and ignorant and unable to negotiate. Suggested that the block residents get together to ask each ward to select a man of virtue and intelligence so that five think and study most suitable plans for their settlement in conjunction with the block managers' assembly and the council. The latter must [not?] be overlooked because they are sensitive of their importance as "leaders."

YAMATO ICHIHASHI TO PAYSON TREAT[81]

IO-H I2-D
Amache, Colorado
Dec. 19, '44

Dear Payson:

First of all let me thank you for the kind Christmas package which will be opened on the proper day; of course, I would like to reciprocate but find it impossible. However, I am happy to report that the WRA announced publicly that Japanese evacuees would be able to return to their west coast homes from January 2, 1945 on. . . . We will return to our campus home as soon as I am satisfied with various plans the people make for their resettlement in the west and elsewhere.

There now follows the first part of a report on the *Wei Chih*. [Omitted here are two pages on Ichihashi's research, including a translation of passages from the Chinese historical text.]

Wishing you a very merry Christmas and a Happy New Year, I remain,

> Very affectionately yours,
> [Yamato Ichihashi]

DIARY

Wednesday, December 20

Somewhat overcast but not very cold. More cloudy as the day advanced and a strong wind developed kicking up some sands. Began to snow at 9:00 P.M.

. . . .

[Lectured this evening] on Laoism [Taoism] and Confucianism.

Some of those who wish to remain as "wards" applied for repatriation or expatriation in the hope that they be sent to Tule Lake and kept there for the duration!!! If true; it may be a rumor. A manifestation of the *kojiki* [beggar] complex.

Thursday, December 21

It snowed a little at night, but the morning is clearing; somewhat overcast; and cold somewhat with some snow on the ground.

Received a Xmas card from Miyake who married the Nakata girl.

Received two books from the [Book of the Month?] Club with a bill of $2.00 for a 2nd book.

George Miyama called and said that shops [on the outside] are empty and it is impossible to buy anything. The war boom must have created an unusual demand for goods which cannot be [met] with a normal amount of stocks. The mail-order houses are in the same plight—unable to fill orders. The situation has resulted from the regimentation (restriction) of production of civilian goods on one hand, and inflated wages caused largely by war industries and the shortage of laboring man power. The purchasing power of the laboring class has increased tremendously—hence an increased demand for goods.

Sakais sent us an invitation to their Christmas dinner and asked Kei to send my regrets; this she did in the morning.

Monday, December 25

Overcast and cold; gradually cleared and in the afternoon the sun shone but a cold wind almost kills the warmth. Then the wind died, and it became warm.

A very quiet Christmas day; the nature is kind in making it a pleasant day, or at least, afternoon. No callers to bother me; Yuhora came to see the [model sailing] boat and the cane;[82] the former object interested him very much because he is a *kishū* man and remembers his childhood and boats and ships because he lived in the picturesque Katsuura or its vicinity.[83]

Michiko Machida brought me a box of candies.[84]

Tuesday, December 26

A cloudy, windy and cold morning, rather gloomy; in a trip to the post office, I experienced the coldest weather and my feet almost froze; later the sun warmed up a little, though still very cold. It became mild in the evening, though still cloudy.

I went to the post office and got the package and a card from Stoltenbergs.

. . . .

Kurahashi called in the evening to inform me that *udon* will be tomorrow instead of Thursday due to the death of an old man in his block, whose *otsuya* [wake] will be held on that day and his funeral next day: a man of 80 without any relatives so that the block people will take care of the services. . . .

. . . .

Wednesday, December 27

Overcast but a relatively mild morning though with frost, as compared with yesterday; it is clearing up with the sun shining.

. . . Kuramatsu thinks nobody will move out unless he is given a lump sum of, say, $200.00 per capita, or if given less that amount, he will.

. . . [A young nisei, Takashima] interviewed [camp administrator Melvin P.] McGovern who said that the residents were "uncooperative" as regards their attitude towards the WRA personnel or its policies. The schools would be closed in June as well as all the recreation activities for the purpose of discouraging the residents to linger on here. These and other "attractions" would be done away to stimulate their departure from this center and elsewhere! All this is negative; what are their positive inducements or encouragements? So far there is no indication.

Thursday, December 28

Overcast somewhat and cold, the kind of weather for last several days. Cleared up and the sun is out, but rather cold with a strong breeze.

Attended the Council's dinner held by its outgoing and incoming members with invited guests from the personnel and the residents. Four blocks still have representatives. The dinner consisted of sushi, chicken, sashimi, etc. with beer and wine. The following were called upon to speak: Lindley, Halliday, Ichihashi, Johnson, McClelland and McFarling: none said anything. Forget past disagreements and face the problem of cooperating on the basis of 50–50. The people need help, help without seeking any compensation.

. . . .

Saturday, December 30

Clear and sunny, though somewhat cold, but later became more cloudy and a strong, cold wind developed making [it] rather cold.

The New Year number of the "Pioneer" is out; it contains a number of items relating to the reopening of the West, including a brief summary of immediate reactions of its own staff: "Don't know what to do" is the key-note.

Kid's wife [Woodrow's wife, Alyce] sent the New Year card and kid's photo with his baby; kept away from K.

. . . .

Sunday, December 31

Clear and rather cold with frost, but the sun shines brightly, though it remained cold.

The block is engaged in *mochi-tsuki* [making rice cakes for New Year's].

. . . .

SPECIAL DATA

In the afternoon of the 17th which was a Sunday, the block managers were assembled by the WRA order for a special purpose: the announcement of the removal of the military order of excluding Japanese, aliens and citizens, from the "military zones" of the three states of the Pacific Coast. Later in the same evening, the "Pioneer" "Extra" was distributed among the residents, giving Myer's statement in full: it said, "removal" effective January 2, 1945; the continuation of the centers from 6 months to 1 year from the date; financial aid to those aged who are incapable of self-support, etc.

The immediate reaction of residents appears to be an unpleasant surprise! Whereas the WRA presented the policy as a "gift" to be welcomed generally by those to whom it is given. There are reasons for these conflicting views: 1) many of the residents have no home to return to in the West Coast as they had so thoroughly been uprooted from their various enterprises or had had no foundation of any kind but had been of a floating-labor category. These appear to constitute the majority and to them the newly announced policy seems to cut off their present accustomed life now for 2 1/2 years with which they had to put up, or considered quite satisfactory or not satisfactory. Nonetheless, there has been security which will disappear with their "relocation" outside; this thought creates anxiety in their minds. Hence a shock and a disappointment appears to be their immediate reaction; 2) to these may be added the peculiar psychology developed or intensified since the evacuation—namely, a "bread-line complex." The Japanese have been famous as non-seekers of public charity, a fact not to be disputed. Yet since the evacuation, many have lost the sense of self-reliance, self-respect and responsibility and have become willing or even desirous of taking advantage of any external benefits small and big, and have been satisfied to be "wards" of the government, and perhaps wish to remain so as long as possible, for then there is security as regards elementary needs of living. They have become lethargic both physically and mentally. Has the evacuation been wholly responsible for this corruption (degeneration)?

RESEARCH ESSAY [85]

Attitudes and Needs That Hinder Resettlement

   1. The traumatic shock caused by evacuation and assembly center experience producing:
   Inability to organize oneself to take the necessary steps, even when the wish to do so is present. Obsessive fear of a hostile outside world holds many in the Center. An inability or unwillingness to face reality even so much as considering the question of resettlement.
   2. Negative resistance: Resentment resting on the fact of evacuation, property losses, discomfort in assembly centers, selective discrimination (as against German and Italian enemy aliens), organization and administration of the Center takes the form of resistance to WRA proposals. The present WRA relocation policy is not looked upon as a service to the evacuees, but rather as a means of forcing the evacuees out of the Center "in order to save the government money."

The Issei in American Life

It is an essential fact that the Issei have been denied American citizenship and are citizens of Japan. Many are Americanized in spirit (especially so among the Los Angeles people) and all are Americanized to some degree in behavior. But it is not to be expected that all sentimental ties to Japan have disappeared. Their rejection by our government[86] and people has thrown them back on their sentimental ties to their country of origin and has resulted in extensive dream fantasies of the beauties and virtues of their home of long ago. Without being overtly disloyal, they cannot help feeling that their destinies are tied to the fate of Japan.

Consequently, some Issei have taken the position that they cannot go out to play a productive role in the war effort. They maintain that this would get them listed as traitors in Japan. They are not yet thoroughly convinced that they will not be deported to Japan after the war, so they do not wish to take the chance and prefer "to remain in the Center and be neutral."

Others have been waiting in expectation of a Japanese victory, which would result in the imposition of favorable indemnities on their behalf by the Japanese government.

It has been widely rumored that Tokyo instructions were for the Issei to remain in the Centers. That indemnities would be paid those who do so, but not to those who relocate.[87]

Social and Economic Blocks

Roughly, those who have sufficient savings, property, or investments to make their way without loan or subsidy. Some of these are faced with problems of frozen funds or leases on their property for the duration.

Those who retained a few hundred or a few thousand dollars. They may have enough to make the plunge but because of their advanced age, they are exceedingly cautious about doing so. They hope desperately for government "guarantees" against the wiping out of their last savings through business or farming failures. They do not have any specific ideas as to how the government might do this. Yet they feel that the government, which was powerful enough to uproot them and perform economic miracles of war production, is able to rehabilitate them economically—if it will.

6

Amache–Stanford

January 1, 1945–
April 30, 1945

I chihashi had buried himself in his research work during the closing months of 1944 and despite his eye troubles read regularly, even tackling Tolstoy's *War and Peace*. But try as he did to follow a disciplined routine, the demands of camp life constantly intruded. His advice was sought daily; he was asked to give lectures and talks to camp residents; and ever-changing government policy kept people in turmoil. Just as the uproar about drafting nisei men began to die down in late 1944, news about the federal government's allowing Japanese to return to the West Coast introduced a new predicament. As Ichihashi recorded in his diary, on December 18, 1944, the WRA announced that as of midnight January 2, 1945, the exclusion of persons of Japanese ancestry as a group from the West Coast was removed by the federal government. The imposition of a large number of exemptions, however, still meant that thousands of people people whom the army deemed potentially dangerous could not yet return.[1]

Ichihashi devoted attention to analyzing the residents' reactions, which were not uniformly enthusiastic about the prospect of returning to the West Coast for a number of reasons. For one thing, local reaction to the end of exclusion was frequently hostile and intimidating. Mass anti-Japanese sentiment, inflamed in some cases by local political figures, still ran high. For another, many of the evacuees had few or no resources and were at a loss over how they might restart their lives on the "outside." (The government offered to pay for transportation plus $25 per person.) Ichihashi himself delayed returning to his home because of his interest in observing the closing days of relocation. He anticipated returning to Stanford in the early spring and wrote to his tenant to vacate the house by March 1.

Yamato and Kei occasionally received news about Woodrow from friends, but Yamato refused to establish ties with him, Alyce, and their newborn infant. ◗

1945 DIARY[2]

Monday, January 1

Clear and cold with frost as it has been in the closing days of the last year; it is rather a nice New Year, though the block people are apparently gloomy as they were at the last New Year Day. Later cloudy and cold.

Shogatsu ya meido no tabi no ichirizuka ureshiku mo ari, ureshiku mo nashi.*

Young boys and girls volunteered to wait on tables and wash dishes to relieve the regular crew. Otherwise nothing happened, except Okubo extended greetings on behalf of the mess crew and Miura replied thanking the crew.

The following called: Kuramoto, Kayashima, Sakai, Kitazumi, Kuramatsu and Kurahashi.

The last named invited K.Y. and me to *udon* supper tomorrow.

---

*A possible rendering may be: "My feelings are mixed this New Year's Day—a day of celebration, but also another step toward the end of life. I feel both happy and sad."

Kei reminded [me] that we are to go to the Kuramotos at noon tomorrow.

No news of importance otherwise.

Thursday, January 4

Started cloudy and very cold with frost but later clears up and sun shiny; however remains cold. 2 degrees in the morning (coldest) but at 1:40 P.M. it rose to 81 degrees; thus winter and summer in the same day! Cold with a breeze from 5:00.

No news except that they [the residents] began to do a little thinking more rationally as I anticipated, though still nebulous in most cases; it will take more time. Wild dreams will gradually subside and evaporate perhaps.

The day was quiet and without any disturbances as there were no callers.

. . . .

Friday, January 5

Clear and cold with a bright sun-shine and a chilly west wind but which died by noon and became a nice warm day as in the spring. A mild evening.

. . . .

Mrs. Kuramoto called bringing with her a New Year card from Murata at Heart Mountain and a letter from her oldest son; the latter said that Woodrow had been ordered to go overseas and had left Shelby, but later ordered that his name be canceled from the shipping list; Toru [Kuramoto] is arriving here on the 15th. It may be that Woodrow's departure is postponed.

. . . .

Saturday, January 6

Clear and cold as it has been since the 1st, but soon became overcast with thin clouds, which became thicker and thicker as the day advanced and then also developed a wind. This is the first somewhat gloomy day of this year. My stomach is upset with a slight case of indigestion, though whose cause I cannot tell. Had no lunch. Went to bed at 7:00 and stayed till the following morning; it is a cold which causes pains.

The "Pioneer": 1) no rush to West Coast; 2) some communities still anti-Japanese; 3) evacuee reception on West Coast "hot and cold"; 4) new council is sworn in; 5) census taking tomorrow; 6) college students relocation interviews; 7) Ickes: evacuees are law-abiding.

Sunday, January 7

Clear and cold with a breeze and frost. The sun is out shining brightly. Last year, it snowed.

Kurahashi came bringing some *gobō* [burdock root] and *takenoko* [young bamboo shoots] cooked which I had for lunch with rice.

In the afternoon Sakais sent by their daughter some venison.

My head-ache worse and no *tsūji* [bowel movement] despite a *gezai* [purgative medicine] pill taken.

Monday, January 8

Some clouds scattered in different directions, but the sun kept shining; later it turned out warm though a strong [wind] developed but without kicking up sands.

My cold and head-ache condition remain the same and I stayed in bed most [of the] time.

. . . .

Received a letter from Kenji [Ito]:[3] he is going to Sacramento to effect a compromise in several cases of income tax, later he will go to Seattle. Asks me to inform him about reactions of the residents in regard to the new policy.

The Army, the Immigration and Naturalization [Service], and the WRA are still making "investigations" simultaneously; if they are for different objectives, they are creating unnecessary confusions and irritations doing these at the same time. Bureaucratic stupidities.

Wednesday, January 10

Clear and cold (but not very), and again developed into a very nice, warm day and a mild evening and night.

Could not sleep all night; what caused this I do not know. I feel stupid, though I had my breakfast in the mess hall.

Mrs. Kuramoto called on behalf of her husband as a member of the board of directors of the Blue Star Service Club which is to hold its annual meeting next Sunday, at which two *katō* [low-lifes] are scheduled to speak and asked me to translate their talks. My answer was no and gave reasons for it candidly as follows: 1) officers incapable to perform necessary functions should not remain in office; 2) they should not try to make tools of the capable because the latter would not be so stupid as to help out such fools' political ambitions of social climbers (there are too many of these among the Japanese); 3) their mistaken idea about our own status; though our sons are in the U.S. armed services, [the Blue Star Service Club?] violates my fundamental principles and is unethical, and they are not worthy of association; 4) their attempt to capitalize on the fact (of their sons being in the service) to their advantages is despicable, even if the organization can be made to function as an effective weapon (it involved 600 families in this camp, therefore its membership can claim, at least 1,000) as it is already a "powerful" (and the most powerful) organization in the camp, which even the WRA cannot ignore or trifle [with], as it has been [toward] all the other organized bodies political, social, religious or what not, provided it is properly led. (There are no such men in the camp.)

At any rate, some are smart enough to realize possibilities of this club being rendered (or even as it stands) into a powerful tool to satisfy their political ambition and therefore began to struggle to attain positions in it! They want to show off everything they have got at the coming gathering: speeches, committees and their chairmanships, refreshments, entertainments for 1,000 spectators; but they created their own stupidity—the invited *katō* guests—none of them can handle their speeches and of course it is dangerous for them to rely on any, who like them is politically ambitious, because he will capitalize on every opportunity to his own; hence they have picked me for two reasons: 1) I have no political ambition or desire to share such an honor or have even contempt, and 2) they know that the residents have a universal respect for me as for no one else; in other words, it is good dramatization in regard to the public and yet politically harmless!!! But this is why their proposal or request has been turned down even if they were clever enough to use a woman who sincerely respects me as the "negotiator." What stupid fools! Watch Sunday, the 14th.

Sunday, January 14

Clear and chilly as usual; soon a strong wind developed, kicking up some sands, but subsided in late afternoon; mild with the sun.

. . . .

The Blue Star Service Club elected (?) its new officers with [K] as head: it held its circus meeting to attract the public—in fact everybody was invited! He likes to make himself conspicuous under every opportunity; pose as a "big man." Watch, he will make political capital of the organization to create economic advantages to himself if possible. Another *meiyokyō* [person crazy for prestige?]! A "talent show" was the attraction of the meeting!!!

Monday, January 15

Clear and cold with frost; a strong wind developed, kicking up sands and in the afternoon it became overcast.

. . . .

Miura reported and warned the residents that thefts (3 cases so far) had been committed; one old woman was robbed $350[?] while she was out attending the Blue Star Service Club's entertainments last night. The people should be more alert now that departures began and the ultimate closing is fixed; evil ones are apt to become active.

Went to Kuramoto's for dinner: Junior informed [that he was] "pfc" = private first class. Several thousand nisei are in Europe: 3,000 in the 442nd [Regimental Combat Team] and 1,000 in the 100th [Battalion],[4] while the rest are replacements; some are in the Pacific, India, etc. Casualties are rather heavy.

Junior spoke of the Blue Star Service Club. Another memorial service to be held on the 20th. The [casualty?] lists [are] black, gray and white. Relatively few departures immediately are expected. The September closing is not definitively fixed as far as he knows. I think he expects to capitalize [on] the club as a "political" tool.

Kuramoto Jr.: soldiers 26 years and over and disqualified physically for overseas services are now given 90 day furloughs to work in factories as mechanics, technicians, etc. to overcome industrial labor shortage.

YAMATO ICHIHASHI TO KENJI ITO [5]

Amache, Colorado.
January 15, 1945

Dear Ito kun:

Thank you very much for the Christmas gift, the copy of the "Ir-rigator," and the letter.[6] What you say about the immediate reaction of the Minidoka people as regards the newly announced policy [on returning to the West Coast] is not at all surprising. In fact, I have been anticipating such a reaction, at least, in the beginning. A simi-lar reaction must have manifested itself in all the other centers; it is certainly true here in Amache. However, I am more interested in what lies behind it—cause or causes. As far as I can understand, no matter how camouflaged, the fundamental reason is the issei's desire for the continuation of "camp life," unnatural but irresponsible, de-grading but easy, devoid of true living but secure. It is born of their newly (?) acquired "bread-line" complex. They have lost their guts and have become habituated to look upon the struggle for the exis-tence as a thing to be dreaded and avoided. That is the reason why they "fear" or indulge in "fear," and let out a piteous cry: "We are too old and our young sons have been taken away from us, and we can no longer face a hostile world." (There are in this camp nearly 500 men and women who are 65 years old and over; more than 700 boys from some 600 families have been taken into the Army; and we are all "enemy aliens.") Nonetheless, it is a philosophy of despair unworthy of the Japanese people in America with their historical background: During the past half a century they have lived a life menaced constantly with threats and, indeed, even with violent deeds, and yet they have successfully endured it and have even emerged victorious. This view sounds cold but is a realistic one.

What the people need most is intelligent guidance at this critical hour. There have been and still are "leaders" aplenty, but they lack intelligence, social-mindedness, sincerity; they are not trustworthy. They indulge in an avalanche of words and phrases: Most popular among these is *Kyōryoku-itchi* [Unite into one], but there can be no unity where there is no mutual interest. But in truth, the so-called "leaders" are selfish as are the people themselves; they are *gari-gari* [beggarly]. The former scheme and the latter try to avoid being vic-tims. It is a sad battle of wits: Observe the management of camp co-operatives; political leaders or demagogues and business managers, or rather enterprisers, are not trusted because they scheme with their own profit-motives.

Where else can we look for true leadership? Religionists? My knowledge of them in four different camps makes me shiver; they are no better than the average farmer or tradesman and possess no qualifications of leadership. Educators? They simply do not exist; only *hōgo-sensei* [Japanese language teachers] were given financial support by the Japanese in America, and these are no better than religionists. Both of these had to cater to whims and fancies of the unintelligent people because they had to depend on the people for their bread and butter. This is also true of other issei professionals. It is truly a sad state of affairs. Yet I wonder whether we oldsters can just vegetate for the rest of our lives, even if they last only a decade or two.

There may be a few issei with guts and a few mature nisei with intelligence, who are sincere and broadly interested in life problems. These ought to get together to plan for the future of the people. A number of things must be created and made functioning, if they are to regain a normal life for the Japanese group as a whole. The fundamental principle of guiding such planning must be based on enlightened self-interest; apart from this, nothing is likely to succeed. I am going to remain in the camp until I find out what the people actually propose to do in order to resettle and regain a normal life.

You ask me about the probable, future distribution of Japanese in America, and of course, I can only guess at present: The future distribution is likely to follow the old line (geographical) of distribution. For instance, in a number of localities (in California), the Japanese possess farms and houses, and it may be assumed that these farmers will return to their farms and homes. They will constitute the nucleus in each of such localities, to which others such as farmhands will be attracted and will thus develop an expanded community. Religionists, tradesmen, professionals will follow and render their various services to the community. I think as far as issei are concerned, no matter where they are located at present, they are likely to find their way eventually to such communities. Young nisei, most of them are still young, must follow issei to be protected or supported; there are relatively few mature and independent nisei (minus those in the armed services at present), whose future residence is difficult to forecast. They may find it advantageous to remain outside the West Coast States; if so, there is no reason why they should not remain there and become integrated. But this still

remains to be seen. Further speculation on the subject is superfluous; the foregoing is an attempt to answer your question.

You have moved about and continue to do so according to your
report; please let me know your own experience in, and observation
of, the outside world, whenever you can. I am in need of information for myself and also in order to help others more intelligently.
With highest regards to you and your family,

> Very sincerely yours,
> [Yamato Ichihashi]

DIARY

Thursday, January 18

Overcast by mist but not so cold. At 2:00 P.M. it began to rain lightly
and then [changed] to snow (just a few flakes) for an hour or so; then
both ended, but it remains cloudy and gloomy. It snowed during the
night.

Visited Kuramatsu's studio in the morning and afternoon; he
painted [some] small pictures.

A block meeting was called to hear Uragami:[7] 1) He would advise
the block to name its councilman and 2) "Sit tight" until we hear
from Myer as regards the "seven point" inquiry presented to him by
the Council (?).[8]

No other news of importance.

Oki called and said that he was trying to get 50 men to work in
the hemp factory; he would be lucky if he gets 20 I said. Pay is 65
cents per hour and 8 hours per day and 6 days per week hence about
$38 per week minus $2 per room per week and $1.00 for meals per
day and income tax. Balance is about $20.00 per week. Overtime
1 1/2 the rate.

Friday, January 19

Cloudy but not very cold; partly cleared up though remained cold.
It was not gloomy as yesterday.

Went to Kuramatsu's studio where, among others, Haratani was
found, who asked me about the same relocation problems in the customary general and meaningless manner. I told him the first step is

to get information on the basis of individual families in order to know the nature of problems. Then think out ways and means to help the most helpless first. And don't wait but start the work right away by blocks or from the pulpits. When necessary information is at hand, find most specific ways of [how to] approach individual cases classified into groups.

. . . .

Rumored that 80% of the residents agreed to sit tight?

Saturday, January 20

Cloudy, misty but not very cold; about 9:30 A.M. it began to *snow* steadily and it is piling up. The heaviest since our arrival here, about eight inches deep.

Went to Kuramatsu's studio and then went with him to K's for lunch.

Previously had met Miura who said as a result of Uragami's report that in his own Block 8-K 98% voted not to move out of the center under the "stated conditions" of the WRA; similar votes are being attempted in all the other blocks. Then representatives of this center will meet those of the other centers in a conference in order to make demands on the U.S. government. The idea is to get the people to agree to stay while such a procedure be effected. My own idea is to let the people alone who wish to relocate and let the rest undertake whatever they desire; above all, no agitation of any kind [should] be permitted. We don't want the innocent and help-less to suffer for nothing. There is no harm for them to plan their relocation.

Are these "leaders" (self-appointed) confident of success of what they propose to do? It is wondered whether they realize the worsen-ing consequences of the prolongation of the camp life both for adults and minors? They are thinking exclusively of their own cases or all [their] deductions are based on such. The "Pioneer" has sev-eral new items of information. The Miyakes (5 adults and 5 kids) left for their Atwater farms, the 1st from this block.

Sunday, January 21

Continues to snow, but stopped about 10:30; then the sun began to shine rather faintly. Became cold from the evening on.

Kenji took my picture in snow, working in front shoveling snow.[9]

. . . .

Miura canvassed every unit in the block and found that the people would not move out before June; probably a true index because that is the first deadline set up by the government policy, but their reasons might differ considerably. What I fear is this delay is merely to postpone the inevitable and painful operation without any plans.

. . . .

Monday, January 22

Overcast and very cold (8 degrees) with a good deal of snow on the ground. Soon cleared up and the sun shines brightly; but cold with a chilly wind. Thus it remained all day; the moon and stars are out in a clear sky but rather cold.

In the morning read a monograph.

Received a card [from] Hamatani from San Francisco: "So far so good." Also income tax forms to be returned, from the University.

. . . .

It appears that a few people only are departing from the center, for a while at any rate; the majority will "sit tight"; they find no reasons to hurry whether they have definite plans or not, as it is out of the "season" for farmers.

Some anti-[Japanese] agitations in the State Legislature seem to be inevitable. [Evacuees may be threatened by] alien land law violations and occupational restrictions, even against nisei, so the *Palo Alto Times* reports. . . .

Tuesday, January 23

Clear but very cold with westerly wind and with plenty of snow on the ground. The sun shines brightly but a cold wind makes it still very chilly. It became cloudy in late afternoon and it so remains after the sunset.

. . . .

Mrs. Kuramoto called and said that Corky Kawasaki,[10] who is prohibited from the coast areas east and west, and her husband have a scheme: an agricultural colony somewhere outside the coast areas and in order to make their [plan] materialize are preventing or discouraging people from relocating because it needs farmers and other workers. The inducement they put up is that the government or its agricultural agents will furnish capital or credit to launch and conduct their proposed schemes (enterprises); they would organize a consumer cooperative to meet all the needs of the colonists. It is to be wondered that financing is forthcoming as is expected. At any rate, they are making the people confused and hesitant in making their individual plans of relocation. Similar schemes are apparently being formulated by other men of the same type. Such schemes have many doubtful and dangerous elements and points and are likely to result in failure [rather] than success; if this guess is correct, there will be many victims. Money-making schemes attract, but individual life is far more important; the people should beware, but alas!

Thursday, January 25

Clear with a bright sun. Turned out a nice, warm day and melted the snow on the ground, but sands would absorb water and made the roads slushy and dirty. After the sunset it will freeze.

Visited Kuramatsu's studio and saw some attractive works rather unusual in color schemes.

A big canvas reached [us] from Ando in New York; it is agreed to cut it into three pieces. More paints are needed by Kuramatsu and we have to [get] them for him.

Oki: As a labor recruiter, he is getting unpopular with the so-called "leaders," who would insist that the residents sit tight; a rather stupid stand. Obviously the majority will gain nothing by following such a stand. The leaders are not working for the good of the people but for their own benefits (at least they think that they can make their schemes materialize). We will see.

Saturday, January 27

The 2nd heavy snow, which started last evening about 8:00 P.M., continues this morning, but the wind which blew early completely subsided by the dawn. *Mizore* or sleet. It is the 2nd *ginsekai* [landscape of silvery snow] of the year; while snow of the previous Saturday partly remained unmelted in spots or patches.

It seems ironical: since every general festival, service or performance is scheduled, the nature frowned so far with rain, wind or snow, often violent in character. Snow continues to fall, but does not pile and melts because the weather is not cold enough; it began to pile up slowly as it became cold.

Yoshiharas came back from their Chicago and Louisville (Camp Knox) [trips]. Ky. and Mrs. Y called and told us about their experience.

The "Pioneer": 1) the California district attorney asks law enforcing officers to protect evacuees returning; 2) reception in San Francisco Bay Area "good"; 3) graduate 68 from the Amache high school; 4) information on social security benefits; 5) three nisei return to Hood River despite its hostility (Japanese section).

Sunday, January 28

Slightly overcast with scattered clouds but largely clear and cold with snow on the ground. Soon the sun began to shine and snow on the roof began to melt.

Mr. and Mrs. Sakai with Shirley called in the afternoon and brought some things—chicken.

· · · ·

Takahashi and Sakai (son and Koga), the latter having visited various localities in California, including San Francisco, Los Angeles, Sacramento, Petaluma, Livingston, the Peninsula reported O.K. everywhere; Sacramento alone [had] bad atmosphere. Koga saw more Japanese in Palo Alto and vicinity.

Monday, January 29

Clear, cold with piled snow everywhere. Thin, scattered clouds. Remained thus throughout the day and most the night.

· · · ·

No news of general importance except gossips and rumors relative to the return to the West Coast continue. Yoshihara visited. Takahashi informed [me] that his bank safety deposit box as well as the safe in his house had been opened by the F.B.I. (?) and the contents examined; but whether some of the papers had been removed or not, his son [was] not informed in his recent visit there in Livingston. But as far as the locality is concerned, it is absolutely safe. So far only the Dois have been menaced in California; they have been unpopular in the community because of their selfishness and their failure to make contributions to the good of the community common interest.* Miyake (Livingston) is of the same type, [yet] he has been free from hostility.

YAMATO ICHIHASHI TO JESSIE TREAT [11]

10-H 12-D
Amache Colorado
Jan. 29, 1945

Dear Mrs. Treat:

Miss Westbrook (who had been notified of our possible return in March) wrote me under the date of Jan. 22nd by air mail, but it reached me by the last and only delivery Saturday noon (27th), and [she] informs me that she will leave the house by Feb. 1st—not any later than [the] 15th. She stated that a copy of the letter is being sent to you and so I need not repeat its contents. As far as we are concerned, it does not matter when she vacates the house, but if I had known this earlier, we could have arranged [matters] without making any impositions on you. We have bothered you too much and this imposition adds more and we are very sorry. As to her suggestions I replied: 1) Have the gas and electricity shut off; 2) retain the telephone if possible; and 3) leave the keys with you or Misses Stoltenbergs.

I asked her to have the gas and electricity disconnected because I am still uncertain when we can start [out] for the campus: 1) The WRA has failed thus far in making anything definitive relation to the restoration of evacuees to the Coast States (those who returned had made applications directly to [the] Army Command before the announcement of the new policy);[12] apparently the local agents are not hurrying to get rid of residents here, perhaps being anxious to

---

*A clipping from the *Palo Alto Times* that Ichihashi inserted in his diary contained the following information. On January 18 and 19, 1945, four men in the Auburn, California, area committed arson and attempted "to intimidate and dynamite a human being." "The men are accused of firing at a packing shed at the home of Sumio Doi, 26, Japanese-American who returned from an evacuation camp at Lamar, Colo. early in January with his aged parents, and then firing shots over his house and placing dynamite under the packing shed a night later."

hold their jobs as long as possible. 2) The so-called "leaders" among residents insist that they "sit tight" with many, but empty, promises. But we are hoping to depart here in March or April, if possible. The majority of residents stand askance, worrying much, and yet I can not do much under the existing circumstances, but am hoping for the clarification of the situation. It has been snow-bound for more than a week, but we are well. Hoping that this note will find you and Payson in the best of health, I am,

> Very affectionately yours,
> Yamato Ichihashi

DIARY

Tuesday, January 30

Slightly overcast and very cold (5 degrees); later, the sun shone but remained rather cold, and thus throughout the day.

Visited Kuramatsu's studio and found the official aspect of arrangement for this exhibition had been completed; Kuramatsu was working on new pictures to be exhibited. Kurahashi came and insisted that we go to his place for lunch and we did. . . .

We are having chicken sukiyaki for dinner at home; Yuhora was invited as usual. After the dinner, Kuramatsu came.

Later younger Ono accompanied by K [Ono] came to say goodbye; he is leaving for Alamosa tomorrow morning.

Miura still holds up his instruction to inquire into amounts of lumber needed by the block residents for boxes and crates since he is afraid that that would tend to cause the people to move thus breaking the sit-tight attitude. . . .

· · · ·

Wednesday, January 31

It is not as cold as yesterday morning, though overcast and gloomy; 8:15 it began to snow (fine and light), but it lasted only for a very short while. The day remained gloomy; the sun shone faintly every now and then.

· · · ·

The "Pioneer": 1) 3rd exchange of internees is being considered by Japan because of the Tule Lake situation announced by the State Department; 2) Boycott proposed in Auburn;[13] 3) 5,000 renounced citizenship in Tule Lake; of these 70–80 are "vicious" said Biddle; 6) open hostel in Pasadena for evacuees; 7) the American Legion of California voices: evacuees should stay away from the West Coast for the duration.

SPECIAL DATA

The opening of the West [Coast] announced earlier became operative on the 20th [of January]. Though individually and privately the people, except a relative few, began to think seriously [about returning], despite their publicly defiant attitude—[their] "sit-tight" attitude [is] because of their dissatisfaction with the WRA "conditions," especially "financial conditions." [14] In the meantime, leaders or schemers got busy; one of their favorite schemes being what appears to be "agricultural colonizations." They say, if the people sit tight, they will get from the government or its agencies $5000 credit per capita or per family to start agricultural colonies or communities on the land also to be leased from the government—these are their hopes, but whether anything is expected to materialize is doubtful. Anyhow, to negotiate, it is necessary to have the appearance of universal dissatisfaction. Thus as their [first] step, they are doing everything legitimate and illegitimate to prevent them from departing from the camp. The schemers are mostly from among block managers and councilmen . . . and their like who had been middlemen tradesmen, *tanben[?]*,* etc., but not farmers who are to work under the management of the schemers, who would get soft but well-paid jobs. They call the schemes "cooperative enterprises" (producers and consumers), comprehensive in character. But will "dumb" farmers bite? In either case, the above schemes are bad and fraught with danger for "farmers," the majority, who will be exploited by a minority—unhealthy.

---

*The meaning of *tanben* is not clear.

DIARY

Thursday, February 1

The morning started overcast and with slight *kirisame* [drizzle]; the ground is very slippery, like glass and rather cold. Later it became warmer and made roads slushy.

Did some writing in the morning and visited the studio for a short while in the afternoon.

At the supper, Miura announced that there would be a block meeting to discuss a 17 point something, as had been rumored for the past few days "as regards the unsatisfactory conditions of relocation in view of the existing conditions outside and that there would be a conference of center delegates from the various centers—3 from each center at Denver." The matter was presented rather vaguely. Will see what happens at the meeting; it is a matter of interest for those who cannot relocate and who don't want to relocate under the stated conditions—the main point being the $25 per capita grant, I think.

Friday, February 2

Clear but not cold as yesterday morning; but soon became overcast, gloomy and cold. Partially cleared up and the sun shines warm and melts the snow on the ground so that roads and paths are slushy.

. . . .

Kimi Miyake [of Livingston] wrote saying the neighbors are kind and considerate; the kids are back in school; everything is O.K.

RESEARCH ESSAY [15]

The Problem of Resettlement

THE WRA PROGRAMS: FINANCIAL AIDS AND PROCEDURES
ADOPTED, PLANS OF RESETTLEMENT AND MONEY GRANTS
($25 PER CAPITA)

Categories:

1) The aged single men and women; widows and widowers with minor children.

2) Businessmen and tradesmen and white-collared workers.
3) Professional men: religionists, doctors, dentists, technicians, engineers, lawyers, etc.

I shall resist from reporting on my research work and will write on recent developments in the camps. Through the camp paper, "The Pioneer" Extra dated December 17, the local WRA announced 1) the West Coast will be reopened to evacuees, and they will be free to return to their homes on January 2 and after, and 2) that the relocation camps will be closed in six–twelve months, and 3) that the government reached this decision because sons and husbands of the camp residents have rendered loyal services as soldiers to this country. The news was welcomed more or less by the majority of residents as they are anxious to live in their homes; that was the immediate reaction. Then followed official information relative to the WRA procedure of restoring the people to the West Coast and elsewhere; the information given out to date is specific in some respects, but vague and confusing as a whole.

For instance, the government will bear transportation costs and will allow evacuees a sum of $25.00 per capita upon having reached their respective destinations on the following conditions: a) each family or individual to submit his plan how he expects to provide for his own livelihood, (and to support his family, if he is a family-head); and b) if such a plan is approved by the WRA. The above procedure creates difficulties. The majority was uprooted economically, financially, occupationally or residentially or else in an all-embracing manner. Some doubtless still have parts of their savings but many have foolishly spent all of their savings because of the enforced, unnatural mode of living. As a financial aid, they cannot see much in the proposed grant of $25.00 per capita in their planning for livelihood, and they don't know what to do.

In this category are found businessmen and white-collared gentlemen—workers as well as professionals who have depended and have to depend on Japanese communities (urban districts) and agricultural enterprises (farming communities). The more active and less fortunate financially have become "leaders" in the camps; they are "adventurers" perhaps more unscrupulous and irresponsible, and now they have turned out planners, enterprisers, schemers for their own benefits but in the name of the Japanese public interest.

They are dreaming to exploit their own people; it smells that way. They have launched their subterranean campaigns—"in unity lies the strength" and "nobody should move out of the camps." None of their schemes has yet assumed a definite shape though I know one of them to be the agricultural "colonization" scheme.

The most helpless are widows and widowers with minor children and the aged single men and women. These [?] elements probably constitute 10% or more of the camp population; they [?] roughly number several thousands. They have to be handled as cases of public charge. This is the most tragic aspect of the picture. The Japanese people despise to seek public charity of any kind; they have never sought it in the past except in a very insignificant number. The Japanese privately took care of the needy, but this they no longer can [do] because of their own financial status. The WRA says that Congress appropriated special funds to aid such cases but the procedure adopted in regard to these cases is rather complicated. The Federal funds are to be used apparently in conjunction with county and state aid organizations. We have not been given as yet definite information on the subject. Many are fearful of being forced to live in the old people's' homes—institutions for the aged.

Those who have the best prospect of re-establishing themselves in the West Coast are land-owning farmers who kept their properties by leasing them individually or in groups; they even made money due to high prices paid for horticultural and agricultural produce in 1942–1944, during their absence.[16] But in most cases, the leases have been renewed for the year 1945 because of the WRA failure to make public [in time] the proposed new policy, removal of the exclusion (due to ignorance or the lack of foresight). This means that the farmers in question cannot return even to their homes which have been leased along with farms and their equipments. They have to wait. Besides it is useless to put up with inevitable discomforts and inconveniences in case they return; they need not look after their farms until about September as far as next year's crops are concerned. Hence they are not in a hurry to depart.

Another group (laborers) which can resettle in the West Coast are those who work by the day, house-cleaners and "gardeners," and other miscellaneous workers, provided such types of work are made available to them. Their chief problem is that of "housing"; to solve this problem the WRA and the local communities must get together. The former is supposed to be anxious to resettle the camp residents outside while the latter need performers of such services as mentioned above. At any rate, unless "housing" is provided it is of no use of talking of relocation (an unfortunate term), in reality resettlement; it cannot be effected. The explanation that other people are occupying their (evacuees') residences does not solve the real problem.

As far as industrial jobs are concerned, the Japanese face many difficulties in filling them; racial prejudice is employed against them by the interested. The Army plants willing to employ them have no housing provisions for families of their workers; besides they cannot earn enough to financially support their families residing elsewhere. In the past, these families continued to live in the camp, but this practice is no longer possible. Here is another hitch, a dilemma.

INFORMATION RELATING TO THE REMOVAL
OF THE MILITARY EXCLUSION ORDER

Information which has been made public to date, is chronologically as follows: 1) Myer's notification to Lindley was announced to the camp residents on Dec. 17, 1944. It was as follows: The military authorities will remove the Exclusion Order to the West Coast, effective on Jan. 2, 1945. This was accompanied by the Western Defense Command's "Notice for all Residents of the Center," which classifies the residents into the following three categories: 1) a group of persons "free to move about or reside in any part of U.S."; 2) a group of persons "considered potentially dangerous to the military security" and continue to be excluded from the coast states East and West; 3) and a group of persons whose status has not yet been determined. And on December 20 an Army team of four men arrived here to notify individually those who are to be excluded from the Western and Eastern coast states. To date nobody knows the exact number of persons who have been placed in this exclusion list; it is rumored here that they [number] from 70 to 80. If true, these being all men, the number will increase considerably since their families will likely remain with them.

On Jan. 3rd the WRA made public its "program of resettlement" in detail: 1) all the centers will be closed in 6–12 months, 2) those who expect to "relocate" must formulate and present to the WRA their individual "plans of resettlement" for its approval; without such approved plans, relocatees will receive no financial aid from the WRA—which consists of railway transportation costs of persons and properties directly to their destinations, plus costs of meals while traveling and $25.00 per capita upon reaching their destination. In this connection, 3) the WRA's policy as regards indigent cases touched upon in the Dec. 17 statement is to quote:*

---

*Ichihashi did not fill in the "WRA's policy" here.

Some of the persons in this category have been receiving from the WRA as social grants a sum of $8.50 per capita per month; these have been told that the same amount of money will be granted after their resettlement outside.

KEI ICHIHASHI TO JESSIE TREAT [17]

Amache, Colo.
February 5 [1945]

Dear Mrs. Treat:

Since January 21st, we all Japanese are free to go back to the West Coast, but it seems to me that very few people have decided to move. In our block two families—eleven members altogether and they are relatives—left for Atwater, California, near Merced on the 20th of January. This is the only group moved to the West in this block so far. And I have just received a letter from a young woman in that group. She has two children seven and five, and her husband is in the hospital somewhere about France, he [was] wounded in the recent action. The letter says: our trip was very pleasant. And everyone around her is same as we left them. The neighbours bring in milk and eggs to help us out, so far everything is going along swell. The children start going to school today; they enjoy it very much and the teachers and the pupils are really nice and so on.

When she came to our apartment to say goodbye, I made tea for her and her sister-in-law, so that she appreciated [it] and wrote the letter to thank for [it]. I think they are all enjoying the life at their home town now.

Another group is an old couple, who came from Washington. They had decided to go back home, and planned to see their sons before they leave for the west coast, and went to Chicago about two weeks ago. Their elder son is working at one of the largest stores in the city; they also went to Kentucky to visit the fort to see the other son in the army. The old couple had a nice trip and returned to the center a couple days ago. I think they will leave here soon. One family [who] used to live in Sacramento is planning to go back to California also. But their tenants are still not able to find a house to move into, so they are just waiting to receive a letter from the tenants and they are ready to go home. And I have heard that in our block this family is the only one who was very much pleased, when the people in the center got the notice of the ban is lifted. However all Japanese people will gradually move out. I know, but they are still afraid and hesitating.

I am sorry to hear [about] Professor Duniway's death and also Professor Lesley's, especially young Bussett's sad news.[18] When I think [of] his old parents' grief I feel so sad. I am just wondering which son was William, the younger one who graduated [from] the medical school a few years ago or the other one?

The story of your "Jury Duty" is interesting to me, but I am sorry that you spent so much time for that case when you were enough busy without any extra jobs. It seems to me [that] most female labourers are aggressive and especially emigrants: they always try to take some advantages as much as they could.

My "simple living and high thinking" life is ending rapidly. Now I am going to a dentist and preparing to go back to sunny California. I have heard that in the outside world even dentists are scarce and they are so busy. So I have decided to fix my teeth in the center. At the hospital in the center, as a rule, dentists handle emergency cases only. But I asked one of the dentists to fix my teeth and I am going to the hospital once a week. In 1944 I had so much physical trouble from spring to late autumn, but I am very well now so that when I go back to California I shall be able to enjoy everything.

I am so very sorry to know that Prof. Treat was attacked by his old enemy.[19] I think it will be a sort of warning. Please tell Prof. Treat, Kei says, we are all in, or almost in the rank of retired persons, so please do not work so hard.

Thank you for the sweet present for Valentine's. I always very much appreciate your kindness.

Affectionately yours,
Kei Ichihashi

DIARY

Wednesday, February 7

Cleared up at midnight and the morning was clear and warm, but in the afternoon scattered clouds covered the sky; still is nice and warm for the season.

. . . .

Mrs. Kuramoto came and stated that a small, interested group is discouraging everybody from relocating from the center in order to effect its own schemes, which are being kept secret, but their intended petition [is] to the government to get money or credit in the name of the residents who are all, according to these schemers, incapable of earning their livelihood unless such financial aids [are given]; this necessitates the sit-tight attitude of the people. Block managers are refusing to give any information, saying that the people can read the "Pioneer," along with some councilmen! "The Japanese government said the people should remain in the centers and that the West Coast is dangerous," but no such information is made public. They intend to ask the Spanish consul to find out the government stand on this point! Stupid: they don't realize their own status. She said that Kuramoto said to the committee of eight on the problem that "I [Ichihashi] would not publicly interest myself in this matter," so had informed Uragami who said that he had interviewed me. This is an absolute lie; he has not called on me nor has he ever asked me about my stand on the subject or for that matter on any other subjects. Why these interested people lie about others and in particular about me puzzles and irritates me. If they want to scheme, why don't they do it on their own responsibility? All [I] said to those who inquired [is] that I will help, if possible, in making suggestions as to ways and means of resettlement; they can't stay in the camp. But they twist!

Thursday, February 8

Somewhat overcast and cold, clearing though; while it remained more or less cloudy, it turned a rather warm day.

Komatsu[?], one of the block managers, is being ousted by his colleagues who made J.S.[?] order him to quit; apparently he is not with the gang of "plotters," but his block residents want him to stay on the job. Another case of Ed versus block managers? Mrs. Kuramoto said, she is worried about the doings of her husband who along with his group is apparently hoping to create "an opportunity for himself of making money" by scheming! It is a strange psychology these individuals are developing.

· · · ·

A block meeting was held to present and discuss such requests to be made of the Spanish Consul who is expected to visit presently.

Miura announced that Myer would address residents next Sunday in the high school auditorium.

Friday, February 9

More or less cloudy as usual and cold, clearing up somewhat and the sun is shining. Later rather a strong wind but no sands (being wet) flying.

Kawashiri (chairman of the council),[20] Furuya (treasurer),[21] and Uragami called and said that they were selected as delegates to the Salt Lake Conference which is to begin its session on the 16th.[22] They want me to go over their proposals and if need be, make suggestions; I consented to go over them. They are coming this evening.

Went to Kuramatsu's for *udon* with K. in the evening.

The three council delegates came bringing with them various documents relative to relocation, including the one in which are compiled problems and questions submitted by center residents (17 points) reduced to 15. This list they will discuss with Myer and also at the Salt Lake Conference. There are many points which need clarification and whose English should be improved. This they asked me to do and I consented. In the name of the Council, they presented me a box of cigars.

Saturday, February 10

As usual, cloudy but not very cold; and it practically remained thus, though cleared up more or less.

Formulated a summary of problems and questions at the request of the three delegates and handed it back to Kawashiri as promised at 1:00 P.M.

. . . .

The Pioneer: 1) Myer to speak to residents at 2:30 tomorrow; 2) to date 732 in the Army; 3) new regulations on short-term passes; 3) handicapped to be interviewed; 4) family interviews without appointments; 4) local atmosphere news; 5) [J.S.?] movements of the center population: December 7, 567 to 6,039 by January 29; births: 350 and deaths: 80. Of the 6,000, 2,000 are expected to return to the West Coast states; 6) *senryō* [military occupation?] on the closure; 7) the 3 delegates to the Salt Lake Conference and an outline of the agenda of this center.

Sunday, February 11

Clear and rather cold and frost aplenty. Turned out a nice warm
day and remained so until 4:00 P.M. when it became cloudy and
windy.

Mrs. Yoshihara came to say good-bye; they are leaving early tomorrow morning.

. . . .

Blue Star Service Club will ask [for] special aid for its members!
Myer's talk was postponed until 6:30 this evening. Okubo and Tanji
came and we went to hear Myer. When I got there, Kawashiri and
Takata asked me to translate the high-lights, I refused. (Takata did
it as had been prearranged). Why should I mix with these schemers.
Myer's talk was homely and to the point.

Monday, February 12

Started somewhat overcast, but turned out to be another warm day
in the early summer, though became more or less overcast in late
afternoon.

Myer met block managers this morning and will meet the councilmen to discuss the problems and questions submitted by center
residents; then the Blue Star Service Club which will ask for special
financial aid to those who are related to the men in the armed service! A manifestation of the bread line complex. . . .

. . . .

Thursday, February 15

Essentially clear with thin, scattered clouds and warm; a strong
north wind developed, but no sands, just more cloudy.

Mrs. Kura reported that when the Blue Star Club asked for its
members a special monetary aid, Myer replied that such a request
tends to hurt the feeling of nisei soldiers and therefore should not be
made. I anticipated it—it is [at?] the best no more than a manifestation of *kojiki konjō* [beggarly disposition].

No news in particular.

Observation: the attitude towards resettlement is already changing and more serious thinking is [being] done to their individual

plans as the day dreams fade away which were created and stimulated by the so-called "leader," or schemers.

Monday, February 19

Overcast as usual but not so cold as yesterday; it has thus remained throughout the day but with a wind making it colder.

Looked into the tax-returns.

Yoso [Kuramoto], PFC, Headquarters and Service, 171st Infantry Battalion (Separate) Camp Shelby, Mississippi paid a long visit. He is a truck driver, while W[oodrow?] is a bugler. They get $4.00 more per month than privates.

. . . .

Thursday, February 22

Clear and not so cold; later it became warm, though the sky is covered with thin, scattered clouds. It thus remained into the night.

. . . .

We went to Kuramotos for supper because Yoso was leaving tomorrow morning. Kuramoto showed me the list of questions presented by block managers to Martin, Spanish Vice Consul: mostly stupid, including whether Spain [can] find out the attitude of the Japanese government as to what the center residents should do as regards the WRA's closure policy, etc. He confirmed his wife's report on Myer's reply to the request of the families with men in the armed services. He seemed hopeful of getting loans (en masse); individually quite possible, if tests are met satisfactory. "$25 per capita not enough," when boiled down. He and his group are still working with that desire; hence are apt to exaggerate facts and rumor unfavorable for relocation. For instance, he was positive that the "sit-tight" determination is universally true in Gila and Rohwer!

The Shibatas left for Livingston and the Kobayashis, for Sacramento, except the husband.

Friday, February 23

Overcast and mild; a cold wind, though [later] cleared up and sunny.

Two pictures came from Kuramatsu. Yuhora helped by Takemura prepared boards to make frames; they helped Fukuyama's exhibition.

Went out [with] K. for *misoshiru** supper at Kurahashi; returned his book on *ōyōmei-gaku*† in Japan.

Partly prepared the tax returns.

The residents are beginning to depart from the center though slowly.

· · · ·

Saturday, February 24

Thin clouds cover the sky, cold with frost. More or [less] cleared up and the sun shines through the clouds and warm.

· · · ·

Tom wrote that he and Woodie were made sergeants, the latter with "T." [23]

Monday, February 26

Clear and cold with snow-covered grounds and some scattered clouds. The sun shines brightly, but a cold wind renders it cold even though the snow melts late in afternoon; it became mild when the wind died.

Received a note from Tom Bailey, the chairman of a committee [in the Stanford history department] to find candidates to succeed to the chairs of Ichihashi and Treat, asking me to recommend those who may be considered for my chair. Borton, Fahs and Biggerstaff of respectively Columbia, Pomona, and Cornell. Borton is o.k. Fahs is primarily a political scientist. Borton is primarily an economic historian, but I think he can develop cultural history of Japan. Spinks should be considered; his qualifications are well-known though still inexperienced as an academic teacher. I consider him as the safest bet among those whom I have trained. [24]

· · · ·

Called on Okubo; he told me that he had been summoned by the hospital director in re: his false-teeth making, but apparently he is

---

*Traditional Japanese meal featuring *miso*. bean-paste soup.
†The doctrines of Wang Yang-ming, a neo-Confucian scholar in China.

let alone. . . . Tanji came later; he is going to Texas to look around, but would eventually return to Livingston when his children decide to do so. The talk turned on resettlement; it is felt that from April on, the people will begin to move out.

. . . .

Tuesday, February 27

Partly overcast and sunshine but cold and windy. Thus it has remained throughout the day, save the wind became stronger in the afternoon.

Takahashi finished the gourds; they will be souvenir-curios.

McFarling called in the afternoon and talked in general about resettlement problems. Johnson still sticks to his "pets," the block managers, but Lindley is gradually shifting towards the council. The two bodies, if placed under two different officials, it would be better, he opined. He hoped that Lindley would have full confidence in the council, which [would] greatly improve the relationship between the Administration and the residents. He characterized block managers as "conservative" while the council is positive and constructive. He would like to meet Buddhist representatives in re: resettlement. Promised me to have a copy of his reports made for my own reference.[25] The delegates returned on Sunday. The conference finally adopted a resolution on the maintenance of the centers for the duration of the war; this was fought for by the delegates from Gila, Poston and Heart Mountain, and the rest finally joined them. So reported to McFarling by one of our delegates (Kawashiri?). The residents of the 3 centers must be largely from cities and those rural districts (farmers who do not own land). The churches in Livingston (Methodist) and in Cortez (Presbyterian) are both independent and are not under the control of boards of missions and therefore ministers have no control over them and their belongings; there are others in the came category. In order to convert churches into hostels not simple.

Wednesday, February 28

Overcast, gloomy and cold; thin clouds partly clear up and the sun came out, and in the afternoon it became warm despite a breeze.

Wrote to Bailey in re: candidates for the chairs of Ichihashi and Treat: Biggerstaff, Borton and Fahs; nominated Spinks.

The "Pioneer": 1) short wave sets (several) had been seized here;[26] 2) Ickes on the closure of the relocation centers; 3) census shows 6,197 residing [here], an increase of 603 since the last October; 4) exchange boat unlikely; 5) anti-Japanese agitation in California; 6) seven teenagers arrested for breaking high school windows by rocks—charged with juvenile delinquency; 7) news along the West Coast, Japanese section.

1) Ickes: since January 2, 539 resettled in the West Coast: 413 in California, 43 in Washington, and 33 in Oregon. Also 32 in Arizona, 352 in Illinois, 120 in Ohio and 85 in New York, 78 in Michigan, 68 in Colorado, 63 in New Jersey, etc. a total of 1,200. . . .

. . . .

SPECIAL DATA

Livingston, Cortez and Cressey Japanese farmers own 3,000 acres of vineyards and are organized in a producers' cooperative; these 3,000 acres are "leased" to one Momberg to manage, at the time of evacuation. He got a salary of $500 per month plus 20% of gross profit (a big inducement was necessary to get him to accept the job). The growers made a lot of money during the past three years (but of course not as much as they could have made under their own management). The vineyard on the average produced 8 tons per acre. The grapes sold so far about $100 per ton, or 3,000 × 8 or 24,000 tons; if @ $100 per ton = $2,400,000. The number of land-owners: Livingston 64, Cortez 28, and Cressey 17. Each made money according to the amount produced on his vineyard (Y. with 60 acres cleared $7,000 last year, '44). Besides the individual profit for about 100 units or 30 acres, the cooperative has accumulated $500,000 which is described as a common fund to be distributed as dividend among its members (details of the individual allotment yet to be worked out). All the mortgages have been paid and the vineyards are maintained in an excellent condition. The contract will expire at the end of 1945. Momberg has made lots of money for himself but legitimately. The bookkeeper, Mrs. Austin and the lawyer, Calden, hired by the co-op, are checking the management. An example of the farsighted and well-considered case among Japanese farmers with profit to everybody involved.

DIARY

Thursday, March 1

Clear though with scattered clouds and rather mild. A strong wind developed [and] became stronger, kicking up sands just before noon. Sand-storm.

Mailed the tax returns to San Francisco office.

Invited the Kuramotos to dinner: chicken *sukiyaki*, *sunomono* [vinegared salad], *ebi* [shrimp], *tamagoyaki* [fried egg], *kamaboko* [fish cake]; very good. They stayed for a long while. Kuramoto said Woodrow is promoted to the rank of corporal. Tomlinson turned over $150 confiscated from gamblers to the Blue Star Service Club. Freight will be delivered to residences instead of by depots except in Chicago. Express?

Personally, he [Kuramoto?] is stuck because unless farm communities are re-established, he cannot do his former business (handling). His partners set up machinery for handling agricultural produce in Ontario, Oregon. Washington is politically hostile and it is therefore better to resettle somewhere in the mid-West or East to take advantage of the propinquity of main markets. But there are only two forms of agricultural enterprises: family and capitalistic; my own thought is that most of the people will resettle in their hometowns and communities. It is the question of *time*. He is puzzled as are most of the men formerly engaged in that [line] of business. They have to be constructive to promote their mutual interests with producers, if they are to succeed at all.

Saturday, March 3

Clear, cold with frost; turned out a sunny day though with a cold wind.

Broke up the coal box to make packing boxes with Y; T. helped a little.

The "Pioneer": 1) Japanese section prints in full the resolution passed by the Salt Lake City conference of 7 centers (Manzanar not participating) February 16–22, pages 1 and 3. English: 2) nisei's house shot at in Lancaster, California; 3) during February, 160 left the camp, 46 to the West Coast and the rest elsewhere; 4) the Supreme Court refused to review the Korematsu [case] (a nisei at San Leandro who refused to evacuate); 5) the case of 2 arrested and sentenced to "unlawful activities;" 6) James R. Young gave an anti-Japanese talk at Fresno;[27] 7) a nisei girl was put on probation for the theft of $600 in Chicago, named [K] (18 years old); 8) another nisei [S] in Oakland threatened by phone; 9) hostel in L.A. The boy who broke a window (high school) suspended from school while the remaining 6 deprived of the gate-pass privilege for 30 days.

Received canceled check (insurance) from Bank of America.

Saw the talent show: the auditorium was filled to the capacity for this variety show; the scenery was excellent considering the circumstances; the performance was just as expected in the amateur-performers. The *manzai* [comic dialogist] rendered a take-off on the "relocation conditions" in the form of a *kagōuta* ["sing-songy" poem]; 1–10 was most outstanding. The kabuki was mediocre. Dances were mostly by children. Yuhora, Takemura and I went, but Kuramatsu changed his mind at the last minute!

Sunday, March 4

Clear and mild, a regular spring day. But a wind began to blow at noon. It thus remained. The wind in the evening.

Mrs. Kuramatsu called and stayed for a while.

[Masachika] Yonemura followed and stayed till 9:00. Talked things in general and relocation in particular. I told him to call tomorrow about 2:00 P.M. so that we [could] call on McFarling together, as he has expressed his desire to meet representatives of the Buddhist group which has no official connection with the Administration as such, despite the fact that this group is the largest group in the center population. It is, however, politically inarticulate and for that reason it is ignored as a group.

Monday, March 5

Started with slight snow (soon stopped) and a cold wind [started]. Thus it has remained throughout the day and into the evening. Snow again at 10:00 P.M.

. . . .

Took Yonemura to call on McFarling in regards Buddhist group about resettlement. I suggested that Buddhists form their own com-

mittee on the subject and that the committee in turn select representatives to a center-wide committee which may include various organizations, groups interested to secure and disseminate information
among the residents. The council should take the initiative in forming such a committee, including representatives of 5 wards plus.
McFarling will talk to the councilmen.

. . . .

Report meeting of the 3 council delegates at the Salt Lake City
Conference at 7:00 in high school auditorium; it is held at Terry
Hall instead. The attendance was poor, about 150 persons, mostly
old men. The reports were informative on the whole—Kawashiri:
the work of the conference [was described day by] day. Furuya: interpretation of the conference work and observations: [railway] de-
pots, hotels and difficulties; prices of meals twice as high as before;
jobs plentiful and sentiment favorable. Uragami complained of residents' indifference; center people's conduct inside and outside—
darashinai [slovenly]; kids: no schools after June.

Saturday, March 10

Started somewhat overcast but soon cleared up and turned out a
warm, sunny day.

Kay Hamatani, who with 6 others, had spent 3 weeks in San
Francisco and Sacramento called and reported that the situation existing in the 1st visit has reversed favorably to returning evacuees
with all kinds of employment opportunities open to them; the sentiment favorable. The situation in Topaz was bad due to misguidance:
the "sit-tight" attitude was being stimulated. The Council of [Bud-
dhist?] churches proposed with Friends to finance in converting the
San Francisco Buddhist Church into a hostel; the Topaz Buddhist
Board does not favor it. Hamatani found some embezzlements committed by those responsible; the [account?] book has been destroyed
($18,000–20,000 involved) plus insurance premium [of] 10% added
by the agent (Japanese) [in] conjunction with board members. The
crookedness runs through the financial management of the temple.
At the time of evacuation, member properties were deposited there
for storing @ $1.00 a piece; none of these has been [returned?] to
their owners (resettled or at Tule Lake) despite WRA efforts to get
them out. Anything that tends to reveal the real state of financial affairs has been fought against by those who are responsible. . . .

The "Pioneer": 1) [J. Edgar] Hoover: "the FBI has nothing to do with returning evacuees"; 2) the Salt Lake City Conference resolution is outlined; 3) 171st Infantry Battalion, Separate, at Shelby, Mississippi [will be] "inactivated" as such on February 18; its members will be distributed elsewhere, including overseas service; 4) more than 200 nisei working in Washington, mostly in government services; 5) another case of violence at Visalia [in California's Central Valley].

Sunday, March 11

Started clear and bright and mild. Later windy but warm.

Went to Kuramotos with Kei for lunch (chicken and sashimi); the latter I did not like.

Kuramoto: hereafter the Granada will be a flag-station for west-bound trains.

Tuesday, March 13

Started somewhat overcast but clearing off and rather mild; it so continued throughout the day (overcast but very warm).

. . . .

. . . Two men went recently to Fresno to investigate the existing conditions there; one, who contracted to take 50 men to work on a large farm, insisted that he had seen no Filipinos threatening them, which the other insisted upon it as a fact. . . .

. . . .

Wednesday, March 14

Overcast and mild. Turned out to be a warm summer day.

. . . .

Found out what I had to do to obtain release from the status of a parolee.[28] [Takata] suggested items of facts to include and write to

Honorable Edward J. Ennis
Department of Justice
Alien Enemy Control Unit
Washington, D.C.

. . . .

The Pioneer: 1) Information regarding property storage; 2) an Oregon court ordered return of a nisei farm leased to a Caucasian couple to the owner; 3) returnees attacked with fire and bullets— San Jose, Alviso, the first case in Santa Clara County. . . .

Thursday, March 15

Somewhat overcast and cold with frost. But as it cleared, it became rather a warm day; in afternoon a strong wind—sand-storm.

Prepared a note to Ennis requesting release from the status of a parolee.[29]

Mrs. Kuramoto came bringing a walking-stick which her husband and a friend of his made for me; it is a cedar cane. Stayed till lunch time talking on usual subjects and asking me many questions relative to the resettlement. I was to take Kuramatsu to the relocation office but the sand-storm made him refuse to go like a spoiled child; he is painting.

. . . .

Friday, March 16

During [morning?] a strong gale continued and the morning started overcast and with a strong wind and sand-storm worst as yet. Rather warm.

Kuramatsu was to go with me to the Relocation Office but wished to postpone. Is he afraid, if so, of what? I am puzzled.

Went to [Donald T.] Horn's office but he was out attending a meeting; I left my letters to *Ennis* with the Yamazaki girl to have it glanced [at] and if o.k., seal it and mail at Post Office. O.K. and mailed.

The sand-storm became terrific with the development of a gale in the afternoon.

Went with K to K[uramatsu']s place despite the storm and had a good, *misoshiru* [family-style] supper.

Saturday, March 17

Somewhat overcast and chilly; later cleared up and late in the afternoon a strong wind developed and a sand-storm. But it became rather warm.

. . . .

The "Pioneer": 1) a nisei soldier killed in France (Sakamoto);
2) 63 nisei who had refused to report for induction sentenced to
serve 3 years in penitentiary; 3) again Hood River returnees;*
4) check WRA property before the departure; 5) resettlement financial aid of "needy" evacuees assured; 6) Horn resigns effective
April 1. Japanese section: 1) block managers requested the Spanish
Consul to find out the attitude of the Japanese government in regard to the closure of relocation centers in the name of "日本臣民一同
[the Japanese residents together]"; but who authorized them?
2) statistics relative to the movements of center evacuees; 4) Good
Neighbor Movement organized (East and West) in the West Coast
with Pearl Buck as its head; Japanese problems, its present focal
point.

Sunday, March 18

Overcast and cool; cleared up [and] turned out to be a warm day
but a cold, strong wind (no sand as yet). Overcast again and a
stronger wind.

Sakais with Shirley called in afternoon and brought a chicken and
a large bottle of sake; stayed for quite a while. Told them, we are
leaving here in about a month.

Woodrow sent a telegram to Kei asking for $200.00! At [Fort]
Meade, Indiana.

KEI ICHIHASHI TO JESSIE TREAT [30]

Amache, Colo.
March 19 [1945]

Dear Mrs. Treat:

Thank you for your kind letter dated the 3rd of March.[31] One after another something happens so that we are still in Colorado, and
don't know yet exactly when we shall be able to start for California,
although we applied for Pullman [train] reservations today, so it will

---

*Many of the evacuees who returned to the Hood River area in Oregon faced open
hostility from the local residents. In January, the local American Legion Post removed the
names of sixteen nisei servicemen from the Hood River honor roll. Only after national
attention and a direct order from the national commander of the Legion were the names
restored, on March 12, 1945.

be sometime in April, I think, and we shall write you the date of our departure has been fixed.

Ichihashi is quite active now, and doing something for people in the center and trying to help these helpless people. We have visitors almost every day, and sometimes twice or three times a day. Yesterday morning a woman came and stayed till twelve noon. She used to live in the same block at Tule Lake and she visited our place very often. In the evening right after supper, two persons came and talked about all sorts of problems, from the problem of the resettlement to the latest war news, and stayed until nine o'clock. As you know I don't do any cooking or wash dishes, shopping or marketing, but still don't have much time to do my own work.

During [the] last two months, five families went back to the west coast from our block, and a few young men and women went to Chicago and other big cities to seek jobs. Most families will start to move after June when schools in this center are closed. And at the present there are not much works on any farms until June. So people are still thinking about their plans for the future and sit still. I have received a letter from a woman in Milwaukee, Wisconsin. She went there last fall with her boys who were in a high school. She was brought up at Mayfield[32] and went to Sacramento and lived there till the evacuation, as her husband was doing an automobile business there. Since they were evacuated they didn't see much hope in Sacramento and finally decided to stay out in the Midwest. She wrote me that they were still in a hotel, because they could not find a suitable house to live in. And it said "If finding homes were easier, this city would be a nice place for people to resettle." I have heard that many Japanese families moved into that city already, and they are having the same difficulties.

You said in your last letter "The blossoming trees are blooming and daffodils are dancing in the wind." It sounds like Paradise to all of us. Here we had a warm day today, but a week ago it was very cold and snowed a little. We have no grass, no green leaves yet, and everything is naked. Then the famous Colorado wind has started to blow, so that sands are flying in the air. This is a typical spring weather in Colorado. It will be about the Easter vacation at Stanford. I hope you will enjoy a nice spring weather.

> Affectionately yours,
> Kei Ichihashi

◘ The war in the Pacific at this time focused on the Philippines, where Allied and Japanese forces were engaged in ferocious fighting. After several months of combat, the Japanese had lost almost 200,000 soldiers. During February and March, American and Japanese forces clashed on Iwo Jima, with both sides suffering heavy casualties. In mid-March, American fliers began regular bombing of Okinawa. And on April 1, American troops landed on the southern tip of Okinawa. The planned invasion of the Japanese home islands had begun.

During the last month of his own internment, Ichihashi decided to devote himself actively to helping his fellow evacuees plan on their re-settlement out of camp. He spent hours counseling individuals, attending committee meetings, deliberating with camp officials, and speaking publicly to encourage evacuees to leave camp expeditiously. He became an informal adviser to the Community Council, and his help in encouraging resettlement inspired a camp official to describe him as "pure gold" in an internal memorandum to the WRA office in Washington.[33] His efforts were not universally welcomed by the residents of Amache, some of whom tried to organize more collective ways to return to the outside and to gain increased federal government support for the internees. Ichihashi, whose own attitude might be described as a combination of Japanese self-reliance and American "rugged individualism," continued to denounce these attempts up to the day of his departure from Amache. ◗

DIARY

Monday, March 19

Started with light snow and cold. Soon cleared with sun shine, but a strong wind developed—sand-storm.

Saw Lindley who ok'd Pullman for us; he so told [Relocation Program Officer Walter J.] Knodell. The latter arranged everything needed as preliminary steps for my and Kei's resettlement: notification to Denver Immigration and Naturalization Office for the permit to return as a parolee—it takes 3 to 4 weeks. This is aside from the release application to Ennis. Three sponsors named: Wilbur, Robinson and Treat. Applied for the Pullman reservations (lower and upper) to Los Angeles (Santa Fe) and from L.A. to Palo Alto (the Lark) Southern Pacific. A requisition for boxes and crates made via [evacuee property officer Herbert J.] Vatcher. [?Camp agriculture chief John N.] Spencer in charge will send a man to estimate the need. Pullman for April, 19–20, a day or two before or after. Called on McFarling concerning [my] proposed resettlement course, which he thinks good; also the work of the [Resettlement?] Bureau. He and I will attend the Council meeting tomorrow morning.

. . . .

Tuesday, March 20

A clear, cold wintry morning; it turned out to be a nice, warm day without a customary wind and sand.

Attended the Council session in the morning. . . .

During my absence the chap who estimates lumber [needs] came and said [there were] no army boxes save two, which he promised [us]. But men (Japanese) in charge delivered in afternoon one Army box and another and 4 small boxes and 500 feet of lumber. The head man said, if I needed more, apply at the office for I will be given what is necessary. Boxes are poor and varied[?], fit only [for?] *kojiki* [beggars'] moving. Damned!

Wednesday, March 21

Another nice, clear morning. Turned out to be a rather warm day and remained so until evening when a wind developed.

. . . .

Invited Okubos for chicken sukiyaki dinner. Later Koda dropped in; they stayed till after 10:00. They talked on resettlement. Koda: Block heads versus Council; proposed Horn's send-off party; the necessity of creating a $100,000 fund to meet the problem of Japanese after relocation (co-op funds as a source). As usual, the talk in general and not in particular. Neither has any concrete idea about any specific problem.

. . . .

Monday, March 26

Started as a beautiful morning but a gentle wind soon developed, which became stronger as the day progresses and a result was a bad sand-storm.

Kuramatsu left with the Onos for La Jara [Colorado].

Fixed three cartons (books and printed matters) to be crated; the book-case is emptied.

To the letter written on March 16, a reply came dated 22nd from Ennis saying that "no change will be made at this time in your parole status."

. . . .

Tuesday, March 27

Started again as a nice day but later in morning, a gale developed and caused rather a bad sandstorm (perhaps worst so far).

Wrote the speech and then Yonemura dropped in and told me that Buddhist temples in the hands of faithful are financially mismanaged, but in conjunction with priests, a few of whom are really religious men. He encounters troublesome Shinto [priests?] here even in this camp. Money causes mischiefs of all kinds.

Shūkyō kai no daraku! [corruption of religious groups]

Wednesday, March 28

Started as another clear, beautiful morning, and remained so all day with no wind and no sandstorm.

Fixed most of my things to be shipped, boxed or crated.

Kawashiri came to inquire into the subjects I was to speak on at the mass meeting tomorrow evening: 1) my own opinion on *jikyoku mondai* [current problems or issues] and the Council's new plan on resettlement (*kaisetsu*) [explanation].

. . . .

Thursday, March 29

Started again as a clear, nice morning, but became overcast in spots in the afternoon, though no wind; it is rather warm and if it remains so, it will be lucky for the mass meeting; it so turned out.

Made boxes and crates. Read some.

Attended and spoke at the mass meeting of residents, more than a thousand of them filled the auditorium. [Community Council member Thomas] Kofu reported on the replies to the conference resolution and was followed by Furuya and Uragami both of whom spoke at length. Uragami blundered and heckling by some in the audience, but they kept attention when I spoke. Kawashiri did well as the chairman. Furuya made a flowery speech, while Uragami was full of *temaemiso* [boasting] and unsuccessful. The meeting as a whole was a success.[34]

Friday, March 30

Another nice day, later became overcast in spots but no wind. Nice all day long.

Mrs. Kuramoto came with a vase and canned soups to warn that the block manager, bearded Furukawa,[35] came to her husband and said that his colleagues were insulted when I asked them to cooperate with the council! Fools, and they [can] come if they want, in a body. I will tell them a thing or two. What [do] they think they are anyway; I suppose that they are still dreaming of running the show. That is why they have lost their face with residents and they should know it; if they don't acknowledge it, they will be worse off. Damned fools!

. . . .

Saturday, March 31

Another clear, nice day, though somewhat cool. Turned out to be warm. But a strong wind developed in afternoon and some sands a flying.

. . . .

Learned that Shima had attacked my speech at the mass meeting as "an insult" as the block manager!!!

Kiyohara: There are 4,000 persons 65 and over; of these those who are unable to earn a livelihood will be placed in a center (Manzanar) and will be looked after as charity objects according to Myer, but not by Congress; appropriations will be annual, which will invite politics. Charity OK.

The "Pioneer": 1) Japanese graves desecrated in a Fresno cemetery; 2) property mailing instructions; 3) most of Amacheans relocate in East; 4) the mass [meeting] briefly reported; a detailed report in the next issue. "Extra": the hitherto anti-Japanese elements (Native Sons of the Golden West, American Legion, the Hearst papers) will welcome returning Japanese to the West Coast.

Sunday, April 1

Clear and warm but quite windy. The wind stronger as the day advanced and sands are blowing. This is Easter Sunday and children below 18 were given some candies.

No news of importance. Many persons inform me that most residents began to think more seriously (since my talk [at the mass meeting]) about resettlement and in fact hesitants are now determined to relocate instead of waiting for improved conditions (financial) which for the most part are likely to dissolve into a mere dream. Thus they are becoming more constructive or positive from negative in attitude.

Monday, April 2

It snowed a little and the morning is chilly and miserable as in winter; rains a little. It remained miserable throughout the day into night.

Kozō [kid, i.e., Woodrow] wrote, among other [things], saying for what objects he wanted $200. This should have been [done] before his wire. At any rate, the rest is a complaint over the failure to recognize his wise choice, of which he is proud and condemns our part as an unjustifiable wrong! Yet he begs for money; has he lost his sense of shame? Interprets our part as if it is born of our miserly[?] meanness. We will see.

Called on McFarling and talked over the mass-meeting and the foolish attitude of block-heads. The council is bound to become articulate.

. . . .

Tuesday, April 3

It snowed during early morning and there was an inch of it on the ground at the dawn, cloudy and cold; icicles on eaves. Snow is falling at 8:00 A.M. Snowing continues but does not pile up because of a warm atmosphere.

Kei and [I] discussed *Kozō*'s case with a usual result: no agreement.

Yuhora and I had *udon* for supper, which Kuramatsu had brought last evening.

Kawashiri, Nakamura and Kofu came and requested, as a resolution of the council yesterday, that I undertake to explain the council's new plan to assist resettlement at meetings by districts, 5 in
number (from next Monday). It was accepted with a suggestion that
the audience is free to ask questions and make suggestions to improve [?] the plan so that it can more effectively meet desires of the
residents. The meeting will be arranged accordingly.

Kawashiri brought a copy of the "Pioneer"; the section which
contains an account of the mass-meeting by Konno and another by a
Block Head Fujino,[36] which distorts the talks in order to abuse them
in a manner which manifests block-managers' dissatisfaction, born
of envy and jealousy of the council and due to their own lost face
with residents in general and the WRA. They have done nothing
helpful to the people or committed acts beyond their own jurisdiction. . . . The poor devils; they are making asses of themselves.
Just ignore them for that is the best way of dealing with them. They
are not worthy of any consideration. McFarling: "They are losing
their ground as far as the residents are concerned; their influence
will continue to diminish as time progresses." The people know it
generally.

Monday, April 9

Overcast and mild morning, but soon a gale started, causing the
worst sand storm and continued into the night.

"An appointment has been made for you with Miss Elizabeth
Evans" at 10:30 A.M.; there was no interview to speak [of] and
proved to be a more of social call. Found her an amiable middle-
aged woman. She is a graduate of Minnesota University, later doing
some graduate work there when she had furloughs. 29 years in the
Seijo-Jo-Gakko [Seijo Women's School] in Sapporo. Her friend
Reisner at Kanazawa for 20 years; she was born in Niigata. The
evacuation, a disgrace, she said. Viccio [administrative staff member
Mario Vecchio] dropped in to tell me that we can be cleared [to
leave] because my permit from San Francisco Immigration Office
is on the way. . . .

. . . .

Spoke about the Council's new [resettlement] plan in 7F mess
Hall; more than 50 men and women came despite the terrible sand-
storm. But they remained inarticulate save a few; that was to be
expected as they are not accustomed to speak in public. The net

result—a support. A drunken fool (Sakamoto), a block-head, tried to interfere with my talk but was chased away after severe denunciations from the people. The Block manager of 7F expressed regrets!!!

Wednesday, April 11

Clear and cold with frost; later turned out a nice day. Then it became overcast in the afternoon. But no sandstorm to speak of.

Yonemura called and stayed for quite a while and talked on many things in general and Kuramoto in particular, pointing out his suffering from his superiority complex; he has no confidence of his block residents.

Gave Kei $100.00.

. . . .

At the meeting in 11-E, I did the usual explanation of the new [resettlement] plans and made a report on the leaflet (the handbook)[37] to be distributed. Then took up the Fujino attack and sailed into it to a great satisfaction of residents and the council men.

The "Pioneer": 1) the block managers' attack on Sasaki Sasaburo[?] in a childish manner; they are getting desperate, but they are suffering more and more at their own invitation. Who cares?

President Roosevelt passed away, and funeral is to be held Saturday.

Thursday, April 12

Started clear and warm, but later became overcast and windy. Thus it remained throughout the day and night.

Yonemura called and stayed over for lunch; he said that they are happy over my talk because of their dissatisfaction with the misconduct of "leading" block managers and Kuramoto in particular. The meeting [yesterday] was a great success.

. . . .

Kei sent a wire to Woody [asking] whether he has time to buy what he wants.

The meeting was well-attended, though not as many in the preceding one. Among the audience, at least, one or two block-heads were present: in 7-H, Fujino, in 11-E, Kuramoto; but these remained absolutely silent. Fujino, however, made nasty remarks about the councilmen and I took him up in Kuramoto's block and gave him

what he deserved. In 9-κ, Shima came and started what amounted
to heckling; I saw him for the first time. I took him up and gave him
what he needed. Handled him in a manner to stand up like a man,
but he has no guts; all he could say was that he was "proud" to have
his sons in the Army. Said what is the *legal status*? He thinks, he is
a "leader," but he has not even an elementary understanding of human problems such as are being faced by residents. As McFarling
has predicted, "they" are fast losing their influence, if they have had
any! Poor fools!

Friday, April 13

Started clear and delightful and so remained until late afternoon
when it became overcast and a gale—sandstorm developed. Rain
started about 7 P.M.

Went to the Relocation Office and signed the forms applying
for ration books. Met Lindley who thanked me for what I am doing; he will write to Myer and a copy of it will be sent to me for the
scrap book.[38]

. . . .

The last of serial sessions held in 11-H; perhaps due to hale, sand-
storms and rain, attendance was not as good as in the previous two
sessions. But Furukawa (bearded) (72) did everything to help; an old
man resembling Uragami in many ways: boisterous but straightfor-
ward and harmless. It now appears that the worst of the bunch [of
critics] are K and F and Kayokata[39] and another. These are without
moral guts and principles; little men anxious and ambitious to adver-
tise themselves by heckling. But they have lost out, as it has been
anticipated, but their own stupid moves.

At any rate, the district meetings proved a success in reaching and
making the residents understand and appreciate the Council's work
and new plans: effected good relationships all around.

Saturday, April 14

Overcast, raining, some scanty snow on roofs: what weather! Snowing and miserably cold and windy.

The "Pioneer": 1) Lindley warns against rumors: the closing
date, what I said in re: relocation is true; 2) news along the coast;

3) Japanese section: six men to California to investigate; Sasaburo replies to block managers; 4) Myer: surplus household goods will be loaned to hostels which accommodate 20 persons or more.

No other news of importance except the funeral for the late President was held.

During the night it snowed and a strong gale raged.

Sunday, April 15

Snow on the ground and cold and miserable. It snowed lightly and intermittently all day.

Sugita of the *Shokumin Kyōkai* [settlement association]: Louisiana: 40 acres per family: 100 families; vegetable [production?] hopeful. But lumber for houses (100) is not available; could I help him? The answer was no. Get men who can handle such matters. Sugita who is an illiterate can hardly do it! Apparently nobody is available. The plan is destined to flop.

Fixed crates and boxes.

Again during the night it continued to snow and a gale raged; the rattling of barracks disturbed the sleeping.

Monday, April 16

Started clear but a strong wind continues from the [previous] night: the snow is melting. A gale developed and the ground is growing dry. Improved towards the evening though rather cold with a north wind.

Fixed crates, boxes, etc.

Mrs. Okubo called, thinking we are departing soon.

Went to Kuramatsu's for *udon* supper; there was Watanabe, the chief cook of the block.

No news of importance.

Kofu and Kawashiri called and reported that Myer sent his reply to the Salt Lake Conference "requests and recommendations." A reading of it impresses me that it is about all Myer could say, at least, for the time being. Besides, it leaves chances for further communications on the subject; Myer is willing to discover best means to meet the desire of evacuees. . . .

Tuesday, April 17

Clear but cold with frost; turned out to be a nice, warm day and thus it has remained into the evening.

Went [to] the Relocation Office and got my own clearance, i.e., the Immigration and Naturalization permit. Kei needs a gate pass! Made applications for "grants" for both of us; informed that the procedure was simplified as a result of the telephone conversation between Myer and Lindley (Myer at Tule Lake) so that everybody will be given the $25 grant upon application. No attempt will be made [to distinguish] between the needy and others. Cash will be handed a day before his departure, along with the necessary documents! Later called on Lindley and told him that what Myer said in reply to the "Conference Recommendations" relative to parole release is meaningless.[40] Showed Ennis' identical rejection of the release applications. He copied mine in order that he might request Myer contact with Ennis ("they know each other well") with a view of getting a real "reconsideration" of my application. Lindley was somewhat shocked because mine was rejected, [mine being] the case of a "detainee." I reported these two points to the Council meeting.

Then I saw Vatcher about property shipment, M.W. for pickup. Called on Kiyowara at McFarling's office and spent a couple of hours with him: [we discussed] the general resettlement problems and some of the obstructing block managers; in fact, Lindley mentioned Kuramoto by [name?] (an acquaintance from Tuke Lake on) as one of them.

But I said nothing; they have gone down in the eyes of the Administration and residents as a whole. Not they but the Council will run the show from this time on. They blundered but unintelligent to realize. If they should continue their cheap[?], insinuating opposition, they would get in trouble. They had better be on guard!

Secured a short leave pass to visit Sakais' April 20–24 for both Kei and myself; [administrative staff member Lewis] Fanslan was very gracious about the passes!

Wednesday, April 18

Overcast and cold; this it remained all day, though the [clouds] cleared off in spots.

Okubo called to get the instruction relating to how to label crates and boxes; stayed for a while and talked about the general situation in the camp. Yonemura followed: to show the feeling of the block against Kuramoto, one Yamamoto was elected as its councilman! It gets worse as time passes.

Finished packing and the boxes, crates, suit-case are ready for shipment: 11 pieces by freight and 6 pieces by express (to residence).[41]

. . . .

Thursday, April 19

Clear but cold with a wind; turned out a nice warm day. Thus it has remained throughout the day.

. . . .

Received from Fanslan, the necessary documents and railroad tickets (Granada to Palo Alto) and the Pullman reservations with a government "check" covering the cost to be handed to the Pullman conductor. "Grants and meal money" will be mailed to Stanford in a check. Dropped in at Okubos; he was out. A card of notification of our return was sent to Stanford University post-master.

. . . .

. . . [McFarling] had made a mistake about the "grants." Cash will be given before our departure. Please come a day or two before and get it. So he told me!

Wrote to Treats and Stoltenbergs, [and] Robinson.

YAMATO ICHIHASHI TO JESSIE AND PAYSON TREAT [42]

10-H 12-D
Amache, Colorado
April 19, 1945

Dear Friends:

Many apologies for my long, long silence for which I have no real reasons to offer except that I have been preoccupied with my efforts to help the helpless hundreds, maybe, thousands how to meet problems of resettlement. I have been meeting these individually [and] in groups large and small; I now feel confident that they know how to solve their problems. I am no longer needed here.

Therefore we have decided to depart from this camp. I am able to report definitely that we are to take the California Limited [from] here (Granada) on Friday the 27th (evening) to San Francisco which is to reach the latter at 10:15 P.M. on the 29th Sunday. But it will [probably?] get there several hours later, and therefore we are likely to reach Palo Alto sometime in the morning of Monday, the 30th; we are hoping that it will be so. We are not attempting to catch the [late-evening] theater train from San Francisco. We will let you know from San Francisco when we [will get] to Palo Alto. This was the best arrangement we could make due to the stupidity of the WRA man in charge of railroad transportation.

May we ask you to have the Pacific Gas and Electric Company, to turn on gas and electricity sometime during the next [week]. Sorry again to trouble you, but we have [forgotten] the address of the company. Thank you.

We have many things to tell you when we see you in person, but in the meantime, hoping that you are in the best of health. I am

Very affectionately
Yamato Ichihashi

DIARY

Sunday, April 22

Overcast somewhat and is rather disagreeable. It improved somewhat in afternoon.

Sakai will come for us in the morning; came at 11:30 and reached his house about 12:30. The family was glad to see us, and had a nice lunch. Little too cold to sit outside. Had a nice dinner. . . . A strong wind blew all night and rattled. Did not sleep well.

Monday, April 23

Started overcast and gloomy and rather cold; it rained off and on all day.

Spent the day mostly in [Sakai] parlor; Shirley monopolized everybody; she is a spoiled child, being the last in the family. Talked about everything, but in particular my travel experiences during my life.

Tuesday, April 24

Started more or less cleared up but gloomy; it remained thus throughout the day and night.

The Council holds a dinner in my honor at the 10-H Mess Hall— 7 o'clock P.M.

Left the [Sakai] house at 2:00. In the morning. Okubo telephoned asking me to obtain 3 ducks or 4 chickens to be used for Tuesday dinner in my honor; Sakai, of course, supplied 4 chickens and 2 ducks. A rather funny proposal! Reached the camp about 4:00 as the women wanted to stop at Lamar. Distributed the fowls at the Okubos and they stayed here for a short while.

The Council members and I were photographed at 6:30. The dinner which followed was a success; other than the Council members were present by invitation. Everybody was happy: several from 10-H; a few from 9-H, the "Pioneer" and other blocks. The Council presented me a box of cigars—a token of appreciation. Japanese cops [came] in regards baggage, but ignored them.

Wednesday, April 25

It rained rather heavily in the morning; but stopped near noon and remained thus; a clear moon-lit night.

The Okubos, Kiyowaras, Kayashimas invited us to a dinner at Okubos' room.

Yuhora was visiting but left when Okubo came to tell me that McFarling will call for us at 5:00 to go to his house for dinner. Later old Washizu[43] came to say good-bye, thinking that we were leaving tonight.

Had a hair cut. Also the first shower since the last Saturday.

Packed up everything to be ready for checking.

Matsuoka took the baggage and checked them o.k.; they go by coach train, as the Pullman, which is different, has no baggage cars.

McGovern, Jackson and Terami came to say good-bye.[44]

McFarling came to take us to Okubos for a farewell dinner. Present were Kiyowara, Kayashima, Tanji, Shibuya and McFarling besides the Okubos. Came back at 9:30.

Thursday, April 26

Somewhat overcast and mild; it continued to be overcast and windy and cold.

Yuhora came and then Mrs. Yamiji and talked about her desire to return to her Mountain View home now leased till November.

Kurahashi came and asked me for supper; accepted. Yonemura and Mrs. Nakata paid their calls.

Went to the Relocation Office and got ration books. From the cashier-agent received $62 ($50 grants and $12 for meals en route). Saw Evans and Vatcher. Called on Lindley to advise him what block managers might try to do: he is responsible to see to it that the Council continues to function along the established line. Had lunch at the Workers' Mess Hall; at 1:30 met a group of parolees (60 in number in Town Hall) till 4:00 o'clock. Got photos and a list of re-location offices in the West. Two reported that they were told by the Army representatives that they were excluded from the West; some from Zone A in the West.[45]

Had *misoshiru* supper at Kuramatsu's; Watanabe chef was there too.

Friday, April 27

Overcast and somewhat cold and windy. It started to rain at 10:30. Rain stopped. But thunder and shower followed.

Koda, the co-op chief (9-H) brought an enlarged print of the Council photo.

Kawashiri brought a box of cigars (50), the present from the fol-lowing: Kofu, Uragami, Tani, Koika (Grace), Kitamura (Betty), Nakamura, Kawashiri, J. Ralph McFarling.

Tamiyasu who was in "73" Tule Lake paid us a visit and photoed us; he went to Heart Mountain. Mori came to say good-bye.

Paid $12.00 for canvasses.

Kuramoto came to say good-bye. [Ditto?] Komatsu[?] and Wa-tanabe, Kurahashi; sushi from Miyamotos, Kuramatsu's friends [from?] 7-G.

Many came to the apartment to say good-bye from 6:00 on. M. said that the Council has 2 cars and arranged for our transportation from the camp to the Granada depot; many were at the [train sta-tion?] too. The Council *kanbu* [leading members] came to the De-pot. The train came [at] 10:05. . . .

Saturday, April 28

The morning was clear (New Mexico) and remained so throughout the day and rather warm.

Kei got ill and missed both breakfast and supper, but had sushi and sandwiches purchased at Aqua[?]; my breakfast [was] 75 cents and supper $1.60. Talked to a number of people. Mostly soldiers and sailors who are friendly as usual—both officers and men. The country we passed thru is desolate and uninteresting. The service is fair, but that is all. The porter is a jolly old man.

Sunday, April 29

Clear and hot.

The train was on the schedule until we reached Barstow where, however, it remained 3 hours before the switching took place. Afterward the train became slow and "local." Though due in San Francisco at 10:15 P.M. on Monday, the 30th, it reached Oakland at 3:00 A.M. Stayed on the sleeper until 6:30 A.M. Took 7:45 bus to Frisco, and then a taxi to Southern Pacific depot. The taxi service is unimaginably bad; it took us more than a half hour to find one through the efforts of a colored porter at the bus depot; we had to share with a solider and his girl to our destination (3rd and Townsend, S.P. Depot) and paid 45 cents.

Monday, April 30

Clear and sunny. Hot in the afternoon in the campus home!

Reached Southern Pacific Depot and took the 8:20 train to Palo Alto; telephoned to Treats, and Jessie came to meet us. She gave us somethings to eat for lunch.

Payson [Treat], Edgar [Robinson] and Tom [Bailey] came; Edgar invited us to supper and Nelson [Spinks] will be there. They all looked well but aged somewhat.

Our luggage was not at the depot, but delivered later in early afternoon.

[Saw Charles] Fahs and Kent of Yale,* the men connected with

---

*Unidentified.

the strategic board responsible for the planning of administration of occupied countries: Japan. Asked whether a revolution will follow the occupation. My immediate answer was no revolution. Fahs felt there might [be]; Kent thought so, but he does not know Japan. Fahs does not think properly trained men will be enough, but make the best of them. That is all! Doubtful whether they can influence the Army men. Will write from time to time; O.K. though I have no information to calculate reactions. Religious beliefs must be carefully handled I said.

Reported to the District Parole Office at San Francisco 5:00 P.M. . . .

◻ The following letter, the last document reproduced in this collection, describes the reaction of the Ichihashis to their long-awaited return to their Stanford home. ◗

YAMATO ICHIHASHI TO SAKAE KAWASHIRI [46]

> 523 Salvatierra Street
> Stanford University, Cal.
> May 30, 1945

Dear Kawashiri san:

Exactly one month has elapsed since our arrival here in our campus home, and now I have no excuse for further delay in writing to you. First of all, let me sincerely apologize for my failure to communicate sooner at least to express my gratitude for many kindly considerations you and your colleagues had given me before my departure from Amache.

The inside of the house was not in a bad condition, but required a good deal of work before it could be rendered livable. But the garden had gone wild with trees overgrown and with weeds covering the entire ground and no help is available. We could almost weep at these awful sights. Thus my wife and I have been laboring like devils since our return; yet we are far from being settled. This was the reason why you did not hear from me sooner. I wish to extend my sincere thanks and greetings to you and through you to all of your colleagues, especially the officers and staff of the Council and Mc-Farling and others. Please also remember me to Mr. Lindley.

I shall now tell you what I have experienced since my departure from the camp. First as regards the trip: the train reached Barstow almost on the scheduled time (26 minutes behind to be exact), but there our train remained for three hours before it was switched. Moreover, from this point on the train became "local" and slow; though scheduled to arrive in San Francisco at 10:15 P.M. of the same day, it actually reached Oakland (the Santa Fe terminal) at 3 o'clock A.M. of the following morning. In the meantime, many passengers, mostly strangers to this region and inexperienced travelers, began to worry: What were they to do at 3 A.M. I knew, however, that at least under the normal condition, the Pullman Company was under obligation to allow its passengers to remain in their births until normal hours of the morning. We were so informed by the conductor very late that night; he should have informed them sooner, but alas in war time negligence is the rule. What did he care about [the] inconveniences of the passengers? By the way, the passengers, especially several men were very friendly.

We took the 7:45 A.M. bus to San Francisco (the Greyhound Depot); there we got stuck again as taxis were very difficult to obtain. Through persistent efforts of a colored porter, a taxi already occupied by a soldier and his girl was finally made available for us; this kind of sharing with others, I have discovered since, is a common practice among the local taxi drivers; however, charges are not reduced thereby. We took the 8:20 train and reached the familiar Palo Alto Depot an hour later; there we had a cup of coffee, our first drink of the day. A friend met us there and brought us home, our home, from which we had been absent for three, long years; we almost wept.

Visitors streamed in to welcome us; flowers were sent; lunches and dinners were provided by our friends. We started to work.

Our luggage were delivered early in the same afternoon. The same day, I reported to the parole officer at San Francisco; in the post office I found the Bills of Lading. On May 2nd, a card dated 2nd from the American Railway Express Company was received; on the 8th, the property shipped by freight was delivered to our house free of charge, while the property shipped by express was delivered on the 10th (also of course free of charge). These facts are presented in order that those who are planning to relocate may be informed accurately of what they are likely to encounter in their trips.

Next I wish to inform you what I have to do as a parolee after the relocation: First, I had to report to the district parole officer within 24 hours after my arrival here. Several days later I received from the parole officer a letter which in part reads as follows:

[Ichihashi apparently planned to quote from the letter here, although this space was left blank in the draft. What follows apparently are Ichihashi's comments about sections in the parole letter.]

1) The foregoing is self-explanatory and requires no elaboration.
But though I have submitted along with my first report on the form
furnished me, dated May 5, 1945, the names of five persons, one of
whom may be "appointed as a sponsor," none has been as yet appointed. Thus I continue to make a weekly report, the form for
which is very simple:

"I reside at . . . . ."
"I am employed at . . . . ."
    Signature.

2) The "agreement" is as follows:

"I, the name, a national of Japan, the (new) address, in consideration
[blank]"

This is all a parolee has to do after the relocation, if my own case
is typical; I have nothing more to add on this subject. Finally, I have
contacted Miss Isenberg, the local Chairman of the American Principles and Fair Play Committee,[47] who is doing all she can to assist
the resettlement of Japanese in this area which embraces San Mateo
County and Santa Clara County as far as San Jose. Jobs confined
to domestic service and garden work are plentiful; the former pays
usually $100 a month plus board and room and $150 in exceptional
cases while the latter pays $1.00 per hour. There are no white-collar
jobs in this residential area. The main problem here as elsewhere is
that of housing, and thus families with children or with disabled old
people cannot be resettled unless they have their own homes. Employers [are] not willing to take in such families. Moreover, many
nisei aspire for jobs that are not locally available and that is a dilemma faced by the Committee Chairman. She is sympathetic with
the young people's aspirations, she feels that they should resettle
with the available jobs temporarily at any rate, and then plan for the
return of their parents. If there are those who desire to resettle in
this area under the stated condition, she will be happy to help them.
But in order to facilitate her part, applicants must give information
as to their ages, experiences, abilities, marital state, etc. so that she
can properly negotiate for jobs. I have stated the gist of our interviews as was given me without comment.
    [The draft letter ends here.]

See, the morning glories faded

While I drew a picture of them.

—Shiki (1867–1902)

Epilogue

On the morning of Monday, April 30, 1945, the Ichihashis' dear friend, Jessie Treat, picked up the couple at the Palo Alto train station and drove them the short distance to their campus residence. It had been three years almost to the day since they had last seen Stanford and been in their own home. They were exhausted and joyous in returning. That evening they went to the Edgar Robinsons for dinner; the next evening they ate at the Treats'.[1]

For the next several weeks, the Ichihashis worked on their home to restore it to the order they wanted. Yamato labored outside on the garden, which was wildly overgrown. Inside the house, he waxed the floors, fixed broken furniture, and repaired rotted window frames. (In a later claim to the federal government, the Ichihashis calculated that their loss in income and damage to their possessions amounted to over $3,600 for the time they were in camp.)[2] Together, Yamato and Kei tended their flowers, especially the morning glories of which they had become so fond in camp. When they received seeds of various morning glory varieties from friends still at Amache, they immediately prepared soil and pots and set them out. They were thrilled when the first sprouts appeared just three days after planting. Yamato kept a detailed record of their growth, the shape and color of their flowers, and the number of blossoms they sent forth. With new blooms every morning, though they lasted less than a day, the morning glories had become something the

Ichihashis could look forward to in their sad and turbulent lives. They learned to their amusement that back in Amache the morning glories continued to bloom in front of their old barracks. These flowers were one of the few things that still could give them simple pleasure, beauty, and constancy.[3]

Word quickly got out that the Ichihashis had returned. Friends and colleagues came steadily to welcome them back to campus, bringing flowers and home-grown fruits and vegetables, precious in wartime. Jessie Knight Jordan, widow of Stanford's first president, sent flowers. Even the weather seemed to be a homecoming gift: "delightful" was the word Ichihashi used to describe the days immediately following their return.

As the Ichihashis tended to mundane matters such as fixing the water heater and reconnecting the telephone, hoping to recapture some sense of normality, the world-at-war constantly intervened. On May 7, Yamato read the newspaper report that Nazi Germany had finally surrendered, ending the European conflict. "Here the students are celebrating with the band and a parade," he wrote in his diary. "All is good so far." He must have known that the end of the Pacific War would not be long in coming. The continuing prohibition on traveling on highways and other restrictions placed on what the Department of Justice called "alien enemies" regularly reminded Yamato, though, that he was still linked to the hated Pacific adversary. The Department of Justice required him, as a parolee, to make a "personal report" on his activities to his sponsor twice a month and make a "written report" once a month to the regional chief of the Alien Control Division. Payson Treat, as his sponsor, accepted the stipulated responsibility to "undertake to keep in close touch with [Ichihashi], observe his conduct and activities, and maintain knowledge of his whereabouts to the end of assuring his compliance with the terms of parole." Ichihashi was not released from his parole status until November 15, 1945, three months after Japan's surrender. In September 1946, he heard from a close friend that, according to the government attorney who had presided over his immigration hearing during his stay at Sharp Park, the reason behind the government's arrest of Ichihashi and its belief he was a "dangerous enemy alien" was that he had a brother in the Japanese army. That had not been the entire reason why the FBI had taken him into custody, interned him at Sharp Park for two months, and placed him on parole after his release. It was, however, the closest Ichihashi ever got to an official explanation.[4]

Stanford was a very different place from the one he had known before internment. There were new faces and new ways of doing things. Ray Lyman Wilbur, president of Stanford since 1916, had retired in 1943. His successor, Donald Tresidder, a businessman who had directed the concessions at Yosemite National Park, quickly became unpopular among many of Ichihashi's friends and colleagues. He was seen as a corporate man, tied in with a bureaucratic clique uninterested in traditional scholarship and the gentlemanly ways of the past. There was transition in the history department too; Thomas A. Bailey began to assume the responsibilities of the chair and eventually replaced Edgar Robinson, who had held the position since 1929. Although a friend of Ichihashi, Bailey also represented the new forces assuming leadership at Stanford. Bailey, a Stanford Ph.D. and a historian of American diplomatic history whose first book was on the America-Japan crises of the early twentieth century, was a tireless professional and an aggressive administrator. Payson Treat himself became emeritus in 1945 and retreated to his campus home and its abundant garden. He was embittered by the war, feeling that he, the senior Asianist in the United States, had been deliberately snubbed by some Stanford colleagues and Washington officials because of his reputation as being "pro-Japanese." And the department had already started to look for Ichihashi's replacement.[5]

Ichihashi received invitations to attend campus functions, such as the annual receptions for the campus emeriti, for the Phi Beta Kappa honor society, and for department faculty members. He turned them all down. Even though his departmental office was only a ten-minute walk from his home, it was not until January 1946, nine months after his return to campus, that Ichihashi finally mustered the energy and will to visit his old haunts. He found his office dusty, stuffy, and stripped of the hundreds of library books that he had once kept there, but otherwise as he had left it. The Japanese American Citizens League asked him to be an adviser to their organization, but he refused. He did, however, perhaps because it was Treat who asked, agree to translate for the Hoover Library some Japanese army material captured on Iwo Jima.[6]

Although they would later become recluses, Yamato and Kei in the months after their return kept up an active social life with close campus friends. They also received a steady stream of visitors, former students and fellow internees they had come to know over the years in camp. Yamato corresponded regularly with Kenji Ito, his closest associate in camp, about conditions in the relocation centers in their last days and the progress of Japanese resettlement on the outside. After leaving camp, Ito moved to Los Angeles, where he became a prominent business attorney in the Japanese American community. The two friends remained in contact for years after the war, with Ito helping the older man with legal and financial problems. Ichihashi worried that the camp residents would not be able to handle the transition well and that they were susceptible to all sorts of unscrupulous schemes; he continued to receive the Amache newspaper and tried to keep track of his many acquaintances from camp—about 44,000 Japanese were still living in the relocation centers at war's end. Amache itself did not finally close until October 15, 1945.[7]

"Started misty but soon clearing, and became warm," is how Ichihashi's idiosyncratic ongoing weather report reads in his diary for Monday, August 6. He wrote that he devoted himself "to research and reading." But a terse note added at the end of the brief entry highlights the news of the day: "An atomic bomb on Hiroshima."

Ichihashi wrote little in his diary the next several days. On Wednesday, August 8, he simply noted that Payson Treat informed him that "Russia had declared war on Japan." On August 9, the United States dropped an atomic bomb on Nagasaki, but Ichihashi mentioned nothing about the event. Then on Tuesday, August 14, a warm day with "a gentle breeze," he wrote:

> At 4:00 P.M. the war ended & announced by sirens in Palo Alto and gun-shooting in the campus. "The war is over" is heard everywhere. The University siren is blowing now. What a tragic end for J[apan] after a stupid, stupendous folly—a bad dream. Whistles, sirens, auto-horns are blowing. Good for the innocent people; they are saved from a hell.

Other than branding the use of the atomic bombs as "criminal" acts more than a year later, Ichihashi wrote nothing in his diary of his feelings about the bombs or the end of the war.[8]

A few months after Japan's surrender, Ichihashi wrote Kenji Ito about a visit from a former graduate student of his, now army major, who inquired whether he might be interested in helping advise the U.S. army in the postwar occupation of Japan. His student told him that General Douglas MacArthur had organized a team that would investigate the status of Japanese education and "formulate a program of 'democratic' reforms." "Will I be willing to join the group," he wrote Ito, "if necessary protective measures are provided? Another Japanese might jump to avail himself of such an opportunity, but not I because I am bound to encounter embarrassments of all sorts, if not certain dangers."[9]

Ichihashi's diary became a place where he noted trivial events around the household and composed meticulous summaries of the day's international news, gleaned from newspapers and radio broadcasts. One day he read in the paper that Colonel Don Nugent, one of his former graduate students and a Japan specialist, had become the first prosecution witness in the war crimes trial of former Japanese premier Tōjō Hideki and 27 other high-ranking officials. (In another strange twist, Ichihashi learned later that the federal attorney who had presided over his own hearing when he was at Sharp Park had joined the prosecution team at the trial.) Tōjō and six others were later hanged, in December 1948. Postwar international developments, especially the increased influence of the Soviet Union and communism, depressed Ichihashi and left him deeply pessimistic about the future of world politics. The prospect of nuclear war also worried him. "I wonder whether the so-called statesmen of the powers realize the meaning of the much heralded atomic age," he wrote Kenji Ito in early 1946. "Are they really determined to have no more wars? Thinking men must think and speculate." [10]

But if he was embittered by the war and its aftermath, it was not yet evident to his friends and colleagues immediately after the end of the war. Emery Fast, Lisette Fast's brother, who worked for the WRA helping resettle Japanese Americans out of the camps in northern California, visited Ichihashi several times in the closing months of 1945. After one such occasion, Emery wrote his wife, Ethel, who was still working for Dillon Myer in Washington, D.C., that the Ichihashis seemed "on the whole to be getting along fairly well," despite being "very much concerned" about not hearing from family members in Japan. Ichihashi groused about the new Tresidder administration at Stanford, which actually pleased Fast. "It makes one feel good to hear [Ichihashi] identify himself so completely with Stanford," he wrote his wife. "And I was touched by his expression of hope that the Stanford Alumni Association in Tokyo, of which his sister is a member, might be able to put him in touch with her." [11]

In November 1945, Ichihashi learned to his great relief that his sister Shizuko had indeed survived the war. According to a secondhand report, she had been seen at a Stanford alumni gathering in Tokyo in October and was still working as the secretary to the president of Tokyo University. But it was not until mid-February 1946 that Ichihashi finally received confirmation from someone who had seen her in person. A Dr. S. V. Christianson, Stanford class of 1917, sent a photograph of Shizuko to Ichihashi, who began to send her letters, food, soap, and clothing through another former student in the U.S. Army. Shizuko, who remained single, had suffered greatly through the bombing of Tokyo; she had had no contact with her other brothers, all of whom were still alive. In her first letter to Ichihashi after the war, she expressed great remorse for the war and the "great wrong and sins we [Japanese] had committed which would never be pardoned by God." She pledged to "accept the consequences bravely and honestly" and devote herself to building an "entirely new yet healthy clean society." Ichihashi's reply letter, written in an affectionate and intimate tone that was reserved for Shizuko alone, praised her courage and example. "The country needs more of your kind," he wrote Shizuko. He continued, "The people must get together in performing this fundamental task [of rebuilding the country materially and spiritually]. Those of us who are abroad must stand helpless for the present and can join you only in spirit and prayer. I am sure some of us are prepared to do what we can when an opportunity presents itself. I wish that I could be there just now sharing in the task, but alas in vain!" He added that "as to those who caused the national ruination, justice will be done as they deserve, for their stupid crime and sin." As to his own experiences during the war, all he wrote was that he and Kei had suffered greatly physically and mentally and had lived lives like "prisoners of war." [12]

Despite his closeness to Shizuko, he did not confide in her about his serious family problems; he gave no indication at all that anything was amiss. Relations between Yamato and Kei continued to be terribly strained, especially by continuing differences over their relationship with Woodrow, now stationed in Germany, and his wife and baby, who were in Chicago where the family made their permanent home. "What an impertinent demand!" Ichihashi had written in his diary after Woodrow, who had made contact with Kei in May 1945, asked for some money, with "the condition that his wife and kid [be] recognized." Ichihashi refused the request. He did not see Woodrow again for almost twenty years, until his son visited from Chicago just a few months before Ichihashi's death in 1963. He never met any of his four grandchildren. [13] And even more than he did in camp, he often complained in his diary about what he felt was Kei's outspokenness. To him, she no longer seemed to be a quiet, obedient wife. He dated her new attitude to the disagreement they had at Amache over Woodrow's marriage. From his diary descriptions, it appears that their arguments over household matters were frequent, bitter, and never resolved. The shadow of internment lay over the Ichihashis for the rest of their lives. [14]

In March 1953, Ichihashi traveled alone by freighter for a last visit to Japan. After an unpleasant journey, he arrived in Yokohama and was met by his sister, George Mizota and his wife Fujie, who was Kei's sister, and a few other friends. Mizota had grown up in southern California and attended Stanford Law School before he returned to Japan, where he worked for the Japanese navy before becoming a prominent attorney. Ichihashi remained in Japan, staying with his sister for eight months, ostensibly to work on his cultural history manuscript. [15]

As on his prewar trips, Japanese Stanford alumni and old friends sought him out, wanting to honor him. Even a white staff member from Amache who had taken one of his classes on Japanese culture in camp looked him up when he learned Ichihashi was in the country. In his pub-lic talks, he encouraged American-Japanese cooperation, as he had in the past. He threw his support to the American-backed political reforms that were transforming the country, although he criticized those of his countrymen who he felt were too eager to adopt American styles of life. He advised his American friends in Japan not to take too seriously the anti-American sentiment that had flared up in the early 1950's. Those feelings "will fade away as the anti-Japanese sentiment in the U.S. has," he told the press. When asked by a reporter if he would become a natu-ralized American citizen under the McCarran-Walter Act of 1952, which finally granted that right to Japanese immigrants, he replied dis-ingenuously, or perhaps sarcastically: "In all the years I spent in the United States I have never suffered inconvenience because of my alien status. Why should I bother about citizenship now?" He never became an American citizen.[16]

On September 25 before a luncheon meeting of the America-Japan Society in Tokyo, the group he had addressed sixteen years earlier on his previous trip, Ichihashi delivered what would be his last major public address. Some of the old admirals who had been at the 1922 Washington Conference came to see him for the last time. In a lengthy talk, he re-viewed the complicated history of Japanese-American relations over the past hundred years, freely drawing on his own personal experiences, from his life as a schoolboy in San Francisco to his three years in "veri-table concentration camps," in his words, to illustrate his points. The views he expressed sharply contrasted with those he advocated before the war: in talking about the rise of militarism in Japan in the 1930's and its effect on U.S.-Japan relations, he described the "blundering adven-tures" of the militarists, starting with the creation of the "puppet state" of Manchukuo; the Sino-Japanese conflict begun in 1937 "developed into a war of so great a magnitude" that they were "utterly incapable" of coping with it; and the attack on Pearl Harbor was "the worst and most stupid act." Abroad, the militarists "behaved like barbarians"; at home, "they treated civilians like slaves, confiscating their money and other properties, forcing them to wear rags, and pushing them to a starvation diet. They destroyed the national wealth and undermined the spiritual life of the nation." In contrast, he described the American Occupation authorities who brought food to starving Japan as "compassionate." The Japanese people, he claimed, accepted the aid that came to them from America "with a deep and sincere gratitude."[17]

On January 8, 1954, Ichihashi arrived back in San Francisco. Kei was at the dock to meet him, with an old friend from camp, Kurihara.[18]

As the months and then years passed, Ichihashi retreated increasingly to his home office to read the daily paper and listen to news broadcasts. He spent his time recording the international events of the day in his journal, and while he claimed to be working on his study of Japanese cultural history, he seems to have made little progress on it. He stopped attending department functions altogether, as he saw his familiar world gradually disappear. Ray Lyman Wilbur, under whom he had worked for 30 years, had died in 1949. Neighbor Clara Stoltenberg, who with her sister had watched over the Ichihashi home during the war, died in her Salvatierra residence in 1950. Edgar Robinson retired from the university in 1952. New neighbors moved into the homes around the Ichihashis, replacing old acquaintances. Jessie Treat, Kei's closest friend, gradually slipped into senility (possibly Alzheimer's disease), and in 1958 Payson, unable to care for her any longer, reluctantly committed her to a state hospital. He regularly visited her there until she died in 1961.[19]

Colleagues and friends of the Ichihashis remember the couple during the 1950's with respect and sadness. Yamato grew increasingly cranky and eccentric. He would rise at 5 A.M., put on a scarf and gloves against the morning cold, and set about mowing his lawn, angering his neighbors with the racket. They believed he behaved this way because, class-conscious as he was, he did not want to be seen doing manual labor. He generally avoided talking about the camps, but when he did so he spoke bitterly of the experience and gave people the impression he resented that the university had not done more for his family during the war. Kei retreated as well and never spoke of her wartime experiences. Those who knew her sensed there was little affection between her and Yamato, but knew few details about the relationship. In 1953, after her husband had left on his voyage, Kei exclaimed to her neighbor, "Ichihashi's gone to Japan—pure heaven without him!" But her strongest feelings were reserved for the four grandchildren whom she did not see until 1958, when she traveled to Chicago by herself for a visit. Her friends recall that she was heartsick at being separated from them, and that in consolation to herself, she doted over the youngsters of her good friends. Gordon and Louise Wright describe their own sons as having been Kei's "surrogate grandchildren."[20]

In December 1962, Woodrow Ichihashi and his father finally reconciled. Woodrow, then in his mid-forties, came out alone to Stanford from Chicago to recuperate from an eye operation and exhaustion. Woodrow recalls that he and his father drank together and had some nice conversations during the several weeks of the visit. He still wonders why they could not have made up earlier and laments the many years of alienation.[21]

A few months later, in the spring of 1963, as he neared his 85th birthday, Yamato Ichihashi entered the hospital for exploratory surgery. The doctors found advanced liver cancer. Nothing could be done, and he died a few weeks later, on Friday morning, April 5, 1963, at his campus home. Lisette Fast telegraphed the news to Woodrow, who flew out immediately to Stanford and made arrangements with a mortuary. A few days later, a service was held at a Palo Alto funeral home. It was simple, without music, and presided over by a Stanford chaplain. Kei arranged the memorial flowers. A group of Ichihashi's colleagues came to pay their last respects.[22]

Ichihashi's death left Kei deeply, and noticeably, disturbed. She turned to her women friends for support and help, but she began to behave strangely almost immediately—Woodrow had detected nothing odd in her behavior during his December visit. Kei borrowed a hat and coat to wear to the funeral from Edgar Robinson's wife and attached herself to Lisette Fast, who helped her decide what to do with Ichihashi's personal possessions, his manuscripts, books, and journals—including 40 years of issues of the *American Historical Review*. After the funeral Kei began to call Lisette repeatedly, up to six times a day, and Lisette became increasingly worried about her friend's mental state. To add to Kei's troubles, the university decided within weeks of Yamato's death that it wanted to take control of the Ichihashis' house, which like all faculty housing on campus was on leased Stanford land. Officials pressured Kei to sell the house back to the university, prompting Louise Wright and Lisette Fast to protest the callous treatment to the president's office. The effort failed, and Kei faced the agony of having to break up her house and quickly dispose of the family property. She became angry that selling her furniture, which she thought valuable even though most of it had been purchased before World War I, brought in very little money. It was all too much for her. The family attorney called Woodrow, informed him that his mother was becoming irrational, and advised him that she needed help. In early June, Alyce, Woodrow's wife, and Nan, their daughter, came out to bring Kei back with them to Chicago. Within days, Kei left Stanford for good, never to return.[23]

Kei lived with Woodrow and his family for a few weeks, but she became hostile and violent and, Woodrow feared, dangerous to his wife and children. On August 6, 1963, a Cook County court judge declared Kei "mentally ill" and committed her to Elgin State Hospital. She died there seven years later at the age of 78.[24]

The Ichihashi house remained standing for a few more years and was used by the University for various purposes, the last of which was as a social center for Chicano students. By the late 1960's, it too was gone, torn down to make way for a new law school building. The chair in

Japanese studies held by Yamato Ichihashi slipped into obscurity and went vacant until 1992, when the university in auditing its books discovered the oversight. The endowment income had been used for purposes other than its donors had intended. Fifty years after Yamato Ichihashi retired, the chair in Japanese history and civilization that he had once occupied with distinction was formally renamed in his honor and filled.[25]

Appendix

Selected Writings of Yamato Ichihashi

Listed here are Yamato Ichihashi's doctoral dissertation and, in chronological order, a selection of more significant published works and reviews. Several unpublished manuscripts and sets of lecture notes are cited within the endnotes.

DISSERTATION

1913. "Emigration from Japan and Japanese Immigration into the State of California." Ph.D. diss., Harvard University.

PUBLISHED WRITINGS

1907. "Japanese Students in America." *Outlook* 87, 6 (12 Oct.): 295–97.
1909. "Hagoromo, the Winged Robe: A Japanese Folk-Tale." *Pacific Monthly* 21 (April): 354.
1913. "The California Alien Land Law." *American Citizen*, June, pp. 257–58, 287–88.
1913. *Japanese Immigration: Its Status in California*. San Francisco: Marshall Press; rev. ed., 1915.
1917. "Tokio Imperial University." *Stanford Sequoia* 27, 3 (Dec.): 94–96.
1919. "Address: California University." *Semicentenary Celebration of the Founding of the University of California with an Account of the Conference on International Relations*, pp. 357–58. Berkeley: University of California Press.
[1919]. "The War and Japanese Intellectuals." *The New World*[?] n.d.
1919. "Westernized Japan." *Japan* 8, 5 (Jan.): 7–11.
1921. "Westernized Japan" [in Japanese]. *Stanford* 1 (Jan.): 10–25.
1922. "Results—What Was Accomplished for the United States and Japan at the Washington Conference." *Japan* 11 (July): 32–33, 45.
1922. "Admiral Baron Kato, New Premier of Japan." *Japan* 11 (Aug.): 28–30, 52.
1923. "Count Yamamoto, New Prime Minister of Japan." *Japan* 13, 2 (Nov.): 24, 30.
1923. "Japanese Catastrophe and American Humanitarianism." *Japan* 13, 3 (Dec.): 24, 55.
1925. "Westernized Japan." *The Mid-Pacific* 30, 6 (Dec.): 531–34.
1927. "The Eventful Era of Taisho: Japan's Advance During the Reign of the Late Emperor Yoshihito, a Tribute." *Japan* 16 (Feb.): 10–11.
1928. "The Record of the Centuries: The Historian Looks Backward." *Japan* 17 (May): 19–20, 77–83.
1928. "Viscount Eiichi Shibusawa." *World Unity* 2, 3 (June): 189–93.
1928. *The Washington Conference and After: A Historical Study*. Stanford, Calif.: Stanford University Press.
1929. "Limitation of Naval Armaments—Washington to Geneva." *Proceedings of the Annual Meeting* (1928), vol. 23, pp. 67–75. Los Angeles: American Historical Association, Pacific Coast Branch.
1931. "Economic Life in Japan, 1600–1868." Review essay on *The Economic Aspects of the History of the Civilization of Japan* by Yosaburo Takekoshi. *Journal of Economic and Business History* 4 (Nov.): 156–67.
1931. "International Migration of the Japanese." In W. F. Willcox, ed. *International Migrations*, vol. 2, pp. 617–36. New York: National Bureau of Economic Research, Inc.
1931. "Political Developments in Japan." *Institute of International Relations, Proceedings Vol.* 7 (1930), pp. 138–43. Los Angeles: Institute of International Relations.
1932. "Beikoku no kinkyō to saikin no nichibei-kankei" (Current situation in the United States and recent developments in the U.S–Japan Relationship). In *Watashi no mita Amerika no kinkyō* (2 essays). Tokyo: Taiheiyō Mondai Chōsakai.
1932. *Japanese in the United States: A Critical Study of the Problems of the Japanese Immigrants and Their Children*. Stanford, Calif.: Stanford University Press.

1932. "Watashi no mita Amerika no kinkyō" (My observations of the current situation in the United States). In *Watashi no mita Amerika no kinkyō* (2 essays). Tokyo: Taiheiyō Mondai Chōsakai.

1933. "Gendai Amerika wo ronzu" (America of today). *Osaka Asahi Shimbun,* Jan. 1, 3, and 6, 1933, and *Tokio Asahi Shimbun,* Jan. 3, 1933.

1935. "The Far East and World Peace." *Bulletin of the Second America–Japan Student Conference* (1934), pp. 23–24. Washington D.C.

1935. "Japan's Foreign Trade Expansion." *Proceedings of Institute of World Affairs,* vol. 12 (1934), pp. 125–31. Los Angeles: Institute of World Affairs, University of Southern California.

1935. "Living Art," *Vo-Mag* [Pasadena, Calif.] 3, 3 (May): 3–4.

1936. "Japan's Rights and Obligations in the Pacific." *Proceedings of Institute of World Affairs,* vol. 13 (1935), pp. 73–77. Los Angeles: Institute of World Affairs, University of Southern California.

1936. "The Problem of Naval Bases in the Pacific." *Proceedings of Institute of World Affairs,* vol. 13 (1935), pp. 101–4. Los Angeles: Institute of World Affairs.

1937. "Japanese Studies in American Universities." *America Japan Society Bulletin* 1, 1 (4th quarter): 7.

1953. "Japanese–American Relations." *America-Japan Society Bulletin* 4: 33–37.

BOOK REVIEWS

1927. Of *International Rivalries in Manchuria* by P. H. Clyde. *Stanford Illustrated Review* 29 (Dec.): 122–23.

1929. Of *The Documents of Iriki: Illustrative of the Feudal Institutions of Japan* by K. Asakawa. *American Historical Review* 35 (Oct.): 95–96.

1931. Of *Food Supply and Raw Materials in Japan* by E. F. Penrose. *Pacific Affairs* 4 (March): 252–53.

1931. Of *Japan's Economic Position* by J. E. Orchard. *Historical Outlook* 22, 3 (March): 128.

1931. Of *The Japanese Population Problem* by W. R. Crocker. *Japan* 20 (Oct.): 36.

1932. Of *The Basic Industries and Social History of Japan* by U. Kobayashi. *Political Science Quarterly* 47, 1 (March): 159–60.

1932. Of *Japan: An Economic and Financial Appraisal* by H. G. Moulton. *American Economic Review* 22 (March): 93–94.

1932. Of *The International Legal Status of the Kwantung Leased Territory and Japanese Jurisdiction in the South Manchurian Railway Area* and *Japan's Special Position in Manchuria,* both by C. W. Young. *Pacific Historical Review* 1 (June): 262–64.

1932. Of *Japan and America* by H. Taft. *Pacific Affairs* 5 (Dec.): 1087–88.

1936. Of *The Manchu Abdication and the Great Powers, 1908–1912,* by J. G. Reid. *Pacific Historical Review* 5 (Sept.): 277–78.

1936. Of *Eastern Industrialization and Its Effect on the West, with Special Reference to Great Britain and Japan,* by G. F. Hubbard. *American Economic Review* 26 (Dec.): 740–41.

1937. Of *Diplomatic Commentaries* by Kikujiro Ishii; trans. W. R. Langdon. *Pacific Historical Review* 6 (March): 83–85 (In Japanese *Gaiko Yoroku,* 1936).

1937. Of *Japan's Feet of Clay* by F. Utley and *The Industry and Trade of Japan* by S. Uyehara. *American Economic Review* 27 (June): 351.

1937. Of *Japanese Trade and Industry, Present and Future* by Mitsubishi Economic Research Bureau. *American Economic Review* 27 (Sept.): 569–70.

1938. Of *Early Japanese History, c. 40 B.C.–A.D. 1167* by R. K. Reischauer. *American Historical Review* 44 (Oct.): 129–30.

1942. Of *The Maker of Modern Japan: The Life of Tokugawa Ieyasu* by A. L. Sadler. *Pacific Historical Review* 11 (March): 88–89.

Reference
Matter

Notes

Complete authors' names, titles, and publication data for sources cited in short form in the notes are given in the Bibliography; Ichihashi's works are listed in the Appendix. Archival abbreviations are explained in the Abbreviations list, pp. 11–12.

INTRODUCTION

1. There are only a few publications that contain substantial first-person, firsthand accounts of internment. The best-known is Charles Kikuchi, *The Kikuchi Diary: Chronicle from an American Concentration Camp; the Tanforan Journals of Charles Kikuchi*, ed. John Modell (Urbana: University of Illinois Press, 1973). Kikuchi, a second-generation Japanese American, worked for University of California sociologist Dorothy S. Thomas during World War II. He kept diaries as a self-conscious contribution to Thomas's study of evacuation, as well as other private journals for himself. The public journals cover a few months in the Tanforan "assembly center" before Kikuchi left for the Gila River Relocation Camp in Arizona. (In April 1943 Kikuchi was able to leave the camp and go to Chicago. He eventually entered the U.S. Army.) A much briefer account of assembly center life is Zuigaku Kodachi and Jan Heikkala, trans., and Janet Cormack, ed., "Portland Assembly Center: Diary of Saku Tomita," *Oregon Historical Quarterly* 58, 2 (Summer 1980): 149–71. A different sort of work is Takeo Ujo Nakano, *Within the Barbed Wire Fence: A Japanese Man's Account of His Internment in Canada* (Seattle: University of Washington Press, 1981); Nakano's daughter Leatrice Nakano assembled this short account from her father's camp poetry and diary. A slim volume of memoirs and diary excerpts is Takeo Kaneshiro, comp., *In-*

ternees: War Relocation Center Memoirs and Diaries (New York: Vantage Press, 1976). Lengthy contemporary reports can be found in Nishimoto, *Inside an American Concentration Camp*. Richard Nishimoto, a Stanford engineering graduate who had taken at least one class from Ichihashi, was interned in the Poston, Arizona, camp. While there, he wrote reports for academics studying the internment experience. I am not familiar with the literature in Japanese on relocation and therefore cannot write confidently about where this work will fall within it.

The Ichihashi story is part of the wartime drama of the vast majority of Japanese in America who were interned in camps run by the War Relocation Authority. Several thousand other Japanese who were considered potentially dangerous were held as "enemy aliens" in detention camps run by the Department of Justice. This book speaks only marginally to the latter experience.

2. Some of the principal books on the subject are: Alexander Leighton, *The Governing of Men: General Principles and Recommendations Based on Experience at a Japanese Relocation Camp* (1945); Carey McWilliams, *Prejudice: Japanese Americans: Symbol of Racial Intolerance* (1944); Dorothy Swaine Thomas and Richard Nishimoto, *The Spoilage: Japanese-American Evacuation and Resettlement During World War II* (1946); Leonard Bloom and Ruth Riemer, *Removal and Return: The Socio-Economic Effects of the War on Japanese Americans* (1949); Morton Grodzins, *Americans Betrayed: Politics and the Japanese Evacuation* (1949); Dorothy Swaine Thomas, *The Salvage* (1952); Jacobus N. tenBroek, Edward N. Barnhart, and Floyd W. Matson, *Prejudice, War, and the Constitution* (1954); and Leonard Bloom and John I. Kitsuse, *The Managed Casualty: The Japanese-American Family in World War II* (1956).

3. See for example, Allan P. Bosworth, *America's Concentration Camps* (1967); Audrie Girdner and Anne Loftis, *The Great Betrayal: The Evacuation of the Japanese-Americans During World War II* (1969); Edward H. Spicer, Asael T. Hansen, Katherine Luomala, and Marvin K. Opler, *Impounded People: Japanese-Americans in the Relocation Centers* (1969); Dillon S. Myer, *Uprooted Americans: The Japanese Americans and the War Relocation Authority During World War II* (1971); Roger Daniels, *Concentration Camps U.S.A.: Japanese Americans and World War II* (1972); Jeanne Wakatsuki Houston and James D. Houston, *Farewell to Manzanar: A True Story of Japanese-American Experience During and After World War II Internment* (1973); and Michi Weglyn, *Years of Infamy: The Untold Story of America's Concentration Camps* (1976). Recent histories include Sandra C. Taylor, *Jewel of the Desert: Japanese American Internment at Topaz* (1993) and Page Smith, *Democracy on Trial: The Japanese American Evacuation and Relocation in World War II* (1995).

4. This literature is almost wholly in the form of memoirs or oral histories drawn from interviews long after the fact. See for example, Daisuke Kitagawa, *Issei and Nisei: The Internment Years* (1967); Arthur A. Hansen and Betty E. Mitson, *Voices Long Silent: An Oral Inquiry into the Japanese American Evacuation* (1974); Yoshiko Uchida, *Desert Exile: The Uprooting of a Japanese American Family* (1982); Eileen Sunada Sarasohn, ed., *The Issei: Portrait of a Pioneer; An Oral His-*

tory (1983); John Tateishi, ed., *And Justice for All: An Oral History of the Japanese American Detention Camps* (1984); and Harry S. Ueno, *Manzanar Martyr: An Interview with Harry Y. Ueno*, ed. Sue Kunitomi Embrey, Arthur A. Hansen, Betty Kulberg Mitson (Fullerton: California State University, 1986). Also see the testimonies in *Personal Justice Denied*, the report of the United States Commission on Wartime Relocation and Internment of U.S. Civilians. A related, but much smaller body of literature concerns the Japanese who were held in Department of Justice camps as suspected dangerous enemy aliens. Accounts of this experience include Yoshiaki Fukuda, *Yokuryu Seikatsu Rokunen* (1957; reprinted as *My Six Years of Internment: An Issei's Struggle for Justice*, 1990), and Tetsuden Kashima, "American Mistreatment of Internees During World War II; Enemy Alien Japanese," pp. 52–56, in Roger Daniels, Sandra C. Taylor, and Harry H. L. Kitano *Japanese Americans: From Relocation to Redress* (1986).

   5. See the extensive writing of Roger Daniels on the camps, as well as Daniels, Taylor, and Kitano, eds., *Japanese Americans: From Relocation to Redress* (1986). See also Peter Irons, *Justice at War: The Story of the Japanese American Internment Cases* (1983); Richard Drinnon, *Keeper of Concentration Camps: Dillon S. Myer and American Racism* (1987); Thomas James, *Exile Within: The Schooling of Japanese Americans, 1942–1945* (1987); and Yuji Ichioka, ed., *Views from Within: The Japanese American Evacuation and Resettlement Study* (1989).

   6. S. Frank Miyamoto, "Resentment, Distrust, and Insecurity at Tule Lake," in Ichioka, ed., *Views from Within*, p. 127.

   7. On this point, see Hayashi, *Japanese Brethren*, p. 153.

   8. Sugimoto, *Daughter*, p. 217.

   9. The name of the flower is used as the title of a study of the Japanese navy, which ironically had interested Ichihashi for much of his life. See Howarth, *Morning Glory: A History of the Imperial Japanese Navy*.

   10. Sugimoto, *Daughter*, p. 138; also see 218–19.

   11. Eaton, *Beauty Behind Barbed Wire*, pp. 25, 52, 166. The Merced Assembly Center had an area called "Morning Glory Lane"; See V. J. Matsumoto, *Farming the Home Place*, p. 106.

   12. Lady Chiyo is among Japan's most celebrated female haiku poets and was a favorite of Ichihashi's. He kept a copy of this poem, Chiyo's most famous, in his lecture notes (IP, B2, F7), reproduced it in his essay "The Record of the Centuries: The Historian Looks Backward" (1928, p. 20), and cited it in at least one lecture ("The Imperial Family of Japan," n.d., IP, B2, F7). Ichihashi believed that the Japanese as a people were unique in their high appreciation of beauty and nature. This may explain his fondness for this piece, in which Lady Chiyo expresses reverence for a morning glory that has entwined the bucket to her well. Not wanting to disturb it, she asks for "gift-water."

   13. Moritake was one of Japan's most famous haiku poets. This piece is known as his "death verse." Quoted in Reischauer and Fairbank, *East Asia*, p. 652; and see Miyamori, *Anthology of Haiku*, p. 113.

PART I, CHAPTER 1

The title of this chapter paraphrases a statement by David Starr Jordan: "A man of whom Stanford has a right to be proud" (Jordan to T. Kuma, Sept. 10, 1912, DSJ, B82, F751).

1. Ichihashi to Reginald George Trotter, n.d., IP, B7, F3. Trotter was a Canadian academic who wrote about North American politics.

2. A major problem in writing about the forced relocation of the Japanese is terminology. The terms the federal government used at the time were often simply distortions. "Evacuation," for example, was the euphemism given by the federal government to refer to the mass round-up and incarceration of Japanese Americans. The Ichihashis usually used the terms employed at the time. In my voice, I usually use the term "internment" and sometimes "relocation."

3. Yuji Ichioka, a leading scholar of Japanese American history, discusses Ichihashi's work in *The Issei* and elsewhere observes that "general histories of American immigration rely heavily upon Ichihashi's work for their treatment of Japanese immigration" (Ichioka, "'Attorney for the Defense,'" p. 192n).

4. See note 1 to the Introduction.

5. The only other study of Ichihashi is Ichioka, "'Attorney for the Defense,'" which focuses on Ichihashi's early Stanford career.

6. For an introduction to the literature on Asian Americans, see three texts by leading scholars in the field: Sucheng Chan, *Asian Americans: An Interpretive History*; Roger Daniels, *Asian America: Chinese and Japanese in the United States since 1850*; and Ronald Takaki, *Strangers from a Different Shore: A History of Asian Americans*.

7. Family Register in Japan provided by Yuji Ichioka. Passenger arrival list, vol. 2, p. 132, National Archives, Pacific Sierra Region. Ichihashi's Lowell High School transcript gives 1882 for his birth date; his application for admission to Stanford, dated June 6, 1902, gives his birth date as April 15, 1882; his Stanford transcript has Aug. 20, 1883; and his Harvard transcript has April 15, 1884. All these dates make Ichihashi younger than he actually was. The clearest indication of deliberate falsification appears in the introduction to his doctoral thesis, where he states that he landed in San Francisco in 1899. Ichihashi prided himself as a man careful with the facts, and he was not likely to make a mistake on such an important matter as the day he arrived in America. Many years later, on Aug. 2, 1944, he in fact noted in his diary that he arrived in the United States in 1894 at 16 years of age.

8. Duncan I. McFadden to J. E. Wallace Sterling, Jan. 5, 1954, History Dept. Files, B2, F79.

9. Autobiographical note, n.d., IP, B1, F1; completed WRA questionnaire, IP, B5, F8, and B7, F3; Ichioka, "'Attorney for the Defense'"; and author's interview with Woodrow Ichihashi, April 5, 1992.

10. Ichihashi registration, March 29, 1943, WRA, Ichihashi Case File; FBI Report, June 10, 1942, Ichihashi FBI File.

11. Autobiographical note, n.d., IP, B1, F1. Passenger arrival list, vol. 2,

p. 132, for Yamato Ichihashi, National Archives, Pacific Sierra Region. According to Japanese records, Ichihashi was issued a passport in July 1894 to travel to the United States for "academic study." This information is from material shared with me by Seizo Oka of the Japanese American History Archives, San Francisco.

12. FBI report, June 10, 1942, Ichihashi FBI File.

13. See Ichioka, *Issei*, pp. 12, 16, 18, 27.

14. Ichihashi, *Japanese in the United States* (1932), p. 88.

15. *Fukuinkai Enkaku Shiryō* (Gospel Society Historical Record), Period III (B), May 1893–Aug. 1895, p. 8, and Period III (C), Oct. 1895–Dec. 1897, p. 19; Japanese American History Archives, San Francisco.

16. Lowell High School, 1902 *Ledger*, p. 84. I thank Yuji Ichioka for sharing the Lowell High School material with me.

17. Ichioka, *Issei*, pp. 7–9, 117.

18. The bubonic plague scare occurred in March 1900 and the anti-Japanese rally was in May 1900. Ichihashi gave the correct year in his book, *Japanese in the United States* (1932), pp. 230–31.

19. Phelan quote from Daniels, *Politics of Prejudice*, p. 21. Ichihashi, "Emigration from Japan and Japanese Immigration into the State of California," Ph.D. diss. Harvard University, 1913, pp. 266–67. Ichihashi was a high school, not grammar school, student at the time of the rally.

20. Ichihashi's Stanford application form, Registrar's Office, Stanford University. Beginning in 1859, San Francisco segregated Chinese students from whites. Agitation for similar treatment of Japanese had begun as early as 1892 and reached a peak in the spring of 1905, when the San Francisco Board of Education presented to the Board of Supervisors a budget that allocated funds for the expansion of the Chinese school facilities to include Japanese students. Bailey, *Theodore Roosevelt*, p. 14.

21. Wilbur, *Memoirs*, p. 123.

22. Mirrielees, *Stanford*, pp. 99–102. Also see Weinberg, *Ross*.

23. Mirrielees, *Stanford*, pp. 59, 61; Wilbur, *Memoirs*, pp. 134–35; and author's interview with Toichi Domoto, June 23, 1992. Also see the records and memorabilia of the Chinese and Japanese clubhouses held at the Asian American Activities Center, Stanford University.

24. Ichihashi to David Starr Jordan, Sept. 16, 1907, DSJ, B56, F542; and Ichihashi transcript, Registrar's Office, Stanford University. Mirrielees, *Fifty Years*, p. 79.

25. Shizuko Ichihashi transcript, Registrar's Office, Stanford University. The first woman of Japanese ancestry to graduate from Stanford was Minnie Ruth Kimura, who was born in Carson City, Nevada, and graduated from Stanford in 1914. Kimura had been orphaned at the age of three and was adopted by Mary Gallagher Kimura; Cline, "The Twain Meet" and see note 82 to this chapter.

26. Jordan to Editor, *San Diego Union*, May 13, 1913, DSJ, B89, F791. Also see Jordan, *War and the Breed*, pp. 25–33; and Degler, *In Search of Human Nature*, p. 43.

27. See Burns, *Jordan: Prophet of Freedom*; and Fowler, "Some Aspects of Public Opinion," pp. 80–81.

28. Ichihashi to Jordan, March 8, 1907, B54, F527; Sept. 4, 1907, B56, F541; Sept. 16, 1907, B56, F542; Jan. 31, 1908, B58, F558; Feb. 24, 1908, B58, F561, all in DSJ. Fowler, "Some Aspects of Public Opinion," p. 80.

29. A version of the essay in Japanese also appeared in print, although it is not clear where. See clipping in B1, F3, Records of the Japanese Student Association, Stanford Special Collections, Green Library. On *The Outlook*, see Lewis, *DuBois*, pp. 122, 206, 207, and 224.

30. Quoted in Bailey, *Theodore Roosevelt*, p. 4.

31. Ibid., pp. 27, 327.

32. The editors of *The Outlook* rewrote important sections of what appears to be Ichihashi's manuscript, entitled "The Man From the East," n.d., IP, B2, F6. Most of the changes were stylistic, even though Ichihashi's written English was very good. In his draft, Ichihashi makes several positive references to the spiritual value of Christianity for Japan and to the inspiration of the "character" of America, its "manhood," embodied in Americans such as Theodore Roosevelt and David Starr Jordan: "We discover that America has a thing more valuable for us [than just a practical education] to learn. It is manhood. We have seen it, we want it, we will have it." These comments do not appear in the published version.

The Outlook's coverage of the Russo-Japanese War had been sympathetic to Japan. Its correspondent was George Kennan, who later also wrote essays on the condition of Japanese in San Francisco. See Kennan, "The Japanese in San Francisco Schools."

33. Ichihashi to Jordan, Feb. 24, 1908, B58, F561; Feb. 26, 1908, B58, F562; April 17, 1908, B59, F568; all in DSJ.

34. Harry Alvin Millis (d. 1948) received his doctorate from the University of Chicago and taught at Stanford from 1903 to 1912. He later joined the faculties of the University of Kansas and the University of Chicago, where he headed the Economics Department from 1926 to 1938. He specialized in labor economics and industrial relations. In 1934 President Franklin D. Roosevelt appointed him as one of the first three members of the National Labor Relations Board, which Millis headed from 1940 to 1945. He was the author of *The Japanese Problem in the United States* (1915).

35. See U.S. Senate, *Abstracts of Reports of the Immigration Commission*. Although 42 volumes were planned, only 41 were published.

36. Ichihashi, *Japanese Immigration*, rev. ed., 1915, p. 2.

37. Kathie O. Nicastro to author, Dec. 27, 1993. Ichihashi's name does not appear in the Commission reports, but there is no formal listing of all the agents. In the introduction to his report on Japanese immigrants, Millis acknowledges: "The Commission is placed under special obligation to four Japanese students who at different times have served it as interpreters and translators." He gave no names. U.S. Senate, *Reports of the Immigration Commission*, p. 4. On the other hand, Woodrow Ichihashi recalls his father's showing him an immigration commission badge; author's interview with W. Ichihashi, Feb. 22, 1995.

38. Ichihashi to Jordan, April 17, 1908, B59, F568; July 2, 1908, B60, F578; April 9, 1910, B67, F640; all in DSJ. In his letter of July 2, 1908, Ichihashi wrote: "I have been lately appointed a temporary assistant to that Immigration Commission headed by Prof. Mitchell of U.S. through the kind effort of Prof. Millis. Dr. Millis and I expect soon to start investigation of Japanese engaged in agricultural pursuits. This is the field assigned to us. The work will not only acquaint me with Prof. Mitchell's new method but also help me financially."

39. Ichihashi, "Emigration From Japan" (1913), pp. ii, iii.

40. Ichihashi to Jordan, April 28, 1910, DSJ, B67, F642.

41. Ichihashi to Jordan, Feb. 16, 1911, B71, F671; Feb. 22, 1911, B72, F679; April 10, 1911, B72, F682; all in DSJ. Ichihashi's Harvard transcript and Taussig to Haskins, March 27, 1911, both from University Archives, Pusey Library, Harvard University.

Before he became known as a political economist, Ripley was a professor of sociology at MIT, where he specialized in ethnography, the study of "race," so-called. His 1899 book *The Races of Europe: A Sociological Study* was a 600-page exploration of the relationships of racial "types," culture, politics, and geography in Europe, with comparisons to other "races" in the world. Carver was also interested in "ethnology," the comparative study of races heavily influenced by social Darwinist assumptions. See Degler, *In Search of Human Nature*, pp. 3–33, 61–81.

42. Ichihashi to Jordan, Nov. 5, 1911, DSJ, B75, F708.

43. Ichihashi to Jordan, Feb. 22, 1912, DSJ, B78, F724.

44. Ichihashi to Jordan, Feb. 16, 1911, B71, F671; March 16, 1911, B71, F677; March 25, 1911, B72, F679; Feb. 22, 1912, B78, F724; and Jordan to Ichihashi, Feb. 28, 1912, B78, F725; all in DSJ. For more on the history of the endowed chair, see Ichioka, "'Attorney for the Defense.'" E. D. Adams to Numano Yatsutarō, Nov. 5, 1913, and Payson J. Treat to E. D. Adams, April 29, 1914, B1, F49; both in History Dept. Files.

45. Ichihashi to Jordan, Sept. 7, 1912, DSJ, B82, F750.

46. Jordan to Iwasaki, Sept. 9, 1912, B82, F751; Jordan to Y. Fukukita, Sept. 10, 1912, B82, F751; and Jordan to T. Kuma, Sept. 10, 1912, B82, F751; all in DSJ. These are only three of many letters, which included several to the presidents of the leading universities in Japan. Fukukita Yasunosuke, a business leader, was president of the Stanford Alumni Association of Japan in the early 1930's; Fukukita to Wilbur, Sept. 27, 1933, Hoover Wilbur Papers, Box 47, Japanese.

47. *San Francisco Chronicle*, April 19, 1913, p. 4; April 27, 1913, p. 52.

48. See clippings in IP, B2, F1.

49. Ichioka, "'Attorney for the Defense,'" pp. 200–205.

50. Ibid.; "Report of the President," n.d., PJT, B24, 1951 Misc., Hoover Institution; Ichihashi to Jordan, May 20, 1913, DSJ, B89, F792. The link between the timing of the donation to Stanford and the Alien Land Act agitation did not go unnoticed even at the time. Treat to Adams, April 29, 1914, History Dept. Files, B1, F49. Today, most universities, including Stanford, seem to have little

difficulty accepting donations from foreign governments as long as the terms of the gifts do not violate academic integrity.

51. Ichihashi to Jordan, April 7, 1913, B88, F785; May 23, 1913, B89, F793; both in DSJ. Numano to Treat, March 4, 1914, B6, F2, John C. Branner Presidential Papers. Ichihashi to Jordan, Oct. 25, 1913, Hoover Jordan Papers, B24, Ichihashi.

52. Woodrow Ichihashi recalls his father working on a long manuscript, but it is nowhere to be found. It may have been destroyed with other papers after they were donated to the Hoover Institution. It seems not even excerpts were ever published.

53. Ichihashi, "Emigration from Japan" (1913), pp. 259, 396, 403.

54. Ichioka, *The Issei*, pp. 248–50.

55. Ichihashi, "Emigration from Japan" (1913), pp. 290–95, 417–18.

56. Adams to Ichihashi, June 2, 1913, History Dept. Files, B1, F49; *Annual Report of the President of the University, 1914*, pp. 31, 42, 54–55. There appears to be no material on Ichihashi in the Turner papers at Harvard or in the Turner Papers at the Huntington Library in San Marino, Calif.; Martin Ridge to author, Oct. 7, 1993.

57. After the passage of the 1882 Chinese Exclusion Act, Japanese were generally considered "aliens ineligible for citizenship." But because of the ambiguity of the term "white person," some lower courts allowed a few Japanese to become naturalized citizens before the Supreme Court definitively ruled on the racial and, thus, legal status of Japanese in 1922. In that year, in the case of Takao Ozawa, the Court declared that since Japanese were neither free white persons nor persons of African ancestry, the two classes of people Congress had explicitly recognized as possessing the right, Japanese could not become citizens of the United States. Not until 1952, with the passage of the McCarran-Walter Immigration Act, which ended discrimination on the basis of nationality or race in naturalization, could Japanese obtain U.S. citizenship. Children of Japanese immigrants, if they had been born on American soil, had always been considered U.S. citizens.

58. Ichihashi to Jordan, Oct. 25, 1913, Hoover Jordan Papers, B24, Ichihashi; Treat to Adams, April 12, 1914, PJT, B4, 1916–17/Special.

E. D. Adams received his doctorate from the University of Michigan and came to Stanford in 1902. He first taught European history, then American history and the history of British-American relations. He was head of the department from 1908 to 1922 and was instrumental in organizing what became known as the Hoover War Library (later the Hoover Institution). He was distantly related to Herbert and Henry Adams.

59. Ichihashi to Jordan, Oct. 25, 1913, Hoover Jordan Papers, B24, Ichihashi.

60. Sindo to Jordan, Jan. 30, 1908, DSJ, B58, F558. Sindo had assisted Jordan on two scientific essays, "A Review of the Japanese Species of Surf-fishes or Embiocidae" and "A Review of the Pediculate Fishes, or Anglers of Japan" (both 1902); he is explicitly acknowledged in the citation information.

61. Ichihashi to Adams, April 11, 1914, History Dept. Files, B1, F49.

62. Treat to Adams, April 29, 1914, History Dept. Files, B1, F49.

63. Adams to Ichihashi, March 5, 1914, History Dept. Files, B1, F49; Ichihashi to Jordan, Oct. 25, 1913, Hoover Jordan Papers, B24, Ichihashi; and Treat to Adams, April 29, 1914, History Dept. Files, B1, F49.

64. Ichihashi to Jordan, Aug. 18, 1914, DSJ, B91, F810. *Annual Report of the President of the University, 1915*, p. 63; and Ichioka, "'Attorney for the Defense,'" pp. 205–6.

65. Ichihashi to Adams, Feb. 14, 1914, April 11, 1914, May 19, 1914; Treat to Adams, April 12, 1914; all in B1, F49, History Dept. Files.

66. Jansen, *Japanese Studies*, p. 14. Treat to Adams, June 11, 1914, History Department Files, B1, F49. Ichihashi to Anesaki, June 5, 1924, IP, B2, F4. Anesaki later wrote, in English, *History of Japanese Religion*. In a letter to Jordan in 1915, Ichihashi describes Anesaki as a "very good friend" (March 3, 1915, Jordan Hoover Papers, B24, Ichihashi).

67. Jordan to Treat, May 24, 1913, DSJ, B89, F793. Treat (1879–1972) wrote a number of books, the best-known being a two-volume study entitled *Diplomatic Relations Between the United States and Japan, 1853–1895* (1932).

68. See Treat, "California and the Japanese."

69. Ichihashi to Treat, July 18, 1914, PJT, B2, 1914–15 E–M.

70. Ichihashi to Treat, Sept. 7, 1914, PJT, B2, 1914–15 E–M.

71. "Address: California University (1919).

72. Ichihashi to Numano, May 25, 1915, in Uyehara, *Checklist of Archives*, reel 746.

73. Ibid.

74. There are numerous documents related to the history of the gift from Japan in the Ray Lyman Wilbur Presidential Papers; the John Casper Branner Presidential Papers; and the Stanford History Dept. Files, all in Stanford Special Collections.

75. During the American occupation of Japan following World War II, the United States examined the archives of the Japanese Ministry of Foreign Affairs. Eventually the Library of Congress and the Department of State jointly supervised the microfilming of two million pages of archival documents. The material is described in Cecil H. Uyehara, comp., *Checklist of Archives in the Japanese Ministry of Foreign Affairs, Tokyo, Japan, 1868–1945*, pp. viii–xii, 25. The material described here is located on reel 746. Coincidentally, one of the individuals principally responsible for selecting documents for filming was the economic historian Thomas C. Smith, whom Stanford had hired to replace Ichihashi after World War II.

76. FBI report, Aug. 19, 1944, Ichihashi FBI File.

77. Ichihashi to Numano, Jan. 6, 1916, and Ichihashi to Acting Consul General, Dec. 28, 1915, Uyehara, *Checklist of Archives*, reel 746.

78. Ichihashi to Numano, Jan. 6, 1916, in ibid. Ichihashi was not alone among Japanese in his negative assessment of Japanese in America. See Iriye, *Pacific Estrangement*, pp. 107–50.

79. Ichihashi to Acting Consul General Yamasaki, May 17, 1916, Uyehara, *Checklist of Archives*, reel 746.

80. *Annual Report of the President of the University, 1915*, pp. 45–46, 63–66; *Annual Report, 1916*, pp. 64–65, 84; *Annual Report, 1917*, pp. 66, 69.

81. Adams to Wilbur, March 6, 1919, RLW, B30, F1.

82. Kiyoshi K. Kawakami, a prominent journalist and friend of Ichihashi, published extensively on Japanese foreign policy. His books include *American-Japanese Relations* (1912), *Asia at the Door* (1914), *Japan in World Politics* (New York, 1917), *Japan and World Peace* (1919), *Japan's Pacific Policy* (1922), and *The Real Japanese Question* (1921); Kawakami came to the United States in 1901 to study political science at the University of Iowa, where he earned a master's degree. He became a prominent leader in San Francisco's Japanese community. Although he served as an active, unofficial publicist for the Japanese government for much of his career, he became critical of Japan after Pearl Harbor. For more on Kawakami, see Ichioka, *Issei*, esp. pp. 190–91.

Toyokichi Iyenaga was also a prolific writer in English on international relations and Japanese foreign policy. His books include *How Shall We Keep Peace with Japan?* (1915), *Why Europe Is at War* (1915), *Japan's Real Attitude Toward America* (1916), *The Imperial Japanese Mission* (1917), and, with K. Sato, *Japan and the California Problem* (1921).

Jiuji G. Kasai arrived in the United States in 1903, completed high school in Seattle, and earned a bachelor's degree from the University of Chicago and a master's degree from Harvard. In 1913, the University of Chicago Press published the text of his speech delivered as an undergraduate under the title *The Mastery of the Pacific*. The speech had won the Julius Rosenwald Prize for Excellence in Oratory of the University, and university president Harry Pratt Judson wrote an introduction for its publication. While in the United States, Kasai wrote on Pacific affairs. After returning to Japan, he became a leading member of the Diet, but was arrested by the military police before the attack on Pearl Harbor because, he suggests, of his attitude toward the United States. He collected an extensive Abraham Lincoln library, which, to his great sorrow, was destroyed in the May 26, 1945, bombing of Tokyo. After the war, he became president of the Japan-American Cultural Society. His prize-winning lecture, with his own brief introductory material, can also be found in Jiuji G. Kasai, *To My Alma Mater: The University of Chicago, In Appreciation* [1973?].

"Inui" is apparently Kiyosue Inui, who had been a political science and law student at the University of Michigan and had distinguished himself as a lecturer in the Chautauqua circuit. He was the general secretary of the Japanese Association of America in 1912 and later became a lecturer at the University of Southern California and Occidental College; see Inui, *A Peace Tour Around the World* (1914). After returning to Japan in the early 1920's, Inui continued to write about Japan-U.S. relations. In 1915, he married Minnie Kimura, the first Stanford graduate of Japanese ancestry and the adopted daughter of Mary Gallagher Kimura, to whom Inui dedicated his book, *The Unsolved Problem of the Pacific* (1925). Gallagher was an interesting figure herself: in 1886 she married Kimura Jun, a University of Michigan student from a prominent Japanese family, and went to Japan with him. Kimura's family, however, did not accept the marriage, and Mary returned to the United States after teaching in Japan for several years. She moved to Palo Alto and became well known for her civic, church, and campus activities. Cline to author, Sept. 27, 1993, and Cline, "The Twain Meet."

83. Flowers, "The Third Conflict." Flowers also devoted pages of his earlier book, *The Japanese Conquest of American Opinion*, to attacking Ichihashi: "Japanese, employed in colleges, are teaching the subjects of 'Immigration' and 'American Foreign Relations.' Dr. Ichihashi, of the Leland Stanford University, is a case in point. He teaches the general subject of 'immigration.' I recently had a conversation with one of the students who had taken his course. She was a sweet-minded young lady, of possibly eighteen or nineteen; I found her *en rapport* with the Japanese singly and as a nation, and wholly persuaded that California was wrong and that the Japanese should be permitted to come into this country on equal terms and in numbers with all other people. She stated that the whole of Leland Stanford University is as highly sympathetic as herself. I asked her what reasons lay in her mind for this sympathy, both on her part and that of the University. Her answer is a revelation, 'I do not know where I got the idea, whether Ichihashi gave it, or which of the Professors gave it, but Stanford is grateful to the Japanese for the part they played in the establishment of the University. You see Stanford was founded by Senator Stanford, who made his money in constructing railroads, and it was the Japanese labourers, who worked for him in building the railroads, that enabled him to make the profits with which the University is now endowed!' Seven mature persons besides myself heard this statement made. Is it not appalling? The fact is that, at the time when Senator Stanford had finished all of his railroad construction, there were not a total of a thousand Japanese in the United States. Thus, stopping up or poisoning with false sentiment the very springs of our national life—*the schools*—Japan proceeds on her conquest of American opinion" (pp. 131–32).

Ichihashi also came under attack from an eccentric Japanese instructor at UC Berkeley, Yoshi Kuno, who accused him of being a propagandist for Japan. See the 1920 correspondence between Kuno and Wilbur in RLW, B40, F4, and Ichioka, "'Attorney for the Defense.'"

84. Author's interview with W. Ichihashi, Oct. 29, 1992.

85. Okei Maki listed her birthplace at Aomori-shi, Aomori-ken, Japan, and incorrectly transliterated a part of her school's name as "Zyoshi." Biographical information from author's interview with W. Ichihashi, Oct. 29, 1992, and relocation camp registration material. Also see Scheiner, *Christian Converts*, pp. 7–40. There is some question about Okei Maki's name. In the usual Japanese practice, "O" is used before a person's given name to suggest informality or affection. Mrs. Ichihashi, however, used the name "Okei" in her legal documents, although Yamato and her American friends regularly called her "Kei," perhaps became it sounded like a common American name. She referred to herself as "Kei" as well.

86. Etsu Inagaki Sugimoto, *A Daughter of the Samurai*, pp. 24, 131, 97. It is unclear to which character in Japanese "kinoji" refers. Also see Baroness Shidzué Ishimoto, *Facing Two Ways*, which is another autobiographical account of a woman's upbringing in Japan and her travel to America in the first decades of

the twentieth century. Romantic love was not seen as a principal ingredient in marriage by most issei; Yanagisako, *Transforming the Past*, p. 108.

87. Sugimoto, *Daughter*, pp. 139–44.

88. Author's interview with Nancy McLean, July 14, 1993.

89. Kikumura, *Harsh Winters*, p. 112.

90. Passenger arrival lists, National Archives, Pacific Sierra Region; *Japanese Who's Who in America, 1922* (1922), p. 477. Seizo Oka brought the latter item to my attention.

91. Marriage license, Book 164, Page 243, San Francisco City and County Marriage Bureau. Most ceremonies involving picture brides were conducted on the docks immediately after the women disembarked.

92. Iriye, *Across the Pacific*, p. 153. Many in the Stanford community mistakenly believed that Woodrow's middle name was Wilson.

93. Reynolds, "Oriental-White Race Relations," p. 128; Lukes and Okihiro, *Japanese Legacy*, pp. 50–52, 70–72.

94. See clippings from local newspapers in the "Japanese" file compiled by the Palo Alto Historical Society in the main branch of the Palo Alto Public Library.

95. Treat to his father, Dec. 20, 1915, PJT, B38, With Father, 1912–21; Jessie Jordan to Whom It May Concern, May 5, 1942, Hoover Jordan Papers, B87, F1. Payson Treat, "A Stanford Anecdote," *Stanford Alumni Almanac* 6: 8, May 1968. Nakasawa died in relocation camp in Nov. 1942.

96. Fowler, "Some Aspects of Public Opinion," p. 79.

97. *Palo Alto Times*, Dec. 16, Dec. 17, 1920. According to one study, the Japanese in Santa Clara County attracted much greater public interest than did the Chinese during the same period. From 1912 to 1923, one researcher wrote, an "amazing total of 2,877 items and 20,453 inches of space" in Santa Clara County newspapers were devoted to articles on Japan and Japanese in America. Most of the coverage was antagonistic in point of view. Typically, the articles were "complaints concerning their economic behavior, agitation in favor of legislative discrimination against them, [or expressions of] fear concerning their growing numbers or power" (Reynolds, "Oriental-White Race Relations," pp. 286–87, 295).

98. William C. Smith, "Interview with Prof. Y. Ichihashi of Stanford" [1925?], Survey of Race Relations, B32, Document #337, Hoover Institution.

99. Adams to Wilbur, March 6, 1919, RLW, B30, F1.

100. Ichihashi to Jordan, Oct. 7, 1919, DSJ, B98, F874.

101. *New York Times*, Sept. 29, 1919, p. 15; Nov. 9, 1919, IX, p. 4. International Labor Conference, *Delegates' Guide*.

102. League of Nations, *International Labour Conference*, pp. 52, 159–60, 166. International Labor Organization, League of Nations, *Report on the Eight-Hours Day*. The Japanese government delegates were Kamada Eikichi, president of Keio University and member of the House of Peers, and Oka Minoru, ex-director of the Bureau of Commerce and Industry of the Department of Agriculture and Commerce. The "employer's delegate" was Mutō Sanji, the "worker

delegate" Masumoto Uhei. No material revealing Ichihashi's thoughts about the conference and his role in it has been found.

103. New York FBI Report, Sept. 26, 1921, in Ichihashi FBI File. On the Vanderlip delegation see Taft, *Japan and America*, pp. 3–108. Taft misspelled Ichihashi's name as "Ishihase." Taft's book was reviewed by Ichihashi in *Pacific Affairs* (Dec. 1932).

104. Taft, *Japan and America*, pp. 48, 83–85.

105. *Annual Report of the President of the University, 1920*, pp. 180–81; *Annual Report, 1921*, pp. 153–54; *Annual Report, 1922*, p. 154. Ichihashi, *The Washington Conference* (1928), p. 6. Ichihashi had an interest in an Englishman named Will Adams, who in 1600 was the first from his country to visit Japan. An undated Ichihashi lecture shows that he conducted research on Adams in London, Rotterdam, and Tokyo. "Will Adams, the English Pioneer in Japan," n.d., IP, B2, F6.

106. League of Nations' Association of Japan, *Activities*. Though of humble origins, Shibusawa was one of the first Japanese to travel to Europe, visiting Paris in 1867, even before the Meiji Restoration. His impressions of the West are discussed in Keene, *Japanese Diaries*, pp. 76–89. Shibusawa first visited the United States in 1902 and then again in 1909 as head of a commercial commission. In a memoir of those visits he fondly recalled meetings with David Starr Jordan, but also recounts the discrimination faced by Japanese in America, including one particular insult: Shibusawa stated that an indoor swimming pool in San Francisco's Golden Gate Park bore a sign declaring "Japanese not admitted." Shibusawa, "Japanese-American Relations and Myself," in Masaoka, ed., *Japan's Message*, pp. 19–36.

107. Ichihashi remained close to Shibusawa and even wrote a flattering essay about him that so pleased the financier he had it translated into Japanese. Shibusawa to Jordan, Feb. 6, 1929, and May 25, 1929, Hoover Jordan Papers, B79, Shibusawa.

108. Adams to Wilbur, Aug. 20, 1920, DSJ, B89, F790; Summaries of the "Report of the President," n.d., PJT, B24, 1951 Misc.; *Annual Report of the President of the University, 1920*, pp. 180–81; *Annual Report, 1921*, pp. 153–54; *Annual Report, 1922*, p. 154; Ichioka, "'Attorney for the Defense,'" pp. 208–10.

In 1954, Duncan I. McFadden, University Controller, conducted an exhaustive investigation into the history of the funding of the chair Ichihashi had held. In his report to J. E. Wallace Sterling, Stanford's president at the time, the controller stated that in all the documentation he consulted, "no mention is made of any of the names of the Japanese individuals who contributed to the fund except that of Viscount E. Shibusawa." McFadden also cited an Ichihashi letter that stated Ichihashi had been informed by Shibusawa himself about the collection of the money, though Shibusawa did not identify specific funders. McFadden to Sterling, Jan. 5, 1954, History Dept. Files, B2, F79.

109. Ichihashi normally traveled under regular Japanese papers. FBI Reports, Sept. 9, 12, and 13, 1922, Ichihashi FBI File.

110. Office of Naval Intelligence to State and Department of Justice (FBI),

Nov. 8, 1921; L. McNamee and R. E. Ingersoll to State and Justice, Oct. 5, 1921; and W. J. Burns, FBI Director, to E. J. Brennan and Frank M. Sturgis, Oct. 11, 1921, all in Ichihashi FBI File.

111. FBI Report, Sept. 13, 1921, Ichihashi FBI File.

112. Washington FBI Report, Sept. 15, 1921; Baltimore FBI Report, Sept. 14, 1921; Chicago FBI Report, Sept. 17, 1921; San Francisco FBI Report, Sept. 20, 1921; all in Ichihashi FBI File.

113. New York FBI Report, Oct. 6, 1921, Ichihashi FBI File; and Walker to George Price, Sept. 22, 1921, Wilbur Personal Papers, B37, Ichihashi. This latter memo requests information about Ichihashi for the Department of Justice, which, according to the memo, was "surprised to find that whereas he was previously using a passport as a student or investigator, he now has a diplomatic passport." The response was highly favorable of Ichihashi. The source, who because of the FBI's document eliding is not identified except as a "confidential informant on Japanese matters," stated that Ichihashi was "a good teacher, a scholar and a gentleman. As far as I know there has been no suspicion of propaganda in regard to him. I think that he is a very high-minded Japanese who understands America and its attitude on Oriental problems. I feel that he can be of the greatest of service at the Conference on Limitation of Armaments." A copy of a letter Wilbur sent to the FBI appears to be the source of these comments; see Ichioka, "'Attorney for the Defense,' " p. 222, n. 65.

114. *Annual Report of the President of the University, 1920*, pp. 180–81; *Annual Report, 1921*, pp. 153–54.

115. Material on the Washington Conference can be found in IP, B1, Folders 3, 4.

116. U.S. Senate, *Conference on the Limitation of Armament*, p. 37; *Annual Report of the President of the University, 1922*, p. 154. Also, see translated speeches and notes from meetings in IP, B1, F2 and 3.

117. Clipping in Ichihashi FBI File.

118. U.S. Senate, *Conference on the Limitation of Armament*; Player, *Arms— and the Men*; Ichihashi, *Washington Conference*, p. 31.

119. Ichihashi, *Washington Conference*, pp. 340–50; Raymond Leslie Buell, *The Washington Conference*, pp. vii, 328–68; Iriye, *Across the Pacific*, p. 143; and Bailey, *Diplomatic History*, pp. 636–48. For a different contemporaneous view of the Conference by another Japanese in America see Kawakami, *Japan's Pacific Policy*.

PART I, CHAPTER 2

The title of this chapter is taken from that of an editorial in the *Stanford Daily*, Jan. 6, 1938.

1. See DeConde, *Ethnicity*, pp. 91–93; and Lauren, *Power and Prejudice*, pp. 76–101.

2. Mears, "California's Attitude," p. 199.

3. Iriye, *Pacific Estrangement*, chaps. 1, 2.

4. Quoted in Ichioka, "'Attorney for the Defense,'" pp. 208–9.

5. Jordan to W. H. Taft, April 12, 1910, National Archives, Records of the Dept. of State, RG 59, Numerical File, 1906–10, Doc. #12050/3; Wilbur to Ichihashi, April 18, 1913, RLW, B50, F3. Ichihashi, *Japanese Immigration* (1915).

6. Ichihashi, "Americanizing the Japanese," manuscript, [1920?], UCLA Special Collections 2010, B158, F4. Ichihashi to Jordan, March 3, 1915, Hoover Jordan Papers, B24, Ichihashi. On Abiko, see Ichioka, *The Issei*, pp. 60, 146–50, and "'What Manner of Man?'"

7. Ichihashi, "Fourth of July Speech at San Jose," manuscript, 1917; "Japanese Appreciation of American Diplomacy" manuscript [1918?]; "The War and Japanese Intellectuals" [1919]; "Westernized Japan," *Japan* (1919); all in IP, B2, F5. For an American perspective on the political climate in Japan, following World War I, see Dewey, *China, Japan, and the U.S.A.*

8. Iriye, *Across the Pacific*, pp. 151–53.

9. For example, Ichihashi frequently wrote during the 1920's for *Japan*, which called itself "The Magazine of Overseas Travel." It was a monthly magazine published in English in San Francisco and distributed for tourists throughout the United States and other Pacific countries. The publisher was Tōyō Kisen Kaisha (Oriental Steamship Company), a Japanese company whose president had early discussions with David Starr Jordan about funding the chair in Japanese studies at Stanford.

Ichihashi's articles in *Japan* include, "Results: What Was Accomplished for the United States and Japan at the Washington Conference" (July 1922); "Admiral Baron Kato: New Premier of Japan" (Aug. 1922); "Count Yamamoto, New Prime Minister of Japan" (Nov. 1923); "Japanese Catastrophe and American Humanitarianism" (Dec. 1923); "The Eventful Era of Taishō" (Feb. 1927); and "The Record of the Centuries: The Historian Looks Backward" (May 1928).

10. Ichihashi, "Japanese Catastrophe" (1923), pp. 24, 55; "Westernized Japan," *Mid-Pacific* (1925), pp. 531–34.

11. Ichihashi, "Results" (1922), pp. 32–33, 45; "Some of the More Obvious Changes I Saw in Japan," manuscript [1923?], IP, B2, F6.

12. Ichihashi, *The Washington Conference*, pp. 155–56.

13. Ichihashi, "Admiral Baron Kato," p. 28; *The Washington Conference*, pp. 289–90. Also see "The Reign of Emperor Yoshihito: The Era of Taishō," manuscript, n.d., IP, B2, F7.

14. On this point see Ichioka, "Japanese Immigrant Nationalism."

15. *The Stanford Book-Worm* 1, 1 (Jan. 1929): 4 and 1, 3 (July 1929): 1–2, 4. I thank Cindy Gammer of Stanford University Press for bringing this to my attention.

16. FBI report, June 10, 1942, Ichihashi FBI File; Iriye, *Pacific Estrangement*, pp. 233–34, and *Across the Pacific*, pp. 153, 211.

17. Ichihashi, "Japanese Catastrophe" (1923), pp. 24, 55; see also manuscript version, IP, B2, F6.

18. Unidentified clipping, n.d., B1 F1; and Ichihashi, "The London Naval

Conference," lecture, n.d., B2, F5; both in IP. On how whites regarded Ichihashi, see Fowler, "Some Aspects of Public Opinion," pp. 153, 156.

19. In 1954, when the federal government investigated the IPR, J. Edgar Hoover brought Ichihashi's relationship to the organization to the attention of the CIA. Hoover to Director of the CIA, Feb. 15, 1954, Ichihashi FBI File.

20. Iriye, *Pacific Estrangement*, p. 233; and Ichihashi to Anesaki, June 5, 1924, IP, B2, F4.

21. *Annual Report of the President of the University, 1925*, p. 185; Wilbur, *Memoirs*, pp. 317–23; materials from the IPR Conference, IP, B1, F5 and F6. Also see Ichihashi, "The Asiatic Nations as They Are Today," lecture [1926?], B1, F7; and "Japan's Influence and Interests in China," lecture, March 1928, B2, F5; both in IP.

22. FBI reports, Aug. 12, 1922, and Sept. 9, 1922, Ichihashi FBI File.

23. Quoted in Kitano, *Generations*, p. 28. Kawai earned his Stanford B.A. in 1926, an M.A. in 1928, and a Ph.D. in 1938 (Kawai transcript, Registrar's Office).

24. Hayashi, *Japanese Brethren*, pp. 42–43.

25. "Tentative Findings of the Survey of Race Relations," March 21–26, 1925, pp. 1–5, B5, Tentative Findings; clipping from *Palo Alto Times*, March 24, 1925, B5, Clippings; "West Coast Oriental Survey," Sept. 12, 1923, B5, Minutes and Progress Reports; and "Suggested Plan for a Survey of the Japanese Situation in California," Sept. 3, 1924, B6, Cooperating Institutions (Ichihashi worked with his old friends Kiyutaro Abiko and Harvey Guy in the project); all in Survey of Race Relations Papers, Hoover Institution. Ichihashi, "The Awakening of the Orient," manuscript, 1925, IP, B2, F6.

26. See Millis, *The Japanese Problem in the United States*; Mears, *Resident Orientals* and "California's Attitude."

27. See Strong, *Japanese in America*; *The Second-Generation Japanese Problem*; and *Vocational Aptitudes of Second-Generation Japanese in the United States*.

28. Thomas A. Bailey (1903–1983) completed his undergraduate and graduate education at Stanford, receiving his doctorate in 1927. He was chair of the History Department from 1952 to 1955 and from 1957 to 1959. He was the author of seventeen books on diplomatic history and was elected president of the Organization of American Historians and the Society of Historians for American Foreign Relations.

29. See Lasker, *Filipino Immigration*, p. 7, n. 1. Strong, Bell, and Reynolds were all considered specialists on the Japanese in California; see "Speakers Foresee Race Trouble From Laws Irritating Asiatics," *Palo Alto Times*, March 15, 1935.

30. See, for example, Reynolds, "Oriental-White Race Relations"; Arthur G. Butzbach, "Segregation of Orientals in the San Francisco Schools," M.A. thesis, Stanford University, School of Education, 1928; and Fowler, "Some Aspects of Public Opinion."

31. *Annual Report of the President of the University, 1928*, p. 238; and *Annual Report, 1929*, p. 371.

32. Ichihashi, *Japanese in the United States* (1932), pp. 56–61, 112–15.

33. *Ibid.*, pp. 147–50, 174–76, 201–4, 351–52. Ichihashi's papers include far more notes and reports of local conditions than are reflected in his published writings. See, for example, the material in B2, F1 and F2 for notes from his research from 1927–30, which includes his own observations as well as transcripts of interviews. This material also suggests that he had once begun a major study, never completed, of the Japanese flower growers of the San Francisco area.

34. Ichihashi, *Japanese in the United States* (1932), pp. 362–63.

35. Ibid., pp. 347–63.

36. See Daniels, *Asian America*, pp. 275–76.

37. Ichihashi, "American Feeling Toward the Japanese in Los Angeles," notes [1929?], IP, B2, F1.

38. Reviews include, Andrew W. Lind, *Pacific Affairs* 6 (1933): 117–18; and Charles E. Martin, *American Journal of International Law* 27 (1933): 373–74. Edgar Robinson, then the chair of the History Department, praised the book to his friend when it was published: "May I congratulate you on its scholarship," Robinson wrote Ichihashi. "But that is to be expected. In particular do I admire the fine balance and rigid finality with which you have presented a most difficult subject. It must be destined to stand as a landmark in the literature on this subject" (Robinson to Ichihashi, Nov. 2, 1932, EER, B7, F46).

39. *Annual Report of the President of the University, 1931*, pp. 200, 286–89; Program of the PCB-AHA 1930 Meeting, PJT, B11, 1930 Misc.; Program of the PCB-AHA 1934 Meeting, PJT, B14, 1934 A–F; Program of the PCB-AHA 1936 Meeting, PJT, B15, 1936 Misc.; and Program of the PCB-AHA 1939 Meeting, PJT, B17, 1939 Misc.

40. Ichihashi, "Japanese Studies in American Universities" (1937), p. 7; Ichihashi to an unnamed Stanford colleague [1937?], IP, B2, F4.

41. Arthur Wright and Ichihashi corresponded when the former was a student at Oxford University (IP, B2, F4). Gordon Wright has affectionate recollections of Ichihashi, whom he came to know well when he was a graduate student; he drove Ichihashi to conferences and had Ichihashi as a member of his doctoral orals committee in 1939. After the war, Gordon Wright became a member of the Stanford history department and the Wrights and Ichihashis were neighbors on campus; author's interview with Gordon and Louise Wright, July 21, 1993 and G. Wright to author, Oct. 12, 1991. Meribeth Cameron recalls, "In the 1920's California was a hotbed of anti-Japanese propaganda and to come out of that atmosphere to the calm, thoughtful, scholarly atmosphere of Mr. Ichihashi's classes was a revelation. I know that I liked, respected and admired [Ichihashi] and found him an excellent teacher" (Cameron to author, March 31, 1995). Cameron's 1929 doctoral thesis, "The Reform Movement in China, 1898 to 1912," was later published and became a classic study in the field.

42. Ichihashi to Wilbur, May 31, 1937, IP, B2, F4; and clipping from *Nippon Times* attached to diary entry of Aug. 5, 1953, IP, B11. For a description of the state of East Asian studies on the West Coast in the 1930's, see Treat to Evarts[?], Feb. 23, 1931, PJT, B12, 1931 G–Q.

43. Ichihashi, "Political Developments in Japan" (1930).

44. Ichihashi to Robinson, Sept. 12, Sept. 27, and Nov. 16, 1932, and April 3, 1933; all in EER, B7, F46. Ichihashi to Treat, Nov. 14, 1932, PJT, B13, 1932 G–O and April 3, 1933, PJT B13 A–J. See also Borton, *Japan's Modern Century*, pp. 322–42. Some of the notes from Ichihashi's Tokyo University lectures are found in IP, B1, F2.

Edgar Eugene Robinson (1887–1977) had been an undergraduate student of Frederick Jackson Turner at the University of Wisconsin but never completed a doctorate. He joined the Stanford faculty in 1911 and taught a course on western American history until his retirement in 1952. A major force at the university throughout his 65 years there, he headed the Stanford History Department for 24 years and occasionally filled in for Wilbur as acting president. He attended the Washington Disarmament Conference in 1922 as a representative of the Hoover Library and published several books on the American presidency. See Robert De Roos, "Edgar Robinson Held Sway as Teacher, Author, Administrator," *Campus Report*, Sept. 9, 1992, p. 10.

45. Ichihashi, "Watashi no mita Amerika no kinkyō" (My observations of the current situation in the United States) (1932), pp. 1–24. In the same volume is "Beikoku no kinkyō to saikin no nichibei-kankei" (Current situation in the United States and recent developments in the U.S-Japan Relationship), which contains similar comments. Ichihashi's papers contain two lectures, "History of Japan-U.S. Diplomatic Relations" and "Japanese Immigration to the U.S.," which he apparently delivered at Tokyo University; IP, B1, F2. Also see the report on his activities in *Annual Report of the President of the University, 1932–1933*, pp. 340, 530.

46. Although Ichihashi frequently spoke on Japanese culture, he published virtually nothing about it. The only two examples I could find are a brief retelling of a Japanese folktale, "Hagoromo, the Winged Robe" (1909), and "The Record of the Centuries: The Historian Looks Backward" (1928).

47. See Ichihashi, "Gendai Amerika wo ronzu" (1933).

48. Clipping, "Ichihashi Is Commentator On Doctrine," [*Palo Alto Times?*], April 26, 1934; and clipping, "Defense Plans Forced on Japan, Says Ichihashi," *Palo Alto Times*, Aug. 6, 1934; both in IP, B1, F1; Yamato Ichihashi, "Japan's Rights and Obligations in the Pacific" (1936).

49. Ichihashi to Treat, Nov. 17, 1935, PJT, B14, 1935 G–M. Also see Ichihashi, "The Far East and World Peace" (1935).

50. Ichioka, "Japanese Immigrant Nationalism," p. 260. Also see Hayashi, *Japanese Brethren*, pp. 104–9.

51. Hall, "Kan'ichi Asakawa: Comparative Historian," pp. 3–21; Asakawa to Bloch, Jan. 8, 1930, in Committee for the Publication of Dr. Kan'ichi Asakawa's Letters, *Letters*, p. 45. Asakawa also once suggested that Yale University Press might approach Ichihashi to write a book about the Japanese in the United States; Asakawa to Chitoshi Yanaga, Feb. 2, 1942, *Letters*, p. 128. Ichihashi had a high regard for Asakawa's work; see for example, his review of Asakawa's translation and editing of *The Documents of Iriki* (1929).

Payson Treat, comparing the lecturing abilities of Ichihashi and Asakawa, concluded that Ichihashi was more effective. Ichihashi "knows how to present his material in an attractive and forceful way" (Treat to Greene, May 16, 1917, PJT, B4, 1916–17 G–M).

52. Clippings, Cedric Larson, "Viewing the News," *Stanford Daily*, Oct. 30, 1934, Jan. 25, 1935, IP, B1, F1; clipping, "Prof. Treat Tells of Japan's Plan to Advance Peace," *Stanford Daily*, March 4, 1936, PJT, B15, 1936/misc. In 1933, Treat sent a long letter to his friend Nelson T. Johnson, then American ambassador in Peking, that presented his ideas about the Sino-Japanese conflict and defended himself from allegations he was "pro-Japanese":

> But what I very much resent is the now long-persistent effort of Chinese and their American sympathizers to involve the United States in a controversy—preferably war—with Japan. I would not see the blood of a single American doughboy shed in defence of *China*. If it is shed, it must be in defence of vital *American* interests.
>
> These interests, in Asia, are as you describe them—the right to trade peacefully and on a basis of equality with the peoples there. By equality I would mean the American theory of qualified most favored nation treatment. Unless the ruling class of Japan at any given moment goes quite mad I do not envisage any impairment of our interests in this direction." (Treat to Johnson, Sept. 16, 1933, PJT, B13, 1933/A-J).

53. *Annual Report of the President of the University, 1933–34*, pp. 237–331; *Annual Report, 1934–35*, pp. 316–18; *Annual Report, 1935–36*, pp. 313–15, 506; *Annual Report, 1936–37*, pp. 341–45, 545; Wilbur, *Memoirs*, p. 603; materials from the Second America-Japan Student Conference provided to the author by Caitlin James, Japan-America Student Conference; Woo, "Japanese Educator Denies 'Invasion'."

54. Robinson to Ichihashi, June 13, 1936, History Dept. Files, B2, F68.

55. Delmer Brown to Treat, Aug. 23, 1937, PJT, B16, 1937 A–G; *Bulletin of the America Japan Society*, 1, 1 (1937): 3.

56. Ichihashi to Robinson, Nov. 4, 1937, EER, B11, F119; Ichihashi to Treat, Nov. 15, 1937, PJT, B16, 1937 H–O.

57. Announcement, Jan. 4, 1938; clipping, "China Began Asiatic War: Ichihashi," Jan. 5, 1938; both from *Stanford Daily* in IP, B2, F5.

58. Clipping, "Son of the Rising Sun," *Stanford Daily*, Jan. 6, 1938, IP, B2, F5.

59. See various clippings from the *Stanford Daily* in IP, B2, F5; *Annual Report of the President of the University* for the academic years 1938–39 through 1942–43.

60. Author's interview with Kazuyuki and Soyo Takahashi, Aug. 2, 1993. Ichihashi's colleagues recall his isolation and bitterness in the late 1930's; author's interview with Gordon and Louise Wright, July 21, 1993.

61. Author's interview with W. Ichihashi, Feb. 22, 1995; Ichihashi to Treat, Oct. 27, 1935, and Nov. 17, 1935, both in PJT, B14, 1935 G–M.

62. The following account of Ichihashi's home life is drawn largely from interviews with Woodrow Ichihashi on April 5, Oct. 29 and 30, 1992, and Feb. 22, 1995. His comments reflect his days at home from the mid-1920's through the late 1930's.

63. Program of Japan Society of America dinner for Tsuneo Matsudaira,

March 6, 1925, PJT, B8, 1925 E–M; dinner invitation from S. Nakase, Manager of Nippon Yūsen Kaisha, Nov. 24, 1931, PJT, B12, 1931 G–Q.

64. See material in Japanese Student Association Files, Stanford Special Collections. Author's interview with Kazuyuki and Soyo Takahashi and Kenzie and Mary Nozaki, Aug. 2, 1993.

65. Author's interviews with W. Ichihashi; interview with Gordon and Louise Wright, July 21, 1993. "I am a Christian myself," Ichihashi once wrote David Starr Jordan (March 3, 1915, Hoover Jordan Papers, B24, Ichihashi).

66. Author's interviews with John Johnson, Sept. 8, 1992; Yoshio Okumoto, Sept. 9, 1992; W. Ichihashi, Oct. 30, 1992; Kenji Ito, June 18, 1992; Gordon and Louise Wright, July 21, 1993; Nancy McLean, July 14, 1993; and George Knoles, June 11, 1992.

67. Lisette Fast graduated Phi Beta Kappa from Stanford in 1919. After graduate study at Bryn Mawr and the University of Washington she returned to Stanford, where she spent the rest of her life. She worked as the social secretary for Marguerite Blake Wilbur, wife of the Stanford president, in the early 1920's before moving to the History Department. She married Edgar Robinson in 1970 after the death of his first wife; the three had lived for many years in the same residence on campus. Lisette Fast died in 1992 at the age of 94. Her brother Emery Fast, a Stanford alumnus and a friend of Ichihashi, worked for the WRA helping camp residents resettle in California in 1945–46. Interview with Emery Fast, Oct. 3, 1993.

68. Author's interviews with Kazuyuki and Soyo Takahashi, Aug. 2, 1993; Nancy McLean, July 14, 1993; and Yoshio Okumoto, Sept. 9, 1992; Delmer Brown to Ichihashi, Aug. 1, 1945, IP, B7, F2; and Marguerite Wilbur to Dillon Myer, May 12, 1943, RLW, B123, History.

Ethel Barker married Emery Fast, Lisette's brother, and began working for Dillon Myer when he was at the Dept. of Agriculture in 1935. She and Emery visited Ichihashi after the war. Interview with Emery Fast, Oct. 3, 1993.

69. Interviews with Gordon and Louise Wright, July 21, 1993; and Nancy McLean, July 14, 1993.

70. George Yoshida, unpublished ms. on Japanese Americans and jazz, p. 41; author's interview with Kazuyuki and Soyo Takahashi, Aug. 2, 1993.

71. Quoted in Nee and Nee, *Longtime Californ'*, p. 383.

72. Ichihashi, "Japanese Studies" (1937); Ichihashi to Robinson, Nov. 4, 1937, EER, B11, F119.

73. Park, "Human Migration and the Marginal Man." Park is also quoted by Ronald Takaki, *Strangers from a Different Shore*, p. 13.

74. Bailey to Sterling, April 9, 1953, History Dept. Files, B2, F78. Handwritten note on Wright to Bailey, Nov. 20, 1953, History Dept. Files, B2, F79. Bailey believed that the terms of the endowment of Ichihashi's chair required it be filled by a professor of Japanese ancestry.

75. Ichihashi, "Japanese Studies" (1937) and "Japanese-American Relations" (1953). On race and uniforms, also see Chang, "'Superman is about to visit.'"

76. Lewis, *DuBois*, pp. 199–201.

77. See for example Chinn, *Bridging the Pacific*. Ichihashi also does not fall

neatly into what Robert E. Park called "the marginal man" in "Human Migration and the Marginal Man." Ichihashi's attitude toward Japan and his interest in "personal diplomacy" may perhaps best be compared with that of fellow historian Kan'ichi Asakawa; see Hall, "Kan'ichi Asakawa."

78. Quoted in Hayashi, *Japanese Brethren*, p. 122. Kawai later published *The Boxer Protocol Negotiations* (Stanford: Stanford University Press, 1938) and *Japan's American Interlude* (Chicago: University of Chicago Press, 1960).

79. Ichihashi to Anesaki, June 5, 1924, IP, B2, F4. Ichihashi usually spoke from the Japanese "point of view" in his talks, but on occasion he assumed an American vantage point. One such occasion was in an address to an academic audience in the 1930's in which he ostensibly spoke from an American perspective, even using the terms "we" and "our" in reference to such matters as the colonization of the Philippines and of U.S. interests in Asia. "Common Sense in International Relations," n.d., IP, B2, F6.

80. Ichihashi to Donald Nugent, May 21, 1946, IP, B7, F3.

81. Ichihashi, "Japanese-American Relations" (1953), p. 33.

82. Author's interview with Yoshio Okumoto, Sept. 9, 1992; Treat to Eleanor Hadley, Feb. 11, 1937, PJT, B15, 1937 H–O; Program of the Third Annual Northern California Intercollegiate Advance Conference at Stanford, April 9, 1938, PJT, B16, 1938 Misc.; and Sugahara, "Nisei." I thank Valerie Matsumoto for bringing this clipping to my attention and Caitlin James for sending copies of conference material from the 1935 and 1937 America-Japan Student Conferences. Ichihashi was a member of the National Advisory Board of the AJSC. On issei attitudes toward nisei, see Leighton, *The Governing of Men*, pp. 70–74.

83. A reviewer of *Japanese in the United States*, while praising the work overall, observed that the tone of Ichihashi's writing "diminishes its scientific value. It is quite clear that the author is playing the role of the attorney for the defense." The reviewer characterized the writing in different places in the book as "emotional." R. D. McKenzie, review, *Pacific Historical Review* 2 (1933): 347–48. Also see Ichioka, " 'Attorney for the Defense'."

84. Author's interview with Toichi Domoto, June 23, 1992. Domoto attended Stanford for a couple of years in the early 1920's, but his family, pioneering flower growers in the Oakland area since the late 1890's, had known Ichihashi for some time. The Ichihashis and the Domotos all were relocated to Amache during the war.

85. Baer to Ichihashi, Sept. 7, 1942, and Smith to Ichihashi, Oct. 26, 1942; both in IP, B5, F1.

86. Letters and interviews in possession of the author.

87. Tamotsu Shibutani to author, July 24, 1993. The gist of Shibutani's comments is endorsed by the description of the same event in the diary entry of Frank Miyamoto, Aug. 3, 1942 (Miyamoto diary, R21.03, JERS, 67/14, Bancroft Library, University of California, Berkeley). Robert Billigmeier, who earned his doctorate in history from Stanford in 1957 and later became a professor of sociology at UC Santa Barbara, wrote the following in 1992: "Yamato Ichihashi was a Stanford professor who was sent to Tule. The S.F. papers portrayed him

as the secret ruler of Tule Lake. But he was an aristocrat with no interest in Japanese-American farmers. Tom Shibutani, Frank Miyamoto and I were allowed to go with Professor Dorothy Thomas during one of her visits [to him]. We were not even introduced or noted as we stood in the living room while the seniors talked. Finally Mrs. Ichihashi directed us to seats in the dining room—away from any chance to follow the senior professor. He held himself to be a man of great academic position—certainly having no concern with the plight of Japanese barn farmers. He certainly did nothing to help the ordinary evacuees. But to the newspapers he was the secret leader" (Billigmeier to Jeannette Rust, quoted in Jeannette Rust to author, Dec. 29, 1992, in author's possession). As a product of a strict and formal academic tradition, Ichihashi expected deference from young academics, Billigmeier recalls; author's conversation with Billigmeier, Aug. 12, 1995.

Another assistant to the Thomases was Richard Nishimoto, a 1929 Stanford engineering graduate. After the war, Nishimoto was instrumental in helping publish several studies on relocation and was co-author of *The Spoilage* with Dorothy Thomas. Nishimoto's Stanford transcript shows that he took at least one course on Japanese history from Ichihashi. Like Ichihashi, Nishimoto was born in Japan, attended Lowell High School in San Francisco, and had a Stanford degree. He died in the mid-1950's. See Ichioka, ed., *Views from Within*, pp. 17, 65–94, and Nishimoto, *Inside an American Concentration Camp*.

88. Shirai, *Kariforunia nikkeijin kyōsei shūyōjo* (Concentration camps for Japanese Americans in California), pp. 17–19. Shirai was also one of the two witnesses to Ichihashi's signing of his formal will in September 1943. Ichihashi Probate File, No. 59701, Santa Clara County Municipal Records; and author's interview with Toichi Domoto, June 23, 1992.

89. See O'Brien and Fugita, *Japanese American*, p. 16.

90. Lewis, *DuBois*, pp. 196, 206, 209–10.

91. Ichihashi, *Japanese in the United States* (1932), pp. 18, 156.

92. Ibid., p. 156.

93. Ichihashi, "The Racial Superiority," n.d., IP, B1, F6.

94. Ichihashi, *Japanese in the United States* (1932), p. 209.

95. FBI Report, June 10, 1942, Ichihashi FBI File; author's interview with Gordon and Louise Wright, July 21, 1993.

96. See Fiftieth Anniversary Papers, SC 2, Stanford Special Collections, Green Library.

97. Cyclone Covey, "Farm Professors Hold Lively Debate in War Issues Panel," *Stanford Daily*, Oct. 3, 1941, p. 1, in Fiftieth Anniversary Papers, B11, F123; and *Palo Alto Times*, Oct. 3, 1941, p. 4.

98. FBI Report, June 10, 1942, Ichihashi FBI File.

99. Author's interviews with W. Ichihashi, Oct. 30, 1992; and Gordon and Louise Wright, July 21, 1993.

100. I am not disclosing the name of the student or providing other specific information that may identify her. FBI report of June 10, 1942, in Ichihashi FBI File; letter of Oct. 4, 1993, in author's possession; and conversation with a Stanford alumnus.

It was unthinkable for a woman raised in traditional ways, as Kei had been, to consider divorce. Baroness Shidzué Ishimoto, who wrote about her life in Japan and America and who was a contemporary of Kei's, stated, "It is an unwritten code that a Japanese woman shall have only one man in marriage in her lifetime. . . . To break the marriage tie on her own initiative is unthinkable for any well-bred Japanese woman" (*Facing Two Ways*, p. 101). It is likely that Kei knew of this book, since Payson Treat had favorably reviewed it in a professional journal.

101. Ichihashi to Jordan, March 3, 1915, Hoover Jordan Papers, Box 24, Ichihashi.

102. Draft letter, Ichihashi to Shizuko, Oct. 1945[?], in Japanese, B6, F8.

103. Author's interview with W. Ichihashi, Oct. 30, 1992.

EDITOR'S NOTE

1. Hansen to Thomas C. Smith, Jan. 18, 1968, and handwritten reply Smith to Hansen, IP, B4, F7.

2. The following are the first paragraphs of the unedited Ichihashi diary material. The reader may compare them with the edited version that appears in Part II Chapter 1. Similar editing was often necessary for other diary material, although relatively little was done on the correspondence. It is not clear why the quality of the English is so much poorer in the diary material, other than the fact that Yamato Ichihashi most likely devoted greater attention to the composition of his correspondence. He prided himself on his English ability, which was significantly better than Kei's.

Through Hideo Furukawa of the P.A. Service Committee learned the evacuation announcement Saturday morning (May 23,1942) at 11:00 A.M. Summoned for registration at San Jose (S.J.S. College gym) at 8 A.M. When learned learned Tuesday as the day of evacuation, I tried to negotiate for one day postponement; the office personel were unanimous in approving, including Liut. Holmes, Jr, the military provost, but the Central Office at S.F. said nothing doing.

So K & I busied ourselves in packing our luggage and arranging the house which was left in care of the University. A complete set of keys was left with Stoltenbergs & Lois Ruth Bailey. Left the house at 11:00 A.M. Tuesday (May 26th); Sam Anderson drove us to Mayfield where we assembled at the J.L.School, 472 Sheriden Ave. We were supposed to leave there at 12:00, but due to the inadequacy of trucks to carry luggage, we were detained until after 1 P.M.; we did not reach San Jose until 2:00. A medical examination was held and we did not get on the train until 3:00. It was a hot day, but we had to walk quite a distance with heavy luggage; it was cruel hardship on old people like ourselves. All this was done at the S.J. Freight Depot.

We entrained at 3:00; the cars composing this train were all old day coaches, dirty and smelly – no light in Laboratory which people, especially children dirtied in no time. Upholstered chairs showed moth-eaten spots. Basket-supper sandwiches, 2 cup-cakes, an orange and ¼ pt [?] milk at 6:00 P.M. This was repeated for breakfast (Wednesday). At night, heat was turned and it got too hot, so that electric fans were turned on; thus passengers suffered either from heat or draft. This was the worst-managed train experienced in U.S. in addition to the above characteristics. Each car was guarded by an armed soldier. Beside him there was a doctor and a nurse. All these people were nice and sympathetic. The train was supposed to reach the destination at 6 or 7 A.M. the following morning. But alas it did not reach S.A.A.C. till 12 : 30. It was a most trying trip – hot, dirty, very uncomfortable. But who were responsible for all this remains a question. At any rate, the delay was in part over detention at Los Angeles when an electric motor had to be substituted for a steam engine; we reached L.A. 7:00 A.M. but detained until 11 : 30. We missed lunches. K & I got exhausted in finding luggage and to have the same delivered to our woodshed. We had to stand in heat 2 1/2 hrs. When we got to our dwelling to be after 3 hrs, we were shocked to discover that it was empty except *mutsuki* drying which belonged to the next door. Luggage was piled up; at 5:00 much hoped for "supper" was to be had. We were assigned to the Mess Hall (Red) in the Main Building. As we approached it, we heard a terrific noise (later found the handling of used meal apparatus – metal plate designed like Stanford Union Blue Plates, a cup, a tea-spoon & a fork. Here thousands are at 3 intervals. For our supper we got Cherries Comport (white) 1/2 doz. a small quantity of baked spaghetti, a small boiled potato, rice and water to drink. Thus far we saw the shed and food both which made us feel very sad; it was an awful come-down. But when we returned to the shed, we found two dangerously wooden cot and we were told to pack bags with straw for mattress. This was too. By negotiations, I succeeded in obtaining two iron cots with mattresses, which are de luxe equipments as compared with the former. Having not slept a wink the previous night, we slept soundly in this hideous sleeping place, if it is fit to so designate.

3. Miyoshi, *As We Saw Them*, p. 108.

4. For a recent study of Japanese diaries, see Keene, *Japanese Diaries*.

5. I thank Gary Mukai for providing the Tule Lake directory and Paul Rodriguez for the Amache directory.

PART II, CHAPTER 1

1. Diary entry of Lisette Fast, Dec. 7, 1941, according to author's conversation with her niece, Lynn Bonner, Oct. 1993.

2. Girdner and Loftis, *The Great Betrayal*, pp. 10, 98; handwritten draft letter in Japanese, Ichihashi to Ichihashi Shizuko, Oct. 1945[?], IP, B6, F8. Ichihashi continued to buy bonds until November 1942, when he asked the Stanford payroll office to discontinue purchases; bond purchase receipts and memorandum, Stanford financial vice president to Ichihashi, Nov. 9, 1942, both in IP, B5, F1.

3. Edgar Eugene Robinson (1887–1977) joined the Stanford History Department in 1911 and became an institution at the university. Although he never completed a doctorate, he was head of his department for 24 years, beginning in 1929, and occasionally served as acting president of the university in Ray Lyman Wilbur's absence. Robinson came from the University of Wisconsin, where he had been a student of Frederick Jackson Turner, who had pioneered studies of the American frontier. As a representative of what became the Hoover Library, Robinson, like Ichihashi, attended the Washington Disarmament Conference of 1922.

4. Ray Lyman Wilbur, as president of Stanford University, devoted considerable attention to the fate of the relocated Stanford students and worked with

other educators to see that they eventually were able to complete their education. In April 1942, he wrote the House Select Committee Investigating National Defense Migration (known as the Tolan Committee), "It has been impossible for me to answer the many questions put to me by the [Japanese American] students as to *why* [they must relocate]. Everything that they have learned from babyhood up in this country is negatived by their present experience" (Wilbur to Tolan, April 13, 1942, RLW, B118, Japanese). It must be said, however, that Wilbur did not publicly oppose the general policy of forced evacuation. As he wrote in his memoirs, he did not agree with those "inclined to raise a hubbub" about evacuation since, "from a practical standpoint I think that in no other way could the safety of the Japanese people [on the West Coast] be assured if parachute troops invaded California" (Wilbur, *Memoirs*, pp. 606–7). Wilbur also did not favor an early mass return of Japanese to the coast, but did support student resettlement out of the camps. See Wilbur to Gerda Isenberg, June 12, 1944, Hoover Wilbur Papers, B47, Japanese Relocation. It is not clear whether Ichihashi knew the details of Wilbur's position.

5. Robinson diary entry of Dec. 8, 1941, EER, B66, 1941 Diary. Wilbur to Robinson, Dec. 9, 1941, EER, B15, F220. Ichihashi to Robinson, Dec. 10, 1941; Wilbur to Ichihashi, Dec. 19, 1941; Ichihashi to Wilbur, Dec. 26, 1941; all in RLW, B118, History.

6. *Palo Alto Times*, Dec. 8 and 9, 1941; Daniels, *Asian America*, p. 202. Even as the Palo Alto newspaper called for fair treatment of the Japanese, it referred to alien and citizen alike with an inappropriate term.

7. *Palo Alto Times*, Dec. 9, 1941; Yoshiro Oishi, President, and Peter Ida, Secretary, Japanese Student Association of Stanford University, to Dr. Wilbur, *Stanford Daily*, Dec. 11, 1941; Wilbur address to student body, Dec. 10, 1941, Wilbur Personal Papers, B48, 1941. Wilbur sent a personal letter to the president of the University of Oregon to ask him to watch out for the well-being of Ichihashi's son and wife, Kei, who were in Oregon at the time; Wilbur to Donald M. Erb, Dec. 26, 1942, RLW, B118, History.

8. Ichihashi to Don Nugent, May 21, 1946, IP, B7, F3.

9. Author's interview with John Johnson, Sept. 8, 1992. Johnson was a colleague of Ichihashi's and lived in the adjoining unit after the Stoltenbergs; Clara Stoltenberg to Ichihashis, Aug. 8, 1942, IP, B5, F1. Clara S. Stoltenberg (1865–1950), a professor of anatomy who had received her degrees from Stanford and had become emerita in 1930.

10. *Stanford Daily*, May 26, 1942. In Sept. 1942, the director of Stanford's library, in response to a military request for materials on Japan, arranged to recover 270 volumes from Ichihashi's office, some of which had been in his possession for "as long as twenty years." Much of the material was in Japanese, but the borrowed books also included a copy of Shakespeare's *A Midsummer Night's Dream*. Nathan Van Patten to Wilbur, Sept. 16, 1941, RLW, B124, Japanese; Ralph Lutz to Wilbur, Oct. 21, 1942, RLW, B123, History. The Department asked the Library to send "a light truck and two men" to retrieve the books from Ichihashi's office. Lutz to Van Patten, Sept. 17, 1942, EER, B17, F248. And see

Wilbur to Frank S. Walker, May 26, 1942, RLW, B118, History; Erwin to Wilbur, March 20, 1943, RLW, B123, History.

11. C.R. to Wilbur, May 25, 1942, RLW, B118, History. The Army took over Santa Anita race track on March 20, and the first residents began to arrive on April 3. Milton Silverman, "Assembly Centers: Santa Anita," [1942], JERS, B9.01.

12. Irwin Abrams to author, Nov. 1, 1992, in author's possession. Abrams and his wife, Freda Morrill Abrams, were members of the local meeting of the American Friends. Abrams taught in the History Department at Stanford from 1938 to 1943 and is now Distinguished University Professor Emeritus, Antioch University.

13. Recollection of Wat Takeshita. Japanese American Alumni Information Sheet, 1993. Collection of Stanford Asian American Activities Center.

14. *Stanford Daily*, May 26, 1942; Ichihashi to Wilbur, April 18, 1913, RLW, B50, F3. Katzuzo Nakasawa worked in the Jordan home almost continuously for 40 years, from Dec. 1902 until evacuation. He died in camp in Nov. 1942 at the age of 66, from complications of a prewar stroke; Jessie Knight Jordan to Whom It May Concern, March 5, 1942, Hoover Jordan Papers, B87, F1. A woman named Fusako worked as a maid for the Treats. Y. Ichihashi to J. Treat, June 9, 1942, PJT, B38, Ichihashis.

15. Yoshida to Treats, May 4, 1942, PJT, B19, 1942 A–J.

16. Beecher Kellogg, "144 Japanese Say Goodbye to Homes Here," *Palo Alto Times*, May 26, 1942, clipping in Japanese file, Palo Alto Public Library.

17. Blue book diary, "Evacuation to the Santa Anita A. Center," IP, B5, F2. This undated entry appears to have been written by Ichihashi a few days after his arrival at Santa Anita.

18. Hideo Furukawa graduated from Stanford in 1939.

19. Lois Ruth Bailey was a Stanford graduate and a secretary in the History Department.

20. Sam Anderson was affiliated with the American Friends.

21. A report on Santa Anita written in mid-April 1942 mentions that 2,216 "apartments" had been made from converted horse stalls. The army constructed 600 other buildings, including 585 barracks. The center was designed to hold 16,000 persons, although the actual number climbed to some 18,400. (Silverman, "Assembly Centers: Santa Anita,") JERS, B9.01.

22. Regulations at Santa Anita were typical, if somewhat stricter than at other centers. Girdner and Loftis, *Great Betrayal*, p. 169.

23. Treat Faculty Record, Feb. 9, 1945, PJT, B20, 1945 Misc. Treat spoke out against discriminatory laws against Japanese and Chinese in the 1920's and 1930's. He opposed all racial considerations in the immigration and naturalization laws, and actively supported the Citizens Committee to Repeal Chinese Exclusion in 1943. He later supported the NAACP. Richard J. Walsh to Treat, May 17, 1943, PJT, B20, 1943 K–Z.

24. PJT, B19, 1942 A–J.

25. "Chief" was a long-standing affectionate form of address used by various

members of the Stanford History Department with faculty senior to themselves. Treat used the term himself in earlier letters to the department chairman.

26. This word is indecipherable in the original text but may be "marvelous," which can mean either "exceptional" or "indescribable."

27. PJT, B38, Ichihashis.

28. J. Treat to Y. Ichihashi, June 2, 1942, PJT, B19, 1942 A–J. Jessie Treat's letter was primarily concerned with efforts to rent the Ichihashis' house. For various reasons, the house remained vacant for most of the war years and fell into disrepair. I omit subsequent letters and most references to the rental issue in the Treat-Ichihashi correspondence.

29. Yamato Ichihashi had enjoyed fishing expeditions into the California wilderness.

30. Blue book diary, "Evacuation to Santa Anita," IP, B5, F2. Ichihashi completed diary entries for May 26–June 5 but these largely repeat information included in his correspondence and so are not reproduced here.

31. Elections were held on June 5 for 49 positions on a "self-governing" council for Center residents.

32. The *issei* were the first or immigrant generation of Japanese in America. The *nisei*, or second generation, were the children of the issei, born in the United States and hence U.S. citizens. Until 1952, federal law prohibited the issei from becoming naturalized citizens of the United States.

33. IP, B5, F1.

34. Immediately after receiving the requests from the Ichihashis, the Treats spent two days shopping for the items, which they sent parcel post. P. Treat to Y. Ichihashi, June 4, 1942, PJT, B19, 1942 A–J.

35. The Wartime Civil Control Administration (WCCA) was created by the Western Defense Command on March 11, 1942, to take charge of the evacuation and to establish and run 15 assembly centers as temporary gathering places for the evacuees. The federal government later transferred responsibility for the evacuees to a civilian agency, the War Relocation Authority (WRA).

36. Two days later, Ichihashi wrote to Jessie Treat to tell her that the Ichihashis had forwarded to the Treats' former maid a magazine, soap, and a note the Treats had sent her. He again expressed his gratitude for the things sent by the Treats and said they had all been inspected by the camp authorities. "Despite inevitable hardships, we are learning to readjust our living to the best of our ability," Ichihashi wrote and concluded his letter, "We are suffering from stomach troubles" (Y. Ichihashi to J. Treat, June 9, 1942, PJT, B38, Ichihashis).

37. Blue book diary, "Evacuation to Santa Anita," IP, B5, F2.

38. Presumably, Ichihashi means that he would divide his efforts equally between service and recreation.

39. Ichihashi's PTA effort is mentioned in Lehman, *Birthright of Barbed Wire*, p. 50.

40. PJT, B38, Ichihashis.

41. Payson Treat described the table as one that was designed for "auto camping," stronger and more practical than a regular card table; the chairs

folded and had canvas backs. P. Treat to Y. Ichihashi, June 4, 1942, PJT, B19, 1942 A–J. I have not been able to find the June 9 letter.

42. After being placed on probation at Reed College for allegedly spending too much time on social activities, Woodrow Ichihashi had transferred to the University of Oregon in Eugene in 1940 to study architecture. Among the last Japanese Americans to leave Oregon, he was sent in June to Tule Lake Relocation Center in northeastern California. Author's interview with Woodrow Ichihashi, Oct. 30, 1992; Earl Pomeroy to Gordon Wright, Aug. 4, 1992, in author's possession.

43. Blue book diary, "Evacuation to Santa Anita," IP, B5, F2.

44. Lynn White, Jr. was a native San Franciscan and had received his undergraduate education at Stanford. A historian of medieval Europe, he taught at Princeton for several years, then joined the History Department at Stanford in 1937. He would later serve as president of Mills College, a women's college in Oakland, California, from 1943 to 1958 and finished his distinguished academic career at UCLA, retiring in 1972. He was president of the American Historical Association in 1973 and was particularly interested in the history of religion and of technology. He died in 1987.

45. Karl Yoneda, a former leading member of the Communist Party, USA, characterizes those who beat Shuji Matsui at Santa Anita in 1942 as a "pro-Japan group." *Ganbatte*, p. 173.

46. PJT, B19, 1942 A–J.

47. The strike is described in Girdner and Loftis, *Great Betrayal*, pp. 179–82.

48. Blue book diary, "Evacuation to Santa Anita," IP, B5, F2; this blue book concludes with the entry for June 23.

49. The center newspaper reported that approximately 600 parents and teachers attended the meeting. Ichihashi was quoted as saying, "As individuals, we must watch our daily living habits, as children cannot distinguish good from bad, and learn to a great extent by observation of people about them" (*Pacemaker*, June 25, 1942).

50. Blue book diary (2), 6/24–[July 15], IP, B5, F2.

51. PJT, B38, Ichihashis.

52. EER, B15, F220. Soon after receiving this letter, Robinson wrote a note to Ichihashi offering his help; EER, B15, F220.

53. A copy of the article by Ted Nakashima, "Concentration Camp: U.S. Style," *New Republic*, June 15, 1942, can be found in IP, B5, F1.

54. PJT, B19, 1942 A–J.

55. On June 25, H. Russell Amory, the Center Manager, issued "Administrative Notice Number 13: Procedure Governing Meetings Held Within the Santa Anita Assembly Center," which included the following provisions. Meetings (defined as any "assemblage of residents for any length of time, for any purpose, held at any place within the Center") were prohibited for the discussion of (1) international affairs; (2) national, state, county, or city politics; (3) the war with Japan. Written applications, "with an agenda complete in every detail," to

hold any other meeting had to be submitted to the Center administration for approval, and "one or more Caucasian American citizens representing the management must be present at all meetings to act as an observer." A "complete stenographic transcription of the proceedings must be made, including the names of all speakers" and submitted to the management within 24 hours after the meeting, and "no language other than English, written or spoken, shall be used." A copy of the notice can be found in IP, B5, F4.

56. One account says that Matsui was of mixed Japanese and Korean ancestry. Lehman, *Birthright of Barbed Wire*, p. 63.

57. A brief discussion of what appears to be this incident and its aftermath appears in Irons, *Justice at War*, pp. 114–16.

58. IP, B5, F1.

59. The National Japanese-American Student Relocation Council was formed on May 29, 1942, as a result of the efforts of religious, educational, and other service organizations to help college students continue their education away from the assembly centers and relocation camps. By war's end, it had helped place 4,300 students in colleges and universities in the Midwest and the East Coast region. The Council was led by Clarence E. Pickett of the American Friends Service Committee in Philadelphia. See Girdner and Loftis, *Great Betrayal*, p. 336; Daniels, *Asian America*, p. 244. The records of the Council from 1942 to 1946, which include considerable correspondence with students and the papers of Thomas Ray Bodine, a field director of the Council, and other individuals linked to the Council's efforts, are held in the Hoover Institution Archives at Stanford.

W. O. Mendenhall, president of Whittier College, personally thanked Ichihashi for the help he gave the Council during its visit to Santa Anita. Mendenhall to Ichihashi, July 31, 1942, IP, B5, F1.

60. Blue book diary (2) IP, B5, F2.

61. Ichihashi is referring to the San Gabriel Mountains and the communities around Pasadena.

62. Some internees decided they wanted to return to Japan. In June 1942, the ship *Gripsholm* of neutral Sweden made the first of several wartime voyages to exchange American and Japanese nationals. Fifteen hundred persons of Japanese ancestry, mainly issei, were on board for the first trip, which began in New York and ended in East Africa. There, Americans on a Japanese ship were exchanged for the *Gripsholm* passengers. The number of repatriates and expatriates (those who renounced their American citizenship) who left for Japan numbered several thousand by war's end. Girdner and Loftis, *Great Betrayal*, pp. 450–51.

63. PJT, B38, Ichihashis.

64. PJT, B19, 1942 A–L.

65. On July 7, G. W. Wilbur, Acting Center Manager at Santa Anita, announced "Administrative Notice No. 15 Designating Literature Printed in Japanese as Contraband." This directive, issued from the San Francisco WCCA office, declared that "Japanese print of any kind, such as newspapers, books, pamphlets, periodicals or other literature, with the exception of approved Japa-

nese religious books (Bibles and hymnals) and English-Japanese dictionaries, are not authorized in the center at any time." Residents were given four days to turn in any and all "such contraband" to the Center administration. In late June, the WCCA began tightening regulations governing all centers. A copy of Notice No. 15 is in IP, B5, F4.

66. Ichihashi described his research materials to the center management as comprising some 50 books and monographs "in Japanese, Chinese and some western languages" on Japanese cultural history of the sixth through eighth centuries. Some belonged to the Stanford Library. Ichihashi to L. W. Frader, July 10, 1942, IP, B5, F1.

67. Ichihashi's Stanford salary for 1942 was $4,725.00, or $394.00 a month. Ichihashi to Wilbur, March 17, 1942, RLW, B118, History.

68. Wilbur to Robinson, July 8, 1942, RLW, B118, Japanese. Robinson to DeWitt, July 8, 1942; DeWitt to Robinson, July 16, 1942; Wilbur to Ichihashi, July 17, 1942; Robinson to Ichihashi, July 23, 1942, all in RLW, B118, History Department.

69. PJT, B38, Ichihashis.

70. RLW, B118, Japanese.

71. Wilbur had helped the Ichihashis leave Santa Anita and had responded to all of Ichihashi's notes with messages of encouragement and solicitude.

72. Soon after the opening of the relocation centers, Professor Paul R. Hanna of Stanford's School of Education proposed to the WRA that the university might help in planning the schooling of the internees' children. After visiting Tule Lake and meeting with representatives from the centers, Hanna and his graduate students played the principal role in developing the educational program. Despite his involvement with attempts at schooling at Santa Anita, it does not appear that Ichihashi had any role in the Hanna effort. Hanna to Wilbur, July 28, 1942, RLW, B118, FI. See also James, *Exile Within*. Independent of Hanna, Ichihashi asked Grayson Kefauver, Dean of the School of Education at Stanford, to convey his interest in helping with educational development in the camps. While WRA authorities thanked Ichihashi for his overture, nothing formally developed as a result of it. Robert E. Gibson to Kefauver, Aug. 4, 1942, and Gibson to Ichihashi, Aug. 12, 1942, both in WRA, Ichihashi Case File.

73. K. Takahashi to P. Treat, July 8, 1942; M. Taoka to P. Treat, July 8, 1942; G. Taoka to P. Treat, July 22, 1942, all in PJT, B19, 1942 K–Z. Yoshiro Oishi to C. H. Danforth, June 18, 1942, Hoover Wilbur Papers, B47, Japanese (Relocation).

74. Tamie Tsuchiyama, "Preliminary Report," July 31, 1942, JERS, B8.05; *Pacemaker*, July 25, 1942.

75. *Daily Tulean Dispatch*, Aug. 4, 1942, p. 3. The newspaper first mentioned Ichihashi's arrival in its issue of July 31, 1942, p. 2.

76. EER, B15, F220; also in PJT, B19, 1942 A–J, which is a typewritten copy of Ichihashi's handwritten original to Robinson. A shorter, draft version can be found in IP, B5, F1.

77. Klamath Falls, Oregon, is near Tule Lake.

PART II, CHAPTER 2

1. W. Ichihashi to P. Treat, Aug. 24, 1942, PJT, B19, 1942 A–J, with hand-written notations by Treat. Two days later Woodrow wrote to Jessie Treat, thanking her for her help, informing her that his parents' baggage had finally arrived at Tule Lake, and asking the Treats whether they might be able to visit his father. Woodrow recalls that the FBI agent stationed at Tule Lake had no information about the reasons for his father's arrest, which left him and his mother in confusion. Woodrow's residence was at one end of the camp, and his parents' at the other; he saw them only occasionally. W. Ichihashi to J. Treat, Aug. 26, 1942, PJT, B38, Ichihashis; author's interview with W. Ichihashi, Oct. 30, 1992.

Woodrow also wrote to Edgar Robinson and Ray Lyman Wilbur, both of whom immediately replied to him and sent letters of support for Ichihashi to the Immigration Service. W. Ichihashi to Robinson, Aug. [24, 1942]; Wilbur to W. Ichihashi, Aug. 25, 1942; Robinson to W. Ichihashi, Aug. 26, 1942; all in EER, B15, F220.

2. FBI reports, Nov. 5, Dec. 1, 1941, and June 10, 1942; and N. J. L. Pieper to Hoover, June 10, 1942; all in Ichihashi FBI File.

3. Hoover to Biddle, July 3, 1942; Edward J. Ennis to Hoover, Aug. 19, 1942; Hoover to San Francisco FBI, Aug. 26, 1942; all in Ichihashi FBI File. *Daily Tulean Dispatch*, Aug. 29, 1942, p. 6.

4. The state of California constructed the Sharp Park Camp in the late 1930's for the rehabilitation of "alcoholic indigents." The federal government took it over in March 1942 to hold questionable aliens, particularly those from enemy nations. It held as many as 2,500 prisoners at one time, nearly all of them men. [Milton Silverman?], "Internment Centers: Sharp Park," n.d., JERS, B9.01. Today virtually nothing remains of the camp, now the site of the San Francisco Rifle and Archery Range. A 1966 newspaper article on the camp carried this description:

> It was a huge complex, neatly tended, well kept. It had a hospital, a recreation hall, a PX, quarters for guards, quarters for men and for women—plus a "fumigation center" for clothing which some of the arrivals wore.
>
> It was not a happy place, of course. But it was not as grim as Alcatraz. There were fire [sic] guardhouses where U.S. Immigration Service officers stood with rifles and spotlights ready. (*Pacifica Tribune*, Dec. 21, 1966, in Sharp Park clipping file, Pacifica Library).

5. Author's interview with W. Ichihashi, Feb. 22, 1995.

6. PJT, B38, Ichihashis.

7. Lisette Fast was born in 1898 in Colorado and graduated Phi Beta Kappa from Stanford in 1919. She returned to Stanford after earning a Master's degree in business administration from the University of Washington. She was an active university staff member for decades, serving at one time as social secretary to Marguerite Blake Wilbur, wife of Ray Lyman Wilbur. For most of her career, she worked in the History Department and on projects with Edgar Robinson

that related to the department. She lived with Robinson and his wife for many years; after his wife's death she and Edgar married in 1970. She died in 1992. *Campus Report*, Oct. 21, 1992, p. 2.

8. Apparently, the reference is to Sylvia Dean, daughter of the president of the University of Hawaii and the wife of historian Thomas A. Bailey. She had been thrown from a horse and suffered serious head injuries.

9. Robinson diary entry, Aug. 25, 1942, EER, B62, F67. Wilbur to W. Ichihashi, Aug. 25, 1942; Robinson to W. Ichihashi, Aug. 26, 1942; and Wilbur to INS, Aug. 25, 1942; all in EER, B15, F220.

10. The formal name of the body was the Alien Enemy Hearing Board No. 2. U.S. Attorney General Francis Biddle formed such boards in early 1942 to hold informal hearings for aliens regarding their loyalty. Three to six civilian members, most of them lawyers, served without pay on the boards. They were run without formal rules of procedure and evidence, and had not been authorized by existing federal law or presidential proclamation. The boards heard cases of arrested German and Italian aliens in addition to Japanese. See Irons, *Justice At War*, pp. 23–24.

11. E.L.F. to Wilbur, Aug. 29, 1942, RLW, B118, History; E.L.F. to Wilbur, Sept. 2, RLW, B123, History; E.L.F. to Wilbur, Sept. 5, 1942, RLW, B118, Japanese. A copy of "Instructions for Visitors" to Sharp Park is located in PJT, B38, Ichihashis.

12. PJT, B38, Ichihashis.

13. Not located.

14. George Bliss Culver, Dean of Men at Stanford before the war.

15. PJT, B38, Ichihashis.

16. Not located.

17. Presumably the Japanese attack on Pearl Harbor, December 7, 1941.

18. The military placed curfews and travel restrictions on Japanese in America immediately following Pearl Harbor.

19. PJT, B38, Ichihashis.

20. The date of receipt was presumably added by Jessie Treat. She and Payson regularly dated the correspondence from the Ichihashis. Their notations are reproduced only when the Ichihashis neglected to date a letter.

21. The relocation camp in Wyoming was at Heart Mountain, so named for an unusually shaped hill nearby.

22. There were two relocation camps in southeast Arkansas, Rohwer and Jerome.

23. "From the Arrest & the Sharp Park," n.d., IP, B5, F2.

24. This letter has not been located, although Wilbur apparently attached a copy of it to a letter to the immigration authorities. Wilbur to INS Chief, San Francisco, Aug. 25, 1942, RLW, B118, History 1941–42.

25. The sentences omitted here concern the general purposes of different agencies in the Justice Department as described by Saunders.

26. Presumably hot air balloons or dirigibles used for port security.

27. Here, Ichihashi gives additional details about the physical makeup of Sharp Park and the arrangement of the living quarters.

28. Here, Ichihashi includes a table listing 16 Japanese, 39 Italians, 36 Germans, and nationals of 15 other states, including 9 Chinese and 19 Mexicans.

29. Treat reported the name of the Stanford alumnus as Alfred Ehrman; E.L.F. to Wilbur, Sept. 4, 1942, EER, B15, F220. Ehrman was a member of the Alien Enemy Hearing Board and Louis Mercado an assistant U.S. attorney, according to the Report of the Hearing on Yamato Ichihashi, Sept. 3, 1942, in Ichihashi SF INS File.

30. Ichihashi wrote Treat immediately upon hearing the news of his approved release. He believed he would be able to return to Tule Lake within a week. Ichihashi to Treat, Oct. 13, 1942, PJT, B19, 1942 A–J.

31. These items are with the Research Essay (IP, B5, F2) but are not reproduced here.

32. Ichihashi to Treat, Oct. 13 and Oct. 30, 1942, both in PJT, B19, 1942 A–J; Ichihashi to Edgar Robinson, Nov. 22, 1942, EER, B17, F248. Ichihashi's Stanford colleagues regularly informed former students and mutual friends about his situation. See for example, Delmer Brown to Treats, Dec. 16, 1942, PJT, B19, 1943 A–J.

33. White to Ichihashi, Oct. 19, 1942; Carolyn Strouse Baer to Ichihashi, Sept. 7, 1942; and Olive Cole Smith to Ichihashi, Oct. 26, 1942; all in IP, B5, F1. White deplored relocation and observed that perhaps the "sole virtue" of the camps was that they helped prevent outbreaks of "anti-Japanese violence in places like Stockton where the Chinese and Filipino elements might start trouble and irresponsible Americans join in." He told Ichihashi, "Here at Stanford you have many friends, and they wish that you were here to see this agony [of the war] through with us." White also asked Ichihashi for his opinion about a proposal to start "Pacific Basin studies" at Stanford.

34. Report on Ichihashi Hearing; Francis Biddle order, Oct. 9, 1942; and Report of Enemy Alien, Dec. 12, 1945; all in Ichihashi SF INS File.

35. PJT, B38, Ichihashis.

36. Woodrow helped organize an eight-piece band called the "Down Beats." According to the camp newspaper, their debut performance was actually in late September 1942. They continued to perform at dances throughout the fall and winter. *Daily Tulean Dispatch*, Sept. 25, p. 3; Oct. 3, p. 3; Nov. 25, p. 4; Dec. 19, p. 3. George Yoshida to author, March 15, 1994.

37. Woodrow Ichihashi became interested in jazz in high school by listening to the radio and recalls seeing Cab Calloway's and Duke Ellington's bands play in San Francisco. He took up the trumpet, tenor sax, and then guitar, but his father was unhappy with his interest and preferred that he study European classical music. Woodrow did not acquiesce to his father's wishes, though, since the rhythm, freedom, and spontaneity of jazz appealed to his spirit. Author's interview with W. Ichihashi, April 5, 1992.

38. PJT, B19, 1942 A–J. On Nov. 22, 1942, Ichihashi also wrote a long letter to Edgar Robinson (IP, B5, F1); since it contains no additional information, it is not included here .

39. Treat to Y. Ichihashi, Nov. 13, 1942, IP, B5, F1. In this letter, Treat playfully kidded his friend about becoming the father of the "Big Jazz King" of

Tule Lake, "acquir[ing] more merit than all your academic distinctions!" Treat also informed Ichihashi of curricular and administrative changes taking place at Stanford.

40. Immediately upon receipt of the message, Treat sent Ichihashi's books and a letter that commented on Ichihashi's views of the camps and described recent campus events, including the annual "Big Game" against UC Berkeley. Treat to Ichihashi, Nov. 24, 1942, IP, B5, F1.

41. PJT, B38, Ichihashis.

42. PJT, B38, Ichihashis.

43. Not located.

44. H.M.I., "Sweetness & Light: Dr. Ichihashi," *Daily Tulean Dispatch*, Dec. 13, 1942, p. 2; ellipses in original. Dr. Harold Jacoby thoughtfully brought this article to my attention.

45. Y. Ichihashi to Treat, Dec. 19, 1942, PJT, B19, 1942 A–J.

46. All diary material for 1943 in this chapter is from Yamato Ichihashi's entries in a commercially published yearbook sent by Payson Treat; IP.

47. Possibly Satoru and Ryo Kuramoto, from Auburn, Washington. Mr. Kuramoto became a friend and frequent visitor of Yamato's and a community leader in camp. The Kuramotos later transferred to Amache, where they continued their association with the Ichihashis.

48. The *Daily Tulean Dispatch* was the camp newspaper published by the residents.

49. Yuji and Tosa Kumasaka and their two sons were from Seattle, Washington. The camp directory lists many families with the name Yokota.

50. Frank Matsumoto was manager of block 73, where Kei and Yamato lived, and although much younger than Ichihashi, became a good friend of his. He came from Vashon, Washington, and later moved from Tule Lake to Chicago. Subsequent references to "Frank" are assumed to be to Matsumoto. Letters from Matsumoto to Ichihashi can be found in IP, B5, F8.

51. In 1992, Harvey M. Coverley's recollection was that he had gone to the Ichihashi residence out of deference, rather than request that the professor go to the administration building. The reason for his overture was his wish to improve administration ties with camp residents; Ichihashi, in Coverley's words, was a person of enormous prestige among them.

Coverley recalls that he took several courses from Ichihashi as an undergraduate at Stanford, including one seminar in which he wrote a long paper about the 1922 Washington Conference that pleased his professor. He graduated with distinction in 1924. After the outbreak of war in 1941, Coverley, who was involved with the construction of defense housing in California for the Department of Agriculture, was recruited by Milton Eisenhower for the newly created War Relocation Authority. Coverley said he was a "trouble-shooter" and helped straighten out disorganized administrations at Manzanar and then Tule Lake. He accepted a commission in the army in the spring of 1943 and left the WRA, eventually participating in the invasion of Normandy. He had considerable contact with Ichihashi at Tule Lake, but recalls their relationship as being formal and not particularly warm. The two men did not keep in touch after Coverley's departure. Author's interview with Harvey Coverley, Aug. 17, 1992.

Another person who knew Coverley at Tule Lake, Daisuke Kitagawa, wrote this about him after the war: Coverley "was an extremely honest and just man. He had no ill will or bad intentions, but he was also a man who followed directives from above to the letter. One always knew exactly where he stood, what he meant, and how one stood with him. But he obviously was not the man to handle people in a complex and morbid state of collective mind" (Kitagawa, *Issei and Nisei*, p. 115).

52. Harold S. Jacoby was head of internal security at Tule Lake. He had taught sociology at the College of the Pacific; he returned there after the war and later became dean. He recalled he was very upset by the relocation order. After the registration crisis, he tendered his resignation to Coverley but ultimately did not resign until late 1943. Author's interview with Harold Jacoby, March 23, 1993.

53. Arthur G. Ramey was supervisor for teacher training during the first year of Tule Lake High School, after which he moved to University High School in Los Angeles. See his "Student Activities in a Japanese Relocation High School," published in 1943 in *The Clearing House*, a journal for professional educators.

54. Noboru Shirai was born in Hiroshima and graduated from Hiroshima University. He came to the United States in 1934 and, after attending other universities, entered Stanford, where he received a M.A. in sociology in 1939. He was still engaged in graduate work at Stanford in 1942. After the war, he briefly attended Princeton, then taught at the University of Pennsylvania for a short while before returning to Stanford, where he studied mining. After moving to southern California, he became a successful businessman and journalist. In 1981, he published a memoir in Japanese entitled *Kariforunia nikkeijin kyōsei shūyōjo* (Concentration camps for Japanese Americans in California), in which he devoted several pages to describing Ichihashi's career and personality (see pp. 16–19). An FBI report derogatorily described Shirai as Ichihashi's "right-hand man" at Tule Lake; FBI report, Dec. 17, 1943, Ichihashi FBI File. Shirai was executive secretary of the Community Council in Tule Lake in 1943. Author's conversation with Akiko Shirai, Aug. 15, 1995; *Daily Tulean Dispatch*, Jan. 4, 1943, p. 1.

55. A teacher at Tule Lake

56. Robert Billigmeier, a young researcher on the staff of Professor Dorothy Thomas's project studying relocation, recorded the content of a talk given by Ichihashi at Tule Lake. Billigmeier's notes are undated, but their content suggests they may have been of the talk given by Ichihashi on January 7 or another one soon after. According to the notes, Ichihashi spoke to what was called the "Cultural Assimilation Group" and began by describing the origin and development of Shintoism and the transplanting of Buddhism to Japan from China. He then addressed problems of the nisei and their cultural identity. Billigmeier took detailed notes on Ichihashi's comments about the camp administration, paraphrasing them as follows:

One of the most important things for people in responsible positions to learn is this, do not promise when you can't deliver. I talked to Coverley on this subject. I told him that frankness is much better than promises which cannot be realized. Such promises constitute one of the sources for so many under currents in the community. I want to do everything I can to help the people but I want to remain an impartial observer. I want to suppress evil influences I find in the community and to stimulate the good. I will help Coverley as a friend, but will not affiliate myself with the administration. In the long run that is best. If you have an interest to protect, you then have something to defend and you lose impartiality and objectivity. I won't take a job for that reason. Why should I? I am still being paid by Stanford University.

Another difficulty in the administration comes from too much insistence on authority and jurisdiction and too little emphasis on duty towards the people. Through the block manager of my block, for example, I asked the head block manager for access to block statistics. The head of the block managers said, "Why should he (Ichihashi) have them? Why didn't he come and beg me for them?" (Ichihashi made his voice harsh and assumed an arrogant stance in imitation.) I went to see Coverley. He said there was nothing confidential in those figures, "If you can't get anything, let me know and I'll get them for you." (Billigmeier, "Notes on the Meeting Cultural Assimilation Group," n.d., Billigmeier Diary, JERS, 67/14, R20.03)

Ichihashi's diary notes that he was to meet Billigmeier personally on January 8 and that he met Thomas and three unnamed assistants on January 14. He had met Thomas previously on August 3, 1942, at Tule Lake. Recollections of that encounter can be found in Part I of this book. After the war, Billigmeier completed his doctorate in history at Stanford but had little contact with Ichihashi. Author's conversation with Robert Billigmeier, Aug. 12, 1995.

57. An assembly center in Central California.

58. Probably George Akamatsu, who graduated from Stanford in 1927 with a degree in zoology. He became a physician.

59. Daisuke Kitagawa, an issei Christian minister from the Seattle, Washington, area. After the war, he wrote a memoir of his experience, *Issei and Nisei: The Internment Years*, and other books on religion and racial minorities in America.

60. Ichihashi turned down the request, saying he did not have the time. Note from Kitagawa to Ichihashi, Jan. 6, 1943, IP, B5, F7.

61. Ralph Lutz, a Stanford history department colleague.

62. The Taika Reforms dramatically changed the politics and economics of seventh-century Japan.

63. The study eventually produced several major books on the wartime internment of Japanese Americans: Thomas and Nishimoto, *The Spoilage* (1946); Thomas, *The Salvage* (1952); and tenBroek et al., *Prejudice, War and the Constitution* (1954). See also Ichioka, ed., *Views from Within*.

64. Diary entry for Jan. 14, 1943.

65. In 1992, after rereading a copy of his letter to Wilbur, Coverley wrote that he was "convinced" he had not written it, or at least most of it, and he guessed that staff members had actually composed it over his signature. Coverley to author, Oct. 27, 1992.

66. Coverley to Wilbur, Jan. 9, 1943; Wilbur to Coverley, Jan. 11, 1943, both in RLW, B123, History.

67. Presumably "Aristotle's dictum," *dictum de omni et nullo*: whatever may be affirmed or denied of a class may be affirmed or denied of every member of it.

68. Without consultation with those named, the Japanese government compiled a list of Japanese in America for repatriation. Ichihashi received a copy of such a list dated January 14, which included his name; he signed a formal "Declaration of Declination" on January 26. The completed form read: "I, Yamato Ichihashi, declare that I have been informed that I am under consideration for exchange to the Empire of Japan by reason of the request of the Japanese Government. I further declare that I desire to remain in the United States and that I do not desire to go to the Empire of Japan, nor otherwise to be repatriated to Japan." Notice, and Jacoby to Ichihashi, Jan. 22, 1943, IP, B5, F7; diary entry, Jan. 23, 1943; and Declaration of Declination, Jan. 26, 1943, WRA, Ichihashi Case File.

69. World War I flying ace Edward V. Rickenbacker was president of Eastern Airlines when he was asked to make a tour of American military bases in the Pacific. On Oct. 21, 1942, the plane he was on ran out of fuel and had to be ditched in the South Pacific. Rickenbacker and other crew members survived 21 days on open rafts before being rescued. *Life* magazine made his dramatic personal account its cover story for the Jan. 25, 1943, issue and completed it in the Feb. 8 issue.

70. Donald B. Tresidder became Stanford's fourth president in 1943. He had been president of the university's board of trustees, but Ichihashi had not known him. Treat included the report in a letter to Ichihashi.

71. The camp newspaper regularly announced Ichihashi's lectures and other cultural activities.

72. Apparently Kenneth Yasuda, who had come to the United States after attending high school in Japan. He attended the University of Southern California and then the University of Washington, where he studied poetry. *Who's Who in American Poetry, 1939–1941* recognized him under the pen name Ken Bysen. He worked on a book entitled "Aesthetic Analysis of Japanese Poetry" at Tule Lake and regularly published poetry and literature studies in the camp magazine. See *Daily Tulean Dispatch Magazine*, Aug. 2, 1942, p. 2; Nov. 1942, p. 4; Feb. 1943, p. 9; March 1943, p. 13. He remained at Tule Lake throughout the war years, then returned to the University of Washington after 1945 and pursued graduate work at Columbia University and Tokyo University, where he earned a doctoral degree. Yasuda was deeply interested in Japanese literature, especially poetry. With help from Ichihashi he published his first translation of *haiku* poetry right after the war: *A Pepper-Pod* (New York: Knopf, 1947). (See correspondence between Yasuda and Ichihashi in IP, B7, F3.) He became a leading authority on Japanese literature in the United States, received an imperial decoration from Japan, and retired as a professor of East Asian Languages and Cultures from Indiana University. He wrote poetry and plays, including one in the *nō* style honoring Martin Luther King, which is published in his *Masterworks of the*

Nō Theater (Bloomington: Indiana University Press, 1989). He first met Ichihashi at Tule Lake and visited him often. They had little contact after the war, but Yasuda continued to have kind feelings toward Ichihashi. Author's telephone conversation with Kenneth Yasuda, Jan. 23, 1995.

73. See the discussion of Japanese American service in the armed forces in the next narrative section.

74. The following material appears in a diary section designated "Special Data" for January; such a section follows the last calendar day of each month. It is unclear when Ichihashi actually made this entry.

75. Daniels, *Asian America*, pp. 249–53; author's interview with W. Ichihashi, April 30, 1992.

76. For more on the registration crisis, see Girdner and Loftis, *The Great Betrayal*, pp. 267–95.

77. Kenji Ito became one of Ichihashi's closest friends at Tule Lake. The two, who had met before the outbreak of war, saw each other almost every day. They continued their association in the postwar years, with Ito serving as Ichihashi's attorney.

Ito was a University of Washington Law School graduate, nisei, an attorney, and a prominent member of Seattle's Japanese community. At 2:00 A.M. on December 8, 1941, the FBI arrested the 32-year-old Ito at his home and took him from his wife and infant daughter. Unlike most others of Japanese ancestry rounded up after Pearl Harbor who were eventually released after questioning, Ito was indicted by a grand jury on December 23 for "subversive activity." His public addresses that endorsed Japan's aggressive policy toward China (some two hundred in number given in the late 1930's), probably were the reason for the government's suspicions. When he finally came to trial in March 1942, the charges were reduced to having been an unregistered agent for a foreign government. No evidence was produced during the trial to show that he had had any formal ties with the Japanese government, and he was acquitted of all charges. During the much publicized trial, Ito testified that his speeches were simply expressions of his personal opinion and that he regretted the support he had given to Japan's actions against China. His views had been wrong, he admitted. During and after the trial, Ito expressed his loyalty to America and pride in his citizenship.

After spending time in Tule Lake, Ito and his family moved to Minidoka Relocation Center in Idaho, where they lived for the duration of the war. After the war, Ito became a prominent attorney in Los Angeles, specializing in international business. One of his daughters married a Chinese American Stanford graduate, Emory M. Lee. Ayleen Ito Lee, "United States vs. Ito"; author's interview with Kenji Ito, June 18, 1992.

78. Many issei, especially men, married late in life since it took them many years of hard work before they felt they were sufficiently secure financially to begin families.

79. The WRA required all residents of the camps to complete extensive questionnaires that included questions of a political nature. Ichihashi describes

the ensuing crisis below and later summarizes the events in a long letter to Treat on May 4, 1943, which appears in Chapter 3.

80. Manzanar Relocation Center was the site of a riot on Dec. 6, 1942, that resulted in the army killing two residents and wounding at least ten others. Residents conducted a general strike in protest and left the camp unsettled for weeks following the incidents. The riot was unrelated to the registration issue.

81. In addition to the title of the registration form, two particular registration questions created problems for internees 17 years and older, all of whom—men and women, citizen and alien—had to respond:

> 27. Are you willing to serve in the armed forces of the United States on combat duty, wherever ordered?
>
> 28. Will you swear unqualified allegiance to the United States of America and faithfully defend the United States from any or all attack by foreign or domestic forces and foreswear any form of allegiance or obedience to the Japanese emperor, to any other foreign government, power or organization?

Conditional answers were not permitted, although several thousand, nevertheless, did give qualified responses.

82. The numbers Ichihashi gives following a name refer to a residence block address, not a person's age.

83. Apparently, the man had renounced his Japanese citizenship at one time. Japan recognized dual citizenship.

84. The Japanese American Citizens League (JACL) advocated full cooperation with the WRA to demonstrate loyalty to the United States in the hope that suspicion of Japanese Americans could thus be reduced and discriminatory policies ameliorated.

85. Presumably, Kazuo Isozaki from Elkhorn, Washington. Wardens were residents charged with maintaining security within the camps.

86. A draft or copy of this letter kept by Ichihashi reads, in part: "As to your information as regards my *alleged* conduct, I was very much shocked in view of the fact that I had called on you for the opposite purpose, namely, for clarification of the 'registration' in order to help and calm down the agitated people because of the lack of intelligence and understanding. This sort of allegation should not be lightly passed by; from my own standpoint, it is vital. Therefore I am naturally anxious to know the source of information from which [you] have learned. If you are willing to give information on this point, I shall be happy to come and receive it in person" (Ichihashi to Coverley, Feb. 18, 1943, IP, B5, F7).

87. Michi Weglyn describes the incident in detail in *Years of Infamy*, pp. 147–51. She reports that 35 nisei were arrested by 24 soldiers, and as the conflict continued, many other Tule Lake residents were arrested. Weglyn states that although the WRA required all camp residents to complete the registration questionnaire, the War Department regarded it as voluntary, and the whole crisis was therefore unnecessary.

88. Milton Silverman, "Life at Tulelake—Rumors and Riots Spread Like Wildfire—'Jap Against Jap,'" *San Francisco Chronicle*, May 27, 1943, p. 12.

89. PJT, B38, Ichihashis.

90. Lynn White, Jr., Ichihashi's former history department colleague.

91. Probably the wife of Percy Alvin Martin, a professor of Latin American history in the Stanford History Department.

92. In a letter dated February 22, Payson Treat gently chided Ichihashi for his infrequent correspondence; the last letter from Ichihashi had been in mid-December. Treat described the shortages in Palo Alto and developments on campus, and informed Ichihashi that he had sent his friend a diary, "the largest obtainable." Treat included a copy of a recent *Stanford Daily*, which reported on the university's new president, Donald Tresidder, and expressed hope that Tresidder would become a great educational leader. IP, B5, F7.

93. PJT, B19, F1943 A–J. On March 22, 1943, Treat responded to the following letter and playfully criticized his friend for writing in "such a miniature script that sometimes even a reading glass fails to clarify the letters." He also described recent developments on campus and in the History Department. IP, B5, F7.

94. These essays were not located in Ichihashi's papers, which contain little material in Japanese, most of it on nineteenth-century Japanese diplomatic relations.

95. Promotion to emeritus status, or retirement, was considered an honor that capped one's academic career. Ichihashi never enjoyed receiving the tribute in person. Copies of the letters mentioned by Ichihashi are in RLW, B123, History.

96. A trade periodical that Ichihashi subscribed to.

97. Presumably, this is a reference to camp stores purchasing goods in bulk.

98. George O. Danzuka was the father of Woodrow's first roommate at Tule Lake, Norman Danzuka. According to the camp newspaper, George Danzuka and Lorraine Bruno, a member of the Wasoo Tribe, had nine children and lived on the Warmsprings Indian Reservation in The Dalles, Oregon, where George was a cook and butcher. Lorraine and her children left Tule Lake in Aug. 1942. *Daily Tulean Dispatch*, Aug. 22, 1942, p. 2.

99. Woodrow recalls the rumor may have had something to do with gambling, but Ichihashi's diary suggests it was tied to his relationship with Alyce Sakumura, Woodrow's future wife. Author's interview with W. Ichihashi, Oct. 30, 1992.

100. Ichihashi had the name wrong; it was Sakumura.

101. The Civil Liberties League was organized by internees to protect "the civil rights of Japanese Americans" and was patterned after the American Civil Liberties Union. *Daily Tulean Dispatch*, April 8, 1943, p. 1.

102. George B. Sansom, a British diplomat and leading authority on Japanese history, and Kenneth Scott Latourette, a prominent historian of Asia. Sansom spent his later years at Stanford, where he wrote his three-volume *History of Japan* in the late 1950's and early 1960's. It is not known whether he and Ichihashi ever met.

103. The Ichihashis did not respond to question 27 about willingness to serve in the United States armed services and answered "yes" to question 28, which had been revised to read, "Will you swear to abide by the laws of the United States and to take no action which would in any way interfere with the war effort of the United States?" Y. Ichihashi, copy, "Application for Leave

Clearance," IP, B5, F8; O. Ichihashi, "Registration," March 15, 1943, WRA, Okei Ichihashi Case File.

104. PJT, B38, Ichihashis.

105. Ba Maw, a Burmese political figure, led a mission to Tokyo in March 1943, ten months after Japan had completed its conquest of Burma. During Ba Maw's trip, the Japanese government announced that it would recognize an "independent Burmese state" within the year. Apparently, Ichihashi had access to a short-wave radio, which was banned by camp authorities; the radio is mentioned again on March 29 and several other occasions.

106. In March 1940, the Japanese established a puppet Chinese government in Nanking headed by Wang Ching-wei, a former leader of the Kuomintang, the Chinese Nationalist Party.

107. The reference is to the 442nd Regimental Combat Team, the volunteer nisei combat unit announced on January 30, 1943. Ichihashi, who had little regard for Stimson, had sharply disagreed with the then Secretary of State's 1932 condemnation of Japan's occupation of Manchuria. The Poston camp was in Arizona, not Colorado.

108. Anna Seghers (1900–83) was a German Jew and communist. *The Seventh Cross*, a fictional account of life in fascist Germany in the 1930's, was first published in the United States in 1942. It was an immediate best-seller and a Book-of-the-Month Club selection. It was later was made into a Hollywood movie starring Spencer Tracy.

109. PJT, B38, Ichihashis.

110. In late March, a Liberty transport ship named for Stanford's first president was launched at a Marin County shipyard, north of San Francisco. Because of ill health, Mrs. Jordan asked Jessie Treat to take her place at the christening. In a March 22 letter (IP, B5, F7), Payson Treat described the event, reported on campus news, and commented on matters raised in Yamato Ichihashi's Feb. 26 letter.

111. Yokosuka had been one of the Japanese Imperial Navy's major naval bases and shipyards since 1872. Several of the battleships and aircraft carriers used in World War II were constructed there.

112. Apparently the wife of David Harris, a historian of Central Europe and a Stanford colleague of Ichihashi's.

113. Radio Tokyo, apparently. The broadcasts occasionally included sensationalized reports on the mistreatment of the Japanese in the relocation centers.

114. Y. Ichihashi, "History (Survey) of the Tule Lake, II," IP, B6, F4; "Calendar of Events," IP, B5, F8.

115. Kitagawa, *Issei and Nisei*, pp. 89–91. Also see V. J. Matsumoto, "Japanese American Women During World War II."

PART II, CHAPTER 3

1. In April 1943, Dillon Myer asked Edgar Robinson for his opinion of Ichihashi. Robinson reported that he had known Ichihashi for 30 years, that he was

"outstanding as a teacher and distinguished as a scholar, [and that] Mr. Ichihashi came to be accepted as one of the most distinguished members of our academic community" (Robinson to Myer, May 12, 1943, EER, B17, F248). See also note 20 to this chapter.

2. All diary excerpts in this chapter are from Ichihashi's commercially published year book for 1943, IP.

3. Apparently, Ichihashi added this entry at some later date.

4. *Liberty Magazine*, a popular weekly of news and commentary that regularly carried condensed versions of current books. Vanya Oakes, who also went by the name of Virginia Armstrong Oakes, reported on her experiences in Asia in *White Man's Folly*, published in 1943. It is not clear whether Ichihashi received an advance-dated copy of the periodical or entered his comments some time later on the April 12 diary page. Coincidentally, Oakes spoke in person at Stanford later in the year, calling for an end to racial prejudice at home as part of the struggle for democracy in the world. *Palo Alto Times*, Dec. 15, 1943; clipping in Ichihashi 1943 diary.

5. A brief account of Myer's meeting at Tule Lake is in Kitagawa, *Issei and Nisei*, p. 123.

6. "Accepted repatriates" were those who wanted to return to Japan and were accepted by the Japanese government.

7. During a meeting of the House Naval Affairs Subcommittee in San Francisco on April 13, General DeWitt went into a tirade against Japanese Americans and emphasized his opposition to their release from relocation camps and return to the West Coast. "There is no way to determine their loyalty," he said in addition to the remarks quoted by Ichihashi. Extensive portions of Dewitt's testimony were read into the Congressional Record; and his remarks were widely publicized in the press. These generated some criticism, including a *Washington Post* editorial. A week later under pressure, DeWitt retracted his position and announced that nisei servicemen could enter the Western Defense Command. For more on DeWitt's comments, see Girdner and Loftis, *Great Betrayal*, pp. 277–79.

8. Ichihashi's reminder to himself of a meeting.

9. Probably Dr. George Akamatsu '27; Dr. George Hashiba '15 and M.D. '17; Fukuzo Obayashi '10; Noboru Shirai M.A. '39; and Frank Nakamura M.A. '27. Ichihashi mentions Obana several times, but neither he nor Hara has been identified.

10. Dr. Reese M. Pedicord, the camp's chief medical officer. George Hashiba, who was a prominent San Joaquin valley physician and surgeon, was the chief assistant medical officer at the camp. In early November 1943, a California state investigator accused Hashiba of being a leader and instigator of the rioting then occurring at Tule Lake, during which Pedicord was beaten. Ichihashi's diary records some of the tensions in the hospital over Pedicord's conduct, which led to the rioting. [*Palo Alto Times?*], "Stanford Man Held Leader at Tule Lake," n.d., and other newspaper clippings in Ichihashi's 1943 diary, IP.

11. In conveying Ichihashi's reply to Johnston, Coverley described him as a "personal friend of mine for approximately twenty years" and a former professor

of his at Stanford. Coverley gave a copy of the letter to Ichihashi. Coverley to Johnston, April 19, 1943, IP, B5, F7.

12. Senator Harry S. Truman headed a U.S. Senate committee formed in 1941 to investigate the costs of military-related production activities. Controversy arose when the Committee released figures of ship loss that were disputed by the Navy.

13. Possibly Ushizo Oyama from Sacramento.

14. The *San Francisco Examiner* article reported on the battle in the Bismarck Sea, off the coast of New Guinea, which was part of the Allied campaign to isolate the Japanese-held Solomon Islands.

15. IP, B5, F7.

16. IP, B5, F7.

17. On April 28, Treat had written a letter to Dillon Myer in strong support of Ichihashi, testifying to their 40 years of friendship, to Ichihashi's integrity as a scholar, and to his fitness for use in the current war effort. Treat also wrote letters in support of Woodrow. PJT, B19, 1942 K–Z. See note 1 to this chapter for Robinson's letter to Myer.

18. In his quick reply to this letter, Treat said he "was very glad" to learn of Ichihashi's reaction to the stories about him. "Now I can categorically deny the two rumors which I mentioned in my last letter." The letter also included the following poignant paragraph, which conveyed to Ichihashi some sense of the attitudes of the "outside" world toward Japanese Americans: "It is impossible for individuals to make plans in the midst of this gigantic struggle. In the year that you have been away the reality of the war has been brought face to face with every one in our country. The lives of scores of millions have been changed, as families have been broken up and cherished plans cast aside. Conditions change so rapidly that unexpected factors crowd in to destroy a hoped-for development. Thus, I was looking for a great improvement in the policy of the WRA when reports from overseas fanned the dormant fires. Of course decent people were not affected, but government must operate to meet the passions of the ignorant masses. And we know that these passions subside almost as fast as they rise. There is a strong minority who keep the cause of our fellow citizens before the public. The "safety valve" of the S.F. *Chronicle* carries as many letters for the Japanese as against them. Our newspapers publish sympathetic, as well as critical articles about the centers. The *Palo Alto Times* prints regular letters from John Kitasako in Heart Mountain. And the best magazines, such as *Atlantic* and *Harpers* have discussed the problem intelligently. Of course Americans who never knew any Japanese are ready to believe anything, but Americans who have friends in the centers miss them very much and deeply regret that conditions for which they were in no way responsible should have brought such hardship upon them" (Treat to Ichihashi, May 9, 1943, IP, B5, F7).

19. EER, B17, F248.

20. In a letter dated April 28, 1943, Robinson informed Ichihashi that he had just received an inquiry from Dillon Myer about Woodrow and his father. Myer's letter stated that they had applied for "employment, education, or residence elsewhere," and Robinson therefore wanted information about Ichihashi's

plans so that he could write the reference letter. Robinson to Ichihashi, April 28, 1943, IP, B2, F7. Robinson's reply to Myer is quoted in note 1 to this chapter.

21. The very supportive letters from Ichihashi's colleagues appear in his relocation file. All testified to his professional credentials, scholarly abilities, and even political inclinations. Ralph Lutz, then Chairman of the Board of the Hoover Library, concluded his letter saying: "In my opinion, Professor Ichihashi could be trusted to leave the relocation Center for residence elsewhere. In my opinion he would not obey a summons to return to Japan even if he received one" (Lutz to Myer, May 5, 1943, WRA, Ichihashi Case File).

22. Location of the army camp where the nisei combat team trained.

23. These jobs were in the Tule Lake Center.

24. PJT, B38, Ichihashis.

25. Not located.

26. Possibly the wife of Boynton Morris Green, a professor of mechanical engineering, who lived on Salvatierra Street, as did the Ichihashis.

27. Letters from Jessie Treat, Ray Lyman Wilbur, and Clara Stoltenberg for Kei appear in her evacuee case file. All strongly testify to her personal integrity and character as a cultured lady and homemaker. WRA, Okei Ichihashi Case File.

28. Typewritten ms. of a talk to nisei [summer 1943?], IP, B6, F7.

29. Ichihashi diary, May 12–14, 1943; "Introduction" (Spring 1943), IP, B5, F7. Ichihashi's papers (B6, F5) contain a couple of manuscripts for *Tule Lake Interlude* with his comments.

30. The camp newspaper did not publicize these films. The WRA produced several public-relations documentaries on relocation and the camps.

31. Milton Silverman (b. 1910), a native of Piedmont, across the Bay from San Francisco, graduated from Stanford in 1929. As an undergraduate he had been editor-in-chief of the *Stanford Daily* and had ruffled some feathers as an aspiring investigative journalist. He recalls that he may have met Ichihashi briefly while at the university. He earned his doctorate in biochemistry from Stanford in 1938 and worked for the *San Francisco Chronicle* from 1933 to 1959, mainly as its science editor. At Stanford, Silverman had also met Karl R. Bendetsen, who became a colonel and chief aide to the army Provost Marshal General and one of the principal architects of relocation. Bendetsen briefly hired Silverman away from the *Chronicle* to observe the process of relocation for the army. Coincidentally, Silverman wrote reports on Santa Anita and Sharp Park, where Ichihashi was also incarcerated. Later in his career, Silverman worked in medical research and health administration for the federal government and was on the faculties of the Medical School at the University of California, San Francisco, and its School of Pharmacology. He was the author, coauthor, or editor of 21 books. See Milton Silverman, Mia Lydecker, and Philip R. Lee, *Bad Medicine: The Prescription Drug Industry in the Third World* (Stanford, Calif.: Stanford University Press, 1992), pp. xv–xvii; author's interview with Milton Silverman, Dec. 2, 1994.

32. A Tule Lake resident had to apply to a special board to purchase shoes, with a limit of one new pair a year.

33. On April 18, American pilots shot down the plane carrying Admiral Ya-mamoto Isoroku, commander of the Japanese Combined Fleet and chief plan-ner of the attack on Pearl Harbor.

34. Possibly a reference to William L. Holland, international research sec-retary of the Institute of Pacific Relations (IPR), with which Ichihashi was affili-ated from its founding in 1925. Holland began work for the IPR in 1929 and became its secretary general in 1946. He defended the IPR during the Senate internal security investigations of the organization in the early 1950's. See W. L. Holland and Kate Mitchell, *Problems of the Pacific, 1936* (Chicago: University of Chicago Press, 1937?) and William L. Holland, *Truth and Fancy about the Insti-tute of Pacific Relations* (New York: American Institute of Pacific Relations, 1953).

35. Kawakami to Ichihashi, May 19, 1943, IP, B5, F7. Kawakami wrote from Washington, D.C., about the "infamy of Pearl Harbor," inquired about Ichiha-shi's condition, and said that his own son was planning to help the army in translation work. After Pearl Harbor, Kawakami was detained in Baltimore for two months before he was cleared by federal authorities. Kawakami to Treat, April 15, 1943, PJT, B20, 1943 K–Z.

36. An "isolation" or "detention" camp where dissidents were sent by the WRA.

37. *San Francisco Chronicle*, May 25–29, 1943. The series was reprinted in edited form in the *Palo Alto Times*. Silverman recalls that he had heard rumors about an unidentified "emperor" or "chief man" at Tule Lake from internees at Manzanar and elsewhere before his visit, and was surprised to discover that Ichi-hashi was the alleged kingpin. Silverman says he bumped into Ichihashi while walking around the camp and then arranged the interview. Author's interview with Silverman, Dec. 2, 1994. Lending some support to Silverman's view was the practice of the vice-consul of Spain in San Francisco, who was responsible for representing Japan's local interests, of addressing correspondence to Ichi-hashi as the "spokesman for the Japanese" at Tule Lake. In August 1943 Ichi-hashi chaired a meeting of camp representatives with the consul; Antonio R-Martin to Ichihashi, Aug. 26, 1943, with minutes of meeting of war represen-tatives, Aug. 20, 1943, IP B5, F8. Harvey Coverley recalls that Ichihashi's bar-rack was "luxurious," with rugs, chairs, and drapes, but rejects the notion that Ichihashi, though very highly regarded by his fellow internees, was any sort of "emperor." He recalled no rumors about Ichihashi having fascist sympathies or exercising any special power within the camp; author's interview with Coverley, Aug. 17, 1992. Robert Billigmeier calls the articles "outrageous" and without foundation, since, in his recollection, Ichihashi was not a camp leader or activist; author's conversation with Billigmeier, Aug. 12, 1995.

38. PJT, B19, 1943 A–J. A typewritten version of this letter is also in History Dept. Files, B4, F108. Treat presumably had the original handwritten letter typed and distributed to his colleagues; see the following note.

39. On June 2, Treat replied to Ichihashi's letter, saying that the Silverman article made him "very sad and very indignant." Treat informed Ichihashi that Silverman was known to be a "reckless journalist whose unreliability is well

known," and that he used his Stanford doctorate "for commercial purposes." Treat wrote:

> I shall correct [Silverman's] report wherever possible. I made a copy of your letter for Robinson to read and, with my approval, he took it over to Dr. Wilbur. The Dr. was well aware of Silverman's reputation. There is nothing one can do with a creature like this, except keep as far away from him as possible.
>
> However, do not let it disturb you too much, unjust and indecent as it may be. Your friends will not believe it, and all others will promptly forget all about it. (Treat to Ichihashi, June 2, 1943, IP, B5, F7)

40. PJT, B38, Ichihashis.

41. Herman Goebel to Captain Astrup, July 16, 1942; JERS, B2.08.

42. A copy of the petition can be found in IP, B5, F1. It appears that Ichihashi helped translate it into Japanese. The petition charged Pedicord with incompetence, endangerment of the health of the residents, and authoritarianism, earning him the "hatred" of the hospital's staff and patients.

43. Ichihashi diary entries, June 15, 23, and 29, 1943. See Spicer, et al., *Impounded People*; and by Opler, "Cultural Dilemma of a Kibei Youth," "Japanese Folk Beliefs and Practices, Tule Lake, California," "Senryu Poetry as Folk and Community Expression," and "A 'Sumo' Tournament at Tule Lake Center."

44. Treat to Ichihashi, May 9 and June 24, 1943, both in IP, B5, F7. Treat to Ichihashi, July 29, 1943, IP, B5, F8. It is not clear what Treat meant by his comment, about Ichihashi becoming emeritus, quoted above. Stanford records show that Edward M. Hulme, a long-standing member of the History Department, became emeritus several years before Ichihashi.

45. Woodrow recalls that he had discussed leaving the camp with his parents before this day, although they hoped he would leave just temporarily. Woodrow wanted to get out of the camp for good. Author's interview with W. Ichihashi, Oct. 30, 1992.

46. The newspaper reported that on July 7, 1943, Chinese held at Sharp Park Detention Camp flew banners as part of a commemoration protesting the start of Japan's invasion of China. Most of the 47 Chinese had been seamen on British ships and were being processed for deportation since they had no immigration papers. Some of the camp's 172 alien Japanese reacted hostilely to the banners, and camp authorities feared rioting. They brought in a platoon of army soldiers, armed with machine guns, in 25 jeeps. To avoid trouble, immigration authorities transferred all the Chinese to the Alameda County Jail in Oakland. "Japs at Sharp Park Menace 47 Chinese; Troops Balk Rioting," and other clippings in IP, B7, F5. On July 9, Ichihashi wrote in his diary that the *Examiner* had made "a mountain out of a ——; what is surprising is the fact that there are as many as 172 Japanese in the camp as contrasted with 11 men & 12 women when I left in September; these must be gathered in connection with the Feb.-March registration rumpus."

47. On segregation, see Daniels, *Asian America*, pp. 262–74; and Weglyn, *Years of Infamy*, pp. 153–58.

48. Ichihashi diary entries for July 15 and Sept. 22, 1943.

49. PJT, B19, F1943 A–J; a handwritten draft can be found in IP, B5, F8.

50. PJT, B19, F1943 A–J.

51. Immediately after receiving this letter, Treat responded to Ichihashi to express his sympathy. "I need not tell you how my mind reacts to every deviation from right and justice and fair play. But these foul things are spawned in war time just as toad stools are bred in manure heaps. I like to think that there are less of them in this country than in some other lands—but there are too many here." Treat denounced the hostility toward Japanese Americans that continued to infect the country. Even in the Stanford community, "the ignorance is appalling" (Treat to Ichihashi, July 29, 1943, IP, B5, F8).

52. PJT, B38, Ichihashis.

53. PJT, B19, F1943 A–J.

54. Many of the *kibei* (nisei educated in Japan) developed strong sympathies with Japan.

55. Senate Resolution 166, passed on July 6, 1943.

56. The Japanese American Joint Board was made up of representatives from the WRA, the Provost Marshal General's office, and Army and Navy intelligence. It was established on January 20, 1943, to decide on the eligibility of evacuees to depart from relocation camps.

57. The new director was Raymond R. Best. Educated in Los Angeles and a Marine veteran of World War I, Best had worked previously in establishing Moab Isolation Center, Utah, and Leupp Isolation Center, Arizona, for suspect Japanese aliens and dissidents.

58. Treat had written Ichihashi on July 29 that Ralph Lutz had suffered a severe stroke. IP, B5, F8.

59. Treat made the inquiries Ichihashi requested and passed along what he had learned. He also told Ichihashi that his recent letters about the segregation program had given him "the best survey of the situation" he had found (Treat to Ichihashi, Aug. 18, 1943, IP, B5, F8).

60. PJT, B38, Ichihashis. Jessie Treat apparently misdated the letter as arriving in 1942; its contents indicate it was written in 1943.

61. Ichihashi noted the same information in his diary. For example, on August 6, he wrote that many of those who had moved out of the camp had been misled about the conditions they could expect and thus found themselves "stranded and in sad plight." One former camp leader, Ichihashi recorded, "returned here because of the impossibility of finding satisfactory living conditions outside."

62. Ichihashi diary entries, August 9–23, 1943. "Addenda," Aug. 18, 1943; Ichihashi, Tsuda, and Mayeda to Best, Aug. 24, 1943; both in IP, B5, F8. Ichihashi also compiled research material and notes on segregation, all undated; see, "A Chronology of Events Relative to Segregation," "A History of the WRA Policy of Segregation," and an untitled essay, all in IP, B5, F8.

63. Ichihashi wanted to travel to Amache by individual arrangements to avoid being moved with hundreds of other residents.

64. The usual WRA practice was for the dead to be buried in cemeteries just outside the camp fence.

65. As has been noted, Spain was responsible for representing Japan's inter-

ests in the United States during the war. Its vice-consul Antonio R-Martin visited Tule Lake in August 1943 and met with Ichihashi and other leading residents. Minutes of meeting of war repesentatives, Aug. 20, 1943, IP, B5, F8.

66. PJT, B38, Ichihashis.

67. Gasoline, because it was rationed during the war, was a valuable commodity.

68. Author's interview with Harold Jacoby, March 23, 1993. Best to Lindley, Sept. 3, 1943, and Kenneth M. Harkness to R. B. Cozzens, Sept. 2, 1943; both in WRA, Ichihashi Case File. Ichihashi diary entries, Aug. 1–30, 1943.

69. PJT, B38, Ichihashis.

70. Although the Ichihashis hoped they would be able to leave Tule Lake before the other residents, they did still did not have a firm departure date when Kei wrote this letter. They were given only a day's notice before they actually left, on September 4.

71. Ichihashi diary entries, Sept. 5–6, 1943.

PART II, CHAPTER 4

1. [Mid-October 1943], IP, B6, F1. The observations, sentiments, and opinions Ichihashi expressed in the essay, which was typewritten, correspond to those in his daily diary for this period.

2. An estimated 20,000 evacuees had to move in or out of Tule Lake as a result of the segregation decision. It is not clear where Ichihashi "already indicated" the numbers.

3. This and subsequent quoted material apparently came from orientation literature prepared by the camp administration.

4. James G. Lindley, Project Director of Amache from 1942 to 1946. A metallurgical engineer by training, he was smelter superintendent of the Phelps Dodge Corporation, in Clifton, Arizona, before working for the WRA,

5. The identification of many Amache residents mentioned by Ichihashi was made possible by reference to *Amache* by Dr. Paul Rodriguez, who thoughtfully sent me a copy of the book. Among other items, it reproduces a camp directory, listing the last names of male residents in rough alphabetical order, with a brief entry for each, providing age, barrack number, the names of family members, if any living at the same address, and place of residence before relocation. The original directory was published sometime after late 1943.

Gihachiro Yuhora, then in his late fifties, was from the farming town of Livingston in California's Central Valley. His wife was Kusu and his son, Hiro. Yuhora and Ichihashi became good friends in camp and engaged in common hobbies such as gardening. Hiro Yuhora and Ichihashi also became close. After Hiro joined the Army, he continued to write Ichihashi regularly about his experiences, according to the notations in Ichihashi's diary, but correspondence between the two has not been located. Takahashi's identity is unclear; the camp directory lists many people by that name.

6. The Sakai family, Ichihashi's relatives through marriage, lived near the relocation center; see Yamato's letter to the Treats, Oct. 21, 1943, below. They did not have to relocate since Colorado was outside the designated defense zone. Members of the Sakai family continue to reside in the area to this day. Approximately 2,800 persons of Japanese ancestry lived in Colorado in December 1941.

7. Many of the numbers in this document are very faint or illegible.

8. Amache was located outside Military Zones 1 and 2.

9. Probably Henry F. Halliday, assistant project director at Amache.

10. The Amache directory does not list anyone with the surname Kiyohara, although it does include a 63-year-old man named Danzo Kiyowara from Los Angeles. Ichihashi's diary shows that he and Kiyohara met regularly.

11. For another description of life at Amache, see V. J. Matsumoto, *Farming the Home Place*, pp. 119–48. A transcript of a long firsthand report on Amache that was broadcast by a Denver radio station July 5–9, 1943, can be found in "KFEL News Hour," University of California, Los Angeles, Manuscript Collection, #2010, F10, B120.

12. PJT, B38, Ichihashis. Yamato and Kei sent several postcards to the Treats during and after their move to Amache to keep their friends abreast of their welfare and address and to thank them again for all their help. Postcards of Sept. 5, Sept. 11[?], and Sept. 19, 1943, all in PJT, B19, F1943 A–J.

13. Kei may be referring to a postcard she sent on Sept. 21. PJT, B38, Ichihashis.

14. Jessie Treat's letter has not been located, nor the identity of the presumed renter determined.

15. All 1943 diary entries in this chapter are from the commercially published yearbook for 1943, IP.

16. PJT, B19, 1943 A–J.

17. The handwriting of Edgar Robinson was notoriously indecipherable.

18. George Mizota was born in Japan but raised in Brawley, California, by a Caucasian family. Mizota attended Stanford as an undergraduate in the early 1920's and later went to Stanford Law School. He became a successful commercial and international business attorney in postwar Japan. Author's interview with Toichi Domoto, June 23, 1992.

19. A copy of Ichihashi's letter to Ito is in IP, B5, F8. It contains information Ichihashi included elsewhere and is therefore not reproduced here.

20. Ryo Kuramoto. She and her husband, Satoru, had also transferred from Tule Lake. Satoru became block manager for 11-E at Amache.

21. Lisette Fast wrote the Ichihashis after their arrival at Amache. Ichihashi's reply contained material repeated elsewhere and is not reproduced here. A copy of his letter is in IP, B5, F8.

22. The Japanese imperial government granted so-called independence to the Philippines from United States rule, but continued to occupy the islands. Jose Laurel, a 1920 graduate of Yale Law School, was made president under the Japanese, and his government joined Japan in the war against the United States. His son Salvatore became vice president of the Philippines in 1986.

23. Aichi was Ichihashi's home prefecture. Ichihashi and Ono regularly visited in Amache and kept in touch after the war.

24. In mid-October, the death of a Tule Lake resident in a farm truck accident touched off two weeks of unrest. Residents believed that WRA negligence had played a part in causing the accident and that the victim's widow had been callously treated. The unrest brought other grievances to the surface, resulting in a ten-day work stoppage at the camp farm. The level of anger among residents was still high when Dillon Myer visited Tule Lake on November 1, which ignited a week of new disturbances.

25. Ichihashi had the name wrong. The deceased was Kanetaro Domoto, one of four brothers from Japan who helped pioneer the flowering growing industry in the United States. The family also founded the first company to import provisions from Japan. The Domotos had emigrated to California in the 1880's. Eventually they established a large operation in Oakland for growing cut flowers; they introduced many flower, shrub, tree, and fruit varieties to the United States and shipped their cultivated products across the country. Kanetaro became "one of America's most respected flower growers," according to Gary Kawaguchi, author of *Living With Flowers*. When he was an undergraduate at Stanford, Ichihashi came to know the Domotos and later referred to them, although not by name, in his book, *Japanese in the United States* (pp. 201–2). Kanetaro's son, Toichi, attended Stanford from 1921 to 1923. Author's interview with Toichi Domoto, June 23, 1992. For more on the Domoto family, see Kawaguchi, *Living With Flowers*.

26. The identity of Tanji is unclear. The Amache directory lists three large families named Tanji, all from the California Central Valley; they may have been related. The second named individual may have been Hisashi Kayashima from Los Angeles.

27. PJT, B19, F1943 A–J. A faint carbon copy can also be found in IP, B5, F8.

28. The age groups as Ichihashi wrote them add to 197.

29. Treat responded in a letter dated November 11, in which he discussed the recent troubles at Tule Lake. He feared that they fueled the anti-Japanese sentiments in the state and caused "a great deal of harm to the interests of all persons of Japanese ancestry in this country." Before the events, he had harbored some hope that restrictions might be loosened to permit some of the Japanese to return home, but now he was pessimistic about a change for the better. Treat also discreetly suggested that Ichihashi rent out his home, now vacant for seventeen months, since it was suffering from neglect and there was a great demand for campus housing. Ichihashi did not reply to Payson for almost two months, and while the reason for his lapse is unclear, a comment he made in his diary entry for Nov. 16, 1943, about Treat's November 11 letter implies that he might have been unhappy with Treat's characterization of the Tule Lake events.

30. A carbon copy of the letter to Marvin Opler is in IP, B5, F8. In it, Ichihashi describes the trip to Amache and their impressions of the camp and its staff. The information repeats that given in other material included in this chapter. The tone of the letter is very friendly, and it even ends with a request that Opler "remember us kindly to Mr. Best," the camp director.

31. Possibly Hisaro Yoshihara, wife of Mitsutaro, from Shelton, Washington.

32. Not located.

33. In late October 1943, U.S. Secretary of State Cordell Hull met British Foreign Secretary Anthony Eden and Soviet Foreign Commissar V. M. Molotov in Moscow, the first high-level meeting of the so-called Big Three. During the sessions, Stalin promised that the Soviet Union would join the Allies against Japan once the conflict in Europe was ended. The Moscow Conference also saw agreement on the creation of a postwar organization for peace, what later became the United Nations. The Conference was enthusiastically hailed in the United States. The "pronouncement" mentioned by Ichihashi revealed only general information about the meeting.

34. Jessie Treat's letter has not been located.

35. The identity of Fujita is not clear. Suematsu Yasukazu was a Japanese historian of Korea.

36. Dr. Thomas A. Storey, who had founded the School of Hygiene at Stanford, died in Atlanta in October 1943.

37. Ichihashi attached a clipping from the *Palo Alto Times* of Oct. 28, on the work stoppage at Tule Lake. The article mentioned that 300–500 "loyal Japanese" from other camps had volunteered to help harvest the crops at Tule Lake.

38. Tule Lake was renamed a "segregation center" after resettlement of the "loyal" residents out of the camp.

39. PJT, B19, 1943 A–J. This letter was handwritten.

40. PJT, B38, Ichihashis.

41. Ichihashi notes on Tule Lake events, Nov. 11–12, 1943, IP, B5, F8; Ichihashi diary entries, Nov. 12–24, 1943; and "The Tule Lake 'Riot' And Its Background," IP, B6, F4. Ichihashi collected numerous newspaper articles on Tule Lake in his 1943 diary.

42. Ichihashi apparently expressed interest to the camp administration in helping advise his fellow evacuees about resettlement out of the camps. A letter from John A. Rademaker, a community analyst at Amache, to central WRA authorities in Washington, D.C., raised Ichihashi as a possible member of a proposed Relocation Information Bureau and counselor. Although Rademaker expressed high regard for Ichihashi's professional qualifications (he had "more information on the past occupations and social relationships of the Japanese in the United States than any other person I know"), he also cautioned his superiors about Ichihashi's personality. "His egoism (apparently an intrinsic aspect of the personality of full professors at Stanford!)," Rademaker wrote, "indicates that he is not wholly trained and prepared for objective counselling." The Relocation Information Bureau did not come to be. Rademaker to Crays, Nov. 22, 1943, WRA, Microfilm Records, M1342, Reel 15.

43. Possibly Ichiro Konno from Honolulu. Santa Fe was the location of a federal internment camp for enemy aliens and evacuees believed to be especially dangerous.

44. When Ichihashi first arrived in San Francisco in the mid-1890's, he joined the Japanese Gospel Society, or Nihonjin Fukuinkai, the first Japanese

immigrant organization in the city. Ichihashi's older brother, Shun'nosuke (b. 1871), had also been a member of the society. Elsewhere in his diary, Ichihashi wrote that his lecture was entitled, "Asia Shōminzoku no Kōbō" ("The struggle of Asian minorities").

45. Club members were mothers of nisei in the U.S. armed services.

46. Ichihashi diary entries, Nov. 16–Dec. 6, 1943; Y. Ichihashi to J. Treat, Nov. 16, 1943; Alice Westbrook to Ichihashis, Sept. 10, 1943; and Westbrook to Treats, Oct. 7, 1943; all in PJT, B38, Ichihashis. Kazuyuki Takahashi to Treat, Nov. 10, 1943, PJT, B20, 1943 K–Z.

47. Kazuyuki Takahashi was a graduate student at Stanford at the time of relocation. He and his new wife, Soyo, who had grown up in Palo Alto and had known the Ichihashi family, first went to Santa Anita, then to Manzanar. After moving out to St. Louis to try to continue his studies, Takahashi actively kept in touch with his Stanford friends, including the Treats. He and another alumnus, Henry Tani, published the "Stanford Nisei Alumni Newsletter" during the war years. After the war, Takahashi earned his medical degree from Stanford and became a prominent physician in the Oakland area. His long, frequent, and thoughtful correspondence with Payson Treat provides further interesting insights into Japanese American experiences during the war years; these letters are in the chronological files of the Treat Papers at the Hoover Institution. Author's interview with Kazuyuki and Soyo Takahashi, Aug. 2, 1993.

48. Buddy Tsuneo Iwata, from Turlock, California, graduated from Stanford in 1939. He was active in student affairs as an undergraduate and had taken Ichihashi's courses. After leaving relocation camp, he taught Japanese at the University of Colorado Navy Language School and the Army Language School at Northwestern University. He also did translation and broadcast work for the Office of War Information in Washington, D.C. After the war, he became a prominent community leader in the Modesto area and was general manager of the Livingston Farmers Association for many years. The Association was descended from the Yamato Colony, one of the first agricultural associations of Japanese farmers in the United States.

49. PJT, B38, Ichihashis.

50. This letter was handwritten.

51. The *Kojiki* (Record of ancient matters), compiled in 712, and the *Nihongi* (or *Nihon shoki*, History of Japan), compiled in 720, are two of the most important sources on the origins of the Japanese and the formation of the Japanese state. *Fūdoki* are local records and historical materials compiled in the eighth century by imperial authorities.

52. Ichihashi refers here to the American and Japanese nationals who had recently been exchanged on the Swedish ship *Gripsholm*; see note 62 to Part II, Chapter 1.

53. Ichihashi used the diary space devoted to "Special Data" at the end of November for the following entry, which he dated.

54. On December 9, Attorney General Francis Biddle testified before a congressional committee investigating the WRA and asserted "the WRA has no legal technical right of interning any American citizen. They (the centers) were

set up to afford these people a place they could go before they found some place to live." He added, "I know of no authority in any executive order to hold a citizen in a center." He also suggested that American citizens of Japanese ancestry who declared loyalty to Japan could be deprived of U.S. citizenship. Japanese authorities, he told the committee, were closely watching the treatment of its nationals in the United States. Unidentified clipping in Ichihashi diary, Dec. 9, 1943.

55. Possibly Ryo Kurahashi from Yuba City.

56. Hanji and Yukino Okubo, from Los Angeles. Hanji, in his mid-sixties, was the manager for Ichihashi's block and was a dentist by profession.

57. A carbon copy of this letter is in IP, B5, F8. In the letter, which principally concerns his historical research, Ichihashi also thanks Treat for a 1944 diary book. "Every page of the Diary Book will be of historical value," Ichihashi told his friend.

58. Ernest Kuramatsu, who apparently lived alone, was an amateur artist in his late fifties from Carmel, California.

59. The significance of these November dates is unclear.

60. This and subsequent diary entries for 1944 are from Ichihashi's 1944 diary book, IP.

61. Presumably Seiichiro Takahashi of Livingston, California, a man in his late fifties. His wife was named Sei, and his children include Kazuo.

62. After requesting repatriation in 1943, several thousand evacuees changed their minds and wanted to retract their statements.

63. PJT, B38, Ichihashis.

64. Unidentified. This individual regularly visits Ichihashi and is an important source of information about camp affairs, but the camp directory does not list anyone with the surname Kujo.

65. IP, B6, F7. This was a carbon copy and not signed.

66. *Kun* is a term of familiarity for a younger male.

67. According to his diary, Ichihashi received a letter from Shirai at Tule Lake on January 6, 1944.

68. Kenji Ito wrote from the Minidoka camp in Hunt, Idaho. A letter from him dated Jan. 7, 1944, made reference to an earlier letter Ichihashi had written him in Japanese. There is no copy of that letter in the Ichihashi Papers.

Ito also wrote to Ichihashi on January 11 and 22, reporting on developments at Minidoka and agreeing with Ichihashi's negative evaluation of the Japanese relocatees. Both Ito and Ichihashi believed their fellow Japanese lacked courage and were a disgrace to their national traditions. Ito's letters and an Ichihashi response of January 16, which repeats much of the letter to Shirai, are found in IP, B6, F7.

69. IP, B6, F7. Though it contains information similar to that in the letter to Shirai, this letter's milder tone and omission of specific observations about camp life contrasts with those in Ichihashi's letters to Japanese friends.

70. In a letter dated Jan. 4, 1944, Treat described recent visitors to his home, campus events during the holiday season, and news of Stanford acquaintances who were working for the WRA in other relocation camps; he encouraged Ichi-

hashi to continue with his research and translations of Japanese texts, and reported on his own career plans. Treat wrote that because he would turn 65 in September, his current sabbatical leave would be his last. He asked his old friend to keep him informed of his "researches," so that when he gave his "last course of lectures on the Far East they will be up-to-the-minute" (Treat to Ichihashi, IP, B6, F7).

71. Ichihashi's harsh criticism of his fellow internees was shared by others. The January 29, 1944, issue of the camp newspaper reprinted an article from the Heart Mountain camp paper, "Bread-Line Complex" by John Kitasako, that contained a view similar to Ichihashi's. The *Palo Alto Times* also regularly published Kitasako's reports.

72. Possibly the wife of Hango Uratsu, from Loomis, California.

73. IP, B6, F1. This is a handwritten draft of a letter; it is unclear whether it was ever sent.

74. Lou Henry Hoover, Herbert Hoover's wife, died on January 7. A memorial was held for her at Stanford on January 14.

75. The identity of Hattori is not clear, The camp directory lists several families by that name. He and Ichihashi became friends, and the two visited regularly, sharing hobbies such as gardening.

76. Possibly Toyoji Konno, a man in his late fifties from Livingston, California.

77. PJT, B38, Ichihashis.

78. Ex-wife of Paul Clyde, a former student of Ichihashi's.

79. In September 1942, the Selective Service Board decided to assign all persons of Japanese ancestry, citizen and alien, to the IV-C draft category, which was supposed to designate only unacceptable aliens.

80. John A. Rademaker, a community analyst for the WRA at Amache, submitted a confidential report on this meeting to his superior in Washington. The following excerpt provides a vivid sense of the atmosphere in the camp: "Tonight a mass meeting is to be held, at which [a statement regarding the draft] will be considered, and approved, or corrected. This meeting has *not* been called by the Community Council, but by a small group of nisei who are anxious to arouse objections to the situation, and who operate sub rosa. The mass meeting was not cleared through the policy department by 2 p.m. this afternoon, and is hence illegal. I went to Mr. Lindley and conferred on the matter. I asked that he instruct the Internal Security chief not to interfere with the meeting, despite its illegality, on the ground that it would only rouse greater determination to push it through, and would probably lead to considerable disorder. I did this because I feel that if the police accidentally happened to tumble in on it and tried to adjourn it there would certainly be trouble. . . . I agreed to go to the meeting (uninvited by the sponsors, but quietly invited by some Council members, who were invited to attend by the sponsors), and at an opportune moment if possible to secure the floor and speak as one nisei to the others, trying to review the whole situation calmly. . . . Mr. Lindley agreed to this program. . . . Feeling is high, tempers are short, and people are sensitive and on edge most of the time.

Slight rubs create many symptoms of friction. A mass meeting with a good agitator could go a long way in formulating extreme demands" (Rademaker to Edward Spicer, Feb. 16, 1944, IP, B6, F7). Rademaker apparently felt on sufficiently close terms with Ichihashi to give him a copy of this and other confidential reports to the WRA. It is not clear what Rademaker meant about speaking as "one nisei to others." See Ichihashi diary entry, March 4, 1944.

81. Presumably the "Seventeen-Mile Drive," a scenic route along the rocky shore in Pebble Beach, near Carmel, California.

82. Rademaker earned a doctorate in sociology from the University of Washington in 1939, with a dissertation entitled "The Ecological Position of the Japanese Farmers in the State of Washington." He minored in Oriental Studies. He also had published "The Japanese in the Social Organization of the Puget Sound Region," *American Journal of Sociology* 40 (1934): 338–43 and an essay called "Japanese Americans" in Francis J. Brown and Joseph S. Roucek, eds., *Our Racial and National Minorities* (1937), in which he expressed a view sympathetic to the Japanese in America. Arguing against Japanophobes, Rademaker pointed out that the Japanese had come to America for the same reasons as other immigrants. He taught at Bates College in Maine from 1939 to 1943, when he went to work for the WRA. At Amache, he and Ichihashi became friends, with Ichihashi eventually reading and commenting on Rademaker's thesis. Rademaker and his wife, Elizabeth Spencer, both enrolled in Ichihashi's cultural history class at Amache. After the war, Rademaker taught in Hawaii and then at the Willamette University in Oregon, where he became a local celebrity because of his liberal political activism. Author's conversation with Elizabeth Rademaker, Sept. 1993.

83. Rademaker described the second meeting in a Feb. 17 postscript to his Feb. 16 letter to Spicer. It read: "The meeting was held without violence, and with little if any disorder. . . . The spearhead of the effort is evidently a group of 50 or 60 kibei, 10 or 12 of whom are active leaders, many of whom have recently asked for repatriation. They think they will be sent to Tule Lake, and that the army will find them non-acceptable, so they will get out from under—or if they don't, they won't be any worse off if they raise a fuss than if they don't. They're trying to spread the idea of sending the War Department demands with the statement that if the demands are not granted they will not serve in the army. This will obviously be considered as obstruction of the draft, and as such punished by the FBI. Many nisei are pretty immature, and are being influenced by this sort of pressure. The majority, however, seem to be level headed enough to want to avoid spending the next twenty years in Leavenworth Penitentiary. Some are conscientiously willing to suffer such martyrdom in order to advance the cause of the nisei, as they think of it. However, the result will probably be the opposite, which only a few clear-thinking leaders can see. These leaders are on the spot, and most of them are not talking. Some way of stopping the agitation is what we need, and repression is not the answer. Can you give us some suggestions? The first induction date is February 22 in the local board. My talk helped and hindered. I doubt that any real headway will be made, but there is

some chance that the threat of the penitentiary will be clouded by the zealots and a stampede of confused youngsters result. I'm going out again to see what we can do to rally the opposition."

84. Treat's letter not found; reference to notices unclear.

85. W. Ray Johnson, Assistant Project Director. Before working for the WRA, he had been the regional chief for community and family services for the Farm Security Administration, U.S. Dept. of Agriculture, in Denver.

PART II, CHAPTER 5

1. Diary entry, March 17, 1944; Minutes of the Special Joint Committee for Giving Information to Draft-Age Nisei, March 17, 1944, IP, B6, F7; Lindley to Dillon S. Myer, July 7, 1945, WRA, Ichihashi Case File.

2. Diary excerpts in this chapter are from Ichihashi's diary for 1944, IP.

3. PJT, B38, Ichihashis. Kei had once organized an exhibition of Japanese dolls on Girls' Day at Stanford. ("Ichihashi to speak," *Stanford Daily* clipping, n.d., IP, B1, F1.)

4. Harold Ickes, Secretary of the Interior. On Feb. 16, 1944, jurisdiction of the WRA was transferred from the War Department to the Department of the Interior.

5. The Japanese-American Student Relocation Council was organized largely by the American Friends Service Committee in May 1942 to help college-aged nisei leave camp to pursue their studies in the Midwest and eastern United States. The group's national headquarters was in Philadelphia, and it was supported by a distinguished group of church leaders and educators, among them Ray Lyman Wilbur of Stanford.

6. Ichihashi may be referring to the United States attack on the island of Truk, which had been one of Japan's most important naval bases in the south-western Pacific. In mid-February, American fighters attacked airfields, planes, and ships on the island, effectively neutralizing Truk as an operational base. In addition to warships, the Japanese lost 24 freighters. These losses were a major setback for Japan.

7. Japanese Imperial Army Headquarters News Release. Apparently, some Amache internees were able to listen to shortwave broadcasts from Japan. It is not clear what Ichihashi meant by "'Amache' D."

8. George was the son of Orichi and Tome Oki from Yuba City, California.

9. In late February 1944, after the attack on Truk, U.S. forces landed on Eniwetok and Parry Islands in the Marshalls. After heavy fighting, they took the islands.

10. The camp directory lists George Miyama, in his late twenties, his wife, Sakaye, and two children occupying the barrack given by Ichihashi. They were from Lodi, California. Miyama regularly visited Ichihashi; later in the year, after he left camp, he sent reports about the "outside."

11. PJT, B38, Ichihashis.

12. Not located.

13. Presumably, Susan Kennedy Branner, the wife of Stanford's second president, John C. Branner. Mrs. Lyon has not been identified.

14. George Bliss Culver was Dean of Men at Stanford before World War II.

15. Kay Kitagawa, a Stanford alumnus and undergraduate student in Ichihashi's classes, was serving in the U.S. military.

16. Lecture notes that may have been prepared for his course can be found in Ichihashi's papers; for example, see "Problems of Cultural Assimilation," n.d., B6, F1.

17. For example, on April 9 Yamato spoke to a gathering of young Buddhists in the camp. A letter from the group respectfully thanked him for the talk and observed that he, as a senior professor at Stanford, had been familiar to nisei "in and out of university campuses." The group expressed appreciation for the chance to now "have you to guide us, especially in this chaotic epoch in the lives of niseis" (Richard Iseri to Y. Ichihashi, April 14, 1944, insert in his diary for 1944).

18. The Jerome, Arkansas, center was being closed, and internees there had to transfer to other camps.

19. Leupp Isolation Center was located on Navajo Indian land in Arizona.

20. Paul Yamamoto was a Stanford student who was one quarter away from graduating from Stanford when he was relocated from campus in 1942. He later entered the Army Military Intelligence School at Fort Snelling, Minnesota.

21. This letter has not been located.

22. A description of the educational system at Amache written by the superintendent of education of Colorado can be found in Lloyd A. Garrison, "Education at Amache," *Colorado School Journal*, March 1943, pp. 15–18.

23. PJT, B38, Ichihashis.

24. There were many Japanese flower growers in the Stanford area before the war. See Kawaguchi, *Living with Flowers*.

25. The reader may recall that the time described by Kei was when she and Yamato were not speaking to each other.

26. PJT, B20, 1944 A–J.

27. Probably Homer B. Hulbert (1863–1949), an authority on Korean history.

28. Possibly Ryo and Satoru Kuramoto.

29. The 4,000-acre WRA farm was associated with the center.

30. Interior finishing material.

31. George B. Sansom, *Japan: A Short Cultural History* (New York: Appleton-Century, rev. ed., 1944).

32. Presumably Masachika Yonemura, a Buddhist minister in his sixties, who received his education in Japan and lived in Marysville, California, before the war.

33. According to the description in the guide to the Thomas Bodine Papers at the Hoover Institution, in 1941 Bodine worked with the American Friends Service Committee, which then sent him to assist Japanese Americans in the Seattle area after Pearl Harbor. In December 1942, Bodine became West Coast

director of the National Japanese-American Student Relocation Council. He later became its Field Director, traveling to various relocation centers as the liaison between counselors, students, and the main office in Philadelphia. His papers contain much correspondence with college-age nisei. It is unclear which individual named Oki Ichihashi refers to here and subsequently.

34. Nichiren-shu was a major Buddhist sect in Japan, named after its thirteenth-century founder.

35. Langdon Warner, *Japanese Sculpture of the Suiko Period* (1923).

36. The Japanese community newspaper of Utah.

37. PJT, B38, Ichihashis.

38. Mountain View is located directly south of Palo Alto.

39. From 1882 until 1943, when the Chinese exclusion acts were repealed, federal law prohibited Chinese from becoming naturalized citizens. Korean aliens, as well as Japanese, remained barred from U.S. citizenship.

40. PJT, B38, Ichihashis.

41. Apparently Daisuke Kitagawa. Rev. Clarence Gillett had been a missionary in Japan and a leader of the American Board of Foreign Missions.

42. By the end of the war, religious and local civic groups had established over 100 hostels across the country to help internees resettle after leaving the camps. On the hostels and Christian involvement in trying to ameliorate the effects of relocation, see T. Matsumoto, *Beyond Prejudice.*

43. On July 1, 1944, President Roosevelt signed Public Law 405, the so-called "denaturalization bill," which permitted renunciation of citizenship on American soil in time of war. Administration officials hoped nisei would avail themselves of the opportunity, thus making their continued internment less problematic legally.

44. Laurence E. Davies was a correspondent for the *New York Times* and a friend of Dillon Myer.

45. Retired General Koiso Kuniaki and retired Admiral Yonai Mitsumasa, whom Ichihashi had met before the war, headed the Japanese cabinet following the fall of the Tōjō government in July 1944.

46. PJT, B38, Ichihashis.

47. Paul Clyde was a former doctoral student of Ichihashi's and an Asia specialist. He was the author of several books on Asia, including *International Rivalries in Manchuria, 1689–1922* (1926), *Japan's Pacific Mandate* (1935), *A History of the Modern and Contemporary Far East* (1937), *United States Policy Toward China* (1940), and *The Far East* (2d ed., 1952).

48. Maxwell Hicks Savelle was a member of the History Department who specialized in American colonial history. He went through several marriages, to the perturbation of some of his colleagues.

49. Henry Lanz, professor of Slavic languages and philosophy, taught at Stanford from 1918 to 1945, the year of his death. His son, Henry, Jr., graduated from Stanford in 1936.

50. The letter from Mrs. Storey has not been located.

51. The author was probably Frederick Seymour Hulse.

52. In 1935 at Reed College and in 1937 at Stanford, Ichihashi had participated in the America-Japan Student Conferences that brought American and
Japanese students together to promote mutual understanding, but it does not
appear that he was deeply involved in their planning. The conferences have been
held regularly since 1934, except during the war years. See "The Japan-America
Student Conference: Celebrating Sixty Years, 1934–1994," compiled and published by the Japan-American Student Conference, Washington, D.C., 1994.
(The organization altered its name after World War II.)

53. The agent's report of this interrogation is in Ichihashi's FBI file and is
consistent with Ichihashi's description. A portion of the report reads as follows:
"Subject was also questioned as to whether or not SHIOZAKI or the Japanese Consul in San Francisco did not aid him financially in 1937. It should be noted at
this point subject became antagonistic and stated that his truthfulness had never
been questioned before and that he was a man of honor. He advised the Agent
he had previously informed that he had never been on the payroll of the Consul
and that the Agent was attempting to intimate that he had been paid by the
Japanese Consul. At this time Agent advised subject that the Bureau had been
furnished definite information that subject had been paid by the Japanese Consul
in 1937. [Here the FBI elided two lines from the released document.] As previously stated, Subject denied this as being true" (Report, Aug. 19, 1944, Ichihashi
FBI File).

54. PJT, B38, Ichihashis.

55. Not located.

56. Possibly Takashi Terami, a man in his mid-fifties from Walnut Grove,
California, and Lowell M. Jackson of the administrative staff. S. I. Hayakawa was
a linguist, whose best-known works are *Language in Action* (New York: Harcourt
Brace, 1941) and *Language in Thought and Action* (New York: Harcourt Brace,
1949). He was president of San Francisco State University in the late 1960's and
served as U.S. Senator from California from 1976–82. Hayakawa knew of Ichihashi and recommended to the WRA that Ichihashi might help in language
training. Because he resided outside the Western Defense Zone, Hayakawa was
never interned. "Community Analysis Report No. VIII[?]," WRA, Granada
Community Analysis Reports.

57. PJT, B38, Ichihashis.

58. The Treats' former maid, who had been at Santa Anita with the Ichihashi's but later was able to leave internment.

59. The note apparently was from Woodrow's wife, Alyce. Woodrow was
first placed in the 171st infantry battalion, which was all Japanese Americans,
except for two Korean Americans. He was sent to Europe in early 1945 and
was finally discharged in July 1946. Author's interview with W. Ichihashi,
Oct. 30, 1992.

60. PJT, B20, F1944 A–J.

61. Not located. Ichihashi's diary notes that he received a letter from Treat
on Sept. 21.

62. Ethel Barker Fast, wife of Emery Fast and sister-in-law of Kei's friend, Lisette Fast. A letter from August Fast to Mrs. Emery Fast, Sept. 20, 1944, Emery Fast Correspondence, Stanford Special Collections, comments on her report about visiting Yamato.

63. Ichihashi's diary indicates a stronger interest in the possibility of returning to Stanford than this letter to Treat suggested. He felt, however, that Stanford had to make the first move in formally requesting his return; it does not appear that Stanford ever did so. Diary, Sept. 22, 1944.

64. Possibly Iwakichi Haratani from Livingston, California. The camp directory also lists his wife and six children.

65. Apparently the letter dated Sept. 22, 1944.

66. Presumably the American Civil Liberties Union (ACLU).

67. Newspaper of the Tule Lake segregation center.

68. Apparently Edward Kitazumi, from Sacramento, California.

69. The use of the term "blockheads" to refer to the block managers seems to have been a deliberately derogatory pun. See Nishimoto, *American Concentration Camp*, pp. 167–68.

70. The rule of Shōtoku in the early seventh century brought about far-reaching changes for Japan, including the confirmation of Confucian ethical concepts for the ruling elite, the goal of centralized political institutions, and regularized relations with China. His "constitution" was not a formal document but an expression of his precepts.

71. PJT, B38, Ichihashis.

72. PJT, B20, F1944 A–J.

73. Letter not located.

74. In August 1944, Stanford approved the hiring of fourteen Japanese-language instructors from Manzanar.

75. An ancient Chinese historical text of the Wei dynasty that contained important descriptions of Japan in the third century A.D.

76. B. R. Stauber to Lindley, Oct. 6, 1944, and Lindley to Stauber, Nov. 14, 1944, WRA, Ichihashi Case File.

77. The name given to seventh-century reforms in Japan, along the lines advocated by Prince Shōtoku.

78. PJT, B20, F1944 A–J.

79. PJT, B38, Ichihashis.

80. PJT, B38, Ichihashis.

81. IP, B6, F7.

82. The model boat was a gift from the students in Ichihashi's class and the walking cane, with a carved warbler on the handle, was a Christmas present from a friend. Along with these gifts, Ichihashi also received some candies and cookies from friends outside the camp and a blank diary book for 1945 from Payson Treat.

83. "Kishū" refers to Wakayama Prefecture, which has many small fishing villages along its southern coast. Katsuura is a well-known hot spring resort in Wakayama.

84. The Machida family was from Covina, California.

85. IP, B6, F8. What follows is part of a brief undated report, probably written in mid- or late 1944.

86. It was unusual for Ichihashi to speak of the U.S. government as "our government," although he had occasionally done so in public talks in the past.

87. For more on the isseis' views about Japan and the war, see Hayashi, *Japanese Brethren*, pp. 141–45.

PART II, CHAPTER 6

1. About 5,000 men continued to be excluded from the Coast, and another 5,000 were to be kept under detention and not allowed to relocate anywhere. Girdner and Loftis, *Great Betrayal*, p. 381.

2. This and subsequent entries for 1945 come from Ichihashi's 1945 diary book, IP.

3. Letter not located.

4. The predominantly-nisei 442nd Regimental Combat Team was joined by the Japanese-Hawaiian 100th Battalion.

5. IP, B7, F2.

6. "Minidoka Irrigator," newspaper of that camp. According to Ichihashi's diary, he received a letter and the newspaper clipping from Ito on Jan. 12, 1945. This letter too has not been located. Ito had sent candies to Ichihashi for Christmas.

7. Roy Eiji Uragami, from Los Angeles and in his mid-sixties, was vice-chairman of the Community Council.

8. Presumably questions raised by the Community Council about the return to the West Coast.

9. Although Ichihashi's diary notes that his photograph was taken on several occasions by various people during his relocation and that he was given prints of some of these pictures, none of these photos have been located.

10. Corky Kawasaki was the executive secretary of the Federation of Co-operatives of the internment camps.

11. PJT, B38, Ichihashis.

12. Several hundred individual internees had quietly been allowed to return to the West Coast before January 2. These included spouses of non-Japanese, of nisei servicemen, and of nisei soldiers on furlough, among others.

13. Calls for boycotts of produce and flowers produced by returning internees were raised throughout the West Coast in early 1945.

14. Many internees believed the WRA should have provided greater financial support for them than it did. As Ichihashi often implied in his diary, he apparently felt that the internees should be as self-reliant as possible.

15. According to Ichihashi's diary, he began writing the following draft report on February 4, but it is unclear when he completed it. It was handwritten, and some marginalia are not reproduced here. IP, B6, F7.

16. Ichihashi is referring to the arrangement worked out by farmers in the Cortez, Cressey, and Livingston area of California's Central Valley. The farmers, who had a long history of cooperative agriculture, established an association and hired non-Japanese operators to maintain and operate their farms in their absence. Most of these farmers had been relocated to Amache. Ichihashi describes the arrangement under "Special Data" for February 28, 1945, below. Also see V. J. Matsumoto's history of Cortez, *Farming the Home Place*, chaps. 3 and 4.

17. PJT, B38, Ichihashis.

18. Clyde A. Duniway had been a professor of history at Stanford and president of Colorado College, the University of Montana, and the University of Wyoming. He had been retired for several years. Professor Everett P. Lesley was a mechanical engineer and had been at Stanford since 1907. William Bassett was the son of Professor Lee Emerson Bassett. William graduated from Stanford in 1936 and taught drama at the University. He died in the sinking of the destroyer *Monaghan*.

19. A reference to conflicts within the History Department.

20. Ichihashi used the spelling Kawajiri here, but the council president was Sakae Kawashiri, a commercial artist from San Francisco in his late twenties who had attended San Francisco City College. His wife was Chizuru. He became chairman of the camp council and was known as the "mayor" of Amache. He and Ichihashi became good friends. Kawashiri entered the army during the closing months of the war. After the war, he returned to live in Berkeley. *Kansas City Star*, Sept. 9, 1945, p. 4C, University of California, Los Angeles, Special Collections, Collection 2010, Box 120, #10.

21. Shinichi Furuya, treasurer of the Community Council, in his late fifties, was from South Central Los Angeles.

22. On February 16, 1945, an all-center conference of internee representatives was held at Salt Lake City to discuss the return to the "outside." Thirty representatives from seven centers attended the week-long meeting. According to Richard Nishimoto's report on the conference, the discussion focused on three issues: monetary reparations for losses and damages; special support for the elderly and needy; and a full guarantee of the rights and safety of individuals. Nishimoto, *American Concentration Camp*, pp. 164–67.

23. "T" stood for "Technical." Woodrow reports that he made only corporal, not sergeant.

24. Hugh Borton was the author of *Japan Since 1931* (New York: Institute of Pacific Relations, 1940) and *Japan's Modern Century* (New York: Ronald, 1955) and other books on Japanese history. Before the war, Fahs published work on Japanese government and politics, including *Government in Japan: Recent Trends in Its Scope and Operation* (New York: Institute of Pacific Relations, 1940). Knight Biggerstaff became an authority on the government of imperial China. His books included *The Far East and the United States* (Ithaca: Cornell University Press, 1943) and *China: Revolutionary Changes in an Ancient Civilization* (Ithaca: Cornell University Press, 1945). Charles Nelson Spinks received his degree from Stanford in 1936; his doctoral dissertation is entitled "A History of the

Anglo-Japanese Alliance, 1902–1922." He published *Japan's Entrance into the World War* (1936?). He was a member of the United States Strategic Bombing Survey group that after the war studied the effects of the Allied bombing of Japan. He later published several books on China, Japanese foreign relations, and art in Southeast Asia.

25. Ichihashi's papers include official material from the Amache administration, including analyst reports. See Boxes 6 and 7.

26. See Part II, Chapter 5, n. 7.

27. James R. Young was a reporter for the Hearst newspapers who regularly wrote sensational, hostile articles against the internees.

28. Ichihashi had been placed on parole after his release from Sharp Park.

29. Ichihashi retained a draft of the letter his diary indicates he sent to Ennis on March 16, 1945 (IP, B6, F7). The letter described in general terms where he had lived since relocation and his life in America after arriving in 1894. He ended his request to be released from parolee status with the following:

> I have had no connection with any Japanese organizations, though I have been a member of several American learned societies; in fact, I have been isolated from Japanese communities and activities during my residence in this country.
>
> I have never applied for repatriation to my native land; I have my interests and friends concentrated in this country. Our only child Woodrow, a son, was inducted into the Army last August, and is now serving as a corporal. Though myself denied the privilege of becoming a U.S. citizen, I am content for I am now old and have no ambition of a youth.
>
> However, I am hoping to complete a piece of research work in the field of cultural [history] with the view of publishing a book. For this I need facilities of a university library. The status of a parolee is a social stigma and therefore I would like to be relieved from such a status, if possible, so that I may live as a free man pursuing a scholarly life.
>
> Thanking you, for your kind and sympathetic considerations of the request, I remain
>
> Very respectfully,
> Yamato Ichihashi

30. PJT, B38, Ichihashis.

31. Not located.

32. Presumably a reference to a Palo Alto neighborhood just south of Stanford.

33. Handwritten note, B. to B. R. Stauber, n.d., WRA, Ichihashi Case File.

34. In a report to Dillon Myer, James G. Lindley, the project director of Amache, described Ichihashi as the "principal speaker" of the March 29 meeting and a speaker also at the five follow-up district meetings. Lindley wrote, "Considerable discussion has been evoked at all these meetings and it is my feeling that the meetings have been well sponsored and well conducted. I am particularly grateful to Dr. Ichihashi for the firm stand that he has taken on behalf of relocation" (Lindley to Myer, April 19, 1945, WRA, Ichihashi Case File).

35. Presumably, Tatsuzo Furukawa of the Block Managers Assembly.

36. Ichiro Konno and Shinshichi Fujino, both men in their fifties, worked together on the Japanese section of the *Granada Pioneer*. Konno was from Honolulu, and Fujino from Upper Lake, California.

37. This refers to a guide to resettlement that the camp administration, with Ichihashi's help, compiled for the residents.

38. James G. Lindley wrote Dillon Myer about Ichihashi's activities at Amache in July 1945. Lindley's observations offer an interesting perspective on Ichihashi's life in camp. The most substantive part of his letter, a copy of which he sent to Ichihashi, reads: "Shortly before Dr. Ichihashi left the center on April 27, 1945 to return to his home in Palo Alto I had a long talk with him. I had noted that although he was looked up to by a large number of the residents who were aware of his attainments in the educational field he had assumed little or no leadership in the center. He told me that he had so conducted himself advisedly because in attempting to show some leadership at the time of segregation in Tule Lake his motives had been questioned. He had resolved that after his transfer to this center he would lead a quiet and self-contained life and leave the leadership to more politically minded people. Just before he left, however, he served as an Advisor to the Community Council during the time that that body was coming to the front in helping the residents work out their relocation plans. He was the principal speaker at many mass meetings of evacuees and threw all of his influence toward relocation and the speedy closing of the centers. I am very grateful to Dr. Ichihashi for the firm stand he took on behalf of relocation and also for the fact that he showed his belief in his precepts by his own example" (Lindley to Ichihashi, July 23, 1945, with enclosure, Lindley to Myer, July 7, 1945; IP, B7, F2). In addition, Lindley endorsed Ichihashi's request for release from his parole status.

39. Presumably referring to S. Kuramoto, vice-chairman, S. Fujino, treasurer, and Joe Kayokata, chairman of the Block Managers Assembly.

40. Lindley wrote directly to Myer the next day to report on the conversation with Ichihashi. Ichihashi had argued that the WRA had given what at best had been perfunctory attention to requests for release from parole status, using his own case as evidence. Lindley to Myer, April 19, 1945, WRA, Ichihashi Case File.

41. The Ichihashis shipped eleven pieces of freight that came to 1,350 pounds and six express pieces that weighed 452 pounds; these included some pieces of furniture.

42. Handwritten letter, PJT, B21, F1945 A–J; a letter to Edgar Robinson containing similar information is in EER, B17, F305. In a March 9 letter, Robinson offered to do whatever possible to help welcome the Ichihashis back to Stanford, noting "Your office is just as you left it" (Robinson to Ichihashi, March 9, 1945, EER, B19, F305).

43. Presumably Yukichi Washizu, in his late sixties, of Isleton, California.

44. Presumably Melvin McGovern and Lowell Jackson, members of the administrative staff, and Takashi Terami.

45. The reference may be to Military Zone 1, which extended 200 miles inland along the length of the Pacific Coast and the borders of Canada and Mexico.

46. Handwritten draft, IP, B7, F2.

47. Gerda Isenberg, a German-born naturalized U.S. citizen, was a founder of the Palo Alto Fair Play Council. She had actively helped Japanese Americans throughout the relocation ordeal.

EPILOGUE

1. This and several following paragraphs are based on entries in Ichihashi's diary for 1945, IP.

2. The claim was in response to the federal Japanese American Claims Act of 1948, which offered to compensate some of the monetary losses of the Japanese who had been relocated. Kenji Ito to Ichihashi, Feb. 1, 1952, IP, B7, F4.

3. Ichihashi diary entries, June 29, July 2–7, Sept. 22, 1945, and April 18, 1946.

4. Dept. of Justice, "Conduct to be Observed by Alien Enemies," July 11, 1944, and Sponsor's Agreement, June 2, 1945, PJT, B20, F1945 Misc. F. O. Seidle to Treat, Dec. 6, 1945, PJT, B21, 1945 K–Z. George Mizota to Ichihashi, Sept. 5, 1946, IP, B7, F3.

5. Treat to Wilbur, May 21, 1943, and Wilbur to Treat, May 24, 1943, RLW, B123, History. Robinson to Ichihashi, March 9, 1945, EER, B19, F305. Thomas Bailey, Memorandum of conversation with Claude Buss, April 24, 1945, Donald B. Tresidder Papers, B24, F4.

6. Ichihashi to Ito, Oct. 7, 1945, IP, B7, F2; Ichihashi diary, June 1 and 19, 1945.

7. Ichihashi to McFarling, June 25, 1945; Ichihashi to Ito, Aug. 19, Sept. 24, Oct. 7, and Nov. 13, 1945, and Jan. 22, Feb. 13, 1946; Ichihashi to Kawashiri, Aug. 3 and Sept. 4, 1945; all in IP, B7, F2 and F3. Daniels, *Asian America*, p. 285.

8. Ichihashi diary entry, Nov. 4, 1946, IP.

9. Ichihashi to Ito, Feb. 12, 1946, IP, B7, F2; Ichihashi diary entry, Feb. 7, 1946, IP.

10. Ichihashi to Ito, Feb. 13, 1946, IP, B7, F2; Ichihashi diary entry and clipping, June 17, 1946, IP.

11. Emery Fast to Ethel Fast, Sept. 2, Sept. 4, Nov. 6, and Nov. 12, 1945, all in Emery Fast Correspondence. Author's interview with Emery Fast, Oct. 3, 1993.

12. Ichihashi diary entry, Feb. 19 and 20, 1946. Christianson to Ichihashi, Feb. 18, 1946; Ichihashi to Shizuko, Feb. 21 and draft letter, [April] 1946; Shizuko to Ichihashi, Aug. 28 and Sept. 12, 1946; Ichihashi to Lt. Colonel [Bielefeldt], May 21, 1946; all in IP, B7, F3. Handwritten draft letter in Japanese, Ichihashi to Shizuko, Oct. [1945], IP, B6, F8.

13. Ichihashi diary entry, May 19, 1945, IP; author's interview with W. Ichihashi, Feb. 22, 1995.

14. Ichihashi diary entries, Aug. 1, Aug. 20, Sept. 27, and Dec. 11, 1945, and May 21 and July 23, 1946, IP.

15. Ichihashi diary entry, March 31 and April 16, 1953, IP. Mizota to Ichi-

hashi, Sept. 5, 1946, IP, B7, F3. Author's interview with Toichi Domoto, June 23, 1992.

16. Kinoshiguri[?] to Treat, Nov. 30, 1953, PJT, B12, 1931 G–Q. Ichihashi diary entries, April 21, 23, and 24, 1953; newspaper clipping from the *Nippon Times* attached to the entry page for Sept. 26, 1953; clipping attached to the entry page for Aug. 5, 1953; all IP.

17. Ichihashi, "Japanese American Relations" (1953).

18. Ichihashi diary entry, Jan. 8, 1954, IP.

19. Treat to Helen, Nov. 23, 1958, PJT, B29, 1958 A–I.

20. Author's interviews with John Johnson, Sept. 8, 1992; with Nancy McLean, July 14, 1993; with Gordon and Louise Wright, July 21, 1993; and with George Knoles, June 11, 1992.

21. Author's interview with W. Ichihashi, Oct. 30, 1992.

22. Author's interview with W. Ichihashi, Oct. 30, 1992; clippings of obituaries in PJT, B33, 1963 Misc.; author's interview with Rixford Snyder, August 17, 1993; and Robinson diary entries, April 5–10, 1963, EER, B69b, 1963 diary.

23. Author's interviews with Gordon and Louise Wright, July 21, 1993, and with George Knoles, June 11, 1992; Robinson diary entries from April 10–June 8, 1963, EER, B69b, 1963 diary.

24. Author's interview with W. Ichihashi, Oct. 29, 1992; Yamato Ichihashi probate file, #59701, Santa Clara County Municipal Records, San Jose, California.

25. Author's interview with John Johnson, Sept. 8, 1992. In 1992 Stanford appointed Jeffrey P. Mass, a distinguished authority on medieval Japan, the first occupant of the Yamato Ichihashi Chair in Japanese History and Civilization.

Bibliography

PRINCIPAL MANUSCRIPT COLLECTIONS AND ARCHIVES

Hoover Institution on War, Revolution and Peace, Archives, Stanford, California

Thomas R. Bodine Papers
David Starr Jordan Papers
Survey of Race Relations
Payson J. Treat Papers
Ray Lyman Wilbur Papers

Japanese American History Archives, San Francisco, California

National Archives, Pacific-Sierra Region, San Bruno, California

Passenger Arrival Lists

National Archives

Records of the War Relocation Authority, Record Group 210, Suitland, Maryland

San Francisco County Vital Records, San Francisco, California

Santa Clara County Probate Records, San Jose, California

Stanford University, Green Library, Special Collections, Stanford, California

Thomas Andrew Bailey Papers
John Casper Branner Presidential Papers
Emery Fast Correspondence
Fiftieth Anniversary Papers
History Department Files
Yamato Ichihashi Papers
Japanese Student Association Records
David Starr Jordan Presidential Papers
Edgar Eugene Robinson Papers
Donald Bertrand Tresidder Papers
Ray Lyman Wilbur Personal Papers
Ray Lyman Wilbur Presidential Papers

University of California, Berkeley, Bancroft Library

Japanese American Evacuation and Resettlement Records

University of California, Los Angeles, University Library, Special Collections

Manuscript Collection 2010, Japanese American Research Project

University of the Pacific, Stuart Library, Holt-Atherton Department, Stockton, California

Guy W. Cook Papers
Harold S. Jacoby Papers

AUTHOR'S FREEDOM OF INFORMATION REQUESTS
RE YAMATO ICHIHASHI

U.S. Department of Justice

Civil Rights Division
Federal Bureau of Investigation
Immigration and Naturalization Service

U.S. Department of the Navy

INTERVIEWS, CONVERSATIONS, AND
CORRESPONDENCE WITH THE AUTHOR

Formal Interviews

Delmer Brown, Sept. 6, 1993. Lafayette, California
Harvey M. Coverley, Aug. 17, 1992. Sausalito, California

Toichi Domoto, June 23, 1992. Hayward, California
Emery Fast, Oct. 3, 1993. Washington, D.C.
Woodrow T. Ichihashi, April 5, Oct. 29, Oct. 30, 1992, and Feb. 22, 1995. Morton Grove and Chicago, Illinois
Kenji Ito, June 18, 1992. Los Angeles, California
Harold S. Jacoby, March 23, 1993. Stockton, California
John Johnson, Oct. 30, 1991, and Sept. 8, 1992. Stanford, California
George Knoles, June 11, 1992. Palo Alto, California
Nancy McLean, July 14, 1993. Menlo Park, California
Yoshio Okumoto, Sept. 9, 1992. Stanford, California
Jeannette Rust, July 28, 1993. Palo Alto, California
Milton Silverman, Dec. 2, 1994. Menlo Park, California
Rixford Snyder, Aug. 17, 1993. Stanford, California
Kazuyuki and Soyo Takahashi, and Kenzie and Mary Nozaki, Aug. 2, 1993. El Cerrito, California
Gordon and Louise Wright, July 21, 1993. Stanford, California

Informal Conversations

Robert Billigmeier, Aug. 12, 1995
Lynn Bonner, Oct. 1993
Mollie Coleman, May 11, 1992
Elizabeth Rademaker, Sept. 1993
Akiko Shirai, Aug. 15, 1995
Wat Takeshita, Oct. 1, 1993
George Taoka, Oct. 1, 1993
Kenneth Yasuda, Jan. 23, 1995
Dwight Wilbur, Aug. 18, 1993

Correspondence

Irwin Abrams, Nov. 1, 1992
Meribeth Cameron, March 31, 1995
Laura Cline, Sept. 27, 1993
Harvey M. Coverley, Sept. 10 and Oct. 27, 1992
Harold S. Jacoby, April 16 and May 24, 1993
Caitlin James, March 28 and May 15, 1995
Frank Miyamoto, April 23, 1993
Kathie O. Nicastro, Dec. 27, 1993
Earl Pomeroy, Aug. 13, 1992
Elizabeth Rademaker, Sept. 4, 1993
Martin Ridge, Oct. 7, 1993
Jeannette Rust, Dec. 29, 1992
Elmo Sakai, Sept. 27, 1992
Tamotsu Shibutani, July 24, 1993
Mitsue Takahashi, May 28, 1993
Wat Takeshita, Oct. 4, 1993
Gordon Wright, Oct. 12 and Aug. 18, 1992
Louise Wright, July 24, 1993
George Yoshida, March 15, 1994

PERIODICALS

Daily Tulean Dispatch
Granada Pioneer
New York Times
Palo Alto Times
San Francisco Chronicle
San Francisco Examiner
Santa Ana Pacemaker
Stanford Daily
Stanford University Campus Report

BOOKS AND ARTICLES

Anesaki, Masaharu. *History of Japanese Religion*. London: K. Paul, Trench, Trubner and Co., 1930.

Asakawa, Kan'ichi, ed. and trans. *The Documents of Iriki: Illustrative of the Development of the Feudal Institutions of Japan*. Tokyo: Japan Society for the Promotion of Science, 1955.

————. *The Russo-Japanese Conflict*. Boston: Houghton Mifflin, 1904.

Bailey, Thomas A. "California, Japan, and the Alien Land Legislation of 1913." *Pacific Historical Review* 1 (March 1932): 36–59.

————. *A Diplomatic History of the American People*, 9th ed. Englewood Cliffs, N.J.: Prentice, 1974.

————. "Japanese Protest Against the Annexation of Hawaii." *Journal of Modern History* 3 (March 1931): 46–61.

————. *Theodore Roosevelt and the Japanese-American Crises: An Account of the International Complications Arising from the Race Problem on the Pacific Coast*. Stanford: Stanford University Press, 1934.

Barnhart, Edward N., ed. *Japanese-American Evacuation and Resettlement: Catalog of Materials in the General Library*. Berkeley: University of California General Library, 1958.

Beach, Walter G. *Oriental Crime in California: A Study of Offenses Committed by Orientals in That State, 1900–1927*. Stanford: Stanford University Press, 1932.

Bell, Reginald. *Public School Education of Second-Generation Japanese in California*. Stanford: Stanford University Press, 1935.

Bloom, Leonard, and John I. Kitsuse. *The Managed Casualty: The Japanese-American Family in World War II*. Berkeley: University of California Press, 1956.

Bloom, Leonard, and Ruth Riemer. *Removal and Return: The Socio- Economic Effects of the War on Japanese Americans*. Berkeley: University of California Press, 1949.

Borton, Hugh. *Japan's Modern Century*. New York: Ronald, 1955.

Bosworth, Allan P. *America's Concentration Camps*. New York: Norton, 1967.

Buell, Raymond Leslie. *The Washington Conference*. New York: D. Appleton, 1922.

Burns, Edward M. *David Starr Jordan: Prophet of Freedom*. Stanford: Stanford University Press, 1953.

Chan, Sucheng. *Asian Americans: An Interpretive History*. Boston: Twayne, 1991.

Chang, Gordon H. "'Superman is about to visit the relocation centers' and the Limits of Wartime Liberalism." *Amerasia Journal* 19, 1 (1993): 37–59.

Chinn, Thomas W. *Bridging the Pacific: San Francisco Chinatown and Its People*. San Francisco: Chinese Historical Society of America, 1989.

Cline, Laura. "The Twain Meet." Chapter on Minnie Kimura from an unpublished biography of Mary Gallagher

Committee for the Publication of Dr. Kan'ichi Asakawa's Letters. *Letters Written By Dr. Kan'ichi Asakawa*. Tokyo: Waseda University Press, 1990.

Coolidge, Mary Roberts. *Chinese Immigration*. New York: Henry Holt, 1909.

Cormack, Janet, ed. Zuigaku Kodachi and Jan Heikkala, trans. "Portland Assembly Center: Diary of Saku Tomita." *Oregon Historical Quarterly* 81 (1980): 149–71.

Daniels, Roger. *Asian America: Chinese and Japanese in the United States since 1850*. Seattle: University of Washington Press, 1988.

———. *Concentration Camps U.S.A.: Japanese Americans and World War II*. New York: Holt, 1971.

———. *The Politics of Prejudice: The Anti-Japanese Movement in California and the Struggle for Japanese Exclusion*. Berkeley: University of California Press, 1962.

Daniels, Roger, Sandra C. Taylor, and Harry H. L. Kitano, eds. *Japanese Americans: From Relocation to Redress*. Salt Lake City: University of Utah Press, 1986.

DeConde, Alexander. *Ethnicity, Race, and American Foreign Policy*. Boston: Northeastern University Press, 1992.

Degler, Carl N. *In Search of Human Nature: The Decline and Revival of Darwinism in American Social Thought*. New York: Oxford University Press, 1991.

Dewey, John. *China, Japan, and the U.S.A.: Present-day Conditions in the Far East and Their Bearing on the Washington Conference*. New York: Republic, 1921.

Drinnon, Richard. *Keeper of Concentration Camps: Dillon S. Myer and American Racism*. Berkeley: University of California Press, 1987.

Eaton, Allen H. *Beauty Behind Barbed Wire: The Arts of the Japanese in Our War Relocation Camps*. New York: Harper, 1952.

Flowers, Montaville. *The Japanese Conquest of American Opinion*. New York: George H. Doran, 1917.

———. "The Third Conflict in Japan's 'Peaceful Invasion' of California Scheme Now On." *The Grizzly Bear*, Dec. 1919, pp. 6–7.

Fowler, Ruth Miriam. "Some Aspects of Public Opinion Concerning the Japanese in Santa Clara County," M.A. thesis, Stanford University, Sociology Department, 1934.

Fukuda, Yoshiaki. *Yokuryu Seikatsu Rokunen*. Okayama, Japan: Tamashima Kappansho, 1957. In English, *My Six Years of Internment: An Issei's Struggle for Justice*. Trans. Konko Church of San Francisco and the Research Information Center of the Konko Churches of North America. San Francisco: Konko Church, 1990.

Furuki, Yoshiko. *The White Plum: A Biography of Ume Tsuda, Pioneer in the Higher Education of Japanese Women*. New York: Weatherhill, 1991.

Girdner, Audrie, and Anne Loftis. *The Great Betrayal: The Evacuation of the Japanese-Americans During World War II*. New York: Macmillan, 1969.

Grodzins, Morton. *Americans Betrayed: Politics and the Japanese Evacuation.* Chicago: University of Chicago Press, 1949.

Gulliford, Andrew. "The Granada Papers and Japanese-American War Relocation." *People & Policy*, Summer 1980, pp. 5–14.

Hall, John Whitney. *Japan: From Prehistory to Modern Times.* New York: Dell, 1981.

———. "Kan'ichi Asakawa: Comparative Historian." In Committee for the Publication of Dr. K. Asakawa's Works, comp. and ed. *Land and Society in Medieval Japan.* Kanda, Japan: Japan Society for the Promotion of Science, 1965.

Hansen, Arthur A., and Betty E. Mitson, eds. *Voices Long Silent: An Oral Inquiry Into the Japanese American Evacuation.* Fullerton: California State University, Oral History Program, 1974.

Hayashi, Brian Masaru. *"For the Sake of Our Japanese Brethren": Assimilation, Nationalism, and Protestantism Among the Japanese of Los Angeles, 1895–1992.* Stanford: Stanford University Press, 1995.

Hosokawa, Bill. *Nisei: The Quiet Americans.* New York: Morrow, 1969.

Houston, Jeanne Wakatsuki, and James D. Houston. *Farewell to Manzanar: A True Story of Japanese-American Experience During and After World War II Internment.* Boston: Houghton, 1973.

Howarth, Stephen. *Morning Glory: A History of the Imperial Japanese Navy.* London: Hamish Hamilton, 1983.

Ichioka, Yuji. "'Attorney for the Defense': Yamato Ichihashi and Japanese Immigration." *Pacific Historical Review* 55 (1986): 192–225.

———. *The Issei: The World of the First Generation Japanese Immigrants, 1885–1924.* New York: Free Press, 1988.

———. "Japanese Associations and the Japanese Government: A Special Relationship, 1909–1926." *Pacific Historical Review* 46 (1977): 409–37.

———. "Japanese Immigrant Nationalism: The Issei and the Sino-Japanese War, 1937–1941." *California History* 69, 3 (1990): 260–75.

———. "*Kengakudan*: The Origin of Nisei Study Tours of Japan." *California History* 73, 1 (Spring 1994): 30–43.

———. "'What Manner of Man?' A Portrait of Abiko Kyutaro Through Selected Letters." *Nichi Bei Times*, Supplement, Jan. 1, 1995, pp. 2–4.

———, ed. *Views from Within: The Japanese American Evacuation and Resettlement Study.* Los Angeles: Regents of the University of California, 1989.

International Labor Conference. *Delegates' Official Guide.* Washington: Government Printing Office, 1919.

International Labor Organization, League of Nations. *Report on the Eight-Hours Day or Forty-Eight Hours Week.* London: Harrison, [1919].

Inukai, H., ed. and comp., *Tule Lake Directory and Camp News, May, 1942 through September 1943.* Hood River, Ore.: Inukai Publishing, 1988.

Iriye, Akira. *Across the Pacific: An Inner History of American–East Asian Relations.* New York: Harcourt, Brace, 1967.

———. *Pacific Estrangement: Japanese and American Expansion, 1897–1911.* Cambridge, Mass.: Harvard University Press, 1972.

Irons, Peter. *Justice at War: The Story of the Japanese American Internment Cases.* New York: Oxford University Press, 1983.

Ishimoto, Baroness Shidzué. *Facing Two Ways: The Story of My Life.* New York: Holt, 1935. Reissued, Stanford: Stanford University Press, 1984.

James, Thomas. *Exile Within: The Schooling of Japanese Americans, 1942–1945.* Cambridge, Mass.: Harvard University Press, 1987.

Jansen, Marius. *Japanese Studies in the United States: Part I, History and Present Condition.* Tokyo: Japan Foundation, 1988.

Japanese American National Museum. *The View From Within: Japanese American Art from the Internment Camps, 1942–1945.* Los Angeles: UCLA Asian American Studies Center, 1992.

Johnson, Melvyn. "At Home in Amache: A Japanese-American Relocation Camp in Colorado." *Colorado Heritage* 1, 1 (1989): 2–11.

Jordan, David Starr. *The Days of a Man,* 2 vols. New York: World Book, 1922.

———. *War and the Breed: The Relation of War to the Downfall of Nations.* Boston: Beacon, 1915.

Kawaguchi, Gary. *Living with Flowers: The California Flower Market History.* San Francisco: California Flower Market, 1993.

Kawakami, K. K. *Japan's Pacific Policy: Especially in Relation to China, the Far East, and the Washington Conference.* New York: E. P. Dutton, 1922.

Keene, Donald. *Japanese Diaries: The Japanese at Home and Abroad as Revealed Through Their Diaries.* New York: Henry Holt, 1995.

Kennan, George. "The Japanese in San Francisco Schools." *The Outlook* 86, 5 (June 1, 1907): 246–52.

Kikumura, Akemi. *Through Harsh Winters: The Life of a Japanese Immigrant Woman.* Novato, Calif.: Chandler & Sharp, 1981.

Kitagawa, Daisuke. *Issei and Nisei: The Internment Years.* New York: Seabury Press, 1967.

Kitano, Harry H. L. *Generations and Identity: The Japanese American.* Needham Heights, Mass.: Ginn Press, 1993.

Lasker, Bruno. *Filipino Immigration to Continental United States and to Hawaii.* Chicago: University of Chicago Press, 1931.

Lauren, Paul Gordon. *Power and Prejudice: The Politics and Diplomacy of Racial Discrimination.* Boulder, Colo.: Westview Press, 1988.

League of Nations. *International Labor Conference, First Annual Meeting, October 29, 1919–November 29, 1919.* Washington: Government Printing Office, 1920.

League of Nations' Association of Japan. *Activities of the League of Nations Association of Japan, January–June 1921.* Tokyo: Kojimachi, 1921.

Lee, Ayleen Ito. "United States vs. Ito." Research paper, Mills College, 1977.

Lehman, Anthony L. *Birthright of Barbed Wire: The Santa Anita Assembly Center for the Japanese.* Los Angeles: Westernlore, 1970.

Leighton, Alexander H. *The Governing of Men: General Principles and Recommendations Based on Experience at a Japanese Relocation Camp.* Princeton: Princeton University Press, 1945.

Lewis, David Levering. *W. E. B. DuBois: Biography of a Race, 1868–1919.* New York: Holt, 1993.

Lukes, Timothy J., and Gary Y. Okihiro. *Japanese Legacy: Farming and Community Life in California's Santa Clara Valley.* Cupertino, Calif.: California History Center, De Anza College, 1985.

Lurie, George. "Return to Amache." *Denver Magazine,* May 1982, pp. 33–38.

Masaoka, Naoichi, ed. and comp. *Japan's Message to America: A Symposium by Representative Japanese on Japan and American-Japanese Relations.* Tokyo: n.p. 1914.

Matsumoto, Toru. *Beyond Prejudice: A Story of the Church and Japanese Americans.* New York: Friendship Press, 1946.

Matsumoto, Valerie J. *Farming the Home Place: A Japanese American Community in California 1919–1982.* Ithaca: Cornell University Press, 1993.

———. "Japanese American Women During World War II," *Frontiers* 8, 1 (1984): 6–14.

Mayer, Robert Stanley. *The Influence of Frank A. Vanderlip and the National City Bank on American Commerce and Foreign Policy, 1910–1920.* New York: Garland, 1987.

McWilliams, Carey. *Prejudice: Japanese Americans, Symbol of Racial Intolerance.* Boston: Little Brown, 1944.

Mears, Eliot Grinnell. "California's Attitude toward the Oriental." *The Far East*, vol. 122 of *Annals of the American Academy of Political and Social Sciences* (Nov. 1925): 199–213.

———. *Resident Orientals on the American Pacific Coast: Their Legal and Economic Status.* Chicago: University of Chicago Press, 1928.

Millis, H. A. *The Japanese Problem in the United States.* New York: Macmillan, 1915.

Mirrielees, Edith R. *Fifty Years of Phi Beta Kappa at Stanford, 1891–1941.* Stanford: Stanford University Press, n.d. [1942?].

———. *Stanford: The Story of a University.* New York: G. P. Putnam's Sons, 1959.

Miyamori, Asataro, trans. and comp. *An Anthology of Haiku: Ancient and Modern.* Tokyo: Maruzen, 1932.

Miyoshi, Masao. *As We Saw Them: The First Japanese Embassy to the United States (1860).* Berkeley: University of California Press, 1979.

Modell, John, ed., *The Kikuchi Diary: Chronicle from an American Concentration Camp, the Tanforan Journals of Charles Kikuchi.* Urbana: University of Illinois Press, 1973.

Myer, Dillon S. *Uprooted Americans: The Japanese Americans and the War Relocation Authority During World War II.* Tucson: University of Arizona Press, 1971.

Nee, Victor G., and Brett de Bary Nee. *Longtime Californ': A Documentary Study of an American Chinatown.* Stanford: Stanford University Press, 1986.

Nishimoto, Richard. *Inside An American Concentration Camp: Japanese American Resistance at Poston, Arizona.* Ed. Lane Ryo Hirabayashi. Tucson: University of Arizona Press, 1995.

O'Brien David J., and Stephen S. Fugita. *The Japanese American Experience.* Bloomington: Indiana University Press, 1991.

Opler, Marvin K. "Cultural Dilemma of a Kibei Youth." In Georgene Seward, ed. *Clinical Studies in Cultural Conflict.* New York: Ronald, 1958.

———. "Japanese Folk Beliefs and Practices, Tule Lake, California." *Journal of American Folklore* 63 (1950): 385–97.

———. "Senryu Poetry as Folk and Community Expression." *Journal of American Folklore* 58 (1945): 1–11.

———. "A 'Sumo' Tournament at Tule Lake Center." *American Anthropologist* 47 (1945): 134–39.

Park, Robert E. "Human Migration and the Marginal Man." *American Journal of Sociology* 33, 6 (1928): 881–93.

Player, Cyril Arthur. *Arms—and the Men.* Detroit, Mich.: Evening News Association, 1922.

Ramey, Arthur G. "Student Activities in a Japanese Relocation High School." *Clearing House* 18 (1943): 94–96.

Reischauer, Edwin O., and John K. Fairbank. *East Asia: The Great Tradition.* Boston: Houghton Mifflin, 1960.

Reynolds, Charles N. "Oriental-White Race Relations in Santa Clara County, California." Ph.D. diss., Stanford University, Economics Department, 1927.

Ripley, William Z. *The Races of Europe: A Sociological Study.* New York: D. Appleton, 1899.

Rodriguez, Paul, ed. *Amache.* Garden City, Kans.: Aurora Publishing, 1992.

Sarasohn, Eileen Sunada, ed. *The Issei: Portrait of a Pioneer; An Oral History.* Palo Alto, Calif.: Pacific Books, 1983.

Sawada, Mitziko. "Culprits and Gentlemen: Meiji Japan's Restrictions of Emigrants to the United States, 1891–1909." *Pacific Historical Review*, Aug. 1991, pp. 339–59.

Scheiner, Irwin. *Christian Converts and Social Protest in Meiji Japan.* Berkeley: University of California Press, 1970.

Shirai, Noboru. *Kariforunia nikkeijin kyōsei shūyōjo* (Concentration camps for Japanese Americans in California). Tokyo: Kawade shobo shinsha, 1981.

Smith, Page. *Democracy on Trial: The Japanese American Evacuation and Relocation in World War II.* New York: Simon & Schuster, 1995.

Spector, Ronald H. *Eagle Against the Sun: The American War with Japan.* New York: Free Press, 1985.

Spicer, Edward H., Asael T. Hansen, Katherine Luomala, and Marvin K. Opler. *Impounded People: Japanese Americans in the Relocation Centers.* Tucson: University of Arizona Press, 1969.

Stanford University. *Annual Reports of the President of the University,* 1913–1945.

Strong, Edward K., Jr. *Japanese in California.* Stanford: Stanford University Press: 1933.

———. *The Second-Generation Japanese Problem.* Stanford: Stanford University Press, 1934.

———. *Vocational Aptitudes of Second-Generation Japanese in the United States.* Stanford: Stanford University Press, 1933.

Sugahara, T. Roku. "Nisei . . . Naughty or Naive? Local Lights Become All Ears as Authority from Stanford Discusses Nisei; A Study of Dr. Ichihashi, Author, Educator." *Kashu Mainichi,* April 15, 1934.

Sugimoto, Etsu Inagaki. *A Daughter of the Samurai.* Garden City, N.Y.: Doubleday, 1931.

Suzuki, Peter T. "Anthropologists in the Wartime Camps for Japanese Americans: A Documentary Study." *Dialectical Anthropology* 6 (1981): 23–60.

Taft, Henry W. *Japan and America: A Journey and A Political Survey.* New York: Macmillan, 1932.

Takaki, Ronald. *Strangers from a Different Shore: A History of Asian Americans.* Boston: Little Brown, 1989.

Tateishi, John, ed. *And Justice for All: An Oral History of the Japanese American Detention Camps.* New York: Random House, 1984.

Taylor, Sandra C. *Jewel of the Desert: Japanese American Internment at Topaz.* Berkeley: University of California Press, 1993.

tenBroek, Jacobus, Edward N. Barnhart, and Floyd W. Matson. *Prejudice, War, and the Constitution.* Berkeley: University of California Press, 1954.

Thomas, Dorothy Swaine. *The Salvage*. Berkeley: University of California Press, 1952.

Thomas, Dorothy Swaine, and Richard Nishimoto. *The Spoilage: Japanese-American Evacuation and Resettlement During World War II*. Berkeley: University of California Press, 1946.

Thompson, William Takamatsu. "Amache: A Working Bibliography on One Japanese American Concentration Camp." *Amerasia Journal* 19, 1 (1993): 153–59.

Treat, Payson. "California and the Japanese." *Atlantic Monthly* 127 (1921): 537–46.

———. *Diplomatic Relations Between the United States and Japan 1853–1895*. Stanford: Stanford University Press, 1932.

———. *Japan and the United States, 1853–1921*. Stanford: Stanford University Press, 1928.

Tule Lake Committee, ed. *Kinenhi: Reflections on Tule Lake*. San Francisco: Tule Lake Committee, 1980.

Uchida, Yoshiko. *Desert Exile: The Uprooting of a Japanese American Family*. Seattle: University of Washington Press, 1982.

United States Commission on Wartime Relocation and Internment of U.S. Civilians. *Personal Justice Denied: Report of the Commission on Wartime Relocation and Internment of Civilians*. Washington: Government Printing Office, 1982.

United States Senate. *Abstracts of Reports of the Immigration Commission*, 61st Cong., 3rd sess., 2 vols. Washington: Government Printing Office, 1911.

———. *Conference on the Limitation of Armament*, 67th Cong., S. doc. 124. Washington: Government Printing Office, 1922.

———. *Reports of Immigration Commission: Immigrants in Industries; Part 25, Japanese and Other Immigrant Races in the Pacific Coast and Rocky Mountain States*, 61st Cong., 2nd sess. Vol. 1. Washington: Government Printing Office, 1911.

Uyehara, Cecil H., comp. *Checklist of Archives in the Japanese Ministry of Foreign Affairs, Tokyo, Japan, 1868–1945*. Washington: Library of Congress, 1954.

Varley, H. Paul. *Japanese Culture: A Short History*. New York: Praeger Publishers, 1973.

Weglyn, Michi. *Years of Infamy: The Untold Story of America's Concentration Camps*. New York: William Morrow, 1976.

Weinberg, Julius. *Edward Alsworth Ross and the Sociology of Progressivism*. Madison: State Historical Society of Wisconsin, 1972.

Wilbur, Ray Lyman. *The Memoirs of Ray Lyman Wilbur, 1875–1949*. Stanford: Stanford University Press, 1960.

Woo, Fred G. "Japanese Educator Denies 'Invasion.'" *Chinese Digest* 2, 7 (Feb. 14, 1936): 8.

Yanagisako, Sylvia Junko. *Transforming the Past: Tradition and Kinship Among Japanese Americans*. Stanford: Stanford University Press, 1985.

Yoneda, Karl. *Ganbatte: Sixty-Year Struggle of a Kibei Worker*. Los Angeles: UCLA Asian American Studies Center, 1983.

Young, Peter, ed. *Atlas of the Second World War*. London: Weidenfeld and Nicholson, 1973.

Index

In this index "f" after a number indicates a separate reference on the next page, and "ff" indicates separate references on the next two pages. A continuous discussion over two or more pages is indicated by a span of numbers. *Passim* is used for a cluster of references in close but not consecutive sequence.

Many persons named by Yamato Ichihashi have not been identified, but most of those he mentions are listed here. A surname alone indicates that no information has been found and the name may apply to more than one person. Tentative identifications are indicated by placing the given name in parentheses.

Bailey, Thomas A., 21, 59–60, 77, 143,
420, 422, 444, 451, 482n28
Balfour, Arthur, 50, 56
Barker, Ethel, *see* Fast, Ethel Barker
Bassett, William, 415
Beach, Walter Greenwood, 60
Bell, Reginald, 59, 65
Bendetsen, Karl R., 510n31
Best, Raymond R., 251, 254, 285, 513n57
Biddle, Francis, 141, 154, 296, 409, 498n10,
518n54
Biggerstaff, Knight, 420, 422, 528n24
Billigmeier, Robert, 82, 487n87, 501n56,
511n37
Bloch, Marc, 69
Blue Star Mothers Club (Amache), 291,
308, 325, 352, 379, 398f, 418, 423
Boas, Franz, 24
Bodine, Thomas R., 339, 523n33
Borton, Hugh, 420, 422, 528n24
Brandt, Karl, 85
Briand, Aristide, 50
Bricker, John William, 331f
Brown, Delmer, 65
Bryan, William Jennings, 52
Buck, Pearl, 428
Buddhism, 170, 200, 264, 270, 308, 340,
348, 350, 359, 369, 381, 421–25
passim, 432, 524n34; and Ichihashis,
74, 216, 378, 523n17; study of, 178,
337, 376, 501n56

Cameron, Charles R., 71
Cameron, Meribeth, 65, 483n41
Camp Shelby, Miss., 200
Carver, Thomas Nixon, 23, 30, 473n41
Central Intelligence Agency (CIA), 482n19
Chan, Shau Wing, 85
Chapman, Everett, 114–18 *passim*, 128
Chin, Frank, 76
China, 54–55, 65, 68–71 *passim*
Chinese, 61, 83, 347, 370, 381, 471n20,
478n97, 499n33, 512n46, 524n39;
at Stanford, 17f, 41
Chinese Exclusion Act of 1882, 474n57,
524n39
Chiyo, Lady, 469n12
Christianity, 42, 57, 101, 264, 269–70,
308, 340, 348, 350, 369, 524n42;
and Ichihashis, 16, 21, 39ff, 74, 81,
366f, 472n32, 486n65
Citizenship renunciation, 238, 300, 409
Civil Liberties League, 194
Clyde, Mildred, 312, 353, 360
Clyde, Paul, 65, 353, 359

Colorado Japanese Language School, University of Colorado, 207, 290, 294
Columbia University, 18, 24, 33, 40, 420
Combat team, 217-18, 318. *See also* 442nd
Regimental Combat Team
Commonwealth Club of San Francisco,
57, 70
Concentration camps, 122n. *See also* Internment *and individual relocation
centers by name*
Conference on the Limitation of Armament, 46–50 *passim*, 54, 56, 60, 71,
141, 144, 455
Congressional Joint Commission on Immigration, 22–23
Cook, John D., 172
Coolidge, Calvin, 58
Coolidge, Mary, 59
Cortez, Calif., 421f
Coverley, Harvey M., 167ff, 171–72, 178–
83 *passim*, 188–96 *passim*, 203,
207–8, 216–21 *passim*, 227, 229,
500n51, 511n37; and camp government, 212, 238–45 *passim*, 500n51
Cressey, Calif., 422
Crystal City, Tex., 122n
Culver, George Bliss, 145, 224, 329

Danzuka, George O., 5, 191, 195f, 200,
212, 230, 506n98
Davies, Laurence E., 351
Dewitt, General John L., 99, 135, 139,
206, 213, 222, 508n7
Diary keeping, 95, 165
Discrimination, *see* Racial prejudice
Doi, Sumio, 407
Domoto, Kanejiro (Kanetaro), 281, 288,
516n25
Domoto, Toichi, 314, 487n84
Doolittle, James H., 209f
Draft (selective service), 175ff, 307–30
passim, 338, 342, 347, 354, 372
Du Bois, W. E. B., 21, 23, 78, 83
Duniway, Clyde, 415

East Asian Studies, 13, 33, 375f
Edge, Walter Evans, 331
Ehrman, Alfred, 214
Eisenhower, Milton, 138n
Elberson, Irving D., 232
Endo, Mitsuye, 371
England, Edward J., 114–15, 124, 147
Ennis, Edward J., 426f, 430, 432, 439,
529n29
Erb, Donald, 86